Heroes with Humble Beginnings

Heroes with Humble Beginnings

*Underdogs
On the Diamond,
At the Movies,
In the White House*

F.M. Kail

Heroes with Humble Beginnings
Underdogs On the Diamond, At the Movies, In the White House

Copyright © 2019 F.M. Kail.

All rights reserved. No part of this book may be used or reproduced by any means, graphic, electronic, or mechanical, including photocopying, recording, taping or by any information storage retrieval system without the written permission of the author except in the case of brief quotations embodied in critical articles and reviews.

The author gratefully acknowledges the permission granted by the Baseball Hall of Fame for use of its copyrighted images of the ballplayers and by Photofest for permission to use its studio images of the movies stars.

iUniverse books may be ordered through booksellers or by contacting:

iUniverse
1663 Liberty Drive
Bloomington, IN 47403
www.iuniverse.com
1-800-Authors (1-800-288-4677)

Because of the dynamic nature of the Internet, any web addresses or links contained in this book may have changed since publication and may no longer be valid. The views expressed in this work are solely those of the author and do not necessarily reflect the views of the publisher, and the publisher hereby disclaims any responsibility for them.

ISBN: 978-1-5320-7228-4 (sc)
ISBN: 978-1-5320-7230-7 (hc)
ISBN: 978-1-5320-7229-1 (e)

Library of Congress Control Number: 2019903622

Print information available on the last page.

iUniverse rev. date: 05/07/2019

To my family

Contents

Foreword ix
Introduction xi

Part One: Setting The Stage 1

Part Two: Underdog Greats 16
  I. On the Diamond 17
      Josh Gibson 18
      Mickey Mantle 27
      Stan Musial 35
      Ted Williams 42
      Henry Aaron 53
      Babe Ruth 61
      Roberto Clemente 71
  II. At the Movies 80
      Kirk Douglas 81
      John "Duke" Wayne 88
      Gregory Peck 96
      William Clark Gable 104
      James Francis Cagney 110
      Cary Grant 122
      Sidney Poitier 135
  III. In the White House 148
      William Jefferson Clinton 149
      Ronald Wilson Reagan 161
      Lyndon Baines Johnson 170
      Andrew Jackson 181
      Dwight D. Eisenhower 190
      Abraham Lincoln 206
      Barack Hussein Obama 220

Part Three: How Beginnings Mattered 236
I. On the Way Up 236
    A. The Ballplayers 236
    B. The Movie Stars 244
    C. The Presidents 250
    D. Wrap-Up 261
II. At the Top 264
    A. The Ballplayers 265
    B. The Movie Stars 265
    C. The Presidents 266
III. Special Sauce 267
IV. The Bottom Line 272

Part Four: What of The American Dream? 274
I. Where It Came From 274
II. Whether It Has Worked 275
    A. For Our Greats 276
    B. For Others 286
III. What the Polls Say 294
IV. Why It Endures 295

Appendices 301
    A. Listing of Notable Underdog Films By Decade 301
    B. Chart on the Colonization of North America 303
    C. Description of Social Class in the U.S. 304
    D. Ballplayers Rankings 305
    E. Presidents Rankings 306
    F. Demographic Profiles of the Top 20s 307
    G. Earnings Details of the Ballplayers and Movie Stars 318
    H. Occupations of the Top 5% of Male Wage Earners, 2000 325
    I. Intergenerational Mobility Study, 2006 325
Bibliography 327
Acknowledgments 345
Endnotes 347

Foreword

A love of sports, movies, politics – and underdogs. Those are prime among the many things Mike Kail and I have in common, and they all fit together somehow into a shared vision of the American story. The best aspects of our country derive from the sensibility of the underdog, and the worst moments in the nation's history invariably involve the times when underdogs were killed, ignored, dismissed, and segregated against.

In this engaging book, Mike has taken his obsession with underdogs and followed it down many trails. By introducing the reader to one fascinating story after another, he shows us how those underdog narratives connect and helps us understand the backgrounds, talents, and flaws that drive people to overcome the odds. A book that is prodigiously researched and both fun and illuminating – what could be better?

David Maraniss

Introduction

When I think back on it, I first really understood what it meant to be an underdog after reading a biography of Glenn Cunningham for a high school English class. Cunningham grew up in Elkhart, Kansas. When he was eight his brother died, and he almost did, in a fiery explosion. All the flesh on his knees and shins was burned off along with the toes on his left foot and most of his traverse arch. The doctor recommended amputating his legs. When his parents refused, the doctor told them that he doubted their son would ever be able to walk normally again. For two years after the fire Glenn was unable to walk at all, and it appeared that he never would. But as a result of his parents' care and his determination, he did learn to walk. Then he learned to run. And in February 1934, in Madison Square Garden, Glenn Cunningham established the world indoor record for the mile. Throughout much of the 1930s, the boy who was supposed to spend his life in a wheelchair was hailed as America's premier middle-distance runner.

The underdogs who populate this book are also underdogs in the game of life, not because of any physical limitations, but due to their humble beginnings. Perhaps the first encouraging words children of my generation heard in grammar school was that any boy, even a poor one, could grow up to become President of the United States. However oversold the idea may have been, the notion that the sky is the limit has remained one of this nation's most compelling and enduring boasts, not just to its youngsters, but to generations of poor immigrants whose successes continue to brand this country as a promised land.

I was drawn to the baseball diamond, the movie screen and the White House to find my stories of underdog greats. I suppose my interest in ballplayers began over the recurrent October "sick days" I took as a kid when the Yankees were perennial World Series participants. As to politics, I can pinpoint the spark to a drab September afternoon in 1960 when I waited on Sunrise Highway to get a glimpse of a very-tanned John Fitzgerald Kennedy as his motorcade sped by. My love of movies, especially old ones, came years later, after I got married, and found out how fond my new wife was of classic films.

Within these fields, how do you decide which underdogs to feature? To begin with, I restricted myself to men. That was how it had to be with the ballplayers and, to date, the Presidents and how I chose to do it when it came to the movie stars. The choice with the actors partly reflected a desire for consistency, but more importantly came from a belief, recently reinforced, that gender presents a unique set of issues, wholly apart from socio-economics, that has an impact in virtually every workplace. To do justice to the stories of iconic American women requires a comprehensive and separate telling, and one by a story-teller better suited to the task than I.

Among the male candidates for consideration, there were those figures so towering that they could not be ignored: Babe Ruth, John Wayne, Abraham Lincoln. There were others who commanded admiration by dint of their extraordinary drive or grit – Ted Williams, Sidney Poitier, and Andrew Jackson – and others still who stood out because of their sheer and undeniable talent – Henry Aaron, Cary Grant and Barack Obama.

Admittedly, it was a subjective process, and I had some favorites going in. My purpose is not to argue that those I have picked are the most accomplished male underdogs that history has served up, though I would argue they belong in that group. Rather, each of the men profiled was a mountain climber in his own way, and each mountain offered its own set of unique perils. What drew me most to those I chose was what they had to navigate in the challenging initial phases of their remarkable ascents.

F.M. Kail
March, 2019

PART ONE

Setting The Stage

The Merriam-Webster dictionary defines an "underdog" as "(1) a loser or predicted loser in a struggle or contest."[1] The word is said to derive from nineteenth century dog-fights and the fact that the loser would roll over on its back and permit the winner to tower (and slobber) over him.[2] Over time, the term has come to signify a person or team that is likely to lose, rather than one that has already lost. Indeed today, many associate "underdogs" with winners, and not with losers at all.[3]

That shift in common understanding is not surprising. It reflects the grip on popular imagination of true stories like that of the "Miracle on Ice," where in defiance of the odds, the underdog did come out on top. The prospects for the American Olympic hockey team could not have been more dim. The U.S. coach was no better than the third choice of the selection committee. His squad, made up of collegiate amateurs who had never played together, was pitted against older, seasoned Soviet veterans who had been a unit on the ice for years. An American team had not beaten a Russian team in any international contest in two decades, and our current Olympians had been routed in the warm-up game less than a week before the opening ceremonies. Yet when the competition was over, this ragtag band of lunch-bucket misfits had won the gold medal.

While to some the 1980 U.S. victory at Lake Placid is "the" classic underdog story, there is room for debate. For avid baseball fans, the "Amazin' Mets" of 1969 are the standouts. After seven losing seasons – during which they never rose above ninth place in a 10-team league – they went on to beat the heavily favored Baltimore Orioles in the World Series. For avid football fans, earlier that same year another New York expansion team defied the oddsmakers in Super Bowl III, when "Broadway Joe" Namath made good on his prediction that his upstart AFL Jets would top another Baltimore team, the NFL's powerful Colts. Other surprises include Muhammad Ali's victory over Sonny Liston in 1964, 8th seed Villanova's wresting the 1985 NCAA basketball crown from defending champion Georgetown and the Vegas Golden Knights making it to the Stanley Cup finals in their maiden season.

For those enamored of the world of entertainment, the picks would differ. Many would single out the rise of the Beatles as the most compelling underdog story. The triumph of these four Liverpool boys, whose status was middling at best, first over English snobbery and then over American parochialism, changed the landscape of popular music, as they became the first-ever foreign group to dominate the U.S. Billboard Charts. Other singers who, like the Beatles, came from humble origins, horrified an older generation and revolutionized the music of their era include Elvis Presley in the Fifties, with his unique blend of white country and black blues, and a collection of hip-hop artists and rappers like the Notorious B.I.G., 2Pac, Eminem and Jay-Z who, in the Nineties, introduced their novel mix of beat and rhyme. Not to be forgotten was the stout, frumpy, 47-year-old Scotswoman who, wearing what looked like a fright wig, took the stage midway through the inaugural episode of *Britain's Got Talent*. Her appearance was greeted with catcalls, until she opened her mouth to sing the first bars of "I Dreamed A Dream" from *Les Miserables*. Then, a stunned audience broke into rapturous applause and leapt to its feet, joined by the astonished judges. At that instant, Susan Boyle epitomized the underdog's wondrous appeal.

For lovers of public affairs, there is still a consensus, even after Trump in 2016, that Harry Truman's upset of Thomas Dewey in the 1948 presidential election is the best underdog story. For Truman not only had to cope with a lack of enthusiasm among his own Democrats, but with two splinter parties, one on the left and one on the right, that credibly threatened to throw the election into a Republican-controlled House of Representatives. Worthy of honorable mention is Barack Obama's feat, less than four years after he burst on the national scene, of stealing the nomination and the White House from the self-proclaimed heir apparent, former First Lady and incumbent two-term New York Senator Hillary Rodham Clinton. And deserving at least a footnote are a number of improbably successful also-rans: Gene McCarthy, George McGovern and Gary Hart.

We are conditioned from our earliest days to expect Lake Placid miracles and Beatles' invasions and Truman-esque upsets, no matter what Merriam-Webster says. We are taught as children to root for the underdog and to believe that he or she can confound expectations and come out on top. We all heard tales growing up that revealed that the biggest, strongest and fastest, or the richest and highest born, or the most beautiful and handsome, did not always win. Our parents, perhaps without even being aware of what they were doing, were letting us know early on not to believe the conventional wisdom about how the world really works. They were inoculating us against the notion that size, strength, speed, wealth, status and appearance were always virtues and that those who had them were always better and would inevitably prevail.

SETTING THE STAGE

For most of us, just reading the titles of the classic underdog stories brings smiles to our faces: *Cinderella, Beauty and the Beast, The Little Engine That Could, The Ugly Duckling, The Tortoise and the Hare, Br'er Rabbit and the Tar Baby, David and Goliath*. Their collective moral is to have faith when confronted with adversity, to avoid despair in the face of bullying or condescension or jealousy, to stand up to those flaunting their physical or social advantages. Who knows at what level or to what extent we absorbed these lessons when we were little? The important thing is that as grown-ups we remember them and their message that underdogs can and do succeed. We recall that the servant girl married the prince; the beast wed the beauty; the little train made it up the hill; the speckled duckling became a swan; the turtle outraced the rabbit; the rabbit outsmarted the fox; and the young boy felled the giant.

These childhood fantasies are not left to founder when we get older. They are replaced and reinforced by grown-up stories of other underdogs who have also overcome adversities or have coped with them in a way that stirs our admiration.[4] As adults, our exposure mainly comes from television, theater, books and movies.

While television reaches by far the greatest audiences, it does not consistently or significantly or intentionally air material with underdog themes. There have been a few notable exceptions, with Alex Haley's monumental, 1977 eight-part mini-series *Roots* still representing the best of the lot. Though from time to time, a situation comedy features underdogs as central characters – *Gimme a Break* (1981-1987) about a black housekeeper; *Murphy Brown* (1988-1998) about a female reporter; *Will and Grace* (1998-2006) about a gay lawyer; *Mike and Molly* (2010-2016) about a plus-sized couple – their "differentness" is generally incidental to the weekly plot.

By contrast, over the years Broadway has provided lots of splendid underdog entertainment. Much has been in the form of musicals, some standouts being *Porgy and Bess* in the Thirties, *My Fair Lady* in the Fifties and *Phantom of the Opera* in the Eighties.[5] There are also many straight plays with underdog themes, *A Raisin in the Sun*, *Fences* and *Boys in the Band* to name a few.[6] Nor is there a shortage of books that tell underdog stories. There are classic novels, like Charles Dickens' *Great Expectations*, Victor Hugo's *The Hunchback of Notre Dame*, Jane Austen's *Pride and Prejudice* and John Steinbeck's *The Grapes of Wrath*. And there are more contemporary offerings, too, such as Bryce Courtenay's *The Power of One*, John Irving's *A Prayer for Owen Meany* and Robert Ludlum's *Bourne* series.[7] Nor are underdog books limited to works of fiction. There are also "real-life" underdog stories running the gamut from natural disasters (*Alive: The Miracle of the Andes*) to high school sports (*Friday Night Lights*) to all manner of biography (*Walk the Line, Seabiscuit*).[8]

However, the mother lode of underdog offerings can be found at the movie house. Every one of the shows and books mentioned in the text and accompanying notes had a second life[9] with a greatly expanded reach when it was translated from its original form into a feature film.[10] And the range and types of underdog motion pictures is vast. There are, of course, the classic "Cinderella stories," movies about romance between un-equals, generally in terms of social or economic status. "Standard" Cinderella stories, like the fairy tale, involve the rich guy falling for the poor girl (*Sabrina, Love Story, Pretty Woman*), though quite a few reverse the plot to have it the other way around (*Roman Holiday, Good Will Hunting*). A variant of the "standard" Cinderella story involves people who are at a disadvantage in life, often because of class, but nonetheless succeed, sometimes spectacularly, but not by taking a trip to the altar. Sometimes the protagonist is a total invention; sometimes a fictionalized version of a real person. *The Farmer's Daughter, Coal Miner's Daughter* and *Erin Brockovich* dealt with struggling women who surpassed expectations. *Sergeant York, Walk the Line* and *Pursuit of Happyness* dealt with struggling men who were similarly underestimated.

Among the most effective and affecting underdog films are those about individuals who have had to deal with serious disabilities, either mental (*Rain Man, Forrest Gump*) or physical (*The Miracle Worker, My Left Foot*). Then there are the movies about individuals who are made to suffer because they are identified with a disfavored group, frequently a minority. The "usual suspects" of such discrimination are race (*Driving Miss Daisy*), religion (*The Diary of Anne Frank*), gender (*Sister Kenny*) and sexual orientation (*Boys Don't Cry*).

Schoolyards (*Lean on Me*), battlefields (*Braveheart*), and courtrooms (*A Few Good Men*) are often a backdrop for stories of underdogs' success. Even more common are sports venues, ranging from baseball stadiums to football fields to running tracks to ice rinks to basketball courts to boxing rings to soccer pitches. The disadvantages faced by the central contestants cover the spectrum: class (*Rocky*), race (*The Great White Hope*), gender (*Million Dollar Baby*), age (*The Natural*).

There are, too, a host of movies about the lives of people from the lower classes, movies that show what it is like to be on the bottom rung of the socio-economic ladder. These pictures provide a glimpse into the everyday experiences and ups and downs of those less fortunate, and are among the most memorable and stirring underdog films ever made, films like *On the Waterfront, I Remember Mama* and *How Green Was My Valley*.[11] Outlaws, outcasts and misfits are in a sense "per se" underdogs, though their difficulties are generally self-inflicted. The central characters are not uniformly admirable, nor do they necessarily come out on top, but their stories are good. *Catch Me If You Can, Bonnie and Clyde* and *Edward Scissorhands* are three that fall into this category.

All the movies mentioned above, and dozens of others, were among the most important entries in their year of release. Each of them was ranked in the top 50 in gross ticket sales[12] or was listed in AFI's "100 Greatest American Films of All Time" or was up for a Best Picture, Best Actress or Best Actor Oscar. By my count something like 225 notable underdog movies were released between 1930 and 2009,[13] meaning on average at least three underdog films a year were seen by large numbers of movie-goers and/or were critically acclaimed.[14] It is because in virtually all of them the underdog prevails or ought to prevail or at least makes a good showing that we have come to think of underdogs as winners, despite the law of averages.

While the prevalence of significant films about successful – or nearly successful – underdogs helps to answer one question, it raises others. Why is it that year after year the studios made these films? And why, once released, did audiences flock to them and did critics write positive reviews?

As to the first question, the social backgrounds of the movie hierarchy offers a clue, at least during the early days of the movie industry. As chronicled by Neal Gabler, Hollywood was created and run by a small group of Eastern European Jews. The principal players were Harry Cohn of Columbia Pictures, William Fox of Fox Film, Carl Laemmle of Universal Pictures, Jack and Harry Warner of Warner Brothers and Adolph Zukor of Paramount.[15] To the extent these men felt empathy for underdogs it was not simply or necessarily because of any religious discrimination they had faced. Rather these men, who were not uniformly devout, were to a person proud of and devoted to the country that had given them the chance to escape their humble beginnings. As Gabler wrote: "Above all things, they wanted to be regarded as Americans, not Jews."[16] That these poor immigrants were able to achieve fame and fortune undoubtedly made them amenable to scripts about other underdog strivers and led them to celebrate the promise of America on their backlots and soundstages.

The Cohns and Foxes and Laemmles and Warners and Zukors routinely invested in underdog pictures not only because the plot lines resonated with them, but because they would be good box office. They understood that American audiences liked watching movies about improbable successes. Part of the reason is conditioning, the fairy tales and fables and Bible stories we recall from our childhood. Part of the reason is the appeal of the notion that if these fictional and fictionalized people can hit the jackpot, despite their modest starts, so can the rest of us. And part of the reason may have something to do with the remarkable extent that underdogs figure in our nation's founding. In an historical sense, our soft spot for underdogs comes naturally.

To begin with, the vast preponderance of those settling here were underdogs at the moment they set foot in the New World. As a premier scholar on colonial demographics wrote:

> For the first two centuries of the history of British North America, one word best characterizes the status of the vast majority of immigrants – servitude. From the founding of Jamestown until the Revolution, nearly three-fourths of all immigrants to the thirteen colonies arrived in some condition of unfreedom.[17]

The "unfree" immigrants fell into three categories: indentured servants, slaves and convicts.[18] As to the first, the written contract of indenture enabled voyagers to the West to travel at no cost in return for agreeing, upon arrival, to be bound "in service" for four to seven years.[19] As a formal matter, the treatment of indentured servants was regulated by statute. While they had the right to pursue legal action in the courts, to be fed and clothed and to receive medical attention for serious illness, their movement was restricted, they could be whipped for insubordination, they were forbidden from obtaining liquor, they could not be married without their master's approval, and they were precluded from voting or holding public office. Some colonial laws authorized captured runaways to be placed in iron collars and for their term of servitude to be extended by 10 days for each day they were gone. Servants in England had it better than servants in the colonies. Servants in the Middle Colonies and New England had it better than servants in the South.

Once the indenture contract had been fulfilled, the servant became a free man or woman. Though there are some heartwarming examples of the success achieved with that freedom,[20] instances of upward mobility were rare. Most of the newly emancipated remained as tenants of their former masters or were compelled to resettle in remote and unsafe areas. Overall, indentured servitude in British North America was a status to be avoided if at all possible.

Far worse, of course, was the lot of the slave, though it was not so at first. During much of the 17th century, when Africans were only 8% of the immigrant tide, slaves were treated little different than their indentured counterparts. They were freed after a set term and thereafter could own land, travel without restriction, obtain firearms, testify in court and even vote. That began to change in 1674, when slave ships were no longer routed through the West Indies. But the real differences came with the turn of the century. Between 1700 and 1775, the slave population exploded – representing nearly 45% of all arrivals – a reflection of the fact that the cost of purchasing a slave for life became the same as the cost of renting a servant for eight years. As slave numbers increased, their situation declined. They could no longer assemble. The workday was extended. Food rations were cut back. Housing deteriorated. Masters became more brutal. And Southern colonies passed laws adding to the terrors and indignities.

The forced emigration of convicts to North America started with the passage of the Transportation Act by the British Parliament in 1718. That legislation gave courts the option of shipping to North America those found guilty of "clergyable offenses" and petty larceny.[21] More than 50,000 came over in the first 75 years of the 18th century,[22] 80% of them ending up in Virginia and Maryland, where they generally worked in the tobacco fields. The usual term of service was 14 years, double or quadruple the typical term for indentured servants.

As to the remaining immigrants, the roughly 25% who arrived as free men and women, the fact that they could afford the three- to six-pound fare did not mean they were wealthy. Nor did it suggest their existence had been easy before they left home. The voyage across the Atlantic was arduous and nightmarish, and few embarked simply because they had a sense of adventure.

The trips, which lasted between four weeks and four months, were often storm-tossed. Each adult was allotted a space below deck of six feet by two feet and would only be allowed to enjoy the fresh air a few hours a day. There was no privacy, no ventilation, no sanitation and likely no change of clothes. Depending on the time of the year, it was either stifling or frigid in the hold, and it was damp and lice-infested irrespective of the season. The food and drink were of limited quantity and poor quality. The biscuits often contained worms or spiders' nests, and when the rations ran out, rats and mice were sometime substitutes. The water was fetid. The sounds of moaning and shrieking were inescapable, as was disease and death.[23] The willingness of the "fare paying" emigrants to endure these hardships en route to an unknown destination is a measure of how unsatisfactory their lives must have been.

Many of these "fare paying" emigrants, who came principally from England, Germany, Ireland and Scotland,[24] felt impelled to leave to better their standard of living. In England, the population had expanded far faster than the economy, and its most important manufacturing sector, the cloth industry, languished in the face of competition from the continent. Wages declined as rents and food prices rose. In the countryside, where four-fifths of British families lived between 1530 and 1630, half were fenced out by their feudal masters under a policy of "enclosure."[25] Surveys of passengers leaving England for America in the 1770's reveal that fewer than 8% described themselves as being in categories at the top of the occupational scale, as contrasted with 20% describing themselves as "Labor" and 44% acknowledging they were tradesmen or craftsmen with only ordinary skills – bakers, plasterers, waiters, button makers.[26] "[M]any, perhaps the majority, who came . . . lived near the margin of British society."[27]

Religious intolerance provided another push for some who left England. For example, English Catholics were precluded from holding public office and subject to criminal penalty for openly practicing their faith, the root of the enmity being their suspected allegiance to their co-religionists in France and Spain, Great Britain's mortal enemies. Many landed in Maryland, founded in 1634 by Lord Calvert as a Catholic refuge. While the English Catholics objected to the Church of England for not being Catholic enough, the English Puritans found the Church of England to be *too* Catholic. During the 1630s thousands of them fled to New England in the so-called Great Migration, driven out by a crown-sanctioned reign of terror authorizing the dismissal of Puritan ministers, the prosecution of Puritan laypeople and the censoring of Puritan tracts. The Quakers were also victims of English bigotry and found a haven in the late 1600s in William Penn's new colony.

Like the English, the emigrating Germans, Irish and Scots were peoples who "could not stand further oppression whether in poverty or persecution."[28]

As had happened in England, the growth of the population in the Germanic states outstripped the demand for labor, creating a surplus of agricultural workers and unskilled craftsmen, the "poor and middling" at the lower end of the socio-economic scale.[29] In addition, many of the rulers of the German principalities fined and imprisoned those who did not subscribe to their religious beliefs. As to the Irish, with the ascendancy of William of Orange, the largely Presbyterian Ulstermen[30] were punished simply because they were not Anglicans: barred from civil and military positions, removed from certain other posts and heavily taxed to support the Church of England. Further, the Crown's discrimination against key elements of the Irish economy – wool, cattle and linen – caused financial hardship and another motivation for leaving home. It was basically economics that prompted the Scots to travel West. They were poorer than the English, made up of Lowlanders, who were struggling artisans and farmers, and Highlanders, who were coping with rising rents that depressed an already failing rural economy.

In short, during the period from 1600 to 1775 the British colonies of North America served as "a refuge for the victims of religious, political and economic oppression."[31] At the same time it was a dumping ground that meant servitude for arriving Africans, minor criminals and those who could not afford the price of passage. All in all, the overwhelming majority of the early immigrants were underdogs when they left home or when they got off the boat or both.

Against this backdrop it is not surprising that among the key figures in the struggle for independence were some whose beginnings were extremely harsh. Still the most famous of them is Benjamin Franklin: statesman, politician, scientist and philosopher. His achievements are legion: inventor of the stove and discoverer of electricity; publisher of the *Pennsylvania Gazette* and *Poor Richard's Almanac*; president of the American Philosophical Society and of what would become the University of Pennsylvania; first Postmaster General; Minister to France and Sweden; "President" of Pennsylvania; signer of the Declaration of Independence.

Franklin was born on January 17, 1706. One of 17 children, he was the eighth child and youngest son from Josiah Franklin's second marriage. Enrolled initially in the Boston Latin School, he was soon withdrawn from that college preparatory program and sent to a Boston teacher to learn more basic skills, a course of study that came to an abrupt and early end when he failed to master mathematics. His formal education over, at the age of 10 Benjamin began working for his father, a candle-maker in the Massachusetts Bay Colony. After two years of "cutting wick for the candles, filling the dipping mold and the molds for cast candles, attending the shop, going of errands, etc,"[32] with a minimal detour in the cutler's trade, he entered into a nine-year unpaid apprenticeship with his brother James, a printer. While the printing business took, Benjamin's relationship with his brother foundered. As Franklin recounted, James frequently "demean'd" and "often beat[]" him.[33] When at the age of 17 "a fresh difference" arose between the two, Benjamin left his brother's employ.³⁴ James responded vindictively by insuring that no local printer would hire him. Nor was his father a source of much support. The precocious 19-year-old came to the attention of the Governor of Pennsylvania, who promised to "procure me the public business" of his colony if the elder Franklin set him up in a shop; Josiah refused.³⁵ Though he hardly had the wind at his back, he went off to London to perfect his craft and begin the process of transforming himself into America's first international celebrity.

If Benjamin Franklin was the consummate polymath, Thomas Paine was the ultimate one-trick pony. His celebrated revolutionary pamphlet *Common Sense* became an immediate best seller, with 150,000 copies in circulation soon after publication.³⁶ John Adams once said: "Without the pen of the author of *Common Sense*, the sword of Washington would have been raised in vain."³⁷

Born 21 years after Franklin, on January 29, 1737, Thomas's parents were the former Francis Cocke and Joseph Pain. While his mother's family was middle class, his father's was no better than upper lower class. The Pains rented a modest, thatch-roofed cottage near the jail in a parish 80 miles northeast of London. Joseph owned a small farm and was a staymaker, supplying the body armor 18th century women wore to cinch in their waists and prop up their busts.³⁸ Thomas attended the local grammar school on funds borrowed from his unmarried aunt. At 12 or 13 his formal education stopped, and he became apprenticed to his father.

Paine spent the years until he turned 20 helping Joseph out in his shop, making stays in London and signing on as shipmate on an English privateer. At 20 he was back in the capital city and, having squandered the prize money from his sea-faring adventure, was without funds and much sense of direction. While Paine's mind prospered over the next 18 years, nothing else in his life did. Overall it was a period of instability, disappointment and failure. For the first three years he made stays in London, Dover and Sandwich. He also got married, but his wife, a maid and an orphan, died in childbirth. After her death, he decided to become an Excise Officer. His first stint ended in 1765, when he was dismissed for falsifying an inspection. After a hiatus spent stay-making and teaching, he was re-instated in 1768. His second stint ended six years later, with a warrant for his arrest for taking an extended, unauthorized leave from his post. During this latter period he also bankrupted a grocery business he inherited from his father-in-law and became separated from his second wife.

In 1774, Paine returned to London virtually penniless, unattached and without prospects. While there he presented himself to an American agent he had met during one of his earlier spells in the City. For all his haplessness, Thomas Paine was intellectually impressive, and the agent described him "as an ingenious worthy young man" in a letter of introduction to the Governor of New Jersey.³⁹ The agent was Benjamin Franklin.

Like Thomas Paine, John Paul Jones grew up in the British Isles. Though Paine's time at sea was an adventurous detour, for Jones the sea defined his life. Best remembered for his daring naval exploits, Jones engineered the capture of scores of British vessels during the War of Independence.[40] These victories earned him the title of "The Father of the American Navy."

"Jones" was born in Arbigland, Scotland on July 6, 1747 to John and Jeannie Paul and, like his father, he was named simply "John Paul." John Paul Sr. was the head gardener, what today would be called a landscape architect, on the estate of William Craik. Though undoubtedly extremely skilled and "indispensable" to his master, John Paul Sr. nevertheless was a member of the servant class.[41] Jeannie Paul worked as a housekeeper for William Craik, and at least one serious biographer has speculated that John Paul Jr. may have actually been an illegitimate son of the master.[42]

The Pauls lived in a small, whitewashed, stone, "gardener's cottage."[43] While their house may well have been neat and convenient, it was at most times cramped, as the Pauls had five children. Little is known about Jones' childhood.[44] It is guessed that he went barefoot most of the year and wore rough woolen clothes that had belonged either to his older brothers or to one of the boys from the manor house. There is no information about what kind of education he may have had. What is clear is that in 1761, when Jones was 13, he left home and signed a seven-year apprenticeship as a "ship's boy" on the brig *Friendship*.[45] Jones would rather have gone to sea as a mid-shipman – a "young gentleman" – in the Royal Navy, but neither he nor his family had the "social connections" or funds to pursue that course.[46]

By the terms of his indenture, Jones received no pay but did master the skills of his chosen career. In 1764, at the age of 17, he was released from the remainder of his apprenticeship. In 1768 he was made captain of the *John*. In 1771 he was made captain of the *Betsy*. Both commands involved commercial travel from England to the Caribbean, and each resulted in murder charges being brought against him. In the case of the *John*, Mungo Maxwell, the ship's carpenter, was flogged by Jones for being lazy or careless or disrespectful. When Mungo died en route home, Maxwell's father attributed his death to Jones' flogging and had Jones arrested and jailed. Though Jones was eventually cleared, the episode was humiliating. In the case of the *Betsy*, Jones was attacked with a bludgeon by a man he dubbed "the Ringleader," for refusing to immediately pay the crew for the completed first leg of the journey to Tobago. In apparent self-defense, Jones picked up his sword and killed the advancing mutineer. On the advice of friends, who feared Jones would not receive a fair trial on the island home of his victim, he fled.[47] He left with only 50 pounds in cash.

The 20 months following his flight are a blur. We know Jones' Tobago friends never sent him the money they had promised. We know he was in Virginia, probably in the winter of 1774, and discovered that his brother who had settled there had died and left his entire estate to their sister in Scotland. We know that his peril was such that he had been advised to travel "Incog" and that he was using the name of "John Jones."[48]

SETTING THE STAGE

As with Thomas Paine, at this low point in his life John Paul Jones managed to impress a prominent American, in his case, Joseph Hewes. Hewes was a partner in a ship-owning concern, a fellow Mason, and North Carolina's representative at the Second Continental Congress. He was also an "influential member" of the seven-man Maritime Committee charged with building a Continental Fleet and choosing its officers.[49] In this capacity, Hewes was instrumental in having "John Paul Jones, Esq." commissioned on December 7, 1775, as a first lieutenant on the *Alfred*, the appointment marking the beginning of his service to the revolutionary cause.[50]

In terms of breadth of achievement, Alexander Hamilton was more like Benjamin Franklin than Thomas Paine or John Paul Jones. During the Revolution Hamilton raised and commanded an artillery company which took part in the fighting in and around New York City, served for four years as General Washington's aide-de-camp and participated heroically in the Battle of Yorktown. After the War, he was elected a delegate to the Constitutional Convention, wrote 51 of the 85 *Federalist Papers* and became the nation's first Secretary of the Treasury. He also founded the Bank of New York and the *New York Post*.

Nevis, a tiny island in the British West Indies, is generally accepted to be the place where Alexander Hamilton was born on January 11, 1755.[51] Ten years before his birth, his mother, the former Rachel Faucette, had married Johann Michael Lavien. They settled on St. Croix and had a son they named Peter. Lavien, a fortune hunter, was already in debt when he met Rachel and during their years together he recklessly spent most of his wife's money. In 1750 Rachel walked out on her feckless husband and young son and decided to start a new life on St. Kitts. This decision was both bold and rash. It not only led to her immediate arrest, but meant that after her release she could not legally remarry and, therefore, that any other children she might subsequently have would be deemed illegitimate.

Rachel met James Hamilton in 1750, shortly after she left Lavien. Though Hamilton's father was the laird of a massive estate in Scotland, as the fourth son, none of this property would devolve to him. James failed to master the textile trade in Glasgow or to succeed as a planter or merchant on St. Kitts. At the time he and Rachel began keeping company, James was reduced to working as a watchman or weighman By 1752 they were presenting themselves to the world as man and wife. In 1753 Alexander's older brother James Jr. arrived, but James' economic fortunes did not improve as his young family grew. Fifteen years into the relationship, in 1765, James abandoned Rachel and their boys.[52] To support herself and her sons, Rachel leased a two-story house, using the upper floor for lodging and converting the lower floor into a small grocery.

Over the next 48 months Alexander and his brother suffered an unspeakable cavalcade of tragedies. In 1766 their aunt Anne Lytton died, in 1768 their mother Rachel died, and in 1769 their cousin (and guardian) Peter Lytton and their uncle James Lytton died. None of the prosperous Lyttons made any provision for the Hamilton boys in their wills. As to Rachel's estate, because of the unrefuted allegations of illegitimacy underlying the divorce proceedings brought by Lavien in 1759,[53] all of her assets were awarded to Peter Lavien, the son whom she had not seen in 18 years.

Alexander Hamilton was 14 in 1769, without parents or close relatives, without a home and without any source of income. As with Thomas Paine and John Paul Jones, at this critical juncture Alexander's drive and ability attracted a group of older admirers. They included Thomas Stevens, a successful businessman, who gave him a home and a family;[54] "Beekman and Cruger," New York-based merchants, who provided him with a job; his cousin Anne Lytton, who offered him emotional ballast; and Hugh Knox, a Princeton-trained school teacher *cum* minister, who supervised his education. And these patrons were likely the principal source of the funds collected to send Alexander to British North America, where he would have the chance to make for himself a new and better life.[55]

These four heroes of the Revolution were all born into obscure families with limited financial resources. They grew up in very different places: one in colonial America, one in rural England, one in coastal Scotland and one on the Islands of the British West Indies. And, along the way, each faced additional, and very different, impediments to their success: Franklin, an indifferent father and a mean-spirited brother; Paine a succession of mind-numbing, dead-end jobs; Jones, legal entanglements attributable in part to his volatile temperament; Hamilton, social stigma, financial and emotional instability and abandonments. They also had much in common. They all entered into apprenticeships when they were barely teenagers. They all were avid readers, adept writers and essentially self-taught. They all acquired well-placed mentors. And they all were determined to defy the limited expectations about how far they would get in the world. Fortunately, they lived in a century where fierce determination was encouraged, an "Age of Enlightenment" whose central premise was that success would be based on merit, not the accident of birth.

The lives of these four men are, in a way, a microcosm of the Revolution which became such a central part of their legacies. At the beginning, what were the odds that either they or their cause would succeed? On paper, there is no question that the English were the prohibitive favorite to win the war instigated by their North American colonies. However, like baseball, battles are played out on grass, or a reasonable facsimile thereof, where paper advantages often matter little.

In 1775 the world was a dozen years into a mostly peaceful period, ushered in by Britain's defeat of France and Spain in the Seven Years War. At that moment England was the preeminent nation on earth, *the* global super power. It had a strong central government and a functioning bicameral legislature. It had a standing army made up of officers and enlisted men who chose soldiering as their life's work. And it had a Navy that ruled the seas. The English forces were well-trained, well-armed, well-clothed and well-fed.

SETTING THE STAGE

On the other side of the Atlantic were the 13 English colonies. With their differing economies and diverse populations, they were not united in 1775 and never had been. The one attempt at creating a structure for coordinated action, sponsored by Benjamin Franklin on the eve of the French and Indian War, had gotten nowhere. They had a few men who had served in that war, among them a young George Washington, but there were no professional soldiers and those in the local militias were the 18th century equivalent of weekend warriors, amateurs who played army only part-time. As the first battle was about to take place these Americans had a pronounced distaste for establishing a "sovereign national government" and little appetite for creating a professional military.[56] Moreover, more than half of the colonists were indifferent to independence or actively supported the King.

There were a host of reasons why, despite all this, Great Britain did not win in a rout. To begin with, the British government misconceived its colonial enemy in two fundamental ways. First, a combination of poor intelligence and wishful thinking led to the belief that the desire for independence was localized, essentially confined to New England and, even within that region, limited to a small subset of the population.[57] Second, whether out of the unhappy experiences during the French and Indian War or as a result of sheer arrogance, the ragtag rebel forces were regarded as hopelessly and totally outclassed by the spit and polish English regulars.[58]

The British also did not fully appreciate the challenges of attempting to suppress an uprising thousands of miles away. Because they had underestimated the extent of the rebellion, they overestimated their ability to live off the land, counting on a mass of still loyal subjects to provide forage, nourishment and shelter. Over time they realized that the only reliable supplies would come from home, tethering them to the coast and making them hostage to the vagaries of transatlantic shipping. They also failed to recognize that to put down a colonial revolt "required a numerical superiority on the order of three to one, or greater."[59] As one English scholar explained: "Britain had an army of conquest, but not an army of occupation. It conquered every major city during the war, but there were insufficient troops to retain and police large areas of territory against a popular rebellion."[60]

In this connection, England relied too much on Hessian mercenaries and too late or too little on indigenous resources. The problem with the Hessians was that they did not speak the language, which meant they could not communicate with the colonial population. Moreover, the very resort to hired guns was resented and had the effect of galvanizing the rebels. With respect to free local talent, the English did not arm the Tories until about 1780, when some of their initial enthusiasm had waned, and they did not arm the African-American slaves at all, using them mainly behind the lines and doing that only sparingly.

There were also complications in applying and adapting the established English command structure to the distant American war. Top-level responsibility for operations was divided among several ministers based in London, meaning that the decision-makers had to reach a consensus before they could do anything and were always weeks behind on what was really going on across the ocean. Moreover, the British army and navy had separate hierarchies and, particularly within the army, there was a lack of effective coordination, in part because of the personal enmity among some of the senior officers.

The Americans had two ultimate advantages: George Washington as their commander and France as their ally. "[F]ortune smiled on the infant nation when Washington was selected to lead it into this war."[61] Through failure, as much as success, George Washington had learned much and continued to grow over time. He was without fear, largely selfless, an excellent judge of talent, a superb administrator, a deft politician and a dedicated patriot. The French, who intervened on the rebel side in 1778, provided funds, personnel, armaments and a naval fleet, permitting the Americans to continue to fight even after their economy was in ruins. They supplied, as well, superb senior officers who were content to work in concert with and under the direction of their colonial counterparts.

The net of all this is that the odds in favor of the British were not as lopsided as they first seemed. It did not mean the rebels were likely to win. It did mean that they had a sporting chance.

What is striking about the Revolutionary War is how often timely rebel victories followed decisive rebel defeats. Just when it seemed that the English had the upper hand, the Americans would somehow rebound and reassert themselves.

- The British prevail at Lexington and Concord, but are virtually routed by American snipers on their way back to Boston.
- The British gain control of New York City, yet almost the entire American force manages to flee to New Jersey and Delaware.
- The British successfully besiege Charleston, decisively defeating the Americans, only to see them regroup and win at King's Mountain and Cowpens.

At the time of the pivotal showdown at Yorktown, a full six years after the firing of the "shot heard 'round the world,"[62] it was still anybody's war. Had it ended in a stalemate, it is not apparent how much longer the British Parliament or the French king would have carried on. Ironically, neither of the commanding generals – George Washington for the Americans or Henry Clinton for the British – was enamored of having a climactic encounter in Tidewater Virginia.[63] Nonetheless, it was at Yorktown in the latter part of 1781 where it all came together for the rebels and all fell apart for the English.

SETTING THE STAGE

There were in effect two battles of Yorktown, one on the water in early September and one on land in mid-October, and England could have won them both. As to the marine phase, the British vastly underestimated the size of the French fleet and issued contradictory signals as to the rules of engagement. When the cannons stopped firing, the British had suffered 336 casualties to France's 209, and six of the 19 British ships were rendered unfit for further action, as compared to just four of France's 24.[64] More significantly, the British dawdled getting their fleet back to shore, allowing the French to blockade the coast, thereby depriving the English army of an escape route to the sea if it were besieged.

As to the land phase, the Americans succeeded brilliantly in coordinating with their French allies and executing an overland march[65] of 8,000 men to supplement the rebel forces already in place. By contrast, the two English generals were unable to work together, and the relief force of 7,149,[66] which would have essentially equalized the size of the two armies, failed to be shipped from New York on time.[67] The result was that by the end of September, the rebel forces numbered 16,650, and the British forces numbered 7,400, a numerical advantage that would not change and was determinative.

By mid-October, after days of emplacing fortifications, diversionary feints, bloody skirmishes and fierce fighting, it was plain that a rebel victory was imminent. Cornwallis saw one possible last chance to evade the inevitable: cross the York Creek on the north of town, break through the American lines and make way to New York and safety. At 10 or 11 pm on the night of October 16, Cornwallis managed to ferry a British contingent across the river. Then Mother Nature chose sides, unleashing a terrible storm that scattered Cornwallis' small flotilla of vessels and made another crossing impossible. The next morning Cornwallis initiated a cease fire.

It took another two years, until September 3, 1783, for the parties to sign the Treaty of Paris and formally end the hostilities. Almost exactly two months after that, on November 2, 1783, George Washington voiced his "astonishment" that the Americans had won, saying it was "little short of a standing miracle."[63]

The fact that we are a nation of immigrants, that most who came here were no strangers to struggle, and that from these raw materials emerged a country that is the envy of the world; the fact that among the heroic and iconic figures who helped birth our republic were men who emerged from that improbable pool; the fact that this undistinguished populace with its citizen soldiers managed to defy the odds and make history by wresting its independence from an implacable, vastly superior foe; somehow all of this, whether at a conscious or subliminal level, bears on why we as Americans root so hard for underdogs and take such pleasure when they succeed or even when falling short have fought the good fight. Whatever the psychological mechanics, there is little question that our devout fondness for underdogs is baked into our collective DNA.

PART TWO

Underdog Greats

The stories which follow deal with underdogs who made it to the pinnacle of three glamorous, long-shot, quintessentially-American careers. They recount the early years of some of the greatest ballplayers, movie stars and Presidents of all time. What these men have in common is what they lacked growing up: economic comfort and social status. Some of them were truly disadvantaged, others merely *un*-advantaged; none was wealthy. And not one had parents who were "professionals" or had what could be reasonably regarded as a significant calling. Most had to cope with other adversities, as well: alcoholism; the loss of a mother, a father or both; racial or religious discrimination; severe illness; abuse. All were what I think of as underdogs in the game of life.

These biographies stop where most begin in earnest, at about the 18th year, the point at which these young men were in some form or fashion "on their own," or just about to be. The narratives detail their humble beginnings – where they lived, what they wore, the food they ate, their parents' occupations. Though all were un-privileged, that did not mean they were unhappy or that they saw themselves as poor. That said, their standard of living was extremely basic and uniformly without frills. In order to paint a complete and rounded portrait, there is much on the relationships these boys had with the significant people in their lives, on what their schooling was like and on the things they did outside the classroom, particularly those activities and experiences that bear upon the paths they would ultimately take. Because I wanted to choose from the absolute best ballplayers, movie stars and Presidents and to be utterly objective on that score, I relied entirely on the opinions of knowledgeable authorities to come up with rankings in each of these fields. And because the odds of succeeding in one of these fairy-tale careers seem like the odds of winning the lottery, I thought it would be interesting to take a stab at calculating what the mathematical probabilities really were.

I. On the Diamond

Because baseball lends itself to statistical analysis, many students of the game have tried to assess the relative performance of major league players. In arriving at a list of the 20 all-time great ballplayers, I used 12 sources, although there are obviously countless others that could have been consulted.[1] Some of these sports scholars numerically rank the top 100, others just rank the top 10, others just name a small group of those they deem elites, without ranking them at all. Listed below is the top 20 based on these dozen sources.

1. Babe Ruth*	11. Joe DiMaggio
2. Willie Mays	12. Rogers Hornsby
3. Henry Aaron*	13. Christy Mathewson
4. Ty Cobb	14. Barry Bonds
5. Ted Williams*	15. Cy Young
6. Lou Gehrig	16. Tris Speaker
7. Honus Wagner	17. Jimmie Foxx
8. Stan Musial*	18. Mike Schmidt
9. Mickey Mantle*	19. Josh Gibson*
10. Walter Johnson	20. Lefty Grove

The six players with asterisks after their names will be the subject of the biographies which follow, starting with Gibson and proceeding in reverse ranked order. In addition, I have included a seventh biography, one of Roberto Clemente, who ranked 28th in the composite study. He was added as a "Wild Card" in order to recognize one of the first and most prominent ballplayers of Hispanic origin.

Three of the seven men profiled spent all or most of their careers in the American League, three in the National League and one in the Negro League. Putting aside Babe Ruth's stint as a pitcher with the Boston Red Sox, all were position players by the time they got to the majors.[2]

Josh Gibson
December 21, 1911-January 23, 1947
Career span: 1929-46
Catcher: Crawford Giants; Homestead Grays
Key Statistics: BA: .351; HR: 224; H: 1,010
Signal Honor: Hall of Fame, 1972.
Miscellaneous: "the Black Babe Ruth"

UNDERDOG GREATS

We know almost nothing about Josh Gibson's ancestry except that he was named after his paternal grandfather, who had been born a slave. Josh's father, Mark, lived in southwest Georgia, close to Atlanta, in a rural town with the picturesque name of Buena Vista, Spanish for "Good View." It is said that Mark Gibson's house, a wooden shack with no plumbing, was on Pineville Road in Puttville, a part of Buena Vista situated two miles southwest of the town limits. Whether Josh's grandfather lived in the same area is unclear, although former slave cabins still exist in these flatlands in the shadows of now-restored manor houses.

Mark Gibson married Nancy Woodlock. No wedding date is reported and little is known about her, except that she was large, like her husband. Josh, the first of their three children, was born on or about December 21, 1911. A second son, Jerry, was born in 1914. A daughter, Annie, was born in 1917. Mark and Nancy Gibson were sharecroppers.

Josh's childhood in Georgia is largely a mystery. He attended segregated schools from the first to fifth grades, where the quality of education, like the facilities, was poor. It appears that Josh, "a squat chunky boy with quick legs and strong wrists," began to play baseball even back then, likely shoeless, on dusty fields and with no equipment to speak of.[3]

In 1921, when Josh was nine, Mark Gibson left his family in Buena Vista and joined the many blacks who migrated up North to find a better life. He chose "the Smoky City" – Pittsburgh – where some of his relatives had settled. At the time, roughly 50,000 blacks lived in Pittsburgh, making up almost 10% of the population. Mark found a job as a steelworker at the Carnegie-Illinois mills, sending a portion of his paycheck back home to his family. Three years later, he had saved enough money to retrieve his wife and children. Their move was the turning point in Josh's life. As he put it, in one of the few comments he ever made about his feelings, "The greatest gift Dad gave me was to get me out of the South."[4]

By the time the Mark's family rejoined him, he had bought a brick house on the North Side of Pittsburgh, across the Allegheny River from the downtown. The address was 2410 Strauss Street in a section known as Pleasant Valley. Like "Buena Vista," "Pleasant Valley" was a misnomer: the air was polluted by the soot from the mills and the homes, built right up to the sidewalks, were sited on an elevated series of steep hills.

Josh was 12 years old when he got to Pittsburgh, and he was enrolled in the sixth grade in the electrical studies program of the Allegheny Pre-Vocational School. A year later, he transferred to a similar program at the Conroy Pre-Vocational School. Josh spent most of his young life in the streets and playgrounds, where he developed his athletic skills. When he first arrived in town one of his favorite pastimes was roller skating up and down the neighborhood inclines. He also liked swimming and diving, and won several contests at the local public pools. And though he was stocky, he was a good runner, winning track awards, as well. As to team sports, he showed no interest in either football or basketball, though both were popular in the area. But baseball was different. It appealed to him in part because he was good at it and in part because it was a career that even then provided a way for a person of color to make a decent living and achieve a measure of respectability.

Josh left school after ninth grade, at the age of 16, to help support his family. He began working as an apprentice electrician at Westinghouse Airbrake, a supplier of railway equipment. A short time later he joined his father at the Carnegie-Illinois mills. By this time, Josh had been transformed from a flabby boy to a broad-shouldered, six-foot-two-inch man. He had a thick neck and strong legs, physical attributes suited to – and enhanced by – his backbreaking job at the mills. He was uniformly described as a dutiful, effective, friendly and even-tempered employee.

At 16, Josh not only had to take on more responsibilities outside the house, but also inside it. His father, who was as physically imposing as his son, had begun to feel listless, to the point that he frequently could not go to work. It is now thought that he was suffering from high blood pressure, or hypertension, a condition that, at the time, was neither diagnosed nor treated by a doctor. His mother, a domineering woman when sober, was even more difficult to handle after the frequent parties she held, where liquor was freely flowing. Often in the morning, Josh found both his parents in bed, dead to the world, his father because of his illness, his mother due to a hangover. It fell to Josh to make breakfast for his younger brother and sister and send them off to school. It made him hate being home.

Baseball provided relief from the turmoil and burdens. As early as 1927, while still in school, Josh began playing for a local sandlot team, the Pleasant Valley Red Sox. Once he began working, he played for company teams, initially for Westinghouse Airbrake and then for Carnegie-Illinois. Josh's first turn at "organized" baseball was with an all-black recreational squad sponsored by Gimbels department store. Because of his size, strength and quickness he was initially installed as the catcher, but after being moved all around the diamond, eventually landed at third base. While his fielding was only adequate, he hit the long ball with enough frequency and power that Gimbels hired him as an elevator operator just so he could continue to wear their colors.

In the world of Negro baseball in the Pittsburgh of the late Twenties, the "hot team" was the Crawford Giants. It had been founded by the Crawford Bath House, a community center located in the Hill district where Josh lived. In the early years its players, mostly black teenagers, performed community service, such as delivering holiday baskets at Christmastime, in keeping with the center's mission. Because the Crawfords were not funded by a manufacturing plant or a steel mill or a department store, the team's survival depended on the generosity of the black businessmen in the area, which by the mid-Twenties was beginning to wane. As the club was on the verge of collapse, William Augustus "Gus" Greenlee stepped into the breach. A flamboyant mobster, Greenlee owned a successful night club located on the Hill and ran the area's numbers rackets. Greenlee supplied the capital that saved the team from oblivion, and by 1926 the Crawfords had become the pre-eminent semi-pro organization in the city. They were only "semi-pro" because the players were unsalaried, their earnings limited to the money collected by passing the hat during games.

Josh's life changed forever when Harold "Hooks" Tinker, the Crawford center fielder, discovered him. In 1927, Tinker had also become the Crawford's player-manager, when the previous skipper found better prospects as a runner in Gus Greenlee's gambling empire. Sometime the following Spring, Tinker attended an industrial league all-star game because two of his Crawford teammates had been named to the squad. Though only 16, Josh had been named to the squad as well. As Tinker recalled years later, that was the day that he first saw Josh on the diamond:

> He was playin' third base, and he was very mature in his actions. . . .[H]e was a power hitter even then. His last time at bat he hit one over the top of the mountain in back of center field. I'll never forget that, because that's when I knew we had to have him with our Crawford team.[5]

After the game, Tinker asked Josh whether he would "'like to play with a real baseball team?' and Josh replied 'Yes sir.'"[6] Upon joining the Crawfords, Josh was moved from the "hot corner" to behind the plate to avoid displacing their talented and popular third baseman. There is disagreement as to how good Josh was as a catcher. Some said he was ham-fisted, more like a "boxer" than a fielder, at least at the outset. Tinker saw it differently, describing Josh as a "natural" from the beginning: "He came in as if he had been catchin' all his life. Good arm, good head."[7]

But there was never any disagreement about Josh's skills as a hitter. From the time of his arrival, he was rocketing the ball over the fences during batting practice, standing on the right side of the box using an extra-heavy bat. As to the source of his skills, no one can improve on Tinker's take:

> He had quick wrists. He could hold that bat down on the end, with his pinky over the handle, and wait on the pitch. Then he'd just meet the ball right; he wouldn't need to try and kill it 'cause if he met it his muscle would do the rest. That was the key for him, mak'in the contact. . .
>
> That's why his stride was short, like Joe DiMaggio's was. He spread out real wide, which made him even more balanced and his vision on an even line, no bouncin', no twistin'. He didn't move a muscle 'til the ball was almost in on him. That's why you couldn't fool him with a curveball, and you

couldn't get a fastball by him. He was like a reflex, a nerve jumpin' all at once. I'm tellin' you, the Lord made the boy to hit a baseball.[8]

One of the best examples of this God-given talent was again provided by Tinker. The Crawfords were playing a team from nearby McKeesport, Pennsylvania, and they were leading 3-2 in the third inning. The Crawfords were clawing back and had runners on first and second, when Josh came up to bat. Because he already had a reputation as a power hitter, the McKeesport manager decided to intentionally walk him, even though it would load the bases. After looking at two outside pitches, Josh asked the umpire for a timeout so he could visit Tinker, who was on second base. Josh whispered, "Hooks, I can hit the pitch he's throwin'."[9] The manager told him to just take the base on balls. Josh continued to insist, and Tinker finally relented. The rest is the stuff of legend. Josh was thrown another outside pitch, and he stepped into it, driving it over the center field fence. Recounting the story when he was a much older man, Tinker still spoke with amazement: "Damn. It was one of the most tremendous home runs I ever saw him hit, and the people there almost fainted. I couldn't believe it myself."[10]

By 1928 Josh had chosen baseball as his life's work, though he still ran the elevator at Gimbels on his days off. Because the Crawfords could not charge admission, he likely made little more than a few dollars a day for his efforts on the field. But with a summer season that could produce as many as 100 games, those dollars were adding up to the beginnings of a livelihood. Frequent playing also helped Josh learn his craft. Whether on the bench or in the field, he always carefully observed his teammates and opponents. He watched what players did when they had the ball and when they did not. He took in how they concentrated, talked to their teammates, argued with umpires. He learned the way catchers crouched, threw and called pitches, and the way batters moved, stood, waited and swung. He became a serious student of the game.

Off the field, despite the temptations and dangers of the Hill District, Josh was said to be a "fine boy," still young and unaffected, still preferring an ice cream cone to a stiff drink.[11] In 1928 he had met Helen Mason, a pretty girl of 16, who lived around the corner from Ammon Field where the Crawfords played. Helen had two sisters, Dolly who was older and Rebecca who was younger. All three of the girls attended Schenley High School. Their father, James, repaired pipes for the city water company. Rebecca recalled that her dad "thought a million dollars" of Josh, because he was so nice, manly and respectful.[12] She also observed that Josh "seemed to want to be with our family more than his own."[13] And so he was. On March 7, 1929, Josh married Helen. He moved in with the Masons on his wedding night and never lived with his parents again.

The Crawfords were "taking on the look of a pro operation" by the time that Josh joined them.[14] Gus Greenlee used his muscle to encourage other Hill big shots to become backers. The result was the players got real uniforms, free motorized transportation to and from the games (on a dedicated ice truck), regulation baseballs and new bats, like the 40-inch, 44-ounce edition made-to-order for Josh. The Crawfords' popularity was such that the 5,000-seat stadium often overflowed with fans. The turnout on Memorial Day 1930 reportedly hit 6,000. While the money was pitiful – even that Memorial Day crowd netted the team only $6 – the competition was first rate. In mid-June, W.O.W., the winner of the Greater Pittsburgh Semipro Tournament, journeyed to Ammon Field to play the Crawfords.[15] When it was all over, the black amateurs had beaten the premier white semi-pros 9-8 in a thriller. The contest, treated by the *Courier* as big news, listed Josh "Gipson" as catcher. It failed to mention that the teenage cleanup batter hit a pair of doubles and a pair of singles in his first four plate appearances.

The Crawfords' big dream was to take on the Homestead Grays for hometown bragging rights. The Grays' owner, Cumberland "Cum" Posey, had little interest in a match with amateurs: there was little money in it, and it violated protocol. However, the Crawfords had undeniable talent, which the Grays could use. So as early as 1928 Cum intimated to Hooks that a showdown at 40,000-seat Forbes Field might be arranged. This tantalizing possibility was enough to dazzle Hooks into agreeing to be the "feeder" for Posey, turning over to the Grays any Crawford player they asked for.[16] To make sure Cum had a clear view of Hooker's best prospects, in 1929 Cum embedded his brother Seward – "See" – into the Crawfords' management. When by mid-1930, Cum had still not committed to the Crawfords/Grays showdown, Tinker was wise to the fact that there would be no such game until his most promising acquisition, Josh Gibson, had switched uniforms.

Hooks was torn about what to do on the inevitable day when Josh was given the option to become a real professional. On the one hand, he wanted the best for Josh, and a steady income with the Grays would certainly be a good thing for a young man with a new wife. On the other, Hooks truly believed that Josh, like many of his players, were happy where they were because they got to do what they enjoyed most at a high level with people that really cared for one another. The Crawfords "gave them a family they didn't have at home."[17] It would not be the same with the Grays. Though Posey was shrewd enough to portray Homestead as "arrow straight," the truth was anything but.[18] Cum was a philanderer, and his players were "rough guys," hard-drinkers and serious carousers off the field.[19] And on the field, they did whatever they could to gain an advantage: wearing blousy shirts to get hit by a pitch, stealing bases with spikes high, cursing and name-calling, doctoring the baseball with whatever substance was available. The Grays were a mean and nasty bunch, and Tinker was genuinely worried about what would happen to Josh if he took his big break.

In July 1930 the moment arrived when the Grays needed an extra catcher. The Crawfords were playing against a white team in Ingomar, Pennsylvania, and had built up a 15-run lead. Josh had had another of his impressive performances, smashing two triples and a homer. See Posey, who seldom attended away games, was there and offered Josh a spot with the Grays. Josh asked Tinker what to do, and Tinker, despite his qualms, told him to go. All Tinker got for his trouble was a commitment that the long-postponed Crawford-Grays match would get played.

There are a variety of stories about the circumstances surrounding Josh's actual "debut" with the Grays. The most dramatic had Josh in the stands watching a portion of a night game, pitting the Grays against the Kansas City Monarchs. The poles on which the new-fangled lights were strung were not particularly tall, creating shadows in which the ball could get lost. Recognizing this limitation, the pitcher, Smokey Joe Williams, said he would only throw fastballs and curves, and the catcher, Buck Ewing, should point his glove up for a fastball and down for curve. After a few innings, the simple signals got crossed, and Buck injured his hand because of the mix-up. Cum asked for backup from his outfielder Vic Harris, who refused, having no interest in getting hurt himself. Cum spotted Josh, eating hotdogs near the Grays dugout, still in his work clothes from the Edgar Thomson steel mills. Josh agreed to be put in, and he caught the rest of the game, not letting a single ball get by him. His last-minute stand-in performance was deemed "an incredible entry into the big time." [20]

Another version had Buck injuring his finger, but during an afternoon game while Josh was in Ingomar. In this one, Buck soldiered on, despite the injury. It was not till the next evening, at a game that *was* under the lights that Josh got in, changing from his Crawfords uniform into the Grays.' Josh had no impact on the game, failing to get a hit his two times at the plate.

A third version sets the scene at a twilight doubleheader with Dormont, a white semi-pro team as the opponent, not the black Monarchs. Buck Ewing did split a finger and Vic Harris agreed to fill-in as the catcher until Josh could be fetched by Vic's brother from the Crawfords. Josh was inserted into the lineup when they got back. His first start with the Grays occurred on the night of July 25, he and Buck both played, and each had a couple of at-bats.

Though by the end of July 1930 Josh's career with the Crawfords had ended, he did not immediately become a phenomenon with the Grays. The first week or so, the major challenge was learning how to pull his weight in the battery and adjust to the different throwing styles of the Grays' pitchers. Some said that in those early days he was more of a "blocker" than a "catcher," though from the beginning his throwing arm was true. Always seeking to improve his game, he adopted Judy "Jing" Johnson as his mentor, continually asking him to tell what he did wrong.[21] Though Jing was a contemporary of Josh's, he took to the role and helped the eager kid, talking through the games, teaching him the angles, discussing strategies and coaching him on the little moves that would make him a better player. Whatever his weaknesses, Josh was there to stay, and even after Buck Ewing's finger healed, he shared the catching duties, entering late in the game or playing the second half of doubleheaders. From time to time he was slotted in the outfield, rather than behind the plate. Given the powerful Gray hitters, he tended to be placed at sixth or seventh in the batting order.

Two and a half weeks after Josh was promoted to the Grays, on August 11, 1930, he received an urgent call at the ballpark from his sister-in-law, Dolly Mason. Dolly told him to go right to the hospital: his wife Helen, eight months pregnant with twins, had gone into premature labor. Helen had become unconscious at home, and by the time she had arrived at the hospital one of her kidneys had ruptured, causing poison to flood through her body. The doctor told the family that he could save the babies or, possibly Helen, but not both. Helen's mother left the decision to the doctor, who chose to deliver the twins. Josh arrived, screaming that he wanted to try to save his wife. But it was too late.

When it was time to bring the infants home, Josh made it clear that he did not want them to be with his parents. So when Josh Jr. and little Helen were discharged from the hospital, they went straight to the Masons where they were looked after by their maternal aunts and grandmother. Josh rejoined the Grays, and he was soon back on the road. While he provided funds to his in-laws, Josh made no commitment to having a role in the upbringing of his children. He ended up being "an absentee father," seeing Josh Jr. and little Helen on the infrequent occasions when he was in town.[22] Josh's sister-in-law Rebecca later said, "I just thought that when Helen died, it looked like it took some of the energy out of him. That enthusiasm he had for life was gone. I don't think he was ever the same."[23]

On August 27 the long awaited showdown between the Grays and the Crawfords finally took place at Forbes Field. Despite the fact that the Grays were boasting a 33-game win streak, the Crawfords were their equal. The score was 3-2 in the seventh, and the Crawfords threatened in the eighth. The game was called because of darkness before the last inning was played, and the Grays escaped by the skin of their teeth. No one disputed Hooks, when after this premature ending, he said, "We shoulda won that game."[24] Or as the *Courier* headlining the "classic" contest wrote, "The losers clearly demonstrated the fact that they are dangerous contenders in the ranks of big-time colored baseball."[25]

Having barely survived his in-town rivals, Posey spent the next few weeks preparing for the self-described "championship match" with New York's Lincoln Giants.[26] Cum's "warm-up" took the form of a 14-day swing through the Midwest playing three of the Negro National League's best-known teams. It was during this tune-up that Josh began to hit his stride.

Posey's idea – his hope – was to demolish the competition on the tour and thereby gain the psychological edge for the encounter with the Giants. The

Grays performed to Cum's script in the first two games, beating the Detroit Stars by margins of 11-3 and 16-5. While the *Courier* trumpeted the lopsided scores, there was also a brief mention that the Grays' young black catcher produced four singles. Josh rode the bench in the first two contests with the next opponent, the St. Louis Stars, and the teams split, the Grays winning the opening game 10-6, the Stars winning the second game 9-1. In the rubber match, Josh finally made an appearance, batting seventh in the order. Though he did not heroically produce a victory – the Grays lost 6-5 – he did hit his first professional home run. While the shot was barely noted by the press, it was long remembered by Cool Papa Bell, the St. Louis center fielder, who said it cleared the short 250-feet porch in left field by some "four hundred and some feet."[27] Cum gradually found a regular spot for Josh in the field and, over time, moved him slightly up in the batting order. In mid-September, he caught both games in a doubleheader against the Baltimore Black Sox and recorded three hits.

The 10-game championship series with the Lincoln Giants began on September 20. To insure the world noticed, eight of the games were in major league parks, with the finale taking place in a weekend series at Yankee Stadium on September 27 and 28. Attendance ranged from 8,000 to 20,000.

During the course of the championship series, Gibson did not disappoint. He caught every game and his timely hitting contributed to the Grays' winning six of the 10 games. His batting average was a healthy .386 and included five home runs. The penultimate blast became known in the annals of Negro baseball as the "shot heard round the world."[28] Though at the time the feat was buried in the news, the Grays' victory being the main story-line, all who saw it agreed it was a monster blast. Some claimed that the ball was still rising when it went over the left field fence into the visitors' bullpen, others that it was the longest ball hit at Yankee Stadium that season and perhaps the longest ball *ever* hit there. Measurement estimates ranged from 460 to 600 feet, depending on whom you listened to.[29]

In the September 27 edition of the *Courier*, Rollo Wilson, their main scribe, used all but a third of his column to write about Josh Gibson. The content was all fanciful, with invented quotes – "a homer a day will boost my pay" – talk of the boy's Ruthian eating habits and made-up examples of his wicked repartee.[30] Nonetheless, it was favorable and substantial coverage.[31] Subsequent articles described Josh as the youngster "who had wrecked the Lincoln Giants."[32] Hometown reporters wrote that "the Lincoln boys still have headaches when they hear his name."[33] That one September series and single momentous home run had made Josh Gibson into a "sensation."[34]

But, it was just the beginning. Josh Gibson had been a real professional for a little more than two months. And that autumn, when the "Negro World Series" was over, he left town to travel the country playing exhibition games. He would not turn 19 until December 21.

Mickey Mantle
October 20, 1931-August 13, 1995
Career span: 1951-68
Center Fielder: New York Yankees
Key Statistics: BA: .298; RBI: 1509; HR: 536; H: 2,415
Signal Honors: Hall of Fame, 1974; Triple Crown, 1956; American League MVP, 1956, 1957, 1962; All-Star Appearances, 1952-65, 1967, 1968.
Nickname: "The Mick"

HEROES WITH HUMBLE BEGINNINGS

Mickey Mantle's great-grandfather, George Mantle, lived in Brierly Hill, a coal mining town in the West Midlands of England. In 1848, George and his family emigrated to the United States, landing in New Orleans and then taking a riverboat to St. Louis. Although he and his boys initially got jobs in the mines, after three years the family headed to the western part of Missouri to try their hand at farming and the grocery business. George's son Charles, Mickey's grandfather, moved to Oklahoma where he found work as a butcher. Charles and his wife Mae had four children. The eldest, born on March 16, 1912, was christened Elven, but forever was known as Mutt. Mutt Mantle was Mickey's dad.

When Mutt's mother died of pneumonia a month after giving birth to her fourth child, the infant was sent off to live with an aunt and uncle, and Mutt, at eight, was given the responsibility of helping to care for his younger brother and sister. When Mutt was around 12, he left school to take a job on a road gang. By the time he was 18 he was married.

Mutt's bride, Lovell Thelma Richardson Davis, eight years his senior, had been recently divorced and had two small children. It is said that Mutt was actually courting Lovell's younger sister, when Lovell took control and nabbed him for herself. She liked his looks – he was tall and handsome – and thought that beneath the tough exterior lay a true gentleman. She was also tall, with reddish blond hair and gray eyes. In terms of personality, they were opposites: Mutt was quiet and passive, Lovell was "a hellcat" and dominant.[35] Though Mutt could occasionally feign a social side, Lovell was an unreconstructed loner.

Mutt and Lovell Mantle began their life together in a two-room unpainted house on an unpaved road outside Spavinaw, Oklahoma, a town with a population in the hundreds. Spavinaw is in the northeast corner of the state, near both the Missouri and Kansas borders. It was a desolate place, part of the infamous "Dust Bowl," and it was a desolate time, the start of the Great Depression. Mutt had lost his job grading roads and had become a tenant farmer, attempting to make a living planting someone else's 80-acre spread. It was against this backdrop that on October 20, 1931, Mickey Charles Mantle was born.

Some say that before Mickey's birth Mutt told folks that if he had a boy he would become a ballplayer. He had already decided that the boy's first name would be after Mickey Cochrane, the starting catcher and star of the Philadelphia Athletics.[36] The boy's middle name, Charles, was after Mutt's father, a miner who pitched for his company team. Mutt, who also played semi-pro ball, was a baseball fanatic, and that fanaticism was the story of Mickey Mantle's childhood and the engine that propelled him to success.

Mickey Mantle's first baseball cap had arrived in Spavinaw before he had. He had a baseball not a stuffed animal for company in his crib, and Mutt and grandpa Charlie were working on the baby's hand-eye coordination, rolling baseballs to him, before he could walk. Years later, after Mutt was dead and his dreams for his son had come true, Mickey Mantle had this to say about his father's passion for the game:

> Baseball, that's all he lived for. He used to say that it seemed to him like he just died in the winter, until the time when baseball came around again. Dad insisted on my being taught the positions on the baseball field before the ABCs. He was that crazy about baseball.... I was probably the only baby in history whose first lullaby was the radio broad cast of a ball game.[37]

Lovell, too, contributed to the program by converting one of Mutt's old uniforms into sliding pads and having a shoemaker make a pair of worn-out shoes into pint-sized cleats.

By 1935, drought had driven Mutt from the farm to Commerce, Oklahoma, a town of roughly 3,000 people about 50 miles to the northeast of Spavinaw. Commerce was in the heart of mining country. And Mutt was now employed by Eagle-Picher Zinc and Lead Company, starting as a shoveler and eventually graduating to the position of ground boss.

The day of a mineworker began at 7 am and ended at 4 pm. Miners rode buckets down a five-by-seven-foot shaft to reach their underground workplace. On an average shift, they filled between 45 and 60 of the cannisters, each weighing 1,250 pounds. There was no ventilation or means of absorbing the dust or the dampness or the smells from the rock face and the men and the mules. Not surprisingly, silicosis and tuberculosis shortened the life spans of many who were forced to earn a living in this way. Accidents ruined or ended many lives, as well.

The mining activities created a hellish landscape aboveground. There were huge mountains of mineral waste (called "chat"), the largest containing 13 million tons and rising to a height of 20 stories.[38] There were scores of sludge ponds, and there were hundreds of abandoned shafts and tunnels hidden beneath a hazardous camouflage of grass. There were deep craters and alkali flats. And putting aside the bizarre topography, there was chemical contamination. The land was laced with cadmium, copper, magnesium, lead and zinc.

Mutt's obsession in making his son into a ballplayer stemmed partly from a desire to realize his own stunted fantasy. But it stemmed equally from a determination that his son would never be faced with the prospect of making his living underground.

The Mantle house in Commerce was located at 319 South Quincy Street. The clapboard structure was one-story high, had three rooms and a kitchen and was 750 square feet in area. The Mantles moved there when Mickey was three and remained for 10 years, during which time the family grew with the birth of three boys and a girl. Given the cramped quarters, at times four slept in one bed. During those years Mutt's income rose to a respectable $75 a week, but there were eight mouths to feed when Mickey's step-sister was there. Lovell took in laundry to make ends meet. One of Mickey's friends said, "They could just barely eke out a living."[39] Though the Mantles lived on the edge of poverty, there was always enough to eat, and as a matter of principle they never bought on credit.

During the decade in Commerce Mutt taught Mickey how to play baseball. When he returned from work in the late afternoon, Mickey had to be there, ready to learn. The backstop for batting practice was a falling-down, humpbacked metal shed. Mutt devised an elaborate system for determining what was an "out" and how to distinguish singles from doubles, doubles from triples and triples from home runs. The sessions continued until it was dark and the two could no longer see the ball.

Years later Mickey told his wife that by the age of five, when he was still practicing with a tennis ball, he "knew . . . he wanted to be a ballplayer."'[40] At six, Mickey graduated to a hardball. Around this time, about 1938, Mutt started converting Mickey into a switch-hitter, with Mutt pitching lefty when Mickey was batting right-handed and grandpa Charlie pitching righty when Mickey was batting left-handed. In teaching Mickey to switch-hit Mutt was clearly ahead of his time, since these lessons began when there were only 11 switch-hitters in all of the majors. This baseball immersion continued at night at the dinner table, with Lovell doing the play-by-play of the Cardinals games she had heard on the radio during the day.

All of the hard work paid off, and early on it was clear that Mickey was a special talent. But the process put a whole lot of pressure on a very young boy. Mickey knew how much time and energy his father devoted to him after long, grueling days in the mines. For this reason, Mickey adored Mutt. Mickey also knew how important it was to his father that he do well. He knew, too, how terrifying his father could be when he felt his teaching had not been absorbed or, worse, was being ignored.

At 10 Mickey started playing catcher in the Peewee League. He was two years younger than his teammates and relatively small. On one particular day, Mickey was facing a very able right-handed pitcher and, batting from the left side of the plate, he struck out the first three times he was up. When he was up the fourth time, Mickey stepped into the right side of the batter's box, ignoring Mutt's rule that you only bat righty when facing southpaws. With no concern that he was humiliating his son in front of other parents and the older boys, Mutt yelled that Mickey should go home and not return to the ballfield until he was prepared to play properly.

When his father was angry with him, Mickey could not expect to get any comfort from his mother. While Lovell was fiercely protective of her children, and would literally bash anyone who was hurting her boys, she was extremely cold and never affectionate with them. When she thought Mickey was out of line she was not averse to administering a whipping.

Unfortunately, that was not the worst that Mickey had to endure as a little boy. When he was four or five, his half-sister, Anna Bea, who by then was a teenager, began to molest him, often in the company of her sniggering girlfriends. The abuse did not stop until Anna Bea moved out of her mother's house. Mickey was also fondled on more than one occasion by an older neighborhood boy. His parents never knew; he was too traumatized to tell them. Against this backdrop of enormous and relentless pressure to succeed, parents who were emotionally distant and shameful sexual abuse, it is not entirely surprising that he wet his bed until he was well into his teens.

Despite all this, Mickey wrote in his first autobiography that "I had a lot of fun growing up. I had a happy boyhood."[41] As the saying goes, "Mickey was all boy," and at five would make a game of lighting the trash and trying to douse it with a bucket that had a hole in it or tying himself to the back of a calf to see whether, and for how long, he could survive its bucking and kicking. He liked country music and playing pool. He enjoyed it when Mutt took him and his friends to the neighborhood bars to absorb the atmosphere. He looked forward to Saturday afternoons when he could go to a movie and then have "the twenty-five cent blue plate special" at the Black Cat Café.[42]

In 1944 the Mantles left the house on Quincy Street and relocated to the country, so that Mutt could get out of the mines and so that his father, who was dying, could be in a place where there was fresh air. The house was a shambles, with no indoor plumbing and gaps between the floorboards that let the heat out and the wind in. There were 160 acres, a horse, some cows and a tractor, and Mickey loved being there. He loved the spring planting and the milking, loved that he was nearer to the hunting and fishing and loved that he got to ride a horse to school. As to school itself, well, education was never a big focus in the Mantle household or high on Mickey's personal list of priorities.

Charlie Mantle died shortly after the move, and a summer of unrelenting rain and flooding forced Mutt to give up farming and return to the city and the mines. The Mantle's next house, in a crummy town called Whitebird, was old and dilapidated. It had neither a kitchen nor a bathroom, and Mickey, Mutt, Lovell and his sister slept in a single bedroom.

Amidst all the scenery changes and ups and downs, there was baseball. In 1941, when Mickey was 10 and weighed less than 100 pounds, he helped his Douthat team win the Peewee League championship. A year later he was recruited for the Picher team, sponsored by Mutt's employer, in the Junior Cardinal League. Since Mickey was only 11, he had to be granted a waiver of the rule requiring the boys be at least 12. In Mickey's second year in the Cardinal League, the Picher coach shifted him from catcher to second base. On special occasions, when they could put together enough money, Mutt and Mickey drove the 300 miles to St. Louis to watch their beloved Cardinals. The most memorable of these excursions was in the fall of 1946, when Mutt surprised Mickey with tickets to see the Cardinals play the Red Sox in the first two games of the World Series.

It was around this same time, at the beginning of his sophomore year in high school, that Mickey defied Mutt and tried out for the Commerce football team. In a scrimmage in early October, he was accidentally kicked in the left shin by a teammate and went to his cousin's house to rest. No one thought anything of the injury until the next morning, when he ran a fever of over 103. Overnight his leg had swollen tremendously and had turned beet red. He was first taken to Picher hospital, where the local doctors regarded the situation as acute enough to consider amputation. Mutt and Lovell reacted by driving Mickey 200 miles to Crippled Children's Hospital in Oklahoma City. Lovell applied for public assistance in order to pay for his treatment. Ultimately Mickey was diagnosed as suffering from osteomyelitis, a bacterial infection of the bone. He was treated with massive doses of penicillin, at times as many as 50 shots in a 30-hour period, and the treatment saved his leg and maybe his life. Over 13 months he was in the hospital five times and a total of 40 days.

Mickey's high school career was not marked by academic distinction. Many years later, one teacher from an indeterminate grade, had this to say to a visiting newsman:

He was no angel. But he was a good, clean boy, alert, quick and willing to learn. Sometimes he'd skip school and we'd have to go find him and bring him back.[43]

Despite his occasional wanderings, all in all, Mickey was a success at Commerce High. He was an assistant editor of the school newspaper and a member of the Engineers Club. He took part in the senior play. And he was listed in the Commerce Yearbook as the "Most Popular" boy in the class.[44]

When it came to sports, Mickey proved to be a gifted athlete. He had begun playing on the Midget basketball team as a freshman and had moved up to the varsity level by the time he was an upperclassman. He scored 10 touchdowns in seven games and was named to the all-district football team during his injury-plagued sophomore year, and as a senior he was asked by scouts from the University of Oklahoma to visit the Norman campus.[45] In fact, his football coach thought that baseball was his "second-best sport," saying Mickey was "the best high school football player I ever saw."[46]

But Mickey was bred to play baseball. In the summer of 1947, when he was still recuperating from osteomyelitis, Mickey was invited to join Barney Barnet's Whiz Kids, a semi-pro team in the Ban Johnson League made up of all-stars from Kansas, Oklahoma and Missouri. At 15, he was the youngest player on a team composed mainly of 18-year-olds. He was also the slightest, having lost as much as 30 pounds when he was sick. While there was no uniform small enough to fit him, he was thrilled to make do with the oversized pants and shirt he was assigned. More than two decades later, on the occasion of his induction into the Baseball Hall of Fame in 1974, Mickey spoke of getting that first Whiz Kids uniform as a landmark moment in his life, "the most proud I ever was."[47]

In the spring of 1948, toward the end of his junior year, Mickey continued to impress on the diamond. In one game he was asked to take the mound and struck out 14. In another, he stroked home runs from both sides of the plate. That summer, as a rising senior, there were further glimmers of the great athlete he would become. Some combination of natural maturation and after-school jobs – digging graves and lugging tombstones – had re-made Mickey's upper body. He had gained 40 pounds and grown four inches. In the Whiz Kids home stadium, Mickey frequently crushed the ball nearly 400 feet. In one August or September game, he hit three monstrous home runs, two as a righty and one as a lefty.

By the time of Mickey's graduation in the spring of 1949, he and his father were poised to realize the dream of a career in major league baseball, a dream that Mutt had formed before Mickey was born. Three scouts had shown an interest in him that year: Runt Marr of the St. Louis Cardinals, Hugh Alexander of the Cleveland Indians and Tom Greenwade of the New York Yankees. As every scout knew, there was an absolute prohibition against even approaching potential recruits until they were finished with high school.

The Commerce High School Commencement ceremony was held on May, 16, 1949. By then, the Cardinals' scout, Marr, seems to have lost track of Mickey or the Commerce graduation schedule. And the Indians' scout, Alexander, had lost interest in Mickey, when he was told by the Commerce principal, Bentley Baker, that the school had no baseball team and, in any event, Mantle had been injured playing football and was suffering from arthritis. Why Marr of the Cardinals did not follow up with the Mantles is a mystery. Why Baker misled Alexander of the Indians is anybody's guess. But whatever the reasons, Greenwade of the Yankees had no competitors by the time it was appropriate to negotiate with Mickey. That gave him an unfair advantage, which he fully took.

Taking unfair advantage seemed to be Greenwade's *modus operandi*. In clear contravention of the rule proscribing contact with prospective recruits while they were still in high school, Greenwade had already "unofficially" talked to Mickey during his junior year. Greenwade had also "personally brought" Mickey to a Yankee tryout camp during his senior year.[48] What happened next was a classic mismatch of city slicker vs. country bumpkins.

The evening of graduation Mickey was not in Commerce, but in Coffeyville playing a game for the Whiz Kids. Some combination of Mutt and Greenwade had convinced the principal and the school superintendent to give Mickey his diploma in the afternoon before the formal exercises, so that he could be in uniform and play baseball that night. Mutt and Greenwade drove Mickey to the game and then went off to negotiate a minor-league contract. By its terms, Mickey would be paid a monthly salary of $140 – roughly equivalent to what he would have made as a miner during the week and playing semi-pro ball on Sundays – and he would receive an $1,100 bonus. As they were bargaining, Greenwade told Mutt that Mickey's small size and inconsistent fielding prevented him from offering more. But years afterward, he admitted to Mickey that from the beginning he "knew he was going to be one of the all-time greats."[49] Greenwade was, quite simply, a scoundrel, capitalizing on the absence of rivals from other clubs and on the Mantles' desperation and lack of sophistication.

In June of 1949, Mutt took Mickey to Independence, Missouri, home of the Yankees' Class D team. Mickey was not yet 18, and he had never before been away from his parents for an extended period.[50] He confided in his teammates his worries about a recurrence of the bone disease and his fears about dying young. In the first month or so, Mickey was plagued with errors at shortstop. He was also not yet hitting for power or much at all; his batting average was an unimpressive .230. He was convinced he would never be good enough to make it in the Big Leagues and wanted to go home.

Mutt showed up in Independence with Mickey's twin brothers in the middle of the night of July 16. Mutt was disappointed and angry with Mickey and said he was ready to take him back to Commerce to work in the mines. Somehow, Mickey's teammates calmed Mutt down, and he left without his oldest son. Shortly after the midnight visit, Mickey went on a hitting tear. By the end of his rookie season his batting average had climbed over 80 points to a more than respectable .313.

Mickey's manager filed this evaluation of Mantle's first season in professional baseball and of his future potential:

> Can be a great hitter. Exceptional speed. Just an average shortstop. Has a fine arm and a good pair of hands. Lets the ball play him too much. Attitude excellent. Will go all the way. He has everything to make him a great ball player. I would like to see him shifted to third or the outfield.[51]

Stan Musial
November 21, 1920-January 19, 2013
Career span: 1941-44, 1946-63.
Outfielder, First Baseman: St. Louis Cardinals
Key Statistics: BA: .331; RBI: 1,951; HR: 475; H: 3,630
Signal Honors: Hall of Fame, 1969; National League MVP, 1943, 1946, 1948; All-Star Appearances, 1943, 1944, 1946-63.
Nickname: "Stan the Man"

Donora, Pennsylvania is a small industrial city located 28 miles south of Pittsburgh. It is sited on the Monongahela River and was the home of American Steel and Wire Company, a U.S. Steel subsidiary established around 1900. It was named by Andrew Mellon, the owner of American Steel, to honor W.H. Donner, who organized the town for him, and Nora McMullen Mellon, his new bride. Despite its esteemed etymology, Donora was hardly a garden spot. The pollution from the smoke stacks coated the houses in gray soot and killed any vegetation. And the Donora Zinc Works, which opened in 1915, added an inescapable and acrid odor. In season, it insured yellow-tinged snow. The Zinc Works produced 70,000 tons of zinc and sulfuric acid; the Steel and Wire Company produced barbed wire, screws, nails and cables for suspension bridges.

Lukacs Musial, Stan Musial's father, worked in the shipping department of American Steel and Wire, muscling 100-pound bales of wire into freight cars. He had come to America in 1910, at the age of 19, from a Polish village that at the time was part of the Austro-Hungarian Empire. During the first 10 years he was employed as a "machine helper" and hotel porter.[52] He had virtually no formal education, and when he arrived he spoke very little English. Lukacs apparently ended up in Donora (population 8,174) because one of his cousins was already there. Although his naturalization papers listed his height as 5'7" and his weight as 150 pounds, in fact he was only about 5' tall and considerably lighter. More likely accurate was the description of his hair as blond and his eyes as gray.

Mary Lancos, Stan Musial's mother, was born in New York City and was of Czech descent. She was tall, between 5'8" and 6,' big boned and athletic. Her family was large – she had eight brothers and sisters – and poor. Mary's mother took in 16 boarders, who somehow fit with the 11 members of the Lancos family in a five-room house. Mary's father was a coal miner, earning 90 cents a day. By the age of eight, Mary hired out as a maid. In 1910, the year Lukasz Musial arrived in Donora to work at American Steel and Wire, Mary began working there as well, sorting and taking the "whiskers" off nails.[53] They met at a dance, and though they were a physical mismatch – she at least eight inches taller than he – and despite a nearly seven-year difference in age – he was almost 23 and she just 16 – they were married on April 14, 1913.

Over the next six years, Mary Musial gave birth to four daughters. Then, on November 21, 1920, she had her first boy, Stanislaus, always called Stashu at home. A second boy, Ed, was born two years later, and it was not until then that Stashu was baptized.[54] The Musials lived in a rented house, likely without indoor plumbing, in the center of town until 1927 or 1928. After that, they moved in with Mary's mother. While the Lancos house was an improvement, it was in an undeveloped part of Donora and located on an unpaved road that always smelled of raw sewage. Built in 1903, it was gray, box-like and clad with imitation brick shingles and perched on a rugged hillside over an abandoned coal seam which the boys mined for heating. There were only two bedrooms for Stan, his brother and four sisters, his parents and at least one grandparent.

Lukasz earned $11 bimonthly, from which he had to pay $4 a month in rent. Mary and the girls found jobs as maids, Stan's oldest sister scrubbing her first floor when she was just eight. In order to economize on food, Mary made bulk purchases every two weeks: 50 pounds of potatoes, 100 pounds of flour, 25 pounds of sugar and 15 pounds of coffee. She would bake 10 loaves of bread at a time, but they would last only two days. Mary would can her preserves from blackberries and elderberries picked by the children. The standard menu almost always included various forms of cabbage as the vegetable and bologna – "coal miners' steak" – as the meat.[55]

Stan was nearing nine when the stock market crashed in 1929. The Depression hit Donora hard, worse than Musial later remembered or described. The Steel and Wire works were essentially shut down, with one day being the typical "work week" for most laborers. Lukasz was either laid off or on a drastically reduced schedule. One of his neighbors described him as "the poorest guy in town."[56]

In order to survive, people were reduced to knocking on doors for food, stealing from the common garden plots and relying on local charities to provide shoes, coal, groceries, clothing and seeds. The Musials suffered along with their neighbors and verged on destitution. Their basic necessities came from the Red Cross and other charitable organizations. During this period Mary was employed cleaning one of the movie houses. Lukasc, who had been prone to stop off for a beer or so and a shot when he was working, indulged even more in these times when he was not. His excessive drinking only added to the financial and emotional strain on the family, though Stan would never talk of it.[57]

What Stan did talk about was how in 1929 or 1930, when he was nine or 10, his father introduced him to gymnastics. Three times a week he and Lukacs would go to the Polish Falcons Lodge, where Stan learned how to vault the horse, swing on the parallel bars and tumble. When the weather was good, the Falcon coaches would take the boys to compete in outdoor track and field meets.

Musial credited the three years he worked out with the Falcons as giving him the strength to be a better ballplayer, enabling him to throw the ball harder and hit the ball farther. As he recalled it, he had wanted to be a major league ballplayer from the time he was eight, even before he began at the Falcons Lodge. Stan's first baseball was made by his mother from spare rags and string. When she had time, she played catch with him. But it was his neighbor, Joe Barbao, who taught him the rudiments of the game and spent hours practicing with him and his brother and making suggestions to improve their skills. Joe, who was 30 when they met, was a former minor league pitcher and outfielder and still played semi-pro ball. He had the time because he was a "short shifter" at the zinc mill, working only three hours in the morning.[58]

Soon Stan was not only watching local teams, but putting his lessons into practice in pick-up games with his friends, wherever they could find a flat surface. When he and his pals were unable to field a full team, they would hit bottlecaps with a broomstick to improve their coordination.

Because there was no organized Little League, in the summer of 1935, when Stan was 14, he and his friends assembled a Donora team that they called the "Heslip All Stars." Their lopsided 24-2 victory over Cement City attracted coverage in the local press, in an article noting that Stan hit three doubles and struck out 14 batters in a five-hour game. Like his mentor, Joe Barbao, Stan pitched and played the outfield, but unlike Joe, Stan was a southpaw who modeled himself after Lefty Grove.

During the summer of 1936, when Stan was 15, he again played for the Heslip All Stars, which came in first in its eight-team league. The press observed that "the slender and rather frail looking Musial" – he was 5'4" and weighed 140 pounds – was "probably the outstanding player in the local circuit."[59] When the Heslip season was over, Stan got his first opportunity to test his stuff on 20- and 30-year-olds. By this time Joe Barbao was the manager of, and Stan the batboy for, the Donora Zincs, a semi-pro squad in the eight-team Industrial Mon Valley League. In early August, when the starting pitcher got roughed up, Stan made his debut as a reliever. With a good fastball and an active curve, Stan struck out between five and 13 batters – estimates vary – in between four and six innings of work.[60]

Stan was an all-around athlete. In early 1936, before his initial appearance with the Zincs, he made a name for himself as a basketball player for St. Mary's in the City League which, like the Mon Valley League, pitted him against older players. After commenting on his scrawny appearance, a local sports columnist wrote that Stan handled and shot the ball well and predicted that Stan's name "should find its way into the headlines" within a couple of years.[61]

Stan entered Donora High School as a sophomore in the fall of 1936 when, for the first time, he played sports for a school team. Athletics was really the only thing in school in which Stan had any interest. Always dutiful – his attendance record was excellent – he was at best an average student and studied very little. That pattern had been established when his formal education began at Castner elementary school. The most notable thing about those early years was that his teachers, fixated on uniformity, forced Stan, a natural lefty, to write with his right hand. Their zeal was likely responsible for the stammering which occurred when he was excited.

While teachers were not impressed by Stan's academic performance – he mostly got "Cs" – they all liked him personally. They found him to be friendly, good natured, well-mannered, humble and respectful of adults. They seem to have been won over by his rosy cheeks, his sunny smile and his shy, somewhat awkward, manner. As Jim Russell, Stan's High School basketball coach, summed it up: "He never gave anyone any trouble."[62]

During Stan's first year at Donora High, he mainly rode the bench on the school basketball team until the post-season tournament. Playing for the Donora Cubs, made up exclusively of juniors, he led all scorers with 10 points in their championship game. When the summer of 1937 came, thanks to his sister's husband, Stan got a job as a gas-station attendant in Pittsburgh. But he still found time to play baseball. He had a second season with the Zincs, where he began to pitch nine-inning games, and he played for a team sponsored by the Eugene V. Debs American Legion Post. His growing reputation as a promising prospect attracted the attention of Andrew French, the business manager of a St. Louis Cardinals' farm team located in nearby Monessen. French invited Stan to try out for the Monessen Club and handed him off to the team's player-manager, Ollie Vanek.

Stan appeared one Saturday at Monessen's Page Park, a flimsy wooded stadium, dressed in jeans, a white tee shirt and his Zincs baseball shoes. Though 16½, he was still gangly and very young looking. French's scouting report, dated June 5, 1937, said the "green kid" had a good arm, was fast and aggressive and was worth pursuing.[63] Stan worked out three or four more times at Monessen, and French and Vanek visited the Musials on multiple occasions to express their hope that Lukasc and Mary would give their underage son permission to become a professional baseball player. When in late August French and Vanek returned, this time with a contract, Lukasc refused to sign. Looking back on it, Musial explained that his father saw college on a basketball scholarship as the best way to keep him out of the mills. Two of his biographers are dubious. They maintain that Stan was not a basketball standout at that point in time, and that Lukasc *did* want Stan to go to the mills and to start making money and thought he was wasting his time on a longshot dream.[64] In the end, after tears from Stan, Mary saved the day. She reminded her husband that they had come to America for freedom, and that Stan should be free *not* to go to college. Lukasc relented and signed the agreement. It provided that Stan would report in the spring of 1938 to a farm team in the St. Louis Cardinals organization and be paid $65 a month.

Shortly after this momentous decision, Stan began his junior year at Donora High School. By the time basketball season rolled around, he had shot up to six feet, weighed 145 pounds and had perfected his left-handed hook, his outside set shot and his ball handling. He was slotted in as a starting forward. The 1937-38 "Dragons" were the best Donora had ever seen, winning 11 of their 12 league games and, for the first time, earning the title of Section champions. At 10 points per game, Stan was the Dragons' second highest scorer and was named to the "all section" team.

In the district tournament hosted at the University of Pittsburgh, the Dragons won the first round in an upset, but lost round two in overtime. According to coach Russell, Stan, who almost did not make the trip because he had been laid up with the flu, "played a wonderful game."[65] As memorable as Stan's on-court performance was his reaction to an off-court drama. The

Dragons had two black players and the management of the Schenley Hotel, where they were staying, refused to let them into the public dining room. Stan and his teammates said they would not play if the hotel excluded their Negro friends. The hotel capitulated.[66]

Stan's 1937-38 basketball season was significant in one other respect: through it, he met the love of his life, a pretty 5-foot blonde named Lillian Labash. Dick Ercius, a senior on the team, was dating Lil's sister Ann, and he introduced Stan to Lil either at the drugstore or in a skating rink or after a basketball game. Lil already knew who Stan was, having watched him play sandlot baseball and high school basketball. They soon became an "item," the school newspaper reporting Stan was "keeping Lillian Labash company after school hours."[67] Lil's father, Sam, who had played baseball himself, liked Stan and was happy to feed the growing boy from the shelves and cooler at his neighborhood grocery store.

In part because the basketball season had gone so well, Stan faced pressure from his high school teachers and coaches to reconsider his decision to forgo higher education in order to play minor league baseball. He heard arguments about the importance of college to future success, the difficulty of making it into the majors and the real possibility that he could get a basketball scholarship. But he also heard from an unlikely source, the school librarian, that he should make up his own mind and follow his heart. And there was no question that Stan loved baseball best.

At the end of his junior year, Stan showed Donora High how good a ballplayer he was, dominating on the baseball diamond even more than he had dominated on the basketball court. Donora High had not had a baseball team for 13 years, but Ki Duda, Stan's seventh grade English and Civics teacher, convinced the powers that be to field a team and to let him coach it. Duda, another poor boy from a large immigrant family, took a special interest in Stan and was a combination guardian angel and father figure. Stan proved himself worthy of Duda's attention. On opening day he pitched a three-hitter, striking out 17 in a seven-inning victory over nearby rival Monessen. His record for the season was 4-2, and it would have been 5-1 had the position players not committed five errors in one of the losses. As a batter, he had a .455 average, his most memorable hit being a grand slam off a low-inside fastball that made it to the right field fence, 450 feet away, on a single bounce. With a 7-3 league record, Donora High finished in second place in its division. Stan was selected for the "all section team" as an outfielder.

During the spring of 1938, Stan not only wavered about whether to leave school after graduation, but also about whether he should go with St. Louis. Part of this uncertainty was caused by the Cardinals' failure to keep in touch with him after he signed his contract in August. And part of it was caused by baseball commissioner Kenesaw Mountain Landis censuring Branch Rickey, the Cardinals general manager, for violating the farm system rules.

Into this breach stepped a couple of "interested parties" who thought it was not too late for this hometown boy to affiliate with the hometown Pittsburgh Pirates. Stan was softened up by a Donora sports columnist who took him to Forbes Field to see his first-ever professional baseball game, the Bucs vs. the Giants. Thereafter he returned to Forbes Field with a Donora merchant and rabid Pirates fan, for a tryout. In fact, he tried out three or four times, and Pittsburgh's manager, Pie Traynor, said he would give Stan a chance with his organization if St. Louis did not come through.

But St. Louis did come through, and in the late spring of 1938 Stan boarded a bus for Williamson, West Virginia, the Cardinals farm team in the Class D Mountain States League. Williamson was a small coal mining town on the West Virginia-Kentucky border, 240 miles from Donora, and Stan was incredibly homesick, being so far away. Fortunately, his manager took an interest in helping this very young 17-year-old boy.

Stan lost the first game he pitched, pulled out after several innings and a series of balks. But he won his second game with a three-hitter. This seesawing performance defined the season which ended with an even 6 and 6 record and an undistinguished ERA of 4.66. Stan walked 80 batters and struck out 57 in 110 innings pitched. His hitting was decent, but not earth-shattering: he had a .258 batting average with three doubles and a home run among his 16 hits. The scouting report filed on Musial after that first year read: "Arm Good. Good fast ball, good curve. Poise. Good hitter. A real prospect."[68]

That was at the beginning, when Stan was not even 18. Near the end, when his career was winding down, Bob Burnes, a local sports columnist had this to say about how well the "real prospect" had turned out: "[He] will go down in baseball history as the most beloved, the most honored, the most admired, the most complete player the game has ever known."[69]

Ted Williams
August 20, 1918-July 5, 2002
Career span: 1939-42, 1946-60
Left fielder: Boston Red Sox
Key Statistics: BA: .344, RBI 1,839; HR 521; H: 2,654
Signal Honors: Hall of Fame, 1966; Triple Crown, 1942, 1947; American League MVP, 1946, 1949; All Star Appearances, 1940-42, 1946-51, 1953-60.
Nicknames: "The Splendid Splinter," "Teddy Ballgame"

UNDERDOG GREATS

In his autobiography, Ted Williams launched the myth that his father, Samuel Williams, served in the Spanish-American War and that his mother, May Venzor, was part French. It is not known whether he did this to make his father seem more heroic and his mother less Hispanic, or whether he was simply misinformed. There is no question that Sam Williams was enamored of Teddy Roosevelt and did nothing to disabuse folks of – and may have even fostered – the notion that he charged up San Juan Hill with the Rough Riders. Similarly, at least some of May's Venzor relatives insisted that her family, who happened to live in Mexico, was partly – if not entirely – Basque or French Canadian. Whatever the explanation, until 2013 when Ben Bradlee, Jr. published "The Kid," the myth launched by Williams was perpetuated, with varying degrees of skepticism, by his earlier biographers.[70]

As to the facts, Samuel Williams, Ted's father, was born in a New York City suburb in either 1886 or 1888 to Nicholas Williams and the former Elizabeth Miller. Sam's father was a barber. After Sam's parents divorced, Nicholas Williams remarried and had three daughters, Sam's half-sisters. According to Sam's birth records, he would have been 10 or 12 in 1898 when the Spanish-American War was fought. More to the point, military records show him enlisting at the end of 1904, six years after the four-month war had ended. Sam was initially deployed to the Philippines to help quell the Moro Rebellion and served under Major General Leonard Wood, who had commanded Roosevelt's troops in Cuba. So there was at least some link to his fanciful tales of derring-do, made real by the sabre he kept as a souvenir and the pictures of him in uniform, standing at attention with a bugle at his side or sighting his rifle over the rump of a horse. Sam reached the rank of corporal shortly before his first tour was over, and he decided to re-up. He spent the three years from 1908 to 1911 stationed in Hawaii, where he remained after he was mustered out.

May Venzor, Ted's mother, was born in 1891, the second child of Pablo Venzor and Natalia Hernandez. According to genealogical research, the Hernandez family had lived in Mexico for three generations, which is as far back as the records go. While there were no similar written records on the Venzor family, interviews with surviving members of May's parents' generation do not provide any basis for concluding that the Venzors' roots were not firmly planted in Mexico as well. Moreover, there is no evidence of Basque or French heritage on either the Venzor or Hernandez side of May's family. The Venzors moved to Santa Barbara in 1907 when May was 16. There Pablo, Ted's maternal grandfather, found work as a stone mason and shepherd. Natalia, Ted's maternal grandmother, who never learned English, stayed home, to raise her eight children.

May Venzor moved to Chicago at 18 to enroll in the Salvation Army's training college. Upon graduation in 1911 she was sent to Hawaii with the rank of lieutenant. There she met Sam Williams. We know little about what attracted them to one another. Williams describes Sam as having straight black hair and May as having "one of those infectious Eisenhower smiles."[71] Sam was not quite 5'6," and May was either "short and lithe" or "lean and tall – about 5'10."[72] At the time they became acquainted, he was either 25 or 27, and she was 20. He was from the East Coast and of Welsh and English descent, while she was from the West Coast and claimed Mexican and Basque descent. Aside from Sam's brief stint in a Salvation Army training program, which he may well have entered to ingratiate himself with May, the two had nothing in common. Nonetheless, after a two-year courtship they were married on May 13, 1913, in Santa Barbara, California.

The newlyweds first set up housekeeping in Los Angeles, where Sam was employed as a street-car conductor. Two years later, in 1915, they moved to San Diego, where they lived in a series of apartments. San Diego at the time had a population of roughly 55,000 and was located 120 miles south of Los Angeles on a branch line of the Southern Pacific Railroad. Its claims to fame were as the site of the 1915 Panama-California Exposition, an international fair held to mark the finishing of the Panama Canal, and as the coaling station that became the home base for the Navy's Pacific Fleet. Edmund Wilson once said San Diego was the destination for "every loose marble in the country."[73]

After two miscarriages, on August 30, 1918, May had her first child, listed on his birth certificate as "Teddy Samuel Williams."[74] In 1920 May's second child, Danny Williams, was born. At this point, Sam had taken office space above a restaurant in downtown San Diego and set up a photography shop. His business consisted of taking pictures of sailors and their girlfriends and producing passport photos. Sam earned at best "a modest living" and was away from home until long after dinnertime, either tied up in his studio or at a neighborhood saloon.[75]

Although May initially helped out with Sam's work, ultimately she went her own way, resuming her service in the Salvation Army. For May, the Salvation Army was not a pastime but a calling. Founded in England in 1865, its mission, as its name implies, was to save those who had lost their way: alcoholics, drug addicts, prostitutes, the homeless. Its doctrine, set forth in the "Teaching Manual" was humorless and exacting:

> Try to put a screw into wood by turning it the wrong direction and it will never go in; plane the wood against the grain and there will be trouble; use the plane on the wrong kind of surface and the blade will suffer. Be selfish, but suffer for it.[76]

May's territory extended as far north as Los Angeles and as far south as Tijuana. She began work at dawn and did not return till long after dark. She was fearless, going into jails, bars, red-light districts and boxing arenas to spread the gospel of healing and to exact donations, always dressed in her blue uniform and blue bonnet. Sometimes she sang, sometimes she played the coronet or shook a tambourine and sometimes she did magic tricks – whatever it took to get the attention of the fallen and to fill her coffers. She knew everyone, from the highborn – mayors, police chiefs, business tycoons – to the lowliest of the low. She was called "Salvation May," "the Sweetheart of San Diego" and "the Angel of Tijuana."[77] For a time she held the world sales record for the Salvation Army magazine, *The War Cry*. Had she not married Sam, who was not a member of the Army, she might have risen to the pinnacle of the organization.

May Williams could revel in the reputation she had developed of tireless dedication to the cause. In at least one respect, it paid tangible dividends. In 1923 May bought a small frame house on 4121 Utah Street. It was a modest six-room California bungalow, with low ceilings, cramped rooms and a small backyard. She borrowed the $4,000 asking price, agreeing to pay $20 a month plus interest until the loan was satisfied. In 1924 John D. Spreckles, the wealthy publisher of the local newspaper who was well aware of May's charitable activities, quietly discharged the note.

While May was a treasured public figure, her family saw her differently. May's nephews on the Venzor side got to know her when they were sent down for a couple of weeks to help with the chores. She treated them like the hired help, instructing them not to call her "Aunt" and telling any neighbors who asked that they were Danny's Mexican friends. Sam's half-sisters thought she was an absolute horror, in part because she was such an overbearing wife. Williams cringed, as well, at the way she browbeat Sam. He also thought, when it came to her religion, that she was "domineering" and "narrow-minded".[78]

Ted Williams later said that he "loved" his father, that his mother was "a wonderful woman" and that he regretted that he had so little to do with his brother.[79] In fact he felt some combination of anger at, embarrassment with and disappointment in all three. The problem with Sam was, essentially, he was not there. He was a quiet, unsmiling figure, who did not "push very hard."[80] While Williams disputed the notion that Sam "wandered" off and "deserted" the family, he admitted that the two of them were not close and that Sam never once provided advice when Ted needed it.[81] Sam was no more than a "peripheral figure" in his son's life.[82]

In some respects, the problem with May was just the opposite of the problem with Sam. She pushed very hard, was always willing to give advice, even if unsolicited, and sought to be the central figure in Williams' life, but only if he was willing to be a convert to her crusade. May "dedicated" Ted to the Salvation Army at an unspecified "early age," much as her parents had early on dedicated her.[83] As a result, he became a "Corps cadet," participating in Bible study programs, in group meetings and in Sunday services. In addition, May frequently took him on her solicitation rounds, since little boys were catalysts for contributions. Williams, "a gawky introverted kid," hated those times.[84] He hated the attention she attracted – and the jeers she was subjected to – because of her prim uniform, her loud music-making and her confrontational tactics. Seventy years later he wrote how he was "embarrassed that my mother was out in the middle of the damn street all the time. Until the day she died she did that, and it always embarrassed me . . ."[85]

In some respects, however, May and Sam presented the same problem: they were never home. In May's case it was because she had this "higher calling." In Sam's case it was because he wanted to avoid May's hectoring. The net result was that the Williams boys did not see their parents very much and were on their own well into the evenings. Ted recalled, "Many nights my brother, Danny, and I would be out on that porch past 10 o'clock waiting for one of them to come home. I was maybe eight at the time, Danny was six."[86] His parents' half-hearted solution was to hire maids, but they did not stay very long and did not help very much, since they were taken from "the bottom of the barrel."[87] Aside from being terrible "caregivers," Sam and May were terrible housekeepers. Their place was filthy. May, who did not know how to cook, had no intention of learning. The only semblance of a normal homelife occurred when May's younger sister Sarah came to stay with the boys, make their meals and straighten up.

Just as May and Sam were mismatched, so were their two sons. Ted was tall and athletic, and Danny was short and hopelessly uncoordinated. Ted had light coloring, while Danny was dark. Ted respected authority, and Danny flouted it. They shared nothing other than their absentee parents. They had virtually no relationship with one another. As Williams observed, "There wasn't the closeness between us there should have been."[88]

One consequence of all this was a deep and yawning need for a father figure, was someone to fill the role that Sam did not or could not play.[89] Someone who was there physically and emotionally and who cared about him. Ted was fortunate that there were a number of men from his neighborhood who acted as "surrogate fathers."[90] Williams was acutely aware that without these other men "taking an interest . . . things would not have worked out as well as they did."[91]

Chick Rotert was a former game warden who lived next door. He exposed Ted to the joys of fishing, which became his second favorite sport. Rotert taught Williams to cast and took him on his first fishing trip. John Lutz had a poultry store and lived across the street. He was a competitive marksman, who shot skeet and trap with the best of them and got Williams interested in guns. Lutz also took him on field trips down to Mexico to hunt and out on the Bay to fish.

Les Cassie, Sr., another across-the-street neighbor, superintended construction for the San Diego schools. Cassie opened up his house to Williams and treated him like a member of the family, always happy to set another place for Ted at the supper table. Les Sr. was always available for a game of checkers and always willing to have Williams tag along when he went surf casting till the wee hours of the morning. Ted became so close with Les Cassie, Jr. that they thought of one another as brothers.

When Williams was in his teens, Floyd Johnson, the principal of San Diego High School, befriended him. The two definitely did not talk about academics, since, as Ted acknowledged, he was "a lousy student."[92] His approach to course selection was to find the subject with the least homework. His scholastic claim to fame was in typing class. Williams would regularly drop by Johnson's office, sit down in a chair, prop his feet on the desk and "shoot the breeze." Johnson did not regard Ted as disrespectful in showing up without an appointment or in making himself comfortable once there. Rather he saw Williams as one of those rare creatures who treated teachers and kids exactly the same: informally and directly. Johnson and Ted shared fish tales and talked about the national pastime.

Well before Williams reached high school, baseball had become his passion, and there were other men around who acted as mentors as he pursued his goal of being the best hitter possible. That is not to say that baseball stopped Williams from taking part in the typical diversions of All-American boys. He played marbles when he was young, spending hours on his knees shooting *aggies* and *immies* and *puries*. He hiked the several miles to Mission Valley, where the San Diego River runs, to hunt jack rabbits, or at least to spot them, since shotgun shells were expensive. He played tennis, until May said it was too costly to keep on replacing the strings he consistently broke. He hung around the fire station to play pinochle with the volunteers, joining the action when the alarm went off. He engaged in the usual mischief, climbing the local water tower and greasing the streetcar tracks when it was Halloween. Occasionally he went to the movies, especially when Olivia de Havilland was on the bill, and he frequently spent time at the pool hall, followed by a stop at the drugstore for a malt. On the weekends he listened to USC games and Benny Goodman on the radio.

There were two things that typical All-American boys did that Williams did not: go on dates or play football. In both cases it was at least partly because he felt he was too thin, either to attract girls or to hold his own on the gridiron. He was very self-conscious about being underweight.[93] The school nurse was also concerned, as she frequently told May. To bulk up Williams did scores of fingertip pushups and became a milk shake addict, with no immediate or evident effect.

While being skinny kept Williams from dating and football, it did not keep him from baseball. From the time he was a little boy he went at it with a single-mindedness of purpose and a tirelessness akin to May's devotion to the Salvation Army. Whether Ted's drive and ambition was genetic or learned is a question for experts. What is clear, though, is that Williams was his mother's son when it came to the way he relentlessly pursued the game which was to define his life.

According to John Lutz, it all began when Williams was five and would drag his bat across the street and ask to be pitched to. When he was eight May's brother, Saul Venzor, got into the act. Saul, who had been a minor league pitcher, played catch with Williams when the family visited Santa Barbara. Saul, who was a towering 6'5," would position himself at the top of his sloping driveway and challenge Williams, stuck at the bottom, to hit any of the 19 pitches in his repertoire. While Saul would not let his nephew pitch to him, he did teach Ted how to throw.

Interestingly, Williams never mentioned his uncle Saul as a factor of any sort in his autobiography. He seems to date the onset of his baseball obsession with his fifth-grade year at Garfield Elementary. This jibes with the recollection of his fifth grade teacher who remembered that ". . . even then he loved his baseball with a passion."[94] Williams recalled that as a fifth grader he got up early so he could get to school around the time the janitor opened the equipment cupboard and be the first to get a bat; under school rules, he could keep the bat – and continue hitting – so long as no one caught the ball. He would get in another quarter hour of practice at the tail end of the lunch recess. After school, he would go to the North Park playground, which was a block and a half from his house. Because it was lighted, Ted would usually stay there until it closed at nine. Williams and his pals played a game called Big League, which involved hitting a softball against a backstop, the scoring dependent on whether their shots hit above, below or right on the bar in the middle of the screen.

It was around this time that Williams met Rod Luscomb, the director of the North Park Playground. Luscomb was about 21 and had played baseball at the University of Arizona and briefly in the Class D California State League. He was blond, 6'3" tall and weighed about 200 pounds. Williams called him "my first real hero" and until he went to high school was with Luscomb constantly.[95] Roy Engle, who would captain the Hoover High baseball team, said "Luscomb and Ted worked on hitting five, six, seven hours a day, five, six, seven days a week, for seven years."[96] They would pitch to each other, simulating nine-inning games, each of them at bat three innings at a time. The scores were close and the victories pretty evenly divided. And these one-on-ones taught Williams that while there were nine men on each side, the individual pitcher-hitter duels were at "the real crux" of the game of baseball.[97]

When Luscomb was not available, Williams played ball with his friends. He was fanatical about hitting practice and estimated that between the time spent with Luscomb and his buddies he likely was at the plate 100 times a day. Though he hung around with Joe Villarino, Roy Engle, Swede Jensen and Ted Laven, Wilbur Wiley was his "first real boyhood pal."[98] The two would often play together in vacant sandlots, rotating the roles of pitcher and batter, hoping there would be little kids around to retrieve the balls. For years their routine was to announce the pitch – fastball, curve, slider – in advance of the throw. One day, when Williams was 14, he told Wilbur *not* to call the pitch, and found he could still hit whatever Wilbur threw. It was a milestone, what Williams described as ". . . the biggest thing that ever happened to me in baseball. . . I knew right then I was a good hitter."[99]

UNDERDOG GREATS

Not too long after the Wiley breakthrough, in February 1934, under the staggered schedule adopted in San Diego, Williams advanced from Horace Mann Junior High to the new Herbert Hoover High School. Shortly before the transfer, baseball tryouts were held for the high school team. Williams watched the workout, but was ineligible to try out because he had not yet finished the ninth grade. He kept pestering Wos Caldwell, the coach, to let him hit. After a while, when Caldwell took the mound, he told Williams to pick up a bat. Williams hit the coach's first pitch on top of the lunch arbor behind the right field fence, some 350 feet from home plate. According to Les Cassie, Jr., "[N]obody had hit it anywhere near there all day long."[100] Williams repeated the feat on the next pitch. The coach asked the kid his name. "My name's Ted Williams. I graduate from Horace Mann Junior High on Friday. I'll be here next Monday."[101] True to his word, Williams returned and made the varsity. He later wrote that Caldwell was "the first strong influence I had to continue in baseball, to make it my life's work."[102]

Caldwell did not make things easy for his new prodigy. Speed was not among Williams' strengths, and the coach made him run the bases, spurring him along with a switch. Nor did he make Williams a varsity regular his sophomore year, putting him in only a half dozen games.

During the summer of 1934, Williams also appeared for a variety of non-school baseball clubs. He played for the Padre Sierra Post of the American Legion, as well as for various county and independent teams. He also started for semi-pro teams with names like San Diego Market, Central, Walter Church Service Station and Cramer's Bakery. The pay for Sunday games was $3 plus refreshments and transportation.

Though Williams was mostly at first base and in the outfield, he also pitched. This is not a surprise given the hundreds of hours of one-on-one contests with Luscomb and his friends at North Park during which he was "on the mound" half the time. Williams was the number two starter his junior year at Hoover High, compiling a 4-2 record. He became the number one starter his senior year, going 12-1, undefeated in league play. In a game against nearby Redondo, he set a school record with 20 strikeouts. On another day he pitched both ends of a doubleheader, lasting 19 innings, fanning 21 and allowing only three runs. In the championship game against arch rival San Diego High he pitched a three-hitter, striking out 13 in a 6-1 victory. Ted had a strong arm, a good curve, an excellent palm ball and pinpoint control. The school paper dubbed him "Hoover's Dizzy Dean."[103]

For all his pitching prowess, Williams' performance was even more remarkable at the plate. In his abbreviated sophomore year his batting average was .333. It jumped to an astonishing .502 his junior year, and settled down to a still spectacular .402 when he was a senior. His three-year average was .430. Younger kids from the neighborhood were awestruck by how high he could loft the ball. His contemporaries were amazed at how he could reach base even when his opponents put on a shift.

Williams hit his first home run in a game situation when he was only 15 in a Sunday contest at North Park, facing pitchers at least 25 years old. In a subsequent North Park game he homered off future Hall of Famer Grover Cleveland Alexander. In a game between Hoover High and Santa Monica, delayed because of a hitting exhibition by major leaguer Babe Herman, a .393 batter, Williams belted two homers that went farther than anything the Dodgers' slugger had hit. At an annual two-day post-season tournament, Williams stroked seven home runs in three games. In his senior year he hit two home runs in the same inning in a game against Monrovia.

Near the end of the 1936 season Hoover was invited to an Easter vacation competition held in Pomona and featuring all the best high school teams in southern California.[104] Ted remembered it because his father showed up. Sam may have been there because the Governor was in attendance, and he was now state inspector of prisons.[105] More likely he was there because he sensed there might be money in it for him if his son turned pro.

Others remembered the competition for a different reason:

> There was an orange grove in right field, and a ground rule that anything hit into the orange grove was a double. Ted hit one so far that the outfielder didn't move. It was so far that nobody bothered to look for the ball. It must have gone 450 feet . . .[106]

During the five-game tournament, Williams blasted four home runs.

Why was Williams such a good hitter? North Park director Luscomb was taken by his smooth hip turn and the fact that he always made contact with the meat end – the sweet spot – of the bat. His best pal Wiley believed that the key was Williams' strong hands and wrists. Others were struck by his uncanny ability to know what opposing pitchers would throw him before the ball left their hands. Williams himself thought the advantage was his eyesight, so good that he could see the ball flattening out when it hit the bat.

Williams' baseball world, like May's Salvation Army world, extended from the border with Mexico to the south to Los Angeles in the north. Ted estimated that his high school team played about 64 games his senior year, and he probably played in another 64 semi-pro games. The Hoover varsity not only competed with other high schools, but with Navy teams, teams from the Marine base and even college teams like San Diego State.

As Williams approached graduation, five professional baseball organizations presented themselves as possible options, some having followed his progress since he began high school. The Los Angeles Angels disappeared as a possibility because Sam, who appointed himself his son's agent, was offended that their manager wanted to talk to Ted and not him. The Tigers took a pass, telling May that they liked Ted's moves, but he was so skinny – at 6'3" and 147 pounds – that they worried he would literally get killed if he were in the Big Leagues. The Cardinals had been watching and speaking with Williams for several years. Despite Ted's having had a poor tryout, they came up with an offer. Though Williams was very fond of the Cardinals' "bird dog," he was concerned that he would be sent to Oshkosh or Peoria and get lost in their huge farm system. The Yankees, who had first seen Williams as a 15-year-old, also tried to sign him and thought they had a deal, which either Sam or May tried to improve upon at the last minute. There is some dispute as to whether the proposed new terms spooked the Yankees, but in the end it did not matter, for another option presented itself when San Diego built a stadium and obtained a franchise in the Pacific Coast League.

The new team, called the Padres, was owned by Bill Lane, a wealthy businessman and former semi-pro ballplayer himself. The club got its first close look at Williams when he and some other high school stars attended an informal Padres workout the third week of June. In a scene reminiscent of Ted's Hoover High debut, San Diego's manager was pitching batting practice and told Williams to get into the batter's box. Williams stroked six or seven balls, launching at least one home run distance, a feat few on the team could match. After his performance one of the veterans predicted Ted would be signed within the week, and he was. The monthly pay was less than that offered by the Yankees, but Lane promised May that her son would not be traded until he was 21.[107] As Williams said, his mother "liked the idea" of his playing for the Padres "because she wanted me close to home.[108]

The summer of 1936 was a momentous one for Williams. Not quite 18, it was a time of adventure. He took road trips to cities like Portland and Seattle, playing from Tuesday to Sunday, Mondays reserved for travel. He got to play with new balls, wear a new uniform and order new bats. His manager, Frank Shellenback, was another surrogate father, "a wonderful, wonderful man, I respected as much as any I've known in baseball."[109]

Williams continued his fanatical obsession with hitting, swinging rolled-up pieces of paper or pillows or imaginary bats while he looked at himself in the mirror to make sure his mechanics were perfect – and stylish. He obviously was doing something right, as confirmed by Lefty O'Doul, manager of the San Francisco Seals and reputed to be the best hitting teacher in the league. After watching Willliams for a week, he took the unusual of step of nabbing this rookie from a rival team after batting practice and telling him, "Never let anyone change your swing."[110]

It is not at all clear when and why Williams first became a Padres regular. According to Williams, it happened when skipper Shellenback asked him to pitch in Los Angeles in a game already out of hand: the Padres were trailing the Angels by 10 runs in the sixth inning. Williams was inserted as a pinch hitter and doubled, starting a five-run rally. After holding the Angels scoreless, he hit another double in his next at-bat, closing the gap to one run. Shellenback called in a new reliever, and moved Williams to left field for the rest of the game, and he remained there for the rest of the season.

One Williams biographer tells a slightly different story. He agrees that Williams pitched and had two-hits – his first as a professional – in a game against the Angels. However, he contends that Williams did not immediately become the Padres everyday left fielder. Rather some weeks after the Angels game, in late August, Williams was moved to the outfield when one of their veterans unexpectedly quit.

Williams finished the '36 season with a respectable, but not remarkable, .271 average, based on 107 at-bats in 42 games. During that summer he met two men who were to become central parts of his life. The first was Bobby Doerr, the Padres young second baseman, whom he got to know well on the week-long road trips. They were two young players on a team filled with old-timers. They both loved fishing and hunting and Western movies. They would later become Red Sox teammates and great friends.

The second was Eddie Collins, general manager of the Red Sox. Collins had come to the West Coast to scout Doerr and while there got to see Williams in action. Though Ted's numbers were not great, Collins saw something he liked and wanted to sign him on the spot. As Collins later said, "It wasn't hard to find Ted Williams. He stood out like a brown cow in a field of white cows."[111] Lane told Collins of his agreement with May that he would keep her son in San Diego for at least two years. Collins asked to be notified when the two years were up. Lane did not forget to do so, and the rest, as they say, is history.

Henry Aaron
February 5, 1934-present
Career span: 1954-76
Left fielder: Milwaukee and Atlanta Braves
Key Statistics: BA: .305; RBI: 2.297; HR: 755; H: 3,771
Signal Honors: Hall of Fame, 1982; National League
MVP, 1957; All-Star Appearances, 1955-75.
Nickname: "Hank"

Henry Aaron's grandfather and namesake was born in December 1884 in a part of Alabama known as the "Black Belt." According to the 1910 census, Henry was 25 and living in a rented cabin with his 23-year-old wife Mariah. The cabins in the area had once been slave quarters. They were one- or two-room affairs with a four-paned window on each side, propped up unevenly on wooden blocks to mitigate against rot and to provide a crevice into which youngsters could find a bit of shade during the blistering summers. The Aarons lived south of Selma in Camden, Alabama, the county seat of Wilcox County. With nearly 18,000 slaves, Wilcox had been one of the top 20 slave-holding counties in America. The census noted that Henry and Mariah had an 18-month-old son, Herbert, the famous Henry Aaron's father.

The original Henry Aaron described himself as a "general farmer" which meant that he sharecropped for Frank Tait, whose ancestors, the largest slaveholders in the county, may well have owned his ancestors. The elder Henry had never been to school and was illiterate. His wife Mariah had been to school and could both read and write. Despite these differences, "Papa Henry" and "Mama Sis," as their grandchildren knew them, both preached on Sundays, upholding an Aaron family tradition.[112]

Herbert, one of a dozen Aaron children, was not at all interested in farming. Nonetheless, he labored in the cotton fields and operated farm machinery well into his teenage years. But he could not abide the prospect of staying put, working someone else's land and never getting ahead. He was not alone in this sense of dissatisfaction: in the 20 years after his birth in 1908, 30% of the African American population of Wilcox County had left for the proverbial "greener pastures."

Herbert departed from Camden in 1927 when he was 19, taking along with him a local girl, Stella Pritchett, who was pregnant with their first child. Their daughter, Sarah, was born that same year. Herbert and Stella were married in 1929, the wedding ceremony officiated by a justice of the peace in Mobile, Alabama. According to the official documentation, Herbert "Aron" was 22 years old, 5'8" tall and weighed 142 pounds, and Stella Pritchett was 19 years old, 5'7" tall and weighed 115 pounds.

The Aarons settled in Down the Bay, the Mobile neighborhood "where poor blacks resided," filled with maids and cooks and men who sought work on the docks.[113] There were good reasons for the family to choose Mobile, as it was regarded as one of "the more livable cities" in the South for people of color.[114] Some of its "livability" has been attributed to Mobile being a major port, resulting in an influx of diverse people and cultures. Some of it has been attributed to there being a better balance between the races in Mobile – roughly half the population was white – as compared to Wilcox County, for example, where the whites were, and felt, vastly outnumbered. And some of it has been attributed to the French and Spanish influence and the presence of another ethnic group, the Creoles. Whatever the explanation, Mobile had a local college that had been integrated before the Civil War, an NAACP chapter that had been established in the 1930s and a public library system that was open to its black citizens.

But while Mobile may have been relatively less hostile than other Alabama cities, that did not mean that life there was easy if you were an African American. Through law and tradition, segregation was rigidly enforced. Blacks and whites were separated on buses, in eating places, in hotels, in bars, in health facilities and in burial grounds. The separation was a means of reinforcing white superiority over blacks. Herbert knew that as a black male, he could not offer to shake a white man's hand or pay any attention to a white woman or address a white adult as anything other than "Sir" or "Ma'am" or take offense if he were addressed as "boy" or react in any way if forced to surrender his place in line when a late-arriving white showed up. Herbert had to suffer these indignities silently because he had a family to take care of. When his son became famous, it was the memory of this crippling silence which caused Henry Aaron to use his celebrity to give voice to the frustration and inequities he had witnessed.

The rent for the Aaron's first Down the Bay Apartment was $6 a month. To pay it, Herbert hired out as a laborer and later as a truck driver for a coal company. Initially Stella found work as a domestic, scrubbing floors, but soon there was too much to do at home, and so she cleaned house for others only occasionally; when she did, she earned $2 a day. In 1930, three-year-old Sarah got a brother, Herbert Jr. And four years later, on February 5, the day before Babe Ruth's birthday, she got a second brother, Henry. Over the next decade the family was rounded out with two more girls, Gloria and Alfredia, and one more boy, Tommy.

In 1933, when Herbert was 25, he began working for the Alabama Dry Dock and Shipping Company, ADDSCO, at a salary of 16 cents an hour. For a time he served as a boilermaker's assistant, which required him to hold 60-pound plates while a riveter secured them in place. Through the Depression years, Herbert was as often out of work as he was employed, and it was not until the Second World War that he had any job security. In 1942, shortly after America's entry, Herbert was promoted to the position of full-time riveter. But even with the promotion, money was tight for the Aarons, and for a time Herbert supplemented the family income by running a small tavern, serving its own special blend of moonshine.

The Aaron saloon, called the Black Cat, abutted the house that Herbert moved his family to in 1942. By that time, the Aarons had been in Down the Bay for 15 years in four different apartments, and Herbert decided he wanted to stop paying rent and become a home owner. The place he chose was in a formerly all-white area about seven miles northwest of Down the Bay called Toulminville. It was dubbed "Struggleville" by the black dwellers of center city, who regarded it as a step in the wrong direction.[115] It had oak groves, cornfields, watermelon patches and blackberry bushes. Cows, chickens and hogs roamed the unpaved streets, as did the pigs who were relied upon to consume the garbage. Because it was in the country and away from the Mobile "action," it was affordable.

Herbert bought two lots, for $55 apiece, and scrounged ship timbers and boards from abandoned or partially burned buildings to construct a modest house.[116] It had a little kitchen area and a small yard which had a garden, animal pen and outhouse. There were no windows or electricity. Water for cooking, cleaning and washing was pumped from an outside well and heat was provided by burning whatever materials could be stripped from deserted properties. Herbert was proud of the fact that "the only people who owned their own homes were the rich folks and [the] Aarons."[117]

The Aarons' life style bore no relation to that of rich folks. The house itself was ramshackle, so limited in area that the six children always shared a bed. The kids wore nothing but hand-me-downs, with no concern about the gender of the garments. Hardly any food was store-bought, and the family diet was vegetarian for reasons of necessity not fashion. A typical dinner was "homegrown beans and greens and skillet fried corn bread."[118] The half dozen little Aarons were so thin that they described themselves as "six o'clock – straight up and down."[119] Nonetheless, the Aarons did not see themselves as poor: "Everybody else was in the same boat. We didn't know to feel sorry for ourselves."[120]

The six Aaron children spent summers back in Wilcox County on the farm owned by Herbert's parents, Papa Henry and Mama Sis. Young Henry was sent away more than the others, not so much because he needed a vacation, but because he needed to learn how to work. All the Aaron kids took on odd jobs. Sarah, as the oldest, helped with her father's small saloon, and Herbert Jr. clerked at a nearby grocery store. Henry, who admittedly was not a worker, did stints mowing lawns, picking potatoes, mixing cement and hauling ice. Also, often under protest, he helped his mother by cutting wood for the stove and tending to her garden.

For recreation, Henry would read comics or fish for trout or shoot marbles or roller skate or get into friendly fights. He and his friends liked to eat, so catching crayfish to make a stew, topped off with a stolen watermelon, was a treat. It was occasionally improved upon if someone had a spare nickel for buying a cookie with inside icing or, better still, if someone had a whole dime for buying a cookie with icing on the outside as well. Henry enjoyed being a Boy Scout, especially the challenges of finding his way out of the woods and catching snakes.

These pastimes paled in significance to Henry's passion for the game of baseball, a love affair that started when he was a little boy. It was undoubtedly helped by the fact that he lived in Mobile, a city that was baseball mad. To begin with, several major leaguers were born there. On the black side, the most famous was Negro League pitcher Satchel Paige. But when Henry was growing up, everyone from his part of town also knew of "Double Duty" Ted Radcliff, who during a 36-year Negro League career operated on both ends of the battery. On the white side was a set of brothers, Milt and Frank Bolling, who made it to the "Bigs," as well.[121]

Mobile was also a way-point from spring training for the teams that started their seasons in Florida. The Yankees, Dodgers, Cardinals and Reds all barnstormed through town on their way to their home parks up north. As a result of these visits, at eight Henry got to see the Yankees and Joe DiMaggio, his first hero, catching a glimpse of him again when he was 12 and DiMaggio was back from the Army. When he was 14 he got to see the Dodgers and Jackie Robinson, who by breaking the color line made it realistic for little black boys to dream of playing in the Major Leagues. He also undoubtedly got to see the Cardinals and Stan Musial, who was the kind of ballplayer Henry himself would become: a batter who hit home runs, but did not always go for the fences; a man of enormous talent and great accomplishment, who shunned the spotlight and felt when he took the field he was just like any other man doing his job.

Mobile not only spawned baseball-obsessed fans but a substantial number of serious amateur players. Many of the local businesses sponsored their own teams made up mostly of men in their twenties and thirties, men who had day jobs as welders and riveters and boilermakers.

Henry started learning baseball skills before he was eight, when the Aarons lived in Down the Bay. Because there was not very much room in the city, he practiced hitting by swatting bottle caps with a broom, his brother Herbert doing the pitching honors. Henry was serious enough about the game even back then that his dad asked a lady down the street to sew him a uniform.

The move to the wide open spaces of Toulminville in 1942 changed everything. When Henry was alone, he threw the ball up on the roof and either caught it or hit it as it rolled off. With the luxury of open land, the kids in the neighborhood could choose up teams and play until the sun went down. Their equipment was rudimentary. Baseballs were made of nylon stockings wrapped around golf balls, crumpled tin cans or bundles of rags.

A few years after the Aarons arrival in Toulminville, the town of Mobile annexed the village and built baseball diamonds right across the street from the Aarons in a facility named Carver Park. Henry could be found most days playing pick-up games at the park or reverting to broomsticks and bottlecaps in his yard. Henry's first organized play was as a catcher for Toulminville Grammar School, which was part of a Negro recreational league. By the time he was 14 he had gained a reputation as one of the most outstanding softball players in Mobile. He was part of the Central High School fast pitch team that won the championship of the Negro League two years in a row, dropping only three games in the two seasons. Henry caught, played short and third and "hit quite a few home runs."[122]

Henry achieved baseball success despite an unorthodox hitting style. He whipped the bat with wrists of legendary strength and held it cross-handed. He placed his weight on his left front foot and lashed out to meet the ball at the very last second. While Henry was adept in the field, he was brilliant in the batter's box. Henry was a loner, and when he was at the plate, entirely by himself, he was wholly in his element.

Despite his quiet manner, Henry was supremely confident about his ability. When he was barely a teenager, he told a close friend "I'm a good ballplayer. I know I am. I'll make it. I'll make it all the way to the top."[123] He said much the same thing to his father around the same time, telling him he "would be in the big leagues before Jackie [Robinson] retired."[124]

In his sophomore year at Central High, Henry also went out for football. Despite the fact that he only weighed 150 pounds, he was named as starting guard on the all-city squad. But he stopped playing after that one season. There are various theories about why. One is that he preferred baseball and did not want to risk getting injured on the football field. Another is that his mother saw playing football as the route to a college education, and Henry saw college as a needless detour. A third is that there were some "personal things that went on with the football team" – never defined – that Henry did not "care for."[125]

Henry's single-minded devotion to baseball not only ended his football career, but also effectively ended his career at Central High. Though Stella strongly believed in the importance of education, Henry did not. He thought school was boring and entirely unnecessary, and he basically stopped going. After being absent for 40 straight days, he was expelled in the middle of the year.

In addition to playing ball while he was in high school, Henry played on local teams. Because he was so good, he was allowed to join older men on the Braves, a fast-pitch softball club that was part of a city recreation program. The first semi-pro team he played for was the Pritchett Athletics. He was slotted at shortstop or third base and earned $2 or $3 a game.

Henry then was recruited by the even better Black Bears, having caught the eye of the team's manager, Ed Scott.[126] Scott took a real interest in Henry and spent countless hours shagging flies for him at Carver Park. He thought that Henry's ability to consistently make contact with a ball or a bottlecap using a bat or a stick of wood was something very special. Although Stella would not let Henry travel with the Black Bears when they went out of town, she did allow him to play on the Sundays when they were at their home park in nearby Prichard. His position was shortstop, and his pay was around $10.

Scott wanted Henry to develop further and make more money and thought he could do both by moving up to the next level. Since Scott doubled as a scout for the Indianapolis Clowns of the Negro American League, he knew the Clowns' business manager, Bunny Downs. (In fact, he had once played for Downs when Downs had managed the Norfolk Stars.) And so Scott arranged with Downs for the Clowns to play the Black Bears in the late summer of 1951, so that Henry could have a tryout in a game setting. Whether Henry hit a homer and "a double or two" or "two singles and a double," his performance at the plate coupled with his sterling play in the field convinced Downs to sign this 17-year-old kid.[127] Right after the game, Downs offered Henry $200 per month to play for his Clowns.[128] Some combination of Scott and Downs ultimately got a reluctant Stella to agree to let Henry go in the spring of 1952, so long as he promised to finish high school when the Clowns season was over.[129]

In March 1952, a very frightened Henry Aaron left Mobile, Alabama, for Winston-Salem, North Carolina, the home of the Indianapolis Clowns. The Clowns were the Harlem Globetrotters of baseball, complete with a female at second base, an enormous man in a grass skirt as its mascot, a first-base coach who stood on one hand and a "shadow ball routine" during pre-game warm-up.[130] Despite the circus-like novelties, the Clowns played serious ball once the first pitch was thrown.

Having won the Negro League title the preceding two years, the Clowns' veterans did not need a scrawny teenager to help them out, and they hardly brought out a brass band to welcome the kid from Mobile. Most of the players were grown men who were teenagers before Jackie Robinson had made a major league career a real possibility for blacks. As such, they were resentful of the tongue-tied boy with the raggedy shoes and the broken-down glove who might get the chance they deserved but never had.

The Clowns camp was so filled that it had run out of warm-up jackets the first day, and Henry stood there shivering until Dewey Griggs, a scout for the Boston Braves, took pity on him. Henry must have looked pretty good in the batting cage, because he became the Clowns regular shortstop when their veteran infielder got injured early in the spring. Buck O'Neil, the manager of the Kansas City Monarchs, recounted an exhibition match-up in which Henry, who was batting fourth, pasted every kind of pitch from the aces of his staff, predicting Aaron would be gone before he met up with the Clowns again back home in Missouri. In Henry's first plate appearance in the Clowns first regular season game he hit a home run, and followed it up with a single and two doubles.

Ed Scott, Henry's mentor and friend, was also his chief flack, and he began writing to major league clubs before the Clowns' season was a week old. Because Henry's debut was not a fluke, the Braves, Giants, Yankees and Phillies had Henry in their sights within two weeks of opening day. Henry's most spectacular outing was in a doubleheader against the Kansas City Monarchs in Buffalo: in game one, he hit a home run, two doubles and a single; in the nightcap, he had six more hits; in the field, he was at the front end of five double plays; and on the base paths he was credited with two steals. His batting average after the Buffalo contests was an astronomical .467.

With performances like these, the press took notice. The *Pittsburgh Courier,* the principal source of news on black sports, called Henry "a shining light" and described his work in the field and in the batter's box as "a revelation."[131] The *Chicago Defender* went even further. In an article appearing halfway through the season, on June 7, it wrote that Henry had "locked up" the Negro

League batting title with his .483 average.[132] Other pieces gushed that Henry "stands at the plate like a Ted Williams" and was "the best prospect seen in the Negro League since Willie Mays."[133]

The major league clubs were falling all over themselves to sign Henry. After the Buffalo doubleheader, John Mullen, the Boston Braves general manager, instructed his scout Dewey Griggs to pull out all the stops to purchase Henry from the Clowns. The Braves offered to pay the Clowns $10,000 in two installments and to pay Henry $350 a month.[134] Their principal competition, the Giants, offered to pay the Clowns $15,000 in four installments and to pay Henry $250 a month.[135] When Henry asked the Clowns' owner what to do, Pollock, who had always been partial to the Braves, suggested he go with Boston, even though the Clowns might earn more were he to choose the New Yorkers. The suggestion made sense from Henry's perspective. The Giants were offering Henry $100 less a month than the Braves, and the Braves were going to ease him in on a lower-pressure Class C team, while the Giants were going to rush him into Triple A.

Henry followed Pollock's advice and signed with the Braves, influenced somewhat by the fact that the Giants had addressed their telegrammed offer to Henry "Arron."[136] Henry played for another two weeks with the Clowns, during which his average dipped below .400, and he lost the Negro League batting title. Nonetheless, when on June 8 he boarded the train from Chicago to Milwaukee to take his first plane trip, Henry Aaron was on his way to realizing the confident prediction he had made when he was only 14: that he would play professional baseball.

Babe Ruth
February 6, 1895-August 16, 1948
Career span: 1924-46
Pitcher/Outfielder: Boston Red Sox, New York Yankees, Milwaukee Braves
Key Statistics: BA: .342; RBI: 2,213; HR: 714; H: 2,873
Signal Honors: Hall of Fame, 1936; American League
MVP, 1923; All-Star Appearances, 1933-34.
Nicknames: "the Sultan of Swat;" "the Bambino;" "the Big Bam"

For a time Babe Ruth was the most famous man in America. Therefore, it is not surprising that he is the subject of more biographies than any other baseball player, and perhaps any other American sports figure of any generation.[137] Given this intense interest, one which dates back to his playing days, it is striking how little is known about his earliest years. But Ruth did not want to talk about that period once he got famous, and by then both his mother and father, who might have been more obliging, were long gone.[138] His sister, who lived till the ripe old age of 91, was only two when Ruth left home. As a result, and not surprisingly, one of the most thoughtful biographers described his "beginnings" as "a closed book."[139]

This is what can be pieced together. George Herman Ruth Jr. was born on February 6, 1895, in Baltimore, Maryland. He was the first son of George Herman Ruth Sr. and Katherine Schamberger Ruth.[140] The weather that day was frigidly cold. The birth took place in the second-floor front-bedroom apartment of Kate's parents, one of four long (59 feet) and narrow (12 feet) red-brick row houses on an alley called Emory Street. The Baltimore of that era was a major port city, and the Ruths lived right near the docks and not far from the yards of the Baltimore & Ohio railroad, "on the wrong side of Pratt Street, the downtown dividing line for class and economics."[141] "It was," Ruth later recalled, "a rough, tough neighborhood" and was known as "Pigtown" because droves of pigs were "run through the streets" from the stockyards to the slaughterhouses.[142] In addition to pigs, the streets were typically filled with "longshoremen, merchant sailors, roustabouts and water-front bums."[143]

Ruth said, "I hardly knew my parents."[144] We know this. His father, Big George, was born in Baltimore, as was his paternal grandfather, John. John Ruth was a Lutheran and for a time was in the lightning rod business. He eventually became the owner or manager of a restaurant/bar. Ruth's paternal great-grandfather, Peter Ruth, was said to have been from Bucks County, Pennsylvania; his paternal great-grandmother, Karizah Reager, was said to have been from Lancaster, Pennsylvania, the Amish country. The ancestral Ruths were of German extraction. Big George looked just like his son: big, dark-haired, with a swarthy complexion, a flat nose and prominent lips. He always, or often, appeared to be angry.

Big George seemed to have had a hard time holding down a steady job. Before he was married he was employed as a driver, an agent, a salesman, a harness maker and a grip-man on a cable car, though it is unclear what he drove, whom he was an agent for or what he sold. At the time he married Katie Schamberger he was living with his parents and working the counter of their grocery and tavern.

We know nothing of when or how Big George met his future bride. We do know that, like her future husband, she was at least partially of German descent.[145] We know, as well, that like John Ruth, Katie's father Pius, for some years after the Civil War, had been a grocer and saloon-keeper. Around the time his daughter got married, Pius was an upholsterer.

We do not know what attracted Big George and Katie to one another, other than their common ethnic heritage. Nor do we know about their personalities or their interests. We do know that George Jr. was born only seven months after the wedding, which may explain everything.

There were very few tangible milestones during Little George's childhood, but there are some. When Little George was four, Big George and his brother went into the lightning-rod business, as their father once had. When Little George was five, Katie gave birth to twin girls only one of whom, his sister Mary Margaret – Mamie – survived. (Katie delivered, in all, eight children, including two sets of twins; six of them died early.) By 1901, not long after Mamie was born, Big George abandoned lightning rods and bought a bar, relocating his family to an apartment upstairs. On June 13, 1902, when Little George was a bit shy of seven and a half, his parents committed him to St. Mary's Industrial School for Boys.

Overall, during Little George's first seven and a half years his mother was having and losing babies and was not very healthy; his father was shifting from job to job and had not yet found the right one; finances were extremely tight, and tensions were extremely high. And Little George did not help.

The adult Babe Ruth confessed that he had "a rotten start:" "I was a bad kid," "a bum."[146] He admitted that he did not "remember being aware of the difference between right and wrong" and had no "bearings."[147] He said he never went to school, roamed the streets, chewed tobacco, drank beer and stole from his parents. For these and other infractions he was beaten with a horsewhip or a cue stick or bare fists.

There have been a variety of reasons given for why at this particular moment in time the Ruths sent their son away. One, advanced by his sister, is that his parents were simply exasperated by the fact that her brother could neither read nor write and they could not make him go to school. Another, more dramatic, cites a "brawl" at the Ruth's saloon at which "shots were fired," drawing the police.[148] An irate neighbor, who may well have made the "911" call, told the authorities, "There's a young kid living there; it's no place for him."[149] A third is that the Ruths were simply at the end of their rope. When Little George turned six his parents bought the tavern, and both were working all day and well into the evening to make a go of it. Katie had a toddler to contend with and the grief and exhaustion from her "frequent and unhappy pregnancies."[150] Little George was hyperactive, unruly and for the most part out of control. Removing him from the household would make things both calmer and less expensive.

So in late spring 1902, Big George and Little George boarded the Wilkens Avenue trolley and traveled from the city to a semi-rural spot four miles southwest of downtown Baltimore. St. Mary's Industrial School for Boys did not attempt to cultivate a bucolic look. The principal structure was a gray fortress-like building, five-stories tall, of pseudo-medieval design. It was flanked by five similarly grim buildings. Of the 800 "inmates" roughly

50 percent were "remanded" there for delinquency by the local and state courts.[151] George Herman Ruth Jr. was one of those "remand" cases, listed on the enrollment form as an "incorrigible."[152] He was committed to remain at St. Mary's until he reached 21. The 400 "non-incorrigibles" were orphans and boys whose parents were divorced or seriously ill or just too poor to care for them. One of the "strays" who fell into the "non-incorrigible" category was Asa Yoelson, later to be known as Al Jolson and to become as famous as an entertainer as Babe Ruth would become as an athlete.[153]

George was an exception at St. Mary's. At seven and a half, he was one of the youngest boys enrolled. He would also remain there far longer than the two-year average. There is some dispute as to how long his stay was. A letter from the Associated Catholic Charities of Baltimore states he was "resident" at St. Mary's from June 13, 1902 to February 27, 1914.[154] Yet other accounts have him returning home for various stints, so that rather than being there for a dozen uninterrupted years, he may have spent bits and pieces of only seven. But whatever the case, the times at home are blank slates. The place where he was formed was not Pigtown with his parents but in the outskirts of Baltimore with the Xaverian brothers.

There is also a mixed account as to how much George saw his family after he had been committed to the Institute. Louis Leisman, who wrote of George during the St. Mary's years, said no one ever showed up to see him on Sunday visiting days, George always joking that it was because he was just "too big and ugly."[155] His sister Mamie, with her tendency to put a good face on things, remembered trolley trips she made with her mother to St. Mary's "once a month."[156]

The Xaverians were a religious order started in Belgium in 1846 that had spread to the United States after the Civil War. In the 1880s St. Mary's founder, Reverend Spaulding, asked the Xaverians to run his institution. Like priests, the Xaverians took vows of poverty, chastity and obedience. But like nuns, they could neither celebrate Mass nor hear confession. As such, the Brothers, as they were called, operated at the lowest rung of the religious hierarchy of the Catholic Church. The order attracted a broad spectrum of types, "from devout to worldly, from meek to charismatic, from kindly to sadistic."[157] Most were from working-class families, attracted in part by religion and in part by the security of a free place to stay and regular meals. St. Mary's was run by 20 or 30 Xaverians. They housed, clothed, fed and gave comfort to their 800 charges. In addition, they taught classes in religion and secular subjects and provided instruction in a variety of trades. They wore long black cassocks with a cross embroidered at their chests and rosary beads dangling from their belts. They were stern and steady, and they regarded "obedience" as "the number one virtue."[158]

St. Mary's was right out of "Oliver Twist." Two-hundred boys were assigned to each of the four dormitory floors, their beds set out end to end, barracks style, in long rows. There were communal toilets and showers. The boys were awakened at 6 am, attended Mass before breakfast and then made their beds. They were in classrooms or workshops by 7:30 am, where they remained until late in the afternoon. After that they were allowed two hours of recreation until suppertime and were back in bed by 8 pm. The boys were essentially confined behind the St. Mary's gates unless formally released for a special occasion.

Mealtime was a time of silence. Whispering was punishable by the disgrace of standing still at the front of the room and the pain of a whipping. The food was terrible. Breakfast was a bowl of oatmeal or hominy, with a single pat of butter or margarine for a treat on Fridays and three hotdogs for a treat on Sundays. Lunch and supper were the same throughout the week, soup and bread, though on weekends three slices of baloney were offered.

While there was Sunday Mass, baptisms, communions and confirmations, formal religious instruction was not emphasized. Nor was academics: the boys received five hours of daily classroom until they were 12, reduced to three-and-a-half hours a day after that. In terms of class size, each brother was responsible for teaching 40 to 50 students. For the rest of the day, there was vocational training in gardening, farming, tailoring, shoemaking and shoe repair, steam-fitting, woodworking, carpentry, baking and glazing. Using their newly acquired skills, students took care of the grounds, renovated the facilities, prepared the food and made the clothing. For recreation, slotted in every afternoon and all day Sunday (after Mass), there was handball, football, boxing, soccer, volleyball, foot-racing, wrestling and, in season, ice skating.

For George, St. Mary's was an environment exactly the opposite of what he had known before. Regimentation, stringent rules, close supervision and harsh discipline were substituted for an absolute lack of structure. Yet George loved St. Mary's and always looked back at his years there with "warmth and nostalgia."[159] He described it right before he died as "one of the most constructive periods of my life," saying he was every bit as proud of it "as any Harvard man is proud of his school."[160]

George was not enamored of St. Mary's because of its scholastic program, such as it was. He was at best an "indifferent student," though he did develop an "astonishingly graceful" penmanship, all the more remarkable since he was left-handed and was forced to write with his right hand.[161] Nor was it attributable to his theological studies, though he did convert to Catholicism, received his first Holy Communion there, served as an altar boy and regularly went to confession.

Neither did Ruth's gratitude arise because St. Mary's miraculously converted the former hellion into a model of deportment. The Institute surely did tame and root out certain of the boy's anti-social and vaguely criminal tendencies, but for the most part the brothers allowed George to be George. He remained the loud, physical, outgoing kid he was when he arrived.[162] As one of the brothers wrote: "He was livelier than most of the boys, full of mischief. . . He was an aggressive, shouting boy who was always wrestling around with the others."[163] But though George could be annoying, irritating and badly behaved, he had undeniable charm. One of his classmates, Lawton Stenerson, remembered him as "popular, unpredictable, stubborn, reckless and, above all else, generous."[164] George was the one who would buy candy for the small boys, "particularly those who were orphans and had no relatives or friends."[165] He was the one who would take the rap for the scared eight-year-old who had accidentally broken a window. And he was the one who in the coldest weather would go out in shirtsleeves – tough guy that he was – and wander about the frozen little kids, rubbing their hands and blowing on their fingers to warm them up.

Some of Ruth's positive feelings about St. Mary's may have come from the fact that it was there that he gained confidence that he was competent to do something constructive and which might provide him with a means of earning a living. For George took to the vocational training offered at St. Mary's. He was a capable carpenter, and he mastered the art of "cigar rolling." He proved most adept as a tailor, his specialty: putting collars on shirts. For a part of five-and-a-half days a week George could be found on the third – "high city tailor" – floor of the four-story stone workshop, earning six cents for each shirt he made for the Oppenheim Shirt Company.[166]

However, there is no question that the principal reason for Ruth's profound attachment to St. Mary's was Brother Mathias Boutlier. Mathias, who was 30 years old when George first enrolled, was from Cape Breton, Nova Scotia. He was the brother with overall responsibility for the boys' behavior. His formal title was "Prefect of Discipline"; the boys dubbed him "the Boss."[167] Ruth adored him, calling him "the greatest man I've ever known," saying that in all his days he had never met "anyone who was even close to Brother Mathias when it came to manliness, kindness and grace."[168] He thought Brother Mathias "could have been anything he wanted to be in life, for he was good-looking, talented and dynamic."[169]

Brother Mathias became George's "ideal" such that he imitated, as best he could, his habits and mannerisms: "I even learned to walk as he did."[170] So what everyone always took to be "the Babe's" patented walk – pigeon-toed, body leaning forward with each stride – faithfully mimicked his idol. Brother Mathias was more than a hero to this young, troubled boy. "He was," Ruth acknowledged, "the father I needed."[171]

Physically, Brother Mathias was huge: 6'6" in height, weighing 250 to 300 pounds. He was so big that the door to his little room had to be hung swinging outward to accommodate his bed. Though from Ruth's description of this blond-haired blue-eyed titan one has an image of a Rock Hudson or Dwayne Johnson, with narrow hips and broad shoulders, in fact Brother Mathias was "shaped something like a pear, with a relatively slight face and sloping shoulders descending into a heavy body with thick legs."[172] He also had "a somewhat receding jaw and a slight double chin."[173]

What was remarkable about this mountain of a man was his understated presence. He never shouted. He was always calm. He earned respect by being consistent and fair. There is no evidence that he ever resorted to corporal punishment. If a boy did something wrong, he would be deprived of some privilege, like time for recreation. Once the punishment was served, the infraction was never mentioned again.

Brother Mathias' startling powers were in evidence when he was called back from a visit to another Xaverian facility because a bunch of the older boys began fighting in the recreation yard. The "roughhousing" was getting out of hand and beginning to have all the earmarks of a riot. Brother Mathias sped back to St. Mary's. When he got there, Ruth remembered, "[H]e stood on a piece of high ground in the yard, and just looked out over the uprising."[174] According to legend, he did not say a word. As the boys became aware of him "[a] great silence" descended, and "the trouble stopped immediately."[175]

Early on Brother Mathias noticed this mischievous little kid from the docks. It is unclear what made George stand out. Perhaps it was just obvious that he sorely needed some adult to look out for him and to be in his corner. Whatever the trigger, Brother Mathias decided that he would be that person. He was unfailingly patient with George and, despite his broad responsibilities, he would find the time to help him when he had difficulties, whether with his "studies" or with his "tailoring work" or with whatever it was that was not going well.[176] Ruth credits Brother Mathias for teaching him "to read and write" and "the difference between right and wrong."[177] George also was clearly touched with the way Brother Mathias would warmly welcome him back to St. Mary's when he was released to his parents and the release did not work out. There was never even the hint of reproach.

There was one thing more that Brother Mathias could do: "I think I was born as a hitter the first day I ever saw him hit a baseball."[178] That day came in George's first summer at St. Mary's, the summer of 1902, as he watched Brother Mathias play fungo, which he did most Saturday evenings after supper. George would not have been the only one witnessing the performance, as the whole school would invariably come out to see. Brother Mathias tossed the ball in the air with his left hand and, with only his right one holding the bat, he would loft it 350 feet. His stroke was "effortless."[179] Ruth said he stood there in awe, "bug-eyed:" "I had never seen anything like that in my life."[180]

Though it is likely that George had played some form of baseball on the city streets of Baltimore before he came to St. Mary's, it is undeniable that it was at St. Mary's that he became passionate about the sport and began to perfect his skill. The chronology of George's development as a ballplayer is, to say the least, murky. But it without question occurred during his years at St. Mary's, where baseball was every bit as sacred as High Mass.

To begin with, there was no problem with equipment. If St. Mary's could not buy it, they could make it in one of the shops. Nor was there a problem with instruction. Most of the brothers were young enough to play alongside the boys, and those who were older, like Brother Mathias, coached. Getting up games was not a problem either. There were always a couple of boys around, which was a sufficient number for "pokenins," a two-man contest between pitcher and batter which George played by the hour.[181] But there were also all manner of full roster teams, a total of 40 in all.

St. Mary's baseball was divided into leagues, by dormitory floor or age or class or trade. There was also an "elite" league made of the oldest and best players from the various intramural "feeders," the teams named after real major league clubs: Red Sox, White Sox, Cubs, Giants. At the top of the pyramid was the "main" team, the "cream of the crop," which represented St. Mary's in contests against other schools.[182] The season was nine or 10 months long, running from March till November or December. St. Mary's crowds sometimes approached 3,000.

By dint of hard work, George progressed through the system. He took two to three hours of batting practice daily. Brother Mathias worked on his fielding by hitting him grounder after grounder or by playing catch. He made sure George was challenged, always putting him on teams with boys three or four years older than he. When George was eight or nine he played with the 12-year-olds; when he was 12 he played with the 16-year-olds. By the time George was 16 he was on the roster of an intramural "elite" team, and soon thereafter he was drafted for the interscholastic "main" team.[183] Ruth once guessed that while at St. Mary's he played 200 games a season, often appearing in double- and triple-headers. As a teenager he was practicing and playing more baseball than most professionals.

The position George typically played at St. Mary's was catcher. It was somewhat unusual for a southpaw to be behind the plate, and very unusual to play the position the way George did. In the absence of a lefty catcher's mitt, he wore a righties' mitt on his throwing hand, caught the ball, shoved the mitt under his right arm, grabbed the ball with his left hand and threw it back to the pitcher, unless a steal was on, in which case he would throw it to the pickoff man. George also played the outfield and, at times, third base, another odd placement for a left-handed player.

George's first outing as a pitcher occurred when he was 14 or 15, courtesy of Brother Mathias. The St. Mary's Red Sox were in a deep hole because everyone who took the mound was being shellacked. When the last of the pitchers was being hit all over the lot, George went into hysterics. Brother Mathias asked him what was so funny, and George replied, "That guy out there – getting his brains knocked out."[184] Brother Mathias told him to go out there himself and see if he could do any better. Before that day, George had never pitched in his life. He recalled that he did not "know how to stand on the rubber, or how to throw a curve or even how to get the ball over the plate."[185] Nonetheless, he also recalled feeling "a strange relationship" with the pitcher's mound, that it "seemed to be the most natural thing in the world to start pitching."[186] George must have caught on very quickly, because once his toe was on the rubber, no one else got a hit.[187]

While the boys and the Brothers began talking about George's baseball prowess almost from the start, the first reported "ink" he got was when he was 17. A box score in a 1912 edition of St. Mary's *Saturday Evening Star* recounted a game where George caught, played third and pitched (striking out six) and, batting lead-off, registered a double, a triple and the game's only home run. In June of that year, with George pitching for an "outside" team, the Mount Washington Club of Baltimore, he again struck out six in a 4-3 victory over Mt. St. Mary's College of Emmitsburg.[188]

George's name debuted in a "real" newspaper on June 8, 1913, in an article in the *Baltimore American* about a victory of the St. Mary's Stars over the St. Mary's White Sox, 10-3, with "Ruth" listed as "catcher."[189] During the summer of 1913, George was playing weekends for both amateur and semi-pro teams, and the press coverage, while a bit inaccurate, was a little more expansive. One newspaper piece noted that "Roth [sic], the speed boy" was expected to pitch for the St. Patrick's Catholic Club against powerhouse Northwestern AC; in the event, he tossed a one-hit shutout, striking out a dozen and getting a single and a double.[190] The next week he lost 4-3, but struck out 14. "Roth" appeared again for St. Patrick's, winning 2-1.[191] On August 3 "Ruth" is mentioned in an article as a player for the Bayonnes, catching both ends of a doubleheader and getting three hits. He was also in the lineup for the Bayonnes near the end of the month, this time positioned in left field. In an 18-2 thrashing of the Sparrows Point Marines he had a "perfect day," going four for four with a walk, a single, two doubles and a homer.[192] The sports writer said, "Ruth, the Bayonne fence buster, was there with the willow."[193] He played catcher for the Bayonnes in September, homering in a 12-11 victory. In another September game, this one written up in the St. Mary's *Evening Star*, it was reported that Ruth, "one of the Stars star slabmen," threw another one-hitter, notching 22 strikeouts, giving up a single free pass, and registering four hits.[194] There are no official statistics for these years, though Ruth himself says he "kept track."[195] He estimated that during one season he hit over 60 home runs in more than 200 games. As to batting average, he said he "used to hit .450 and .500."[196]

By the fall of 1913 the "incorrigible" George Herman Ruth Jr. "was the absolute king of all of St. Mary's baseball" and was "beginning to earn a reputation for himself around Baltimore."[197] At some point over the next few months he came to the attention of Jack Dunn, owner of the minor league Baltimore Orioles. According to one story, Dunn heard about Ruth from Joe Engel, a young pitcher for the Washington Senators, who shared a train ride with Dunn to D.C. Engel had just watched the freshman team of his *alma mater*, St. Mary's *College*, play the all-stars from St. Mary's *Industrial School*. Engel regaled Dunn with a tale about a kid from "the orphan asylum" who had "real stuff."[198] There are different versions of what happened next. Some say Dunn saw Ruth strike out 22 in a 6-0 thrashing of St. Joseph's College, "the rich school down the road."[199] Others say Dunn never saw George throw a pitch but did watch him "sliding on an ice slick" at St. Mary's and liked his "big, agile, rangy" build.[200]

Whatever the preliminaries, on February 14, 1914, right after George's 19th birthday, he was "paroled" to Jack Dunn. His contract promised him $100 a month for the six-month season. Two weeks later, on February 27, George was released from St. Mary's. His school record contains the brief notation: "He is going to join the Balt. Baseball Team."[201]

Roberto Clemente
August 18, 1934-December 31, 1972
Career span: 1955-72
Outfielder: Pittsburgh Pirates
Key Statistics: BA: .317; RBI:1,305; HR: 240; H: 3,000
Signal Honors: Hall of Fame, 1973; World Series MVP, 1967; National League MVP, 1967; All-Star Appearances, 1960-67, 1969-72; 1963.

Roberto Clemente was the first *bona fide* superstar of Latino origin to play in the American major leagues. Despite the fact that his life was tragically, and unnecessarily, cut short when he was on a mercy mission to Nicaragua, he nonetheless ranks in many listings as among the greatest ballplayers of all time.

Roberto was born on August 18, 1934 in Puerto Rico. His parents lived in the province of Carolina in the rural barrio of San Anton, located 12 miles southeast of the capital San Juan. Both his father, Melchor, and his mother, Luisa, had grown up in Carolina.

By the time Roberto was born, Melchor was the foreman, the *capataz*, of the "brigades" of cane cutters employed by Central Victoria, a sugar cane processing company. Melchor augmented his income by renting out his battered truck to deliver sand and gravel to construction sites. In addition, the front room of the Clemente house doubled as a grocery store, stocking eggs, milk, flour and, on Saturdays and Sundays, meat.

Melchor taught his children that a man "paid his debts," gave and "demanded" respect, held himself in a dignified fashion, took care of his family and helped those who could not help themselves.[202] He drummed into them the significance of his Jibaro roots, how the Jibaro were a proud people who scattered into the mountains rather than become slaves to the Spanish conquerors. He told them that the wealthy owners of the plantations were no better than they were. He stressed the values of honesty and hard work. And he impressed on his sons that he wanted each of them "to become a good man, a serious man."[203] Don Melchor was "hard," but he was loved by his children.[204] Dona Luisa was "idolized" by them.[205]

Luisa had been a widow for about five years with two children, Luis and Rosa Maria, when she married Melchor. Over time they had five children of their own: four sons – Matino, Andres, Ivaldo, Roberto – and a daughter, Ana Iris. Luisa has been described as "dignified," finely dressed and friendly.[206] She was said to have brought "warmth and a sense of the practical" to the Clemente household.[207] Luisa was heavy set in appearance and physically powerful. Her shoulders were so strong that she could, without assistance, lift a slaughtered cow from a wheelbarrow prior to butchering it. Her arm strength was such that at 75 she was able to throw the "opening ball" – with some mustard on it – to launch Puerto Rico's Winter League season.

Luisa needed that energy to meet the demands of her daily life. She was up at 1 am to do laundry and ironing for her husband's employer. When she came back home before dawn, she prepared the daily meals for her family, as well as the lunches for the people working on the plantation. She supplemented the family income further by taking in sewing. Luisa had little time for what she saw as idle pleasures. Roberto said she "never went to a movie [and] never learned to dance."[208]

While one family friend said the Clementes were "almost dirt poor," another said they were not "poor poor" but "a little bit below middle-income."[209]

The fact is that in absolute terms, the Clementes had very little money. But, by the standards of the country, they were not destitute. They had a roof over their head, electricity, clothes and enough to eat.

And Melchor always had a job and an income. According to one study, cutters of sugar cane earned $5.76 a week in 1934, and foremen, like Melchor, earned double that amount, or around $11.50 a week.[210] While not a small salary, given the large size of his family, there was only enough for the basics, no more. There were 12 mouths to feed: his and Luisa's, their seven children's and the three cousins who lived with them.

The Clementes had "a square white frame house" sited "deep in a grove" about five miles from the town of San Anton.[211] It is unclear whether there were a total of five rooms or five bedrooms.[212] Whatever the number, with a dozen people to bed down, some children were always sleeping in the living room. Moreover, conditions were spartan: "Everything plain inside: iron beds, one bathroom, built of concrete; bare white walls, furniture of wood and *pajilla*, rolled corn leaf."[213] The family staples were "pork and rice and pink beans."[214] After the Second World War, chicken was added to the menu. Whether food was sparse or plentiful, Melchor and Luisa always fed the children first and ate the leftovers afterwards.

However tight the economic circumstances, Roberto Clemente had good memories of his years at home He said it was a happy household with no "hate" and with parents who were "lovely."[215] At mealtime, the family would have their food, "make jokes" and talk: "That was something wonderful . . . to grow up with people who had to struggle to eat."[216]

Melchor was 51 when Roberto was born in the summer of 1934. From the time he was a little boy, he was called "Momen." His oldest brother Matino could not recall its origin. His mother said her eldest daughter gave him the name, and it had no particular meaning. But one biographer claims that an older cousin nicknamed him "Momen" because Roberto hated to be rushed and was always crying *"momentito, momentito"* when he felt hurried.[217]

Luisa said Roberto's hands were very "different" from those of her other children and were his most distinctive physical feature.[218] By the time he was an adolescent people were struck by how broad his palms were and the way they tapered into "widely spaced, long fingers."[219] A great friend of his claimed his hands were so huge that with just one he "could wash his face and his head at the same time . . ."[220]

In terms of personality, Robert was pensive, intelligent and extremely good-natured. If his father was ill, he would come home right away to help. If there was a death in the neighborhood, he would go to the house of the bereaved family to see what he could do. He was quiet and well-behaved and, unlike the other boys, "never got whipped."[221]

Roberto was also a hard-worker. From the age of eight, he and his brothers went to the fields with their father, and when they were 10 or so, they would make a few pennies carrying ice water to the cane cutters. The boys also earned a few extra coins by helping Melchor load and unload sand and gravel from his truck.

When Roberto was nine he desperately wanted a bicycle, a luxury his family could not afford. Melchor told Roberto if he wanted one he would have to buy it with his own money. Roberto understood, and he accepted his father's view that to be a "good man" one had to work.[222] So for a penny a day, he lugged a milk can back and forth from a neighbor's house to the local store, getting up at 6 am to do so. It took him three years, but he eventually had $27, enough for a used bike. Years after, when he could afford bicycles by the dozens, he thought back to what it took to get that first one, remarking, "Maybe that is why I don't smile so often."[223]

Melchor also believed in the value of education and made sure that his children went to the nearby Fernandez grammar school. Roberto was an "above average" but not exceptional student.[224] He had a reputation as a well-mannered and respectful boy. He was known, too, for being resourceful. When a teacher complained that the schoolyard was dirty and full of weeds, but that it was too costly to hire a maintenance crew, Roberto organized his classmates, browns and whites, into a clean-up brigade.

Roberto remained a model of deportment during his three years at Vizcarrondo High School.[225] His 10th grade history teacher, Mabel Caceres, recalling the shy boy who took the last chair in the classroom, had three distinct memories of her young "friend:" he had "beautiful hands" that were "[h]uge but gentle;" he was a dutiful son and "would do anything for his mother"; he was devoted and kind, once carrying her "to the doctor's office in his arms" when she had fallen ill.[226]

Though Roberto did not stand out scholastically in high school, he did as an athlete. He excelled at track and field, and could triple jump 45 feet and high jump 6 feet.[227] His premier event was the javelin, which he hurled 190 feet, leading to speculation that he would try out for the Olympics. However, Roberto's great love was baseball, at which he also excelled, chosen three years in a row for Vizcarrondo's all-star team.

Roberto had become obsessed with the sport when he was very young. Both he and his mother are clear that he started to play by the time he was five, before he went to school. Clemente recalled that as "a little kid, the only thing I used to do was play ball all the time."[228] In her memory, Luisa could still could hear the incessant pounding from her young son, lying in bed, bouncing a rubber ball against the walls. As he got bigger, Roberto would scrounge "pick-up" games in the neighborhood and be gone for hours, often missing lunch and frequently not returning until dark.

In a way Roberto's passion for baseball is no surprise. For one thing, it was the dominant sport on the island. It could be played year-round. There was an active Winter League boasting talented locals, Negro Leaguers and major leaguers wanting to stay in shape at the close of their regular season. For another thing, there was not much else for a young boy from Carolina province to do for fun: the beaches were 10 miles to the north, the rainforest was 15 miles to the east, and the Clementes did not have a car. Plus there was the fact that Roberto's brother Matino, seven years his senior, was an avid and accomplished ballplayer, a star in a premier amateur league, renowned for his excellence on both offense and defense. As Roberto's first coach, Matino instilled in his little brother a love for the game. Finally, there is the matter of destiny. In a 1972 interview Clemente said "The more I think about it, I [am] convinced that God wanted me to play baseball."[229] His mother had come to the same conclusion: "Roberto was born to be a baseball player."[230]

At eight Roberto joined his first neighborhood softball team, playing "organized baseball" on the field across the way from his house.[231] The equipment was makeshift. The first balls were fashioned of tightly-knotted rags, though twisted magazines and newspapers or old pairs of stockings were adequate substitutes. The first bats were made from the branches of guava trees. The first gloves were made from coffee bean sacks, which also were the raw material for the bases. For practice, the boys often played fungo with broomsticks and bottle caps.

At 10, maybe younger, Roberto's older brothers brought him along to play in a school-league game. A boyhood friend, Manuel Maldonado Denis, recalled that while Matino was a great first baseman, Lorenzo was a powerful hitter and Andres was accomplished on the mound, "All you had to do was look at Momen to know that he had been born to play baseball."[232]

When Roberto was around 11 or 12 he started taking the bus into San Juan to watch the professionals play at Sixto Escobar stadium. Sometimes his father gave him a quarter to go into town to buy a 15 cent lottery ticket, and he got off a mile before the stop, to hang around the stadium. Sometimes his father gave him a quarter to go into town to buy a 15 cent bleacher seat and go inside.

Roberto's idol was Monte Irvin of the San Juan Senators. During Roberto's formative years, before he turned 15, Irvin was one of the best players in the Winter League.[233] Clemente explained later that he admired Irvin "because not only was he a good hitter, but he had such a good arm."[234] Roberto would wait outside the stadium after the games just to get a glimpse of his hero, though he was too nervous to look him in the eye, much less speak to him. Eventually Roberto did get up the courage to ask Irvin for his autograph, and they struck up a friendship. Irvin would allow Roberto to carry his glove or garment bag and as a "reward" give him baseballs and let him stay to watch the game for free.[235] Irvin talked about their special relationship 50 years after the fact, revealing "I taught Roberto how to throw."[236]

In a family album, a teenaged Roberto wrote of his feelings for the sport:

> I loved the game so much that even though our field was muddy and lots of trees on it, I played many hours every day. The fences were about 150 feet from home plate. One day I

hit about 10 home runs in a game we started about 11 A.M. and finished about 6:30 P.M.[237]

Don Melchor apparently was at that marathon contest and proudly acknowledged, "[H]e played surprisingly well against boys his age and older."[238] Dona Luisa was less enamored of Roberto's ceaseless play, his being continually late, his neglecting family dinners. She became so exasperated one night that, in a fit of rage, she threw his bat into the fire.

And Roberto's fanaticism *could be* exasperating. When he was not playing on his local team, he was throwing a ball against the ceiling or in San Juan at Sixto Escobar watching games or just hanging around the stadium or squeezing a rubber ball to improve his forearm and wrist strength or listening to Winter League radio broadcasts. He even slept with a foul ball that had been hit by his hero, Monte Irvin.

When Roberto was about 14, Roberto Marin entered his life, a man so important to him that upon recording his 3,000[th] – and last – hit, Clemente told a nationwide radio audience, "I dedicate that hit to the person I owe most to in professional baseball, Roberto Marin."[239] Marin first noticed Roberto as the class of a ragtag band "batting empty tomato sauce cans with sticks."[240] According to street rules, a player remained at the plate until he was struck out, and Roberto stayed at bat forever, swatting the cans very far and in every direction. Marin, who as a boy had played the same game with the same improvised equipment, asked Roberto to try out for an All-Star team sponsored by his employer, the Sello Rojo Rice Company. Roberto made the team, and by the time he was 15 he was a regular fixture. Marin, who was both organizer and manager, started Roberto at shortstop, eventually moving him to the outfield to make better use of his rifle arm. Roberto soon gained a reputation for his acrobatic catches and, over time, for his hits to deep right field. In addition to playing for Marin, Roberto had joined the San Juan youth league, and as a 14-year-old – two years younger than most of his teammates – was selected for its "future stars" competition.[241]

At 16 Roberto was recruited from the Sello Rojos by the Ferdinand Juncos, one of the premier teams in the Double A amateur league. Rather than softball, the Juncos played hardball. Roberto's experience at this higher level, mostly as an outfielder, further and dramatically improved his hitting, particularly his ability to pull the ball. He played for the Juncos for the next two years. Marin, who stayed in close contact with Roberto, was convinced that he could do even better than Double A. He told Roberto that he was as good as the professionals who played in the Winter League.

As Roberto was turning 18, there were two significant developments bearing out Marin's confidence in Roberto's potential. While the precise chronology and the details are subject to dispute, no one questions that Marin was involved in each of them.

UNDERDOG GREATS

The first was Roberto's discovery by Alex Campanis, a scout for the Brooklyn Dodgers. Campanis had been a player and manager in the minor leagues from the end of the 1930s to the beginning of the 1940s. He spent the next several years in public relations, showing World Series newsreels to potential season ticket buyers. Then, in 1948, the legendary Branch Rickey, Campanis' mentor, asked him to start scouting the Caribbean for talent.

Campanis arranged for a Brooklyn Dodgers tryout on November 6, 1952, at Sixto Escobar Stadium in San Juan.[242] Seventy-two eager young men and boys gathered to participate, including Roberto who was accompanied by Marin. The first exercise was to throw from the outfield to home plate. One of the 72 threw "a bullet from center on the fly."[243] The throw was so true and hard that Campanis asked the kid to do it again. His second effort was equally stunning and on target. Campanis next timed each of the hopefuls in the 60-yard dash. The kid with the great arm was also fast. He ran the distance in 6.4 seconds, twice, in a bulky uniform, at a time when the world record for the 60 was 6.1 seconds.

Campanis had seen enough and dismissed all but the sure-throwing speedster. He asked him to stay and take a turn in the batting cage. After he stroked a number of line drives, mostly to center, Campanis instructed the pitcher, a seasoned Winter Leaguer, "to keep the ball outside" in order to take advantage of the fact that the kid stood so far from the plate.[244] Pitch placement made no difference; the hits kept on coming. During a 20-minute display, the kid sprayed drives "all over the place," 10 of which had home run distance.[245] Campanis learned that the "kid" was 18-year-old Roberto Clemente. Nearly two decades after Roberto's performance, by which time Campanis had seen thousands of prospects, he still maintained that Clemente was "the greatest natural athlete I have ever seen as a free agent."[246] In his contemporaneous scouting report, which graded each young hopeful on arm strength, fielding, hitting, speed, power, accuracy, reactions, the lowest grade he gave Roberto was an A. Campanis knew he was onto something, but since the budding superstar was still in high school, he could not legally formalize an arrangement with the Dodgers.

The second key development was Roberto's discovery by Pedrin Zorilla, major league scout and owner of the Santurce Cangrejeros – the Crabbers, a local baseball team. There is no consensus as to whether Zorilla's "look" came before or after the Campanis tryout, and there is some indication that Zorilla met Roberto before he actually saw him in action. But at some point, likely in the second half of 1952, and definitely at Marin's urging, Zorilla attended a Juncos game in Manati when Roberto was in the lineup. Zorilla was favorably impressed by Roberto's play, both on the field and at the plate. There are various accounts of Roberto's feats that day. One has him lacing a ball 345 feet, stretching it into a double and making a sensational grab of a long line drive followed by a perfect strike to second to complete a double play.[247] Another has him making *two* great catches and throwing out a runner at the *plate*, as well as notching a solid double.[248] A third, the most dramatic and elaborate, has him hitting a double to score two runs in the second, a triple in the fourth, another double in the seventh and rifling a victory-saving throw to tag a runner in the ninth.[249]

After watching Roberto, Zorilla asked Marin to bring him to his house the next day. Zorilla told Roberto he wanted him to join the Crabbers, offering him a $400 signing bonus and a starting weekly salary of $40 "until he learns to wear a uniform."[250] Though the Puerto Rican teams were apparently not subject to the rules which precluded Campanis from acting, Zorilla still needed Don Melchor to approve any contract with his son. Melchor took Zorilla's offer to a neighbor who advised him to hold out for more, maybe as much as $5,000. Some combination of Marin and the senior Clemente tried to negotiate a better deal with Zorilla, but Zorilla would not budge. Roberto told Marin and his father that he wanted to sign. He said the offer was fair, and he would earn more after he proved himself. Melchor relented, and a formal contract was executed in the fall of 1952.

The Santurce team was the best in the Winter League, filled with many black stars from the U.S. Zorilla's philosophy was not to play the youngsters too early, for fear they would get discouraged by failing to hit major league pitching. He also wanted to avoid alienating the veterans by inserting boys into the lineup who were not even out of high school. Roberto did well in his debut as a ninth-inning defensive replacement, making a good play in the field and producing a timely hit. But his success did not get him off the bench. During the first two months, Roberto saw limited action and became frustrated. After a while he told Marin that he would quit if he did not play more and asked Marin to transmit an ultimatum to Zorilla. Zorilla was unmoved and said it was just Roberto's first year and that he, as the owner, would decide when the time was right to give his young rookie more playing time. Marin, afraid to discourage Roberto, softened the Zorilla message, telling him to be patient and that his day would come soon.

Late in the year, it did. With three men on base, a batter on deck who had trouble with lefties and the Crabbers at the short end of the score, Roberto was sent in to pinch hit. He made the most of it, stroking a double that won the game. More importantly, thereafter he was in the linep regularly. Though he batted only 77 times in the 70-game season, and had only 18 hits – a .234 average – it was not a bad start for a teenager facing high-caliber pitchers for the first time.[251]

Even at this early stage, Crabber manager James "Buster" Clarkson was impressed by Roberto. Though Roberto was by no means perfect, Clarkson was struck by the boy's intensity: "[H]e never made the same mistake twice. He had baseball savvy and he listened."[252] For his part, Clemente never forgot the interest Clarkson took in him: "He insisted the other players allow me to take batting practice and he helped me. He put a bat behind my left foot to made sure I didn't drag my foot."[253]

Clarkson predicted great things for his young, eager outfielder, and when Roberto was in the dumps about his lack of playing time, he offered encouragement. And a prediction. He told Roberto, "Keep it up and you'll be as good as Willie Mays."[254] In retelling this story years later, Clarkson gave his personal assessment of how it all turned out: "And he was."[255]

What are the odds of making it as a major league baseball player? In 2000 there were 30 professional baseball teams, 15 in the National League and 15 in the American League. The maximum roster size permitted for each team, before the September call-up, was 25, meaning that at any one time, there were 750 major leaguers. Since injury and performance issues mean that there are lineup changes during the course of a year, I increased the 750 by 40% to 1050.[256] According to the 2000 U.S. Census, there were slightly over 52 million males between the ages of 18 and 42, the rough range of ages represented in the majors. That means in the year 2000 the chances of a male "making it" as a professional baseball player was about 1 in 50,000 or approximately .002%.[257]

I have also calculated the odds more conservatively. On the one hand, I expanded the numerator to include all significant professional sports leagues: the NFL, NBA, NHL, MLS, USTA, PGA and WBF.[258] On the other hand, I limited the denominator to only include the proportion of boys who played inter-scholastic sports in high school.[259] The overall effect of these changes is to improve the odds from one chance in about 50,000 to one chance in roughly 4,700 or from .002% to .021%. Much better, but still daunting.

II. At the Movies

It is far more difficult to identify the greatest movie stars than it was to name the greatest ballplayers – at least it is far more difficult to come up with a list that seems authoritative. In part, this is because acting, unlike baseball, does not lend itself to objective metrics. There are no "batting" or "earned run" averages; no "on base" or "fielding" percentages. This problem is compounded by a seeming reluctance of movie critics, who might have their own private lists, to disclose them. To be sure, "best actor" polls are conducted, but there are no qualifications for voting and the results tend to snapshots of contemporary popularity.[1]

For my purposes, this dilemma was solved by the American Film Institute ("AFI") which in 1998 asked a jury of 1,800 film artists (directors, screenwriters, actors, etc.), critics, historians and other cultural leaders to choose from a list of 500 the top 50 screen legends of all time. Among the criteria they were asked to consider were star quality, craft, legacy and historical context. The top 20 male actors who emerged from that poll were:[2]

1. Humphrey Bogart
2. Cary Grant*
3. James Stewart
4. Marlon Brando
5. Fred Astaire
6. Henry Fonda
7. Clark Gable*
8. James Francis Cagney*
9. Spencer Tracy
10. Charles Chaplin
11. Gary Cooper
12. Gregory Peck*
13. John Wayne*
14. Lawrence Olivier
15. Gene Kelly
16. Orson Welles
17. Kirk Douglas*
18. James Dean
19. Burt Lancaster
20. The Marx Brothers

The six actors with asterisks after their names will be the subject of the biographies which follow, also presented from the lowest ranked to the highest. In addition, there is a seventh biography, another "Wild Card," this one profiling Sidney Poitier, one of the earliest *bona fide* black movie stars with staying power. Poitier came in at number 22 in the AFI survey.

Kirk Douglas
December 9, 1916-present
Career span: 1946-2003
Major Films: *Champion* (1949); *Ace in the Hole* (1951); *The Bad and the Beautiful* (1952); *Lust for Life* (1956); *Spartacus* (1960); *Lonely Are the Brave* (1962).
Signal Honors: Academy Award Nominee for Best Actor 1949, 1952, 1956; Honorary Academy Award 1995; American Film Institute Lifetime Achievement Award 1991.

Herschel Danielovitch was born in Russia in approximately 1884. Little has been written about his childhood. We do know that he married Bryna Sanglel, the daughter of Ukrainian farmers, and that the couple lived in an impoverished village south of Moscow.

Herschel and Bryna were Jews. As such, they were subject to the legal restrictions and threats of violence sanctioned by the government at least since 1881, when a Jewish student was charged with being complicit in the assassination of Tsar Alexander II. Things got worse after 1903, when an anti-Jewish massacre led by priests in Kishinev left nearly 50 dead, almost twice that number severely injured, and hundreds of homes and businesses destroyed or routed. *The New York Times* graphically described the "[b]abes literally torn to pieces by the frenzied and bloodthirsty mob," the "streets piled with corpses and wounded."[3] Such pogroms became even more commonplace after 1905 and the collapse of the Russian Revolution.

It was against this backdrop of terror that Herschel received training as a tailor. Because he lacked the natural dexterity to maneuver a needle, his instructors tied his thumb to his forefinger to improve his precision. Whether it was the pain of the apprenticeship or the prospect of being drafted to fight in the Russo-Japanese war, Herschel immigrated to the United States in 1908. Bryna remained in Russia another two years, working in a bakery to earn the funds for her passage. Her departure was motivated not only by her desire to be reunited with her husband, but to leave the country which had allowed her brother to be murdered in the street before her eyes.

The Danielovitches arrived on Ellis Island for processing. They were among the droves of poor, illiterate immigrants who believed that in America they would find streets paved with gold. They did not remain in New York City, but traveled 180 miles up the Hudson River to the city of Amsterdam, New York, where Herschel's older brother Avram had settled.

Herschel and Bryna promptly began having children, all of whom were born in December and all of whom, like their parents, had dimples in their chins. The first three children were girls: Pesha born in 1910, Kaleh born in 1912 and Tamara born in 1914. In 1916, Bryna had her first boy: Issur, the future Kirk Douglas. Two years after that she gave birth to twin daughters, Hashka and Sifra. In 1924, at the age of 40, she bore her last child, Rachel. Douglas said later: "We laugh at it now, but it was terrible being the only male in a house full of women. I was dying to get out. In a sense it lit a fire under me."[4]

Douglas's autobiography does not present this entirely female household as all that terrible. He writes about the "tranquility of the kitchen...with the wood-burning stove... No one there but Ma and me and the angels."[5] He writes about his first day at the Fourth Ward School and his fear when his teacher pulled him "away from my sisters, away from my mother."[6] He writes about his older sister Tamara and how they were two "good friends" who "used to stroll through town with our arms around each other."[7] And he writes about his sadness when he was forced to sleep alone on the parlor sofa and how he "missed not being next to the warm body of [Pesha], of having her read to me from *The Bobbsey Twins* or the Frank Merriwell stories."[8] Issur's problem was not with too many domineering women, but with one domineering man. The real tragedy during those Amsterdam years was his relationship – actually the lack of relationship – with his father.

Herschel Danielovitch was a man's man: "a big drinker, [who] spent most of his time in saloons, much of it in fights."[9] In his most celebrated brawl, Herschel took on seven men, throwing one out the window and braining or bruising the other six. He avoided jail because the judge could not believe that a single man could create such mayhem. Other feats added to his "legend,"

> that he popped metal bottlecaps and crushed shot glasses with his teeth; that he would go from saloon to saloon with an iron bar, betting for drinks that he could bend it with his bare hands, and doing it; that nobody could beat him at arm wrestling.[10]

Not only was he physically powerful and utterly fearless, he was also a magnetic figure: "He had a tremendous personality, could hypnotize people with his dramatic storytelling. Wherever he went, he made an impact."[11]

But this huge character was totally illiterate and wholly unskilled. Although Amsterdam, New York, was a leading industrial city, producing carpets, knit goods, pearl buttons, brooms and gloves, Herschel Danielovitch did not work in any of these factories.[12] With few options, he became a peddler, traveling the neighborhoods with a horse and wagon, collecting and then re-selling metal, junk and rags. In terms of status, "Even on Eagle Street, in the poorest section of town, where all the families were struggling, the ragman was on the lowest rung on the ladder."[13]

Regardless of his father's social status, Issur did not look down on him. When Herschel was in the neighborhood, Issur would race after his wagon after school and clamber over the rubbish to sit next to him. While Herschel may have been embarrassed by his son's company, Issur craved these times because he "wanted so much to let him know that I wasn't ashamed of him. I wanted so much to let him know how much I loved him."[14]

But Herschel was seemingly incapable of accepting that love, much less giving it back to his under-sized, sensitive and shy boy. When Issur was eight, he slipped into a deep trench filled with water and would have drowned if his friend Wolfie had not waded in and pulled him out. When Wolfie brought Issur back to Eagle Street, Herschel beat Wolfie up, thinking he had pushed his son into the ditch. When Herschel found out what really happened, he beat up Issur instead. On another night, Issur split his head open during a game of tag. When the neighborhood boys brought him home, bleeding and in tears, his father told him, "That's what you get for going out and playing."[15] When his father was not verbally abusive, he was indifferent.

Douglas summed up his highly conflicted feelings, decades after the fact:

> I loved my father but I hated him, too. He was a ragman who drove a horse and wagon and couldn't read or write. But to me he was big. He was strong. He was a man. I didn't know what I was. But I wanted to be accepted by him, to be given a pat on the back.[16]

One evening, after years of frustration, a teenaged Issur boiled over. It happened during one of those rare occasions when Herschel was at home, rather than carousing at the local bar. The family was sitting around a table, drinking Russian tea. As a scowling Herschel sucked the tea through the sugar cube in his glass, ignoring his wife, his six daughters and his son, Issur could stand his sullen presence no longer. He filled his spoon with hot tea and flicked it across the table into his Herschel's face. His father roared, grabbed Issur and flung him into the next room. Though stunned and terrified, Issur survived. His act of defiance became "one of the most important moments of my life," the moment Herschel knew Issur "was alive," the moment that made him "feel different from my sisters – a man."[17]

The emotional impoverishment of Issur's childhood mirrored its economic deprivation. Herschel's failure as a provider may not have been a source of embarrassment, but it did mean that his family lived on the edge of survival. We know little of the Danielovitch house, except that it was a dilapidated structure at the end of a sloping street, located next to the mills, with far fewer rooms than inhabitants. Insulation from the winter cold was provided, Russian-style, by manure deposited in a trench dug around the base of the foundation. Food was always a problem, and the family often went hungry. When there was enough money to go to the kosher butcher, they would buy meat – usually one pound, but on special occasions, two – making sure there were plenty of bones to make soup. Cornflakes and milk was a luxury dinner. Issur thought it a feast when he and a friend roasted a potato found in the street in a fire they made in the gutter. Recalling this scene, when his life had become one of comfort and plenty, Douglas said: "Unless you've been hungry-poor, you don't know what poor means."[18]

All the children worked to augment Herschel's limited income. When he was a young boy, Issur ran errands and sold candy and soda to the workers at the mill near their house, until the factory decided it would supply the refreshments. When he was older, he delivered out-of-town newspapers, since Jews weren't given routes for the *Amsterdam Evening Recorder*.

The Danielovitches were orthodox Jews, keeping a kosher home, lighting candles on Friday evenings and attending synagogue on the Sabbath. Being Jewish in Amsterdam meant being one of an unpopular minority. It meant Issur was constantly evading or receiving beatings at the hands of the various street gangs that roamed the neighborhood. Ironically, given what he endured because of his religion, he was not at all enamored of its teachings. Although he faithfully attended Sunday school, he did not like the Old Testament God he learned about in class. He did not understand why this God would test Abraham by asking him to sacrifice his son or why he forbade Moses from entering the Promised Land, after spending 40 years in exile leading his people to their fabled destination.

Nonetheless, Issur pursued his religious studies and at 13 was presented for Bar Mitzvah. However, even that joyous event became a source of regret and disappointment. His Bar Mitzvah gifts, when added to the nickels and dimes he had put away from years of menial jobs, had produced a nest egg of $313 – $4,515 in 2017 dollars. Herschel asked to borrow this money to purchase a large lot of copper which he was sure he could resell at a huge profit. Bryna pleaded with her son to say "No," but Issur would do anything to try to please his father. Issur had turned 13 in December 1929, and the copper his father hoped would reap 24 cents a pound fetched only two cents. Herschel had lost his son's entire savings.

While Douglas could never look back at his childhood as "the good old days," it was not a period of unrelenting bleakness. He had friends. There was Wolfie, who had saved him from drowning in the ditch, Pete, whose mother introduced him to chicken cacciatore and spaghetti, and Sonia, whom he would visit in the evenings to talk about his hopes and plans. There were the kids on the street, the Stoshes and Gingas and Yabos. He and his pals would play made-up games like "church on fire," which resulted in a ritualistic "initiation by urination" when shouted by a newcomer perched at a hydrant.[19] His best friend was a large, powerful male dog, part Doberman and part hound, named Tiger. Tiger would race up the street to lick Issur's face, pull his improvised barrel stave sled and growl at anyone who seemed to pose a threat. With so little money, Issur enjoyed few extravagances, but he did get to go to a circus in Amsterdam, hitchhike to Proctor's movie theater in Schenectady and buy a cheap banjo on the installment plan (ultimately repossessed for non-payment.)

It is clear that it was Bryna who instilled in her son the importance of education, and it was at school that Issur learned the joy of performing. At age five, as a kindergartener, he took part in a presentation to parents and teachers, reciting a poem about the Red Robin of Spring. Though he was small and by nature timid, he had learned to use his imagination to escape from the unsatisfying reality of his world. And so, as Issur spoke the words, he was no longer inside a rundown urban schoolhouse but in a sunlit country field serenaded by singing birds. The audience enthusiastically applauded when he finished. Their response gave him confidence and the sense of worth that he so desperately needed. He later said that it also gave him the first inkling of what he wanted to be.

In second grade, Issur had the lead role in *The Shoemaker and the Elves*. His mother made him his costume, and children from all the schools in the area attended the special evening performance. Unbeknownst to him, his father was in the back watching and after the play took him out to buy him an ice cream cone. Douglas wrote in his autobiography, "No award I have ever received has meant more to me than that ice cream cone."[20]

When he got to Wilbur Lynch High School, Issur became the protégé – or project – of Louise Livingston, the tall, patrician head of the English Department. Her impact was life-changing. She opened his mind to the world of poetry and listened to him describe his dream of an acting career. "To be a great actor," Mrs. Livingston said, "you have to be a great person. You must be educated. You must be trained."[21] And with her help and encouragement, he developed a set of goals and a plan of action.

While Louis Livingston's influence was pivotal, her motives were mixed, or at least complex. Douglas makes it plain that this widow, with a son only five years older than he, sought a relationship with her prize student that was more than platonic.[22] He was not offended by her advances. In fact, he was flattered by her attention and remained close to her until she died. Whether or not they were physically intimate is beside the point. For his teacher, like his father, had a duty to look out for him, and neither did. His father did not give him enough attention; his teacher gave him attention of the wrong kind. In each instance an important adult in a position of responsibility had failed him.

In his junior year Issur entered a public speaking and acting contest sponsored by the local Sanford Mills. He chose a poem, *Across the Border*, which recounted the haunting thoughts of a dying soldier. His dramatic rendition won him the gold medal. His employer, Mr. Goldmeer, was so proud of Issur that he asked him to do an encore performance for all the salesmen of his Wholesale Grocery Company. In his senior year, he saw his first real play, an Albany production of *The Barretts of Wimpole Street*, starring Katharine Cornell, Broadway's premier actress.

Issur was 17½ on June 27, 1934, when his high school held its graduation exercises at the Rialto movie theater. He had been elected treasurer of his class. At the ceremony, his mother and sister heard the announcement that he was being honored for his essay, "The Play's the Thing," and for having delivered the Best Speech at Commencement. It was also announced that he had won the Best Acting Prize.

The summer after his senior year Issur found work as a bellhop at the Orchard House on Lake George. The gentiles-only resort catered to young Christian ladies in search of romance. The attractive older woman who managed the hotel told Douglas of her dislike for Jews and how, despite their appearance or their name, "she could spot them in a minute. There was a smell about them."[23] At the end of the summer having satisfied a large number of the younger patrons, Issur was invited by the proprietor to her room for a "good-bye" drink which led to his satisfying her as well. He made it clear, in the midst of their coupling, using language both colorful and graphic, that it was a Jew who was having his way with her.

However gratifying his conquest, Issur returned to Amsterdam in September about to turn 18, with no prospects of getting out of town. It was a desperate period. With his sister's help he was hired to work in the men's section of the M. Lurie Department Store. He had one good suit and a light overcoat that he wore to work each day. The job was numbingly dull. For a time, perhaps to break the monotony, he stole small amounts from his employer, until he had the sense that management was becoming suspicious. He turned down an opportunity to handle publicity for a grocery chain, concerned that he would get trapped by the handsome salary. He played John Barrymore in an amateur theater production of *The Royal Family*. He fended off jealous advances from his former English teacher.

By the next September, now about to turn 19, Issur decided to take a gamble and see if he could get on with his education. After a tearful good-bye with his mother and sisters and a brusque one with his father, he accompanied his friend, Pete Riccio, who was a rising sophomore at St. Lawrence University in Canton, New York. He and Pete began hitchhiking to the school, the final leg of their trip, somewhat appropriately, provided by a driver hauling a truckload of fertilizer.

Issur arrived on campus and went directly to the administrative office with his transcript and records. His grades were good, and he had won several awards. He was ushered in to meet Dean Hewlitt, who was like a film version of a college administrator: "lined face," "steel-gray hair," "gruff voice."[24] The Dean found out quickly that Issur had only $163 to cover both tuition and expenses. After a long moment of silence, and "a whiff of the horse manure," the Dean said, "All right. We'll take a chance on you. We'll work out a college loan. My secretary will show you where to go to register."[25]

It was a happy ending, just like in the movies.

John "Duke" Wayne
May 27, 1907-June 11, 1979
Career span: 1926-76
Major Films: *Stagecoach* (1939); *They Were Expendable* (1945); *Red River* (1948); *The Quiet Man* (1952); *The Searchers* (1956); *Rio Bravo* (1959); *True Grit* (1969).
Signal Honors: Academy Award Winner for Best Actor 1969; Academy Award Nominee for Best Actor 1949.
Miscellaneous: Actor with most years as number one at the box office.

John Wayne was far more complex than the iconic "strong, silent type" he so often portrayed on the screen. The complexities were a direct outgrowth of the unhappy marriage of his parents, Clyde Morrison and the former Mary Brown. Their troubled relationship explains a lot about why he was who he was and why he did what he did.

Wayne's paternal ancestors arrived in the United States in 1799, when his great-great-grandfather, Robert Morrison, emigrated from Northern Ireland. Robert Morrison settled first in South Carolina and then moved to Ohio, where he became a prosperous farmer and a state legislator. Wayne's great-grandfather, James Morrison, also a farmer, began life in Ohio but then moved to Illinois. Wayne's grandfather, Marion Mitchell Morrison, initially took up farming as well, but ended up in the real estate business and found success at it.

Wayne's father, Clyde Leonard Morrison, was born in 1884 in Illinois, but grew up in Iowa. After high school, he spent a semester as a football player at Iowa State and a year as a music student at Simpson College. In 1903, at the age of 19, he changed directions and enrolled at the Highland Park College of Pharmacy in Des Moines. He was described as a "quiet, intelligent, and gentle young man, very easygoing and soft-spoken."[26] He was also thought to be very handsome.

While finishing his training, Clyde met Mary Alberta Brown, known as Molly, likely at the Methodist Church they both attended. Molly, of Scotch-Irish descent, grew up in Des Moines and was employed by the telephone company. Her father was a printer. Her mother ran a dress-making shop. By the standards of the day, Molly's parents were comfortable members of the middle class. Molly was described as "energetic, outspoken and opinionated."[27] She was of medium height and had red hair and green eyes.

After a whirlwind romance, Clyde and Molly eloped and were married by a justice of the peace in Knoxville, Iowa, on September 29 of 1905 or 1906.[28] After the ceremony, they settled in Winterset, Iowa, where Clyde began his career as pharmacist's clerk at Smith's Drug Store. Mr. Smith rented them a small frame house approximately 860 square feet in area.

On May 27, 1907, Molly's first son was born. Molly's pregnancy had been extremely difficult, as had been her labor and the ultimate delivery of her 13-pound baby. Clyde and Molly christened the boy Marion Robert Morrison, the "Marion" in honor of Clyde's father Marion Mitchell Morrison, the "Robert" in honor of Molly's father, Robert Emmett Brown. The boy's nickname was Bobby.

Clyde's first job did not pay enough, especially because he could not refuse friends who needed "a loan." As a result, from the very early days of their marriage Molly often had to ask her parents for help with the finances. A Winterset neighbor remembered Molly as a tough, mercurial woman who, without warning, could "fly off the handle."[29] Clyde was seen as her opposite even-tempered, steady and warm.

After several years of financial frustration, Clyde concluded that he would never be happy unless he owned a pharmacy,[30] and at the end of 1910, with a down payment borrowed from his father, he bought the Rexall Drug Store in Earlham. A year later, he was forced to declare bankruptcy. The problem may have simply been that Earlham's population of less than 1,000 was not large enough to support a drugstore. But Molly thought the problem was Clyde: he gave credit too easily and to the wrong customers. Molly believed her husband was a failure, and she let him know it regularly and loudly.

Molly and Clyde stayed in Earlham until the spring of 1912, when Clyde left for Keokuk to be a pharmacist's clerk, again. Molly remained in Earlham with Bobby to await the birth of her second child. By late summer, at the midpoint of her pregnancy, she told Clyde to take Bobby to live with him. She could not handle or did not enjoy her son, and Clyde could and did. Clyde was patient with the youngster and was able to calm him when he was fussy. He let him spend his days with him at the drugstore. At night he would read him to sleep. Clyde adored Bobby, and Bobby adored Clyde.

The Morrisons' second son was born in December 1912. Molly decided that he should be called Robert and that "Bobby" Morrison would have to get used to being called "Marion." This would seem silly, if it were not so sad. Molly did not like her first son, and never would, even after he became famous. His birth had nearly killed her, or so she had convinced herself.[31] Further, he looked like her husband, and Molly did not like her husband. Moreover, he was a difficult child, crying constantly, hard to put to bed, restless and, even at five, running away, sometimes ending up in another part of town and sometimes on a freight train that took him to another city. It never occurred to Molly that Bobby's behavior was a reaction to the strife at home and his desire for attention. Whatever the root causes of Molly's aversion, it never changed, and it had a fateful impact on the boy who would become John Wayne.

By 1913 Molly, Clyde and their two sons had returned to Molly's parents' home in Des Moines, where Clyde took on a succession of part-time jobs. The continuing bickering between Molly and Clyde and the arrival of a new brother did nothing to improve young Marion's disposition. He suffered from attacks of insomnia, was extremely fidgety and was prone to tantrums. And then, just as Molly's parents had opened their home to their daughter at a time of need, Clyde's father proposed a way that his son could get a new start in life. The elder Marion Morrison had moved to California some years before, and he invited Clyde and his family to come out West and take up farming, as generations of previous Morrisons had done. The idea of a change of scenery appealed to Clyde, not only because it would provide a fresh beginning, but also because he was suffering from a severe cough and shortness of breath, and his doctor had strongly suggested that he relocate to a drier climate.[32] The acreage that Clyde's father purchased fit the prescription: it was on the edge of the Mojave dessert.

Clyde traveled to California in late 1913 to begin to prepare the land and to build a place to live. A year later he sent for Molly, her parents and the boys. The property Clyde's dad owned was part of a small village called Palmdale. The house he and his dad built was a four-room wooden shack with no plumbing, no gas, no electricity and no telephone. It had low ceilings, which made it stifling in the summertime. It was drafty. And there was dust everywhere.

Because money was tight, food was bought on credit. They never had chicken or meat, other than jackrabbit, so their meals were made up of the vegetables they raised, which meant they principally ate potatoes and beans. An exception was the time that the general store had a sale on cases of tuna fish, which became the menu for several months. Wayne later recalled being so hungry that at times he thought his "stomach was glued to my backbone."[33]

Clyde's concept was to grow corn and peas, two crops which could be harvested without heavy machinery. According to the homestead rules, if he could develop the 80 acres he owned, he would be allowed to annex the 560 acres surrounding them. Clyde labored from early morning till nighttime to irrigate, clear, plow, plant and harvest his spread.

Young Marion was only seven when they settled in Palmdale, not old enough to help with anything other than the shucking at harvest time. He did, however, acquire two skills befitting the cowboy roles he would play when he was grown up: how to shoot a rifle and how to ride a horse. He developed these skills not for amusement, but out of necessity. He needed to be able to shoot in order to protect his father from the rattlesnakes which were slithering around while he was tending the fields. And he needed to be able to ride, so he could pick up the mail and the groceries in town and get to the public school situated several miles away.

In the autumn of 1914 young Marion entered second grade at the Lancaster Grammar School. His day started at 5 am, since he had chores to do beforehand. He proved to be both a serious and able student. But the school experience was not a happy one. He was regularly bullied by his classmates because of his sissified name, his odd accent, his gawky build and his timid nature.

Molly liked Palmdale even less than her oldest son and often threatened to go back to Iowa. The first year's corn crop fetched a decent price, and Clyde was convinced he would succeed. But in the second year, the price of corn collapsed, and it became apparent that the farming venture was not sustainable. Clyde's father died in December 1915, and in June 1916, after the school term ended, the Morrisons left the desert.

They re-located to Glendale, a pretty suburb of Los Angeles surrounded by vineyards and orchards, boasting five schools, 15 churches and two newspapers. It was a far cry from Palmdale with its two-block Main Street occupied by a livery stable, a saloon and a blacksmith shop. If Palmdale seemed like a set out of a Western, Glendale was like the backdrop for an Andy Hardy film.

Though the scenery had changed for the better, the unhappy plot line remained the same: frustrated harridan of a wife continually berating her good-natured but hapless husband, ignoring the look-alike older son, and doting on the younger one.

The Morrisons remained in Glendale for nearly a decade. Over that period they lived in as many as a dozen houses, all of them rented, all of them rundown "fixer uppers."[34] Since all of the rentals were in a 10-block area, it is hard to come up with a credible rationale for the moves. The Morrisons might have been evicted for non-payment of rent or they might have left because their continual and noisy fights were an embarrassment.

Upon arrival in Glendale, Clyde's first job was as a clerk at the Glendale Pharmacy. His plan was to prove his worth to the owners so that they would make him the store manager. That never happened. Over nine years Clyde worked in four neighborhood drugstores, not rising above the level of clerk in any one of them. While not a business success, Clyde was well-liked by the clientele. They called him "Doc" because of the valuable advice he dispensed and because he was always a soft touch for a hard luck story.[35] In terms of socio-economics, Clyde's career path in Glendale was one of downward mobility, and "the Morrisons were considered very poor."[36] Clyde's inability to sufficiently provide for his family angered Molly, who would often visit the pharmacy of the moment to publicly upbraid him. In this toxic situation, Clyde, who had always liked "a taste," began to drink even more and to loiter at the local pool halls. Molly believed that Clyde, always known as a bit of a dandy, was more than flirting with his female customers.

While Clyde's relationship with Molly deteriorated, that with his oldest son flourished. Clyde loved football from his days as a schoolboy star and would spend countless hours teaching Marion and his friends how to pass, kick, run, block and tackle. And he shared with Marion his philosophy of life: always keep your word; never intentionally hurt others; do not seek conflict, but accept if it comes; be self-reliant. Marion loved his father, and thought him to be the kindest, most patient man he ever knew. The bond between the two of them undoubtedly caused his mother to dislike them both even more. For his part, Marion admired Molly's toughness and determination but could not stand her volatile and mean-spirited nature.

During the Glendale decade Marion learned to cope with the constant friction and emotional insecurity that defined his life. He dealt with it, in part, by escaping the hard realities through fantasy. At 10 or so he became a fixture at the public library and began reading voraciously, both fiction (Kipling, O. Henry, Conrad, Scott, Cooper, Conan Doyle and Grey) and non-fiction (principally biography). He also began a love affair with the movies. For Glendale was a "movie" town, where a number of studios shot films and where at least one glamorous leading lady lived.[37] Not only did Marion and his friends watch real pictures being made, but they would go through the motions of making pictures of their own, complete with pretend make-up, cameras, props, a director and, of course, actors. He also loved to *go* to the movies, using an unlimited pass from the Palace Grand which he was granted as payment for distributing their handbills three times a week. Marion's taste was deep and broad. He liked period pieces as well as westerns, and was a particular fan of Douglas Fairbanks and Harry Carey. As a measure of the extent of his passion, when Valentino's *Four Horsemen of the Apocalypse* had its week-long run at the Palace, he saw every one of its two-a-day showings.

Around the same time that Marion developed his love of books and movies, he became involved in more traditional youth activities. In 1919, when he was 12, he joined the Boy Scouts and the YMCA. Three years later, in 1922, he joined the Masonic youth fraternity, DeMolay. Not only did these organized, age-limited groups keep him away from his unhappy home, they also freed him from the annoying responsibility, imposed by Molly, of taking Bobby wherever he went. And when Marion was not at the library or movie house or one of his clubs, he could be found wandering down to the blacksmith shop or the livery stables or the sawmill.

School, too, offered a refuge from his battling parents and tagalong brother, and during the Glendale years Marion blossomed there, as well. Two changes, only indirectly related to "education," were key to that blossoming. They resulted from the fortuity that his school route went right by the firehouse. At the time, Marion had a pet Airedale named Duke, who spent the days at the station while his "master" was in class. Since he and his dog were inseparable, the firemen took to calling the dog "Little Duke" and him "Big Duke," and the name stuck.[38] Beyond giving him a manly name, the firemen also helped put an end to the continual thrashings he received from local bullies. When he arrived at the firehouse after one such beating, a volunteer, who had been a professional boxer, began teaching him how to defend himself. The lessons took, he won a few fights and the bullying stopped. For the rest of his life, Wayne could not tolerate bullies and if he saw one in action, he invariably stepped in and "took care of the underdog."[39]

Duke had always done well in school, and that pattern did not change with the relocation to Glendale. His seventh and eighth grade math teacher, who thought Duke was handsome, neat and well-dressed, said he was always prepared, always did his homework and, though he never volunteered an answer, always knew it when asked. She also thought that he looked pale and tired and unwell, and was so worried that she called Molly in for a conference. The teacher learned at that meeting that the Morrisons were poor and that Duke had taken on two jobs to help with the family finances.

It is unclear whether Duke began working at 10 or 12. What is pretty clear is that it was his mother who told him he had to work in order to help make ends meet. So even before he was a teenager, Duke was out of the house by 5:30 am with a morning paper route and was not back at home until at least sundown, after delivering prescriptions. On Saturdays he distributed advertisements for local businesses. As he got older, he also mowed lawns and worked on an ice wagon and on produce farms. The money Duke earned bought clothes for him and his brother, allowing them both to look presentable. Duke appeared not to mind these new responsibilities, since they further minimized the exposure to his squabbling parents. All these efforts might also have in some measure endeared Duke to his mother; after all, they did benefit Bobby. Instead, it embarrassed Molly that she was dependent on a young boy to make up for her husband's deficiencies and caused her to resent the two of them even more.

As Duke progressed from intermediate school through high school, he proved himself to be a phenomenon. He excelled in academics and is said to have earned straight A's, a grade point average in the mid-90s and a ranking of number two in the class. He won the bronze pin for scholarship, while taking every college preparatory course available. On the extra-curricular side, he served as president of the Latin Honor Society and Letterman's Club, on the advertising staff of the yearbook, on the sports staff of the school newspaper, as Chairman of the Senior Dance and Ring Committees and as head of the debate team and Honor Club. He also participated in student government and was elected vice president his sophomore and junior years and president his senior year.[40]

In light of his later career, it is interesting that Duke also found time to appear in both the school and senior plays. When coupled with his love for movies, these activities seem like a foreshadowing of what came next. The fact is that Duke's participation in the theater group was motivated more by his affection for the drama teacher than a love of acting and that he most enjoyed his role on the stage crew, operating behind the curtain building sets and scrounging for props.

Further, Duke later recalled two awful experiences that convinced him that a career in the performing arts was the last thing he wanted. The first occurred at his graduation from intermediate school in 1921 when he was asked to recite an essay he had written about World War I. He remembers that his mind went blank when it was time for him to speak and that he left the stage humiliated.[41] The second was a statewide competition in 1924 or 1925 when he was asked to deliver Cardinal Woolsey's farewell address. The other orators were fashionably dressed, well-spoken and highly sophisticated. He was once again terrified, felt his performance was awful and resolved that he would never become an actor.

Wayne's recollections are no doubt colored by his desire in later life to depict his screen career as sort of an accident of fate. Nevertheless, it is true that at the time he graduated from high school Duke saw himself, and the Glendale world saw him, as an athlete, not a performming artist. While he played sandlot baseball and backyard basketball, his preferred sport, like his father's, was football. His freshman year he was a star guard on the 140-pound team. His junior year he was a star guard on the 155-pound team. And his senior year he was a star guard on the varsity team, a phenomenal squad which had an undefeated regular season and played in the California state championship.

His teammates described him as a hard-driving and ruthless competitor. And the assistant coach thought enough of Duke's ability to recommend that the University of Southern California offer him a football scholarship.

As suggested by his athletic achievements, by the time he was a high school senior Duke was no longer an awkward, gangly kid but a 6'4," 170-pound man. He was also extremely good-looking, with prominent cheekbones, blue eyes and curly brown hair. As one neighborhood girl gushed decades later, "His looks alone could stop traffic."[42] Yet with all his gifts and accomplishments, he did not seem to have any steady girlfriends. One explanation was that he was shy. Another explanation was that he was not ready to have a woman get too close to him, having watched his parents' relationship. A third explanation was that he had neither the time nor the money for serious dating.

And there was a fourth explanation: there was a wild side to Duke Morrison that the nice girls in Glendale, and the parents of the nice Glendale girls, would have found unacceptable. He began drinking when he was a sophomore in high school and thereafter got drunk almost every weekend. He drag-raced, particularly in the flats after a heavy rain. And, on Saturday nights he picked up "a certain type of girl" for a certain type of fun.[43]

Duke had always been part daredevil and part prankster. There was the time when he was cast in a neighborhood "movie" and leapt, Douglas Fairbanks style, out of a second-story window onto a rickety grape arbor; the time when he deflated the tires of a car and then drove it across a train trestle; the many times when he would go "poor boy sailing," taking a big wave and diving onto the slippery mud;[44] the time he was in charge of props and rang a telephone *bell* offstage having "forgotten" to put the telephone *receiver* onstage; the time he pelted passing streetcars with rotten vegetables; and the time when he spread a vile-smelling chemical on a classmate, causing the entire school to be evacuated.

The boy who became John Wayne was enormously talented: a fine student, an excellent athlete and a popular leader. He had a terrible and chaotic home life, dominated by a miserable and unloving mother. This led him to take on a vast array of activities that kept him out of the house as much as possible. Wayne presented at least four faces to the world: the serious boy who studied hard and read good books; the dreamer who endlessly watched and "made" movies; the daredevil who loved dangerous stunts and practical jokes; and the tough guy who drank and swore and hung out with the worst kids in the neighborhood. Watching the film star years later provides not a hint of what a fascinating, complicated and accomplished young life he had lived.

Gregory Peck
April 15, 1916-June 12, 2003
Career span: 1944-93
Major Films: *Spellbound* (1945); *The Yearling* (1946); *Gentleman's Agreement* (1947); *Twelve O'Clock High* (1949); *Roman Holiday* (1953); *To Kill A Mockingbird* (1962).
Signal Honors: Academy Award Winner for Best Actor 1962; Academy Award Nominee for Best Actor 1945, 1946, 1947, 1949; American Film Institute Lifetime Achievement Award 1989.

UNDERDOG GREATS

There is a striking reserve and remoteness to Gregory Peck's performances at the climactic moments of his major films. His heartbreak is controlled when Princess Anna says she must go back to being a royal in *Roman Holiday*. His outrage is contained when his fiancée reveals her sedate bigotry in *Gentleman's Agreement*. And his joy is restrained when his wife decides to support his illegitimate child in *The Man in the Gray Flannel Suit*. It is quite possible that Peck's muted reactions are a function of the way in which he was wired. Or it may be that they reflect the deliberate artistic choices of a seasoned actor. There is a chance, however, that to a certain extent they are the consequences of his experiences during the emotionally trying first 18 years of his life.

Gregory Peck's father, Gregory Peck Sr., was from Rochester, New York, the only child of Samuel Peck and Catherine Ashe. Grandfather Samuel had been born in the United States and was of English descent. Grandmother Catherine had been born in County Kerry, Ireland, and had emigrated when she was 20. In July of 1887, when Greg Sr. was 11 months old, Samuel died of diphtheria, and Catherine took her infant back to the old sod and her family. After a decade in the home country, long enough for Greg Sr.'s brogue to become ineradicable, the two returned to America. Catherine placed Greg Sr. in a Catholic school, while she traveled the West selling ladies underwear. She was successful enough as a saleswoman to buy a 16-room apartment building in San Diego and to send Greg Sr. to the University of Michigan. He returned from college with a degree in pharmacology and got a job as a clerk at the only drug store in La Jolla. After a year of clerking, Catherine gave her son $10,000 to buy out the owner, and in 1910 Greg Sr. was the proprietor of Peck's Drug Store, which stocked medicines, chemicals, toiletries and stationery and boasted a modern soda fountain.

"Doc" Peck quickly became integrated into the social scene of the growing seaside resort. He was not only known for the advice he provided and cures he ministered to his customers, but for his participation in the town band and his play on the local basketball team. "Doc" was extremely fit and handsome, with jet black hair, a cleft chin and a generous mouth. But as of 1915 he had not committed himself to any of the available La Jolla ladies.

In 1915, St. Louis-bred Bernice Ayres was also uncommitted. She had traveled to La Jolla to visit her recently widowed mother, another Katherine, and her sister Myrtle. Myrtle had recently married Charles Rannells, the agent for Railway Express. "Bunny" Ayres was short, blond and vivacious and happy to be introduced to her brother-in-law's good-looking friend, the neighborhood pharmacist. That "Doc" Peck was described as La Jolla's "most eligible bachelor," certainly contributed to his allure.[45]

Aside from the fact that Doc and Bunny were both single and attractive, they had little in common. He was already 29, Catholic, an only child, raised in Ireland and rather low key. She was only 20, Protestant, one of seven, from a family with Mayflower roots and the proverbial "live wire." But there was little to do in La Jolla, opposites do attract, and the two began a courtship that culminated on June 4, 1915, with a church wedding in Bunny's hometown of St. Louis.

After the ceremony, the young couple returned to California and moved into a $4,000 redwood board-and-batten bungalow – named La-Lo-O-Mi – that Doc had constructed for his new bride. The night they got back from Missouri the Pecks were treated to a "Charivari," a noisy "welcome" staged by Charlie Rannells, complete with firecrackers, pistol shots, banging pots and a joy-ride.[46] Five days later Bunny's mom moved in with them. Two months after that Bunny learned that she was pregnant. But before the baby was born, Doc had closed up his shop.

There are a variety of explanations for Doc's loss of the drug store: his preference for outdoor recreation, his good-natured refusal to dun his clients, his crooked accountant, his unwillingness to ask for a rescue from the bank. Whatever the causes, he resented his wife's attempts to save him by going door-to-door collecting unpaid bills, and she resented no longer having a husband who owned his own business. In the immediate aftermath of the sale, Doc continued to work at his former pharmacy, but behind the counter as an employee.

On April 5, 1916, Bunny gave birth at home to a 10-pound boy whom she christened "Eldred Gregory Peck." The origin of "Gregory" was obvious. She plucked "Eldred" from a phone book, where, according to her son, it should have stayed.

Almost nothing is known of the first five years of Greg's life, except that before he was one, Doc had taken a job as the night-shift druggist at Ferris & Ferris in San Diego. The change in employment required the Pecks to give up their little house in La Jolla for a dreary apartment closer to his new place of work. By the time Greg was two, his parents had separated. By the time he was four, his mother had filed for divorce, alleging both emotional and physical abuse directed at both her and her son. By the time Greg was five, the divorce had been finalized. The decree required Doc to pay $50 a month in a combination of alimony and child support. Peck later denied that his father had ever been abusive, attributing the break-up to the nine-year difference in his parents' ages and the increasing financial challenges. But even if the Peck marriage was merely contentious, rather than violent, Greg's early years were basically unhappy ones.

Greg stayed with his father in San Diego until shortly after he turned six, when Doc put him on a train, alone, to make the two-and-a-half-day trip to St. Louis, where Bunny had resumed residence. She had found a job as a telephone operator, her pre-marital occupation, and had rented rooms at a crummy boarding house filled with down-on-their-luck characters. The landlady was a big-bosomed red-head right out of central casting. St. Louis was as bawdy and boisterous as La Jolla was old-fashioned and serene, but Greg adapted. On the twice-a-week poker nights, Greg would spike his five-cents-a-glass lemonade with the gin he had helped mix in the bathtub. He picked up additional small change shining shoes for a dime and selling newspapers at the nearby trolley stop. When Bunny had the time, she took Greg to Creve Coeur Lake, a major recreation landmark, and to the movies, which was the latest form of entertainment.[47]

After half a year in St. Louis, Bunny went to San Francisco, where one of her brothers lived, and enrolled Greg in the local school. But the City by the Bay proved too expensive, and the two of them went back to La Jolla. Bunny got a job as a waitress in a tea room, rented a house for $25 a month, started Greg in yet another school, asked grandma Kate to move in with them and even attempted to reconcile with Doc. But none of it worked, whether because La Jolla was simply too backward – the residents had trouble adjusting to the new-fangled addition of concrete sidewalks – or because she was just not suited to be a wife and mother. In any event, Bunny moved out again, this time to Los Angeles and this time by herself, taking a job answering phones for an advertising agency. Since Doc was still working nights in San Diego and just could not care for a little boy, Bunny's only option was to leave Greg with her mother in La Jolla.

Peck later said that the three years he spent with his grandmother were the best of his childhood. Yet the reality was that at seven Greg was effectively an orphan, but an orphan of the worst kind: an orphan who had living parents. Greg's mother and father were not incapacitated or destitute. They simply would not take the trouble of raising their perfectly normal son. He had to be confused and feel cheated about being deprived of a traditional family life.

Katie Ayres, widowed for over a decade, looked and felt older than her 70 years when her daughter left Greg in her care. As a result, she provided him with more love than supervision. On Sundays she would take him to church and after services join her other daughter, son-in-law and their four children for supper. During the summers Greg would loll around the hayloft in Uncle Charley's barn or go swimming or rafting at the nearby beach. He also liked playing hide-and-seek, riding his bike, making tree-houses and boat-building.

But the three years in La Jolla were not entirely about outdoor recreation. Having obtained his first library card at six, Greg became an avid reader. He became an equally avid movie fan, visiting the local theater two or three times a week. He vividly recalled being mesmerized when he got to watch heavily made-up actors shoot a scene for a silent picture against the backdrop of "his" La Jolla beach. Greg's own acting debut occurred when, as a fifth grader, he was cast in the pivotal role as the opener of Pandora's box. Grammar school was otherwise of little importance to him. Despite his love of reading, he was not much of a student. Nor was he very involved with either his teachers or classmates.

Greg got to see his dad on Thursday afternoons, when Doc would make the 40-minute drive from San Diego. Once a summer Doc had a week-long vacation, and he and Greg would go to Santa Catalina Island, where they swam and hiked and fished and slept in tents. But the perfect moments with his father were relatively few and those with his mother even more rare. As Peck admitted later, he was alone a lot as a kid, and many of his pastimes – reading, swimming, fishing, movie-going – were solitary ones.

In 1926, when Greg was 10, Bunny remarried and moved from Los Angeles to San Francisco. While her finances presumably improved, her new husband was a traveling salesman, and Bunny decided she wanted to go on the road with him rather than be stuck at home with her child. Greg completed La Jolla Elementary School in the spring of 1927. That fall Doc and Bunny enrolled him at St. John's Military School in Los Angeles. At 11, Greg was sent away from Katie Ayres, the only relative who had provided him with the facsimile of home life.

St. John's was run by nuns from the order of the Sisters of Mercy and by retired World War II soldiers. The nuns were in charge of overall administration, academic teaching and religious training, and the soldiers were responsible for military drills, athletic coaching and dormitory supervision. Located in a grim part of LA, most of the students were promising working-class children of divorced parents.

Life at St. John's was as disciplined and structured as life in La Jolla had been relaxed and chaotic. A typical day began with reveille at 6 am and ended with taps at 9 pm. In between the cadets polished their boots, buttons and buckles, mopped the floors, shined the wood, prayed – before and after meals – and attended classes. They wore blue gray tunics and peaked caps and ate their dinners in silence.

Ever the pleaser and ever adaptable, Greg made the best of his new environment. He became an altar boy and three days a week participated in the elaborate theatrics of a traditional Catholic service. He laid out the priest's vestments, donned the lace-fringed black robe, poured the sacramental wine, rang the bells, swung the incense and learned to recite the two-hour Latin Mass. Based on his own superior performance on the drilling field, he became a cadet captain and was put in charge of 60 eight-to 10-year-olds. He was determined that his squad would win the gold medal for excellence and his determination propelled them into a first-place finish.

Greg had other successes. For the first time teachers noticed and liked him. He was chosen to be editor of the school newspaper. The school's unquestioned boy hero, Augustine MacKessy, became his best friend.

The cadets were permitted to leave the campus every Sunday and for the entire weekend on the last Friday of the month. On the Sundays that Greg remained in town he hopped on the trolley with his pals and gorged on movies, often watching several a day. In 1927, he saw Al Jolson in *The Jazz Singer* and the premiere of Cecille B. DeMille's epic *King of Kings*, both of which he later said had a profound impact. When Greg was not at the film "palaces," he was reading a lot, expanding his horizons to include Zane Grey, Charles Dickens, Sir Walter Scott and the Bronte sisters. When he had a two-day pass, Greg took the Santa Fe Railroad 120 miles south to visit his father in San

Diego. During his first year at St. John's, those trips were wrenching, because grandmother Peck had moved in with Doc and was dying of cancer. On the rare weekend that he was not with his father, Greg bunked on a couch at the Rannells' home in La Jolla.

Greg graduated from military school in May of 1930, shortly after his 14th birthday. His tenure had an indelible effect. It taught him self-discipline and persistence, that he had to finish whatever he started. It made him more competitive and instilled in him a sense of duty. It gave him self-confidence.

That confidence was shredded the following fall when he entered the gothic-style public high school in San Diego known as the Gray Castle. He knew none of the students. His hard-won mastery of Catholic liturgy and military regimentation was irrelevant. The city was an unknown urban maze. But he had no choice about moving. Seventy-seven-year-old Grandma Kate was too old to have him return to familiar La Jolla, and his mother Bunny had no interest in inviting him up to San Francisco. So, by default, Doc welcomed his son to the box-like bungalow grandma Peck had left him in her will. The problem was that Doc was still working nights and would seldom be around.

Greg's high school years were bleak. In contrast to St. John's, which was excessively structured, his life in San Diego had almost none. He saw his father in the morning before Doc went to sleep and at dinner before Doc left for work. During the day Greg was entirely on his own. He had no relatives in the area nor did it seem that his father had any friends who might lend a hand. There was no one to offer guidance or direction. At first Greg was depressed and slept a lot. Over time, he developed resilience and became independent, realizing even then that he would to have to fend for himself when it came to his education, his finances and charting his future.

Greg's academic performance at San Diego High was mediocre. During the three years he shot up from 5'4" to 6'2", but he was rail thin and felt awkward and shy. He entered a contest to compose and sing a new school anthem, but froze when his turn came to perform; though he idolized the star of the football team, he was too bashful to even talk to him. With his scrawny build, his athletic pursuits topped out at the intramural level, the sole exception being crew, sponsored by the San Diego Rowing Club. Though girls may have found him attractive, he did not think of himself that way, and he had only occasional dates. Nor did he appear to have made any close male friends. His extra-curricular pursuits were limited to membership in the glee club and a small part in a variety show. He tried out for the lead role in the senior class play and was forever galled by the fact that he did not get it. He had not made any kind of mark by the time he graduated in June of 1933. He had not impressed anyone in any way, such a non-factor that his classmates were stunned by his later success.

Outside of school, the only bright spot was the time he spent with his father camping. But these trips were infrequent and did not make up for the fact that he lacked any semblance of a normal life with Doc and that Bunny seldom even came to see him. Reflective of Greg's barren existence was the Christmas Day he spent walking miles to get to the athletic club where he shot hoops by himself before taking in a movie alone prior to meeting up with his father at a local café for their holiday meal. He never forgot it.

Greg was one of 1,400 day students entering San Diego State Teachers College in the fall of 1933. He was again on his own, but he was less by himself. He pledged a fraternity, became a quarter-miler on the track team and found a group of friends to join him at the movies or when he went to Doc's cabin. While he was not a scholastic standout, he did impress one professor with a reading from *The Emperor Jones* and a presentation of a scene from *Cyrano de Bergerac*. The teacher, who vividly recalled Greg's polite manner, deep tan, black hair and colorful shirts, encouraged Greg to consider a career in acting. Perhaps in response to that encouragement, Greg made it a point to attend one of 1934's hit plays, *Awake and Sing*.

Greg turned 18 on April 5, 1934, and had the ritualistic rite of passage in Tijuana where he drank cheap Mexican beer, watched a blue movie and was at least exposed to the wares in its red-light district. He returned to San Diego, quit the Teachers College and got a job with the Union 76 Oil Company. He started off as a night watchman and then moved up to driving one of its 5,000-gallon tanker rigs. He loved the olive-drab uniform, the cap with the "76" logo and the large red truck. He also loved the $125-a-month salary, which allowed him to buy his first car, a blue Model-A Ford with a white-canvas top, a rumble seat and wire wheels.

Greg wanted the car not just for transportation, but to take his first real girlfriend out on dates. Her name was Betty Clardy. She was from an Irish-American family of five, and Greg likely met her through her brothers. The Clardys took him under their wing, and he got to experience the warmth of a close-knit family. The timing was good, since Doc was about to re-marry, and his future bride and Greg did not get along. Staying in Doc's bungalow was no longer an attractive or realistic option.

The Clardys not only provided Greg with companionship, but gave him a sense of direction and goals. When Greg's Union Oil supervisor told him that in time he could be a manager earning $350 a month, he realized that he wanted more than a routine job, even at a good salary. In part because of the Clardy's influence, Greg returned to San Diego State. Betty and her parents provided study space, reviewed his homework and "quizzed him" before tests.[48] The effort produced results. He was getting A's and B's for the first time. When he applied to the University of California at Berkeley, he was accepted.

Although Greg had clearly turned a huge corner, it did not erase the past. When years later an interviewer from *Cosmopolitan* asked him to reminisce about his growing up, he told her, "I don't care to talk about my childhood because it was so sad."[49] Greg's father and mother were a mismatch from the outset and were living apart by the time he was two. To be sure they had an impact, that was not all bad: he acquired an understated sense of humor and a strict code of decency from Doc, and a sense of creativity and an appreciation of beauty from Bunny. But that did not make up for the fact that he was uprooted so frequently, in the first six years moving from La Jolla to San Diego to St. Louis to San Francisco. Nor did it make up for the fact that between the ages of seven and 14 Greg lived with neither of his parents, that after the age of seven he never lived with his mother at all, and that as a teenager at his father's house the two barely saw each other. There is no question that his grandmothers loved him, as did his aunts and uncle, but their affection was no substitute for a real home life.

Moreover, Greg had no male role models to provide him guidance: his grandfathers were both dead, Doc was not equipped to play that part, his uncle by marriage had a brood of his own to care for and no real mentors stepped into the breach. As a result Peck admitted that during those early, formative years he was "lonely, withdrawn, full of self-doubt."[50] Essentially abandoned by his parents, things ended up all right largely as a result of his of his own resourcefulness and tenacity. Against this backdrop it is not too far-fetched to attribute the reserve that permeates his acting performances as somehow and somewhat related to the deprivation he suffered and insecurity he felt during the unhappy first part of his life.

William Clark Gable
February 1, 1901-November 16, 1960
Career span: 1931-60
Major Films: *It Happened One Night* (1934); *San Francisco* (1936); *Mutiny on the Bounty* (1935); *Gone with the Wind* (1939); *Command Decision* (1949); *The Misfits* (1961).
Signal Honors: Academy Award Winner for Best Actor 1934; Academy Award Nominee for Best Actor 1935, 1939.

Clark Gable's father and mother both grew up in Meadville, a town in the northwest part of Pennsylvania. His father, William H. Gable, had eight or nine sisters and brothers and was of German descent. His grandparents, Charles and Nancy Gable, owned a hotel and farm, though the farmhouse was sold at a sheriff's sale in 1899 after Charles' death. Will Gable was not a farmer, but an oil wildcatter intent on striking it rich and becoming the next John D. Rockefeller. He was a Methodist and a Mason, handsome and well-built, with big shoulders and a narrow waist. Will liked to drink and gamble and, even after he was married, to "visit" other women.

Clark's mother, Addie Hershelman, one of five, was also of German descent and also from a farming family.[51] There any similarity with her future husband ends. While he was unrefined, a physical specimen and a Protestant, she was an amateur artist, frail and a Catholic. Will may have been her first serious relationship when she was proposed to at nearly 30. Addie's parents did not approve of Will's religion or his career, but Addie married him anyway.

In view of the Hershelmans' opposition, Will and Addie Gable moved away to Cadiz, Ohio, a rural Appalachian town 120 miles from Meadville. They first lived on the upper floor of a two-story clapboard house in a two-room apartment accessed by an external stairway. Although Addie's doctor warned her not to have a child, on February 1, 1901, after a very difficult labor, she gave birth to a large baby boy, weighing well over nine pounds. She named him "Clark," after her mother, the former Rosetta Clark. Though Clark was the name on all the official records, before 1925 he was also known as Bill or William or Kid. Will Sr. was thrilled with his big boy, but not with his "sissified" name. Throughout Clark's childhood Will was concerned that his son might be unmanly. The baby had big hands and feet, jug ears, and gray-green eyes, like Addie, and dark hair and dimples, like Will. Clark was plump, quiet, happy and strong.

After Clark's birth, Addie's health got progressively worse. She was in bed a lot, and Will's prospecting meant he was mostly away. Addie was cared for first by her good-hearted downstairs neighbors, then by a hired nurse and finally by her parents back in Meadville. On November 14, 1901, when Clark was nine and a half months old, Addie died, perhaps of epilepsy, as the death certificate said, or maybe of a brain tumor. There can be no question that Addie's death was a trauma for her infant son, perhaps more severe because he could not yet put words to it. Most of Clark's first year had been spent with a loving but sick mother, who was now dead, and a father who was seldom home.

Following the funeral, Will resumed his prospecting in Ohio, looking for oil as well as a new wife. Given the nature of his work, he had no choice but to leave Clark in Meadville, initially in the care of Addie's sister, Josie, and eventually in the care of Addie's brother, Tom. There is no question that Clark was loved by his relatives. There is also no question that his first two years were spent with four sets of "caregivers:" his parents, his grandparents, his aunt and his uncle.

Meanwhile, Will was still drilling in Cadiz, but now living seven miles away in Hopedale, another small Ohio town. He was boarding with the Dunlaps, and ended up "keeping company" with one of their daughters, Jennie. When they met, Jennie was at least 30, so like Addie she was verging on spinsterhood. She was a milliner, so also like Addie she had some degree of refinement. Jennie was tall, always fashionably dressed and had a lively personality. Like most women, Jennie was charmed by the handsome Will Gable, and the two were married on April 16, 1903, a year and a half after his first wife's death.

Around the time of the wedding, Will and Jennie pooled their savings and for $150 purchased four acres of land on the outskirts of Hopedale. The plan was for Jennie's brothers to help Will build a six-room house. Will then travelled to Meadville to retrieve Clark from his uncle and bring him home to his new mother. Clark had enjoyed his time on the Hershelman farm, feeding the chickens, gathering eggs, caring for his pet rabbit and chasing squirrels. He cried when, at not quite two and a half, he was taken away by the father he barely knew. The Hershelmans, who were childless, loved their nephew and would have kept him, had Will not threatened to go to court to establish custody. To keep the peace, Will promised that Clark would return to Meadville for holiday visits. Will kept his promise, and Clark saw the Hershelmans annually. But the interludes were brief, and it was never quite the same for him again.

Jennie was thrilled with Clark from the outset, a joy which only grew when it became clear that she and Will would not have a child of their own. Until their house was finished, Jennie, Clark and Will lived with Jennie's sister Ella and her two coal-miner brothers, John and Edson. They all doted on Clark. Jennie stopped working and threw him lavish birthday parties. His aunt Ella and uncle John scrimped all winter to buy him a hobby horse. And Will, whose economics fluctuated wildly, treated Clark to special gifts when he was flush: one year a bicycle, another year a pool table.

But there was a difference between Jennie's and Will's personalities, in their relationships with Clark and in their aspirations for him. Jennie was warm and affectionate. She wanted her boy to do better than her brother and husband; she did not want him to be a miner or a farmer or a wildcatter. So Jennie worked on Clark's manners and grooming. She always made sure he dressed well, buying him a Buster Brown suit when he was five and long pants, a jacket and a clean stiff-collared shirt when he got older. She read to him and convinced her husband to purchase the 72-volume "Library of the World's Best Literature."[52] She taught him to sing and play the piano and paid for him to have lessons on the French horn.

Until Clark was 16 Will was prospecting in the Scio oil fields and was at home no more than a day and a half a week. He was silent and cold. Will liked to rough-house to insure his boy was masculine. He was proud of the day Clark learned to swim, but embarrassed that Clark sang "Silver Threads Among the Gold" in a local play. Thereafter, Will would hum the song and laugh when his singing made Clark blush. If Will wanted Clark to behave, he called him a sissy and made fun of what he regarded as the girly things he did. Clark confused Will. Why was he unwilling to watch when his friends killed the animals they trapped? And why would he try to talk his way out of any physical confrontation?[53]

Because his stepmother loved and understood Clark better than his natural father, Jennie regarded her mission as running interference between the two. She had to endure Will's criticism that she pampered Clark and that Clark was overly sensitive. For his part, Clark did things designed to please them both. He sang in public, performed in school plays, joined the band, all of which he knew Jennie liked, as she was always there cheering him on. And starting in grade school, he participated in every sport – swimming, running, putting the shot, basketball, baseball – which presumably made his father happy, though Will seldom attended any of his meets or games. Clark not only took part in these activities, he excelled. He was such an accomplished musician that he was invited to join the town band when he was only 13. By eighth grade he was a good enough fielder and hitter that he was used as a "ringer" on the Hopedale High School baseball team.

Beyond the pleasure it was meant to bring to his parents, what did Clark really think of all these activities? More importantly, what did Clark think of Jennie and Will? Growing up he always referred to his stepmother as "Jennie Dunlap," acknowledging years later, "She was a wonderful woman, although I didn't realize it then."[54] He found his father complicated: hard-working, at times generous and thoughtful, but also critical and remote and generally not there.

And what did Clark think of his childhood, surrounded as he was with all these grownups who adored him, both on the Hershelman and Dunlap sides? He knew he was spoiled, but how much did he appreciate that and how much affection did he feel for those who had spoiled him? It appears that, despite the attention showered on him from all his relatives, the instability of it all – the "shuttling" from home to home – left him "never knowing what it was to have a devoted family."[55]

When Clark was nine, Will and his brothers-in-law had at last finished their construction project, and he and his parents moved into their new three-bedroom house. Clark loved cars. He could drive as soon as his father put him behind the wheel of his $175 Ford roadster, and he had no trouble taking its engine apart and putting it back together again. This shared affinity proved to be a bond with Will. So did Clark's toughness and self-reliance when it came to physical labor. At 12 he got his first job, delivering 100-pound sacks of flour from the local mill for 50 cents a week. He also worked summers as a water boy for the coal miners in the sweltering July and August heat.

At 13 Clark was tall, gangly and shy. Regarding his appearance, the consensus seems to be that as a teenager he was more funny-looking than handsome, with his slicked-down hair, stick-out ears and tiny teeth. Clark did have at least one girlfriend, but she recalled decades later that whenever they played post office, Clark opted to be the postmaster to avoid kissing her or anyone else. Gable told the same story when his reputation as a "ladies man" was well-established: he described himself back then as overgrown, clumsy and awkward with girls his age. That said, there was talk that at 16 an older woman lured him into her home and stole his virginity.

In terms of personality, Clark was well-behaved, happy and always smiling. Outside the home, he led a typical small-town life. He went to the local drug store for sodas and the local hotel to listen to the piano player and the local town hall to watch the "flickers."[56] His best friend, Andy Means, was three years older than he, and they would go out into the country to fish and catch frogs or take turns racing bikes.

Little is known about how well Clark did in grammar school, but in high school his performance was strikingly erratic. As a freshman, when he was 14, his grades for nearly all subject were in the 70s. But as a sophomore, they varied widely during the course of the year. In Math, in one month he got a 72 on a test, and in another a 93. In English, the range was from 66 to 88; in Latin, from 48 to 75; in History, from 20 to 98! The one subject in which he consistently excelled was spelling, where he always scored in the 90s and had an average of 95. Clark always liked words, loved to read poetry aloud and enjoyed the Shakespeare sonnets in the 72-volume set of literary masterworks that was likely otherwise untouched.

The Gables' life changed dramatically after Clark's sophomore year, in the summer of 1917. Will decided to give up wildcatting and bought a farm 60 miles from Hopedale in a town called Ravenna. He explained that his decision was spurred by an opportunity to sell his drilling rig at a good price. Others have said it was because Jennie's health was failing or because Jennie wanted a full-time husband or because Jennie wanted to distance Clark from a middle-aged Jezebel whom he was seeing or because the oil wells were drying up or because creditors were on Will's tail. Whatever the reason, in the beginning, Clark enjoyed being in the country and spending time hunting, shooting and fishing with his father. But once school started, he was desperately unhappy. He was 16, and he missed his friends, his sports and his social life. He hated the new school, Edinburgh High, which was a five-mile bus ride away, where he towered over everyone, knew nobody and was treated as an outsider.

Clark quit school in November of 1917, ending his formal education early in his junior year. Jennie was disconsolate; she had worked so hard teaching him manners so that he could escape the life that had stifled her. Will did not object at all; he could use the full-time help of another strong back. For a month or so Clark provided it, but he hated farming, too, every aspect of it: getting up before it was light out, feeding the animals, plowing the fields, harvesting the hay. He found no joy going to sleep every night bone weary.

In January 1918 Clark moved back to Hopedale, financially on his own. He lived with Jennie's relatives, got a job as a water boy at a coal mine earning $5 a day and had soon saved up enough money that he could return home to buy his father's car, which Will sold him for the original $175 sticker price. Clark remained in Ravenna for a while, but having his own vehicle did not make him like farm life any better. His friend Andy Means was planning to go to Akron, which with the onset of the First World War had become the rubber capital of America. Clark was intent on tagging along. Will objected strenuously to the plan, which made Clark like him even less. That Jennie took Clark's part, made him appreciate her more than ever.

Compared to Hopedale and Ravenna, Akron was huge, with a population of 200,000. Clark got a job, first at Firestone Tire and Rubber on the assembly line, then at Miller Rubber Company. He was earning $100 a month, boarding with a pharmacist and living nearby Andy Means. For Andy, the biggest attraction in Akron was female companionship, and for a while he tried to interest Clark in double dating. For Clark, the biggest attraction in Akron was the world of entertainment. It was in Akron that he saw his first real movies, becoming a particular fan of Westerns. And it was in Akron that he discovered live theater.

The first play Clark saw was *Bird of Paradise,* which had opened on Broadway back in 1912. It was a lurid melodrama set in the South Seas prominently featuring a nearly-naked Hawaiian princess – Pauline McClean – who kills herself when she is jilted by her white American lover. Clark was enthralled, and in the days and weeks that followed he hung around the stage door, trailed the actors to their favorite haunts and signed on as an unpaid callboy. While there are discrepancies among his biographers about much in Clark's early life, there is unanimity that *Bird of Paradise* was a turning point.[57]

With the Armistice on November 11, 1918, rubber demand declined and the labor supply in Akron increased as veterans came back from overseas. Both Andy and Clark lost their jobs. While Andy went back to Hopedale to take up farming, Clark stayed on in Akron for the chance to get on stage. His moment finally came at the end of 1918, though it is unclear whether Clark appeared as a non-speaking extra carrying a spear or as a servant informing the leading lady, "Your cab is here, madame."[58] But years later Gable consistently talked about the significance of this first "role": "It was all over then, as far as my future was concerned. I never wanted to be anything else."[59] At just 18, Clark Gable had found his calling in life.

James Francis Cagney
July 17, 1899-March 30, 1986
Career span: 1919-84
Major Films: *The Public Enemy* (1931); *Angels With Dirty Faces* (1938); *The Roaring Twenties* (1939); *Yankee Doodle Dandy* (1942); *White Heat* (1949); *Love Me or Leave Me* (1955); *The Gallant Hours* (1960).
Signal Honors: Academy Award Winner for Best Actor 1942; Academy Award Nominee for Best Actor 1938, 1955; American Film Institute Lifetime Achievement Award 1974; Kennedy Center Honoree 1980; Presidential Medal of Freedom 1984.

James Cagney's childhood taught him how to play the gangster roles he made so famous. It also taught him that the gritty life of the City where the gangsters roamed was the furthest thing from the place he really wanted to be. Yet that gritty life was inescapable, the heritage of both of his parents.

Cagney's father, James Sr., was born in 1875 on New York's Lower East Side in the crime-infested region known as Five Points. James Sr. disliked his sister, had little to do with his brother and for some reason never said much of anything about his ancestors, other than that they hailed from County Leitrim, Ireland, and were originally known as the O'Caignes. James Sr. had dark black hair, a ruddy complexion, a stocky build and was 5'8" tall. In addition, he was said to be "handsome" and "a ladies' man," with a great wit and a remarkable gift of the blarney.[60]

It was likely this combination of good looks and charm that attracted Carolyn Elizabeth Nelson. Carrie, as her future husband always called her, had a mother with Irish roots and a father with roots in Norway. Like her future husband, she was born on the Lower East Side "when poverty ruled there."[61] Her father was the captain, and sole crew member, of a small barge that picked up and delivered coal along the Hudson River. He had one eye, a terrible temper and invariably was on the losing end of scraps. Her mother was a calm counterbalance. Because finances were so tight, Carrie was forced to leave school at 12. Her teacher, who thought Carrie her "most promising pupil," wept when she could not convince Carrie to stay.[62] Carrie never forgot that early trauma, and it produced in her a fierce determination that her own children would not have to make the same sacrifice.

Carrie spent the next six years working at the Eagle Pencil Company. She had matured into an attractive, full-figured young woman with iridescent red hair – her son called it "the truest titian" – that fell down below her waist.[63] It is never said how or where or when she met James Cagney Sr., but the two fell in love and were married in 1896. She was 18. He was 21. After the wedding, she and James Sr. rented a small apartment on the top floor of an old brownstone located in their neighborhood, at the corner of Eighth Street and Avenue D. At the time of their marriage James Sr. was employed as a bookkeeper.

The Cagneys' first son, Harry was born in 1898. Their second, James Jr. – Jim, never Jimmy – was born a year later, on July 17, 1899. By all accounts, Harry was a normal and healthy baby, and Jim was so frail as an infant that he almost died. In terms of appearance, the boys looked much alike, except that Harry's hair was jet black like his father's and Jim's was flaming red like his mom's.

Somewhere around the time of his sons' births, James Sr. was asked by a bartender friend to fill in for him one night. The setting was quite familiar to him, since he was hardly a stranger to saloons, and the principal job requirement, a knack for gab, came naturally. Though James Sr. also had an aptitude for mathematics, bookkeeping was hardly a passion, and he happily turned in his green eye shade.[64] His stint as substitute barkeep began disastrously, when he ordered a large, unruly customer to leave the premises.

For his trouble, he was met with a haymaker to the jaw which cost him 21 teeth. Nonetheless, in early 1901 James Sr. felt he had found his true calling, and the Cagneys moved uptown to Yorkville to be closer to his new place of work. The address of their flat was 429 East 79th Street, a working-class neighborhood that represented a step up from the Lower East Side.

The family was to remain on East 79th Street for six years, from the time Jim was one and a half until he was about eight. It was an eventful period for him. He got a second brother, Edward, in 1902, and a third brother, William, in 1904. A sister Gracie, came in 1905, but died of pneumonia before she turned one. As a little boy, Jim would spend two to three weeks on Grandpa Nelson's barge, delighting in the operation of the coal scoop and in his Grandma's doughnuts. Jim was terrified about starting school and cried all the way to the classroom. His mood changed when he was given a welcoming hug by his pretty young teacher and whiffed her sweet perfume, Heliotrope, which was forever after his favorite fragrance. At five, Jim met his "first love," a neighborhood girl of 10 or 12 called Annie, who would stop by the Cagneys' house to tie Jim's shoes.[65] Around this time, he began sketching, copying illustrations and cartoons from the newspapers. Since Carrie had an artistic bent, Jim's abilities in this regard pleased her greatly.

Despite his timidity at school, helplessness with shoelaces and early love of the arts, little Jim Cagney was not some sensitive and retiring aesthete. To the contrary, out in the streets, he was becoming a tough urban kid. Being so was a matter of survival and prestige. He came to understand, and see, that in a world where everyone was poor, there was "a power hierarchy" not dependent on wealth but on "when and *if* you were handy with your dukes, and could hold your own in a fight."[66] It was the way to establish a reputation and to earn respect. It did not indicate some clinical aggressiveness. It was not exceptional. As Cagney later explained, where he grew up, "street fighting was an accepted way of life."[67]

When Jim was six, an older kid from the neighborhood showed him "how to jab, feint, hook left, cross with a right, *and* a hook . . ."[68] Though he had learned the rudiments early, he was not ready quite yet to fight his own battles, and when a big slugger – "Boo Boo Hayes" – picked on him he went home to tell Carrie, who enlisted an even bigger kid to take Boo Boo on.[69] Carrie often got into the fray herself to protect her brood. She was fiery like her father, but unlike him, she knew how to win the battles she picked. On one occasion, some local kids urinated down the stove pipe into the shack of a night watchman at a building site across the street from the Cagneys. Harry, truly an innocent bystander, was caught and badly beaten by the security guard. Carrie heard of it, put on her coat, grabbed her six-foot long horsewhip and thrashed the watchman so badly that thereafter she was known as "Kill-'Em Carrie."[70] A couple of years later, when Eddie had just started school, his teacher pulled his hair and viciously slapped him across the face for whispering in class. Carrie was livid, particularly because Eddie had badly injured his head and was not fully recovered from a bout of meningitis. Carrie again donned her coat, this time storming the principal's office. The teacher was nowhere to be found. After writing notes of apology to Carrie and the principal, he was inexplicably absent for the next several days in the hopes that this irate parent would cool down.

Carrie understood the law of the slums and did more than simply set an example. She encouraged her sons to stand up for themselves and gave them lessons on how to do so. Two afternoons a week she gathered the boys in the living room and taught them the fundamentals of self-defense. While Jim was the star pupil, all four had to participate in these regular bouts.

During the 79th Street years the East River offered refuge from the hot New York summers. The River was free and refreshing though, in Cagney's telling, not without its hazards:

> It was, quite simply, a cesspool ... because a large sewer close to our street poured its contents right into the river. And we swam there cheerfully right in the midst of all that sewage. Merry *turds* bobbing by. You just ignored them and kept your mouth shut.[71]

Considerably more wholesome and pleasant were the rides on Blank's butcher wagon and the Wild West games in the Cagney apartment.

The highlight of this period, and a turning point in Jim's life, came during the late spring of 1907 when James Sr., who had had a stroke of good luck, hired a fancy horse-drawn "barouche" to transport the family to what was then Green Field – now Flatbush – to the home of Carrie's Aunt Jane and Uncle Jack Nicholson.[72] The area, now occupied by Kennedy Airport, was then a rural spot in Brooklyn. The Nicholsons had a small elm-shaded cottage with a white picket fence and a real farm. Jim saw living things actually growing: red apples, purple plums and fat cherries. There were birds in the trees and cows and sheep in the fields. He and his brothers roamed the countryside, climbing trees and picking flowers. They skinny-dipped in clear ponds. Morning glories, which were everywhere, became his favorite flower. The two weeks in Green Field were transformative. He was in Wonderland. He wanted to live there. Over those 14 days, he later said, "I changed from a city boy to a country boy."[73]

In actuality, Jim was changed from being a city boy to *wanting to be* a country boy, as he realized when they returned to 79th Street in May or June of 1907. In 1908 the family moved further uptown to a rental at 166 East 96th Street between Third and Lexington Avenues. Though the apartment was larger, it was also more bare, and became cramped when Carrie's parents moved in. Harry slept on a bed with Ed in the master bedroom, while Jim slept on the floor with Grandma Nelson. Carrie share the second bedroom with little Bill. Grandpa Nelson and James Sr. had the third bedroom, though James Sr. was home only intermittently and when he showed up, it was generally not until morning.

The move to 96th Street converted Jim from being an observer of his father's alcoholism to being an accomplice. He had seen his dad rocking slowly from side to side, emitting a low moan that always tended to end in a near shriek, and had watched Carrie massage his dad's neck and forehead until he became still. Beginning at the age of nine, when James Sr. would come home after a two- or three-day bender and was in need of a "hair of the dog," it was Jim, his favorite, reliable son, who would be dispatched with two bits to Murphy's saloon to buy a quart of whiskey. And at the times when James Sr. did *not* come home, and Carrie concluded that the economic situation had become desperate, it was Jim, also *her* favorite, reliable son, who would be dispatched to Murphy's or Paddy's or O'Shaugnhessy's to fetch his father or make him cough up enough money to tide the rest of the Cagneys over, at least for a while.

Jim hated these missions, but they never made him love his father less. He came to believe his mother's explanation that the drinking had begun after James Sr. lost his 21 teeth, when the alcohol he sipped to ease the pain became over time an addiction. No wonder: James Sr. was consuming 60 shots of rye every day. However, James Sr. did not justify his vast consumption as a consequence of his dental woes. What he said was that he drank, not to get drunk, but to celebrate, and that he liked to celebrate whenever he could. James Sr. was genial when plastered, just as he was when sober. There were never tales of abuse of any kind. He imbibed quietly, and it was only the angle of his hat – pulled down rakishly from left to right when he was in his cups – that indicated that he had had too much.

Jim always recalled, fondly, how his dad loved to make the boys laugh. How he would sing loudly, and entirely off-key. How he would clog dance. How he would relate the latest joke he had picked up at some tavern. And how he would amuse them with his silly conundrums, dramatically delivered in his reedy Brogue:

> James Sr.: "Say, listen. Why did the sausage roll?"
> The boys (in unison): "We don't know."
> James Sr. "Because it saw the apple turnover."
> The boys: Jeering laughter then heavy applause![74]

As Jim said of his dad: "[H]e was irrepressible. He sailed happily through life, charming everyone, and all the time belting down the sauce that I suppose helped to sustain both his charm and his improvidence."[75]

The joys at home, though tinged with regret, were a counterbalance to the thorough unhappiness in the world outside. Ninety-sixth Street was much sadder than 79th. There always seemed to be people dying or being taken to the hospital. Yorkville was a place of horror and danger. There was the time Jim saw a boy with a butcher knife in his back; the time he heard a boy whimpering, holding his slashed testicle; the time he was hit by a brick in the ribs; the time he got stabbed by a street cleaner's pointed pick.

While Jim was an increasingly accomplished street fighter, he was not part of any gang. Although he never shied away from a battle, he was not an instigator. He described himself as a "combination troubleshooter-backup man."[76] He was the protector, the guy who could always be counted on for rescue from a bully. He was fearless about taking on anyone, no matter his age or size. As a classmate put it, Jim was the loner, the block champion, the one who operated at "the rear guard" and "finished things."[77]

Jim played that role not only for the neighbors but for Harry and Ed, the brothers who were not equipped to do the fighting on their own. When Harry got into an argument with a street fighter called "Bulldog," Harry bragged that his brother could whip him, and Jim did just that, twice. More celebrated was Jim's epic three-round battle in defense of Eddie. It was triggered when Willie Carney, who was a head taller and 20 pounds heavier than Jim, took a golf ball Eddie was playing with and then roughly shoved Eddie to the ground when he tried to take it back. Jim found Carney on another block terrorizing another smaller kid. Despite Carney's height and weight advantages, Jim's footwork proved the equalizer. A crowd gathered as the two went at it, until a cop came to break it up. The next day, same story, though the crowd had grown larger before the same policeman intervened. A day later there was an even larger crowd, including a little old Jewish lady loudly lamenting the fact that the Cagney and Carney mothers were not there to stop the brutality, not realizing that the animated redhead in the front row cheering Jim on *was* his mother. The battle was suspended when Jim broke four bones in his left hand. By the time he had recovered, Carney was nowhere to be found. Some said he had become a professional boxer, others that he had been sent to reform school.

In 1911 it seemed that the Cagney family's luck had changed. With some gambling winnings and the backing of one of his few solvent friends, James Sr. became the proprietor of a saloon, sponsored by the Eards (or Earets) Brewery. It was located on Eighty First Street and First Avenue and was well-appointed, with a long bar occupying most of the interior space. Beer was a nickel, shots a dime, and lunch was free. Even better, James Sr. decided it was time to move the family out of Manhattan. The prime motivating factor was Carrie's deteriorating health. She had a host of ailments, including gallbladder problems, persistent diabetes and hypertension. She also had an insatiable craving for sweets. She weighed 175 pounds when she was just 30, and two years later, right before the bar opened, she was up to 240. Carrie desperately needed a change of scenery and a healthier climate.

And so, at some point in 1912, the Cagneys moved out to Ridgewood, an almost country town located between Brooklyn and Queens. Their modest rental home was one of only nine on a street a quarter-mile long. Jim was ecstatic. He and his brothers could play in their grass front yard or at one of the nearby vacant lots. There were trees to look at and climb. Three blocks away was a movie theater and an ice cream parlor. Jim entered the local Ridgewood school as a sixth grader, and for the first time, he did well academically. He won spelling bees and got A's, bringing home the best report card in the family. His teacher liked him, saying one day, "This is the only boy in the class who knows anything."[78]

However, by the time the Cagneys moved from Manhattan, James Sr. had already lost his saloon. The sumptuous free lunches, the repeated rounds of drinks "on the house" and his own significant consumption were not components of a sound business model. Though he found a decent job tending bar on 76th Street and First Avenue, he eventually wearied of the weekend trips to Ridgewood and thought that Carrie was now well enough to move the family back into the city. So in 1913, after a year and a half in what seemed to Jim like a rural paradise, the family came back to Yorkville to stay. They ended up on East Seventy-eighth Street and lived in various houses on this block until the boys left home years later. The first apartment was the nicest, a second-floor flat with wrought iron railings on the stoop; the rent of $18 a month equaled James Sr.'s weekly salary. A year later they traded down, settling eventually and for good at No. 420.

Jim was re-enrolled in PS 158 for his last year of grammar school. His grades went down, but he enjoyed learning bits and pieces of foreign languages from his first-generation classmates: German, Hungarian, Spanish, Italian and Polish. He especially loved, and mastered, the earthy Yiddish expressions spouted by his Jewish friends: *Gai kocken aufn yahm* ("Go shit in the sea"), *Schlub* ("Jerk"), *Zol vahksen tzibbelis fun pipek* ("Onion should grow from your navel").[79] Jim then entered Stuyvesant High, where he learned real German, while further perfecting his Yiddish to the point that he was almost fluent.[80] Jim not only had a good ear, but a good eye, and he continued sketching, filling his school books with caricatures, sometimes drawing from "life" in the classroom, sometimes drawing from memory at home. Though Jim did not stand out in class, he was never a discipline problem. As to his aspirations beyond high school, he listed his "ideal" occupations, in rank order: "Big league baseball player, boxer, farmer, doctor, go to sea, drive a harness horse and be a philanthropist."[81]

If Jim got his artistic bent from his mother, he got his baseball skills from his father. In his day, James Sr. was a fine pitcher whose fastball earned him the moniker "Jimmy Steam."[82] Jim, who as a teenager was small and wiry, ended up at the other end of the battery, playing catcher for a team called the John Jays. The true class of the neighborhood was a bunch of brawlers known as "The Original Nut Club Team of Yorkville," and on a memorable Sunday the Jays beat the Nut Clubbers 7-4, largely because of Jim and his pal George Mitchell.[83] Their opponents took their defeat with grace, inviting the dynamic Cagney-Mitchell duo to defect to their team. Jim and George accepted the invitation and spent the next few years playing games all around

Manhattan, on Long Island and, occasionally, in New Jersey. Once they even did an exhibition at the Sing Sing penitentiary.

Baseball was not Jim's only social activity. At Halloween, he and his pals would scour the neighborhood for wood so the gang could build a decent bonfire and engage in their version of paint ball: the sock fight. On Thanksgiving, the kids would parade through the neighborhood as Indians or hobos or in whatever costume they could scrounge up.

Jim had guy friends like Peter Hessling, best known as Bootah, who was also a member of the John Jays and was so poor that he took a nickel bet that he could hang from edge of a five-story building and live to tell the tale; he did, and won the five cents. There was Artie Klein, whom he met at 13, a sidekick who was often there to hold Jim's hat and root for him when he mixed it up with some character in the streets.

And there were girl friends like Maud, a southpaw fighter who could "absolutely stiffen" Jim with her left; Sarah, the pretty Jewish girl whom he talked to and held hands with; Nora, who propositioned him at the tender age of 12; and Annie Mularkey, the one he cared for the most.[84] None of these female friendships blossomed into great romances. Jim was too busy with his family and his street life. And without extra money for dates at the movies or the malt shop, his outings were limited to walks through the park or visits on the stoop or rendezvous on the rooftops.

The Cagneys were poor. But they were not as badly off as the Fitzpatricks, who were evicted, or the Hesslings, who were reduced to begging for help from the local parish. Nor were they ever destitute. They always had a place to live, decent furniture, an ice box, a coal stove and even a piano. But they didn't always get "three squares on the table."[85] Jim never had a second suit or more than one pair of shoes. Santa Claus never came by: there was no Christmas tree and a big treat would be to find an orange in the stocking. The problem was that James Sr. was not employed full-time, there were long stretches between jobs, and a good deal of what he earned was spent on liquor and betting at the track. As a result the Cagney boys had to work to make up for the shortfall.

Jim had taken on odd jobs from the time he was very small, selling programs at the Armory, doing pick-ups and deliveries, cleaning and sweeping, whatever could net him a few pennies or a nickel. When he turned 14 in July 1913, he qualified for a work permit and got his first real job as a copyboy for the *New York Sun*. It required him to get up at 5:30 in the morning to pick up heavy bundles of newspapers and advertising proofs at the *Sun* offices downtown on Park Row and to then deliver them to the big department stores uptown. In 1914 the three older boys – Harry, Jim and Eddie – found part-time work at the New York Public Library, putting in 90 hours a month for $12.50. In 1915 Jim had been promoted to the position of book custodian with a corresponding raise in pay to $17.50 a month. When he was not collecting and re-shelving books at the Library, Jim was working evenings as the "discipline orderly (bouncer)" at the East Side Settlement House.[86] And many Sundays he sold excursion tickets for the Hudson River Day Line. At other times Jim made money wrapping parcels, doing stock exchange runs and operating a switchboard.

All of Jim's earnings, and those of Harry and Eddie, went into the "Kitty," a big surplus pot kept in the kitchen which Jim had decorated with a smiling cat. The only competition among the boys was seeing which of them could feed Kitty best. When despite all of their efforts Kitty was low on funds, Carrie would go to Parliament Loan to hock her few prized possessions – her two diamond earrings, her gold watch and her gold chain. The $300 or $400 dollars she received would tide her over for a couple of months, paying for groceries and rent, until some combination of Jim, Harry and Eddie brought home enough to redeem the pawn ticket

A year and a half after moving back to Yorkville, in the summer of 1915, the Cagneys – all but James Sr. – got a break from their bleak routine. Under the auspices of the East Side Settlement House, they attended a family camp, free for the poor. It was held on a large farm in Stepney, Connecticut, 65 miles from New York City. The 20 children were bunked in a large barn, and the mothers stayed in "tent-like concoctions."[87] Meals were communal, served at a long table. For six weeks the boys were in the fresh air. Jim swam in an outside pond adjacent to a field filled with grazing cows, and, for the first time, participated in boxing matches wearing regulation gloves.

As was true when Jim left Flatbush and Ridgewood, the transition from Stepney back to Yorkville was difficult, made worse by the fact that James Sr. was now virtually unemployable. For a while Jim thought he had come up with a way of significantly improving Cagney finances: prizefighting. At camp he had gotten a feel for the ring, and though he did not really like the bulky gloves, he could deal with them if necessary. Irish Patsy Klein and Eddie Fitzsimmons were neighborhood boys who had made good money as boxers. So Jim trained, participating in practice matches at a nearby athletic field, watching professionals spar at the local gym, cutting out sugar from his diet and running a few miles in the morning before school. Observing exhibitions by boxing instructors, he saw that winning was more a function of footwork than arm strength, and he had already shown he could be light on his feet during his many skirmishes on the Yorkville streets. The coaches at the East Side Settlement House, as well as a friend of his father connected with the fight game, encouraged Jim, telling him he had the skills to succeed. He was all set to sign for a four-round bout at the Polo Grounds with a purse of $10, when Carrie asked him why he had been leaving home at dawn. Jim told her his plans and of his confidence that he could beat any of the likely opponents without breaking a sweat. Carrie asked, "Do you think you can lick *me*?"[88] The answer was clear, and Jim's boxing career was over before it began.

In 1916 Carrie became pregnant again and, despite fervent prayers that she be blessed with a daughter, she had her fifth son, whom she named Robert. She had hoped that the arrival of a new child would give her husband a reason to reform, and for a while it did. Robert was a handsome child and became the center of attention. James Sr. adored him. And then, shortly after his first birthday, Robert woke up one night screaming. The doctor was summoned, and the infant died several days later, a victim of tubercular meningitis. Carrie was devastated, and James Sr. reverted to his old ways, devolving into hopeless alcoholism. He was suffering from delirium tremens that were so severe and frequent that Carrie concluded he would have to be involuntarily committed if he were to have any hope of getting better. Though Carrie obtained the court order from the Department of Health, she asked Jim to serve it on him. So Jim, the favorite, reliable son, was saddled with the hideous task of essentially putting his father in prison. Jim did as he was asked, but he believed James Sr. never forgave the family or, more particularly, him.

James Sr. went through the 60-day "cold turkey" regimen at Blackwell Island, and Carrie met him when he was released. He looked rested and fit. Within no more than a week, it was apparent that the cure had not taken. Nonetheless, Carrie stood by him, as she always had and always would. Despite all his frailties and weaknesses, she adored her husband, even at the darkest moments. When her mother once told her that she would not have been able to stand by a man so profligate and irresponsible, Carrie replied, "Oh, yes, you could, Ma. When you see how much fun he gives the kids. And how much fun he brings *me.*"[89] Carrie was sunny and valiant and demonstrative and loving. Her boys idolized her. As her second son wrote on page one of his autobiography: "Without hesitating I can say my mother was the key to the Cagneys."[90]

Jim was due to graduate from Stuyvesant in the spring of 1917. Carrie worked with him to decide what course of study to pursue next. Because her own education had been cut short, she was determined to the point of obsession that her children would not suffer the same fate. She would say often, "I am damned well going to see to it that every kid of mine gets an education," viewing it not simply as an end in itself, but as the pathway out of poverty.[91] And she was wildly successful in achieving her objective: Harry and Eddie both became doctors, Bill became a wealthy businessman, and we all know what happened to Jim. But that was all in the future.

Carrie encouraged Jim to choose a course that would further develop his demonstrated artistic talents. But his love of the country that grew out of the 14 days in Flatbush, the 18 months in Ridgewood and the six weeks in Stepney convinced him that he would like to study farming. Despite her own preferences, Carrie gave Jim a leaflet about the Farmington School of Agriculture that she had found at the East Side Settlement House, and Jim submitted an application. The School evaluated Jim's candidacy, sending a representative to the Cagneys' flat. Whether he failed the interview because of the chaotic and impoverished household or because of his lack of a clear rationale for his interest in agriculture will never be known. What we do know is that Jim never heard from the Farmington School again.

Having graduated from high school without any clear career path, Jim took a job in an architect's office, moonlighting with his brothers as a waiter at Tiffin's Tea Room. One day Harry, who was attending Columbia, told Jim that the college was actively seeking students to participate in the Student Army Training Corps, a precursor of ROTC, and that they had room for skilled draftsmen in their camouflage unit. Enrollment could lead to a Columbia scholarship and a commission as an officer in the Army. Since Jim had always loved sketching he enlisted and, as he put it, in "one fell swoop" became "art student, soldier and college boy."[92]

In 1918, Jim Cagney was veering off in a direction that bore no relation to the career that would define his life. But a year earlier he had his first real encounter with the world he would eventually inhabit.[93] In what seemed like just another random way to fill Kitty, at the beginning of 1917 Jim took a job as a doorman at the Friars Club, the actors' hangout. The salary was bad, but the tips were good. Jim was hardly star-struck. However, he learned that actors were very generous and that even those cast in minor roles earned between $75 and $100 a week. That revelation led him to read plays in the settlement house library and to take advantage of the free passes to both the legitimate theater and movies. One such pass enabled him to watch the fabled *prima ballerina* Pavlova, stirring a sense that dance was in him.

Meanwhile, in her relentless efforts to better her children, Carrie enrolled the shy Harry in a public-speaking course at the Lenox Hill Settlement House. Over time, Harry joined the drama program, and Jim joined the program for arts and crafts that produced the scenery and posters for the amateur productions. Harry was cast in several plays, but became ill before one of the performances and, with no understudy, convinced his younger brother to go on for him. The play was *The Faun*, and Jim was forced to marcel his hair and flit about the stage in little more than a loin cloth, delivering lines about the "wayward wynde."[94] The role could not have been further from Jim's tough-guy street *persona*, and his biographers advance divergent views of its significance. One, quoting Cagney, said it was a near epiphany: that an audience of strangers approved of, or at least was interested in him, that acting was more than a way to make a decent living and that performing might be a way "little Jim" could become a big man.[95] Two others said that Cagney did not regard the evening as either important or happy, citing his recollection that when he left the auditorium he "expected to be attacked on my way home" and feared that "he would never live down the humiliation of it."[96] Putting aside the varying interpretations, Jim's appearance in *The Faun* did mark his theatrical debut.

When he ultimately decided on a career in the performing arts, much of what had come before, skills that were already second nature to him, proved to be both relevant and helpful. Jim's powers of observation, reflected in his sketching, provided an archive of memories of the cavalcade of characters he had encountered on New York's streets. His keen ear, apparent in his easy mastery of languages, enabled him to mimic speech patterns and dialects. And his physical coordination, which made him such a good ballplayer and street fighter, gave him the confidence and ability that directly applied to the body control required for both acting and dance.

It is undeniable, as Cagney himself wrote, that his childhood "was surrounded by trouble, illness and my dad's alcoholism."[97] Yet, as he went on to say, "[W]e just didn't have time to be impressed by all those misfortunes."[98] Jim's great gift was to take it all in stride and to gain strength from the love he felt from his mother, his brothers and even his long-suffering father. As one biographer summed it up,

> On the surface, Cagney is the rock-hard street ruffian displayed on the Warner Brothers screen, but only a thorn scratch beneath the surface dwells a gentle gent with a green thumb and an affection for animals, a sentimentalist in his relationship with family and friends.[99]

Cary Grant
January 18, 1904–November 29, 1986
Career span: 1932-66
Major Films: *The Awful Truth* (1937); *His Girl Friday* (1940); *Penny Serenade* (1941); *The Philadelphia Story* (1941); *None But the Lonely Heart* (1944); *To Catch A Thief* (1955); *North by Northwest* (1959).
Signal Honors: Honorary Academy Award 1969; Academy Award Nominee for Best Actor 1941, 1944.

UNDERDOG GREATS

Cary Grant was born Archibald Alexander Leach in Bristol, England, on January 18, 1904. Bristol was and still is a significant English seaport, and is famous for its sherry, for a university, for William Penn and, now, for a Hollywood legend. Archie's parents had been raised in Bristol. His father, Elias, was from a family of potters, at least on the male side. Elias himself broke the mold and, like his mother, took a job at Todd's Clothing Factory. He worked 10-hour days on the assembly line as a "presser," steaming creases into trousers, jackets and waistcoats. Elias was slim and "delicately" handsome, with curly light brown hair and an "elaborate" mustache.[100] He was quite fond of drinking and was a real charmer, "something of a ladies' man."[101] In May of 1898 when he was 33, he married Elsie Maria Kingdon, who was 12 years his junior.

Elsie was one of five children, the other four – all boys – having moved to Canada by the time of her wedding. Her father, William Kingdon, was a shipwright and in terms of status the Kingdon family was, or regarded itself as being, "a cut above" the Leaches.[102] Elsie, who was spoiled, domineering and a bit of a snob, may have believed that with her support Elias could become – or she could make him into – something more than a laborer. In terms of appearance, Elsie was slight, also had delicate features, with olive complexion, black hair, brown eyes and a distinctive cleft chin. She was a woman of the Victorian age and, as was the fashion, wore "prim, high necked blouses" and "starched petticoats."[103] She did not much like alcohol, tobacco or men. In terms of personality, she and her new husband could not have been more different. Elsie, though seemingly shy in social settings, was determined and strong-willed. Elias was "feckless and irresponsible."[104]

Following the wedding, the new couple rented a semi-detached, two-story house at 15 Hughenden Road, a side street off the main thoroughfare leading out of town. It was constructed of stone and was identical to those on either side of it. With heat supplied by small coal fires in small fireplaces, it was cold and damp in the winter. In the summer, it was "too sweaty."[105] On the first floor were a front parlor that was 12' by 16', a back parlor that was 12' by 12' and a kitchen that was 7' by 10'. On the second floor, reached by a narrow staircase, were three little bedrooms. The toilet was out back, as was the pump for bathing. It was a working-class house in a working-class neighborhood two miles from the center of the city.[106]

However modest the Leaches' circumstances, 15 Hughenden Road was a joyful place on February 9, 1899, when Elsie gave birth to her first son, John William Elias Leach. She was devoted to the little boy and made him the center of her life. From the outset he had little coughs and would run a fever, but he recovered each time as a result of Elsie's devotion and attentiveness. After some months, his intermittent conditions became more constant and worse. He was continually feverish, and he suffered from convulsions. The doctor examined the infant on February 6, 1900. He did not say the child's illness was particularly serious and advised Elsie, who was totally worn out, to get some rest. She followed the doctor's orders and went to bed that night. The next morning she found the baby dead. The cause was tubercular meningitis. He was two days shy of his first birthday. Elsie forever felt that the baby's death was her fault. She believed that had she remained awake, her son would have lived.

Accounts of Elsie as being neurotic and emotionally unstable appear to have their roots in this tragedy. More difficult to time or assess is Elias's return to his bachelor ways of pub-crawling and womanizing. The backsliding might have occurred right after the wedding, when he realized Elsie had no substantial dowry and that no matter how hard he worked her wants would exceed his ability to provide. But it was doubtless exacerbated by his son's death, when Elsie was understandably deeply depressed and not at all able to or interested in satisfying her husband's needs. Elias and Elsie were never a good match, and their relationship grew progressively worse.

At her doctor's urging, Elsie became pregnant again, and on January 18, 1904, roughly five years after the birth of her first son, she had a second. The delivery took place at the Leach home in a second-floor bedroom at about 1 am on a cold and wet morning. A midwife assisted. Archie, as the boy was called for nearly three decades, had dark brown eyes, just like his mother's.

Elsie made Archie her project. As one biographer wrote, "This child would be the only reason for her life."[107] She closely supervised his every activity. She did her best to ensure that his friends were of a suitable type. She selected his wardrobe, keeping him in white girlish dresses, a standard Victorian custom, for more than the standard length of time. She let his curly hair remain in shoulder-length ringlets even after he was out of the carriage. "It was not that she wanted her son to be a girl, it was more that she wanted a doll, a dependent being who would be unable to exist without her love and affection."[108]

Elsie strolled with Archie on the beautiful terraced streets of Clifton, where the rich and successful lawyers and businessmen resided. She clearly hoped that Archie would one day live in such a neighborhood and, to that end, took steps to make him a "little gentleman."[109] She started to teach him to dance and sing. She encouraged him in elocution. She succeeded in moving the family into a nicer house, though Elias was not enthusiastic about the change. Convinced that her son was especially bright, she finagled his enrollment into the Bishop Road Junior School, one of the best in the area, when he was only four and a half.

Bishop Road School was a formidable-looking place. It was housed in a tall building with tiled hallways and high ceilings, situated adjacent to the Bristol prison. Archie, both small and young, was frightened by the new setting. He proved to be skillful at art and language and hopeless at arithmetic. He did not utter a single word to the girl with whom he shared a desk. Over time Archie became more social and discovered he was good at sports. He was agile and fearless enough to be the soccer goalie. Without a net, a chalked rectangle on a jagged stone wall signifying a score, it was a dangerous position. Victory often came at a price: bloodied hands, barked knees, torn clothing. But he loved the approval of his schoolmates, the exhilarating feeling after a game, when he was patted on the back amidst a chorus of "well dones."[110]

Archie was very solicitous of his mother, as she insisted that he be. He allowed her to straighten out his coat and to brush his hair. He put up with wearing Eton collars on weekends, as befitting a "little prince."[111] He was well-behaved, acting politely to strangers, speaking only when spoken to and keeping neat and clean.[112] He understood that he should not ask for money, because it did not grow on trees. He endured, without apparent complaint, her obsessiveness about the household, accepting that when he marred her white linen tablecloth or messed up her cushions his sixpence allowance would be docked.

Yet, for all his patience with Elsie, he was also attached to Elias. From the age of five, Archie went to the pressing factory on weekdays after school to wait for Elias's shift to end and spent Saturdays with him inside the plant. On the walk home there was always some treat, usually candy, and often a life lesson, such as the importance of always dressing well or the logic behind buying goods of high quality.

Archie was able to adapt and please his two very different parents. He found a way to get along with his clinging, high-strung mother, as well as his fun-loving, undisciplined father. It is impossible to pinpoint when he began to understand the nature of the tension between the two, but early on he had to know that Elias and Elsie were unhappy with one another. He could not have escaped their bickering.

The root of the problem was financial: Elias did not make enough to take care of the family or to take care of it in the manner that Elsie thought was required.[113] So Elsie criticized Elias for his lack of ambition and his inability to "better" himself and their situation. Clearly Elsie was also upset by Elias's continual bar-hopping and philandering, but who knows whether her continual nagging drove him to it. As Grant put it decades afterward: "The lack of sufficient money became an excuse for regular sessions of reproach, against which my father learned the futility of trying to defend himself."[114]

All that said, Archie was a normal, even if not an excessively happy, boy. At five he saw his first vaudeville act and may have gotten a glimpse of Charlie Chaplin, whose tours typically made a stop at Bristol. He went to the pantomimes at Christmas, a distinctively English entertainment notable for its spectacular lighting, gorgeous costumes and bizarre takes on classic tales. At six or seven he began making regular visits to the neighborhood cinema, which became the standard Saturday entertainment for him and his mates.

Sometimes Archie's movie-going was with one of his parents, and the experience differed depending on which one he was with. When he went with Elsie, it was to the posh Claire Street Picture House where they watched romances and melodramas, seated on wicker chairs and repairing to the balcony at intermission to be served tea and delicate snacks. When he accompanied Elias, it was to the barn-like and far less expensive Metropole, where the men smoked, the predominant smell was of rubber boots and the hissing and booing competed with the crunching of hard sweets.

In 1911, when Archie turned seven, the three Leaches moved to a larger house in a more desirable location. To help defray the increased cost, Elsie sublet two of the bedrooms to two of her nieces who had just found work as secretaries. Somehow Elsie managed to find money for Archie to take piano lessons from a teacher who seemed to delight in rapping his knuckles. This further attempt to make her son "cultured" just added to the tensions with Elias. He thought piano lessons were not manly and that they were an extravagance. Moreover, he was peeved that the piano had been bought by Elsie's father, which he took as a further slur on his adequacy as a provider.

A year after the move to Seymour Avenue – in 1912 when Archie was eight – Elias took a better-paying job in Southampton, making uniforms for both sides in the Italo-Turkish conflict. Since Southampton was 80 miles from Bristol, Elias decided not to commute but to set up a second household. His motivation for doing so was not simply logistical convenience. While in Southampton he continued his womanizing ways and took up with a younger woman, Mabel Alice Johnson, with whom he ultimately had a child. Grant later said he did not remember his father's departure and speculated that he might have "felt guilty at being secretly pleased . . [to have] my mother to myself."[115] Perhaps Elias's departure did not register because his time away was relatively brief. For Elias was back in Bristol after six months, either because he had been "let go" or because he could not afford the cost of two residences. When he returned, he was re-hired at Todd's. The episode left Elias understandably depressed. Often he did not come home or when he did, sat quietly in the parlor. The estrangement with Elsie only deepened.

Archie's ninth year was relatively uneventful, considering the sorry state of his parents' marriage. He had grown taller and more confident and was continually playing cricket and soccer, being noisy and scruffy and acting as far away as he could from being Elsie's "model boy."[116] He developed his first crush which led him to petition his mother for his first pair of long pants. Elsie decided to economize by making them herself, which led to embarrassment and disappointment: the material was cheap and the trousers fit poorly. At school, he was an indifferent student but well-liked. All in all, he was doing neither great nor too badly.

Meanwhile, Elsie was getting stranger, though Archie was too young or preoccupied to notice. She was locking the doors in the house. She was forever inquiring about the whereabouts of her dancing shoes. She was hoarding food. She was sitting in front of the fire for hours staring at the red coals. After consulting his doctor and town officials, Elias had Elsie committed to the mental institution at Fishponds.

Archie learned his mother was gone when he returned home from school late one afternoon during the spring of his 10th year, and Elsie did not come to the front door as she usually did. His two cousins told him that she had gone away to the seaside for a short vacation.[117] When she did not return after several weeks, and Archie asked Elias when he would see her again, he was simply told that Elsie was fine and sent her love. After a while Archie stopped asking. He was never informed where she was and why she had left.

It was two decades before the then-famous Cary Grant saw his mother again. Grant said he thought that his mother had had a nervous breakdown, precipitated by the ever-present marital strife and her unresolved grief about the death of her first child. Elias may have had been motivated to get her out of the house, in part, because of his ongoing affair. Whatever the real reason, Elsie's leaving was a devastating event for Archie, and at some level he believed that he was responsible.

There was some "acting out" in the aftermath of her disappearance: petty theft, running away, spending hours by himself at the town docks. Around this time, likely during the summer of 1914, the two secretary-cousins moved out of the Leaches' nice house in the better part of town, and Elias and Archie were forced to move in with Elias' mother, sharing her tiny place on Picton Street. Archie largely fended for himself, seeing his grandmother and his father mostly at weekend meals.

During 1914 Archie began studying for a scholarship examination which would enable him to attend an English "public" school free of charge. In early 1915 he learned that his efforts had paid off, for he had won a place at Bristol's Fairfield Secondary School. He was enrolled for the term beginning September 2, 1915. Fairfield had between 300 and 400 students, both boys and girls, and was well-regarded academically. It was the center of Archie's world for the next two and a half years, a period which began aimlessly.

Though Elias did not need to pay for Archie's tuition, he did need to buy Archie's school uniform – ties, caps and blazer – gym gear, bicycle slip and books. These basic "extras" stretched Elias to the limit, and Archie soon concluded that going to university was a pipe dream, "obviously too expensive to consider."[118] Given the tight finances, it is not so surprising that Archie was described by those who remember him as scruffy and poorly dressed. In terms of deportment, he was mischievous and willful, full of pranks and jokes designed to upset discipline and try the patience of his teachers. Though his "minor acts of delinquency" led to frequent canings, there was something about him that was "endearing" and "fascinating."[119] Perhaps it was the big eyes or the big voice or the big laugh or "the aura of pathos" that surrounded him.[120] So, despite all the antics and his unwillingness to do his homework, he was described as "a good scholar" who "could soak things up."[121]

One schoolmate recalled that Archie was "very popular," "clever" at most subjects and "expert" at sports; another that he was "just a nice, ordinary boy" who said he "wanted to join the circus"; a third that his hair was slicked down, he was expert at "fives" (a variant of American handball) and he had a flair for playing piano, music hall songs being his specialty.[122]

Archie's principal activity when he was not in school was as a member of a Boy Scout troop that was sponsored by the YMCA. With Britain's entry into World War I, the Boy Scouts' role became more purposeful. After his first year at Fairfield, during the summer of 1916, 12-year-old Archie volunteered to be a Junior Air Warden. Were there a German aerial attack, his job was to douse the gas street lamps near the Bristol docks. Archie took his responsibility very seriously and made sure his uniform was readily available. After his second year at Fairfield, during the summer of 1917, 13-year-old Archie volunteered to assist as a messenger in Southampton. He did errands and helped in whatever way he could as English soldiers boarded ships bound for the Continent. He issued the servicemen life belts and mailed their last-minute letters, refusing cash tips but gratefully accepting their buttons and souvenirs.

At 13, Archie had grown tall and become quite good-looking, with "black wavy hair," "a dimpled chin," "rich brown eyes" and a "ready smile."[123] His appearance was somewhat marred when he slipped on the ice in the Fairfield playground and broke half of his front tooth. He had the other half extracted which, until his teeth obligingly grew together, allowed him to effectively squirt his classmates by forcing water through this unique gap, further charming the teachers.

As for academics, Archie had difficulty with mathematics and Latin, but liked art, geography, history and chemistry. One afternoon he was in the chemistry lab talking to the very friendly electrician who volunteered as a part-time assistant. The electrician asked Archie if he would be interested in seeing the switchboard and lighting system that he had built for the Hippodrome Theater, a mammoth vaudeville venue that had opened in 1912. Archie enthusiastically agreed, not because of an interest in the performing arts but because of his interest in science. But when he entered the enormous hall, it was not the electronic wizardry which stunned him. Grant described the moment, years later, as "apocalyptic:"[124]

> The Saturday matinee was in full swing when I arrived backstage; and there I suddenly found my inarticulate self in a dazzling land of smiling, jostling people wearing and not wearing all sorts of costumes and doing all sorts of clever things. And that's when I *knew*. What other life could there *be* but that of an actor?[125]

Following that afternoon of destiny, Archie began to hang around the Hippodrome and its sister theater, the Empire, sometimes after school was out, sometimes even when it was in session. His diary for January 1918, for example, records visits to the Empire on the 14th, 17th, 18th, 21st and 22nd. The friendly electrician was able to get Archie an unpaid position at the Empire, where he eventually was promoted to controlling the balcony spotlight. His job ended abruptly and unceremoniously when he was tasked with lighting the performance of a magician known as the Great David the Devant, and Archie let the beam drift to a point on the stage that revealed the secret of one of the illusionist's most famous tricks. Undaunted, Archie shifted back to the Hippodrome, carrying tea to the dressing rooms, discouraging stage door Johnnies and fetching cigarettes for the actors. He also observed and learned some key theater commandments: "Don't milk your bows." "Pick up your cue." "Never walk on the other fellow's lines."[126] He was only 14, but he knew he wanted this to be his world and was trying to figure out how to make that happen.

There are two credible versions of what occurred next, both of them leading to Archie's initial stint with "Bob Pender's Knockabout Comedians," a well-established group of acrobats, dancers and stilt-walkers.[127] In the first version, Pender was appearing at the Hippodrome in Bristol; Archie, who was at the theater that day, asked him for a job; Pender said that there might be an opening if he could get permission from his parents; and Archie forged a letter from Elias saying his son could go. In the second version, Archie heard gossip about Pender while he was backstage doing pickup work at the Hippodrome; he surmised that Pender might be in the market for "new blood" since the war was spiriting away his performers; and Archie forged a letter from Elias with his snapshot asking if there might be work for his "son."

At this point, the two versions converge. Over the ensuing days Archie made sure he was the first to see the mail at home so he could intercept Pender's response. About a week and a half after "Elias's letter" was sent, Pender did answer, enclosing the fare for Archie to come to Norwich for a tryout. Archie snuck out of his grandmother's house in the middle of the night and caught the early morning train.

Once Archie reached Norwich he successfully passed some basic gymnastic tests and immediately began his training with Pender's troupe. At 14, Archie was younger and less experienced than the dozen or so other boys who were already there. He was taught tumbling, eccentric dancing, cartwheels, handsprings, nip ups and spot rolls. He learned how to fall, how to balance, how to react to imaginary blows, how to do backflips and how to apply makeup. Though he had started behind the others in age and skill, he gradually began to see progress "and began to feel the pride and confidence born of accomplishment."[128] He was gaining vital knowledge not only in the "classroom" but by observing performances from the wings.

Roughly 10 days after his arrival in Norwich, Archie accompanied the troupe to Ipswich where Elias caught up with him. Whether his father had been a good "detective" or had been tipped off by the Penders is a subject of dispute. There is also a dispute about how Bob Pender and Elias Leach reacted to one another. One story line has the two of them getting along famously – they were both in their mid-40s, snappy dressers and Masons – and agreeing that Archie should return to Bristol to complete his schooling. The other story line has the two men at complete loggerheads, with Pender wanting Archie to stay on, and Elias threatening to press charges of criminal abduction if Pender resisted in any way. Whatever the temperature of their interaction, the result was that Archie went home to finish up at Fairfield Secondary.

From the moment he got back to school Archie was very unhappy and did everything he could to limit his stay. He made it his business to fail in his academic course work. He was often absent, and when he did go to class he made himself as disruptive and unwelcome as possible. His behavior was not affected by punishment, whether verbal or corporal. His campaign had its desired effect and his tenure at Fairfield ended on March 13, 1918, two months after his 14th birthday.

Archie contended that he was expelled for his role as "lookout" in an escapade to unlock the secrets of the girls' lavatory. Caught in the act, he was summoned to the front of a school-wide assembly as the head publicly excoriated him for being "inattentive," "irresponsible," "incorrigible" – a general "discredit" to Fairfield – and told never to return.[129] Though dramatic, this account is implausible for a couple of reasons. First, the Headmaster, Augustus Smith, was regarded as a "Mr. Chips-like" character who would be unlikely to act so cruelly.[130] Second, there is no real corroboration from contemporaries of what would have been an extraordinary and memorable event. More likely, Archie's repeated and annoying infractions, coupled with his total lack of interest in academics, led a mildly exasperated Headmaster Smith to convince a somewhat reluctant Elias Leach to put Archie, and the school, out of their collective misery.

After the expulsion, consensual or otherwise, any objection Elias may have had to his son's joining the Pender troupe evaporated. Elias may have relented because he could not afford to send Archie to another school or because his absence would allow him to spend time with his common-law family or because it was a relief to have one less mouth to feed. In any event, by the last week in March, 14-year-old Archie was back with "the Knockabout Comedians," and by early August he was under contract. His initial salary was 10 shillings a week together with room and board. The term of the apprenticeship would extend until Archie's 18th birthday.

Archie lived with the Penders in a dormitory-like setting and under strict rules: the boys had to be ready for breakfast by 7:30 am and had to douse their lights by 10 pm. Every day there was morning practice and rehearsal, followed by two or three performances. Archie learned physical skills, like dancing, stilt-walking and pratfalls. He also learned the art of pantomime:

> [H]ow to convey a mood or meaning without words. How to establish communications silently with an audience, using the minimum of movement and expression; how best immediately and precisely to effect an emotional response – a laugh or, sometimes, a tear.[131]

In addition to these wordless skills, Pender also worked on Archie's distinctive but limiting, "West Country Bristol brogue," helping him to develop his own style, whose unique sound and phrasing would one day become a hallmark.[132]

Along the way, Archie received some good "life" advice from seasoned professionals. One piece that he treasured was from Broadway star Florence Reed. Archie had written to request her autograph, asking whether he might enhance his odds of success by moving to America. She responded with a signed picture and her answer: "'Tain't *where* you are makes things happen, but *what* you are."[133]

In June of 1918 Archie was back in Bristol, this time appearing on stage at the Empire as a performer. It was a triumphal moment that made Elias very proud and Archie extremely happy. From Bristol, the troupe interspersed appearances in the English provinces with engagements at a chain of London music halls. After the November Armistice and the return of some of his boys from the service, Pender created two troupes for the Christmas season. The less experienced one, to which Archie was assigned, was relegated to a small and frigid town in north Wales. Archie appeared as one of 10 papier-machéd stilt-walking pantomimists, dressed to resemble an enormous Mother Hubbard.

After the two-month Christmas tour ended, the troupe returned to London where Archie could observe the headliners with whom it shared the bill. He marveled at their timing and apparent confidence, recognizing the years of effort required to achieve such perfection. During 1919 and the first half of 1920, Archie got to perform and further master his craft, travelling throughout England, as well as to major European cities and to the Middle East. By the summer of 1920, Archie "with his handsome face, great smile, easy laugh, and natural athletic ability, had developed a charismatic stage presence that brought him to the front ranks of the Pender touring company."[134] It had not been that long ago that Archie had been playing the back end of a dancing cow.

In July of 1920 Pender held a competition among the 12 members of his troupe to identify the eight who would accompany him on a journey across the Atlantic. Pender had secured an engagement to appear at the Globe Theater in New York in a production staged by American impresario Charles Dillingham. Archie was one of those chosen to make the trip.

On July 21, 1920, the Pender entourage left Southampton on the RMS *Olympic* (sister vessel to the ill-fated *Titanic*), which had been dubbed the "world's wonder ship" when she had been launched in 1911.[135] On board in first class were America's sweethearts, Douglas Fairbanks, Sr. and Mary Pickford, returning from their six-week honeymoon in Europe. Fairbanks made an enormous impression on Archie. His ever-present tan, unfailing affability and easy charm were all to become trademarks of Cary Grant. Despite his fame, Fairbanks joined the Pender group for its morning exercises, a moment memorialized by the shipboard photographer. Grant was forever struck by what a true gentleman Fairbanks was.

At sunrise on July 28, the *Olympic* entered New York harbor, and Archie made sure he was awake to get a glimpse of the Manhattan skyline and the Statue of Liberty. Shortly after its arrival the troupe attended a welcoming reception, to allow the Penders to meet Charles Stone, the star attraction for whom they would open at the Globe. Following the meeting and the first rehearsal, the Penders were told that their act would be moved to the Hippodrome. The stated explanation for the shift was that the low proscenium arch could not accommodate the group's stilt-walking routine. The real reason was that Stone was afraid he would be outshone if the Pender company appeared with him on the same bill.

The New York Hippodrome was a monumental structure, occupying an entire New York City block and seating 5,697. It boasted a huge revolving stage, 48 dressing rooms, enormous facilities for props and wardrobe, cages for live animals and a 960,000-gallon swimming pool. This cavernous theater was the permanent home of *Good Times*, a spectacular revue with something for everyone. The cast numbered over a thousand, with another 800 people working behind the scenes. The show included elephants and horses, acrobats and dancers, soloists and choruses, magicians and cyclists and divers. And, with the addition of the Pender team, stilt-walkers.

Good Times debuted on August 8, 1920. The Pender troupe was slotted into the second of three hour-long acts in a sequence entitled "A Toy Store," Archie appearing on stage as one of the stilt-walking toys that comes to life when the store is closed.[136] The show opened to extremely favorable reviews, *Variety* specifically noting the "very warm reception" received by the "distinctly European" comedy group.[137]

Good Times played two shows a day, six days a week, with a Sunday matinee. As in England, the Penders acted as chaperones for 16-year-old Archie and the rest of the boys, renting them an apartment across the corridor from their own in a hotel for "theatricals" on 46th Street and Eighth Avenue.[138] The boys were responsible, on a rotating basis, for keeping accounts, making beds, cleaning, washing, ironing, mending, shopping and cooking. When it was Archie's turn at the stove, he prepared his "specialty," the beef stew he had learned to make during his days as a Boy Scout.[139]

When not performing or doing household chores, Archie explored the city by subway and, when possible, double-decker bus. He went to the Bronx Zoo and Coney Island, as well as to the tony apartments and mansions on Riverside Drive. He became addicted to American ice cream. He continued his love affair with movies, especially comedies and action films, trying to pick up whatever tips he could from his favorite stars, the likes of Douglas Fairbanks, Charlie Chaplin, Harold Lloyd and Tom Mix. And he developed a huge crush on a blond, blue-eyed ballerina, though he was too timid to do anything more than admire her from a distance.

Good Times ran for 455 performances, concluding its run at the end of April 1921. Archie, who had turned 17, had not only become a "veteran" member of the Pender troupe, but had added to his skillset by learning from the other acts, picking up "special acrobatic tricks, drunken walks, dance steps and illusions," all in an effort to make himself a more complete entertainer.[140]

Following the close of *Good Times*, the Pender group was booked by B.F. Keith's theaters, regarded as the premier vaudeville circuit in America. They shared the program with legitimate stars like Eddie Cantor, the Marx Brothers and the Foy family. They hit the major cities east of the Mississippi, including Boston, Cleveland, Milwaukee, Philadelphia, Chicago and Washington, D.C. The tour happened to be following the same route as the New York baseball Giants, often sharing the same trains and hotels, and Archie, particularly, became a rabid fan. Archie also got to meet current celebrities, like Jack Dempsey and President Woodrow Wilson, and celebrities-to-be, like George Burns and Jim Cagney.

While in Rochester, Archie contracted rheumatic fever and became very ill. He was nursed back to health by Jean Adair, a quite famous vaudeville trouper, whose kindness he never forgot. After a month and a half, Archie had recovered sufficiently to rejoin the group in New York for its grand finale in June 1922 at the Palace Theater, the pinnacle of the Keith's circuit and, for that matter, of the entire vaudeville world. Having reached the heights, the Pender tour ended. The Penders went home. Archie stayed.

There is some confusion about whether the Penders returned to England right away or after a California vacation, and as to whether the return was hastened by some family crisis. There is also some confusion as to whether Archie and Bob Pender ended their four-year relationship on good terms or bad. There is consensus, however, that Pender gave Archie enough money to book a return passage and that Archie used those funds to keep him off the bread lines over the lean months that followed in New York.

With Pender gone and no connections to speak of, Archie did his best to find work. He hung around the National Vaudeville Artists Club, hoping for leads on job openings or short-term pick-up work with traveling groups that were short a man. He managed to get a few auditions, but his obvious good looks could not compensate for an off-putting accent that was decidedly British working class.

Ever resourceful, Archie managed to keep afloat. He found that a day's worth of meals could be had for 70 cents at Ye Eatte Shoppe or for the price of a hairpin at the Automat. He also found that he could dress himself stylishly by searching the secondhand shops. Fate intervened when he struck up a friendship with a 24-year-old Australian named Jack Kelly, who would re-fashion himself as the celebrated Warner Brothers costume designer Orry-Kelly. Kelly, whose day job was as a tailor's assistant, moonlighted by painting neckties he bought for a dollar and sold for three. Archie signed on as Kelly's sidewalk salesman, staking out Broadway as his territory. As Kelly's Greenwich

Village roommate, he earned his keep by doing the cooking, specializing in "fish and chips."

It turned out that as a tall, handsome man with a dark suit, he could be fed at fashionable dinner parties or business banquets, if he were willing to fill out an empty place at the table or serve as an escort. One evening Archie was asked to squire Lucrezia Bori, a world-renowned soprano with the Metropolitan Opera, to a Park Avenue reception.[141] He was seated next to George Tilyou, who took a liking to Archie, especially when he confessed that he was not another upper-class swell, but an unemployed stilt-walker trying to earn an extra buck. Tilyou told Archie that his family owned Steeplechase Park, a famed Coney Island attraction, and a stilt-walking advertiser might be just what was needed.

Tilyou had not been amusing himself with dinner-table chatter, and the next day he hired Archie. Archie was dressed as a Steeplechase doorman, wearing a bright-green jacket trimmed in red, a matching jockey cap and long black pants to cover the stilts. He received $5 each weekday and $10 on Saturdays and Sundays. The weekend rate was doubled as "hazard duty pay," because larger crowds increased the chances of his being upended, with the consequent expense of medical treatment, liniment and bandages. As a bonus for all the indignities, he was able to convince the nearby eateries that the throngs he attracted wherever he stationed himself were worth the price of burgers, fries, corn, hot dogs and frozen custard.

The Coney Island interlude was, mercifully, quite brief, for Charles Dillingham announced he would be staging a sequel to *Good Times*. Archie gathered the members of the Pender troupe still in the States to develop a new act. The group, renamed "The Walking Stanleys," tried out and were hired. The follow-on revue was called *Better Times*.[142] It opened at the Hippodrome on Labor Day weekend, 1922. Archie, who was nine months into his 18th year, was for the first time individually listed in the program. He appeared in two scenes on stilts, in drag as a "Joyful Girl" in a third scene and in period costume as a wordless but "energetic" *Meistersinger* in a fourth.[143] While Archie's performance did not garner specific mention in any of the reviews, the critics were generally enthusiastic, and *Better Times* ran for months.[144]

As he was nearing 19 Archie had accomplished a lot. He had been on his own for nearly five years. He had performed in hundreds of shows, honing his acrobatic skills. He had spent countless hours observing and soaking up the techniques of all manner of performers. But he wanted to be an actor and, as yet, he had not yet uttered a single word on stage.

Sidney Poitier
February 20, 1927-present
Career span: 1950-92
Major Films: *Blackboard Jungle* (1955); *The Defiant Ones* (1958); *A Raisin in the Sun* (1961); *Lilies of the Field* (1963); *In the Heat of the Night* (1967); *To Sir with Love* (1967); *Guess Who's Coming to Dinner* (1967).
Signal Honors: Academy Award Winner for Best Actor 1963; Academy Award Nominee for Best Actor 1958; Honorary Academy Award for Best Actor in a Leading Role 1964; Honorary Academy Award 2001; American Film Institute Lifetime Achievement Award 1992; Presidential Medal of Freedom 2009.

Sidney Poitier was not the first successful black American movie actor. In 1939, when Poitier was 12, Hattie McDaniel had already won the Academy Award for Best Supporting Actress for her performance in *Gone with the Wind*, and between 1929 and 1935 Lincoln Perry, known as Stepin Fetchit, had appeared in 26 films.[145] But Poitier's career differed from those of his predecessors. His roles defied demeaning racial stereotypes and caricatures of blacks as lazy, unintelligent and subservient. In addition, over time, he was cast as the male lead, the number one talent on the call sheet.

That Sidney Poitier was born an American was an accident, and that he did not die as an infant, a near miracle. His parents, Evelyn and Reginald, were descendants of Caribbean slaves. Natives of the Bahamas, they lived on Cat Island, approximately 100 miles to the southeast of the Bahamian capital of Nassau. The Poitiers were farmers who had traveled to Miami because the Produce Exchange there offered the best price for their hundreds of crates of tomatoes. At the time of their boat trip, Evelyn was seven-months pregnant with her seventh child. She went into premature labor and, with the help of a midwife, delivered a baby boy on February 20, 1927.

They named him Sidney. Though he weighed less than three pounds, he was not in the care of a doctor nor was he taken to a hospital. The odds of his survival were not good. The Poitiers had lost other babies through stillbirth or disease, and Reginald visited an undertaker and bought a coffin the size of a small shoebox to prepare for what he felt was the inevitable. Despite their history, Evelyn was not prepared to give up on Sidney, but in light of her husband's pessimism, she sought reassurance from a soothsayer. The elderly clairvoyant, after going through the prescribed rituals, told Evelyn not to worry:

> [H]e will survive and he will not be a sickly child. He will grow up to be [she paused] he will travel to most of the corners of the earth. He will walk with kings. He will be rich and famous. Your name will be carried all over the world. You must not worry about that child.[146]

Who knows how many times the wizened seer had offered the same prophesy? Whatever her track record, as a result of Evelyn's fortitude and care, Sidney did survive, just as the fortune-teller promised. By springtime the Poitier family – mother, father, five boys and two girls – were reunited on Cat Island.

There were two distinct phases to Sidney's childhood and adolescence: an idyllic period of 10½ years on Cat Island, and an often nightmarish, mostly tumultuous period of seven years in the cities of Nassau, Miami and New York.

Though the first nearly dozen years of Sidney's life were happy ones, they were not easy. Cat Island, with its rocky landscape, thin soil and scant waterways, was not the ideal place for farming. "Hurricanes, droughts and disease" increased the risks.[147] To make his tomatoes perfect Reginald raided a cave filled with bat guano and transported hundreds of pounds of the natural fertilizer to his fields. Planting was done by moonlight. The most demanding months were between October and March, when the spent bushes were removed and the new crop was planted. But there was plenty to do the other half of the year, not only in the tomato fields but on the adjacent acre where "string beans, sweet potatoes, navy beans, yams, okra, onions, peppers and corn" were raised for the family.[148] Evelyn worked the land with her husband, as did the children once they reached the age of six. In addition to helping farm, the children had other chores: gathering wood, fetching water, shucking corn, shelling beans, grinding grits, feeding the chickens, slopping the hogs and doing the laundry. The nine Poitiers were housed in a three-room, thatched-roofed stone shack, with an outdoor kitchen and a privy in the back. The standard meal was based on corn, "roasted, toasted, baked, broiled, stewed and ground into grits," leavened with fish, eggs or chicken.[149] Looking back on those early days Poitier did not mince words regarding the family's economic status: "We were poor man! *I mean we were bus-ted!*"[150]

"*Bus-ted*" or not, Cat Island had its compensations. Fifty miles long and four miles at its widest point, the island was rimmed with sandy beaches, blessed with a tropical climate, surrounded by the azure Atlantic and filled with spectacular foliage, including poinsettias, bougainvillea and sapodillas. Because of the proximity of water, Reginald and Evelyn made sure that Sidney could swim before he could either walk or talk. At 10 months, his mother threw him into the ocean and his father scooped him up at the last moment, a routine that was continued for several hours over several days, until he could keep himself afloat. Having acquired aquatic skills, his parents could rest easily when he wandered off. At four, he was allowed to roam the island without restriction, going down to the beaches and feeding himself on berries if he did not return at lunchtime. At five, he walked across the island, hunting turtle eggs. There were no cars, no school and seldom shoes, and Sidney spent parts of his days making mud huts, swimming in the sea and, Tarzan-like, shimmying up trees. He and his brothers would build rafts out of coconut trunks and then go fishing, using thread coated with sap for their lines and bent straight pins for hooks. Sidney was surrounded by caring people who created "a texture of love and warmth."[151] At least as he remembered it, he "was completely free."[152]

This blissful existence came to an end, a casualty of the Depression. In 1936 Florida enacted a protectionist statute precluding imports from the Bahamas, thereby wiping out Reginald's principal market. In the absence of alternatives, the tomato business foundered, and the Poitiers lost their farm. By 1938 Reginald was a very old 51: hollow-faced, white-haired and hobbled by rheumatism and arthritis. In this diminished state, he concluded that the family could no longer survive on Cat Island. Its next stop was Nassau.

Reginald sent Evelyn and Sidney to reconnoiter and find a place to live. For 11-year-old Sidney, Nassau was a culture shock. He had never seen an automobile. He had never seen a camera or a washing machine. He had never seen a clothing store or real stores of any kind. He had never seen electricity in "action." He had never seen ice cream, much less experienced its texture and taste.

While Nassau was exciting and different, it would prove discouraging for a family of tomato-growers from Cat Island. The best housing Evelyn could come up with, given the limited budget, was a dilapidated three-room shanty, with a porous roof and an outhouse in the back. Second daughter, Teddy, her husband and their two kids would occupy the near room, Reginald and Evelyn would occupy the middle room and the four boys – Cedric, Reginald, Carl and Sidney – would occupy the far room.[153] The diet consisted of hominy grits and fish, with rice as a treat on Sundays. Clothes were made from flour sacks, cut into strips, bleached and sewn together.

For employment, Reginald found a job in a bicycle shop, handling repairs, rentals and sales. After three years, he tried his hand at farming, squatting on some government-owned land in the center of the island. The work was tedious and backbreaking and the results were not worth the effort. Evelyn earned 20 cents a day for the eight to 10 hours she spent "beating" 20- to 30-pound rocks into the gravel used by builders to make concrete.[154] She also took in laundry. Despite these efforts, at times she was reduced to asking her daughters for a loan to make ends meet. Poitier's summary of those times: "There were haves and have-nots, and we definitely had very little."[155]

When the Poitiers first arrived, Sidney was enrolled in school and remained there for a year and a half during which he learned "to read a little, write a little, and sing 'Rule Britannia.'"[156] He did not like the structure and had little interest in the curriculum. In addition, given the dire state of family finances, it was more valuable for him to contribute to the kitty.

At 13 Sidney got his first job, serving as a water boy to laborers who were digging a canal across what is now called Paradise Island. Thereafter, he was employed in a warehouse stacking 125-pound bags of flower, rice and sugar. For a time he was part of a crew hired by the U.S. government to expand the facilities at the Nassau airport.

When he was not working, Sidney's most wholesome activity was movie-going. He particularly liked Westerns and "idolized" the "young, well-mannered, straight-shooting, white-hatted heroes . . ."[157] Movies were his escape from the bleak reality of a gritty urban environment.

During his three-plus years in Nassau, Sidney was generally up to no good. Early on he lost his virginity to an "old lady" – a woman in her mid-20s or so – who not only taught him about the joy of sex but also exposed him to the discomfort of gonorrhea.[158] He learned how to bluff his way at cards. He amused himself by tying tin cans to dogs tails and "accidentally" breaking windows with slingshots.[159] He liked the excitement of shoplifting and would wander around the local general store and make off with skates or comic books or food. To earn extra change, he and his pals would swim out to the milk boat and liberate a case of empties, redeeming them for six cents a bottle.

The problem with all these petty criminal activities is that they could have dire consequences if the Bahamian authorities were brought in. Sidney's best friend, Yorick Rolle, was on his own one day and he "borrowed" a bicycle. He was caught and sentenced to four years in a reform school that was not much better than a prison. Reginald reacted, saying "There but for the grace of God goes my son, whom I can't seem to handle anymore – I must get him off this island."[160] Reginald wrote his oldest boy, Cyril, who was settled in Miami, and asked whether he would take Sidney in. Cyril immediately agreed, though a year elapsed between Cyril's reply and Sidney's departure.

In the interim, Sidney was still tempting fate. One night he and three friends made off with a bushel of corn and were happily roasting the ears over an open and highly visible fire when the police nabbed them. All of them went to jail, but only Sidney stayed overnight. Reginald did not have money for bail or to repay the farmer. The fine was $2.50 which made a major dent in the Poitiers' meager finances. Although Sidney felt terrible about the shame and hardship he had caused, two months later he came home drunk on rum. Reginald tried to beat his son, who at 15 was bigger and far stronger than he. It was plain that it was time for Sidney to go.

Cyril sent $10 to finance Sidney's getaway from Nassau. Seven dollars of it was used to book passage and buy Sidney trousers, a shirt, a pair of shoes and a sweater. Reginald shoved the last $3 in Sidney's hand as he saw him off at the dock. In January 1943 Sidney left the only family he knew to live with a brother who was 15 years his senior and a virtual stranger. This black-skinned "cocksure, carefree, stubborn, functionally illiterate fifteen-year old boy with a West Indian accent" was hardly the perfect match for the people he would encounter in his accidental birthplace in America's Deep South.[161]

Sidney lived in Miami for no more than eight months, a fraction of the four years he had spent in Nassau. Yet that brief period was both chaotic and consequential. In moving from Cat Island to Nassau, he had moved from the country to the city, and from happy subsistence to abject poverty. In moving from Nassau to Miami, he moved from a familiar culture to one that was foreign, and from being a member of a downtrodden majority to being a member of a reviled minority. In Nassau, whites did not call blacks "nigger" or "boy" or impose curfews or restrict access to facilities.[162] In Miami, they did. There "Jim Crow" governed and racism was flagrant and rampant. "It was all over the place like barbed wire," Poitier recalled, "And I kept running into it and lacerating myself."[163]

Putting aside the indignities of "colored only" drinking fountains and "whites only" restaurants, Sidney's time with Cyril was awkward. For one thing, his brother had six children and only a three-bedroom house, making the addition of a gangly teenager a strain on accommodations. For another,

Sidney's sister-in-law, Alberta, was "not too thrilled" having him around.[164] There also were differing expectations of what Sidney would do. Sidney had thought he would resume his education; Alberta was insistent that he pull his "own weight" to help with the finances.[165]

When Sidney's job search was not moving fast enough for Alberta, she pushed Cyril to use a connection to have him hired as a bicycle delivery boy for a department store pharmacy. One of Sidney's first deliveries was in an upper class white neighborhood. When he arrived at his destination and rang the front doorbell, the lady who answered told him to "Get around to the back door."[166] When he asked "Why," she repeated herself, more forcefully.[167] Sidney did not understand the "Southern protocol" requiring blacks to only appear at the service entrance, and he left the package on the front doorstep.[168] His ignorance of tradition was not ignored. Two nights later, while Sidney was at the movies, the Klan paraded through his brother's neighborhood, decked out in its traditional robes and hoods. The purpose was to find and teach a lesson to the black boy who had insulted a flower of Florida society.

The scare was enough for Alberta, and she had Sidney shipped 10 miles across town to stay with his Uncle Joe and Aunt Eva, who lived in a tumbledown apartment in a 105 block ghetto called Colored Town. The atmosphere was far better than it was at Cyril's. Joe and Eva liked Sidney, and Sidney liked them. But jobs were difficult to come by for an illiterate Bahamian teenager with no skills. There was the comical day when Sidney decided he would respond to the sea of signs seeking parking lot attendants. Sidney proved adept at touting his skills and his vast experience behind the wheel. The problem was he had no idea how to drive. While he managed to find very temporary employment in half a dozen places, he damaged an equal number of cars – stripping gears, denting fenders, shattering headlights. By day's end he had mastered the art of driving but had been blacklisted by every garage in Miami.

After this fiasco, Sidney did find employment during the weeks he was with his Aunt and Uncle. He washed cars, cleaned rooms at a motel, humped crates in a warehouse and even tried his hand selling Fuller Brushes. The work was menial and uninspiring and the racism that was everywhere proved wearing. He decided that he would try to join the Navy, a process that merely reinforced his dislike for the South.

In order to enlist, he needed a birth certificate and in order to obtain a birth certificate, he needed to get a permission slip from the police. So, Sidney went down to the main police station and when he entered, an oversized and gruff sergeant ordered, "Take off that cap, nigger."[169] Sidney took offense at being called "nigger" and told the sergeant he was "crazy" to address him that way.[170] The sergeant, incredulous, said, "What did you say, boy?"[171] Sidney would not back down: "Boy? My name is Sidney Poitier, you calling me names? Do you know who you're talking to?"[172] Not knowing whether to book Sidney or burst into hysterics at his unheard of sass, the sergeant gave Sidney his pass, Sidney got his birth certificate and went to the recruiting office, only to be rejected for being underage.

After the police incident, Sidney was even more convinced the he needed to run away. So one day after work he went to the cleaners to pick up his few articles of clothing. When he was told that his clothes were still at the cleaning plant some 30 blocks away, he took a bus to the factory to get them himself. For some reason, he was in a great hurry to collect his wardrobe that night. By the time he had gotten his jacket and two pairs of pants it was after 7 pm and the buses had stopped running from this lily-white part of town to Uncle Joe and Aunt Eva's. After walking five blocks, he put out his thumb to flag a ride. A car pulled over, with five of "Miami's finest." After some conversation, Sidney was told to follow the car into an alley and then beckoned to lean over to talk to the cop in the front passenger seat. When he did, a gun was pressed into Sidney's forehead and the muzzle moved around in a circle, as the revolver-wielding officer asked his buddies, "What should we do with this boy?"[173] After a lot more conversation, Sidney was allowed to continue walking home, but warned, "If you turn around we'll shoot you. If you look back just once we'll shoot you."[174] The police car followed Sidney for the "35 fucking blocks" that took him to the edge of Colored Town.[175] Poitier was convinced that had he given the five patrolmen the slightest excuse, he would have been another unexplained and unreported Florida casualty.

Sidney ultimately left Miami, taking a train up North sometime in the late spring or early summer of 1943. His departure was fitful. In his first attempt, Sidney boarded a boxcar, ending up initially on a railroad siding at the other side of the yard and ultimately in Tampa. He visited a relative who lived in a hovel on the outskirts of the city, was fed and sent back to Joe and Eva.

His second attempt involved stowing away on another boxcar, ending up in a small town north of Tampa. He knocked on the door of a well-kept tract home and asked the woman who answered if he could do some chores in return for some food. She invited him into her house, prepared a big meal for him and when he was finished wished him well: "Good luck and take care of yourself."[176] She refused Sidney's offer to work to repay her for her kindness. He spent the next few days mowing lawns, cleaning garages and washing cars, bedding down in the woods at night. Tiring of the routine, he convinced the local police to let him spend the night in jail, rather than being picked up for vagrancy. The officer agreed, but on the condition that he contact his people. Cyril came up by bus to bring Sidney back to Miami, furious that his baby brother was in trouble again. He told him that with his own family to look after, "I cannot, I *cannot* assume responsibility for you – I just simply can't."[177]

After a short stay at Uncle Joe's, Sidney successfully followed up on a suggestion of Cyril's and got himself hired by a rural resort north of Atlanta. Though it was set on a plateau near a mountain top and boasted spectacular views of the surrounding countryside, Sidney's vistas were confined to the kitchen where for 12 hours a day, seven days a week he was washing dishes, scrubbing floors and peeling potatoes. After six weeks and a stash of $39, he resigned, finally having the funds to leave the Deep South. When he got to the Atlanta bus station, he rejected the buses headed for Chattanooga and Birmingham as not going far enough away. He found one heading for a place considerably further, a bus destined for New York. For $11.35 he could put real distance between himself and the failed experiment with his place of birth.

At the end of a 28-hour trip up the East Coast, Sidney arrived at the Greyhound bus terminal in midtown Manhattan. When the porter pulled his suitcase from the storage compartment, it was clear it had been rifled and his jacket, shoes and left-over earnings from the resort job were gone. All he had was $3. He knew of Harlem, vaguely understanding it to be a mecca for black people. So for a nickel he took his first subway ride. He quickly found that Harlem was too rich for his blood: a room in a shabby hotel, the Dewey Square, cost $3 – a night! He rode the subway back to the bus station, invested in a locker for his suitcase and splurged on his first "chocolate malted" and "a big, fat, juicy, hotdog."[178]

Walking down 49th Street at 11 pm, luck, of sorts, was on his side: the Turf Restaurant had a sign in the window "Relief dishwasher wanted."[179] The job paid $4.11 a night, plus two meals, and Sidney took it. He began work immediately, sorting, stacking and shelving the masses of crockery and cutlery spewed out by the huge machine.

At 4 am Sidney had finished his shift and spent that night holed up in the pay toilet at the bus terminal – toilet seat down, legs propped on the door – for the bargain rate of five cents. Within days Sidney had found a "more suitable," and even cheaper, place to sleep: the rooftop of the Brill Building, located on 51st Street, right off Broadway, offering great views of the city (although not yet great pop music). For sheets and blankets he used either *The New York Times* or the *Journal-American*.

Over the next few months, Sidney took on a string of odd jobs. He was a dishwasher at the Crossroads Café, Rudley's, the Savoy-Plaza, the Madison, the Taft, the Edison and the Waldorf-Astoria. He also worked as a butcher's assistant, a drugstore clerk, a salad maker, a chicken plucker, a laborer, a truck driver, a busboy, a porter and a longshoreman. His employment was not steady and the pay was meager. But in time he made enough to abandon the Brill rooftop and rent a shabby room on 127th Street in Harlem for $5 a week. It had "a little cot bed" and a rickety "chiffonier."[180] Lighting was provided by a bare 40-watt bulb that hung not quite from the center of the ceiling. Down the hall was a communal bathroom.

Sidney was surviving, but only barely. He was adrift in a city, having no family and no friends. When things later had gotten good, he recalled those bad times: "Being poor is bad enough, but being poor and a Negro – well, in a city of steel and stone, I was the most miserable young man in the streets."[181]

On August 1, 1943, Sidney got caught up in the Harlem riot. The melee was triggered by outrage over an incident involving a white cop who shot a black serviceman for coming to the aid of a black woman who was being questioned. According to one source, the outrage may have been overblown: the black woman had been "unruly" and the black serviceman who rescued her sustained "only a slight shoulder wound" when he fled after "knocking the white officer to the ground."[182] But it was a hot summer, and there was pent up anger from other incidents that clearly were worthy of indignation. So there were marauding crowds, shattered street lamps, and bricks, bottles and trash thrown at the police from the rooftops. There was also looting. For some reason Sidney was drawn into the fray, entering a department store through a broken window. He heard shots, hid in a storeroom, escaped into the street and was nicked in the calf by a stray bullet. Coating the wound with Vaseline, he limped for weeks and had a scar for life. Sidney was both out of control and at loose ends.

After recovering from his leg injury, Sidney confronted another problem: the weather. On Cat Island, in Nassau and in Miami, the word "winter" did not mean a change in seasons. Up North it did, and it came as a big surprise. Sidney had never seen snow or experienced frigid temperatures. It was disorienting, and he was continually cold. He had all the wrong clothing. He had no gloves, no warm coat, no hat. His only recourse was to wear all his tropical wardrobe at once, adopting the "layered" approach a half-century before it became the rage.

Employment dried up as the thermometer plummeted. Sidney was evicted from his apartment for non-payment of rent. On a night he was forced to sleep on a bench in Pennsylvania station, he was arrested for loitering. He was warned that if he were picked up again, he would be sentenced to "do time." He promised the police he would not be a problem again and told them that he planned to enlist in the Army.

After getting out of jail, Sidney took a short detour, finding shelter in a Catholic orphanage in Brooklyn and washing dishes at yet another greasy spoon. Though the sisters at the orphanage were nice, he was no happier or feeling any less alone. He decided to make good on his spur of the moment promise to the cops and went to the Army recruiting station. Though in late November 1943 he was not yet even 17, he told the desk sergeant he was 18. He was given the once over and was accepted. This time no birth certificate was checked.

Sidney had hoped for a change of scenery, as well as a change in climate, but he did not get his wish. His first stop was Camp Upton, Long Island, for basic training and orientation. From there, he was stationed at a Veterans Hospital in Northport, Long Island. The patients were all shell-shocked GIs. Sidney's duties included physiotherapy, tending to the wards, administering cold packs and assisting with shock treatments. The 150-man company was all black. He was not particularly welcomed by his bunkmates, who were older, more sophisticated and not interested in a country bumpkin from the Caribbean by way of Miami. And he bristled at Army discipline.

Though Sidney was no longer in the South, "Jim Crow" seemed to be unaware of the new geography. One night a couple of MPs, who were chaperoning Sidney and two truckloads of off-duty soldiers, took a road trip to Oyster Bay, a town about a half hour from the hospital. The chaperones got hungry and thirsty and ambled into a restaurant in the white part of town and asked the female bartender for two sandwiches and two beers "to go." She responded, "We don't serve niggers in here."[183] The MPs asked to see the manager, who repeated the statement of policy. The MPs left the restaurant and in a half hour or so returned with about 50 soldiers who tried to place the same sandwich and beer order and met with the same response. The expanded group expressed its unhappiness by completely destroying the premises, breaking every bottle, all the furniture, the works. In a surreal coda, three months later, after the soldiers had served their punishment, they re-visited the roadhouse, and put in a "takeout" order for 50 beers and sandwiches. The same manager, apologizing in advance for the delay, courteously filled the request, neatly boxing the beverages and food.

After about 10 months, Sidney could no longer stand the Army routine. He also felt the patients were mistreated and that the help, both civilian and military, had no real understanding of mental illness or much concern for what these returning veterans were going through. He wanted to leave the Army but, oddly, did not want to simply tell his superior officers that he was underage. Instead, he sought to be dismissed under Section 8, which permitted discharges "at the convenience of the government."[184]

Sidney decided to feign insanity. He asked to meet with the head of the hospital, and promptly threw a chair through the bay window that was two stories above the sidewalk. When he was sent to Mason General Hospital for observation, he underscored his "anti-social" tendencies the night of his first dinner by overturning a huge steam table – the size of a car, holding food for 50 men – sending baked beans, chicken, scalding water and an array of desserts all over the dining hall floor. Sidney's bizarre behavior won him a series of sessions with a psychiatrist, who prescribed a regimen of shock treatments. Sidney panicked and, taking a huge risk, confessed all: that he hated the Army and that he had deliberately acted crazy so he could be let go. Through the conversations with the psychiatrist, Sidney began to look at himself and examine his instability, his aimlessness and the senseless risks he had been taking. The psychiatrist, rather than bringing Sidney up for charges, for some reason decided to grant him his wish. And so, on December 11, 1944, after one year and 11 days of service, two months shy of his 18th birthday, Sidney was released from the U.S. Army. He received several hundred dollars in back pay, which he used to rent a room and buy warm clothing and his first suits.

In light of his reckless ways, it is remarkable that Sidney approached legal adulthood still on the streets and in one piece. Despite a career of petty larceny, he was not sent to reform school in Nassau. Despite flouting the Jim Crow code of behavior, he avoided maiming – or worse – at the hands of the Klan and the rednecks on the Miami police force. Despite joining the looters in Harlem, he managed to escape with a minor flesh wound. Despite insubordinate behavior while in the military, he was discharged without a court martial. In many respects, Sidney Poitier was an extremely lucky young man.

That said, Sidney was virtually illiterate and had no clue about where he was going and what he wanted to be. After being mustered out of the Army, Sidney was resolved to be manly and resilient and to change things. But nothing much improved. He was still drifting from job to job and from apartment to apartment. His attempt to form a relationship with a nice girl foundered. As the winter of 1945 deepened, despite a more suitable wardrobe, he was again thrown off kilter. Sidney decided that he had had enough of the United States and that he would go back home to his family in the Bahamas. He calculated that $100 would do the trick. He could not borrow from his relatives anymore, so he wrote a letter to Franklin Delano Roosevelt asking the President for a loan. He poured out his heart, describing his loneliness, how much he missed his parents and his inability to find his footing in America. Mr. Roosevelt still had a war to win and did not have time to respond.

By the spring of 1945, Sidney was resigned to continue as he had before, finding the menial jobs for which he was qualified. During this period, he worked on the docks, as a messenger and digging ditches. One day, when he was poring over the Help Wanted section of the *Amsterdam News* he noticed an article: "Actors Wanted by Little Theater Group."[185] His reaction: I have done every other kind of job, "but I've never done acting."[186] "[W]hat the hell, the theater must be more interesting than what I'm doing."[187]

Sidney went to the appointed location at the prescribed time and was let in by Frederick O'Neal, a leading force in the American Negro Theater. O'Neal asked if Sidney were an actor. Sidney replied he was. Sidney had never seen, much less been on, a stage. He had never heard of, much less read from, a script. Accordingly, his performance was dreadful. After a few minutes O'Neal told him the audition was over and ordered him to leave the auditorium. Sidney insisted he was an actor. O'Neal said he was not going to waste any more of his time and went on to criticize Sidney's reading, his talking and his thick accent. He grabbed the script from Sidney's hand, took hold of Sidney's arm and shoved him out the door, saying: "Just go on and get out of here and get yourself a job as a dishwasher or something."[188]

Sidney had just been told he looked like a failure, not by a Southern bigot, but by another black man. He was stunned that his limitations were so obvious, but more important, he realized that if he did not take some action he "would be trapped forever as a dishwasher."[189] He reacted to this cold assessment of his worthlessness by refusing to accept it as the final verdict on his life. According to Poitier, recalling that moment 25 years after the fact: "I saw clearly that this was a crossroad and that I had to make a dramatic choice. And I did. I decided that I was going to be an actor."[190] More accurately, as Poitier rephrased it later still, it was not so much that he decided to be an actor, but that he "needed to prove to that man at the American Negro Theater that Sidney Poitier had a hell of a lot more to him than washing dishes."[191]

For the next six months, and for the first time, Sidney had direction and a sense of purpose. His first task was to get rid of, or at least tone down, his accent. He got another dishwashing job, using his entire first week's salary to purchase a $13 radio. He listened to the news, to plays, to commentary "morning, noon and night," repeating everything he heard in the style of an announcer.[192] "How do you do, Ladies and Gentlemen? How do you do."[193] Over time, mimicking what he heard, his "a's" were "lightening" and his speech was becoming less "singsong."[194]

His second task was to learn how to read. His texts came primarily from newspapers and magazines. He boned up during his breaks from washing dishes at a restaurant in Astoria, Queens. A kindly Jewish waiter worked with him every night at around 11 pm when business slowed down. His self-appointed teacher helped him understand what he was reading and coached him on proper pronunciation: which syllables to stress, what letters were silent. After his lessons, Sidney would go home and practice more.

Sidney's second tryout, in the late summer or fall of 1945, was supervised by a three-person panel, consisting of his nemesis, Frederick O'Neal, Abram Hill, the President of the American Negro Theater, and Osceola Archer, head of the School of Drama. Held at the ANT's new facility on West 126th Street, the audition was billed as an "open call" for the ANT apprenticeship program. There were 75 aspirants and an audience of 200, made up of the friends and family of the hopefuls and of theater staff. Despite all his hard work, Sidney once again stood out. The others were dressed casually, but Sidney was decked out in a brown "zoot suit," accented by a brown shirt, tie and socks. The others uniformly selected a passage to perform from a play, Sidney chose one from *True Confessions,* and worse, written from a woman's perspective.

When Sidney's turn came, in a radio-trained, sports-announcer voice, he cried: "I met Frank as I walked down the street going towards so-and-so and there coming towards me is this handsome man and I said to myself 'just look at ---.'"[195] Mercifully, Miss Archer interrupted Sidney's reading and asked him to do an improvisation. She asked him to imagine he was a soldier in the jungle, surrounded by the enemy, and he must make his last stand. Once Sidney had an idea of what an improvisation *was* – he had not gotten that far the first time – he held his arms out like machine guns, made noises to suggest whirring bullets, told the bad guys they were "dirty rats" (in his best Jimmy Cagney imitation), and fell to the floor after a gunshot to the gut, making sure not to fully collapse onto the dirty stage lest he ruin his one good set of clothes.[196] When he finished, he was told, "Don't call us, we'll call you."[197]

A week later Sidney received a postcard accepting him into the ANT program, discovering later that an acute shortage of men was the decisive factor. That point was punctuated when a school representative informed him, "We're going to take you on a trials basis for three months. We don't feel that you'll make it, but we want to give you every opportunity."[198] To make sure there was no misunderstanding, he went on: "If we feel, at the end of three months, that there hasn't been sufficient improvement, we [will] ask you not to continue."[199]

Undeterred by the less than auspicious invitation, Sidney was more determined than ever to prove he could succeed. He quit his nighttime dishwashing job for day work in the Garment District, so he could free up evenings to attend the various courses in acting, speech, movement, voice and stagecraft that were four hours long and held five times a week. Though awkward and shy, his accent still distinct, he now had a reason to remake himself. His determination was breathtaking. Asked to withdraw after the first three months, he convinced the management to let him stay, in return for his performing janitorial services. As one biographer wrote:

> Acting gave him a goal – a career rather than a job. Acting gave him an identity – a creative outlet and a sense of self-worth. Acting gave him human contact – true friends and exciting romances. And acting gave him an education – not only in his craft, but in racial politics.[200]

What are the odds of a male making it as a movie star? In the year 2000 374 movies were released.[201] After eliminating the 21 that were animated, foreign language, documentaries or re-issues of old films, the total drops to 353. For our purposes, a movie "star" is the actor who is featured most prominently in the film and listed first in the credits. Assuming that each of these 353 movies had one male "star" and ignoring the likelihood that some actors might have had two starring roles in a given year, 353 actors were "movie stars" in 2000. According to the 2000 U.S. Census, there were slightly over 92,700,000 males between the ages of 18 and 70, the approximate range of years represented by film actors. That means that in the year 2000 the chances of a man becoming a movie star was about 1 in 260,000 or .0004%.

Again, I have also calculated the odds more conservatively. On the one hand, I expanded the numerator to include all performing artists, adding television and stage actors, as well as singers, and I have broadened the actor definition to include players in featured, as well as starring roles.[202] On the other hand, I have limited the denominator to only include the proportion of boys who were in a high school play, musical or music group.[203] The overall effect of these changes is to improve the odds from one chance in about 260,000 to one chance in approximately 4,200 or from 0004% to .024%. Enormously improved, but still a very long shot.

III. In the White House

In 1948, before the Truman election, Arthur M. Schlesinger asked 55 leading historians to rate U.S. Presidents in terms of their overall quality. Since his inaugural poll, many others have been conducted, including a 1962 follow-up by Schlesinger and a 1996 reprise by his son. It is not much of a surprise that Washington, Lincoln and Franklin D. Roosevelt are in the top three in nearly all polls or that Pierce, Harding and Buchanan bring up the rear. Over the years the stock of some Presidents has been on the rise (e.g., Eisenhower), and that of others has declined (e.g., Cleveland, Hoover). That said, based on an average of 22 scholarly – as opposed to "popular" – surveys, the following is a list of the Presidents ranked from one to 20:[1]

1. Abraham Lincoln*
2. Franklin D. Roosevelt
3. George Washington
4. Thomas Jefferson
5. Theodore Roosevelt
6. Woodrow Wilson
7. Harry S. Truman
8. Dwight D. Eisenhower*
9. Andrew Jackson*
10. James K. Polk
11. John F. Kennedy
12. John Adams
13. James Madison
14. Lyndon B. Johnson*
15. James Monroe
16. Ronald Reagan*
17. Grover Cleveland
18. William McKinley
19. John Quincy Adams
20. William Jefferson Clinton*

The six Presidents with asterisks after their names are the subject of the biographies which follow, once again beginning with the biography of the lowest ranked and moving upward. In addition, there is a seventh biography, a final "Wild Card," profiling Barack Obama, the nation's first African American President. Though he comes out with an average ranking of 10, based on the four surveys that have considered him, the small sample size and the lack of historical perspective make it seem a bit premature to regard him as a fixture in the top 20 quite yet. Nonetheless, his story clearly should be told.

William Jefferson Clinton
August 19, 1946-present
President: January 20, 1993-January 20, 2001
Other Government Experience: Attorney General of Arkansas,
1977-1979; Governor of Arkansas, 1979-1981, 1983-1992.
Major Achievements: A Thriving Economy; North
American Free Trade Agreement; Welfare Reform.

Bill Clinton's most significant and relevant blood relations were on his mother's side of the family. His maternal grandfather, James "Eldridge" Cassidy, was born on August 19, 1898, on a cotton farm near Bodcaw, Arkansas, the youngest of five children. Eldridge's father died when he was eight, the family farm was sold shortly thereafter, and he and his mother moved in with her brother, Bill Russell, a widower with 10 children of his own. After finishing fifth grade, Eldridge left school to help his uncle with his farm.

On January 3, 1922, 23-year-old Eldridge Cassidy married 17-year-old Valerie Edith Grisham, who had grown up on a neighboring farm. Eighteen months later, on June 6, 1923, Edith (known as "Edie") gave birth to their only child, a daughter, Virginia Dell Cassidy, Bill Clinton's mother. At the end of 1923, at Edie's urging, the three Cassidys moved 12 miles west to Hope, "a rough, busy, dirty, smelly town" with a population of 8,000 and the distinction of being the county seat.[2]

Eldridge's first "city job" was with the Ivory Handle Company, grubby and unhealthy work amidst stifling furnaces and stinking chemicals. He made money enough to buy a four-room house, which he lost, along with his job, with the Great Depression. Eldridge then clerked at a small liquor store until the passage of Prohibition. After that, he was employed as a deliveryman for the Southern Ice Company. At first he drove a team of horses and then a refrigerated truck. Once he got to his destination, he would haul slabs weighing as much as 75 pounds – half his weight – from the sidewalk to the ice-box. In the meantime, Edith, who had nearly finished high school, was not content as a housewife or with Eldridge's meager and uncertain earnings. So she took a correspondence course and became certified as a private-duty nurse.

By all accounts, Eldridge Cassidy was an easygoing, warm and friendly man. He was "universally liked, a salt-of-the-earth fellow who let boys ride along with him as helpers and who invariably stopped to assist anyone who needed a tire fixed or an appliance repaired."[3] The same could not be said of Edie, who was strong-willed and extremely moody. Although she was devoted to and tender with her patients and could be charming to her neighbors, she was constantly critical and domineering when it came to her husband and daughter. Her rage was often accompanied by airborne china. When Virginia was young, Edie's whippings sometimes drew blood.

Edie's anger at Eldridge stemmed in large part from his failure to provide at the level she felt she deserved. The two were opposites – her feistiness a foil for his soft-spoken ways – and she was no longer attracted by the difference, if she ever had been. As to Virginia, Edie's anger may have stemmed partly from the similarities with her daughter. Both Edie and Virginia were extroverts. While Edie could be a scold, she also had a "rollicking sense of humor," matching Virginia's lighthearted nature and love of laughter.[4] Edie was thought to be too friendly with some of her doctor colleagues, just as Virginia was a notorious and unabashed flirt. And Edie's theatrical approach to the face she presented to the world – "a daily creation, framed by spit curls, heavily powdered in bright white, with circles of rouge on her cheeks and deep red lipstick, looking somewhat like a stylized character in a Japanese kabuki show" – matched Virginia's early fascination with bright and gaudy clothes and her later identical addiction to "mascara, lipstick, eyeliner, and eye shadow."[5]

For all her flamboyance, in some respects Virginia Cassidy was a relatively normal and responsible young adult. To help with the finances, she waitressed at the Checkered Café. At Hope High School she participated in a host of traditional activities, including the National Honor Society, the science club, the newspaper and the student council. That said, Virginia had a rebellious side. She smoked and went further with boys than was the norm for nice Southern girls, unladylike behavior that was undoubtedly another source of tension with her mother. But, in Virginia's mind, there was no particular point in her conforming to the standards for appropriate behavior, since no matter what she did, she would always be from the wrong side of the tracks. Her parents had neither status nor wealth; they were not regular church-goers; they played cards; they drank. As a result, Virginia Cassidy was regarded as common, not quite white trash, but almost.

In 1941, after graduating from high school, Virginia left home and moved to Shreveport, 90 miles from Hope and Edie. There she enrolled in a nursing program at the Tri-State Hospital, which would enable her to enter her mother's profession, but at a higher level. Two years into her course of study, in July of 1943, Virginia met the first love of her life, Billy Blythe. While at the time she was wearing a boyfriend's ring and he was at the hospital with a female patient whom she thought was his wife, it quickly was established that both felt free to pursue a romantic relationship. She was a little over 20; he was 25 or 26. He was broad-shouldered, with blue eyes and sandy brown hair, full of mischief and fun. And he was charming; even Edie liked him. On September 3, 1943, two months after that initial meeting, Virginia Cassidy and William Jefferson Blythe III were married in Texarkana, Texas.

Virginia had clearly not married "up." Billy Blythe was the sixth of nine children, the (likely illegitimate) son of a poor farmer from north Texas. The Blythes were all crammed into a three-room unpainted wooden house that had neither running water nor electricity. Billy had gotten no further than eighth grade and had begun working at a dairy at 13. His father died three years later. When foreclosure forced the sale of the farm, he became a traveling salesman.

Nor had Virginia married well. While she did not know this during their courtship – indeed, she may not have known it until her son was running for President – Billy Blythe was essentially a gigolo. He had had four wives by the time he made Virginia the fifth, and at least two children born in and out of wedlock.

Whatever the realities, Virginia was a very happy bride when her new husband went off to war five weeks after the wedding. Blythe was stationed abroad, first in Egypt and then in Italy, repairing engines and heavy equipment.

On December 7, 1945, after two and a half years overseas, Blythe mustered out of the service at Camp Shelby, Mississippi. By then, Virginia had completed her nurses' training and had moved back to Hope. The two of them were reunited in Shreveport sometime before Christmas.

Blythe had lined up a job selling machinery for a Chicago company that had employed him before the war, and he and Virginia moved to Illinois, where they spent the first few months of 1946 living in an old hotel. Virginia had learned she was pregnant at the beginning of the year. That fact, coupled with delays in completing their new house in Forest Park and Blythe's need frequently to be on the road, led Virginia to return to Hope in March to stay with her parents.

By mid-May, the Blythes' suburban home was finished, and on the afternoon of Friday, May 17, Billy started the 750-mile drive from Illinois to Arkansas. By 10:30 pm he had reached Sikeston, Missouri, a little more than half-way there; his goal was to get the rest of the way by morning. Three miles west of town, one of his tires blew, the car rolled over twice, and Blythe either crawled or was thrown out of the car, only to drown in the shallow waters of a drainage ditch. That Sunday, May 19, 1946, Billy Blythe was buried. On August 19, 1946, three months after the funeral and eight months after the reunion of Virginia and Billy Blythe, William Jefferson Blythe IV was delivered by cesarean section at the Julia Chester Infirmary.

Given the timing of the birth, the statement of the attending nurse that the seven-and-a-half-pound baby was not born prematurely, the virtually unanimous doubts privately expressed by family and friends about Blythe being the "real" father, the knowledge that Virginia was very much "in circulation" until her husband's return, the comment by the son of one of the doctors who had dated Virginia prior to Blythe's homecoming that Clinton looked just like his father, the fact that Clinton was so smart and Blythe so dumb – all suggest that Clinton was not so much a half orphan as a bastard.

Virginia always denied this suggestion, explaining that she had taken a fall in August, and the doctor determined it would be safest to induce delivery a month before full term. And Clinton, without acknowledging an issue, sought to rebut it as well, by recounting with pride in his memoirs how much he looked like his step-brother, Blythe's other son.

Whatever the truth, it seems likely that at some point this smart little boy overheard the gossip or did the math and either at a conscious or subliminal level had to cope not only with the absence of a father but, to some extent, with the specter of illegitimacy.

The first four years of Billy Blythe's life were spent in his grandparents' rented house on 117 Hervey Street, 100 feet from the Cairo & Fulton railroad underpass. The period was one of turmoil. As one biographer put it, "It is central to understanding the man he would become that he began life in Hope with no father and, in essence, two mothers who competed for his love and attention."[6] The early victor in this contest was "Mammaw" Edie, who was in complete control of every aspect of her grandson's life. She set his sleep schedule, ordered his feedings, chose his wardrobe, determined his church-going and taught him his letters and numbers.

While little Billy was controlled by "Mammaw" Edie, it was "Papaw" Eldridge that he adored. By this time, his grandfather was running a grocery across from a local cemetery, serving customers both black and white. It was less a profitable venture than a place where neighbors could gather and where his grandson could be exposed to people outside of his family. And it was where Billy spent time with a man who was "incredibly kind" and "generous."[7]

Eldridge not only sold canned goods, cigarettes and candy over the counter, but liquor from a cabinet below. The supplier of this bootleg whiskey was a Buick dealer, recently arrived from Hot Springs, Arkansas, named Roger Clinton. It was during one of Roger's under-the-cabinet deliveries to her father's store that Virginia Cassidy met her future husband.

Roger Clinton was known as the "Dude."[8] Like Virginia, he loved to drink, dance and gamble. He liked natty clothes, as she liked flashy ones. Edie Cassidy thought that Roger Clinton was bad for her daughter, and the two women fought about Roger as a suitor as they fought about the right way to bring up Billy, and who knows what else. After a year of this tumult, and at Edie's suggestion, Virginia moved to New Orleans to receive advanced training as a nurse anesthetist and to escape the role of mother that she seemed unwilling or, perhaps, unable to assume.

Virginia's departure, while giving Edie free rein over Billy, did not, as she hoped, end Virginia's relationship with Roger. Though when they were apart each dated other people, one of them often made the 330-mile trip between New Orleans and Hope. Upon completion of her program, Virginia returned home and kept on seeing Roger, despite the knowledge that Roger had a wife and two stepsons in Hot Springs. Edie, at one point, consulted a lawyer to determine whether she could gain sole custody of her grandson.

Against this backdrop, it is not surprising that the Cassidys were not at the ceremony when on June 19, 1950, Virginia and the "Dude" were married at a parsonage across from the racetrack at Hot Springs. Roger Clinton did not adopt Billy Blythe as his own. By the time of the wedding, Billy was almost four years old and seemed a model child – bright, happy, friendly and ever helpful. However, his first nearly four years were hardly ones of perfection: he had no birth father, his mother had abandoned him to the care of his grandmother, and these two dominant female forces in his life fought continually and violently either about him or about his soon to be stepfather.

The new bride moved with her son and new husband to a small three-bedroom bungalow across town from her parents. Over the next 36 months, Roger demonstrated he was not destined to be a successful businessman. He treated the cash box at his Buick dealership as his personal kitty and ran the business into the ground. Although he earned a handsome annual salary of $10,000, he had alimony payments to make and frittered away most of what was left by gambling. In terms of social acceptability, Roger's fine income did not change the fact that he was a loud-mouthed wheeler-dealer and his wife was a free-spirited flirt from the wrong part of town. In addition, Roger's drinking was shifting from a social pastime to an addiction. On at least one occasion, he shot at Virginia because she insisted on leaving the house to visit her dying grandmother. This was not the first incident of spousal abuse: Roger's first wife alleged that Roger had beaten her in the face and bloodied her scalp with one of her shoes.

Roger did not spend much "quality time" with Billy; he was often away from the house, and when home was either arguing with Virginia or alone in his room. Nor, it seemed, was Virginia much occupied with Billy, always seemingly tied up with work. At four, five and six, Billy was overweight, brainy, uncoordinated and desperate to be liked. Donna Taylor, an early acquaintance, said Billy "loved to be wanted" and was "a most obnoxious child."[9] While a kindergartener at Miss Marie Perkins' School for Little Folks, Billy broke his leg tripping over his dungarees during a jump rope game called "hot peppers."[10] Whether he tripped because he was clumsy or because of the "carelessness" of the five-year-olds skipping the rope, Billy was in a cast for two months.

By the summer of 1953, as Billy turned seven, Roger sold his auto dealership and decided to make a new start in his old town of Hot Springs. Hot Springs was Sodom and Gomorrah in the midst of the Bible Belt, the dunghill of Arkansas. It was a resort whose attraction began with the medicinal qualities of its natural waters and which, because of a cooperative constabulary, became a favorite haunt of mobsters and high-flyers.

Initially, the Clintons rented a 400-acre farm west of town, complete with cattle, sheep, goats and an outdoor privy. Billy began second grade at St. John's Catholic School, located in the city proper. In his report cards, other than a "C" in "deportment" for talking too much, Billy received straight A's. His father was not doing nearly as well. Although he had hoped to reinvent himself as a "gentleman farmer," it became apparent within a year that Roger Clinton was no more a farmer than he was a gentleman. Moreover, he had gambled away the proceeds from the sale of his auto business and was once again virtually bankrupt.

And so, as often happened in Roger's life, his older brother Raymond came to the rescue. The successful owner of his own Buick dealership in Hot Springs, Raymond gave Roger the job of parts manager. As to housing, the Clintons found a place at 1011 Park Avenue, on the east end of town. In his autobiography, Clinton described 1011 Park Avenue in idyllic fashion: perched on a hill, two stories, five bedrooms, "a fascinating little ballroom upstairs," painted white with green trim on a large terraced lot, complete with a separate four-car garage.[11] Clinton's description is a bit deceiving. A biographer who visited the property called its style "mock-Tudor," writing that it "looked more imposing from a distance than it really was."[12] He went on: "Its lower half was faced in fieldstone, above which was simple white stucco intersected by half-timbering painted an unusual seafoam green."[13] Moreover, its location, the key factor in real estate, was far from ideal. While the rear driveway exited onto Circle Drive, a tree-lined thoroughfare with elegant brick homes owned by government officials and Hot Springs' professional class, the front of the yard abutted the swimming pool of the Perry Plaza Motel, one of a series of seven similar commercial establishments on the block. Across the street from the entrance was a tin-sheeted garage, a grocery, a laundromat and a barbecue restaurant. Although Roger told Virginia *he* owned the house, she later learned that Raymond was the owner and Roger was just renting it, likely at a below-market rate.

The Clintons lived on Park Avenue for roughly eight years, from the time Billy was seven or eight until he was almost 16. That period marked the steady and inexorable decline of Roger Clinton. He continued to gamble and generally lost. He was drinking more and more and constantly arguing with his wife. He also had a violent streak. One night, while the couple was at a local club, Roger punched Virginia's dancing partner "to pulp," because he thought she was getting too friendly.[14] Ironically, *he* was the philanderer, at least the flagrant one. The evening Roger's father died, he was with a Lake Hamilton woman. He was not found until the next morning, passed out on her bed.

Roger was also physically abusive to Virginia. Twice in 1959 he seriously assaulted her, once kicking and punching her at a public dance hall and another time, throwing her to the floor of their house and stomping her. When Billy was 13, he came home one day to hear Roger screaming at Virginia in their bedroom. Billy "broke down the door" and found Virginia attempting to dodge Roger, pushing chairs in his way, to prevent him from striking her.[15] He forced his father to his feet and warned him: "'Never . . . ever . . . touch my mother again.'"[16] According to the divorce papers filed in the spring of 1962, even after this confrontation, Roger continued to terrorize his wife and, on the eve of the filing, threatened to "mash" his stepson's face if he sided with his mother.[17]

There are a variety of explanations for Roger Clinton's deterioration. He had a wife who had found her calling in nursing and was popular – according to Roger, too popular – with her professional colleagues. He had a brother who was a pillar of the community and a prosperous entrepreneur. And he had a stepson who was proving himself to be an academic, extracurricular and personal standout.

Indeed, Bill Clinton's[18] successes during the years from 1954 to 1962 are the mirror image of Roger Clinton's failures, achievements all the more remarkable against this backdrop of domestic violence which Bill never disclosed to anyone. He stayed at St. John's for third grade and continued to excel in all subjects. From fourth to sixth grades he attended Ramble Elementary and at graduation was tied for third place in the class; he was told that he would have been first, but for bad marks in citizenship. His sixth grade teacher predicted he would either "be governor or get in a lot of trouble," depending on whether he learned "when to talk and when to keep quiet."[19] The pattern of academic excellence was repeated throughout junior high school and into the 10th grade, the last school year the Clintons lived on Park Avenue.

In terms of life outside the classroom, at eight Bill began going to the Park Place Baptist Church. When he was almost 10, Roger Jr. was born, and Bill took on an almost parental role, helping the little boy get dressed in the morning, because Virginia left so early for the hospital, and trying to shield him from Roger's rage. At 13 Bill got his first part-time job at the grocery store across the street from his house. For fun, he and his friends played Monopoly, or went to the movies, or hiked in the forest. Two extra-curricular interests took prominence over these years: music and politics.

Bill's introduction to music came in fourth grade, when he joined the band and learned to play the clarinet. By the time he moved up to junior high he had switched to the tenor sax. He practiced for hours, attended band summer camp and entered and won competitions. In 1956, Bill fell under the spell of the singing truck driver from Tupelo, Mississippi, after watching him on the Milton Berle and Ed Sullivan shows. Like Clinton, Elvis Presley was a Southerner whose family came from the wrong side of the tracks, his father a factory worker living in a federal housing project. In some measure because of these similarities, Elvis Presley became one of Clinton's life-long heroes.

Nineteen fifty-six was also the year Bill's interest in politics was awakened. Although barely 10 that summer, he was transfixed by the televised coverage of the presidential nominating conventions. During the Democratic proceedings, he first saw another rising star: a young, good-looking Senator from Massachusetts waging a valiant, but losing battle for the Vice Presidency against an older, establishment Senator from Tennessee. Unlike Clinton, John F. Kennedy was a Northerner whose family was both wealthy and prominent. Despite the differences, Kennedy also became a hero for life.

Bill's interest in national events deepened in the fall of 1957 as he witnessed Arkansas' Governor Faubus callously preventing nine black students from entering Little Rock's Central High School. Three years later, in 1960, Bill came off the sidelines. He argued the case for John F. Kennedy's election to his high school classmates and joined DeMolay, the Masons' youth organization, committed to teaching leadership skills and civic awareness.

By the end of the Park Avenue phase, Billy had shot up to six feet in height, though he had not outgrown his baby fat, his lack of coordination or his horrible fashion sense. Nor had he outgrown the insatiable desire to be accepted and liked. Over those eight years, his interactions had widened to include grown-ups. Because of his intellect, curiosity and energy – and setting aside his talkativeness – teachers adored him. So did the parents of his friends, whom he sought out to match wits, exchange ideas and, sometimes, to avoid the athletic activities that were not his strong suit. He was not only impressive and earnest when he was with elders, he was also solicitous, often unduly so. Kathy McClanahan, who met Bill when he was 13, said on occasion Bill reminded her of Eddie Haskell from the *Leave It to Beaver* show: "If your mother had shorts on that she'd worn for forty years, he'd say, 'I love your outfit.' He didn't not mean it, but you just wanted to slap him and say, 'Give it a rest.'"[20]

But Bill Clinton was not like Eddie Haskell, because when he paid these compliments he was, at that moment, being sincere. Eddie Haskell was an operator, solely looking out for himself, seeking to charm Mrs. Cleaver and thereafter terrorize Wally and the "Beave." Bill Clinton was not like that. He was unfailingly nice to his peers, and his warmth and interest was not reserved for some special few. He was as good a friend to David Leopolous, a terrible student whose family was even less "well-off" than the Clintons, as he was to Mac McLarty, a "golden boy" – straight-A student, star quarterback, student council president – from a patrician background.[21] And he remained close to both of them throughout his life.

Bill's desperate need for approval had its roots in his atypical and unhappy circumstances. He had never known his real father and may have wondered whether his real father was his father at all. His mother had essentially left him to pursue her career when he was a baby and, once she remarried, was often not at home. Her odd schedule was partially a function of the demands of her chosen profession, which caused her to be gone early in the morning and remain away for long stretches, and partially a function of her continued need for excitement – horse racing, dancing, parties – which kept her out at night. His stepfather was also often away, both with and without his wife. When he was home, most of the time he was drinking or shouting or in a stupor. Family life for Bill Clinton had always been chaotic, with Virginia first at odds with Edie and then with Roger.

Though Bill adored Virginia, despite (or perhaps because of) her eccentricities, she emerges as more of a "pal" than a parent. And though Clinton says Roger was really a fundamentally good man who loved him, it is hard to put aside the alcoholism, whoring, gambling and physical abuse. The case he makes for his stepfather is thin and unimpressive: paying for Virginia's trips from New Orleans to Hope; buying Bill a Lionel train set; taking Bill to see the Cardinals in St. Louis; allowing Bill to help him mow the lawn; involving Bill in the annual parts inventory at Clinton Buick. But what else was Clinton to say in an autobiography written in the wake of his dalliance with Monica Lewinsky, the months of deceit in its aftermath, and his humiliating impeachment? How could he absolve himself if he could not absolve Roger?

On April 9, 1962, Virginia told Roger she would seek a divorce. The next day she and the boys left the house on Park Avenue and moved to a motel. Less than a month later, they found a new home at 213 Scully Street. On May 15, the divorce became final.

But Roger was not out of Virginia's life, nor would he ever be. He begged to be taken back, promising to reform. He had lost weight and looked awful. He would park across the street for hours simply to watch the family that had turned him out. In the end, against Bill's advice, Virginia remarried Roger, less than three months after they had divorced. She did so out of some combination of pity and perhaps doubt that she could survive financially without his salary. In the midst of this latest round of turmoil, Bill went to the courthouse to legally change his name from Blythe to Clinton, despite his ongoing opposition to Roger's return. Bill's timing was bizarre. His motives were confused and mixed: wanting to have the same name as his little brother, wanting to have the same name as his mother, wanting to do something nice for the stepfather who had never adopted him but whose life had fallen apart. When Roger moved back, though he continued to drink, he did so quietly in his room. There was, and would always be, tension in the Clinton household. However, there was no longer terror.

The "rabbit hutch" on 213 Scully Street – what Clinton describes as "one of the new, all-electric Gold Medallion houses with central heat and air" – cost $30,000 and had three bedrooms and two baths.[22] It was much smaller than 1011 Park Avenue. This was the base from which Bill Clinton launched his triumphal junior and senior years at Hot Springs High School.

In terms of academics, Bill completed his third and fourth years of Latin and took courses in world history, calculus, the hard sciences and English literature. Paul Root, who taught Bill during his junior year, likely reflected the consensus view of Bill's abilities: "And I just found him to be an excellent student – he was always pleasant, but always prepared. . . . He just never forgot anything you said. And he always did his reading, and he was interested!"[23] When the class rankings were computed for the 327 members of the Class of 1964, Bill was number four.

Bill's music activities ballooned those last two years. He was a member of the marching band, the concert band, the dance band, the pep band and a jazz trio. In statewide competition he was chosen as first chair on the tenor saxophone and won medals for solos, ensembles and conducting. He was "a brilliant sight reader, as well as improviser, and a tireless manager."[24] As "band major," he demonstrated phenomenal organizational abilities in assisting Virgil Spurlin, the high school's music director, with the band festival held annually in Hot Springs. The challenge was to coordinate the evaluation of thousands of students representing 140 bands on a variety of skills, to arrange myriad concerts and to hire and house dozens of judges from around the country. Clinton met it flawlessly. As a lover of all kinds of music – from classical to jazz to swing to rock and roll – and as a lover of performing and people, "the band culture played to Clinton's personality."[25] Given his prodigious talents Spurlin believed "[h]e might have gone the route of music."[26] But that was not to be.

Bill discovered those last two years, that he loved the world of public service and politics even more than the world of music. During his junior year, he was elected president of his class. He was in great demand on the "speaking circuit," giving inspirational talks to local clubs like the Heart Association, the Optimists and the Elks, which chose him for its Leadership Award. He continued his efforts on behalf of DeMolay, ultimately becoming a Chevalier, the highest distinction the order conferred.

The summer after his junior year Bill attended the American Legion's Boys State Program, held at an old army camp in North Little Rock, Arkansas. Though the greatest honor was to be selected Governor, Clinton's objective was to be chosen as one of the two Senators, so he could go to Washington. To Bill, "Washington was where the action was on civil rights, poverty, education, and foreign policy."[27] He ran an organized and energetic campaign, and he or his surrogates tried to meet every one of the campers. When the results were in, he had won.

In July Bill left Hot Springs to represent his home state on a field trip to the nation's capital. He told a local reporter covering the departure, "It's the biggest thrill and honor of my life."[28] During the week in D.C., the 100 young senators drafted and debated legislation, Clinton ardently advocating laws that would better the lives of America's black population. He also had a memorable luncheon with Arkansas' real Senator, J. William Fulbright, an encounter that made an indelible impression on both of them. But the high point of the visit was an address by President Kennedy in the Rose Garden. On the bus ride over, Bill Clinton asked Daniel O'Connor, the American Legion official chaperoning, whether he could have his picture taken with the President, pressing his point in a fashion that O'Connor remembered even decades later. Upon arrival, the six foot three Clinton, who was in the front of the first bus, power-walked to the front row of seats, so that after the speech, he was perfectly positioned to shake the President's hand. And an American Legion photographer was perfectly positioned to record the moment for posterity.

Although in his autobiography, Clinton unaccountably and disingenuously claims, "I didn't make too much of the handshake,"[29] his mother recalls she had "never seen him get so excited about something."[30] His guidance counselor Edith Irons, the music director Virgil Spurlin, and a former history teacher Paul Root, had the same recollection. Whatever the significance of the photograph, upon his return home after the Kennedy encounter, Clinton decided he wanted to be a politician.

Later that summer, along with much of the country, Bill watched in rapt attention as Martin Luther King, Jr. delivered his "I have a dream" speech. It brought him to tears and furthered his determination to devote his life to public service. Bill began senior year planning to run for class president, but his principal forbade it, saying he was already overloaded with extra-curricular activities. He ran instead for class secretary against his good friend and next door neighbor Carolyn Staley. It was a position he did not really want, and his opponent was both deserving and well-qualified. He lost.

As senior year progressed, Bill began to focus on where to go to college. Having decided on a career in politics, he applied to only one school: Georgetown University. He was attracted by its academic reputation, its

Jesuit rigor and its strong emphasis on international affairs. And it was in Washington, D.C. Although it was risky to so limit his choice, especially since he was not Catholic, in the end he was accepted, though not, as Bill claimed, at the normal mid-April decision date, but quite a bit later, during the summer.[31]

The graduation ceremonies for Hot Springs High School were held on May 29, 1964. In addition to the various music organizations, Bill's activities included the Key Club (a junior Kiwanis organization), the Beta Club (a scholastic honor group), and the National Honor Society. During the spring he had been designated a National Merit Scholarship semifinalist. His name appeared 30 times in the class yearbook. Though the top three students were selected to deliver speeches, Bill was chosen to give the benediction. In light of later events, his words were prophetic.

> Now we must prepare to live only by the guide of our own faith and character. We pray to keep a high sense of values while wandering through the complex maze which is our society. Direct us to know and care what is right and wrong, so that we will be victorious in this life and rewarded in the next. Lord give us the strength to do these things.[32]

Would that his prayers had been answered.

Ronald Wilson Reagan
February 6, 1911-January 5, 2004
President: January 20, 1981-January 20, 1989
Other Government Experience: Governor of California, 1967-1975.
Major Achievements: Ending the Cold War; Restoring National Pride.

Peggy Noonan, Ronald Reagan's friend, speechwriter and biographer, had this to say about the origins of our nation's 40th President:

> Ronald Reagan's beginnings were the most modest and lacking of any president of the past hundred years. And the odd thing about that is it never quite gets said. But Reagan is unique in that his family had no status or standing, was neither of the local gentry nor the middle class, had no profession to claim such as nurse or doctor and owned nothing, no humble farm or small store.[33]

It was in 1878 that John Reagan, Ronald Reagan's grandfather, married a frail young woman named Jenny Cusik.[34] Five years later, in Fulton Illinois, they had a son, Ronald Reagan's father, christened "John Edward" but always called "Jack."[35] Jack and his older sister and brother spent their early years in a two-room frame house. His happiest times, hunting raccoons and foraging the fields, ended when he was six and both his parents died within days of each other. His older siblings were taken in by a nearby uncle, and he was shipped off to Bennett, Iowa, some 60 miles away. Jack's Uncle Orson Baldwin and Aunt Margaret had no children of their own. They operated a general store which, unfortunately, was one of three similar establishments in a town of only 300. Running their business profitably was a challenge.

So was raising Jack. Never a scholar, he was done with school at 12, after finishing 6th grade. He was always a "clown of a boy" and loved pranks.[36] He found tipping over an outhouse nothing short of hilarious. The older he got, the more of a discipline problem he became. In 1899, Uncle Orson and Aunt Margaret, who had struggles enough running their store, had had their fill of their unruly nephew and packed him off to Fulton, Illinois, to live with his aged grandmother and his sister Kate. Kate found Jack a job with her employer, J.W. Broadhead Dry Goods Store. He began in the millinery department, but eventually migrated to shoes. He remained at Broadhead's for eight years, during which time he became known as a handsome dandy with a strong affinity for alcohol. Jack became infatuated with another Broadhead's employee, Nelle Clyde Wilson. She was slight and energetic, had auburn hair and was two years younger than he.

Nelle was the youngest daughter of Thomas A. and Mary Anne Elsey Wilson. Her grandfather, John Wilson, was Protestant and a Scottish patriot who had arrived in Illinois in 1839. Two years later John Wilson wed Jane Blue, whose father was also a Scottish patriot. Eleven years after that John joined his adventurous brother in California in an ill-fated pursuit of gold, and Jane bore him a son, Thomas, Nelle's father. In 1879, when Thomas was 17, he took Mary Anne Elsey, a servant girl, as his bride, and she had her first of seven children in 1867. Like his father, Thomas suffered from wanderlust and abandoned his family to live in Chicago. He did not return until 1894, when his mother, Jane

Blue, was on her deathbed. Six years after his mother's death, in 1900, Thomas's wife Mary Anne also died. Nelle was only 17 at the time and had never gone to high school.

Jack Reagan had arrived in Fulton in 1899, the year before Nelle Wilson became a half orphan. Exactly when the two met at Broadhead's is unclear, but on November 8, 1904, Jack and Nelle were married, despite her father's strong objections. A little more than a year later, in February 1906, the young couple moved 26 miles southeast to Tampico, Illinois, away from Nelle's disapproving father and Jack's hard-drinking brother.

Jack was hired by the H.C. Pitney General Store, and the Reagans set up housekeeping in a two-bedroom apartment above a bakery on Tampico's Main Street. A steep stairway off the dining room led to the toilet, which was located in the backyard. Water had to be carried up the stairs to be heated on a coal burning stove.

Jack and Nelle's first son, John Neil Reagan, was born in their flat on September 16, 1908, and baptized by a Catholic priest. About a year and a half after that, on Easter Sunday 1910, Nelle joined the Christian Church of Tampico, a mainline Protestant denomination, marking the beginning of an ever-deepening and lifelong commitment to religion and good works. Nelle shortly thereafter became pregnant again, and on February 6, 1911, during a howling blizzard, gave birth to Ronald Wilson Reagan. After her difficult labor, Nelle's doctor told her that she should not have any more children.

Upon first visiting his squealing son, Jack Reagan famously remarked, "For such a little bit of a Dutchman, he makes a hell of a lot of noise, doesn't he?"[37] With that, Jack's Scots-Irish son got the improbable nickname of "Dutch."[38] In May 2011 the Reagans moved to a small, white-frame house near the railroad tracks. Nelle was becoming more and more involved in the Christian Church, ministering to those who had fallen on hard times and attending Wednesday and Sunday night services, with her two little boys in tow. At the same time, Jack was becoming more and more involved with demon whiskey, and he lost his job with H.C. Pitney.

The Reagans moved to Chicago in 1913, when Dutch was two. They lived in a small flat lighted by a single quarter-operated gas jet, located near the University of Chicago. Jack worked 10 hours a day selling shoes at one of the major downtown department stores. Because his pay was low, Nelle took in needlework to help with the finances. To further economize, she was reduced to sending Neil to the butcher to ask for free liver to feed a cat they did not have. Neil apparently was also sent by Jack to the neighborhood saloons to supply him with "backdoor beer."[39] While in Chicago Dutch contracted a severe case of bronchial pneumonia and a kindly neighbor gave him a set of lead soldiers to ease his recuperation. In December of 1915, Jack was fired from his job, following an arrest for public intoxication.

The family picked up stakes and moved to Galesburg, a small rural town 140 miles to the west of Chicago. With the help of relatives, Jack got another sales job, this one at O.T. Johnson's. The family lived first in a little bungalow and then in a larger house with its own front lawn. The larger house had an attic where Dutch discovered a large collection of butterflies and birds' eggs displayed in handsome glass cases. This vast treasure trove gave him hours of solitary pleasure and sparked a lifelong "reverence" for "the handiwork of God."[40] It was in Galesburg that five-and-a-half-year-old Dutch astounded his father by reading newspaper headlines, a skill resulting from Nelle's nightly tutoring and Dutch's phenomenal memory. And it was in Galesburg that Dutch began his formal education at the Willard school, impressing his first grade teacher with perfect scores in spelling and mathematics and a final average of 97.

It was also in Galesburg that Dutch became aware that Jack would more than occasionally leave home for days at a time, triggering heated and loud arguments with Nelle upon his return, and that sometimes when Jack was gone the rest of the family would go off on impromptu vacations to one of Nelle's sisters. Dutch did not understand the reasons for these goings-on, but his employers did, and Jack was once again let go shortly after the end of the 1915-1916 school year.

The next stop in the Reagans' journey was Monmouth, a college town less than 20 miles due west of Galesburg. Jack was hired to sell shoes at the town's largest department store. Dutch, who was seven at the time, started second grade at the Central School and was such an academic standout that he was promoted to third grade during the term. Dutch also stood out socially; he had this "air about him" of vulnerability or aloofness that made him a target of the neighborhood kids.[41] An epidemic of Spanish flu hit Monmouth around Columbus Day of 1918, closing all public buildings and nearly killing Nelle. After her recovery, as before she took ill, Nelle was a tireless missionary for the Christian Church, quoting the Bible in her euphonious voice and praying for and with those who were in physical or emotional pain. During the summer of 1919, H.C. Pitney, Jack's former employer, asked him to return to Tampico to manage the Pitney store, with the prospect that, in time, Jack could become a full-fledged partner.

Jack leapt at the possibility of becoming a business owner and shipped his family the 80 miles to the town were Neil and Dutch had been born. They again rented an apartment above the store. After a short while, Jack had concluded that there were too few taverns, too much gossip and not enough customers in this city of fewer than 2,000 and felt a need to leave for bigger and greener pastures.

Dutch felt differently. He was excelling in school, still getting A's in the fifth grade. He led a mischievous gang of ruffians, had become a graceful and adept swimmer and enjoyed his first sandlot football scrimmage. He got to watch all the silent Westerns playing at the Opera House, race Neil's secondhand bike, hike barefoot in the woods and gather strawberries (for pay!) Dutch also got his first taste of performing, imitating KDKA Pittsburgh's veteran radio announcer to informal groups of a dozen or so and, with Nelle's prodding, doing a recitation – the piece was called "About Mother" – to a sizable church assembly. Dutch also found time each day to visit "Aunt Emma" and "Uncle Jim," the elderly owners of the Greenman Jewelry Store that abutted H.C. Pitney's. He would sit in a deep rocking chair in their old-fashioned, overstuffed living room, soaking up the "mystic atmosphere."[42] They would provide him with sweets and a 10-cent weekly allowance for his trouble, though he needed no inducements for his visits.

Nelle seemed content in Tampico, as well. She joined a high school theater group, did some selling and altering of clothes at Pitney's and toured the countryside doing dramatic renditions of the classics. But most of her time was devoted to church work, as Nelle continued to tend to those sick or in despair and to share with them her fervent conviction that, in the end, good would triumph over evil. In keeping with the doctrines of her faith she also proselytized others about the evils of alcohol, while she prayed daily that her husband would be released from its relentless grip.

When sober, there was no one more charming and persuasive than Jack Reagan. He convinced H.C. Pitney that he should invest the proceeds from the sale of the Tampico operation into a small, sophisticated boutique in Dixon, Illinois, 25 miles to the northeast. It would be called the Fashion Boot Shop and would be managed by Jack, with the understanding that over time the shop would become his.

The Reagans moved to Dixon in December 1920. It had a population of almost 10,000 and was bisected by the Rock River. Nearly 50 percent of the workforce was employed by one of the factories: Brown Shoe or Reynolds Wire or Medusa Cement or Clipper Lawn Mower. The other half was involved in agriculture, growing grains that were shipped to market via one of the two railroads or supplying dairy products to the Borden Milk Company. There were no mansions or estates. Wages were below the national average. Eggs and chickens could be bought in town, but not fruits or vegetables. Furniture and farm machinery had to be ordered by mail. Leisure-time activities included a trip to the movie house, an evening at the neighborhood theater or a round at the golf course.

None of this was what the adult Ronald Reagan focused on when he remembered Dixon. To him, it was a place where people knew each other and were there to help in moments of need. If someone was seriously ill or had lost a loved one, a dinner was prepared and brought over by a neighbor down the street. If a barn burned down, the nearby farmers would appear with tools and materials to help raise a new one. People prayed with one another in normal times and for one another in times of trouble.

Dixon was the place where the Reagans finally put down roots, remaining there until Dutch was 21. At the point at which he arrived, he was not quite 10 and had lived in seven houses and five cities. Because of this he had no real friends. He was always the "new kid," sometimes harassed, more often ignored, and if things got better, that was when they were about to leave. All this had an impact. It made him wary of others and protective of himself. Though he was ever amiable and unfailingly polite, he admitted he was reluctant "to get really close to people" and prone to "hold back a little of myself."[43] As a consequence, in the early years in Dixon Dutch spent much of his time in solitary activities. He liked to draw cartoons and caricatures and even thought he might become an artist. His fascination with nature, which started in the attic in Galesburg, continued as he explored the local wilderness, collecting birds and studying wildlife and reading everything on the subject he could lay his hands on. But he read other books as well, including the entire series of *Rover Boys, Tarzan, Frank Merriwell at Yale,* Zane Grey Westerns and even science fiction.

None of this meant that Dutch was anti-social. He loved team sports and was always ready to join a pickup game with the neighborhood kids. But he was too short and light to make much of an impact playing football and, whether in the field or at the plate, he was totally inept at baseball. These athletic troubles, coupled with the familiar challenge of trying to fit in with yet another group of new schoolmates, made Dutch shy and insecure during the early stages in Dixon, a feeling not helped when he compared himself to his outgoing, ever-confident older brother.

If Dixon meant stability for Dutch, it meant opportunity for Jack, the chance to finally succeed in business. Banking on this opportunity, Jack signed a lease on a two-story, three-bedroom house, though at $23 a month the rent was "high by Dixon standards."[44] Notwithstanding the inflated price, the house was quite modest. It had low ceilings. The two boys slept in a room which barely had space for the single bed they shared and a dresser. The staircase to the second floor was narrow, and the dining room was really just an alcove.

To make ends meet, Nelle modified her menu. Chicken was abandoned as the Sunday dinner in favor of liver. The staple meal consisted of soup, potatoes and bread. Soup bones and hamburger were the major purchases at the butcher. Nelle used oatmeal as her version of "Hamburger Helper" to create her "oatmeal meat" which was the standard lunchtime fare.[45] Nelle economized on clothing by recycling Neil's wardrobe for Dutch. At times, Nelle supplemented Jack's salary by taking in boarders or mending clothes, and Dutch caddied at the local golf course.

Why did the Fashion Boot Shop fail to produce the bonanza Jack expected? It was not that Jack was lacking in the skills of a salesman: he was good-looking, glib and knew his merchandise. Nor was Jack afraid of hard work: he had enrolled in correspondence courses to better understand the mechanics of the foot, thinking his advanced knowledge would translate into greater sales. But there were three problems. First, to realize his dream of becoming Mr. Pitney's partner he had to repay him for his initial investment. That meant that any commissions Jack made above his small salary did not come home, but were turned over to Mr. Pitney to reduce Jack's indebtedness. Second, Dixon was not Paris, and Jack's customers were not interested in having the latest-style footwear each year, much less each season. The adults in Dixon's blue collar community had just two pairs of shoes, which they repaired rather than replaced when they got worn; their children made do with hand-me-downs. Third, Jack was still drinking excessively. And his drinking habit was expensive.

Relatively soon after their arrival in Dixon, Nelle explained to her sons that Jack was an alcoholic. She said that was why he was away home for nights at a time, why the boys were suddenly sent to visit relatives, why their parents sometimes quarreled. She described alcoholism as a "sickness" that Jack tried to fight but could not conquer.[46] She made it clear their father's drinking was a disease and not his fault, or theirs. When Dutch was 11, he confronted Jack's illness first hand. Returning from the YMCA one winter evening, he found Jack passed out in the snow, reeking of whiskey. After deliberating about whether to leave him, the scrawny 90-pounder somehow got his dad out of the cold and up the stairs into bed.

Reagan later wrote that Jack's resort to the bottle occurred not when things were going badly, but when things were going well. And though he could be surly and even vulgar, he was not a mean drunk or ever physically abusive. As a result, Dutch loved and respected his father. He learned from him "the value of hard work and ambition" and about individual rights.[47]

Dutch also learned from Jack the importance of tolerance and the evils of bigotry, whether based on nationality or race or religion. Jack often told them of the time that he slept in his car in the dead of winter rather than stay at a hotel where the owner boasted that Jews were not allowed.

Jack's teaching took. Neil's best friend was black, and when they went to the movies Neil would always sit with him in the segregated part of the theater. Several years later, when Dutch was at college, the football squad was en route to an away game, and it had gotten late. The bus stopped at a hotel that refused to admit a black teammate. Dutch told the teammate that the hotel was filled, and the two drove to Reagan's house to spend the night.

While many children of alcoholics are scarred for life, others, like Reagan, survive and flourish. The resilient ones possess an achievement orientation, a caring attitude to others, a positive self-image and a belief in self-help. Reagan had all these traits, and he got them from his mother. While he loved Jack, Dutch was Nelle's boy. He believed it when she said that everything happened for a purpose and that there was no obstacle that could not be overcome. He believed it when she said, "The Lord will provide."[48] He believed it when she said that there was good in everyone.

Nelle practiced what she preached, visiting patients at the state mental hospital and inmates at the local jail, and delivering her religious message with a theatrical verve that made it palatable, even enjoyable. In June of 1922 Dutch was baptized in Nelle's Christian Church and thereafter actively participated in its activities, leading prayer meetings and teaching Sunday school. Through Nelle's faith and example, Dutch developed a quiet self-confidence and sunny optimism that would propel him through childhood and adolescence and would define him as an adult.

While the chronology is a bit muddled, Dutch's life began to change when he was 13 and entered North Dixon High School. That fall he weighed 108 pounds and was 5'3" tall, too small for the freshman football team. But when he turned 14 he started to get bigger and took on highly physical jobs to develop his maturing body. He hired out as a roustabout for the Ringling Brothers Circus, dragging its wagons for 25 cents an hour. He also worked one summer for a residential contractor, six days a week, 10 hours a day, at 35 cents an hour, wielding a pick, laying floors and shingling roofs.

Around this time, one of life's mysteries was solved during a Sunday car trip with his family. His parents were in the front, and he and his brother were in the back. Nelle's glasses were next to Dutch, and for fun he put them on. Suddenly he could clearly see the writing on billboards. Just as suddenly he realized why he always sat at the front of the classroom and had been so hopeless at baseball: he was acutely nearsighted!

In September of 1925, Dutch was 14, weighed 135 pounds and was elected captain of the lightweight football team, playing guard and tackle. A year later Dutch made the varsity, having gained 25 pounds and shot up to a height of nearly six feet. Though he initially rode the bench, once he was substituted for the regular right guard, he kept that position through his senior year. It made him feel good about himself.

There were other developments that boosted Dutch's confidence. He was named drum major of the YMCA band, leading it in holiday parades, twirling his baton, decked out in white pants, a bright tunic and a peaked hat. After sophomore year, he was hired for $18 a week as the lifeguard at Lowell Park. He worked 12 hours every day and was well remembered for his grace, his handsome appearance and the kindness he showed to young and old alike. He was remembered, too, for the 77 bathers that he saved over the seven summers he held the job.

Reagan later admitted that he liked being a lifeguard because everyone looked at him sitting on the high stand, as if he were on a stage in the role of the leading man. As his mother's son, he came by that feeling naturally, since she was a frustrated actress who also loved to be in front of a crowd. When he was a teenager, Nelle again pressed Dutch to do a recitation at one of her readings and after some coaxing he ultimately did. He realized much later that hearing that audience respond to his presentation with laughter and applause was life-changing. This new feeling was reinforced when his English teacher encouraged students to write imaginatively, asking the most original authors to read their work to the class. Reagan was one of those chosen to perform, and again his efforts elicited laughter and applause, this time from his classmates. Since the English teacher was also the advisor to the Drama

Club, he soon encouraged Dutch to become a member. Dutch agreed, spending the remaining years at Dixon High appearing in virtually every dramatic production staged.

Dutch needed little prodding to add the Drama Club to his list of activities, since his first and only high school girlfriend was already a member. Her name was Margaret Cleaver. Her father was the pastor at Nelle's church. By all accounts she was a very attractive redhead, bright, driven and good-hearted. She could do almost anything and, therefore, seemed a perfect match for Dutch. In fact, he was convinced she would become his wife.

By the time of his graduation, in the spring of 1928, Dutch had conquered his youthful shyness and insecurity, though he would never lose his wariness of intimacy. He was an editor of the school yearbook, which contained his drawings and his writings. He was a varsity athlete in both football and basketball. He was vice president of the Hi-Y Club, the boys' service organization, and president of the Drama Club. Despite all this seeming perfection, he was not afraid of a good scrap. He was well-liked *and* well-respected.

To some, Dutch's level of achievement is even more striking because of what Peggy Noonan called his "most modest" and "lacking" of beginnings.[49] Reagan, however, never saw it that way:

> Later in life I learned that, compared with some of the folks who lived in Dixon, our family was "poor." But I didn't know that when I was growing up. And I never thought of our family as disadvantaged. . . [W]e always had enough to eat and Nelle was forever finding people who were worse off than we were and going out of her way to help them.[50]

Lyndon Baines Johnson
August 27, 1908-January 22, 1973
President: November 22, 1963-January 20, 1969
Other Government Experience: U.S. Representative from Texas, 1937-1949; U.S. Senator from Texas, 1949-1961; Vice President, 1961-1963.
Major Achievements: Civil Rights Act of 1964; War on Poverty.

While biographers differ in describing the events and people that shaped Lyndon Johnson's childhood, all paint a similarly unflattering portrait of the young man himself. Putting aside variations in vocabulary and emphasis, Johnson emerges as singularly unappealing, his difficult personality and often bizarre actions neither justified nor excused by his economic circumstances or by the complexity of his relationships with his parents.

The Johnson side of Lyndon's family came to this country around the time of the American Revolution, in which his great-great-grandfather, John Johnson, served as a teenaged soldier. Lyndon's great-grandfather, Jesse Johnson, was a sheriff and a judge and while for a period he prospered as a businessman, by the time of his death creditors had seized all his assets, only partially satisfying his outstanding debts.

The pattern of prosperity and collapse played out again in the life of Lyndon's grandfather, Sam Ealy Johnson, Sr. In the years after the Civil War, Sam and his brother Tom were among the most successful cattle barons in Texas, driving their herds 600 miles for sale at the railhead in Abilene, Kansas. In their best year, 1870, they came home with $100,000, which they promptly spent paying their suppliers (often more than they were owed) and buying up land. But the very next year, a glut of cattle on the market coupled with a national recession resulted in financial disaster: their herd was sold at a loss and five years of real estate holdings were liquidated.

At Sam Sr.'s side for the boom and the bust cycle was his wife Eliza Bunton, Lyndon's paternal grandmother. The Bunton family was even more distinguished than the Johnsons and included a signer of the Texas Declaration of Independence, a governor of Kentucky, a co-founder of the Daughters of the American Revolution and a Tennessee congressman. Eliza's father, Robert Holmes Bunton, was a more prudent businessman than Sam. When oversupply began to plague the cattle market, Robert Bunton avoided catastrophe by pivoting to the business of cattle grazing. His continuing prosperity enabled him to buy the farm in Buda, Texas, that his daughter and son-in-law moved to when their own funds had evaporated.

In moving to Buda, Texas, in 1872 or 1873, Sam Sr. and Eliza Bunton recalibrated their dreams, spending the rest of their lives eking out a living as subsistence farmers. An inkling of their plight: in 1879, less than a decade after Sam had returned with a fortune in $20 gold pieces, he sold his entire crop for $560, netting only $360 after paying the help.

By 1879, Sam Sr. and Eliza had five children, four daughters and a two-year old son, Sam Ealy, Jr., Lyndon Johnson's father. By all accounts, Sam Jr. was a very smart child with an amazing memory and a friendly disposition. He also was, even at a young age, both competitive and ambitious, wanting to be the fastest rider, the straightest with a plow and the best cotton picker. But Sam Jr. wanted to be the best at more than farming tasks, and he did all he could to get an education.

When there was not enough money for tuition at the local school, Sam Jr. taught himself how to butcher the cattle his father gave him and sold meat and soup bones to earn the fee on his own. When the town barber retired, he bought his tools and chair (on credit) and gave haircuts on evenings and weekends so he could continue his schooling. And when he decided to become a teacher, despite not graduating high school, he holed up in his grandparents' cabin to study, passing the special certification exam with a perfect score in history. Sam Jr. began teaching in 1896, when he was 19, but gave it up in 1898 and went back to live with his parents and work the 433-acre farm they had purchased on the Perdenales.

Although farming went well, at least at the outset, it was not what Sam Jr. wanted to do. A farmer was not who he was. He wore suits and fancy boots, not overalls and clodhoppers. His best friends were professionals, lawyers and engineers, not laborers. A striking-looking man – a little over six feet tall with milk-white skin and jet black hair – it was said he "could strut sitting down."[51] The fields just were not his natural habitat. It was, therefore, not surprising that in 1902, when an opportunity presented itself for him to "diversify," Sam Jr. agreed to run for justice of the peace. Nor was it surprising that he won. It was not a surprise either that when a grander opportunity presented itself two years later, Sam Jr. agreed to stand for the state legislature, as his father had 12 years before. Unlike his father, however, Sam Jr. won.

Sam Jr. arrived in Austin in January 1905 and was a natural. He was good with people, loving the business of politics as much as he hated the business of farming. He was a populist, supporting every (unsuccessful) attempt to regulate utilities or limit the workday or tax the big corporations. But he had a practical side, effectively shepherding a bill to restore the Alamo and to ban the cruelty of calf-roping contests. His performance during that first term all but guaranteed his election to a second term, which he won unopposed.

While electoral politics and public service more than satisfied Sam Jr.'s ambitions, it did not pay the bills. State legislators earned only $5 a day during the regular 60-day session and only $2 a day if they had to stay longer. Many of Sam's colleagues supplemented their meager salaries by accepting the largesse of the hordes of lobbyists prowling Austin, who were more than happy not only to pay for meals and hotel bills, but for votes as well. While Sam Jr. liked to drink and carouse and was hardly a prude, he was scrupulously honest, "straight as a shingle."[52] Sam Jr. had to pay his bills from what he earned, and Sam Jr., like Sam Sr., was a gambler. The father gambled on cattle; the son on cotton futures. Like the father, the son had a handful of profitable years.[53] Also, like the father, the son had a year when the market collapsed.[54] The net of it all was that when Sam Jr. returned to Austin to start his second term in the state legislature, he was thousands of dollars in debt.

It was against this backdrop that in 1907 Sam Jr. was interviewed by Rebekah Baines, a blonde, blue-eyed correspondent for an Austin newspaper. The Baines family, like the Johnson and Bunton families, had its share of illustrious members. Rebekah's grandfather, George Washington Baines, was president of Baylor University, and her father, Joseph Wilson Baines, had served as Secretary of State and held the seat in the Texas legislature to which Sam Jr. succeeded. And the Baines family, like two generations of Johnsons, had seen prosperity end up in ruin: Rebekah's father, who over time had amassed a considerable fortune in real estate, lost it all in a single year.

Rebekah Baines' interview of Sam Johnson quickly progressed into a whirlwind courtship, a dashing, hard-charging legislator wooing a refined, college-educated reporter, both of whom had a deep interest in politics. They got married on August 20, 1907, two opposite personalities with no money between them. Apropos of their challenged circumstances, they moved into the Johnson house on the Pedernales River, a shanty with three rooms, each 12 foot square: two bedrooms (one of which doubled as a living room) connected by a breezeway, with a kitchen behind one of the bedrooms, a porch with a sagging roof in the front and a privy to the rear.

As to their marriage, some things are clear. Rebekah had a difficult time with the role of country wife. She had had a relatively privileged childhood which produced aristocratic airs. She loved to read, everything from poetry to biography. She was "a soft-spoken, gentle, dreamy-eyed young lady who wore crinolines and lace – and broad-brimmed, beribboned hats with long veils."[55] Yet, she was thrust into a life of drudgery. There was no indoor plumbing and no electricity. Endless hours were spent scrubbing and hanging the clothes, feeding the stove with wood to heat the flatirons and preparing three meals for her family and the hired hands. Rebekah was often by herself, as Sam was frequently away on business, and her neighbors were hardly soul mates. When Sam was home, he would often stay up late with friends talking and drinking and playing dominoes.

There is no question, as Rebekah herself admitted, that initially she had a problem adjusting to a person who was very different from her and dealing with a way of life that was also foreign. When Sam got drunk, Rebekah likely was upset and may well have blamed the family's perennial "money problems" on his being under the influence, as their oldest son later recalled. But in every marriage there are issues over which – or points in time when – relations fray. Two biographers, Doris Kearns and the team of Irwin and Debbi Unger, conclude that Rebekah and Sam were an unhappy couple. None of the other biographers do. Indeed, Robert Caro emphasizes how much in love Sam and Rebekah were and how those who knew them best rejected entirely the portrayal of their home life as "one of unending and bitter conflict."[56]

On August 27, 1908, 53 weeks after their wedding, Rebekah gave birth to a son, Lyndon Baines Johnson. Both parents were delighted with their firstborn, Sam hiring a photographer to memorialize his looks at age six months, Rebekah beginning at once with his informal education. At a picnic, before he was one, he smiled and reached out to the guests, demonstrating his early political skills, or so his mother remembered. And he was precocious, knowing the alphabet by two, reciting rhymes by three and reading simple words by four.

But Lyndon Johnson was not an easy baby, and from the earliest days he craved attention. When he was about four, he would wander off whenever Rebekah was not looking: once he was found in a haystack near the house and another time in the cornfields, but in both cases it took hours of frantic searching by his parents and others before he was discovered. Then he started running away daily to the local school, a mile from the house. Although he was a year too young, the teacher let him attend, but she had to hold him on her lap before he would read or speak properly, and he insisted on wearing some outlandish outfit – a red Buster Brown suit or full cowboy regalia – when he went.[57] At four, he not only had to be noticed, but had to have his way, and when his seven-year-old cousin was nice enough to carry him to school on *her* donkey, he had to ride up front holding the reins. Or when one of his little classmates had a piece of lemon meringue pie he wanted, he just took it and ate it. Was this all because he now had two little sisters? Who knows?

In 1913, when Lyndon was five, Sam moved his family 14 miles east to Johnson City. With a population of 323, it was hardly a metropolis. It had no electricity, no sewage system, no indoor toilets, no paved roads and no rail connection. The single commercial street was made up of single-story stores – a courthouse, a small restaurant, three groceries, a barbershop, a bank and a post office – fringed by a broken-down wooden sidewalk. While it was some improvement over the farm on the Pedernales, it was not much of one.

But by the time the Johnsons relocated, Sam's economic fortunes had rebounded, and during the Johnson City years he was making money through investments in real estate, livestock and cotton. As a result he could afford a large, fancy car and the hand-tooled boots and pearl gray Stetsons he so admired. And he made sure his improved situation benefitted his wife, as well. He bought her a house, variously described as "a six-room, double ell frame structure" that was "one of the nicest in town" and as "a snug, three-bedroom" affair.[58] Whether grand, in the context of Johnson City, or modest, in absolute terms, it was clearly better than the shanty on the farm, although there was still only gas for the lighting and an outhouse for personal relief. Sam hired young girls to help Rebekah with the housework and purchased the local newspaper, so she could again be a correspondent. Rebekah enjoyed being a reporter and got involved in other activities: starting a Literary Society at school, giving elocution lessons, staging plays and raising funds for worthwhile charities. But she was still overwhelmed by running a house, unwell from all her pregnancies, and toward the end of this Johnson City stay, somewhat of a recluse. And Sam, while earning more, was saving little, constantly finding another scheme to back or another thing he just needed to buy. While life was better, it was still precarious.

Lyndon's close relationship with his mother did not change during the seven years they lived in Johnson City. He felt, indeed Rebekah told him, that she needed him to protect her since she was afraid of being alone when Sam was away on business, which he so often was. At the age of six, the poem he chose to read to his classmates and their parents was entitled, "I'd Rather Be Mama's Boy." Rebekah made him believe he could do anything he set his mind to.

What did change was his relationship with Sam. It changed, and grew, in part because his grandfather was further away and then died and in part because of their shared love of politics. At the age of six, Lyndon was distributing campaign flyers for the gubernatorial candidate his father was backing. At the age of seven, if he was playing with friends at the Courthouse Square, he would leave them flat if a group of men gathered to discuss current events. When local and state officials visited Sam, Lyndon would hide under the dining room table while they ate or sit with them on the outside porch or listen in from his bedroom. In 1917, after a 10-year hiatus, Sam ran again for his old seat in the Texas House of Representatives and won it back. He advocated for the voiceless, supporting bills to provide better roads, drought relief, longer school terms and tick eradication. And this time around, Lyndon was there with him, whether Sam was on the hustings drumming up votes or on the floor of the legislature speaking his mind. Lyndon was so proud and enamored of his father that he tried to mimic his ways: his walk, his idiosyncrasies, his intense and physical approach to persuasion. Mimicry came easily, though, since Lyndon so resembled Sam: they were both tall and thin, with milky white skin and had the same face.

Like any country boy, Lyndon had other pastimes. He was a whiz at marbles and a decent first baseman, principally because of his long reach. When the weather was hot, he liked to go swimming in the raw at the "Baptizin' Hole" under the bridge that crossed the Pedernales River.[59] A favorite entertainment of his crowd was making up dramatizations of early Texas history, always culminating with the siege at the Alamo. Along with all kids of that era he went to the movies, mainly Westerns, and afterwards, to the ice cream parlor.

And, like any country boy, Lyndon took on odd jobs after school and over the summer. He hired out to local farmers and ranchers to plow or harvest their fields and tend to their livestock. He worked as a goat herder. He spaded and raked gardens. He tried his hand as a "printer's devil" at the local newspaper. He shined shoes at the barbershop. He passed out handbills in return for free admission to the local theater. He went with his friends off to the hills to lay traps, so they could catch and then sell fox and raccoon pelts.

But Lyndon Johnson was not really like any country boy. The restless, troublesome behavior evident from his early childhood on the farm became commonplace during the years that followed in the city. Drawn from recollections of relatives, siblings, neighbors and classmates, his behavior forms a disturbing picture.

At the core was the need for attention. Sometimes he simply demanded it, hanging on his mother's skirts until she would look at him or answer his incessant questions. Sometimes he played pranks or was annoying, hiding under the bed and grabbing the legs of passersby or tormenting the little girls in dancing class. Sometimes he did things to get himself in trouble, as when he would steal peaches, or throw rocks at the black kids or stay out all night. Sometimes he just stood out for the sake of standing out, scrawling his name on the blackboard in huge letters when going to the school privy, to set him apart from all his classmates who signed out in the smallest possible hand.

Lyndon had a range of other techniques to get noticed. He would try to dominate, bossing his brother and sister around, or arguing with the men at the barbershop until they agreed with him, or threatening to take his ball and go home if the other boys would not let him pitch. He would make himself pitiable, wailing about a teacher's alleged mistreatment in school, crying as soon as he lost a fight or a game, screaming when his father spanked him, yelling to the doctor "I'm killed" when he fractured his leg.[60] He would be ingratiating, particularly with older women, hugging them, praising their cooking in order to make them like him. And he would be defiant, refusing to wear shoes, not doing his homework and resisting even going to school.[61]

A number of biographers attribute Lyndon's neediness to the conditional love he received from his parents. Rebekah adored Lyndon, even more than her other children. She wanted him to protect her from loneliness, and to a certain extent from Sam; she believed in his abilities; she thought he could do no wrong. Rebekah made Lyndon feel "big and important."[62] But her affection would be withdrawn if he failed to do her bidding. Whether the issue was poor school performance, failing to learn the violin or dismissal from dancing class, if she were displeased, she would pretend he was dead or speak to him in what Johnson called her "terrible knifelike voice."[63]

Sam, who enjoyed having Lyndon as his political sidekick, nevertheless often got angry with him, irrationally so, for not keeping up with his notion of "appearances." When Lyndon was four or five and still had long curls, Sam had them chopped off, because he thought they made him look like a sissy. When Lyndon was 10 and opened a shoeshine business, Sam shut it down, because he was not raising his son to be a shoeshine boy. When Lyndon, a bit older, went hunting for squirrels and rabbits without ever actually using his gun, Sam called him a coward for being the only one in the neighborhood who had not killed an animal. And Sam had a fierce temper, and he did not hesitate to slap Lyndon or use a strap on him when he was displeased.

While it is unclear how bad things really got with his parents, and though his talking about them after the fact may have been for effect, Lyndon's recollections of the turmoil cannot be ignored when trying to understand the roots of his personality. His disposition was plainly affected by the family's ever-changing and sometimes dire financial situation. That situation became catastrophic in 1920.

Sam Johnson was a dreamer, and his dream was to recreate the Johnson fortune. His vehicle was to be his parents' 443-acre farm, which his mother had left to her eight children when she died in 1917. Sam's idea was to make a killing raising cotton, which in 1919 was selling at an unheard of 40 cents a pound. So he outbid his brother-in-law for the Pedernales land, bought or leased equipment, hired help, updated the living quarters and moved the family in from Johnson City. He funded the $40,000 of expenses by selling almost all his real estate, placing a mortgage on the farm and borrowing from the banks. But the very first crop, produced in 1920, was smaller than expected, due to an unusually wet spring and hot summer. To make matters worse, a national recession coupled with a glut in the market for cotton caused its price to collapse to eight cents per pound. Sam lost everything, and for the rest of his life he was in debt.

The family moved back to Johnson City in 1922. Sam's health deteriorated, and he remained in a sickbed for months. His legislative term expired in 1924, and when he was well enough, he worked first as a part-time game warden at $2 a day and then as a foreman of a road-grading crew at $15 a week. His disposition, which was always volatile, had gotten worse.

Rebekah withdrew from most of her civic activities and, to an extent, from reality. She never could manage a household, and without maids the dishes piled up, the laundry went un-ironed and the children were unkempt. There was very little to eat, and what there was often was spoiled.

Moreover, few of the Johnson's neighbors were inclined to help. The townspeople had always resented Rebekah for her airs and inability to cope with domestic life and Sam for his arrogance and his drinking. And while some felt sorry for them, to most they were "the laughingstock of the town," two people who had always been far too proud and had finally gotten their deserved comeuppance.[64]

Lyndon took the change in status very hard. Having grown up hearing stories of his illustrious ancestors, he may have felt his parents' failure was depriving him of his birthright and blamed them for causing him public humiliation. Whatever his inner thoughts, beginning in 1921, when Lyndon turned 13, his outward behavior became even more extreme.

If he did not have a history of self-absorption, some of Lyndon's antics could be written off as typical teenage rebelliousness. He would sneak out of the house after his parents were asleep and get drunk and drive recklessly. He and his friends burned down a barn, just for the fun of it. Continuing to crave attention, he mostly wore slacks and a white shirt and a tie to school to distinguish him from the other "common" boys in their overalls and jeans. On occasion, though, for an opposite effect, he wore clothes so filthy and full of holes that he stood out as the worst dressed student in the class.

But there was more. He would deliberately do what he could to get on his parents' nerves. Rebekah always regarded table manners as a mark of gentility, so Lyndon would stuff food in his mouth and make "loud, slurping noises" when he ate, until he was dismissed from dinner with his mother in tears.[65] Sam would order Lyndon to do his schoolwork and treat his shaving mug as "off limits" when he was away, so when Sam was gone Lyndon would purposely not do his schoolwork and make sure his father's mug was constantly in use.

And there were the things that Lyndon did that were not only defiant, but downright mean. Once he told eight-year-old Sam Houston to haul "a heavy load of wood" from the woodpile, a chore his father had originally assigned to him, knowing full well that Sam would stagger under its weight.[66] Another time he took $11 the same brother had been saving for a second-hand bike and purchased one perfectly sized for him and utterly impossible for the littler Sam to ride. Then there was episode in the summer of 1922, after the cotton fiasco, when the Johnsons had to enroll Lyndon in a private school to avoid his being left back. Sam somehow got the tuition money and gave Lyndon an allowance meant to last for the whole two-month term. Lyndon squandered it in the first week, buying sweets for classmates he barely knew. Or the time Sam wanted to get Lyndon an inexpensive seersucker suit, only to have Lyndon convince the salesman to only show his father the pricey Palm Beach model. Lyndon knew full well that, to avoid a scene, Sam would buy it, though he was in debt up to his ears to every shopkeeper in town.

However unpleasant Lyndon was to his loved ones, he still managed to present a seemingly normal facade to the outside world. Though he never studied, he managed to maintain a B average in school, in part because he was so bright and in part by distracting his teachers. He was taken with interscholastic debate, which was more attention-getting than doing homework, and in 1924 won the county competition. While he was never regarded as particularly coordinated, he played first base on his high school team and threw the discus. By the time of graduation, he was valedictorian and president of his class of five.

Sam and Rebekah were insistent that Lyndon go on to college, Sam because he had not gone and Rebekah because she had. They both had always valued education and in different ways devoted their energies to Lyndon's advancement. When Lyndon had not finished his evening lessons, which was commonplace, Rebekah would read him the textbook at breakfast and, if she was not quite done, would follow him to the schoolhouse door until she was. Sam used the dinner meal for spelling bees, math contests and discussions of current events.

Lyndon was not at all interested in pursuing higher learning, despite his mother's nearly hysterical pleas and his father's incessant insults. Why was he so adamant about avoiding further education? A girl whom he confided in at the time said Lyndon was worried that because he was not well-enough prepared he might stand out, or get lost in the shuffle or be seen as just another, no-account "poor boy."[67]

If Lyndon was not going to college, Sam insisted that he make some money, and Lyndon spent the summer of 1924 doing hard labor. First he worked topping the highway between Johnson City and Austin, wielding a pickax to loosen the gravel from the banks, then shoveling it into mule-driven wagons, then smoothing it with a rake when it was dumped onto the roadbed; he earned $2 a day for his trouble. His next job in a Texas town on the Gulf was even worse, both hotter and harder: for 11 hours a day he fed the boiler in a cotton gin.

In September Lyndon accompanied three of his local friends to the teachers college in San Marcos to take part in a special remedial program, necessitated by the fact that their high school ended at 11th grade. Lyndon returned to Johnson City shortly after he had left, though it is unclear whether he was never registered or had failed his course work or was simply "kicked out."[68] Once home he quickly made plans with some other boys to travel to California. Lyndon was again at loggerheads with his parents, who objected to his going. And once again he defied them.

On a Wednesday in November when Sam was out of town, Lyndon and his pals clambered into their dilapidated Model T Ford and began their adventure. In Lyndon's telling, during the two years they were away they went up and down the coast "washing dishes, waiting on tables, doing farm work when it was available."[69] While there may have been some dish-washing, table-waiting and farm work, Lyndon was not gone for two years and spent much of his time away employed as a clerk in the San Bernardino law offices of his cousin, Tom Martin. Martin appeared to be successful and told Lyndon that in a short period of time he could share in that success. According to his cousin, Lyndon could be admitted to the bar in Nevada by taking an informal oral examination; once admitted in Nevada, he could be waived into the California bar; and once a member of the California bar, he would be welcome to join Martin's firm. Lyndon was excited by the prospect of having a rewarding career without obtaining the undergraduate degree which has parents were so convinced was the key to advancement. It all seemed too good to be true.

And it was. It turned out that Martin was a charlatan, and immoral to boot. During the summer of 1925, when Martin's wife and young son were on a visit to Texas, he invited his girlfriend to move in with him and stopped coming to the office. Lyndon was left in the lurch, practicing law without a license, which was illegal, and making ends meet by taking a part-time job as an elevator operator in Martin's office building. By then Lyndon had concluded he would not want to be in business with his cousin and learned that, even if he retained such ambitions, he would not be able to do so for a very long time. In describing the bar admission process, Martin had forgotten that Nevada had a requirement that a lawyer had to be 21 to even stand for an oral examination and that California would not extend reciprocal recognition unless the lawyer had practiced in another state for three years. Johnson was only 17, so the Martin plan, properly understood, meant Lyndon would have to wait seven years to become a California attorney.

When Martin's wife returned in the early fall of 1925, Lyndon left for home in Texas. He arrived in Johnson City in October or November. His year-long experiment had distanced him from Sam and Rebekah, but had done nothing to resolve his future. An old friend remarked on the difference the time out West had made in him:

> I saw a changed person. Before he went to California, he was just a happy-go-lucky boy. When he came back, well, I saw a serious boy then. I saw a man. I saw what disappointment had done.[70]

The now "serious boy" was still not ready to accede to his parents' renewed pressure to go back to school, though with no money he was once again living with them. Over much of the next 15 months he was on a road building crew, scooping up sand and gravel, pushing wheel-barrows and in the process making himself generally unpopular with his co-workers. He also resumed his semi-delinquent ways, hanging out with an older group known as the "wild bunch."[71] They drank moonshine, held drag races and generally engaged in mischief, like stealing dynamite and setting it off in the middle of the night. Lyndon continued to make himself noticeable, wearing garish silk shirts and strutting around as if he was really somebody, when he and everyone else knew he was not.

Then, one winter evening in February 1927, Lyndon came home and told his mother he was ready to go to college, and she made immediate arrangements to enroll him at Southwest Texas State Teachers College. His awakening may have been triggered by news in January that his highway construction days were over with a change in administration. Or it may have been prompted by the severe beating he received from a German farm boy with "fists like a pile-driver" who had no patience with Lyndon's ever-present sass.[72] Whatever the reason, he was about to see how he would do in the real world.

There is much in Johnson's childhood that foreshadowed his later life. Not only was there a family heritage of government service, but Johnson loved the stuff of politics: the cajoling, the listening, the speechifying, the campaigning. At the time of Lyndon's birth, his grandpa predicted he would be a United States Senator, and by the time he graduated from high school, his classmates prophesied he would be Governor of Texas. Lyndon, as always, thought bigger, telling one of his close friends, "Someday I'm going to be President of the United States."[73] While after the fact it all seems so clear, so foreordained, at the point he left Johnson City, six months into his 18th year, the notion that he would someday be a great man was nothing short of preposterous.

Andrew Jackson
March 15, 1767-June 8, 1845
President: March 4, 1829-March 4, 1837
Other Government Experience: U.S. Representative from Tennessee, 1796; U.S. Senator from Tennessee, 1797; Governor of Florida Territory.
Major Achievement: Resolving the Nullification Crisis.

In the early 1600s, King James, ruler of England and Scotland, established a colony in the Ulster part of Northern Ireland. His purpose was to pacify his Irish subjects. The motivation of the Lowland Scots who agreed to emigrate was to try to better their lives. The Irish, however, did not welcome them and, after 150 years, some got weary of the venture: farming was a challenge, the linen trade was depressed and their Presbyterian faith was under siege. Many of the Ulster Scots looked to the British settlements in North America as offering "greener pastures." Among them were Andrew and Elizabeth Jackson, the parents of the seventh President of the United States.

Andrew Sr. was the youngest son of Hugh Jackson, a weaver of linen. His brother, another Hugh, had joined the army and fought in the French and Indian War, serving in the upland region of the Carolinas. Upon his return, he was full of tales of the beauty of the area and of the great opportunities to become a landowner in the New World. Elizabeth Jackson had been similarly regaled with stories about the promise of the Carolinas from her sisters who had already settled there.

In the spring of 1765 Andrew and Elizabeth Jackson, along with their sons Hugh and Robert, aged two years and six months respectively, boarded a ship at Carrickfergus, a port city near Belfast, bound for North America. Elizabeth was accompanied by her sister Jane and her brother-in-law James Crawford. Two other Crawford brothers, Robert and Joseph, made the voyage as well. The vessel most likely docked in Philadelphia, and the Ulster entourage then probably trekked the roughly 500 miles through what is now Pennsylvania, Maryland, Virginia and North Carolina. Their destination was an area known as Waxhaw, located in the valley of the Catawba River. The region, which had been previously inhabited by the rival Waxhaw and Catawba Indians, straddled the current border between North and South Carolina.

Upon their arrival, the Jacksons stayed with Elizabeth's recently-married sister, Mrs. George McCamie. Elizabeth was soon reunited with two other sisters who were also living nearby. When it came time to stake out a claim, the Jacksons, unlike the Crawfords, did not have the funds to purchase land in the Waxhaw Settlement proper.[74] Instead, they were compelled to settle on a rather marginal red-clay parcel above Twelve Mile Creek, which was six miles – or a three-hour walk – from the center of Waxhaw.

It is uncertain whether Andrew Sr, had clear title to the roughly 200 acres of remote pineland which he struggled to make habitable and arable; a Thomas Ewing may have had a competing claim. It is clear that Andrew Sr. treated the land as his own. He spent the next back-breaking year building a small log cabin and clearing parts of the forest so he could plow, plant, weed and harvest a crop on which the family could subsist. Shortly after their one-year anniversary in America, during the summer of 1766, Elizabeth became pregnant again. Over the winter of 1766-1767, Andrew Sr. worked even harder to increase the amount of farmable property in advance of the baby's birth. In

February he severely injured himself, likely straining to lift a heavy log, and was forced to take to bed. He died shortly thereafter.

Elizabeth Jackson and her two boys left Twelve Mile Creek and their isolated farm and moved into the Waxhaw Settlement to live with her sister, Jane Crawford. Jane was sickly and had eight children of her own, and Elizabeth functioned essentially as her "housekeeper," working at all hours knitting and spinning and caring for a brood that would soon number 11, in return for her family's "room and board."[75] Although James Crawford was prosperous and the Jackson boys enjoyed the benefit of a "well-to-do" household, it was clear that they were living there as the poor relations.[76] Andrew's oldest daughter said her father recalled his childhood as one of "humiliating dependence and galling discomfort, his poor mother performing household drudgery in return for niggardly maintenance of herself and her children."[77]

Elizabeth Jackson gave birth to her third son, Andrew, on March 15, 1767, at the Crawfords' farm in what would become South Carolina. Elizabeth was a religious woman and had aspirations that her husband's namesake, who seemed to be her smartest boy, would go into the ministry. In the 1774-75 and the 1775-76 school terms, when Andrew was seven and eight, his teacher was "Professor Branch," a struggling law student.[78] But in the autumn of 1776, when Andrew was nine, he was signed up for a "select school," presided over by David Humphries, a Presbyterian minister.[79] Elizabeth hoped that Rev. Humphries would lead Andrew to the theological career of her dreams. Andrew excelled in reading, enjoyed geography, mastered "sums" and was at least exposed to the "dead languages." But whatever his native potential, Andrew did not "take" to formal education. He learned but a few Latin and Greek phrases, gained only a minimal knowledge of history, literature and political science and acquired an at best "irregular" familiarity with the rules of grammar and spelling.

While Andrew had little facility for scholarship, he was a natural hellion. Slender, blue-eyed with bushy reddish hair, he was wild and reckless. He liked foot races, jumping contests and wrestling. He was fearless and would fight at the least provocation, and no matter how many times he was subdued, he would invariably bounce back up looking for more. He could be overbearing and act as a bully, unattractive traits which might have been tempered had there been a strong father figure in his life, but Andrew Sr. was dead and his uncle by marriage did not take to that role. Andrew's "acting out" may have reflected the insecurity and defensiveness of growing up in a wealthy environment as the son of the domestic help. Perhaps. In any event, while Andrew enjoyed dominating others and playing jokes at their expense, he did not like it when the shoe was on the other foot. One day some boys dared him to fire a gun, knowing he would be sent sprawling by its recoil. When Andrew took the challenge and was predictably thrown to the ground, he threatened to kill anyone who laughed at him. Andrew Jackson, the boy, was "easily offended, quick tempered" and "difficult to get along with."[80] When upset he would become so enraged that he would succumb to fits of "slobbering."[81]

Andrew had just turned eight when the British engaged the Massachusetts militia at Lexington and Concord and was a little over nine when the Declaration of Independence was signed. For the first three years of the Revolutionary War, the conflict was largely confined to the Middle Atlantic and the northern colonies, and the Carolinas enjoyed a period of relative peace. But in 1780 the British took the war south, in part to exploit the fact that it was home to large numbers of colonists who for reasons of economics and family ties were still loyal to England. In the spring of that year General Clinton laid siege on Charleston, which fell to the English in mid-May.

The victory emboldened the redcoats to widen the hostilities, and the war was brought to the Waxhaw District by one Lieutenant Colonel Banastre Tarleton. Tarleton was ruthless and sadistic and regarded the rebels not only as despicable traitors but as crude, illiterate and thoroughly inferior human beings. On May 29, two weeks after the fall of Charleston, Tarleton descended into the Waxhaw Settlement, leading a force of dragoons and Tories into a massacre of the rebel detachment. His troops killed 113 and wounded 149, many after victory was assured. The Jacksons – Elizabeth, Robert and Andrew – helped minister to the injured at the Waxhaw meeting house. A British force moved into the area and the Jacksons moved out, traveling to North Carolina rather than promising allegiance to the crown. The Jacksons made several trips to and from Waxhaw village as control shifted between the rebels and the Loyalists.

Meanwhile, Hugh, at 17 the eldest Jackson boy, had enlisted and joined the fighting in South Carolina. In late June, the rebels launched an assault at Stono Ferry, and Hugh, who was in a field hospital, left his sickbed to join the fray. The rebels were defeated, and Hugh died shortly thereafter, having relapsed into delirium from the fatigue of battle and the excessive heat.

During the summer of 1780, following their brother's death, both Robert and Andrew became involved in the conflict. Elizabeth, whose hatred of the British had been nurtured by her Ulster forbears, had encouraged her sons to take part in the militia drills. She did not object when 13-year-old Andrew was employed as a scout and courier, riding the country roads to ferry information between the troops and townspeople. In early August Andrew was involved in his "first field" as an observer at the Battle at Hanging Rock.[82] The rebels were under the command of Colonel William Richardson Davies, who was both able and admirable, a truly model soldier. The Americans took the initiative and gained the advantage over the enemy early, only to lose the contest by getting drunk.

Two weeks after the Battle at Hanging Rock, Cornwallis scored a decisive win at Camden. Following the victory, the British marched north to Waxhaw, seizing the house of Robert Crawford to use as headquarters. The Jacksons once again fled, this time to stay with Elizabeth's distant relatives, the Wilsons, who had a farm 40 miles over the North Carolina border near Charlotte. They remained with the Wilsons for nearly six months. While there Andrew helped out with the chores and seemed to be forever amassing or fashioning crude weaponry – clubs, scythes, spears, tomahawks – in order to be prepared in the event of an enemy attack.

The Jacksons were back in Waxhaw by February 1781, after the British departed and it appeared that calm had returned. The period of apparent peace was short-lived. The area became embroiled in civil war, with rebels and Loyalists in a continual state of turmoil. By this time Andrew was an irregular soldier with the militia. Though as Jackson later emphasized, at 14 he had not formally enlisted, he did ride with the troops as "a mounted orderly or messenger," armed with a pistol, courtesy of Colonel Davies, and a "small fowling piece," thanks to Uncle Crawford.[83]

The most significant action Andrew saw began on an evening when he was part of a contingent of eight guarding the house of Captain Lands, a well-known and outspoken rebel. A group of over 100 Tories decided to launch a surprise attack on the Lands residence. Andrew was awakened and told that the Tories were about to enter the Lands' courtyard. He grabbed his gun, perched it in the fork of an apple tree and fired at the enemy when it did not respond to his call. Return fire killed the soldier next to him. Andrew went back to the house and resumed shooting, flanked by two other guards, both of whom were also killed. Seizure seemed imminent, but the Tories, with a huge numerical advantage, retreated when they heard a bugle sounding a rebel cavalry charge. But no cavalry onslaught ensued. The bugle was sounded by a lone unmounted major who happened to be in the right place at the right time and had his bugle and his wits about him.

Not long after the Lands encounter, the British dispatched a troop of dragoons to Waxhaw to aid the Loyalists and "pacify" the area. Andrew joined 40 patriots waiting at the meeting house to repulse the anticipated attack. The dragoons quickly gained the upper hand, capturing 11 rebels and scattering the rest. Andrew, Robert and their cousin Thomas Crawford were among those who escaped. Crawford's horse became mired in the swamp, and he was taken captive, after being struck in the head. Andrew again eluded the enemy, reunited with his brother, and spent the rest of the day and a cold, uncomfortable night in the woods. The next morning the boys left their horses and muskets in a thicket and snuck to the Crawford house for food and rest. Their plan was foiled by a Tory neighbor who discovered their weapons and alerted the dragoons, who occupied the house and took Andrew and Robert prisoner. The soldiers then destroyed the furniture, wrecked the bedding, shredded the clothing and smashed the dishware, while Mrs. Crawford and her small children helplessly watched.

The commanding officer did nothing to control the mayhem, but rather in the midst of the chaos ordered Andrew to clean his muddy boots. Andrew refused, contending that he was a prisoner of war not a servant. The enraged officer responded by striking Andrew with his sword, gashing his head as well as the left hand he had raised to deflect the blow. The officer then issued the same command to Robert, who was similarly uncooperative, and who received an even more serious head wound. Adding the proverbial insult to injury, the officer next directed Andrew to escort him to the home of a "troublesome rebel" named Thompson, threatening Andrew with death if he declined.[84] Andrew complied, but chose a circuitous route to Thompson's house that made the British entourage visible from half a mile away and allowed Thompson to ride off.

Andrew, Robert, their cousin Thomas Crawford and a score of other prisoners were taken on a forced march to the English prison in Camden, South Carolina, some 40 miles away. Having been deprived of both food and drink en route, the Waxhaw rebels arrived famished and exhausted. They suffered more once they got there. They were crammed into cells with 250 other captives. They were not given beds or treated in any way for their injuries. Moldy bread was what passed for food. Once the relationship among Andrew, Robert and Thomas was understood, they were separated. And there was an outbreak of smallpox, which killed 10 percent of the inmates and sickened virtually all the rest, no effort being made to divide the sick from the well or to provide any medical attention.

In April of 1781 salvation seemed possible when the inmates heard that Nathaniel Greene would be launching an assault on the British garrison at Camden. Since the rebel commander had numerical superiority, the prospect of liberation was not fanciful. However, the usually wily and careful Greene was outmaneuvered and was fortunate to flee with his army even somewhat intact. Following the American defeat, Andrew developed a fever and the sweats, the first indications that he too was infected with the smallpox virus. Robert's condition was even worse. He was suffering from smallpox, from severe stomach pain and from an infection in the head wound inflicted when he was captured.

Elizabeth came to the rescue, traveling to Camden with an American captain who negotiated an exchange of his 13 redcoat prisoners for the Jackson boys and five other Waxhaw friends. On the 40-mile trip south, the dying Robert was perched on one of the two horses, the exhausted Elizabeth on the other, while Andrew walked alongside, barefoot and cold, because his shoes and jacket had been stolen while he was imprisoned. When the Jacksons were a few hours from home, they were soaked in a torrential downpour. Two days after their return to Waxhaw, Robert was dead and Andrew was suffering from delirium. With the help of a local doctor and his mother's nursing skills, Andrew began to recover.

In the early fall of 1781 when Andrew was out of mortal danger, Elizabeth sent him to another brother-in-law, Joseph White, to complete his recuperation. Though it would be months before Andrew was entirely well, Elizabeth embarked on another mission of mercy, this one to visit William and James

Crawford, her two nephews being held captive on British ships in Charleston harbor. Elizabeth and two Waxhaw neighbors made the 160-mile journey to Charleston without incident. She was unable to secure William's and James' release, but was permitted to board the prison ships to comfort them. When she had finished doing what she could, she stopped off to see another relative who lived just a few miles away. Elizabeth fell ill from either yellow fever or cholera, contracted when visiting the prison ship. She died on November 1, 1781.

Andrew learned of his mother's death upon receiving a package containing her few possessions. In 1815, after Jackson defeated the British at New Orleans, he spoke of Elizabeth, describing her as "gentle as a dove and as brave as a lioness."[85] And he recounted her last words of advice: to be "honest" and "steadfast," to not "forget an obligation," to be "polite but never obsequious." to "avoid quarrels" but not at the expense of "manhood" and to "never wound the feelings of others."[86]

Andrew fell into a deep depression following Elizabeth's passing. No wonder. He was not yet 15 and had lost his father, mother and two brothers. He had no money, no real prospects and no one to help him chart a course. At first he stayed with his Uncle Thomas Crawford, but Andrew was even more easily provoked and difficult to deal with than he had been before. His volatility was much in evidence when another of Uncle Crawford's house guests, a Captain Galbraith, overheard Andrew – who had forgotten his mother's injunction about not making fun of others – imitate the Captain's pronounced Scottish accent. The former officer took offense that this young boy had so little respect for an elder who had risked his life during the war. Andrew wondered aloud how Galbraith, as commissary during the Revolution, was ever in danger, since the only living things he ever killed were four-legged critters. Galbraith threatened to horsewhip Andrew, and Andrew said if he did he would "send him to the other world."[87] Uncle Crawford told Andrew to apologize, which he did grudgingly. Not long after, Andrew moved out.

The chronology following the Galbraith incident is a little hazy. For some period after leaving Uncle Crawford's house, Andrew was apprenticed to or otherwise boarded with a local saddler. During these months he learned about stable gear, continued to battle illness and gradually came to terms with the tragic and premature deaths of his mother and brothers.

While in Waxhaw, Andrew amused himself by associating with young members of the Charleston gentry, who had fled there when the British occupied their hometown. Andrew drank and gambled with them and joined in on the mischief of the moment. His manic and undisciplined ways endeared him to the wild boys of Charleston and thoroughly alienated him from his remaining relatives. In December of 1782, following the British defeat at Yorktown and their subsequent evacuation of Charleston, he decided to accompany the flood of refugees returning to this sophisticated and exciting city. Shortly after his arrival, Andrew unexpectedly received an inheritance of three to four hundred pounds, most likely from his paternal Scottish grandfather, Hugh Jackson.[88] Andrew was not yet 16 when he came into this small fortune, and with no one to offer guidance, was seduced by each and every game of chance that presented itself. He bet on horses, on dice, on cockfights and on cards. He also acquired the latest tailor-made clothes to look the part of a gentleman. His windfall soon disappeared, and he ultimately was in debt to his landlord. His wanton days suddenly ended – at least in Charleston – when he accepted the challenge to stake his prized horse against a $200 purse, the winner to be determined by a single throw of the dice. Andrew won, paid off his creditors and left for Waxhaw with what he described in later days as having "new spirits infused into me."[89]

He remained at home for a year or two. Initially, he resumed his education, attending the New Acquisition school where he gained further exposure to languages and "a desultory course of studies."[90] Surprisingly, given his less than academic bent, he also spent a term or more as a teacher, holding classes in the vicinity of the Methodist Episcopal Church. And there are indications that he spent some time with the fairer sex, including one of the innumerable Crawford offspring, and that he made use of his keen knowledge of horseflesh by acting as an equine appraiser.

In December, 1784, four months shy of his 18th birthday, Andrew left for Salisbury, a county seat in North Carolina. While there he studied law with Spruce McKay, copying and filing papers, running errands, cleaning the office, reading treatises, finding precedents, tracing statutes and doing whatever else was needed to keep a practice afloat. How much actual instruction was provided by counselor McKay is debatable.

The choice of law as a profession made sense for someone of humble origins who wanted to advance himself. With the defeat of the English, Tory attorneys, who made up a large proportion of the colonial bar, went back to the mother country. Moreover, a new nation meant new laws at both the state and federal level and that the old common law would have to be interpreted against this changing backdrop. These developments generally increased the demand for lawyers and undercut the advantages for seasoned professionals, since the legal landscape was in such flux. Further, pursuing this career in the country, where standards were more relaxed and forgiving, was ideal for someone like Andrew who was more ambitious than studious.

While Andrew may not have been thoroughly dissolute during his Salisbury days, he was hardly a model of deportment. He became the center of a gang of fun-loving teenagers who liked to dance and carouse. He enjoyed horseracing as well as foot racing, anything that was competitive and fast. He drank a lot and supported his habit by shrewd betting, his Charleston oath to forgo such vices notwithstanding. His exuberance at times devolved into delinquency, as when he and his roommates capped a celebration at the neighborhood tavern by smashing the glasses, shattering the tables and chairs, stripping the drapes and then setting the entire wreckage on fire.

And his sense of fun could go haywire, as when he invited Rachel Wood and her mother Molly, the town prostitutes, to the social event of the season, the Christmas ball. His lame excuse – that he thought they would understand it was all merely a joke – could not make up for his thoughtlessness or salve the humiliation he had caused.

It appears that Andrew was popular with the younger set in Salisbury. He was exuberant and stylish and charismatic. The more mature town residents, however, were not taken in or charmed and regarded him as a thorough reprobate. They were convinced that he would amount to nothing and die young. Decades later, when he was running for President, an elderly Salisbury matron – dumbfounded – said, "If Andrew Jackson can be president, anybody can!"[91]

Andrew Jackson's youth was tragic and, perhaps because of that, he was not a particularly admirable boy. As a youngster and adolescent he was fiery, undisciplined and at times cruel. Yet, he was the classic underdog. One biographer summarized it this way:

> By most objective measures, Andrew Jackson's was a deprived upbringing: deprived of educational opportunity, deprived of parental supervision, deprived of more than the most modest standard of living, deprived of much chance to develop self-esteem.[92]

Or, as another biographer put it, Jackson was "the first U.S. President to have sprung from a modest space, from outside the social elite."[93]

Dwight D. Eisenhower
October 14, 1890-March 28, 1969
President: January 20, 1953-January 20, 1961
Other Government Experience: Supreme Commander of the Allied Expeditionary Forces in Europe; Chief of Staff of the Army.
Major Achievements: Ending the Korean War; Establishing the National Aeronautics and Space Administration, Creating Interstate Highway System.

UNDERDOG GREATS

The word "eisenhauer" means "iron cutter," though the family's most famous descendant pointed out it really refers to men with a more refined trade, artists in iron who "literally hewed metal into useful and ornamental shapes, such as armor, weapons, etc."[94] The Eisenhauers, as the name was originally spelled, lived in the Rhineland part of Germany. The earliest members of the clan may have been "medieval warriors" which at least makes a good story given the career path of its great-great-great-great-great grandson.[95] In the 1500s, like many German Protestants, the family became "Mennonites," a new branch of Christianity that believed in a literal approach to the Bible and advocated an "uncompromising pacifism," abjuring all war and killing.[96] Likely to obtain religious sanctuary, the relevant branch of the Eisenhauers fled first to Switzerland and then to the Netherlands. It was from Rotterdam that Hans Nicholas Eisenhauer boarded the *Europa* en route to the New World. He arrived in Philadelphia on November 20, 1741. The choice of Pennsylvania as a destination may have been influenced by a European "speaking tour" made by the colony's namesake and founder, William Penn. Penn described his settlement not only as a haven for all persecuted sects, but as a region blessed with plentiful and fertile lands. The Eisenhauers, like many other émigrés, were farmers, and farmers were needed to balance out the core population of Quaker merchants and craftsmen.

Hans Nicholas was accompanied on his journey by his three sons, Peter, who was 25, and John and Martin, who were both teenagers. They settled in Lancaster County, the domain of the Amish, and a little more than a decade later bought a 168-acre farm. Over the ensuing years the family dealt with Indian troubles and two of Hans Nicholas' sons served in the Revolutionary War.

When Hans Nicholas died, he deeded his property to his eldest, Peter, who made his living not only as a farmer, but as merchant, blacksmith, gunsmith and, for a time, constable. Peter and his wife were prolific, bringing 17 children into the world. Their youngest son Frederick, born in 1802, was Dwight Eisenhower's great-grandfather.

At 14 Frederick joined the River Brethren, an extreme sect of the Mennonites so-called because their flock was baptized in the Susquehanna River.[97] Frederick married a co-religionist, Barbara Miller, and her large dowry enhanced the income Frederick earned from farming and weaving. They had six children, one of whom was Jacob, born on September 12, 1826. A larger-than-life figure, Jacob was Dwight Eisenhower's grandfather.

When Jacob was a little over 21, on February 25, 1847, he wed Rebecca Matter, the great-granddaughter of a Revolutionary War veteran. Jacob purchased and farmed a 100-acre spread in the Lykens Valley, located 25 miles northwest of Harrisburg. He was successful enough to build a large, nine-room manor house in 1854, when he was only 28, and generous enough to open it up to the less fortunate who passed his way. In addition to being an entrepreneur, Jacob was a man of the cloth, delivering fiery sermons in German to better reach his River Brethren congregation. He was tall, bearded and muscular, with long hair, a shaved upper lip, bushy under beard, a stern countenance and flashing eyes. He was "a formidable patriarch."[98]

During the years between 1847 and 1867, Jacob and Rebecca had 14 children, though five sons and one daughter died. In 1863, in the midst of the Civil War, a sixth son was born, and he survived. They christened him David. He was Dwight Eisenhower's father. Although Jacob greatly admired President Lincoln, naming one of his next sons Abraham, he did not serve in the war, presumably as a matter of religious conviction.

In 1878, Jacob along with most of the nearly 500 River Brethren moved from Pennsylvania to an area near Abilene, Kansas, a bold step for a man over 50. Beginning in 1867 Abilene enjoyed a brief period as the Cow Capital of the United States. The town happened to be at the terminus of the Chisolm trail along which Texas-bred cattle moved. It was also at the railhead of the Kansas Pacific Railroad, the origin for goods being shipped through the Plains states to Chicago. Joseph McCoy, an enterprising cattle baron, noticed the overlapping points, as well as the rich grassland and plentiful water supply, and in a two-month period built stockyards big enough to corral a thousand livestock. Quickly the "small, dead place consisting of about one dozen log huts" had a population of 3,000.[99]

Abilene became a magnet for traders, retailers, gamblers, dance hall girls, prostitutes and all sorts of outlaws, who sought to serve – or prey upon – the cowhands who brought cattle on their way to being shipped East. In the early 1870s as many as 10,000 head a week were arriving. Murder and crime were ever present, and Abilene came to signify the "Wild West," a term invented in Kansas.[100] Bad guys, like Billy the Kid, were there, as were good guys, like Wyatt Earp. But it was not long before other towns, like Wichita and Salina, sprang up, and another railroad, the Atchison, Topeka, offered alternatives for the saloon-keepers, merchants, hoteliers and bad and good guys. By 1875 the railroad was extended to Dodge City, shortening the length of the trail and making it easier on the cows and the cowboys. Dodge City became the notorious spot, and Abilene receded into respectability.

Immigration is nearly always a function of factors "pushing" you from where you are and "pulling" you to where you end up. For Jacob and his flock the "push" was the fact that Pennsylvania was becoming more and more "secularized" with an influx of "uncongenial" settlers, who increasingly marginalized fundamentalist religious sects like the River Brethren.[101] In addition, there was a lingering, but real resentment over the failure of most of the Brethren to do their part by serving in the Union Army. The "pull" was the prospect of relocating to a place which had fertile land that could be obtained at virtually no cost through the Homestead Act; 160 acres would be given to each new settler. A delegation of Brethren visited Kansas in 1877 to determine for themselves whether this was, indeed, the new Promised Land. They came back with glowing reports of rich soil for planting, plentiful water for irrigation, vast grasslands for grazing and huge stores of timber for construction. Moreover, credit was cheap, Indians and buffalo were gone and agricultural methods had improved. Kansas also appealed to this highly moral group because it had been settled by abolitionists before the War and had enacted Prohibition soon after the War was over. Kansas was "a haven of right thinking and right living."[102]

On April 9, 1878, Jacob Eisenhower and his family boarded a train in Lancaster and three days later arrived in Abilene, by then a decent-sized metropolis of 8,000. In all, several hundred from the congregation joined the movement west, bringing with them 15 railcars filled with household goods and farming equipment and half a million dollars in cash. While Jacob was deciding where to purchase land, the family lived in a large, frame structure known as Emigrant House, which had been built the previous fall by the first contingent of River Brethren as temporary communal quarters for newcomers. By 1879 he had bought a standard 160-acre plot in a village called Hope at a price of $7.50 per acre.[103] His success in Kansas was, if anything, even greater than in Pennsylvania. In 1879, his first full year in the West, though the crop was meager, he produced 1,000 pounds of butter and gathered 300 dozen eggs. In addition to farming, Jacob became an investor in a local bank, part-owner of a string of ponies, co-founder of a creamery and a real estate mogul. And he continued to be a prominent elder in his church, preaching to the Brethren in his guttural German every Sunday.

Jacob's economic prosperity was such that he was able to give each of his six sons $2,000 and 160 acres of farmland upon their marriage. At the time of the move his oldest son, David, was 15, and it was already apparent he had no interest in a life tilling the soil. He wanted to become an engineer and a businessman. To the extent he would use his hands, it would be to work on machinery, not to guide plows and harvest grain. Given his desire to chart an entirely different course, he was resolved to take his education beyond high school.

In 1883 David enrolled in Lane University, a Nonconformist college located in Lecompton, a town only a few miles from Abilene. The college's most imposing feature was its name, borrowed from the first Kansas Senator, a Lincoln confidant. It was small, having only 10 instructors and a student body of around 200. Hardly a Yale or Harvard, it was probably less demanding than the better high schools back East. None of the faculty had advanced degrees, and the school was never accredited. In terms of facilities, the entire college was housed in "a modest three story building" containing four "recitation" rooms, a laboratory and a minuscule library.[104] It did, however, offer a curriculum that was a mixture of the liberal arts and vocational training, and David took courses in Greek, rhetoric, mechanics, mathematics and penmanship.

David's college years proved life-changing, but not because of the academics. In his sophomore year he met 22-year-old Ida Elizabeth Stover. Like the Eisenhauers, the Stovers had immigrated to America 200 years before "to escape religious persecution and warfare."[105] Ida was born in 1862 near

Staunton, Virginia, in the heart of a major battleground of the Civil War. The traumatic memories of that conflict and the devastation left in its aftermath reinforced the teachings of her religion and made her an ardent pacifist. She was one of four girls among the 11 children of Simon and Elizabeth Link Stover. Her mother died when she was five, leaving a brood ranging in age from nearly three to 17. When Ida was seven her father sent her off to live with William Link, her maternal grandfather. When she was 11, her father died as well, and her grandfather became her legal guardian. Ida was as forward-looking as her guardian was old-fashioned, and she became determined to pursue a formal education as far as she could, a radical ambition for a young woman of that era. At 18 she moved to Staunton to finish high school, memorizing over 1,300 verses from the Bible as part of her course of study. She supported herself first as a housekeeper and then as a teacher in a one-room schoolhouse.

In May of 1883, when Ida turned 21, she received a $1,000 inheritance from her father's estate. She spent $600 – more than most Americans earned in a year – to buy a black ebony-upright piano, a purchase which remained her prized possession for the rest of her life. In June of 1883 she moved west to join her brothers in Kansas, and that fall she started classes at Lane University. She took courses in music, her first passion, as well as English and history.

Ida Stover met David Eisenhower in the autumn of 1884. They were opposites. She was confident, out-going and well-liked, while he was shy, withdrawn and disagreeable. She was fair, slender and pretty, with light brown hair, blue eyes, a small nose and a generous mouth. He was tall, dark and muscular, with black hair, large hands and broad shoulders. She was "warm, pleasant and mild-mannered."[106] He was stern, moody and domineering. A year after they met, on September 23, 1885, they were married in the Lane campus chapel by a River Brethren pastor. While it is undisputed that the couple was a total mismatch in terms of personality, no one disputes their famous son's description of the marriage as "a genuine partnership" based on "mutual devotion."[107]

Six months before the wedding, in March of 1885, David had left college to begin to earn a living in the mercantile and grocery trade. His store was located in a building that Jacob erected on a lot he owned in the town of Hope. It was financed with the proceeds from mortgaging the farm that would have been David's wedding present from his father. Because David had no business experience, he formed a partnership with Milton Good, who had spent two years as a clothing salesman in Abilene. The Eisenhowers and the Goods took up residence in the two apartments built above the store.

While "Good & Eisenhower" enjoyed a brief period of prosperity, the business foundered and was shuttered in the fall of 1888. The failure can be attributed to a variety of factors. The store's principal customers were farmers who bought on credit, and the farmers had several bad years, meaning their credit was no good. David lacked the personality either to be a congenial retailer or a congenial partner. And Good was distracted, trying to perfect an invention – an innovative floor clamp – that he believed would make him rich.

Whatever the reasons, the collapse of the dry goods venture was devastating to David, and in later years an elaborate fiction was fashioned to mask his shame. According to family lore,

> Father continued to extend credit; he carried the farmers to the end. Then his partner proved too weak to go through the ordeal of facing up to the store's own creditors. Taking what little cash was left, the partner departed one night for parts unknown. . . . . Although Father's pride was hurt, he set out at once to find any kind of job and patiently started to pay off his former suppliers.[108]

Contrary to the myth, the Good-Eisenhower partnership was ended by mutual consent in November 1886, when David mortgaged his inventory to his father for $3,500 in order to buy out Good, David himself reporting to the *Hope Dispatch* that his partner had been "released 'from all responsibilities of the late firm.'"[109] Good returned to Abilene and eventually opened another dry-goods store. Once Good was gone, David's brother Abraham was brought into the new "Eisenhower Brothers" enterprise, which was no more successful than its predecessor, since a continuing drought doomed the local farming economy. The only debt David incurred was to his father, who had forgiven it long before the brothers closed up shop.

In October 1886, shortly before the reorganization of the business, Ida gave birth to her first child, Arthur. Two years later, when the business went bankrupt, she was pregnant again. David's reaction to his business setback was to flee Kansas to find employment in another state. He saddled his younger brother with the responsibility of looking after his two-year-old toddler and his wife, who was six months pregnant. Though David could have found something closer to home, he was unwilling to face either the pity or scorn of neighbors who thought he had squandered all the advantages his prosperous and respected father had given him.

David ended up 400 miles away in Denison, Texas, the southern endpoint of the Missouri-Kansas-Texas Railway, known in those parts as the "The Katy." He was hired as an "engine wiper" at a salary of $10 a week, tasked with oiling bearings, filling grease nipples and, as the name implied, wiping with a greasy rag locomotive engines.[110] The work was menial, the conditions were terrible and the days were 12 hours long. David lived by himself in a single rented room in a boardinghouse across the way from the railyard. During his free time, to escape from his dismal existence, he began a lifelong affair with mysticism. He created a chart, which ultimately measured 10 feet by 6 feet, depicting the lines, angles and dimensions of the Great Egyptian Pyramid at

Giza. Its intended purpose was to provide him with answers to all the elusive questions of life.

David remained in this grim and isolated world for six months, until April 1889, when Ida joined him with Arthur, still under three, and a four-month old Edgar. He rented a rundown, soot-covered frame house near the railroad tracks. The scenery comprised stacks of cotton bales and goats trying to find nourishment from the scant vegetation. To reduce expenses, the Eisenhowers shared their shack with a Katy engineer. A "luxury" meal was hot tamales, six of which cost a nickel. They were "dirt poor."[111]

In June 1890 David traveled to Abilene for his mother's funeral. His father had moved there from Hope in January 1889, after the collapse of the dry-goods store and of a bank in which he was a major investor. Ida became pregnant again in 1890, and that October, in the midst of a fierce storm, gave birth to a third son, christened David Dwight, but always called Dwight by his mother – never David, never Ike. One biographer has speculated that the "deeply religious" Ida saw providential significance in this melodramatic entrance, the thunder and lightning foretelling "a life of violence."[112] Maybe.

In the spring of 1891 Jacob visited David in Texas, urging him to come back to Kansas. Within 12 months he did. After three and a half years of self-imposed exile, David returned on the promise of a job at the Belle River Creamery in Abilene, a major concern founded by the River Brethren. David's brother-in-law was the plant's butter-maker and foreman, and there was a need for someone to tend to the refrigeration equipment. Borrowing train fare from the same brother-n-law, his family of five arrived in March of 1892 to the place that Dwight would always regard as his hometown.

At the time of their arrival, David Eisenhower's entire assets were less than $25. All he could afford was a tiny cottage, little more than a shanty, whose only virtue was its location a few blocks from the Creamery. It sat close to, but on the wrong side of, the Southern Pacific Railroad tracks in an area called "Hell's Half-acre," the red-light district of the roaring '70s.[113] As to the job itself, while it had the title of "engineer," in fact David was no more than a manual laborer responsible for maintaining rather simple machinery.[114] At the beginning, he earned $35 a month, about the same as the salary paid to high school students during their summer vacations. The pay reflected the fact that David's duties required little knowledge or skill. He generally worked 12 hour a day, six days a week, leaving the house around 6 in the morning and getting back home around 6 at night.

Abilene in 1892 was fairly primitive, with no sewer system, no paved roads and wooden sidewalks. There was no running water south of the rail line where the Eisenhowers lived, though there was in the wealthy area north of the line. The commercial establishments included grocery stores, drug stores, barber shops and meat markets. There was a one-man police force and a town marshal, at least during the daylight hours. The C.W. Parker Circus made Abilene its base of operations, and it was where merry-go-rounds were built.

Horses and buggies and some bicycles provided transportation. About 4,000 people called Abilene home. In terms of geography, the town was a mile or two north of the Smoky Hill River and basically east of a meandering stream officially called "Serpentine Creek," but named by the residents who knew better as "Mud Creek."[115]

Ida had her fourth son, Roy, the year they moved to Abilene. A fifth son, Paul, was born in 1894, but died 10 months later of diphtheria. In the summer of 1895 Dwight went to visit his Aunt Minnie and Uncle Luther on their farm in Topeka. While roaming their yard, he was terrorized by a noisy and aggressive gander who hissed defiantly at the four-year-old boy whenever he invaded his territory. Uncle Luther gave his nephew a worn out broom to defend himself, and the next time the gander approached, Dwight whacked him. Though the male goose continued to sound off, he did so from a safe distance. Eisenhower said that encounter taught him "never to negotiate with an adversary except from a position of strength."[116]

In the fall of 1896 Dwight began his formal education at the Lincoln Elementary School, a large brick building with no indoor plumbing. Learning was by rote. Writing paper was a luxury. Dwight excelled at spelling and arithmetic, but fell short when it came to penmanship and deportment. Because the Bible-loving Eisenhowers made their boys recite passages from the scriptures, Dwight also distinguished himself with his "ability to read in a loud clear voice and correctly."[117]

Around the time he started at Lincoln Elementary, Dwight had his first – and only – youthful brush with politics. It was the year of the McKinley-Bryan presidential election, and Abilene was the host of a torchlight parade. Although big brothers Arthur (10) and Edgar (eight) promised their parents that they would remain on the sidelines, they were dragooned by the parade managers to carry a torch which, in Dwight's case, equaled his height. The three boys dutifully marched with the band and somehow got back home on time and un-singed.

In a number of ways 1898 was a momentous one for the Eisenhowers. In that year, Ida delivered her fifth baby, a boy named Earl. And in that year David's younger brother Abe decided to abandon his successful practice as an unlicensed veterinarian and travel in a horse-drawn wagon with his wife through western Kansas and the Oklahoma territories, preaching the gospel. Abe's departure meant that his much larger house was available for David and his family. The circumstances of the transaction are a somewhat cloudy. It appears that Jacob had originally bought the property in a bankruptcy sale in 1892 and two years later had sold it to Abe. It also appears that Abe offered to let David have it for $1,000, so long as he would commit to allowing Jacob to move in with him if he ever wanted to. Whether David and Ida first rented and later bought it or they bought it at the outset or Jacob bought it for them, they took possession as soon as Abe left town.

Though small, the two-story white-gabled house with its barn and three acres of grounds was a vast improvement over the shack on Second Street. It was, however, hardly a mansion. Upstairs there were two bedrooms and a windowed closet. David, Ida and baby Earl occupied the first, and Roy, Dwight and Edgar occupied the second, with Roy and Dwight sharing one bed and Edgar having sole possession of the other. As the oldest, Arthur was given the 42-square-foot closet for himself. His "splendid isolation" eventually ended when a high school student, Florence Sexton, came to help out, forcing Arthur to move in with the other boys.[118]

The new house, like the old one, was on the flat, poorer, south side of town, not on the hilly north side with the well-to-do. It had neither running water nor indoor plumbing, meaning that taking a bath involved first heating water in a tub on the kitchen stove. Lighting was provided by kerosene lamps and candles until electricity came in 1905. The boys were dressed in hand-me-down clothes, altered and mended to prolong their usefulness. Shoes were also handed down, though it was not unusual to do without them when the weather got warm. Toys and candy were in short supply, as was cash. As Eisenhower later joked, "[T]he Indian on our penny would have screamed if we could possibly have held it tighter."[119] While the family always had enough to eat and a roof over its head, it was "far from affluent."[120] Whether it is appropriate to describe it as "thrifty" or "respectably poor," is probably making a distinction without much of a difference.[121] As Eisenhower once put it, "I'm just folks. I come from the people, the ordinary people."[122]

Whatever their standard of living, the Eisenhowers were honest, reliable and decent "folks." And David and Ida taught their children good values, like responsibility, concern for others and ambition without arrogance. The boys were also taught to be independent, to sink or swim. Because David and Ida had gone to college, a rarity at that time and place, their children were taught, as well, that their education should not stop at high school.

Despite similarities in outlook, David and Ida were very different personalities and, consequently, they had very different relationships with their sons. David was regarded as "the breadwinner, Supreme Court, and Lord High Executioner."[123] He was humorless, stern and inflexible, and he dealt with juvenile infractions swiftly, such that "the application of stick to skin was a routine affair."[124] It appears, in some ways, that meting out punishment was his principal form of interaction with his boys. He was up early for work and remained away until it was dinnertime. (Though the Creamery was only a block or two from the house, he never came home for lunch.) After a silent supper, he retreated upstairs to his room to read the Bible or some other book and be by himself. David Eisenhower "managed to be absent even when he was present."[125] He had no hobbies that diverted him. He remained strikingly uninvolved with his children. He was not interested in their school life or their friends.

In describing the boys' relationship with their parents, Edgar wrote in his memoirs, "Our love for our father was based on respect. Our love for our mother was rooted in something deeper."[126] By all measures, Ida was a remarkable human-being. Dwight called her "by far the greatest personal influence in our lives."[127] She was serene, gentle, tolerant and continually smiling. While she was anything but an intellectual, she understood each of her boys and adapted her behavior to their particular temperaments. When they did something bad, she was most apt to play the psychologist to ensure that they never did it again. When she occasionally resorted to the rod, it was a lightweight one. She was their tutor, providing Bible instruction and a series of handy phrases to get them through the day: "The Lord deals the cards. And you play them." "There's no rest for the wicked." "Nothing comes easy in life."[128] She spent countless hours with her children, but still always found time to bring a basket of food or a home remedy to a neighbor in need. She had all the homespun talents required on the Prairie and could sew, knit and embroider. She made cushions, tablecloths and bedspreads, as well as clothes for the boys, dresses for herself and shirts for her husband. In addition, she was a role model of whom her boys could be proud: disciplined, fair and moral.

And Ida knew how to run things, playing the role of manager of the household, a skill that enabled the Eisenhowers to make do. Once they took over Abe's house, they had the ability to be virtually self-sufficient: there was a barn for animals, sufficient land to raise crops and an orchard of fruit trees. But to make something of this opportunity required organization, and Ida was organized. While the Eisenhower boys may not have been destitute, they had little free time, because they were, on a rotating basis, constantly performing the daily tasks assigned by their mother. They had to hoe the corn; plant and weed the vegetable garden; prune the orchard; harvest the apples, cherries and pears; and tap the maple trees for syrup. They had to feed the chickens; milk the cows; care for the horses, pigs and ducks; muck the stalls; clean the buggy and harness; and put up the hay. There was also wood to be chopped; kindling to be collected; produce to be stored; meats to be cured; clothes (including soiled baby diapers) to be boiled, laundered and ironed; floors to be cleaned; meals to be cooked; and dishes to be washed. To augment David's meager salary, Ida sometimes loaded a little red wagon with corn, peas, beans, tomatoes and eggs and sent the boys to the north side to sell the produce door-to-door. To earn spending money, each son was given a small plot to grow his own vegetables and sell them. Dwight specialized in corn and cucumbers, though he broadened his inventory to include his own home-made tamales, priced at three for a nickel.

The farm was not only a place for work, but a place for fun. It had space enough to serve as a playing field, a boxing arena and a hobby center. The inside of the barn was a good spot to practice balancing and for doing somersaults into the thick piles of hay. Uncle Abe's Veterinary sign on the barn's roof was great for dares. During spring, summer and fall there was baseball, football, fishing, minor hunting, camping, boating and swimming. During winter there was ice skating and horse-drawn sledding. Given Abilene's relatively recent past as a haven for desperados and gunslingers, the children also invented games with a Wild West theme.

With six boys – Milton would arrive in 1899 – the Eisenhowers had built-in playmates. They differed from one another both in appearance and disposition. Arthur and Roy had dark hair like their father, Dwight had fair hair like his mother, Ed and Milton had chestnut hair and were kind of a cross, and Earl had red hair, a throwback to an earlier generation. Arthur, Roy and Milton were mild-mannered "with tractable natures," while Ed, Earl and Dwight were "hot-tempered and quarrelsome."[129] Despite the differences and usual intramural scraps, they were very close to one another and would present a united front to outsiders. There was an inevitable rivalry between Dwight and Edgar, the two nearest in age and though Dwight's colossal stubbornness would never allow him to admit defeat, Edgar who was older, taller and heavier would always come out on top, whatever the contest. In a letter to Edgar dated April 10, 1944, when Eisenhower was in his mid-50s, he described their relationship this way:

> You were always vastly my superior. You could run faster, hit better, field better, tote the foot-ball better, and do everything except beat me at shotgun shooting. . . . I was just the tail to your kite.[130]

In 1898 there were two more events worthy of mention. The first was the brief and exhilarating Spanish-American War, which captured the imagination of the young Eisenhowers. Remembering the *Maine* and re-enacting the charge up San Juan Hill became a fixture in their games. Ida, who seldom interfered with their play, would have none of it, and lectured her brood on the evils of war, telling them to find other sources of amusement. The effect of her sermon was simply to cause them to move their gallant soldiering elsewhere.

It is ironic that Ida's and David's pacifism was never animated by the endless brawls among her children. Ida felt such fighting was healthy and normal and a good way for her sons to expend their boundless energy. A tomboy herself, having grown up with seven brothers, Ida's only rule was that their fighting had to take place outside the house. David was also never troubled by the tussles. He wanted his sons to be manly and able to defend themselves. One day, David happened to be at home when Dwight ran into the yard, chased from school by a bigger classmate. When his father told him to stand his ground, Dwight stopped in his tracks, knocked the bully down and promised him a daily thrashing if he went after him again. The lesson he took from that experience was "that domination of others in this world often comes about or is sought through bluff."[131]

1898 was also the year that Dwight met Bob Davis, a 50-year-old bachelor who earned a living as a fisherman, guide and trapper. In his autobiography Eisenhower described the gentle, six-foot-tall Davis as his "hero," a key fixture during the formative period from roughly eight to 16.[132] Davis was both a mentor and a father figure, doing all the things with and for Dwight that David did not and maybe could not do.[133] The two spent many weekends together, some on the Smoky Hill River, where Dwight learned to fish, trap, paddle a flatboat, shoot ducks and cook over an open fire. Davis also gave Dwight invaluable lessons on a percentage-based approach to poker-playing, a method that appealed to the mathematically-minded boy and proved to be a great gift later when he needed to supplement his modest soldier's pay. Davis taught using the Socratic method, asking Dwight questions to make him determine the right answer for himself.

Like his father, Dwight had a violent temper and once, in a fit of rage, hurled a brick at his brother's head. In 1900, shortly after his 10th birthday, Dwight flew into another mindless fury. It was triggered by his parents' refusal to let him go "trick or treating" that Halloween with Arthur and Edgar. Dwight's response was to pummel the apple tree in front of the house, bloodying his fists. David thrashed his son severely with a hickory switch and sent him to bed. Sometime later that night, Ida came into Dwight's room. She sat for a while, then washed his hands and applied salve and bandages. She calmly pointed out that the only person who had been hurt by his anger was himself. Paraphrasing from the Bible she said, "He that conquereth his own soul is greater than he who taketh a city."[134] While Eisenhower never could eliminate his temper, he did try to control it and looked back on Ida's intervention that evening as "one of the most valuable moments of my life."[135]

Dwight had two other memorable, searing moments in the early part of the new century. When he was 11 or 12, and Earl was three or four – in 1901 or 1902 – the two were in a workshop attached to the barn. Dwight was making a toy while Earl watched. Dwight had placed his whittling knife on the window sill, away from Earl, but the inquisitive little boy clambered on a chair to grab it and fell, puncturing his left eye. The damage to Earl's sight, which was serious, became irreparable when some time later the youngest brother, Milton, tipped a heavy game board with which he and Earl were playing, and its corner struck the same eye again. Ida and David never mentioned the incident, and Earl ended up doing well both as a child and as an adult, but Eisenhower never could forget the incident or forgive himself.

> I was with him when the first accident occurred and if I had been more alert, it would not have happened. My feeling of regret is heightened by a sense of guilt, even though my parents never charged me with any blame.[136]

In late 1902, not too long after Earl's accident, Edgar and Dwight were eating lunch when David, who never came home at noon, unexpectedly showed up. Edgar had quit school to work for the local doctor, never telling his parents, but the school eventually notified them of his months of absence. David found the boys in the barn and, enraged, grabbed Edgar by the collar and began beating him mercilessly with a leather harness. Dwight shouted for his father to stop, and when he would not, tried to hold his arms. David's response was to threaten Dwight with "some of the same," until Dwight said, "I don't think anyone ought to be whipped like that, not even a dog."[137] The beating ended, Dwight was not punished and an older Eisenhower justified his father's action as necessarily "drastic" because of David's "fear that his boy would seriously damage all the years of life ahead."[138] Yet, David's action was not justifiable, but a window into how violent and unbalanced he could be. Six years before, David had been arrested, pled guilty and was jailed for assaulting a neighbor's son.

In the fall of 1902 Dwight had entered Garfield Junior High School for seventh and eighth grades. His very first day was traumatic, when he was bullied by a bigger boy. He was rescued by his big brother, Arthur, who told Dwight's tormentor to have his fun with someone else. Dwight soon learned to take care of himself, no matter what the size of the antagonist and to never run away from a fight. In that regard, when he had just turned 13 he was egged on by his classmates to take on a boy named Wesley Merrifield. There is a suggestion that the confrontation was based on the hostility between Abilene's south-siders, whom Dwight would represent, and its north-siders, represented by Wes. In any event, in Eisenhower's retelling, it was "short and stocky" Wes against "long and rangy" Dwight.[139] The brawl went on for a while, with neither contestant able to deliver a knock-out punch, and it finally ended in a mutually agreed-upon draw. Though no lasting damage was done, the black eye Dwight earned allowed him to miss a few days of school.

The only other notable event of Dwight's Garfield years had occurred in May of 1903, in the aftermath of the Kansas version of the Hundred Year Flood. Both the Mud Creek and the Smoky Hill River had overflowed their banks and downtown Abilene had become its own waterway. Edgar and Dwight, who always had an instinct for adventure and mischief, decided that a piece of broken sidewalk would serve as a great raft, with no thought that their wild ride would eventually take them to the raging river and a real danger of drowning. Fortunately, a man on horseback saw them and, aware of the hazard, ordered them to get into the waist deep water and wade their way home. As soon as they got there, their worried mother, who had asked two neighbors to go out on a search, sent them off to their rooms. The brothers spent the next several days digging out the house and the yard, pumping the water from the basement and washing the jars and canned fruits that had been covered with mud. Among other things that they never heard the end of was their failure to bring their father that day's lunch.

In 1904, when David was in his 40s, he completed a correspondence course in refrigeration engineering offered by a school in Scranton. It was an important milestone for him, and he proudly displayed the certificate on his bedroom wall. David had never quite recovered from his early business failures and did his best to make his trivial position at the dairy factory seem important. Every day he would go to the Creamery wearing a dark-vested suit, starched white shirt and a watch chain, trying to look like the high-level manager he wished he was.

That autumn Dwight entered Abilene High School. The students were crammed onto the second floor of the Abilene town hall, sharing the facility with the city jail and fire department, which occupied the floor below. The prescribed course load included English, algebra and physical geography. In May of that first year Dwight skinned his knee running down a wooden platform with a group of friends. The injury seemed minor, so he went to school the next day. On the evening of the second day the knee had become seriously swollen and infected. Ida summoned the doctor when she noticed a black streak travelling up his thigh. The doctor concluded that Dwight had blood poisoning and warned that he could die if the infection reached his abdomen. His temperature spiked, and he may have drifted into a coma. Eisenhower recalled overhearing the doctor mention "amputation" and making Edgar swear that he would prevent it – death was better than being a cripple.[140] In the absence of antibiotics, the doctor medicated Dwight and painted a belt of carbolic acid around his body. After several days of treatment, the fever broke. Dwight's condition was weakened enough that he was unable to go back to school that spring, and in 1905-1906 he repeated his freshman year.

By 1907, the beginning of Dwight's junior year, Abilene opened a beautiful modern high school. It was around this time that Dwight became "Ike" to his classmates. Actually, Dwight became "Little Ike" to distinguish him from Edgar, who had returned to school and was "Big Ike," yet another indignity to stoke their rivalry. Dwight's passion was athletics, and during his last two years he played right end for the football team and often center field for the baseball team. He was naturally gifted, with big hands, and he brought a fierce competitiveness and enthusiasm to both sports. He also was fair-minded, a trait he got from his mother. This quality was in full display when he said he would quit the football team if they failed to play against a squad with a black athlete. He reinforced his point by shaking the black player's hand when the game was over. Dwight's leadership abilities were formally recognized when he was elected President of the Abilene High School Athletic Association, established to provide funds for the uniforms, equipment and transportation which was not in the school budget. The dues were a quarter a month. At the risk of putting Dwight's athletic achievements too much in context, his graduating class had only nine boys!

While academics were not his focus, Dwight got good grades, not because of particular diligence, but because he had a logical mind, a good memory and could write clear and effective prose. He had the ability to ask the right question and, when called upon by a teacher, to provide the correct answer. Though not scholarly, he had an insatiable curiosity. During his last two years he did well in all subjects but Latin and in all aspects of school but conduct, which occasionally attracted the attention of the superintendent.

Dwight loved plane geometry and was so far ahead of his classmates that the teachers took away his textbook and created a special advanced course. He welcomed the challenge and the fact that their novel approach meant he had no math homework. So long as the teachers did not abandon the experiment – which they did not – he was assured a mark of A+.

Dwight was also an excellent history student. His interest in the subject developed from reading the dozens of books in Ida's substantial library. He was particularly drawn to accounts of the Greeks and Romans, to the battles they fought and the soldiers who fought them. Of the warriors, he was especially taken with Hannibal, not only because of his daring and his strategic brilliance, but because his exploits had been recorded favorably for posterity by his enemies. When it came to American history, his hero was George Washington. And of Washington's many successes, he was always drawn to his ability to keep the army together and survive the winter of 1778 at Valley Forge. He admired Washington for his "stamina and patience in adversity" and for his "indomitable courage, daring, and capacity for self-sacrifice."[141] Like the fictional Jefferson Smith in Capra's celebrated *Mr. Smith Goes to Washington*, Dwight developed a sympathy for "lost causes" and the underdogs who fought for them.[142]

Dwight did more than go to class. He wrote the "Athletics" piece for the school yearbook, and he even took part in the senior play. His theatrical performance was hailed by the local critic as the "best amateur humorous character seen on the Abilene stage in this generation and gave an impression that many professionals fail to reach."[143] That Edgar also performed to less enthusiastic notices pleased Eisenhower so much that nearly 60 years after the fact he wrote: "For once in our school careers . . . I got more spotlight than Ed."[144]

After school Dwight did odd jobs to earn spending money. He also spent time with Joe Howe, another mentor type, who was the editor of the *Dickinson County News*. Though Howe had no children, he was a school board member with a genuine concern for the well-being of teenagers in town. He organized a club, the Knights of Honor, and provided space behind his newspaper office for the high school boys to play pool, box and engage in other wholesome activities. Since one of Dwight's good pals was a charter member of the Knights, Dwight would be at Howe's office most afternoons, often looking through the collection of newspapers from other cities and countries. It was a broadening experience that made Dwight realize more clearly than he had before that Kansas was not the entire universe.

During his high school summers, Dwight would camp with a group of friends at Lyons Creek, a spot 20 miles outside of Abilene. Each of the dozen or so boys would contribute $5 to cover expenses. They divided up the various tasks: hunting game, fetching wood, building a fire, making meals and cleaning up. Dwight had become a decent cook and that became his permanent assignment. The camp outings were a break from the normal routine of summer jobs which for Dwight had meant picking apples and helping with the wheat harvest. As to girls, Dwight had no time, no money and no clothes for such diversions. Though he was a terrible dancer, his odds of having a girlfriend, if he had wanted one, were strong, since the girls outnumbered the boys by a ratio of two to one.

The commencement ceremonies for Abilene High School were held on May 23, 1909, at the Seelye Theater. At the time of his graduation, Dwight stood 5'11" and weighed 145 pounds. He was popular and handsome, carefree and self-reliant, a strong healthy boy seen as a natural leader. He was comfortable in groups, easy to get along with, and a classic team player. And, putting aside occasional rages, he had a wonderful temperament like his mother and an infectious grin. In *The Helianthus*, the high school yearbook, it was prophesied that he would be a professor of history at Yale, a tribute dampened by the ironic prediction that Edgar would become a two-term president of the United States.

Following graduation Dwight was determined to fulfill his mother's dream that he go to college, but equally determined not to ask for any assistance from his father in getting there. And so he took every job he could. He worked on a farm, for a company manufacturing steel grain bins and at the Creamery, hauling huge blocks of ice. He and Edgar shared a single-minded goal: "to get our hands on every cent we could possibly earn."[145] Beyond that, he had no idea what came next.

While after the fact, scholars would look at Dwight's fascination with soldiers and soldiering, his competitive spirit and his love of teams as foreshadowing his military career, his sole objective then was to get out of Abilene. That he ended up at West Point was as much a fluke as anything. A grammar school pal of Dwight's, Everett "Swede" Hazlett, had returned from military school in Wisconsin in June of 1910. When the Swede asked Dwight of his plans, Dwight said he was thinking of applying to Kansas University. Swede, who was going to try for an appointment to Annapolis, said, "Why don't you come with me?"[146] The idea of a free college education was appealing, since the Eisenhowers could not afford to pay the freight. So Dwight studied for the competitive exam used by both service academies, came in second, and the sitting Senator appointed Ike to the U.S. Military Academy. One biographer says it was because the top scorer failed the West Point physical,[147] another because the top scorer was likely to get a presidential appointment and did not need the Senator's help[148] and a third because the top scorer decided to go to the Naval Academy.[149] So much for destiny.

Abraham Lincoln
February 12, 1809-April 15, 1865
President: March 4, 1861-April 15, 1865
Other Government Experience: Illinois House of Representative, 1835-1843; U.S. House of Representative, 1847-1849.
Major Achievements: Preserving the Union; Ending Slavery.

UNDERDOG GREATS

Because every schoolchild is taught of Abraham Lincoln's modest origins and because he himself described his family as "undistinguished," Lincoln scholars like to start by deconstructing what they regard as the myth about his humble beginnings. They do not take issue with his mother's background because so little is known of Nancy Hanks, other than that she was born in Virginia and grew up in Kentucky. Rather, they focus on his father's circumstances – the Lincoln side of the story.

In 1637 15-year-old Samuel Lincoln sailed from Port Yarmouth for the New World. He left the village of Hingham in the eastern part of England to settle in a town by the same name located 15 miles south of Boston in the Massachusetts Bay Colony. His motives for moving were mixed. Like 13,000 other Puritans who made the so-called "Great Migration" of the 1630s he was drawn by the promise that British North America would offer greater political and religious freedom. As an apprentice weaver growing up as a depression was hitting East Anglia, British North America also seemed to offer better economic prospects. Samuel's hopes were realized as he met success first as a farmer and then as a businessman. He did well enough to erect a substantial dwelling. He was a pillar of the church and the father of 11 children, one of whom, Mordecai, was Abraham Lincoln's great-great-great-grandfather.

Mordecai moved twice, both times within the colony. But Mordecai's son, another Mordecai, traveled farther afield, venturing 300 miles south to the commercial town of Freehold in what is now in the state of New Jersey. Mordecai Jr. "was perhaps the most successful member of the family," making his fortune in real estate and in business.[150] He also married well, taking as his bride Hannah Slater, daughter of a member of the New Jersey colonial legislature and niece of an assemblyman and the acting royal governor. After a time, Mordecai Jr. felt the urge to explore new territory and settled further west in southeastern Pennsylvania. There he acquired more land, constructed a forge and erected a substantial brick house. A member of the "economic and social elite," upon his death his estate included property of over a thousand acres plus an iron business.[151]

Mordecai Jr.'s oldest son, John, though he inherited real estate in New Jersey, initially lived in Pennsylvania, where he wed Rebecca Flower, the daughter of wealthy Quakers. John, like his father, grandfather and great-grandfather before him, could not stay put, and he ended up going south to the Shenandoah Valley of Virginia, where he took up farming in Rockingham County. John was prosperous enough that he deeded his son, the first Abraham Lincoln, and the President's grandfather, 210 acres of prime Virginia land. In 1770, at the age of 26, Abraham married Bathsheba Herring, who came from "one of the leading families of Rockingham County."[152] When the Revolutionary War broke out, Abraham served as a Captain in the Virginia militia. Around the time peace was being negotiated in 1782, the 42-year-old veteran sold his Virginia farm and left with his wife and five children for Kentucky. Abraham was perhaps enticed by the stories his "friend" Daniel

Boone was telling of an "Eden" of plentiful game and fish, tall timbers, clear water and land that was both rich and, at 40 cents an acre, inexpensive.[153] After a trek of 200 miles, Abraham settled his family of seven on the Green River, just outside of present-day Louisville, and filed a claim for over 2,000 acres.

The Lincolns built a log cabin and farmed their new lands. In 1786, Abraham and his three sons, Mordecai, Josiah and Thomas, were planting corn, when they were attacked by Indians. The boys watched as their father fell to the ground and died. Mordecai, around 14, sped to a nearby cabin, and Josiah, about 12, ran to the settlement for help. Six-year-old Thomas was leaning over his father's bleeding body. An Indian was approaching intent on killing or kidnapping Thomas, when he suddenly stopped and fell to the ground. Mordecai had shot him with a flintlock rifle placed at a chink in the logs, aiming at the shining bangle dangling from the Indian's neck.

At the time of his death, Abraham "owned at least 5,544 acres of land in the richest sections of Kentucky."[154] Under the archaic law of primogeniture, Mordecai, as the eldest son, inherited Abraham's entire estate when he reached his majority. Thomas, father of the future president, participated in none of this wealth.

While it is true that once in America the Lincoln family had distinguished itself through its economic success, military service, political involvement, adventurous spirit and notable marital alliances, its most famous descendent knew almost nothing about the generations of his forebears.[155] He was largely unaware of the history of Samuel, the two Mordecais, John and even his namesake, Abraham. Moreover, whatever fortune his ancestors amassed and enjoyed bypassed his immediate family. So when in 1859 candidate Lincoln described his background as "undistinguished," he was not unfairly describing his roots, as he understood them.

After the murder of the first Abraham, his widow Bathsheba and her five children moved to Springfield, Kentucky, to live with one of her cousins. When he got older, Thomas went to work on Washington County farms, at a local mill and for his uncle in Tennessee. He eventually returned to Kentucky and took an apprenticeship in carpentry and cabinet-making. Because he had to fend for himself at such an early age, there was no time for formal education, or indeed education of any kind.

Thomas grew into a stocky man, 5'9" tall and weighing 185 pounds. He had dark hazel eyes, brown or black hair, high cheekbones, a round face and a prominent nose. A neighbor described him as "an uneducated man, a plain unpretending plodding man," who was "quiet and good natured."[156] He was known for his scrupulous honesty and the wry stories he told. At 19 he joined the Kentucky militia, at 24 he was made a constable, at 25 he served on a jury. While not wealthy, Thomas was a respectable member of his frontier community.

Apropos his economics, Thomas was remembered for the fact that he "accumulated considerable property which he always managed to make way with about as fast as he made it," an observation reminiscent of the old saw, "easy come, easy go."¹⁵⁷ Thomas began the accumulation phase in 1803, paying 118 pounds for a 238-acre farm on Mill Creek, seven miles north of Elizabethtown, and purchasing two lots in Elizabethtown proper.

In 1805 Thomas became one of four Hardin County "patrollers" charged with rounding up "suspicious" whites or "roving" blacks.¹⁵⁸ The next year he was employed by local merchants to transport their goods to New Orleans for which he earned 16 pounds in gold and a credit of another 13 pounds. In May of 1806 he bought silk, linen, "cassemere," flannel and "dozens of buttons" in the run-up to his June 12 wedding to Nancy Hanks.¹⁵⁹

Nancy was born in Virginia around 1784. She was the daughter of Lucy Hanks.¹⁶⁰ Her father's identity is unknown. It is also not known whether Lucy was married to Nancy's father. Speculation that she was not arose from the absence of a marriage license, the "several recorded instances of bastardy among Hanks women of her generation" and the indictment of a "Lucey Hanks" for lewd behavior by a Kentucky grand jury.¹⁶¹ One biographer claims that Lucy died when Nancy was "a young girl."¹⁶² Another has Lucy marrying a revolutionary war soldier when Nancy was seven.¹⁶³ One biographer maintains that Nancy was raised in Springfield, Kentucky, by her aunt Rachel Shipley Berry and her uncle Richard.¹⁶⁴ Another contends she was brought up in the home of Thomas and Elizabeth Sparrow.¹⁶⁵ There is no uniform description of Nancy's appearance. She is variously described as tall or average in height, slender or heavy in weight, fair or dark in complexion, beautiful or plain in looks.¹⁶⁶ In terms of personality, there is a consensus that Nancy was quiet, friendly and kind. In terms of intellect, there is a consensus that she was very bright and able to read, though not write.

The Lincoln-Hanks wedding feast was a sumptuous and well-attended affair. The 22-year-old bride wore linen and silk; the 28-year-old groom was decked out in a beaver hat and black suit. The Lincolns' first home was a cabin Thomas built on one of the two lots he owned in Elizabethtown. As a carpenter, Thomas produced cabinets, door frames, window sashes and, from time to time, coffins. Almost exactly eight months after the marriage ceremony, on February 10, 1807, Nancy gave birth to a daughter she named Sarah. The next year Thomas purchased a second farm, a 348.5-acre spread on Nolin Creek, located 18 miles southeast of Elizabethtown. The new property cost $200 and was called the "Sinking Spring Farm."¹⁶⁷ On a little knoll near the spring Thomas built a 16-by-18-foot one-room cabin with a floor of packed dirt, a leather hinged door and either no window or a single tiny one.

The Lincolns were in their new home by February 12, 1809, when their second child was born. He was named after his grandfather Abraham. Nancy was attended by a "granny woman," Aunt Peggy Walters, and, following the delivery, by her aunts Betsy Sparrow and Polly Friend.¹⁶⁸ Dennis Hanks, Betsy's nine-year-old adopted son, showed up as well. He later recalled that after holding the squalling baby for a minute, he turned him back over to the aunts predicting, "He'll never come to much."[169]

Sinking Spring proved to be a very poor farm, a "barren waste," that did not produce enough to support the Lincolns.[170] So in the spring of 1811 Thomas bought and moved his family of four to a 230-acre farm 10 miles to the northeast at Knob Creek, where the bottomland was perfect for raising corn and beans. It was here that his two-year-old son Abe grew and learned to walk and talk. He also learned to do chores like carrying water, filling the wood box, cleaning ashes from the fireplace and using a hoe for planting corn, onions, beans and potatoes, and he ran whatever errands were needed. It was here, also, that he experienced the disappointments and hardships of farm life.[171]

In 1812 Nancy was pregnant again. The new baby, named Thomas, died shortly after he was delivered, when Abe was just three. A few years later Abe and Sarah walked four miles to their first school, attending on days when they could be spared at home. The school house was another log cabin without a floor, filled with backless benches. The first two teachers were Zachariah Riney, "a Catholic," and Caleb Hazel, a former saloon-keeper whose main credential was an ability to "thrash" any student who got out of hand.[172] In these so-called "blab schools" students read their lessons aloud so that the teachers knew they were working. While initially Abe may have been sent just to accompany Sarah on the long walk, he likely learned both to recite his letters and to write them on any surface he could find: shovel backs, wood boards, dirt, sand and snow. Over the five years the Lincolns were in Kentucky Abe may have spent only three or four months at school. When Abe was not in school or doing chores, he liked to hunt, fish and play. A relative said, "Abe exhibited no special traits in k[entuck]y except a good kind – somewhat wild nature."[173]

The Lincolns left Kentucky for Indiana in December of 1816, when Abe was seven, the third move in his young life. When he was a grown man he explained the move as "partly on account of slavery; but chiefly on account of the difficulty in land titles."[174] Regarding the former issue, Thomas and Nancy were personally familiar with slavery: Nancy's close friends the Berrys, who hosted her wedding, owned five, and Thomas's uncle, whom he helped farm in Tennessee, owned six. That familiarity did not make them proponents. To the contrary, the minister they had chosen to marry them was an outspoken abolitionist, and it was "on account of slavery" that they joined a Baptist splinter group that had broken from the established church.[175] Admitted to the union in 1792 as a slave state, slavery was "on the rise in Kentucky."[176]

While slavery may have made Kentucky morally inhospitable, there was also the practical problem that all of Thomas' real estate holdings were snarled in legal disputes. The problem stemmed from the fact that Kentucky had never had a U.S. land survey.[177] As a result, one farm, likely at Mill Creek, had been improperly surveyed, so that it was 38 acres smaller than originally thought; a second farm, presumably Nolin Creek, had a lien on it because of an unknown debt from a prior owner; a third farm, quite definitely Knob Creek, was subject to a dispute lodged by out-of-state claimants who said they were the ones holding the title. Thomas had neither the resources nor the desire to fight these battles in court.[178]

Given the reasons the Lincolns had for leaving Kentucky, Indiana was a sensible destination. First, Indiana was part of the territory governed by the Northwest Ordinance, which specifically prohibited the expansion of slavery. Second, Indiana land had been officially surveyed by the U.S. government and land titles were guaranteed to be valid. So in the fall of 1816 Thomas went off on a reconnaissance mission. He spent several weeks at a spot he found 16 miles from the Ohio River in what is now Spencer County. It had deep, rich soil. Thomas staked out a 40-acre "quarter section" of Congress land, using brush to mark the four corners of its boundary.[179] Several months later, the Lincolns left Kentucky and most of their belongings, taking with them only the irreplaceable essentials: a featherbed, a spinning wheel, cooking utensils and tools. They boarded a ferry that deposited them near Troy, Indiana, and proceeded to hack through the raw and deeply forested wilderness. The region was not only almost impenetrable but untamed, filled with bears, panthers and other wild animals. There were few other settlers in the area, and those that were there were two to three miles away. Their journey ended at a clearing in the vicinity of Little Pigeon Creek.

The Lincolns erected a crude shelter called a "half-faced camp," about 14-feet square and enclosed on only three sides.[180] Over the succeeding weeks, with the help of some of their seven neighbors, they built a real home. It was constructed of logs and measured 18 by 20 feet. Though Abe was only eight, he was big for his age and was likely wielding an ax even then.

That first winter of 1817 in Indiana was hard, described by Lincoln years later as "pretty pinching times."[181] Cold wind whistled through the cabin because the frigid temperatures had made it impossible to dig up the clay and grass for chinking between the timbers. The only source of light came from the burning of logs or pine knots or hog fat. Because the wells that were dug failed, the children had to walk a distance for spring water. It was extremely lonely, since the closest neighbors were still miles away. Since they had not been there the previous spring, they had harvested no crops, limiting the Lincolns' diet to forest game: deer, bear, turkey, ducks, geese.

To get ready for the upcoming planting season, Thomas had to chop trees, clear away brush and plow the "hard unbroken sod."[182] In all this, as well as in splitting fences, Thomas had Abe's help. He had been given an ax to help erect the cabin and, as his campaign biography said, "from [then] till within his twenty-third year, he was almost constantly handling that most useful instrument."[183] Abe also was taught basic carpentry and built a three-legged stool. By this time he had learned how to use a rifle. There is an often-told story of how before his eighth birthday, when his father was away, Abe borrowed a gun to shoot at a flock of wild turkeys that was approaching the cabin. He succeeded in bringing one down, but "never since pulled a trigger on any larger game."[184]

Having survived that desperate period, by October 1817 Thomas was pleased enough with the encampment at Pigeon Creek to make the 90-mile journey to Vincennes to put a $16 down payment on two adjoining 80-acre tracts. He paid an additional $64 in December, leaving a balance of $240 to gain clear title to the land. That autumn Nancy's aunt Betsy Sparrow arrived with her husband Thomas and Nancy's 17-year-old cousin Dennis Hanks.

The promising ending of 1817 was followed by disaster in 1818. Nine-year-old Abe met with a horrible accident, when his horse reared and kicked him in the forehead leaving him bleeding and unconscious, "apparently killed for a time," as he later wrote.[185] Then the community of Pigeon Creek was afflicted by the "milk sickness," a fatal disease contracted by drinking the milk of cows that had eaten poisonous white snakeroot.[186] Among the early victims were Thomas and Betsy Sparrow, who succumbed in September. Nancy Lincoln was stricken, too, and died on October 5. Thomas and Dennis Hanks fashioned a coffin, Abe whittling the pegs, and Nancy was buried next to her aunt and uncle on a wooded knoll a quarter mile from the cabin.

The year 1819 "may have been the hardest in Abraham Lincoln's life."[187] Dennis Hanks moved in with the Lincolns and helped Thomas and Abe clear more land for planting and hunt to put meat on the table. Sarah, just 12, did her best to cook and keep house, although her cousin Dennis remembered that "at times she felt so lonesome that she would sit by the fire and cry."[188] To end the downhill slide, Thomas returned to Elizabethtown, Kentucky, in November. It is said that he went directly to the house of Sarah Bush Johnston whom he had "knowed" "from a gal" just as she had "knowed" him "from a boy."[189] Sarah was a widow with three young children, Elizabeth (13), Matilda (10) and John (9). Thomas was a widower with two children, Sarah (12) and Abe (10). He told her it made sense for them to get married, since she needed a husband and he needed a wife. She agreed. Thomas paid off her debts, and they were wed on December 2, 1819. Thomas was 41 and Sarah 10 years younger.

After the ceremony, Thomas and his new family headed back home, along with a wagon filled with Sarah's possessions: a feather mattress and pillows, a black walnut bureau, a spinning wheel, a large clothes chest, a table and chairs, pots and skillets and all manner of cutlery. When Thomas arrived at Pigeon Creek he introduced Sarah to his daughter and son as their "new mammy."[190] Sarah was a "strong, large-boned, rosy woman, with a kindly face and eyes, a steady voice, steady ways."[191]

With the arrival of the Johnstons, there were eight in the Lincolns' small, unfinished cabin. Sarah had a knack for organization and made the improvement of the living space a priority. With her guidance Thomas and Dennis installed a wood floor, finished the roof, built a real door, cut a hole for a window, added a loft and climbing pegs, made another table and some stools and constructed additional, proper beds. Sarah's neighbors were taken by her "sagacity and gumption," her sewing and mending skills and how spotlessly clean she kept her house and her cooking vessels.[192]

Sarah also had "the gift of love."[193] Abe and his sister had been without a mother for 15 months, and she soaped and scrubbed them clean to make them look "more human" and gave them some of her own clothing to replace the rags they had been wearing.[194] From the outset, she treated Abe and his sister Sarah just like her own. She was able to seamlessly meld the two families into one by being scrupulously fair and never playing favorites.

That said, Sarah had an especial fondness for Abe and had been "warm and friendly" to him from the very first.[195] According to Sarah, Abe never gave her "a cross word" and "never refused" to do anything she asked of him.[196] She felt their minds "seemed to move together – move in the same channel," and so she understood Abe, even his "gloomy spells."[197] Asked to compare her son and stepson after they were gone from her home, Sarah said they "[b]oth were good boys," but that "Abe was the best boy I ever saw or ever expect to see."[198] For Abe, the virtually unconditional love she showed him was "a rich silent force in his life."[199]

In the years after the Johnstons' arrival, there were some notable milestones. In 1821, when Abe was 11, his cousin Dennis Hanks married Sarah's daughter Elizabeth and moved out of the cabin. In 1826, when Abe was 17, his sister Sarah and stepsister Matilda both married neighbors, and they moved out of the cabin, as well.

During this period, as Abe grew, he took on increasing responsibility to help with the family finances and chores. At 12 he worked alongside his father to build a meetinghouse for the Little Pigeon Baptist Church. At 13 or 14 he began to be hired out to other farmers. He sometimes earned cash money, almost all of which he turned over to his father, and sometimes earned board, clothes and lodging. His activities included "clearing timberland for crops, cutting brush and burning it, splitting rails, pulling crosscut saw and whipsaw, driving the shovelplow, harrowing, spading, planting, hoeing, cradling grain, milking cows, helping neighbors at house-raisings, logrolling, corn-huskings, [and] hog killings."[200]

At 16, when Abe was almost fully mature, he had become enormously skilled with an ax. As one neighbor told it, "He can sink an ax deeper into wood than any man I ever saw."[201] Given this ability, he was frequently kept busy from sunrise to sunset building the fences which in pioneer America were in great demand. These barriers served to protect from attack, to corral livestock, to preserve gardens and to define boundaries between neighbors. Finished rails were usually 10-feet long and four-inches wide, made from ash, hickory, oak, poplar and walnut. A skilled craftsman like Abe could fashion up to 400 rails daily for a typical flat rate of 25 cents.

Abe was as wily as he was tough, and in 1826, when he was 17, he and his two stepbrothers-in-law, Dennis Hanks and Squire Hall, thought they could earn more splitting cordwood for steam boats than splitting rails for fences. Their idea was good, but their timing was not. They had hit on their scheme right when "demand was slack and money was scarce."[202] They eventually traded their nine cords of wood for nine yards of "white domestic cloth" from which Abe had fashioned his first-ever white shirt.[203]

After the steam boat disappointment, Abe hired out to James Taylor, who ran a ferry and owned a farm, principally helping on the river, but when that was slow, helping with plowing, slaughtering the hogs and fence-building. The combination of odd jobs, that Lincoln later described as "the roughest work a young man could be made to do," netted him a monthly wage of $6, with an extra 31 cents for those days when hog-killing was involved.[204]

In his spare time 18-year-old Abe built a scow, essentially a small flat-bottomed boat, and one day agreed to row two men and their luggage onto a steamer. He thought he had hit the jackpot when each gave him a silver half dollar for his troubles – one dollar for a few hours of effort as compared to the 20 cents he got from James Taylor for a day's work. Abe's bonanza was short-lived. He was sued by the two Dill brothers, who had the legal franchise to ferry passengers across the river. Squire Pate, who officiated, agreed with Lincoln's argument that he was not ferrying passengers from shore to shore, but only taking them to the middle of the river so they could board their steamboat. Abe felt he had made a friend in the judge and from time to time would observe the Squire hear cases on law day.

In 1828, a local storekeeper sent his son and Abe, now 19, down the Ohio and Mississippi Rivers to New Orleans to dispose of a cargo of meat, corn and flour. It was Abe's first glimpse of a big city and likely his first exposure to trafficking in slaves. Two years later, in March 1830, when he had just turned 21, Abe helped his father and stepmother move from Indiana to Illinois, to a spot on the northern bank of the Sangamon River. That summer he worked with them to clear and fence their new farm. He also made his "first political speech," extolling the virtues of internal improvements, specifically the goal of making the Sangamon more navigable.[205] After working for other farmers during the remainder of 1830 – from this point on keeping what he made –Abe left his father's home for good in 1831.

It was not all work for Abe. Like his peers, he enjoyed sports – wrestling, running, jumping – and proved both fast and strong. He was also not above a scrap, when there was some principle at stake. He would wander the countryside attending "house raisings, log rolling[,] corn shucking and workings of all kinds."[206] Abe was a sight in his coonskin cap and his buckskin pants – always way too short – and could always draw a crowd with his rhymes and jokes and droll stories.

But Abe was not exactly like all the other country boys, or at least our image of what country boys were usually like. He did not hunt. Having experimented once, he did not drink or smoke. And he was enormously kind. There was the time in the dead of winter when, after a full day of threshing, Abe found a drunk man lying in a mudhole, carried him to his cousin's cabin, built a fire to warm him and stayed awake with him through the night. Or the time when he stopped some neighborhood children from heaping hot coals on a turtle to force it out of its shell, telling them "that an ant's life was to it as sweet as our is to us."[207] Or the times he would get up at dawn, before his chores, and trek a distance to be with Matthew Gentry who had lost his faculties, just to sit with him and listen to his "weird disconnected babbling."[208]

Abe was distinctive in two other ways, perhaps interrelated. First, as his friend Nathaniel Grigsby recalled, whenever he was in a group for sport or talk or fun "[h]e naturally assumed the leadership of the boys."[209] Second, he was an intellectual, Grigsby again observing, "His mind soared above us."[210]

When the Lincolns moved to Indiana, Abe had resumed his schooling. In 1820, he and the four Lincoln children went for about three months to a school about a mile away from their cabin. The teacher, Andrew Crawford, was a justice of the peace, who, in addition to the basics, tried to teach his students manners. After a year's break, likely in 1822, James Swaney started a new school that was four miles away. Given the distance and the chores that Abe had to do in the morning, he could attend only sporadically. Swaney's replacement, Azel Dorsey, taught Abe for no more than six months, until Abe reached 15. He never went back. Lincoln estimated that "all his schooling did not amount to one year."[211]

From Lincoln's later perspective, the quality of his schooling was as unimpressive as the quantity. There were no real qualifications for teachers, beyond their having the most rudimentary familiarity with *"readin', writin', and cipherin'. . ."*[212] Lincoln wrote, "If a straggler supposed to understand latin, happened to sojourn in the neighborhood, he was looked upon as a wizard."[213] School would start when a teacher "drift[ed] in," most often in winter, and it ended when a teacher "drifted away."[214] In backwoods areas like Pigeon Creek, school was often out of session for a couple of years.

For all its inadequacies, Abe did learn elementary math, practicing on wooden boards, planing them down when the surface became too blackened with his charcoal markers. But it took, and by the time he was a teenager he could perform elaborate multiplication and long division and solve problems dealing with weights and measures, discounts and simple interest.

Abe also learned to spell, read and write. The basic primer of the time, *Dillworth's Spelling Book*, got things started, at least with respect to grammar and spelling. *Dillworth's* began with the alphabet and then progressed to two-, three- and four-letter words. It built on the basic vocabulary to sentences, ultimately offering examples of both prose and verse. However inefficient the "blab" approach to pedagogy, through "constant repetition and drill" Abe became an excellent speller and the odds-on favorite in the class spelling bees.[215] He also learned to write legibly, a school "sum book" providing an early example of his penmanship, verse and wit.[216]

> Abraham Lincoln is my nam[e]
> And with my pen I wrote the same

> I wrote in both hast[e] and speed
> and left it here for fools to read.
>
> Abraham Lincoln his hand and pen
> He will be good but god knows When[217]

It is not clear how easily these basic skills came to Abe. John Hanks, who stayed with the Lincolns for a while, described Abe as a "somewhat dull," not at all "brilliant boy" for whom learning "was hard."[218] Despite the difficulties, Abe *"worked* his way by toil . . . slowly, but surely."[219] Who knows whether the rudiments of knowledge were, as Hanks said, hard won, though it certainly makes for a good story. But whatever the truth, the learning ultimately stuck, and Abe became a passionate scholar.

He came to love reading, saying, "The things I want to know are in books."[220] According to Dennis Hanks, from the age of 12 on he was always with a book, putting it "inside his shirt" as he went to the fields, reading it under a tree at the noon lunch break and again at night with a piece of corn bread, perched in a chair, "cock[ing] his legs up as high as his head."[221] The recollections of Nathaniel Grigsby were much the same, describing how Abe would "set up late" reading "& rise Early doing the Same."[222] As Abe himself is said to have once put it, "[M]y best friend is the man who'll git me a book I ain't read."[223] If "gitting" the unread book meant going to Rockport, "nearly 20 miles away," he would do it.[224] His hunger was such that he was "reading Evry thing he could lay his hands on."[225]

As to what Abe read, the books Sarah brought from Kentucky may have been among the first. They included the Bible, John Bunyan's *The Pilgrim's Progress, Aesop's Fables* and *Lessons in Elocution,* which included passages from Shakespeare. Friends and neighbors say he also read *Robinson Crusoe, Arabian Nights,* Noah Webster's *American Spelling Book,* Starke Dupuy's *Hymns and Spiritual Songs* and historical works like the *Autobiography of Ben Franklin,* Parson Weems' *The Life of George Washington* and William Grimshaw's *History of the United States.*

As significant as what he read was his desire to get something out of it. Sarah said Abe had to understand everything, "minutely and exactly," repeating things "over to himself again and again," in order that it be "fixed in his mind," after which "he never lost the fact or his understanding of it."[226] Given how "diligent" Abe was for "Knowledge," Sarah maintained that no effort was too great: "if pains & Labor would get it he was sure to get it."[227] She recalled that when Abe found a passage that interested him enough to memorize, he would copy it down on paper, if available, or on wooden boards, if not, so it was handy to look at. The neighborhood farm boys had the same recollection and had images of Abe, book in hand, "picking up a piece of charcoal to write on the fire shovel with charcoal, shaving off what he wrote, and then writing more."[228]

Given young Lincoln's mastery of what he read, biographers have pointed to these early books as influencing his writing and thinking as an adult. The "biblical cadences" that infused his presidential prose are reminiscent of the style of John Bunyan.[229] Abe's 1858 "House divided" speech echoes the *Aesop Fable* of the lion and the four bulls and its moral that "A kingdom divided against itself cannot stand."[230] Grimshaw concluded his U.S. history urging that we "demonstrate by our actions that 'all men are created equal,'" a line later memorialized in the opening sentence of the Gettysburg Address.[231]

To the extent he could, Abe tried to put his abilities to good use, serving as the neighborhood letter writer.[232] He took his job as "ghost" seriously, always making sure he, and the real authors, were clear about what they wanted to say, how they wanted to say it and whether there was another tack that might be taken to make it better. And always intent on improving himself, Abe would travel around listening to educated people speak, whether they were lawyers at the courthouse, politicians on the stump or "wandering evangelists."[233] Having intently listened, he would then see if he had mastered their technique by attempting to mimic them.

Abe Lincoln's capacity for intellectual growth against all odds was extraordinary. It was central to his self-image and, as such, was a major factor in shaping his relationship with his birth father and stepmother.

As to Thomas Lincoln, "In all of his published writings, and, indeed, even in reports of hundreds of stories and conversations, he had not one favorable word to say about his father."[234] Abe's problems with Thomas may have begun at the time of Nancy Hanks' death, when Thomas seemed incapable of providing the warmth and compassion that a motherless 10-year-old boy needed. Those problems grew with Thomas' remarriage, when some said that Thomas preferred his stepson John Johnston to his own flesh and blood. Part of the difficulty between father and son arose from a conflict on the matter of religion. Thomas was a stalwart and devout member of the local Baptist Church, and Abe would never join. Abe was put off by the fiery preaching and the moaning and shaking and hysterics that he associated with organized religion; Thomas was put off by Abe's disrespect when, flawlessly, he would parody the minister's sermons.

But as the years went by, there was a more important divide that arose out of their vastly different attitudes towards "pursuits of the mind." Thomas could only "bunglingly sign his own name," and Abe described him as "a wholly uneducated man."[235] But Thomas was not only uneducated, he was hostile to learning and those who engaged in it. Dennis Hanks, who lived in the Lincoln cabin, said that Thomas believed that Abe was too enamored of books, "having sometimes to slash him for neglecting his work by reading."[236] Hanks' son-in-law believed that "Thos. Lincoln never showed by his actions that he thought much of his son Abraham when a boy."[237] Hanks himself believed the feeling was mutual and doubted that "Abe Loved his father Very well . . ."[238]

There was no doubt about Abe's feelings for his stepmother. As a grown man, he talked of her as "a deep influence in him."[239] A relative recalled his saying that Sarah "had been his best friend in this world and . . . no man could love a mother more than he loved her."[240] His affection for Sarah was obviously in part a function of her love for him. But it also was a function of her understanding of his craving for learning. She supplied him with books. She watched and applauded his meticulous study habits. She fully supported his quest for knowledge and would not let anyone "pester him" or have him "hendered" while he was reading.[241] She "always" said, "Abe was goin' to be a great man some day."[242]

As a self-taught backwoods intellectual, Abe knew he was different from virtually everyone with whom he was in regular contact. And so did they. As Dennis Hanks put it: "There's suthin' peculiarsome about Abe."[243]

Abe's quest for knowledge did make him "peculiarsome" and goes a long way to explaining why Dennis and others felt "Lincoln was lazy – a very lazy man."[244] Sarah acknowledged that Abe "didn't like physical labor."[245] And Abe admitted the same to a friend: "He said to me one day that his father taught him to work, but he never taught him to love it."[246] But who does like physical labor? And who can question, from his rail-splitting and fence-building and hog-killing and plowing and planting that Abe did not work hard. But he liked learning more. Cousin John Hanks, who moved in with the Lincolns when Abe was 14, had it right: Abe was not "lazy," but at times his mind was on books "to the neglect of work."[247]

This passion and gift for learning made Abe desperate to make sense of his ancestry. He needed some explanation for the "ambition, mental alertness, and the power of analysis" that distinguished him from the other members of his family, or at least what he knew of them.[248] Thomas Lincoln had none of these qualities, and though some who knew Nancy Hanks described her as "brilliant" and "intellectual," Abe, who was nine when she died, was not one of them.[249]

But no one had any idea of the identity of Abe's maternal grandfather. While Lincoln never addressed the subject publicly, he did mention his supposition to his law partner, William Herndon. They were on their way to the courthouse in Menard County, Illinois, to litigate a case involving the question of heredity. After Lincoln made the general observation that illegitimate children were often more able than legitimate ones, he cited the example of his mother, whom he described as the "illegitimate daughter of Lucy Hanks and a well-bred Virginia farmer or planter."[250] This phantom Southern aristocrat, he believed, explained how he came to be who he was.

When he was running for President, Abe said the following to the *Chicago Tribune's* John Scripps, tasked with writing his campaign biography:

> It is a great piece of folly to attempt to make anything out of my early life. It can all be condensed into a single sentence,

and that sentence you will find in Gray's elegy, "The short and simple annals of the poor." That's my life, and that's all you or anyone else can make of it.[251]

Lincoln was not exaggerating his poverty, though it may have been no worse than that endured by his relatives and neighbors. But given Lincoln's love of books and knowledge, the impoverishment that was most painful to this extraordinary young man was not material but intellectual.

Barack Hussein Obama
August 4, 1961-present
President: January 20, 2009-January 20, 2017
Other Government Experience: State Senator in Illinois, U.S. Senator from Illinois.
Major Achievements: Affordable Care Act; Ending the War in Iraq; Addressing the Great Recession.
Miscellaneous: Recipient of Nobel Peace Prize, 2009.

Although in his mid-20s Barack Obama depicted his struggle for racial identity as a dominant theme of his childhood and adolescence, as he was growing up, his fractured home life was a more immediate concern than his skin color. Though his white mother and black father were very much alive, he spent much of his early life in the company of his maternal grandparents and they, therefore, take on a disproportionate significance.

Coincidentally, Barack's maternal grandfather, Stanley Dunham, was also largely raised by his maternal grandparents. Stanley's mother had committed suicide when he was eight, likely caused by his father's history of infidelity. After her death, he and his brother Ralph lived with their mother's parents, the Armours, in El Dorado, Kansas Their grandfather Harry worked for Magnolia Petroleum Company as a roustabout and statistician. Their grandmother Gabriella had at one time been a schoolteacher. Because the Armours were not "very well off," their estranged father, Ralph Dunham Sr. took out a $2,500 loan to assist with his sons' upkeep.[252] The boys slept together in a bedroom next to a washing machine on the back porch of the Armours' modest home. For fun they played football, baseball, tennis and golf. To help with the finances, they mowed lawns and did clean-up work around the oil wells. Ralph Jr. was an excellent student and a model citizen. Stanley was a dreamer and a story-teller, who had more imagination than ambition. According to his grandson, Stanley also had a "wild streak" and was expelled from high school for punching the principal in the face, spending the following three years doing odd jobs, hopping freight trains to Chicago, then California, then back to Kansas again, and "dabbling in moonshine, cards, and women."[253]

Barack's maternal grandmother, Madelyn Payne, was quite the opposite, a respectable girl from a respectable family. She was born in 1922 in a farmhouse in Peru, Kansas. The Paynes moved to Augusta, Kansas, where her father R.C. was a warehouse and ledger man for a Sinclair subsidiary, Prairie Oil and Gas, in charge of keeping track of oilfield supplies. Her mother, Lee, had been a schoolteacher and was said to be very smart. Madelyn took after Lee and was a first-rate student herself, always reading books and always having good enough grades to be on the honor roll. Though Madelyn had the intellect and marks to get into a good university, the Paynes lacked the funds to send her to one. As high school was winding down, Madelyn was looking forward – or more accurately not looking forward – to repeating her mother's path and attending the El Dorado Junior College, whose mission was to turn out rural lower-school teachers.

Stanley Dunham, four years out of high school, came to El Dorado, Kansas, working construction for the Socony-Vacuum Company, a forerunner of Mobil Oil. He was "tall and tan with slick-backed wavy brown hair, [and] a quick-flash smile," and he frequented "haunts" in Madelyn's neck of the woods.[254] He was not only attractive, but claimed to be well-traveled and well-connected, having friends like the writers John Steinbeck and William Saroyan. Madelyn, susceptible to being sweet-talked by the romantic stranger, totally bought his routine. Her parents and brother did not. They thought Stanley was impossibly conceited and that his exotic biography was likely made up.

Madelyn was deaf to any and all criticism or words of caution and eloped less than a month before she was to graduate from high school. Shortly after she got her diploma, the newlyweds set out for California, the alleged scene of Stanley's prior conquests. The plan was for Stanley to pursue his muse and write and for Madelyn to deal with putting food on the table. Madelyn accepted the division of labor and got a job tending the counter at a dry cleaner in the Bay Area. The Dunhams had to suspend their adventure after the Japanese bombed Pearl Harbor, moving back to Kansas to live with her parents. Stanley enlisted in the army in mid-June of 1942, shortly before Madelyn was to give birth to their first child.

A daughter, christened Stanley Ann Dunham, was born on November 29, 1942. It was assumed the baby was named after her father, who was finishing up his military training. It may well be that Madelyn chose the unusual moniker, because her favorite actress, Bette Davis, played the role of Stanley Timberlake in a movie released that summer, *In This Our Life*.[255] Not too long after the newborn was back from the hospital, at some point in 1943, Madelyn's parents assumed responsibility for child-rearing as their daughter had gotten immersed in the war effort, hiring out as an inspector for Boeing Aircraft. Madelyn's hours were long, and became longer in 1944, when the model they were building, the Superfortress, was made a national priority. The workday was 10 hours long. The workweek was six days in succession. Madelyn was on the early shift, which ran from 6 am to 4:45 pm.

In the meantime, Stanley had been assigned to an Ordnance Supply and Maintenance Company and sent to a camp in Boston before being shipped to England half-way through the autumn of 1943. Though his unit was responsible for automobile maintenance, newly-promoted Sergeant Dunham was responsible for information and entertainment, organizing parties to keep up the morale of his men, a role that played to his strengths. By the summer of 1945, Stanley had returned to Kansas, unscathed and seemingly unaffected by the War in any way.

A few months after Stanley was discharged from the service, the Dunhams once again headed out West so Stanley could attend the University of California at Berkeley. He enrolled in a hodgepodge of classes – geology, English, economics, French, journalism – courtesy of the G.I. Bill. Madelyn found employment in the university's admissions office. Stanley was as diligent and successful at college as he had been in high school, that is, not at all, and after two years the family headed back to the Midwest. Stanley took a job in Ponca City, Oklahoma, doing something that he seemed suited for: sales. He was one of a half-dozen salesmen on the payroll of Jay C. Paris Furniture Store. He brought to the job not only a gift for gab, but a knack for helping customers come up with an integrated "decorating scheme." It all seemed to be a perfect match.

Yet three years later, the Dunhams were on the move again, this time to Poplar Furniture in Vernon, Texas. The timing of the move – mid-March – towards the end of Ann's third grade, indicates that the change of venue was not entirely voluntary. Ann completed third grade and all of fourth grade in Vernon. She had a group of pals, became a member of the Friendly Bluebirds, a girl scout troop, and the Fourth Grade Rhythm Group, which supplied young dancers for municipal events. Ann proved to be a decent athlete and, but for the jokes about being named "Stanley," generally fit in. As for Madelyn, she worked as a teller at a bank in Witchita Falls and as an announcer at a local radio station.

At least in retrospect, it was during the Texas phase that the Dunhams saw the ugliness of racism. African Americans were barred from the swimming pool and the library and were banished to the balconies of the movie theaters. Of the local eateries, only one served black customers, and it did so only if they came around to the back. It was not uncommon for people of color to be called "nigras" and "niggers."[256] Much later, Stanley told his grandson that it was the racism encountered in Texas which caused this all-white family to leave. Madelyn confided that Stanley was again having difficulties at work. He was also losing money at cards. In any event, for a variety of reasons a change of scenery was again in order.

Ann completed her sixth grade in Texas, her seventh grade in Kansas, and began her eighth grade in Washington State. For her ninth grade, the Dunhams did not move to another state but did change towns, leaving Seattle proper for a suburb called Mercer Island. At this point the Dunhams were in their ninth rental home, and Ann had never been in the same school for more than two years.

During their Washington phase, Stanley sold furniture for Stanard-Grunbaum in downtown Seattle. He continued to be a big talker with "bohemian" pretensions, writing the occasional verse, "grooving" on jazz and hanging out with Jewish men he had met in business.[257] He had great pride and limited ability and became frustrated because he knew, as did his wife and daughter, that he was the least capable member of the family. Madelyn tried to be the steadying force. She ran the household, managed his tantrums and assured they had enough by working at another bank.

Ann was less patient. She found her father to be an embarrassment, however charming and good-hearted he seemed to her friends. She was interested in ideas and the world, and Stanley was not. She was determined not to be suffocated by the "smallness" that he found safe and comforting.[258] She was book smart, making the honor roll all four years of high school, and he had barely managed to graduate.

Ann was regarded by those who knew her at the time as extremely witty and clever, using these gifts to great effect on classmates who were condescending or cruel. She had a nice smile, the best feature of her rather narrow face. She was a little heavy and saw herself as unattractive. While she did not have a steady or serious boyfriend, she was not a wallflower or a loner. She was a member of a service organization, director of the French club and on the staff of the yearbook. She was an amusing addition to slumber parties, with her talent for mimicry, and a loyal and noisy audience member at sporting events. She graduated with a GPA of 3.35 and was all set to go to the University of Washington with a number of her friends.

But her father had other plans. At 42, Stanley was presented with his fourth, or perhaps fifth, "opportunity of a lifetime." Bob Pratt, who had helped run his family's furniture store in Spokane, had decided to break out on his own and start a business in Hawaii, asking the salesman of one of his former competitors – one Stanley Dunham – to come along for the ride. Stanley readily and enthusiastically agreed, searching once again for "that new start."[259] Madelyn went along with this venture, as she had with all the previous ones, and found a position in the escrow department of the Bank of Hawaii. As to his bookish daughter, who wanted to continue on with the first group of friends she ever had, she was informed that she would have to come with them. At just 17, she was far too young to remain in the States by herself. She would have to do what she was told.

And so, in the fall of 1960, Stanley Ann Dunham began her freshman year as a co-ed at the University of Hawaii. She signed up for an array of courses, including Russian 101. An African "exchange student" in his sophomore year at U of H had signed up as well. He also had an unusual name: Barack Hussein Obama.

Barack Obama Sr. was from Kenya. His father, Hussein Onyango, oversaw the domestic staff of a U.S. Information Service officer. In the 1950s Barack worked as a clerk at an Indian law firm headquartered in the capital city of Nairobi. He was bright, arrogant and ambitious. Both he and his father were friends with Tom Mboya, a politically active advocate for independence, who was seeking to fill the vacuum created with the imprisonment of Jomo Kenyatta, the natural leader of the forces pushing for an end to colonial rule.

Barack had married a Kenyan girl four years his junior in 1957. As the decade ended, Barack was caught up in a movement to send Kenyans to the United States for their higher education. It was supported by nationalists, like Mboya, who saw the need to expand the pool of native intellectuals, and American missionary/educators like Betty Mooney, who for more philosophical reasons had come to the same conclusion. Funding was assembled to airlift deserving students to America, and Barack was selected to be in the first wave of emigrants. In anticipation of his selection, Barack had applied to, and been accepted by, several universities, including his first choice, the University of Hawaii. He was attracted by a glowing write-up in the May 1958 *Saturday Evening Post* which touted its spectacular setting, its commitment to cultural diversity and its favorable tuition policies for out-of-state matriculants. Barack arrived in New York in August of 1959 en route to Honolulu, leaving a son and pregnant wife behind.

Barack immediately let it be known to all who would listen that he planned to complete his course of study within three years, go on to graduate school, likely in econometrics, and then return to his soon-to-be-free country to assume a position in the new government. He was at least five years older and far more mature than the average college freshman. For that reason alone he would have stood out. But he also had a charismatic personality and a booming intellect. He had a deep voice and a wonderful accent. He was argumentative and confident and defiant and flirtatious. He enjoyed singing and dancing and laughing and drinking. He smoked a pipe and wore dress pants and a white shirt, looking more like a professor than an undergraduate. By the end of his second semester he had been honored by Phi Beta Kappa, had become President of the International Students Association and had been chosen to be the student chair of "International Week" scheduled to be held during the summer.

At some point in the fall of 1960 the two students taking first-year Russian met. It is unclear who sought out whom, but very soon Ann Dunham and Barack Hussein Obama had become intimate. Ann was clearly vulnerable. She was by herself. Her father was vapid and talked too much. Her mother was practical, but cold. She understood all the differences: in nationality, in race, in age, in sexual experience, in personality. But Ann was a risk-taker, and Barack seemed like a risk worth taking. They were married on February 2, 1961, when Ann was three-months pregnant.

Stanley and Madelyn were opposed to the union, but Stanley's mother had run off with Ralph Dunham at 15 despite her parents' objections, and Madelyn's own marriage to Stanley was contrary to her parents' advice. Barack's father, too, was supposedly antagonistic, either because "he did not want the family blood sullied by a white woman" or because Barack was already married and had a family.[260] The INS was also troubled. It saw Obama as a "playboy" and an apparent bigamist, not overly impressed by Barack's assurance that he was considered single under Kenyan law by virtue of the fact that he had told his Kenyan wife they were divorced.[261]

Barack Hussein Obama II, soon to be called Barry, was born on August 4, 1961. The future president later said that Barack Sr. left Hawaii "back in 1963," when he was two years old, suggesting that his father was around during his infancy.[262] In fact, Barack Sr. left Hawaii in June 1962, when Barry was not yet one.[263] More importantly, Ann and her newborn had already left Hawaii themselves before that, in late August 1961, when Barry was only three weeks old. Mother and son settled in Seattle so that Ann could resume her college career at the University of Washington. Whether her departure was triggered by knowledge of her husband's bigamy, his continued womanizing or some kind of abuse is unknown.

Back in Seattle Ann pretended things were fine with Barack Sr. She and Barry lived in a 500-square-foot apartment. She began her studies with two evening courses and, as she hoped, her grades improved. After completing six courses and auditing one, Ann wrapped things up early in the summer of 1962, and was preparing to return to Hawaii just as Barack Sr. was leaving the island to do graduate work at Harvard.

What young Barry knew or heard or believed about his mother's breakup with his father is not clear. One story he was told was that Ann and he could not go to Harvard with Barack Sr. because Harvard, unlike NYU, had not offered him a scholarship sufficient to support a family. Another was that they could not reunite with him in Kenya after graduate school because Barry's black grandfather was still adamantly opposed to the union and his white grandmother was afraid he would be killed by the Mau Maus.

Neither story was true nor made much sense, except as another in a pattern of tales told to present his natural father in a good, or at least interesting, light. There was the time Barack Sr. and Ann took a day trip with another African student to the Pali Lookout, elevation 1,168 feet. Barack's countryman wanted to try Barack's pipe, and after inhaling his first puff, lost hold of it, and it skittled down the mountainside. Barack picked the terrified student off the ground and dangled him over the fence to teach him a lesson about the value of private property. Or the time Barack was asked to sing some Kenyan folk songs at an International Music Festival, only to find out that the program was filled with semi-professionals. Rather than beg off, he gamely belted out some tunes to the big crowd, winning a big round of applause for his pluck. Or the time he was in a bar and a white customer shouted he should not have to drink "next to a nigger,"[264] causing Barack to calmly talk to him about the evils of racism and the dream he had of equality. Afterwards, the man felt so badly, he gave Barack a hundred dollar bill.

On January 30, 1964, Ann filed for divorce, citing "grievous mental suffering."[265] Barack Sr. could not have cared less. By then he was on to his next conquest, Ruth Baker. Ruth was in some ways Ann's opposite. She was an Easterner, not an itinerant Midwesterner. She was 27, not 21. She was Jewish not Christian. She was upper not lower middle class. But like Ann, Ruth was an only child who was lonely and had a "big social conscience."[266] And like Ann, Ruth fell under Barack Sr.'s spell. She followed him to Nairobi when he left Harvard, and they became man and wife on December 24, 1964.

When Ann returned to Hawaii to continue school, she met Lolo Soetoro, an Indonesian who was attending the University's East-West Center, courtesy of a 21-month visa. To supplement his stipend, Lolo moonlighted as a tennis instructor. Ann was one of his pupils. Barry described Lolo as "short and brown, handsome, with thick black hair and features that could have as easily been Mexican or Samoan as Indonesian."[267] Ann's budding relationship with Lolo likely explained the timing of her divorce. The decree became final on March 5, 1964, and she and Lolo got married ten days later on March 15, 1964. Barry was two and a half.

Shortly after the wedding, Lolo sought an indefinite visa extension, arguing in part that his return to Indonesia would have a traumatic effect on his wife. With the subsequent overthrow of Sukarno's regime, Lolo and Ann reversed course. They decided to go back to Indonesia for a few years so Lolo could perfect the process of formally immigrating to the U.S. and becoming an American citizen.

In June of 1966, Lolo left for Jakarta, having found government employment as a surveyor. Ann remained in Hawaii to complete her undergraduate course work. To economize, she lived with Stanley and Madelyn, earning $425 a month grading papers and tutoring, $50 of which she contributed for household expenses. Barry started school in Honolulu that fall, having just turned five. He was taller and chunkier than the others in his class. He was described as very attentive, though a bit shy.

Ann had hoped to join Lolo in February 1967, when she was due to receive her anthropology degree. However, there were last-minute course-credit issues, and the schedule slipped. She finally graduated in August, around the time of Barry's sixth birthday. Mother and son arrived in Indonesia in October 1967, with Barry determined to protect his mother "from whatever might come."[268] Lolo did not have a car, only a motorcycle. Their rented house was on a narrow, unpaved dirt road in a working class district in Jakarta, a city of four and a half million people. Like the other structures on the block, it was made of whitewashed stucco and had a red tile roof. There were four un-airconditioned rooms and the most basic lavatory. The backyard was a surprise, housing Lolo's menagerie of chickens, snakes, turtles, miniature crocodiles and a small ape.

Barry ran free in Jakarta, careening through the streets, playing in the nearby cemetery, climbing trees, catching crickets, having kite fights and getting thoroughly dirty each day before it was time to go back home. Though he arrived in Indonesia not knowing the language, the customs or the mythology of his new home, within six months, at least as he remembered, all of these mysteries were solved. He began first grade in January 1968, the abbreviated school day running from 7 to 9:30. At the end of the term, he had proved particularly adept in mathematics, and was in the top 20% in all subjects but Bahasa Indonesia, the Indonesian language. In second grade Barry was in Class A and was a lively participant, always raising his hand to be called upon. His third grade teacher was impressed with how bold he was, especially compared to his classmates. But for all his energy and enthusiasm, he was not regarded as a show-off but seen as "a stand-up boy, a leader."[269] Teachers and students recalled that he was a "generous teammate," letting the younger, smaller players get the glory in, for example, throwing at the runner in the baseball-like game they played.[270]

Lolo liked Barry and the feelings were mutual. He taught him to box, to eat raw peppers, dog meat, grasshopper and snake, to change a flat tire and to make the appropriate opening move in chess. On the outside, or to the outside, Lolo was easygoing and gentle and had a winning way. But he had an old-fashioned, misogynistic view that women were basically flawed because they were weak. He counseled Barry against softness in dealing with beggars and servants. Over time, Lolo became remote and sullen, and he increasingly drank.

This caused, or perhaps was a result of, a chill in his relationship with Ann. Lolo hardly talked to her. One neighbor reported that he sometimes heard screaming from the Soetoro home, and not the screaming of a child. Another said that Lolo frequently brought women to his house when his wife was away. Despite it all, Ann remained optimistic and determined to make the best of it. She taught English to Indonesian government employees and businessmen. She became involved with local and foreign women and with Lolo's family. Ann was a survivor.

Despite Lolo's personal problems, his career was prospering.[271] Through family connections he was hired as a "mid-level executive" by Union Oil.[272] This enabled the Soetoros to move in January 1970 to a nicer neighborhood and into a bigger, nicer house. With the move, Barry was transferred to a school filled with children from better families, the sons and daughters of professionals and government people. He was nine and halfway through third grade. Though at school he now mingled with children of affluence, his friends were the sons of the chauffeur of the doctor from whom the Soetoros rented. For fun, they played board games and racket sports.

Barry's typical day began at 4 am, with Ann tutoring him for three hours on an American curriculum supplied by a correspondence course. After a shower he would have a breakfast of pastry or cereal and a glass of milk and then be taken to school by Ann or Lolo or the family servant. He would remain there from 7 am till noon, when Ann would pick him up and bring him home for lunch. In the afternoons, Barry played with the neighborhood kids and would invariably be a sweaty mess by the time Ann got back for a dinner of corned beef or meatballs or, if he were lucky, oxtail soup. The day ended with vitamins, homework and bed. Ann had a routine for herself, as well, working from morning to night on lesson plans, on correspondence with friends and relatives and on recording her thoughts on Indonesian culture. For enjoyment she played tennis and studied batiks.

It was while in Indonesia that Barry became conscious of race and of the fact that he was different from others, reading about the black man who tried to peel off or lighten the color of his skin. Ann tried to make him proud of this differentness, talking of his father as a model, at least in seeking to better himself, and as the source of her son's "brains" and "character."[273] She fed him materials on the civil rights movement, the music of Mahalia Jackson and the speeches of Martin Luther King. She regaled him with stories of black achievers: Thurgood Marshall, Sidney Poitier, Fannie Lou Hamer and Lena Horne. But to Barry her efforts were naïve attempts to romanticize the reality that being an African-American, literally so in his case, was a complication and a burden.

Barry portrayed his mother as being lonely because she was in a faraway place with no friends or blood relations. But Ann loved Indonesia. She was lonely because she was in another bad marriage with another charmer who was unfaithful, unkind and perhaps abusive. Ann and Lolo also had grown more opposite in their outlooks and aspirations. Lolo wanted status and wealth; Ann wanted knowledge and culture. They could not have been less similar.

Barry was sent to Hawaii in the summer of 1970, right before he turned 10. Ann, who had become pregnant around the time of the move "uptown," was in the last trimester of her second pregnancy, and her relations with Lolo were foundering. Madelyn accompanied Barry back to Indonesia after the birth of his half-sister, Maya, but Madelyn was hobbled with a bandaged leg and was not much help with an infant. Stanley stayed back in Honolulu. After two decades selling furniture he had switched to peddling insurance. The product was different, as were the gimmicks, and he liked the slower pace and the freedom it gave him to while away the time with his buddies at the local eateries, telling tales and downing a drink or two.

At 10 Barry returned to Honolulu to live with his grandparents, while Ann, Lolo and Maya remained in Indonesia. A year later, in September 1971, he entered the fifth grade of Punahou, "the oldest, largest, most prestigious private school in Hawaii," its picturesque campus occupying 76 acres and housing 28 buildings.[274] His admission, on scholarship, was a function of a confluence of events and factors that allowed him to beat the one-in-ten odds of acceptance. His mother proved effective working the system, even from overseas; Barry did well in a succession of interviews over the summer; a scholarship program had recently been initiated to admit talented students who would add to the diversity of the student body; and, perhaps most critically, both Stanley's and Madelyn's bosses, who were Punahou alumni, interceded on Barry's behalf.

Stanley and Madelyn, who had once lived in a roomy house, were now cramped in a two-bedroom apartment on the 10th floor of a downtown highrise. It was small and all that they could afford, given Stanley's commission-based insurance job and Madelyn's low salary as a bank employee. The beginning of the school year was a challenge for Barry: his clothes were "old-fashioned," his classmates had been together since kindergarten, most of the students lived near one another in the tonier parts of the city, no one was interested in his sports – soccer and badminton – and he had no skill in theirs – football and skateboarding.[275]

In December 1971, as Barry was beginning to settle in at Punahou, both Barack Sr. and Ann returned to Honolulu, where they spent over a month more or less together. By this point, Barack Sr. had fallen on hard times. He had been involved in several serious automobile accidents, and he had lost his job because of his erratic behavior and heavy drinking. His third wife, Ruth, had filed for divorce, having had her fill of his emotional and physical abuse and flagrant philandering. He looked a bit gaunt and moved shakily.

Barack Sr.'s fashion sense tended toward the foppish, with his ivory-topped cane and scarlet ascot. He behaved as if he were the lord of the manor, appropriating Stanley's favorite chair, sipping beer while Madelyn and Ann prepared meals and cleaned up and bossing Barry around as if he were a regular part of his life. When he spoke, it was to make pronouncements, not to have a conversation.

Barack Sr. had come to Hawaii with a purpose: to convince Ann to reunite with him and for the whole family, including Barry and presumably Maya, to go back to Kenya. His and Ann's complicated marital details were not discussed. His only hope was to mesmerize his 29-year-old ex-wife into ignoring all the difficulties that had only grown since he had lured her teenaged former self to the altar. Fortunately, Ann had the good sense not to be fooled twice and declined Barack Sr.'s nonsensical scheme.

Barry was unaware of the attempt at reconciliation. For him, even with the overall strangeness of the entire visit, the moments of highest tension came in the run-up to his father's appearance before Barry's fifth grade class, triggered by an invitation from Barry's teacher, who had spent two years in Kenya. In the end, the elder Barack performed admirably, lecturing on the importance of education, the grandeur of Africa and Kenya's quest for independence. His final words were filled with praise for his son's upholding the Obama tradition of academic excellence.

Barry then spent the Christmas break with his father. The highlights were a gift of an orange basketball, an outing to a Dave Brubeck concert and a private dance demonstration and lesson. Barack Sr. left the islands sometime in early January. Barry would never see him again.

Ann and Maya, too, left in early 1972, bound for Indonesia, and she was gone for over six months, not returning until the following autumn. As her 11-year-old son began sixth grade, Ann entered the University of Hawaii to begin graduate studies in anthropology. She had been granted a full scholarship and had a part-time job teaching handicrafts at one of the city museums. The three Soetoros – Barry, Maya and Ann – lived in a cramped flat almost adjacent to Punahou and less than two miles from U of H. There was no surplus cash, the refrigerator was often bare and the rooms were not always spotless. Barry helped out by looking after his sister and doing the laundry and grocery shopping.

Not much is written about Barry's "middle school" years. He seemed to be liked by both students and teachers and did not get into trouble. He did well in his studies, though he did not get straight As. He was of mixed race, but that was not unusual in Hawaii during the '60s when one-third of the marriages "were interracial in some fashion."[276] Indeed, at Punahou his teachers went out of their way to celebrate the school's diversity. There is a lovely photograph of Barry and seven of his classmates, posed in front of a blackboard under the caption, "Whether you're a Tamura or a Ching or an Obama, we share the same world."[277]

In his free time, Barry did sports. For the first couple of years, his focus was on tennis, which both his mother and stepfather played. He was good at it, though its significance in memory had nothing to do with his athletic prowess. Instead, it linked to the day that the tennis pro, watching Barry run his finger across a "draw sheet," told him to remove his hands from the schedule because he might get it dirty. A friend who was there said, "Barry's hands weren't grubby."[278] There was no question that the pro was making a crude and cruel racial joke – "that his darker skin would somehow soil the draw" – and it became one of those incidents that Barry recalled as he later grappled with his ethnic identity.[279]

The sport that became Barry's passion, even before high school, was basketball. It was so different from tennis. It was gritty, and urban. It became a link to black America, given the demographics of the game both at the college and professional level. In real time, it was simply a source of fun and exercise and companionship. He was on the courts at nearby Punahou or the Washington Middle School, dribbling and shooting and feinting, before and after classes, during breaks and on weekends. His posse was made up of 10 regulars, that at times swelled to 20. In these early years, Barry was not only unusually tall, but also had greater "body mass" than his mates, and he used these advantages to get to the rim.[280] As he grew even taller and got rid of the extra mass, his love of the game deepened.

When Barry finished the eighth grade, Ann went to Indonesia to do the field work required to complete her degree requirements. He was invited to accompany her, but had no interest in being uprooted and starting over yet again. As he explained it, he had come to an implicit agreement with his grandparents which gave him a palatable alternative: "I could live with them and they'd leave me alone so long as I kept my trouble out of sight."[281] So Barry moved in with Madelyn and Stanley, reclaiming the room which had been his grandfather's study. It was not an ideal situation.

Though his friends loved Stanley, Barry found him sad and depressing. The insurance business was frustrating. Stanley was reduced to making cold calls, asking strangers to meet with him to talk about things they would just as soon ignore. Since he was basically paid a commission on sales, if he could not schedule appointments he could not sell policies, and if he could not sell policies he made no money. There were good evenings, when he was able to fill his calendar. On these occasions he would regale Barry with war stories or the newest jokes or his plans for writing a book of poetry or finishing an oil painting or building a dream house. But those evenings were rare. Stanley's salary did not reach $10,000 in any of these years, and he was no longer the family's principal breadwinner. Madelyn was, having advanced through patience and sheer doggedness to be the first female vice president of a neighborhood bank. As always, she was the practical one, but the burden of practicality had worn her down, and she took refuge in alcohol. Stanley and Madelyn were still a couple, but their relationship, which had been "strained" when they came to Hawaii, had gotten worse over time, as Madelyn lost patience with Stanley's "instability and often-violent temper" and grew "ashamed of his crude, ham-fisted manners."[282] The Dunhams were living largely separate and very lonely lives. At night, Stanley would be propped dozing in front of the television, while Madelyn repaired to her room to read the latest thriller.

From the perspective of those who knew him in high school, Barry Obama was an extremely friendly, capable, untroubled teenager. He was far more attached to his basketball than his books. And he was a truly good kid. Eric Kusunoki, his homeroom teacher, described him as "always well behaved, very courteous, very well-mannered to everybody," not like an "Eddie Haskell" but sincerely.[283] Barry "[a]llways had a big smile" and was "always nice," in a "subtle" and "low key" way that was not designed to attract attention to himself.[284] Kusunoki said he could not remember Barry's "having a bad day."[285]

Of course, Barry did have "bad days." All adolescents do. A classmate two years ahead of him said Barry wondered about his mother's sense of priorities and that he was "upset" that she never seemed to have "time for him anymore."[286] Barry and two other friends, one black and one part Indian, would get together to talk about how they were perceived racially and about discrimination and other social issues. They jokingly referred to their informal gatherings at the edge of a stone staircase on the Punahou campus as the "Ethnic Corner."[287] While their "chats" were serious, they were hardly "radical" or "bitter."[288] To the extent they also talked about their aspirations, Barry's dream was to be "an all-pro basketballer."[289]

Barry belonged to another set that engaged in no "soul searching" to speak of. It was known as the Choom Gang.[290] All its members attended Punahou and shared a love of basketball and/or pot, the bulk of them loving both. Barry definitely had a leadership role in this group, starting trends designed to ensure that not a particle of aromatic smoke was wasted. When the Gang was not in a sealed car getting high, they were playing pick-up ball in a so-called Hack League. The games were on weekends, when school was in session, and any day of the week, when school was out. The style of play was "all out," with flying elbows, hard body checks and constant "trash talking."[291] When the Gang was not smoking dope or running up and down the court, it was body surfing on the beaches or drag racing or listening to music or drinking beer.

As to school itself, Barry preferred history and literature to the sciences. He did well in his courses, without breaking the proverbial sweat, writing papers and studying for tests at the last minute. He was not a member of the National Honor Society nor at the top of his class. He spoke only when he had something to say. He was an effective debater because he had a facile mind and could think on the fly. He did not run for office in student government or seek any leadership positions. Even then, he had a quality of "cool." One of Barry's admirers, and rivals, described him as radiating a kind of "sophisticated detachment."[292]

In the summer of 1978, between Barry's junior and senior years, this "detachment" tested his mother's patience. Ann had come back to Honolulu for a short stay in connection with her studies, though she was largely living with her academic advisor. One of the Choom Gang had been arrested for possession of marijuana, and Ann wanted to know all the details. Barry answered her questions, calmly telling her she need not worry that he would put himself at risk. The inquisition continued, Ann pivoting from Barry's jailed friend to his plans for the future. When Barry said he might stay in Hawaii after graduation and just "stick around Honolulu," she became livid, berating him for acting like "some good-time Charlie."[293] Perhaps Barry was being flippant, but it struck a nerve in his mother who had struggled so hard to get a an education. If Ann's objective was to make Barry more serious, her talk had its desired effect. As Ann told Barry when he reacted to her tapping into his "guilt feelings," guilt is a "highly underrated emotion."[294]

Barry's "detachment" was in evidence everywhere but on the basketball court. Though he was a regular in the Choom Gang's pick-up games, that did not translate into a starting position on the Punahou varsity. To make it to that level meant proceeding from Junior Varsity A to Junior Varsity AA to Varsity A to Varsity AA. Barry did not get to the Varsity AA squad until his senior year and made it then only after the coach demoted two other seniors. While he had good instincts, could "zero in on an opening" and was quick to the basket, he was not an inspired shooter and had trouble elevating off the floor.[295] But Barry, like his mother, had an intense will, and that was what made him stand out and why he was added to the roster.

Barry did not play often on a team with a notable starting five and several stronger bench players. Even so, he treasured "for the first time in his life" being "a member of a cohesive unit with shared goals."[296] The team was coached by Chris McLaughlin, who had already led Punahou to the state championship in 1975, following it up with trips to the state finals in 1977 and 1978. McLaughlin was determined to make it to the finals again in 1979, which was not good news for subs like Barry. On February 2, Barry got on the court, but only because the star shooting guard got cold-cocked by an errant van door. During a tournament later in the season, he was inserted in the second half and scored a half dozen points. And in the state finals, in what Coach McLaughlin called "as good a game as I've ever seen a high school team play," Barry hit a bucket, passed effectively and was strong on defense in Punahou's 60-28 thrashing of its underdog opponent.[297] In an uncharacteristic display of exuberance, Barry made sure that he would be associated with this magic moment, peppering the school correspondent with his take on events and succeeding to get his name in print: "'You know,' said Barry Obama in a quiet moment off to the side, 'These are the best bunch of guys. We made so many sacrifices to get here.'"[298]

In describing his high school years in his autobiography, Obama hardly touched on his basketball career, but as advertised in the subtitle, told his "Story of Race and Inheritance." He recounted the black authors he read his senior year: Baldwin, Ellison, Hughes, Wright, DuBois, Malcolm X. He told of his grandmother's fear of a black man whose odd behavior made her anxious and how "utterly alone" that made him feel.[299] He told of his mother being teased by her classmates as a "Nigger lover" and "Dirty Yankee" for playing with a black girl.[300] He told of his grandfather being informed by fellow salesmen to only deal with black customers after hours. He told of his grandmother being lambasted by a secretary at her bank for addressing an African American cleaning man as "Mister."[301]

The impression is that all these stories were passed on to Obama during his boyhood and that he struggled with them at the time. He said as much in a note to the *Punahou Bulletin* in 1999, recalling that in high school he grappled with his "identity a bit harder than most."[302] But did he? He grew up in Hawaii in a culture that was filled with people of color and diverse backgrounds. He personally encountered very few episodes of racism and none of discrimination. Barack Obama Sr. was not an illiterate no-account but a Phi Beta Kappa intellectual who had gone to Harvard. To be sure, Barry Obama had to cope with a lot: a father who deserted him and a mother who loved him from afar during many of his formative years. It is just not clear that he was wrestling with identity issues when he was growing up.

And if he was wrestling with them, he did a masterful job of keeping these anxieties to himself. His homeroom teacher remarked that if Barry was struggling, "[H]e kept the lid on. . . [I]t never came out in the way he behaved or the way he reacted."[303] A Chinese/Polish friend said he never sensed Barry suffered from "any bitterness, identity crisis, or internal strife."[304] A black friend said that the frequent talks that he and Barry had about their backgrounds were "not agonizing" but were "just sort of for fun."[305] A Filipino/Czech friend said that though they spent lots of time together he "had very little clue" that Barry felt anguished.[306]

Barack Obama II graduated from Punahou on June 2, 1979, two months before his 18th birthday. He did not receive any academic honors, but had been accepted to Occidental College, a small, well-respected liberal arts school located on the outskirts of Los Angeles.[307] In a "dress-up" photo of the class, taken on the eve of the ceremonies, Barry was decked out in a white suit and open shirt à la John Travolta in *Saturday Night Fever*. Though Ann returned for the festivities, Barry's yearbook page thanked his grandparents, the Choom Gang and his drug dealer, but not her.

Over the years to come, Barack Obama would undergo a metamorphosis that ultimately would lead him to the world of politics. But as he prepared to leave Hawaii that change was a ways off. The only clue of what was to come was a poem he had written as a little boy in Jakarta:

> My name is Barry Soetoro. I am a third-grade student at SD Asisi.
> My mom is my idol.
> My teacher is Ibu Fer. I have a lot of friends.
> I live near the school. I usually walk to the school with my mom, then go home by myself.
> Someday I want to be president. I love to visit all the places in Indonesia.
> Done. The eeeeeeeeend.[308]

What are the odds of becoming the President of the United States? According to the 2000 U.S. Census, there were slightly over 40,514,622 males between the ages of 43 and 70, the range of the youngest and oldest men elected President.[309] That means in the year 2000 the chances of a man becoming President was about 1 in 40,500,000 or .0000025%.

Once again, I have also calculated the odds more conservatively. On the one hand, I expanded the numerator to include other significant elected politicians: Vice Presidents, Governors and Lieutenant Governors, U.S. Senators and Congressmen, mayors of cities with populations above 100,000, speakers of state legislatures and state legislators who work relatively full-time and were relatively well-paid.[310] On the other hand, I limited the denominator to include only the proportion of boys who participated in school government or in a public service club in high school.[311] The overall effect of these changes is to improve the odds from one chance in about 40,500,000 to one chance in approximately 2,400 or from .0000025% to .04%. An extraordinary improvement, but still not exactly a sure bet.

PART THREE

How Beginnings Mattered

I. On the Way Up

Obviously, the modest beginnings of the 21 future icons described in this book did not prevent them from achieving greatness. Less obvious, and perhaps surprising, is the fact that their modest beginnings did not negatively affect their choice of career path and had little if anything to do with the major breakthroughs and setbacks they encountered along the way. This point is best made by looking at the milestones and turning points of six of our greats on their way to the top. I have chosen Babe Ruth and Hank Aaron for the ballplayers, James Cagney and Cary Grant for the movie stars, and Abraham Lincoln and Ronald Reagan for the Presidents.

A. The Ballplayers

Babe Ruth and Henry Aaron grew up in separate eras. Ruth began playing professional ball in 1914 with the Baltimore Orioles in the Federal League. Aaron began playing professional ball in 1954 with the Indianapolis Clowns in the Negro League. Ruth spent virtually all of his career in the American League, just as Aaron spent virtually all of his in the National League. Interestingly, as their "swan song," both returned to the city where it all began, but with a team in the *opposite* league. Ruth started as an American League Boston Red Sox and finished as a National League Boston Brave, while Aaron started as a National League Milwaukee Brave and finished as an American League Milwaukee Brewer. Ruth grew up in the Northeast and Aaron in the South. Aaron was an African American, and Ruth was ridiculed for having African American features. Both achieved prominence as home run hitters.

HOW BEGINNINGS MATTERED

Babe Ruth

It is likely that George Herman Ruth Jr. was familiar with makeshift bats and balls while running wild in the streets of Baltimore's Pigtown. However, the first and most critical watershed event on his road to athletic superstardom was his parents' fateful decision to send him at age seven and a half to St. Mary's Industrial School for Boys. As we have seen, St. Mary's approached baseball with the fervor of "a sacrament," and it was there that he fell under the spell of Brother Mathias, a baseball phenomenon in his own right, who functioned as George's trainer, coach and manager. During the St. Mary's years George learned all the skills of a ballplayer: how to hit, pitch, catch, run and slide, spending more time honing those skills than most professionals.

The next milestone was George's acquisition at age 19 by the minor league Baltimore Orioles. To effect the transition, the team's owner, Jack Dunn, formally became George's legal guardian. Dunn was thrilled with the young rookie, writing, "[T]his fellow Ruth is the greatest young ballplayer who ever reported to training camp."[1] George's pitching performance justified Dunn's enthusiasm, as he notched a 14-6 record by the Fourth of July, catapulting the Orioles into first place in the International League. George's wide-eyed behavior off the field also attracted notice, one of his teammates calling him a "babe in the woods," giving rise to his enduring nickname.[2]

While "Babe" was an unquestioned success, both on the mound and at the plate – he was batting .300 – by the second week in July he had become the property of Joe Lannin's Boston Red Sox. Dunn's Orioles could not compete for spectators with the new Baltimore "Terrapins." At games when the Orioles had paid attendance of 20, the Terrapins were drawing 20,000. Dunn was losing $1,000 a day. The only way he could cut his deficit was by selling some players. Lannin, who had previously bailed Dunn out when he could not meet payroll, was the lucky beneficiary of his friend's dire straits. The Red Sox purchased Ruth and two other Orioles for somewhere between $8,500 and $25,000. In a space of less than six months, George Herman Ruth, Jr. had gone from ward of the state to professional athlete.

Boston's player-manager Bill Corrigan immediately saw Babe's pitching potential. While his talent was still raw, Corrigan recalled "he had a barrel of stuff, his speed was blinding, and his ball was alive."[3] Though he started with the minor league Providence team, where his 9-3 record helped the "Grays" displace the Orioles and win the International League pennant, he was promoted to the Big League to stay as the 1914 season wound down.

Over the next three years Babe more than earned his keep as a dominant pitcher on a dominant team, the Red Sox making it to back-to-back World Series in 1915 and 1916 and coming in second to the Chicago White Sox in 1917. In 1915, Babe had a winning percentage of 75%, the best in the American League. The following two years he was the premier southpaw in all of baseball, with marks of 23-12 and 24-13 respectively. His 1.75 ERA in 1916 put him atop the American League, and his 2.04 ERA a year later was nothing to be embarrassed about. But Babe was also hitting well, with an average of .315 in 1915, .272 in 1916 and .325 in 1917. And embedded in these averages were 4 homers in 1915, 3 in 1916 and 2 in 1917. While these home run totals sound meager against what he later accomplished, back then, as Ruth pointed out, "a guy with 10 or 12 homers was called a home-run king," and that guy, unlike the Babe, took the field every day.[4]

In 1918 the game of baseball in Boston changed with America's entry into the First World War and the departure of veterans. Babe, who by now was married and therefore exempt from service, was enlisted to fill gaps in the defense created by the exodus of position players. So Ed Barrow, Boston's replacement manager, slotted Babe into the lineup particularly when a righty was on the mound for the other side. Whether the increase in plate appearances was instigated by Babe or by the new skipper is a subject of debate. Whoever came up with the idea, Babe went from 123 at-bats in 1917 to 432 in 1919. At some point Ruth made it clear that he could not continue to both pitch and play the field and that his preference was to give up the mound. In 1920 Babe got his wish: his regular pitching days were over. So was his affiliation with the Red Sox.

Babe's acquisition by the New York Yankees was the final milestone on his way to the top. The Yankees wanted Ruth because they wanted a pennant, and their manager Miller Huggins told the owners the way to do so was to "[g]et me Babe Ruth."[5] The Sox owner, Harry Frazee, was willing to sell Ruth because he needed money. He was in arrears on a note to Lannin arising out of his purchase of the team. Moreover, his real passion as an investor was not baseball but Broadway theater. The Yankees paid Frazee between $100,000 and $125,000 for Ruth and lent him another $300,000 or so. Frazee satisfied his baseball debts and bought into several theatrical ventures. He justified the sale to irate New England fans, claiming Ruth had to go because his salary demands were excessive and his personal behavior unacceptable. Frazee denounced the Babe as "one of the most selfish and inconsiderate men that ever wore a uniform."[6]

There is no question that the 21-year-old Babe was a handful. Ruth recounted a conversation with Huggins before the Yankee deal was announced, in which his future manager asked "whether you will behave yourself if we do obtain your services for the New York club."[7] Babe provided Huggins with the necessary reassurances, but given his frame of mind as a parolee from St. Mary's, they could not provide much comfort:

> I was a kid with a healthy appetite and a zest for life who had been in a reform school practically all the time since he [sic] was seven years of age. Life looked like a great big lark to me, and after those long hours in St. Mary's tailor shop, baseball was like paradise.[8]

It was paradise for Ruth to eat whatever he wanted when he wanted it, and his capacity for consumption of all manner of meats and sweets was legendary. It was paradise for him to buy expensive, often garish clothes. It was paradise for him to purchase the latest model car and drive it above the speed limit, crack-ups being part of the bargain. It was paradise to drink whiskey and beer and bet on whatever tickled his fancy at the moment. For the first time the Babe had dough, earning $3,500 in 1915 and double that by 1919. And, as his Boston manager pointed out, "He had no idea whatsoever of money. You have to remember his background."[9]

Ruth did not seem to understand or feel that he was bound by any rules or conventions, and he was sometimes – frequently – simply out of control. When he was on the mound in a game against the Senators on June 23, 1917, he was so upset by an umpire's calling a four-pitch walk that he "just went crazy" – his words – rushed the plate and punched him in the jaw.[10] On Memorial Day weekend 1918, while the Red Sox were en route from Washington to Philadelphia, Babe jumped off the train in Baltimore and did not bother to show up until right before the first pitch the next day. His sexual appetite was as unbridled as his appetite for food, and he would often ignore curfews to visit prostitutes or other willing partners, often in multiple numbers, sometimes in sequence, sometimes all at once. His status as a married man was irrelevant.[11]

In 1922, one of Ruth's two "slump" years, he was suspended for nearly a quarter of the season and forced to forfeit his share of World Series earnings for ignoring the Commissioner's prohibition of post-season barnstorming by World Series participants. After he returned, he was ejected for throwing dirt in an umpire's face and fined for vaulting into the stands to challenge fans who were booing him. In a subsequent dispute with an umpire, this one accompanied with threats and "vulgar and vicious language," he received an additional five-game suspension and was relieved of his captaincy.[12] He even got into a fight with Wally Pipp, the Yankees' first baseman. The commotions at the ballpark occurred against a backdrop of Ruth's continuing frivolity off the field. There is a famous photograph, staged by the Babe, of him and his teammates at a Chicago brewery.

1925, the second "slump" year, Babe was even worse. He traded punches with Yankee pitcher Waite Hoyt, and Huggins had to break it up.[13] Towards the end of the summer, Huggins confronted Ruth with a dossier of misdeeds on his return from an all-night stand at a well-known St. Louis brothel. With the approval of senior management, Babe was given a $5,000 fine and suspended for the rest of the season.

While Babe's lack of discipline and reckless behavior soured his relationship with certain teammates, management and baseball's official hierarchy, it did not affect how he played the game. And though his excesses were sometimes attributed by him and others to his "tough going as a kid" and "his unsettled times at home,"[14] that does not mean it can be explained away by his lower-class status. Ruth might have been a better citizen had he had better parents, not wealthier ones. Barry Bonds had an even worse reputation – he was often mean-spirited and generally combatively arrogant – yet he was brought up in a world of affluence.

Henry Aaron

There is a great paradox in the life of Henry Aaron. Race has everything to do with who he was and how he saw himself as both a man and as a baseball player. However, it had no impact on his performance as an athlete, except as a motivating factor. It did not affect his hit production or his fielding ability or his playing time. Nor did his impoverished and anonymous beginnings, as distinct from race, affect his journey from the shack in Toulminville to enshrinement at Cooperstown.

Mobile, as described earlier, was a baseball town, with dozens of teams, formal and informal, for kids and grown-ups; it bred baseball players; it hosted major league exhibitions on the way to and from training camp. It had a veritable "obsession" with the national pastime, and it was both fortuitous and fortunate that a baseball obsessed-boy was one of its sons.[15]

Henry's birthplace apart, the initial turning point for Henry came in 1947, when Jackie Robinson debuted with the Brooklyn Dodgers. As Aaron put it, Robinson "gave us our dreams. He breathed baseball into the black community . . ."[16] His breakthrough gave Henry the faith that he would make it into the majors and would do so while Jackie was still in uniform.

Then, as also described before, Ed Scott appeared on the scene. It was Scott who convinced Mama Stella to let Henry play for his Black Bears. It was Scott who arranged for the game between the Bears and the Clowns that led to Henry's first professional contract. And it was Scott, to a large extent, who interested major league teams in Henry once he began tearing up the Negro League. He, therefore, deserves some of the credit for Henry taking the giant step of becoming a Milwaukee Brave.

Henry's first stop in the Braves' organization was with its farm team in Eau Claire, Wisconsin. It was another watershed event. Until then, virtually all of Henry's social interaction had been with blacks. From there on out, Henry's world would be primarily white. And Eau Claire was lily white, with only 27 people of color among the 35,000 who called the city home.

During that summer of 1952 Henry always felt he was being "watched."[17] His stay was made tolerable because he was "sort of adopted" by a white baseball-loving family[18] and because he roomed at the YMCA with the two other African Americans on the team. His baseball career almost ended a week after it began when he accidentally beaned a runner turning a double play. The player lapsed into a coma, and Henry was ready to quit, until his brother told him he would be "crazy" to even think of "walking out on the best break [he] could ever hope to get."[19] His manager, an Alabaman named Marion "Bill" Adair, said it was hard to tell how smart Henry was because he was so quiet, adding that though he "looked" lazy, he really was not.[20] While Henry was not particularly happy in Eau Claire, he was a sensation in the Northern League, selected to play shortstop in its annual All Star Game and the unanimous choice for Rookie of the Year.[21]

As a result of his stellar performance up North, Henry began 1953 with the Braves' Jacksonville affiliate in the South Atlantic or Sally League. The Sally League was not integrated, and he along with Felix Mantilla and Horace Garner, the team's two other black pioneers, were subjected to racism in its ugliest forms. At the home opener they were greeted with cries of "nigger," "burrhead," and "eight-ball."[22] In Augusta there was rock throwing. In Montgomery there were death threats. At almost every game, the three were treated as target practice by the pitchers. Sally League President Dick Butler recalled that for all the generalized unrest, "most of the focus was on Aaron."[23]

When the three trailblazers were off the field or traveling, Jim Crow laws meant they seldom shared a hotel or a meal or an evening at the movies with their teammates. There were some whites who gave them a break: first baseman Joe Andrews, who stuck up for them by taking on redneck fans; outfielder Pete Whisenant, who found integrated diners where they could all have supper together; and Ben Geraghty, their slight, grizzled manager, who welcomed and schooled them and made sure he found his way to their low-rent and separate lodgings to drink some beer and shoot the breeze. For Aaron, there was also Barbara Lucas, the Florida A&M coed who took him into her home and in October 1953 became his wife.

On the field, Henry was again stellar, winning MVP honors and helping power Jacksonville to a pennant. He also received an invitation from the Milwaukee Braves to participate in spring training to be held in Bradenton, Florida, in March of 1954. Though Aaron was out of the Sally League, he could not escape Jim Crow. Once at camp, he lived in a rooming house, not "at the big, pink Manatee River hotel" with his teammates,[24] had to wait to shower until the white players were finished and could not be out after dark, because the police might take offense. Despite his highly positive advance notices, he was told that regardless of his performance he would be going to the minor league Toledo franchise when spring training was over.[25] For the Braves already had their outfield set. Bill Bruton and Andy Pafko, at center and right, were holdovers; Bobby Thomson had just been picked up from the Giants; and the vastly improved veteran Jim Pendleton – he had flirted with .300 in 1953 – was the odds-on choice as a reserve.

Nonetheless, Henry came prepared and produced whenever he was in the batting cage or in the lineup. When the exhibition season ended, he led the club in several offensive categories. In addition, his competition for a roster spot had melted away: Pendleton hurt his cause by angling for a better deal and then showing up late and out of shape, and the legendary Thomson broke his ankle in a bad slide into second. As a result, when camp broke Henry was offered a major league contract and for the next two-plus decades he would be the Braves' everyday outfielder.

During the first dozen years, from 1954 to 1965, Henry was back in Wisconsin. He loved being in Milwaukee. Though far from perfect, it was better than Eau Claire, which hardly knew what to make of black people, and better than Jacksonville, which knew exactly what to make of them. It was in Milwaukee that he and Barbara had their three children and bought a home in a semi-rural almost all-white suburb called Mequon. And it was in Milwaukee that Henry made a name for himself as a premier player: a perennial All-Star, Gold Glove winner and MVP contender.

But race continued to be a problem. In St. Louis and Cincinnati Henry could not eat with the other players; in Covington he was pulled over by the cops for sitting in the back seat of a sedan with a white couple; in Mississippi local police followed his car until he was beyond town limits. In 1957, the year he was chosen MVP, Henry was invited to speak at an all-white service club in Mobile, but told he could not bring either his wife or his father; he cancelled the speech. Charlie Grimm, the Braves' skipper Henry's rookie year, said his hot new prospect was slow, as in slow-moving and slow-witted, telling the Milwaukee *Journal* he had nicknamed him "Stepanfetchit," because "He Just Keeps Shuffling Along."[26] Warren Spahn, the Braves' pitching ace and the titular leader of the club, also called Henry "Stepanfetchit."[27] And if Grimm and Spahn could make fun of him, then Joe Adcock was free to refer to Aaron as "Slow Motion Henry," and there was no real problem if talk of "niggers" crept into locker room.[28]

Atlanta Journal columnist Furman Bisher did the public hatchet job on Henry in a profile in the August 25, 1956, edition of *The Saturday Evening Post*. Furman, after noting Aaron's "satchel posterior and shuffling gait," favored the reader with direct quotes from the budding star. Regarding Satchel Paige: "I didn't know he come from Mobile, and I never seen him till yet."[29] Regarding hitting .400: "Nobody is hit .400 since Ted Williams."[30] Regarding a spring training slump: "I saving up for opening day."[31] Henry did not dispute the accuracy of Bisher's reporting, but was hurt and angered by his malicious desire to affirm the worst stereotypes of black athletes. As Aaron saw it, the message was plain: "Folks, this is a good ballplayer, but at the same time, we're talking about a dumb country nigger here, you understand."[32]

Henry's evolving reaction to this racism is a key element of his story. At the outset he did nothing or close to nothing. He had just started his career, and the indignities and inconveniences were not unexpected and nothing new. They were part of the life his father had endured and prepared him to face. Nonetheless, Henry was not proud that in 1956 the Mobile *Press* praised him for not "tak[ing] advantage of his peculiar position as a famous Negro player to further any bitterness over race or other questions."[33]

At the end of 1957, around the time his infant son died, Henry began spending time with Father Sablica, an activist priest. As a result of his influence,

Henry became familiar with the writings of James Baldwin and Martin Luther King Jr. and struck up a friendship with Jim Brown, the most outspoken black athlete of the era. By 1958 *The New York Times Magazine* had noted that "Henry Aaron feels deeply" about matters of "race relations."[34] In 1961 *Jet* magazine praised Henry for helping convince the Braves front office to integrate spring training facilities. And in 1965 Henry co-authored an article about the ability of blacks to have managerial roles after retiring from active play.

In 1966 the Milwaukee Braves became the Atlanta Braves, a move Henry had fought from the moment the first rumors swirled.[35] As he told the press in 1964, "I have lived in the South and I don't want to live there again."[36] But Henry did have to live in the South again, and the change was both tumultuous and pivotal.

It was in Atlanta that Henry became a full-fledged participant in the fight for civil rights. As Henry feared, racism had not been eradicated in the capital of the New South. The Aarons frequently received hate letters in the mail, and at Fulton County Stadium there were still cries of "nigger" and "jigaboo" when Henry came to the plate, just like in the old days in the Sally League.[37] Abandoning the "quiet diplomacy" that had been his trademark, he took to heart the urging of Whitney Young, Director of the National Urban League, to use his "big bat" – the influence he had by virtue of being a star – "to hammer out an 'open city.'"[38] He got in contact with key local figures in the burgeoning movement for Negro equality, including Martin Luther King Sr., Martin Luther King Jr. and Andrew Young. He began to speak out when he experienced or witnessed or heard of discrimination. That very first year, as he put it, he "crossed the line and became an agitator," reciting to a reporter for *Jet* magazine the litany of ways that major league baseball discriminated against African American players: "in salary, longevity, managing, the front office, everything."[39] His interview became a cover story under the title, "Hank Aaron Blasts Racism in Baseball."[40]

The Atlanta move also altered the way Henry approached the game of baseball and that, in turn, altered the way the world remembers him. From the time he became a professional, Henry's goal was to be the best "all around" hitter, to be his generation's Stan Musial. After the move he gave up that goal and concentrated on rolling up home runs. As he explained, it all had to do with the fortuities of Atlanta's topography and climate:

> The first time I took batting practice in Atlanta-Fulton County Stadium, I knew that my career was headed in a new direction. Atlanta was the highest city in the major leagues, as well as the hottest, and if you could get the ball into the air, there was a good chance that it wouldn't come down in the playing field.[41]

With that knowledge, Henry put aside the idea of hitting .400: "I changed my batting style immediately, no longer trying to pounce on the ball and whip it in any direction but turning and pulling it toward the seats in left field."[42] That change reflected his new objective: surpassing Babe Ruth's record for the most home runs in a baseball career.

B. The Movie Stars

James Cagney and Cary Grant were born within just five years of one another, at the turn of the 20th Century. Both were school dropouts: Cagney from college, Grant from middle school. Both spent their formative years in New York City, Cagney was born there and Grant took residence in his late teens. Both began as vaudevillians, Cagney focused on dance, Grant on light musicals and operettas. On the personal front, Cagney was from the start a strictly one-woman man, while Grant went through a series of unsuccessful marriages before finding a lasting relationship.

James Cagney

Once James Cagney was famous there was a temptation to point to his Lenox Settlement House debut as the *Faun* and his star-struck reaction to seeing Pavlova dance as a foreshadowing of the future to come. That Professor Mankiewicz, Jim's German teacher at Columbia, was the father of two sons in the movie business also seemed noteworthy.[43] However interesting now, none of this was indicative of anything at the time.

Put another way, who knows what Jim Cagney might have become had his father not been another casualty of the flu epidemic that swept through New York in the early autumn of 1918. At that point Jim was a student at Columbia taking courses in drafting and participating in its Student Army Training Corps, and his father had settled down and was more or less sober, in anticipation of the arrival of a new child.

But James Sr. did die that autumn in the epidemic, and Jim left college. He needed to bring home a paycheck to help support the family and to enable his brother Harry to continue *his* studies. Jim's first job was wrapping parcels at Wanamaker's department store. But when the fifth Cagney was born in March of 1919, the girl that Carrie had always wished for, Jim felt he had to earn more. By chance, a pal at Wanamaker's had a friend leaving a vaudeville act at Keith's theater. The pay was a hefty $35 a week. The bit was called *Every Sailor*, the gobs in the title, six men dressed as women. Jim, always adept at mimicry, picked up the necessary dance steps, learned how to walk in heels, tried out and got hired. It was the eight weeks he spent sashaying on stage in drag that marked the true start of Cagney's career as a performing artist.

After an interlude as a Wall Street runner, which pleased Carrie but not him, Cagney responded to an open call for chorus boys. The new show, *Pitter Patter*, was slated to open in the fall of 1920. Between what he copied from the competition – he made sure he auditioned near the end – and a quick turn of his own invention, he landed a part. Over the course of the run, he moved up to "specialty dancer," supplementing his salary by serving as the star's "dresser" and humping luggage when the show went on the road.[44] He also met the love of his life, Frances Willard Vernon.

Like Jim, "Willie" was short and so the two were usually paired.[45] They were attracted to one another from the start: "both small, wiry, good dancers (she better than he by a bit), intense, witty, and given to volatile displays of temper when crossed."[46] Carrie was unhappy about her son's new lady friend. It was not just that Willie was a country girl but, as Willie told it in 1980: "Mrs. Cagney disliked show business and all it stood for. What it stood for, I guess, was me."[47]

Pitter Patter closed at the beginning of 1921, and for the next four and a half years Jim was a vaudeville "song and dance man." Till the end of his life, that was how he saw himself and was where, he said, he "had the most fun."[48] But it wasn't always fun, because there wasn't always work. When out of work, Jim got frustrated and dejected by the lack of food, the shabby clothes and the crummy furnished rooms. At those times, he told Willie that he wanted to quit show business and get a regular job, as a shoe salesman or street car conductor or whatever. Willie would hear none of it. She believed that Jim had "innate abilities" and, even then, was sure he was destined for great things:[49]

> You're going to dance; you're going to act. You're going to reach the heights, and I don't care how sentimental that sounds. It's the truth. You'd better get used to it. You'd better start working on it.[50]

At first he and Willie put together their own dance routine. Then, for six months, Jim was the third member of a dance and patter trio which had been known as Parker, Rand and Leach, replacing Archie when he left. Willie and Jim got married on September 28, 1922, around the time they were hired for *Lew Fields' Ritz Girls of 1922*, their first "near big time" engagement.[51] The show had run its course towards the end of the year, but by February they were brought back for Fields' *Snapshots of 1923*. A review in the *New York Star* called Jim an obvious "comer:" "Jimmy [Cagney] . . . is a dapper, smiling young chap, full of ambition to rise in his adopted profession. He will. Just watch his smoke."[52]

The smoke did not rise as quickly as predicted, and in the winter of 1923-24 Jim was reduced to sweeping the stage at the Provincetown Playhouse. Desperate for a break, the Cagneys took a flyer in 1924 and went out to California to see if they could get onto the ground floor of the fledgling movie business. They got nowhere. Next it was off to Chicago on borrowed funds in the hope that prospects would be better there. They were not. Jim, unemployed, suffering from stage fright and literally sick to his stomach, again questioned whether he was on the right track. Willie remained determined and unfazed: "I told you that you were going to hit the heights in this business, by God, and by God you will. So no more of that talk. *No more.* You understand me?"[53]

Fate then intervened. Jim encountered an old buddy, Victor Killian, who wanted a partner for a comedy/dancing act. The two came up with a routine that was good enough to get them bookings all the way to New York. Once there, Killian touted Jim's talents to the playwright Eugene O'Neill and the director Kenneth MacGowan, friends of his at the Provincetown Playhouse. Jim had no real interest at all in "straight acting," but agreed to an audition because Killian had gone to such lengths and such trouble to set it up.

After seeing Jim, MacGowan thought there was a part for him in a Maxwell Anderson play, *Outside Looking In,* a character described in the script as "Little Red." Jim was forever convinced he was cast in the role because he was one of two, short red-headed New York actors and, of them, Jim's hair was "a bit redder."[54] As Little Red, Jim played a tough guy on the wrong side of the law. Robert Benchley, the influential reviewer for *Life* magazine, praised Jim as "perfect" in the role, writing that one of his scenes was "something that many a more established actor might watch with profit."[55] The *New York Herald Tribune* was equally complimentary, describing his performance and that of his co-star as "the most honest acting to be seen in New York."[56] After the initial jubilation wore off, Jim doubted the acclaim meant anything: "There were, as far as I knew, no Broadway stars five feet seven and a half inches in height."[57]

Outside Looking In had a decent run of 113 performances, closing in December 1925. Jim was perfectly content with getting back to vaudeville, and the two Cagneys reunited in a sketch entitled *Lonesome Manor,* with Jim playing a wily city boy to Willie's innocent bumpkin. An opportunity to reprise that pairing presented itself with a new show, *Broadway,* scheduled to open in 1926. The male lead was to be "a streetwise song and dance man," and his love interest, "a country-bred girl named Billie."[58] Though Jim was passed over for the starring role in the New York production, he was engaged to headline the London company.

Rehearsals were exasperating, as both author and director insisted Jim play the part as it had been defined by the Broadway lead. Jim had his own ideas, and they were vindicated at the New York dress rehearsal, performed on the eve of his departure for England. He received eight curtain calls and the praise of a slew of actors and producers in attendance. The next night, Jim was slated to star in the Broadway production, a dry-run before he set sail. At the last minute he was informed he would not appear that evening in New York, nor would he be going to London. He had been fired. Jim was stunned, and his confidence was shattered. He told Willie he wanted to enroll in agriculture school. She said she would leave him if he did.

For the next three years Jim alternated between "straight plays" and "song and dance." In September, 1927, he was a "tough kid" in a boarding house drama called *Women Go On Forever*.[59] By the following May, it was back to vaudeville, Jim choreographing and dancing in the 1928 and 1929 editions of *The Grand Street Follies*. In between the two *Follies* runs he did summer stock in Ohio and Massachusetts. As 1929 was winding down Jim got the lead in the optimistically entitled *Maggie the Magnificent*, chosen by the author because he looked like just what he had in mind for the part: "a fresh mutt."[60] *The New York Times* wrote he played "the scapegrace son" with "clarity and spirit," and Robert Benchley, as before, said nice things about him.[61] Despite the praise for Jim, the play was a flop and ran for only a month. Attending the finale was the director William Keighley,[62] who liked what he saw and immediately signed Jim for his newest venture, *Penny Arcade*. As he later told Cagney, he had an image of the lead as "an attractive yet tough young cookie," and Jim once again fit the bill.[63]

In *Penny Arcade* Jim played a young bootlegger, spoiled rotten by his mother, the owner of a local amusement spot. After murdering a rival, he confesses his crime to his mother, a scene one critic hailed as "the high point of the play."[64] The reviewer for *The New York Times* was similarly impressed by Jim's performance, as was Al Jolson, who happened to be in the audience on opening night. Indeed Jolson was so impressed that he secured an option on the film rights to *Penny Arcade* which he then sold to Warner Brothers. Jolson advised Jack Warner to see the play before it closed, and Warner took his advice. He then immediately signed Jim to a three-week contract.

That deal was the turning point in Jim's movie career. With that short-term arrangement, Cagney and Warner began a tempestuous relationship that would define Jim's professional life for decades to come.

Cary Grant

At least in his telling, Cary Grant's love affair with the world of show business began on the Saturday that 13-year-old Archie Leach first saw the inside of the Hippodrome theater. At that instant he says he *"knew"* that life on the stage was the only life for him.[65]

As we know, a year later Archie began his apprenticeship with the Pender troupe and over the next five years mastered the gymnastic arts and the skills of comedic timing. Though by 19 Archie had appeared before thousands of theater-goers across at least two continents, no audience had heard him utter a word.

Over the next couple of years Archie survived by finding spot jobs. He signed on as a "filler" for groups that were a man short, sold neckties on the streets of Manhattan and mounted his stilts to advertise attractions on Coney Island. Along with Tommy Pender, he built a new group, offering a bit of mime along with the usual "tumbling, stilt walking and slapstick farce."[66] He haunted booking agents and when he got really desperate he lifeguarded or hired out as a "barker."[67] He also continued the process of remaking himself into someone urbane and elegant, practicing by squiring attractive women to fashionable Park Avenue soirees.

By the time Archie was 21 he did speak in front of audiences, beginning on a pickup basis as the "straight man" to any comic passing through town.[68] In the process, he got to observe some of the great funny men of the day, including George Burns and Zeppo Marx. Watching them taught Archie a lot: "I learned to time laughs. When to talk into an audience's laughter. When to wait for the laughs. When not to wait for the laugh."[69]

Archie's first salaried speaking part was in a vaudeville sketch called *The Woman Pays,* written in 1926 by Jean Dalrymple. After the playwright had waded through a slew of "Valentino types," Archie auditioned, a bit shy, with an odd walk and a peculiar accent. Dalrymple thought him "absolute perfection."[70] After the close of *The Woman Pays,* and after being fired from a mind-reading act, Archie returned to New York during the summer of 1927. He had begun to dress more conservatively and to stand in a manner that mimicked the natural nonchalance of Noel Coward. As his look and style became more refined, he was in even more demand as a "high class" escort. He continued to scrounge up vaudeville opportunities, doing stand-up at small theaters and clubs around the City. When one evening the other half of his duo showed up drunk, the manager urged Archie to go on solo. The bit required a little singing, and Archie got the idea that if he learned to carry a tune, he might be able to break into musical comedy.

Enter Max Hoffman, a friend of Archie's, who introduced him to Reggie Hammerstein, from the storied show business family. Reggie not only endorsed the notion of singing lessons for Archie, but in September 1927 introduced him to his Uncle Arthur. The celebrated Broadway impresario was about to produce a new operetta and, in what seemed like a major milestone at the time, hired Archie for a part in the show.

Over the next four years, first for Arthur Hammerstein, then for J.J. Shubert, Archie traveled the country performing light musical fare. Reactions to his work ranged from tepid to awful. His English co-star in *Polly with a Past* said "he was completely lacking in talent or skill as an actor, singer or dancer."[71] His American co-star in *Boom Boom* thought he was "absolutely terrible."[72] Critics were not much kinder. For example, in reviewing Archie's part in a knock-off of Strauss's *Die Fledermaus,* one critic called him "woefully unfunny," another found his singing off-key and a third dismissed him as "a mixture of John Barrymore and Cockney."[73]

During this period Archie did a screen test for "Paramount Famous Lasky Corporation" but never heard back. It was just as well. The post-mortem concluded that the nice-looking Englishman would never be a movie star: "bowlegged and his neck is too thick."[74] Nor did Archie's career take off after a second Paramount tryout, a short film called *Singapore Sue*. Archie was asked to wear a white sailor suit, smile handsomely and deliver a few lines to showcase the studio's newest Asian star.

After four years of operettas and little demonstrable progress, Archie and a friend drove out to California in mid-November 1931. Shortly after his arrival, his agent at William Morris introduced him to Marion Gering, a Broadway director who had transitioned into movies. A few days after that, Gering invited Archie to join him and his wife at a dinner hosted by B.P. Schulberg, the head of production at Paramount. The occasion proved to be momentous. Gering's wife was a would-be actress, and Schulberg had agreed to have her tested the next morning. Since there was no one slated to throw her lines, Schulberg asked if Archie would do the honors. He agreed. Mrs. Gering was nervous and ill-prepared. Archie apparently shone.

Following the screen test, Schulberg offered Archie a long-term agreement, with the proviso that he find a new name. Fay Wray, on the cusp of *King Kong* fame, suggested that Archie Leach become "Cary Lockwood," the character he played opposite her in *Nikki,* a short-lived musical which closed right before he went out West. Schulberg was fine with "Cary," but rejected "Lockwood" because Paramount already had a "Harold Lockwood" in its stable.[75] A list of surnames was promptly produced, and all agreed that "Grant" would do nicely. In January, 1932, as Archie Leach was turning 28, Cary Grant signed his first film contract.

Grant's years with Paramount, running from 1932 to 1937, were mostly ones of frustration. During that period he made 25 movies, and they were of a piece: the screenplays were weak and/or the parts Cary was assigned were superficial and/or Cary was a stand-in for the studio's first choice. His first screen role set the tone. It was entitled *This Is the Night,* with Cary cast as an Olympic athlete. He photographed well enough for *Variety* to observe that he "looks like a potential *femme rave*," essentially pigeonholing him as a "heart throb."[76] Thereafter he often appeared in formal clothes and played rich playboys, good-looking naval officers, suave gamblers and wealthy executives. Occasionally critics suggested that Cary was being sold short. As *The New York Times* wrote in a review of a film with a particularly bad script, "Cary Grant is worthy of a much better role . . ."[77]

In 1933 Cary got the "better role," playing opposite Mae West in *She Done Him Wrong.*[78] This time he was not an upper-crust sophisticate, but a lowbrow government agent posing as a "Bowery missionary." His task was to tame West, cast to type as a voluptuous saloon owner. Making use of his vaudeville training, Cary played straight man to West's comic babe, looking quizzical at her bawdy one-liners.[79] The picture was a financial bonanza, earning Paramount $2 million, as was their second pairing in *I'm No Angel,* estimated to have grossed as much as a million more.

Grant's box office success did not cause the front office to give him better parts. Reviewers, however, occasionally saw potential. In *Ladies Should Listen* (1934), *Script* magazine was taken with Cary's "delightful flair for light comedy."[80] In *Wings in the Dark* (1935), *Variety* wrote: "Cary Grant tops all his past work."[81] In *Sylvia Scarlett* (1936), *Time* magazine, gushed that the movie was "made memorable" by "Cary Grant's superb depiction of the Cockney."[82] Years later, long after he was established, the actor said, *"Sylvia Scarlett* was my breakthrough."[83] But Paramount did not notice.

When it came time to renew his agreement, the studio offered to increase Grant's salary to $2,500 a week, over five times what he had been paid at the start. However, it refused to give him the right it gave others to decide which scripts to accept. Zukor, Paramount's single-minded chairman, saw Grant as just another pretty face, a useful option if Cooper or March were unavailable or not in the mood.[84] He also thought Grant was lucky to be making so much money with the country mired in a Depression. Zukor's disdain or lack of interest in Cary was evident when he flatly refused to loan him to MGM to appear with Clark Gable and Charles Laughton in *Mutiny on the Bounty*. *Mutiny* ultimately won the 1935 Oscar for Best Picture and Cary's replacement, Franchot Tone, received a Best Actor nomination.

So, Grant ended discussions with Paramount and beginning in 1937 became a free agent. He quickly entered into lucrative, non-exclusive contracts with Columbia and RKO, each of which gave him the express right of script approval. After this watershed event, Cary "freelanced" for nearly three decades, during which he proved himself to be one of the most talented, durable and versatile entertainers in show business.

C. The Presidents

Abraham Lincoln and Ronald Reagan grew up 100 years apart, Abraham Lincoln in the first quarter of the 19th Century, and Ronald Reagan in the first quarter of the 20th. Both were Republicans and brought up more or less in the Midwest. Reagan went to college, while Lincoln hardly had any formal schooling at all. Reagan seems never to have given a thought to being President until relatively late in life. As to Lincoln's aspirations, as with much else about him, it is hard to say.

Abraham Lincoln

Awkward, ill-kempt, poorly-dressed, generally unprepossessing except as to size, Abraham Lincoln managed to impress and draw all kinds of people into his orbit. There was something special about him, recognized early on, and this almost magnetic pull is central to understanding his improbable rise.

After leaving his father in 1831, Abe settled in New Salem, Illinois, located 20 miles northwest of Springfield. He had first seen the village when a flatboat he was piloting to New Orleans got stuck on a milldam on the Sangamon River, which ran through the town. The boat took on water, and Abe was faced with the seemingly impossible task of saving both the vessel and its valuable cargo. His ingenuity stunned the onlookers:

> Unable to budge the flatboat, he bored a hole in the bow and unloaded enough of the barrels in the rear so that the stern rose up. When the water poured out through the hole, the whole boat lifted and floated over the dam.[85]

Denton Offutt, whose goods Abe was transporting, was on the scene and so taken by Abe's enterprise that he promised to set him up in business when Abe returned. Abe got back to New Salem in July to find, as was often the case with Offutt, a "gasy – windy – brain rattling man," that there was as yet neither store nor goods.[86] So that summer, Abe hired out as a laborer.

Abe remained in New Salem for the next six years, earning the admiration of the locals with his willingness to do any kind of work, his sociability and his "inexhaustible store of anecdotes and stories."[87] He forged a lifelong friendship with Jack Armstrong and his wild "Clary Grove Boys" when he wrestled Jack – reputedly the toughest man in the region – to a solid draw. He also attracted the attention – and interest – of the better educated members of the populace: of Mentor Graham, the local schoolteacher, who helped him improve his skills in mathematics and his knowledge of literature; of Bowling Green, the Justice of the Peace, who taught him how to draft basic legal documents; and of John Rutledge, the founder of the local debating club, where Abe refined his ability to argue extemporaneously.

1832 was a momentous year for Abe. In March, at the urging of the New Salem worthies, he launched a campaign for a seat in the Illinois legislature. He had barely gotten started when the Black Hawk War broke out. On April 21, he volunteered and was sworn into the militia. Each company elected its own officers, and two-thirds of those in Abe's stood behind him, designating him as their choice for captain. Though he made light in later years of his heroic battles "with the Musquetoes," he regarded this first election as one of the proudest moments in his life.[88] When his initial month-long enlistment was over, Abe re-upped twice more. He was discharged on July 10.

Following his discharge, Abe resumed his legislative campaign. His platform focused on local issues, like the development of the Sangamon River and the imposition of restrictions on usury. On the stump he acknowledged his meager beginnings: "I was born and have ever remained in the most humble walks of life."[89] He lost – polling eighth in a field of 13 – but received 277 of the 300 votes cast in his hometown. In 1834 Abe made another run for the legislature, this time winning, his 1,376 votes the second-highest total of any legislative candidate in the state. The election was held in August, but the session did not begin until December 1. In the interim, he was encouraged to study law by John Stuart, who had met Abe during the Black Hawk War. Stuart was a prominent figure in the legal community and an excellent mentor. He was not only a well-regarded Springfield lawyer but also the Whig minority leader in the state house and the odds-on favorite to be the next U.S. Congressman from Illinois. Abe took Stuart's advice and began his legal studies.

Abe was mostly a silent observer during the 1834-35 legislative session and not much of a participant in the session of 1835-36. He spent the summer in between reading law books. Abe ran for a second term in 1836 and won again, this time with the state's highest vote total. His success at the polls earned him the position of floor leader of the Whig caucus, though his maiden speech during the 1836-37 session was not very effective. On April 15, 1837, when the first session of his second term ended, Abe was licensed to practice law. He promptly moved to Springfield, the new state capital, to become the junior partner in John Stuart's firm.

The beginning of Lincoln's legal career marked the end of a dismal period for him in New Salem. Before 1832 was half over, his position as clerk, operating Offutt's small country store, and as manager, running Offut's grist and saw mills, came to an end as Offutt's business "petered out."[90] Abe then entered into a partnership with William Berry, a corporal in his militia battalion. Their little shop, well stocked with tea and coffee, sugar and salt, calico and muslin, hats and a small number of shoes, also failed, a victim of New Salem's stagnant growth and the townspeople's lack of hard cash. On May 7, 1833, Abe was appointed the village postmaster, a position he held for three years. While it provided Abe with a good opportunity to read all the newspapers, it paid poorly. His compensation for the period was a paltry $150 to $175. So Abe borrowed some geometry books, got himself a compass and learned how to do surveys, becoming so good at it that his determination of boundary lines was conclusive when land disputes arose. Then, in the midst of the 1835-36 legislative session, he learned that his former partner, William Berry, had died penniless and that the local court had seized all of Abe's belongings, including his surveying equipment.[91] Though Abe was only liable for half the amount, he undertook to entirely satisfy the creditors, and over time he did. On the personal front there was hardship as well. Sometime during 1835 he had come to a romantic "understanding" with Ann Rutledge, the daughter of a tavern keeper with whom he had once boarded.[92] Tragically, Ann got seriously ill, "probably of typhoid fever," and passed away on August 25, sending Abe into a deep depression.[93]

While Abe's economic prospects improved with his relocation to Springfield, he had virtually no money at the start. Fortunately, Joshua F. Speed, one of the proprietors of the A.Y. Ellis & Co. general store, asked Abe to move in with him and share his room and ample bed. Speed, from a prominent Kentucky slave-owning family, may have been Abe's only intimate friend. His shop served as a place for the eligible town bachelors to gather, talk and tell tales, and Abe quickly became the featured attraction.

With Stuart as his law partner, Lincoln did not have to worry at all about building a law practice. As early as the 1837 summer term of the Sangamon County Circuit Court, Stuart and Lincoln were on the papers for twice as many cases as their closest competitor. Abe viewed the practice of law as consistent with his political undertakings. And so he ran for, and won, his third legislative term in the late summer of 1838. He had become a seasoned hand, having twice been a candidate for speaker (unsuccessfully), serving on over a dozen committees and helping to manage the Whig minority. His party labors included participation in Stuart's 1838 campaign for Congress, helping his patron defeat Stephen A. Douglas, the "little giant," by 36 votes.

In 1839 Abe met Mary Todd, who had come to live with her married sister and brother-in-law, Elizabeth and Ninian Edwards, in their mansion in the heart of Springfield. Mary's father was a socially prominent Lexington banker, and she had spent her childhood in luxurious surroundings, attended by slaves. While their social status could not have been more different, Abe and Mary did have things in common: both were from Kentucky, both loved poetry, and both were Whigs. That said, Mary had a tendency to be haughty and sarcastic, tendencies that Abe neither shared nor particularly liked. Nevertheless, the two were quite serious by the fall of 1840 and became formally engaged around Christmas. A week or so later, on January 1, 1841, Lincoln broke the engagement. His cold feet may have been attributable to a suspicion that he had been led into the relationship by the Edwardses, by a concern that his income would be insufficient to provide Mary with the comforts with which she was accustomed and by the unease caused when his great friend Speed decided that very day to leave Springfield to go back home to Kentucky. After a long break, punctuated by bouts of depression, a pleasant month-long visit with Speed (where he was aided by a personal servant) and attendance at Speed's wedding, Abe and Mary reconciled and were married on November 4, 1842.

Some 20 months before the wedding, in April of 1841, after the completion of the first session of Abe's fourth term in the Illinois legislature, he had entered into a law partnership with Stephen T. Logan. Logan was nine years Abe's senior and "unquestionably the leading figure in the Sangamon County Bar."[94] While his income from Logan and Lincoln was satisfactory, it was not enough, especially once Abe again began to consider marrying Mary. So in the spring and fall, Abe accompanied the Eighth Circuit judge and spent roughly three months riding from county court to county court. Traveling the "circuit" not only increased Abe's earnings, but exposed him to thousands of voters in the central part of the state, an incalculable dividend for a man with a hankering for politics.

After the completion of his fourth term in the Illinois legislature, Lincoln concluded there was nothing to be gained by seeking another. However, the new Seventh Congressional District, which included Sangamon County, was reliably Whig. When Abe's former partner John Stuart, who represented the

Seventh District, decided to retire from Congress, the delegates at a Whig meeting in May of 1843 committed themselves to a single-term rotation system, to accommodate the political aspirations of a number of its party leaders. Under this system, Abe's friend Edward Baker was endorsed as the putative Whig candidate for 1844, with Abe in line to run two years later. Lincoln worked tirelessly to insure Baker's victory and, in so doing, gained a reputation as "the best stump speaker in the state."[95]

Although it took some maneuvering, Lincoln was the Whig nominee in 1846 and soundly defeated his Democratic opponent to become a member of the House of Representatives. What would seem like a major watershed in Lincoln's political career ended up being little more than a paper credential. His single term in the 30th Congress was neither momentous nor particularly successful. During the first session, which began in December 1847, he introduced a series of "spot resolutions" to force the Polk administration to pinpoint where on American soil the attack came that precipitated the Mexican War.[96] It was a silly issue, since the war was generally popular and was virtually over. The President ignored him, the Democratic press was disdainful and his fellow Whigs were largely silent. During the second session, which began in December 1848, he had a muted role in the debate on slavery, the big issue of the time. When it came to voting, he followed the Whig line and supported the Wilmot Proviso, precluding the expansion of slavery into former Mexican territories. His work on a wishy-washy bill abolishing slavery in the District of Columbia never got anywhere.

1848 was a presidential election year, and during the congressional recess Lincoln worked tirelessly for the Whig nominee Zachary Taylor, distributing campaign literature, monitoring political developments in key states, touring New England and stumping in central Illinois. Taylor won, performing well in the Illinois counties where Abe had spoken, but his impact did not result in the plum appointment he had hoped for, commissioner of the General Land Office, with a handsome $3,000 salary and patronage power.[97]

Sorely disappointed, Abe threw himself into his legal business. As he recounted, "From 1849 to 1854, both inclusive, [I] practiced law more assiduously than ever before."[98] As a result, he became one of the best-known lawyers in the state with an income that reached between $2,000, and $5,000 a year. And he acquired another distinguished admirer, Yale-educated David Davis, judge of the Eighth Judicial District. Davis, who got to closely observe Abe as the two made their biannual tour of the circuit courts, described him as a man of "exceeding honesty and fairness."[99] He thought so highly of Abe that he designated him as his substitute when he was unable to sit. It was during this phase that Lincoln earned the nickname "Honest Old Abe – the lawyer who was never known to tell a lie."[100]

In 1854 Congress passed the Kansas-Nebraska Act, permitting the two territories to determine by popular sovereignty whether slavery would be allowed. As such, the legislation repudiated that portion of the 1820 Missouri

Compromise prohibiting slavery in parts of the Louisiana Purchase north of the 36th parallel. The Kansas-Nebraska Act offended and animated Lincoln because it breathed new life into the "peculiar institution" that he believed was appropriately doomed for extinction. That August he described its passage as a "great wrong," and publicly began to articulate the themes that would define his political life and his legacy.[101]

Over the ensuing five years, Abe suffered three defeats that, oddly, did not derail his career, but instead enhanced his stature. In 1854 he ran for the state legislature and crisscrossed the state on behalf of Whigs and Democrats who opposed the Kansas-Nebraska Act. It appeared that the "anti-Nebraska" coalition had gained control of the legislature, and Abe resigned his seat to be constitutionally eligible to become the next Illinois Senator. When the legislature met in February 1855, he led all other candidates on the first six ballots, but withdrew on the seventh to prevent a "pro-Nebraska" Democrat from being chosen.

In 1856 Abe participated in the founding of a Republican Party in Illinois, thereby establishing his status as a leader of this new party in his home state. At the first national convention that June, which chose John C. Frémont as its presidential candidate, Abe attracted a respectable 110 votes in a late and unsuccessful bid to be his running mate. Though he fell short, his showing reflected his growing influence and reputation.

In 1858 Abe was chosen as the Republican candidate for Senate, facing off against the Democratic incumbent, Stephen Douglas. In their seven three-hour debates, Lincoln contended that it was the will of the nation's Founders that slavery die out and, accordingly, be outlawed in all territories and future states. Douglas argued that so long as the decision on slavery reflected the will of the people, it could continue to exist where it was and be expanded into new areas. The sharp contrast on issues mirrored the sharp contrast in their styles. Douglas strove to emphasize his elegance and sophistication; Lincoln made no secret of his homespun roots. When the popular votes for the Illinois state legislature were counted that November, they were almost evenly divided between Republicans and Democrats. However, holdovers and apportionment gave Democrats a numerical edge in legislators, and on January 5, 1859 Douglas prevailed, receiving 54 ballots to Lincoln's 46.

Douglas' victory came at a heavy political cost, given his presidential ambitions. His position on "popular sovereignty" alienated Southern Democrats, setting the stage for a split in the Democratic Party. The Northern Democrats nominated him as their standard-bearer on June 18 in Baltimore; the Southern Democrats nominated John C. Breckinridge as theirs on June 28 in Richmond. Moreover, border state Whigs fielded John Bell to lead a newly-created Constitutional Union party. In light of these developments, if the Republicans fielded a credible nominee, they would win the White House.

The obvious Republican front-runner was William H. Seward, a sitting Senator from and former Governor of New York. His great advantage was his fatal weakness: he was well-known and pegged as an anti-slavery radical. There were other prominent politicians for whom a case could be made, but they had vulnerabilities, as well. Salmon P. Chase, Ohio's governor, lacked charisma and finesse. Edward Bates of Missouri was, at 66, just too old. And John Frémont, who had been the candidate four years before and lost, was damaged goods.

On the strength of his role in creating the Illinois Republican Party and his performance during the debates with Douglas, Lincoln clearly had become a factor and could claim support as Illinois' "favorite son." He broadened and deepened his appeal as everyone's "second choice" on February 27, 1860, with a speech at Cooper Union in New York. Though awkward looking and poorly attired, he stunned the audience with his obvious intellect and his soaring rhetoric, his final words eliciting a spontaneous standing ovation: "Let us have faith that right makes might, and in that faith, let us, to the end, dare to do our duty as we understand it."[102] His triumph in New York was followed by a successful two-week speaking tour of New England, during which he proudly recalled his days as "a hired laborer, mauling rails, at work on a flat-boat – just what might happen to any poor man's son."[103]

The Republicans chose to hold their convention in Illinois, a stroke of luck for Abe. By the time the Party assembled in Chicago in mid-May, Lincoln's supporters were working the delegates, touting his electability and underscoring his "rail-splitter" image, the self-made man who embodied Republican values.[104] His campaign autobiography proudly acknowledged his "undistinguished" ancestry: his boyhood in a bear-filled "wild region," his lack of education, his years of "farm work."[105]

In the end, the arguments made by Abe's handlers took. On the first convention ballot Lincoln came in a strong second. By the third, the nomination was his. In the general election, Lincoln carried every free state but New Jersey. In the Electoral College, Lincoln garnered 180 votes, Breckinridge 72, Bell 39 and Douglas 12.

Ronald Reagan

For Reagan, it is difficult to pinpoint what really started him on his sequential careers of acting and politics. It is hard to ignore the role his mother Nelle had in involving Dutch at a tender age in her church skits, making him feel comfortable in front of a crowd. Though largely motivated by his crush on Margaret Cleaver, he joined and ultimately became president of the drama club at North Dixon High School and had roles in the school plays. His own memories of his summers lifeguarding at Lowell Park focus not on the heroics of his 77 saves but on the fact that perched alone on the stand, "It was like a stage. Everyone had to look at me."[106]

After graduating from North Dixon High, Dutch went to nearby Eureka College, largely to be with his girlfriend. He washed dishes to cover tuition, and continued to pursue his interest in theater. He performed in amateur productions, watched professional ones and participated in a national acting competition at Northwestern University. Though he was pitted against Ivy Leaguers, Dutch came in second and got a special award. As significantly, the school's director of Speech encouraged him to make acting his career.

Dutch's debut in college politics came when he led a protest of the curriculum cutbacks engineered by the school's unpopular president. His speech calling for a strike vote won the unanimous support of students and faculty and led to the president's resignation and the revival of the imperiled programs. Years later he still recalled the pleasure he got from the favorable response of the crowd. In his senior year he was elected to head the student body.

Following college, Dutch was hired as a radio announcer first for the University of Iowa's football team and then for the Chicago Cubs. His warm and soothing voice, coupled with an ability to vividly describe – and at times invent – play-by-play kept him in front of a microphone for four seasons.[107]

Reagan's movie breakthrough was one-part ingenuity and three-parts dumb luck. He convinced his station management to allow him to accompany the Cubs to their 1936 spring training, which was being held close to Los Angeles on Catalina Island. He got nowhere making the rounds of the studios until he happened upon a former station employee, who had become a singer. She introduced him to her manager, who arranged a screen test, and Warner Brothers came back with a contract. Upon hearing the news he wired his agent: "Sign before they change their minds."[108]

Reagan remained with Warner's from 1937 to 1952 and made over 40 largely B pictures. His career advanced because he attracted the attention of two important Hollywood players: the influential gossip columnist Louella Parsons, also from Dixon, and a rising talent agent, Lew Wasserman. Until the Second World War, Reagan was constantly busy. He was nice-looking, versatile, highly competent and quite popular. For a time only Errol Flynn received more fan mail.

In 1940 Reagan married an up-and-coming actress, Jane Wyman. In 1941 he signed a seven-year million-dollar contract with Warner Brothers. In 1942 he was drafted, and spent the war producing recruiting, training and public relations films. In 1945 he was honorably discharged.

Unlike the Stewarts and the Waynes and the Gables, Reagan did not pick up where he had left off when the War ended, and increasingly was cast in smaller parts in generally unmemorable films. As his acting career stalled, Reagan became more involved in the Screen Actors Guild, "SAG," and in 1946 was chosen to serve on its board. As a result of his skillful handling of a strike by the Conference of Studios Union, run by an alleged Communist, in March of 1947 he was elected president of the union. He was re-elected five more times, remaining at the helm until 1953. As SAG's president, Reagan had to manage an organization filled with famous actors with large egos and to represent its membership in negotiations with equally self-absorbed studio heads. In discharging his responsibilities he developed and perfected skills which were to prove invaluable later on. No matter how difficult the issue, Reagan kept his sense of balance and humor. He learned when to hold firm, when to feint, when to stall and when to compromise.

During the post-war period, Reagan got more involved in politics, making speeches for Democratic organizations like the American Veterans Committee. Some of the liberal groups to which he belonged were becoming Communist fronts, and he resigned from them, joining the likes of James Roosevelt and Olivia de Havilland in denouncing communism. But he also took a public stand against blacklisting of suspected communists by the studios. During a time of turmoil, he was a voice of moderation and fairness, neither ducking the issues nor being drawn into the hysteria. In 1947 he became a member of the board of the Americans for Democratic Action, describing it as "the only voice for real liberals." [109] In 1948 he campaigned for Harry Truman.

Over the next four years Reagan started moving to the right. Though he still believed that Hollywood, rather than the federal government, should deal with communism in the motion picture industry, he now felt that the Communist Party should be banned. In 1952 he was a "Democrat for Eisenhower."[110]

By 1948, Reagan and Wyman had divorced. She said it was because Reagan's political pontificating was "exasperating."[111] Friends said it was because Wyman was a "tough broad."[112] Whatever the explanation, Reagan was devastated by what he saw as a very public failure. Fortunately, another young actress, less talented and less driven, was waiting in the wings. Her name was Nancy Davis. She engineered a meeting with Reagan in 1949. He proposed to her towards the end of 1950. They married in March of 1952.

By 1953 Reagan was no longer president of SAG and no longer receiving casting calls. Facing child-support payments to Wyman, as well as the responsibilities of a new wife, new baby and new mortgage, he needed to earn a living. In 1954, with the help of Lew Wasserman, he entered into a contract to host a weekly television show, *General Electric Theater*, at an annual salary of $125,000. During his eight years with GE, what he called his "postgraduate course in political science," Reagan's politics were transformed from somewhat liberal to clearly conservative.[113] He also acquired a new set of skills. The SAG presidency had taught him how to deal with other leaders, "the inside game of negotiation and influence."[114] At GE he learned the "outside game," how to reach "common citizens, not one by one but en masse."[115]

He reached the millions through the show itself, which by the 1956-57 season ranked third in the ratings, exposing vast audiences week after week to this handsome, well-dressed man with the pleasant voice and reassuring presence. He also reached smaller groups as GE's roving "goodwill ambassador," spending as many as three months a year visiting company employees, scattered among 139 facilities in 39 states. Sometimes he would make more than a dozen speeches a day. He would tell Hollywood stories, answer questions and press the flesh. He learned how to handle a live crowd, refining his opening jokes and perfecting a pace that avoided exhaustion and the loss of his voice. He presented himself as a "regular guy" not a stuck-up movie star. He was becoming a politician.

By 1960, when Reagan endorsed Richard Nixon, he had "completed" what he called "the process of self-conversion."[116] In 1962, he formally changed his party affiliation. He explained to a good friend, that he was not abandoning the Democratic Party, the Democratic Party had abandoned him. The same year Reagan became a Republican, General Electric dropped him and the show he had hosted for nearly a decade, some say because of lackluster ratings, some because he had become a political target.

In 1964, as he was preparing to host a new program, *Death Valley Days*, Reagan agreed to be the California co-chairman of Barry Goldwater's presidential campaign, traveling the state stumping for the candidate. Late that summer he spoke to a crowd of around 800 at the Ambassador Hotel. A number of the guests urged him to reprise his talk on television, and on the night of October 27, 1964, it was aired. Entitled "A Time for Choosing," it presented ideas Reagan had been honing for a decade. He said the choice in the election was between "the ultimate in individual freedom consistent with law and order" and the "ant heap of totalitarianism."[117] He gave specific examples of the problems with big government, like an income tax scheme that confiscated 37 cents of every dollar earned and a foreign aid program that spent $2,000,000 on supplying a yacht to an Ethiopian dictator. While his message was stark, his manner was warm. "The Speech" generated millions in contributions, but could not resurrect Goldwater's doomed candidacy. However it did, in one stroke, convert Reagan into a significant political figure. *Washington Post* columnist David Broder hailed Reagan's address as "the most successful political debut since Williams Jennings Bryan electrified the 1896 Democratic convention with his 'Cross of Gold Speech.'"[118] He was immediately besieged by admirers to seek the nomination for Governor of California. After testing the waters, in January 1966 he agreed to make the run.

Reagan entered the race for the Republican nomination for Governor of California as a decided underdog, a 54-year-old Hollywood has-been who had never held public office. Nonetheless, he decisively beat the two-term mayor of San Francisco for the G.O.P nomination and trounced the incumbent, Pat Brown, in the general election. Both opponents underestimated Reagan's skills and tried to typecast him as a right-wing radical. After years of practice, he knew how to present himself effectively both in small settings and large. With respect to ideology, Reagan tacked to the center, pledging to "squeeze, cut and trim" spending, but not threatening well-liked programs.[119]

Reagan's one-million vote margin of victory included independents and nearly 500,000 Democrats. On Election Day, a reporter asked him what he planned to do in office. He responded, "I don't know. I've never played a governor."[120] Some say that on Inauguration Day the sky in Sacramento was dark until the moment that Ronald Wilson Reagan took his oath of office, when a shaft of sunlight appeared "like a halo coming down."[121]

By all accounts, Reagan's two terms as governor of the nation's most populous state were successful. Despite his conservative philosophy, Reagan governed pragmatically and as a moderate. He approved a bill effectively legalizing abortion, abandoned his opposition to a fair housing act, doubled spending on university education, added nearly 150,000 acres to the state parks and approved the toughest rules on automobile emissions in the nation. He exhibited a willingness to deal across the aisle, on the theory that something was always better than nothing. This willingness was the key to his second term during which, working with Democrats, California enacted sweeping legislation to reform the welfare system, both tightening eligibility requirements and raising payments to those who satisfied them.

Reagan resisted pressures that he seek a third term, but came out of retirement in 1976 to challenge Gerald Ford, who had become President when Richard Nixon resigned in disgrace. His disenchantment with Ford was fueled by the chaotic withdrawal from Saigon, the impotent response to inflation and the amnesty offered to Vietnam draft evaders. Reagan's see-saw primary campaign started with a near win in New Hampshire followed by a string of defeats, an unexpected rebound, and a strong finish. Though Ford was shy of the 1,140 votes needed as the convention opened, he quickly made up the difference. However, with 1,070 votes, Reagan had lost his improbable quest by a whisker. Promising his disappointed supporters he would not "go back to sit in a rocking chair," Reagan acted the "good soldier" and campaigned for Ford in 20 states.[122] But the country wanted a change after an eight-year Republican roller-coaster ride, and Jimmy Carter, the peanut farmer from Plains, Georgia, represented that change. He was a Governor, he was an outsider, he was from the Deep South. Carter defeated Ford by over 1.5 million popular votes, and Reagan spent the next three years attending fund-raisers and keeping himself in the public eye with daily radio commentaries, broadcast on 286 stations and re-printed in 226 papers.

By virtue of his strong second-place finish in 1976, Reagan had earned the role of "front runner" for the 1980 Republican presidential nomination. Though he stumbled at the gate, losing the Iowa caucuses to George H.W. Bush, he came back to win New Hampshire and had effectively wrapped things up by mid-March. At the convention, the only suspense was whom Reagan would choose as his running mate. He settled on George H.W. Bush. The Democrats re-nominated Carter, who had been bruised by Ted Kennedy's valiant and quixotic primary opposition. In September, public opinion polls predicted a close race.

Carter's campaign attacks on Reagan as a bigot and a warmonger were without substance and backfired, and he did not help himself by grading his own performance as worthy of no better than B's and C's. Nor was he aided by declaring that the country was in a funk. Reagan did not agree with Carter's bleak assessment: "I find no national malaise. I find nothing wrong with the American people."[123] He did, however, find plenty wrong with the Carter Administration, specifically with the failing economy and the stark decline in military strength. As Reagan toured the country, particularly when he was in the Midwest, he stressed his humble roots: "I grew up in a town with people like you, just across the border in Illinois."[124]

Carter and Reagan engaged in a single debate the week before the election. Despite Reagan's success as a moderate two-term governor, there were lingering questions about his competence, particularly given his advanced age, and lingering fears that he was a "bomb thrower." There are different recollections about the moment during the debate that Reagan had it won, which everyone agrees he did.[125] I believe it occurred even before the first question was asked, when the candidates were setting up at their respective podiums. Reagan strode over to Carter, extending his hand in a gesture of civility and respect. Carter looked stunned and stunted, and the smiling, vital near-septuagenarian looked – and was – in total control.

The debate took place on October 28, 1980. The election was held on November 4. The Reagan-Bush ticket scored a landslide victory, winning 8.5 million more popular votes than Carter-Mondale, and carrying 44 states with 489 electoral votes. It was the largest electoral vote tally by a non-incumbent presidential candidate in the nation's history.

D. Wrap-Up

The Ballplayers

Beginnings, in the broadest sense, affected the career choices made by Babe Ruth and Henry Aaron. Before they were out of their teens each had decided to become a professional baseball player. For Ruth, it occurred because he was sent to St. Mary's, where baseball was almost part of the catechism. For Aaron, it occurred because he happened to be born in Mobile, Alabama, a city which was crazy about baseball in all its forms. In terms of the impact of "socio-economic" beginnings, our focus here, Ruth was not held back, but advantaged by being poor, because St. Mary's only admitted boys from indigent families. It was sheer happenstance that Aaron grew up in a city that was fanatical about America's sport.

Ruth and Aaron were assisted along the way by men who took an interest in them. For Ruth, it was Brother Mathias, who was his surrogate father, practice partner and the inspiration for his swing (and walk); Jack Dunn, who discovered him and gave him his professional start with the minor league Baltimore Orioles; and Ed Barrow, field manager of the Red Sox and front office executive with the Yankees. For Aaron, it was Ed Scott, who helped him move from the semi-pro Black Bears to the Indianapolis Clowns; Ben Garaghty, who looked after him during the trying season in the Sally League; and Mickey Owen, who engineered his shift to the outfield and spent time refining his hitting skills. To the extent the gap they filled stemmed from Ruth's and Aaron's unprivileged beginnings, their lack of privilege was more likely a plus than a problem. That is, modest beginnings may have helped them attract guides and role models.

In both cases the men played in two cities, and their careers blossomed at their second stop. None of these moves had anything to do with their circumstances growing up. For Ruth, the move from the Red Sox in Boston to the Yankees in New York meant his pitching days were over and that he would be in the field every day as a position player, a precondition to his establishing the hitting records which for decades bore his name. For Aaron, the move from Milwaukee to Atlanta meant he was playing in an environment conducive to lofting the home run ball: thin air and high elevation, more warm days and a ballpark with a relatively short porch.

Who these ballplayers were as people is a dominant part of their stories, since in each case they affected their relationships with the baseball community. Ruth's self-indulgent behavior, his rowdiness, philandering and late nights, made him a problem and a distraction to some in the Yankee clubhouse and to the front office. Aaron's race, his lack of sophistication and his languid pace, invited comment, and often derision, and made him feel disrespected and like a loner vis-a-vis almost all the white players and much of Braves' management.

But Ruth's deficiencies as a human being had little if any impact on how he played the game, as his phenomenal achievements attest. More importantly, to the extent his flaws can be laid at the doorstep of his parents, their socio-economic status was not the root cause of his problematic behavior. As for Aaron, the discrimination he faced did not diminish his performance on the field either. It was a function of his skin color, not the lack of advantages during his childhood.

The Movie Stars

If he is to be believed, Archie Leach decided to become an actor when he was barely a teenager and went to the Hippodrome in Bristol to see the lightboards that his chemistry teacher's assistant had installed. That was a moment of pure chance that had nothing to do with the modest circumstances of his birth. The subsequent turning points were similarly not affected by the Leach's place on the social ladder: his signing up with the Penders, their decision to bring him to America, his decision to remain behind when they left, Jean Dalrymple's hunch that he was worth a chance with dialogue, the introduction to Arthur Hammerstein, the whimsical cross-country road trip to Hollywood, the events leading to his fateful screen test, his departure from Paramount to gain artistic control.

To be sure Grant was initially stymied because he could not find speaking roles in the theater and because the critical reception for his stage work was mixed at best. His path to Hollywood was slowed because his first movie screen tests were unimpressive or did not impress the right people at the right time, and his progress once signed was fitful because Paramount and its chief, Adolph Zukor, were content to cast him as his generation's "eye candy." Better family connections in the film business might have helped, but a family's wealth or high standing does not guarantee such connections or get you beyond the front door.

It was not art, but economics, which piqued Cagney's interest in pursuing a career in show business, based on his recollection of the good tips he had received from actors when he worked as a teenaged bellboy at the Friars Club. And, after his father died and his sister Jeannie was born, it was economics which caused him to leave Columbia and to take a flyer in vaudeville, which paid better than wrapping parcels at a department store. For Cagney, had he been more advantaged, he would most likely have gotten a college degree in agriculture or environmental studies and become a farmer. That is, his lack of privilege was a positive and contributing factor to his becoming an entertainer. Once on that course, he "stayed it" in the face of a series of disappointments – like being dismissed from the lead in *Broadway* – because Willie told him that she would leave him if he quit. And it was a series of flukes which got him to the West Coast: theater director Keighley catching the last show of a bad play which resulted in Jim's being cast in a good play which movie star Jolson caught on its opening night which led to Jack Warner making a bet.

The Presidents

Lincoln and Reagan each had a circuitous path to the presidency and each benefitted, in the sense that he learned something, at the stops along the way: Lincoln as farm-hand, store owner, postmaster, surveyor, lawyer, Illinois congressman and Senatorial candidate; Reagan as radio sportscaster, movie actor, union president, corporate pitchman, California governor and 1976 Republican challenger. For Lincoln and Reagan, their modest backgrounds necessitated their entry into the workforce at an early age. But that was certainly not a hindrance to their ultimate success.

Each of them also gained at key points from relationships with "interested parties." For Lincoln there was Sarah Johnston, who encouraged his studies; the Clary gang, who were always in his corner; the New Salem notables, who thought he had the makings of a politician; John Stuart, who believed he could be a successful lawyer; Joshua Speed, who shared his lodgings and got him through the personal rough spots; Billie Herndon, junior partner and ever-faithful cheerleader; and Judge David Davis, who helped burnish his reputation for honesty. For Reagan there was Nelle, who got him before a crowd; his pal from the radio station, who helped get him his screen test; Lew Wasserman, who found roles for him and engineered the GE engagement; his rich Republican business friends, who pushed him to run for Governor; and Nancy, who invariably and no matter what, was at his side. These important helpmates were drawn to Lincoln and Reagan despite or maybe even because of their humble beginnings.

For both of these politicians a key speech was a career milestone. For Lincoln, his address at Cooper Union established him as a serious contender for the Republican presidential nomination. For Reagan, his half-hour television talk on conservatism catapulted him onto the national scene as a compelling spokesman for the right. Beginnings had little to do with the assignment or content or impact of these addresses.

Lincoln and Reagan both benefitted from the fact that their party lost the presidential election immediately before their run and by the fact that the winning incumbent from the "other" party – Buchanan in Lincoln's case, Carter in Reagan's – was not up to the job. Beginnings had no impact on that turn of events.

On their way to the White House neither Lincoln nor Reagan was hurt by his lack of wealth and social standing and in some respects both may have been more appealing candidates because of their modest circumstances. Indeed, in their presidential campaigns Lincoln and Reagan featured their humble backgrounds – Lincoln as the "Rail Splitter" and Reagan as the boy barely from the right side of the tracks. Since they won, it is not a stretch to say their humble backgrounds helped.

A final thought. The irrelevance of these men's humble beginnings may also have do with the fact that most of the managers and scouts who picked the ballplayers were seldom from high society, that Hollywood was invented by Eastern European immigrants and that the majority of voters are – or regard themselves as – underdogs.

II. At the Top

Because the twists and turns on the road to success are unique, and not self-evident, it seemed useful to tell a few specific stories to make the general point that the underdogs who became the greatest ballplayers, movie stars and presidents were not held back by their lack of privilege at the start. Storytelling is not, I think, necessary when it comes to demonstrating that the qualities that made these men great were similarly unaffected by their early difficulties. Put another way, the traits and attributes that made Ruth and Aaron great ballplayers, Cagney and Grant great movie stars, and Lincoln and Reagan great Presidents are to a large extent the same traits and attributes that made their iconic colleagues great. The elements of greatness in these three very public professions are out there for everyone to see.

A. The Ballplayers

In the case of the best ballplayers, favorable genetics gave them the wherewithal to hone the skills that made them such extraordinary athletes. Excellence at throwing, catching, hitting, running, leaping and sliding has nothing to do with status or material wealth. Nor does sufficient stamina to last through nine innings in the heat of summer or the power and coordination to routinely hit the ball over the fence. Neither does eyesight good enough to see the pitcher's grip and the memory to recall his repertoire and anticipate his next offering. Parents' standing in the community or financial wherewithal has no impact on the ability to tune out distractions when on the field or to exercise patience in the batter's box. The great ballplayers were all physically gifted and applied those gifts to master the tasks called for on the diamond. Being un-privileged was essentially irrelevant to their success. As many of them said in one way or another, they were all blessed with talent, a God-given knack.

B. The Movie Stars

The great actors had a fortunate amalgam of natural aptitudes and acquired skills. They all had "looks," or really "a look," that audiences found pleasing or interesting. Their voices were distinct and appealing. To varying degrees they were keen observers and adept mimics, had good memories for dialogue, had enough intelligence to improvise and ad-lib and had a sense of timing and a gift for movement.

While the alchemy is mysterious, the necessary aptitudes and skills have little to do with childhood circumstance. Some of the specific traits – appearance, voice, intellect – are matters of genetics that have nothing to do with socio-economics. Others, like mimicry, memory, timing, observation and movement, are a mix of aptitude and skill. But the aptitude is God-given, and there is no basis for saying that these skills are more readily acquired when parents are well-heeled.

There are three other less obvious qualities often possessed by actors at the top of their game. One is a willingness to draw from experience and to reveal a depth of feeling and vulnerability. Another is a keen sense of professionalism: coming to the set with lines memorized, fully made up, on their marks. The last is respect for their fellow and sister actors, evinced by patient coaching, active listening and sharing or ceding the spotlight. These qualities, like the others, are not dependent on the economic or social circumstances defining the early years of life.

C. The Presidents

The most well-regarded Presidents all had had above-average IQs and brought their intelligence to bear on everything from mastering complex situations to crafting purposeful speeches. Many also had quite extraordinary quotients of emotional intelligence. They could read people well and displayed an empathy that more often than not allowed them to have their way, whether dealing in person one-on-one or with massive and unseen audiences. The great ones used these special qualities in encounters with the press, with their staffs, with legislators and with the electorate. While there can be a debate about how much of "EQ" is a function of nature as opposed to nurture, there is no evidence that socio-economic background is correlated with this trait, one way or the other.

Many were gifted communicators, both in terms of style and of substance. Often they had an active hand in writing what they later spoke, and were capable of inspiring with poetic oratory, as well as imparting dry information with clarity. Overall, they had a feel for the right thing to say and the right way to say it. This feel cannot by attributed to whether they were privileged or un-privileged as youngsters. A good sense of humor was frequently part of the "communication" mix, though the techniques varied: some had an acerbic wit, some had a gift for shaggy dog stories, some were masters at self-deprecation. Again, not a function of early advantages.

The best presidents were seen as truthful and reliable. They were regarded as trustworthy, as men of integrity, and that was critical in their intimate dealings with adversaries, at home and abroad, and in their interactions with the voters both during campaigns and once in office. Humility contributed to or leveraged these elements of greatness, and it is the one trait that might have come more naturally to those who had less in their boyhoods. But that would make their lack of advantage a positive factor, not a negative one.

Finally, virtually all of the most effective and admired presidents were seen as determined, optimistic and confident, attributes that enabled them to take the bold steps that translated into the achievements that in turn earned them their reputations. To the extent their greatness was partly event-driven – coming into office at a time of domestic or foreign peril – their socio-economic status obviously was wholly irrelevant.

For those who made it to the pinnacle of these three unique fields, the traits, attributes and skills which brought them there were either inherited or learned. Of the inherited traits and attributes, they are doled out irrespective of social background. As to the learned skills, none seems in any obvious or substantial way to be class-based or linked.

III. Special Sauce

In 1967, the McDonald's franchise in Uniontown, Pennsylvania, added a new item to its menu called the "Aristocrat." It was introduced to compete with the "Big Boy," a sandwich offered by its rival Eat'n Park. At $.45 the "Aristocrat" – later named the "Big Mac" – was almost triple the price of its basic burger. The upcharge made sense, since the debut item was far heftier, made up of "two all-beef patties, special sauce, lettuce, cheese, pickles, onions – on a sesame seed bun." It turned out that the "special sauce" was just store-bought mayonnaise, relish and mustard, mixed with vinegar and seasoned with garlic, onion powders and paprika. Yet, the sauce did give the Big Mac a singular taste and made it a fast-food favorite for millions.

Is there a "secret ingredient" that helps explain how the Ruths and Aarons, the Cagneys and Grants, the Lincolns and Reagans ascended to the peaks of their professions and remained there? Is there a common trait that spiked their greatness, irrespective of their unique paths and the very different talents and skills required for success in their very different worlds? Malcolm Gladwell, in his provocative *Outliers*, says that for extraordinary achievers the "X-factor" is practice. The idea that "practice makes perfect" has been around for years, as has Edison's reminder that 99% of what passes for genius is "perspiration" not "inspiration." What Gladwell did is provide the empirical evidence behind these adages, describing in detail how the Beatles, Bill Gates and other standouts had to devote thousands of hours to achieve virtuosity in their disparate fields.[126] Though Gladwell demonstrates convincingly that these "outliers" invariably spent years perfecting their crafts, he does not explain what it was that caused them to work so hard. In fairness, he was not trying to answer that question.

Many others have tried to do so, and of them Angela Duckworth has come up with the response I find the most satisfying and convincing. Duckworth, too, believes that "effort" – her word for Gladwell's "practice" – is what turns talent and potential into actual success.[127] But she gives a name to the trait that makes the successful undertake that effort in a sustained and purposeful way. She calls it "grit" and defines it as "perseverance and passion for long term goals."[128] While it is a familiar notion, embedded in the homespun dictum, "If at first you don't succeed, try, try again," Duckworth goes beyond the cliché and provides insight and elaboration:

> Grit entails working strenuously toward challenges, maintaining effort and interest over years despite failure, adversity, and plateaus in progress. The gritty individual approaches achievement as a marathon; his or her advantage is stamina. Whereas disappointment or boredom signals to others that it is time to change trajectory and cut losses, the gritty individual stays the course.[129]

Duckworth reached her conclusions after extensive research. She and her colleagues administered a questionnaire dubbed the "Grit Scale" to individuals engaged in a range of activities and programs that, in one way or another, were designed to winnow out the best participants. Half the questions were about "passion," asking whether the subject retained interests over time or went from obsession to obsession, and half were about "perseverance," asking whether the subject finished what he or she began or gave up when the going got tough.[130] Her objective was to determine how self-assessments of grittiness correlated with performance. Her interviewees included West Pointers about to undergo the rigorous seven-week "Beast Barracks," members of a sales force employed selling vacation time-shares, students attending Chicago's public high schools, participants in a national spelling bee and volunteers for the Green Beret's Special Forces Selection Course. It turned out in each instance that the survivors – those who got through the Beast Barracks, remained in the time-share sales force, graduated from the Chicago high schools, entered the final rounds of the spelling bee and were selected for the Special Forces – were the ones with the highest scores on the Grit Scale.

Each of the six men in our sample encountered setbacks both on their way up and once they got to the top. Their resilience in the face of these challenges – their grit – was another element of their greatness, the "special sauce" essential to fully understanding the secret of their accomplishments.

For the ballplayers, at least when they were in the batter's box, failure was to be assumed in the overwhelming majority of plate appearances. To strike out or ground out or fly out two-thirds of the time, produced a Hall of Fame-worthy .333 batting average.

Babe Ruth showed his grit when he needed to face the music – the fines, suspensions, bad press – caused by his outrageous behavior. It was evident when he rebounded from his major slumps in 1922 and 1925 to produce banner comebacks. It was grit, too, that mid-career enabled him to respond to the chorus of criticism of his notorious excesses on and off the field by moderating his behavior and to react to the physical toll it was taking by subjecting himself to a rigorous multi-year post-season fitness program.

Racial bigotry dogged Henry Aaron's career almost from the start. At least from the time he was in Jacksonville, he was forced to face slurs and taunts and, occasionally, danger. Some of his teammates were rednecks and some just insensitive, but they contributed to making him feel like an outsider. Magazine writers and reporters stereotyped him, cruelly parodying his untutored speech and caricaturing his unhurried style. The venom reached a fever pitch when he was on the cusp of Ruth's career home run record, making what should have been an episode of triumph into a nightmare of death threats and vitriol. Yet despite it all, Aaron pressed on.

Jim Cagney and Cary Grant needed grit to pursue their acting careers, particularly in the years before they got to Hollywood, when they were periodically out of work. During these down times, Cagney considered becoming a shoe salesman and a streetcar conductor, and Grant was reduced to stilt-walking at Coney Island and barking at carnivals. Both of them also had to keep going despite years of anonymity. Cagney had to rebound after his unceremonious firing from *Broadway* on the eve of his London debut. Grant had to repeatedly pick himself up after critics skewered his musical talents and screen tests had pronounced him hopeless. Grant also had to deal with a studio that for five years had him typecast as a "pretty boy," relegating him to second-tier status in B movies.

Abraham Lincoln needed grit to get him through a series of electoral setbacks, including his failure to win his first state race in Illinois in 1832, his failure to win the Republican nomination for Vice President in 1856, and his failure to be selected for the U.S. Senate in both 1854 and 1858. As President he had to deal with a Cabinet filled with better known rivals, a succession of lackluster Northern generals, a string of Union defeats, a restive electorate and opinion leaders who pushed and pulled him on the critical question of emancipation.

Ronald Reagan's grit was tested after the end of the Second World War when his acting career collapsed. His resourcefulness enabled him to re-invent himself first as a television personality and spokesman for American industry and then as a voice for conservative values. It took determination to seek to unseat his party's incumbent president in 1976 and resilience to pivot from that unsuccessful bid to go on and fight another day. He toughed it out through the 1981 recession, the collapse of arms control negotiations at Reykjavik and the Iran-Contra scandal. For Reagan, his finest hour may have been his buoyant reaction to and recovery from John Hinckley's assassination attempt, a display of "true grit," if there ever was one.

Ruth, Aaron, Reagan and Grant had to deal, too, with the embarrassment of very public divorces, Grant more than once. And Lincoln had to endure the tragic losses of his first love and three of his four sons.

Gladwell tells us outliers, exceptional people, had to practice long and hard in order to achieve success. Duckworth says the key to their success is the grit that made them *want to* practice and to continue to do so even when things were not going well. She does not specifically reveal where this desire and drive comes from. Particularly for those who succeed despite challenging beginnings, I wonder whether their resilience in dealing with setbacks as adults derives from the adversity they encountered growing up?

To at least some extent, there was trauma and stress in the childhoods of each of the 21 great underdogs previously described. Five of the men dealt with the death of a parent. Bill Clinton and Andrew Jackson both lost their fathers before they were born. Clark Gable's mother died when he was an infant, Abraham Lincoln's mother died when he was nine, and Andrew Jackson's mother died when he was 14.

Five of the 21 were formally or effectively separated from one of more of their parents. Barack Obama Sr. was gone from the life of Barack II before he was one. Will Gable farmed out Clark to relatives when he was around two. The Pecks sent Greg to live with his grandmother when he was seven. George Ruth Sr. dispatched George Jr. to St. Mary's Industrial School when he was seven and a half. And Elias Leach secretly committed Elsie to a mental institution when Archie was 10. Sam and May Williams were not formally "separated" from Ted and his brother, but they were seldom there.

There was frequent and upsetting bickering between John Wayne's parents, Clark Gable's parents, Cary Grant's parents, Bill Clinton's parents and Lyndon Johnson's parents. Will Gable and David Eisenhower were emotionally remote from their sons, and Molly Morrison was openly hostile to hers, the future John Wayne. Alcoholism, or heavy drinking, was an issue with Josh Gibson's mother and with the fathers of Jim Cagney, Kirk Douglas, Bill Clinton, Ronald Reagan and Lyndon Johnson. Mickey Mantle was sexually abused by his half-sister, and Bill Clinton saw his stepfather physically abuse his mother. Both Mickey Mantle and Dwight Eisenhower faced life-threatening injuries.

Virtually all 21 dealt at some level with economic insecurity. A number had fathers who had low-paying jobs that were also dangerous and back-breaking. Josh Gibson's dad was a steelworker in the Carnegie-Illinois mills in Pittsburgh, and Stan Musial's hauled 100-pound bales for American Steel and Wire in nearby Donora. Mutt Mantle labored in the underground mines of Picher Lead and Zinc Company, and Melchor Clemente worked the cane fields for Central Victoria. Herbert Aaron was employed first as a boilermaker and then a riveter for Alabama Dry Dock and Shipping Company, and Herschel Danielovitch, Kirk Douglas' father, sold metal, rags and junk from a horse-drawn wagon. John Wayne, Gregory Peck, Jim Cagney and Dwight Eisenhower watched, or heard tell about, their fathers' failures when they finally had the chance to run a business of their own. Clark Gable and Lyndon Johnson lived through the feast and famine cycle of the oil business and cotton farming. Many of them endured periods when their parents were simply unemployed.

It turns out that our iconic ballplayers, movie stars and Presidents were not unique among extraordinary achievers in facing hardship at a young age.

Dean Simonton, in his monumental work *Greatness*, surveyed the literature on illustrious men and woman and concluded that "[t]o attain success of the highest order, a person may have to suffer first."[131] In a section called "Building Character: Early Adversity" he cited "orphanhood," parental alcoholism and "economic ups and downs" as among the upheavals experienced by Nobel Prize winners in literature, preeminent scientists and renowned political leaders.[132] Though he does not use the word "grit," Simonton wrote that the success of his distinguished subjects required "motivation of the highest possible magnitude."[133] The Goertzels in their study of 400 "eminences" included a chapter titled "Early Agonies" that similarly recounted the loss of a mother or father or the pain of parental indifference or rejection as not uncommon among their famous men and women.[134] The Goertzels observed: "In many instances, the handicaps are considered by those who experience them as having been motivating factors in their achievements."[135] Anticipating Duckworth, the Goertzels noted, "If there is one trait that all of our subjects had in common, it is persistence in pursuing their own visions and goals."[136]

Did childhood traumas trigger the "grit" these illustrious people showed as they pursued their fabled careers? And if these traumas were a trigger for some, why were they not a trigger for all? That is, why do some react to adversity by buckling and others respond to it by buckling down?

One answer to this question is offered by Paul Tough in his thoughtful and thought-provoking *How Children Succeed*. Tough maintains that "early stress and adversity can literally get under a child's skin, where it can cause damage that lasts a lifetime."[137] He contends, based on research on humans and laboratory studies with animals, that the most "effective antidote to the ill effects of early stress" comes not from drugs but from "[p]arents and other caregivers who are able to form close, nurturing relationships with their children."[138] According to Tough, these relationships "can foster resilience in them that protects them from many of the worst effects of a harsh early environment."[139] Tough variously describes the nurturing parent as "attuned to their child's mood," "responsive to his cues" and "helpful and attentive."[140]

There is evidence that virtually all of our 21 had "nurturers" in their youth. As to the future presidents, all had devoted maternal figures who clearly loved and believed in them. There was no such strong and obvious maternal bond for any of the future baseball superstars. For them the pivotal relationships were highly diverse, from dads to in-laws to coaches to interested neighbors.[141] The picture for the future movie legends is mixed. More than half had faithful and dedicated mothers; the rest were nurtured by grandmothers, fathers, and girlfriends and their families.[142]

In Tough's telling, early adversity without a nurturing relationship will not produce grit. Nor, in his view, will a nurturing relationship, particularly of the over-protective sort, produce grit without adversity. The affluent child who wants for nothing and is shielded from every disappointment by well-meaning parents may be robbed of the challenges that would make him or her a gritty adult. As Tough puts it,[143]

> [W]e know – on some level at least – that what kids need more than anything is a little hardship: some challenge, some deprivation that they can overcome, even if just to prove to themselves that they can.

And so we have the irony, again, that there may be an advantage to being un-advantaged, an upside to facing stresses early, because they permit a child to develop the capacity to rebound in the face of the setbacks and reversals that are an inevitable part of grown-up life.

While grit is a critical component of success, it will not produce it in the absence of some basic aptitude and level of skill. As Duckworth points out, there are situations where the relentless pursuit of an unattainable goal is mindless and self-defeating, occasions when a person should move on and develop a new passion. Moreover, grit is not the be all and end all. It is not a substitute for honesty, integrity and kindness. Grittiness may be necessary for becoming a great success, but it has almost nothing to do with being a good person. Duckworth acknowledged this near the end of her book, "[I]n studies of how people size up others, morality trumps all other aspects of character in importance."[144]

Grit and ability are both required to produce greatness. Ability without grit is not enough, nor is grit without ability. Grit is evident among the best ballplayers, movie stars and Presidents, as they faced challenges both on their way up and once they reached the top. While it seems clear that all of our 21 were extraordinarily able, it is not so clear that they were the absolute grittiest in their fields. Obviously, however, they were gritty enough.

IV. The Bottom Line

Since the humble beginnings of our heroes did not get in the way, and in some sense – and in some instances – actually helped them to the top, why is it that we are so impressed by the success of these underdogs?

Part of it may be that the adversity they faced as youngsters, the lack of material wealth and of status, *was* a lot to endure. Whether it was always wearing hand-me-downs, living in crummy or cramped or cold rentals, going "without" at Christmas-time or birthdays, worrying whether there would be enough to eat or always eating the same thing, watching their fathers cope with job insecurity or unemployment, life was difficult. And it remained so after they left home. Moreover, almost all of them dealt with other difficulties: the loss of a mother or father or both, parental rejection, alcoholism, physical or emotional abuse, significant injuries, racial or religious discrimination.

Part of it may be that even if starting off at the lower end of the socio-economic scale did not directly impede their progress, the road was not easy. At very young ages, virtually all of them had to work after school and during vacations. Their jobs were generally menial, almost always low-paying and often backbreaking. They were employed as errand boys, farmhands, factory workers, dishwashers, bouncers, hod carriers, ditch diggers and runners. Further, the path forward was not straight and took years. And there were setbacks: for the ballplayers, dispiriting slumps; for the movie actors, lack of work; for the politicians, rejection at the polls.

Part of it may be that the details of the rise of underdogs in the worlds of sports, entertainment and politics are not widely known or do not square with our own experiences. That is, there is a general sense that lack of status and lack of wealth *does* make it difficult, or even impossible, to get many kinds of jobs and slows or limits advancement. Sometimes it is a function of sheer and simple snobbery. Sometimes it is because being un-advantaged is often linked with being a member of a minority or an otherwise disfavored race, religion or nationality, resulting in subtle or overt discrimination. Often it is because economic limitations inhibit the academic success which is a precondition for many occupations, particularly white-collar ones.[145]

Part of it may be that these highly glamorous careers are such long shots, that it seems a miracle that anyone can succeed at them. In the face of the almost insuperable odds, everyone is an underdog, the probabilities of success as remote as those of winning the lottery.

And part of it, perhaps the main or most important part, is that the humble beginnings of these heroes made their career choices remarkable, irrespective of whether their backgrounds burdened them once their choices were made. For their lack of status and material comforts – the ramshackle houses, the shoddy clothes, the monotonous meals – not only made life wearying from day-to-day, but defined what they could expect in the future. Everything they experienced foretold their limited horizons. Nothing suggested they could plan, or hope, for more or better. They had no role models at home to show them success was achievable, much less to show them how to achieve it. Yet, somehow these boys defied expectations and refused to trod the expected path, aspiring instead to something both different and grand. We are impressed because these underdogs dared to dream big and then somehow, in astonishing fashion, were able to make those big dreams come true.

PART FOUR

What of The American Dream?

I. Where It Came From

In the Declaration of Independence, Thomas Jefferson wrote it was "self-evident" that "all men are created equal" and that their God-given equality entitled them to certain "unalienable" rights, including the right to the "pursuit of Happiness." The ideas that Jefferson advanced were not new. George Mason and John Locke had to an extent anticipated them.[1] What was new was that Jefferson had elevated these philosophical ideas into principles worth fighting for.

Exactly how much and what kind of "Happiness" Jefferson had in mind was vague. However, it was implicit that this "pursuit" was not a fool's errand, that every man, no matter his station, had a chance not only to seek happiness but to achieve it.

Roughly 150 years after the Declaration of Independence, historian James Truslow Adams gave clarity and content to Jefferson's suggestive language. In 1931, in the midst of the Great Depression, Adams published his *Epic of America* in which he described a concept he called "the American dream," a phrase he liked so much that he used it more than 30 times.[2] He explained:

> [T]here has been also the American dream, that dream of a land in which life should be better and richer and fuller for every man, with opportunity for each according to his ability or achievement. It is a difficult dream for the European upper classes to interpret adequately, and too many of us ourselves have grown weary and mistrustful of it. It is not a dream of motor cars and high wages merely, but a dream of social order in which each man and woman shall be able to attain

to the fullest stature of which they are innately capable, and be recognized by others for what they are, regardless of the fortuitous circumstances of birth or position.[3]

Adams' notion was that "the fortuitous circumstances of birth and position" should not impede attainment of "the fullest stature" or the realization of a "life . . . better and richer." As such, the American Dream has two strands, both of which relate to the opportunity for upward mobility.[4] The first is that humble beginnings do not preclude extraordinary achievement, that a person can move from the proverbial log cabin to the White House, from a position of obscurity to one of fame. The second is that humble beginnings do not prevent material success, that a person can advance from rags to riches, that poor boys from the streets can become prosperous, like characters in Horatio Alger stories.

In this section we will look at whether these two strands of the American Dream have been realized by the men who became the best ballplayers, movie stars and Presidents of all time. With respect to the first strand of the Dream, we have already identified the top 20 in each of these fields, those who in Adams' words attained "the fullest stature." What we do not know is whether the proportion of underdogs in the top 20s matches the proportion of underdogs in our society as a whole. And even if that proportion does match, we do not know how many of the underdogs who attained "the fullest stature" also achieved a "fuller and richer" life, that is, proved out the second strand of the Dream.

We will also look at the extent to which the two strands of the Dream, fame and fortune, have been realized by underdogs in other enterprises and walks of life.

II. Whether It Has Worked

In order to assess whether the American Dream has "worked," we need to estimate what proportion of our society are "underdogs." Sociologists tend to see the United States as stratified into classes, the divisions based on the related concepts of occupation, income, education and prestige. The six-tier structure set forth below is based on two standard sociology texts.[5] The percentages in parentheses are the authors' estimates of the segment of the populace falling within a given tier.

- Upper/Capitalist Class (1%)
- Upper Middle Class (14-15%)
- Lower Middle/Middle Class (30-33%)
- Working Class (30%)
- Lower Class/Working Poor (13-14%)
- Underclass (12%)

Some sociologists lump together the two top tiers, the Capitalist and Upper Middle Classes, and designate them as the "Privileged Classes."[6] By inference, the lower four tiers can fairly be deemed as the "Not Privileged Classes," recognizing that they comprise not only the *under*privileged, but the *un*privileged as well.[7] As indicated above, the four "Not Privileged Classes" add up to about 85% of American society and represent those that I have been calling "underdogs." The remaining 15% of American society fall into the two "Privileged Classes" and represent those who from here on out will be referred to as "overdogs."

Whatever scholarly support there might be for a 15%/85% overdog/underdog split, it just feels more reasonable to adopt a split of 25%/75%. Accepting this breakdown, if the American Dream "worked," so that in Adams terms "the fortuitous circumstances of birth or position" were not determinative of future prospects, then 75% of the all-time great ballplayers, movie stars and Presidents, as well as 75% of great achievers in other careers, would have started life humbly, mirroring the percentage of underdogs in the country as a whole.[8]

A. For Our Greats

Obscurity to Fame

We know who the top 20 ballplayers, movie stars and Presidents are based on expert rankings. We also know from the biographies in Part Two that in each field at least six of the top 20 had a modest start in life. The open question is the classification of the remaining 14. Because there is little hard or consistent family income data, classification is based on parents' employment and their level of formal schooling, as well as on subjective descriptions of their standards of living.[9] I have used a father's occupation as a shorthand for categorization in what follows, providing further detail of their demographics in Appendix F. The parenthetical number is their top 20 rank. An asterisk indicates I am not certain about the proper placement.[10]

The Ballplayers

Underdogs

1. Babe Ruth (1): father owned a small saloon in a working class part of Baltimore, Maryland.
2. Willie Mays (2): father was a Pullman porter and employed in the tool room of a wire mill near Birmingham, Alabama.
3. Henry Aaron (3): father began as a boilermaker's assistant and ended up as a full-time riveter at a dry-dock company in Mobile, Alabama.

4. Ted Williams (5): father owned a small photography studio near the harbor in San Diego, California.
5. Lou Gehrig (6): father was often unemployed; mother worked as a cook and maid in New York City.
6. Honus Wagner (7): father worked in the coal mines in a town near Pittsburgh, Pennsylvania.
7. Stan Musial (8): father employed as a loader of wire bales in a factory outside of Pittsburgh, Pennsylvania.
8. Mickey Mantle (9): father principally worked as ground boss in zinc and lead mines in Commerce, Oklahoma.
9. Walter Johnson (10): father owned and lost a farm in Kansas and ended up as a teamster and loader for an oil company in California.
10. Joe DiMaggio (11): father operated a small boat and fished for bait in San Francisco, California.
11. Rogers Hornsby (12) father had a small farm near Winters, Texas, died young, causing the family to move to Fort Worth, Texas, where the sons worked as meat packers.
12. Cy Young (15): father inherited a small farm in Gilmore, Ohio.
13. Tris Speaker (16): father was a carpenter, farmer and part-owner of a dry goods shop in Hill County, Texas, but died prematurely, and mother took in boarders.
14. Jimmie Foxx (17): father was a tenant farmer in Sudlersville, Maryland.
15. Mike Schmidt (18): father ran a fast-food restaurant in Dayton, Ohio.
16. Josh Gibson (19): father employed as a steelworker in Pittsburgh, Pennsylvania.
17. Lefty Grove (20): father worked as a miner in Lonaconing, Maryland.

Overdogs

1. Ty Cobb* (4): father married into a prominent Georgia family and farmed, founded a newspaper and was elected as a state legislator and town mayor.
2. Christy Mathewson* (13): father saw himself as a "gentleman farmer," having married into a wealthy Pennsylvania family.
3. Barry Bonds (14): father was a major-league ballplayer.

By my tally, there are 17 Underdogs and 3 Overdogs among the top 20 ballplayers, in percentage terms: 85% vs. 15%. If we take into account the uncertainties about the placement of Cobb and Mathewson[11] – that is, leave them out of the equation – there are 17 Underdogs and 1 Overdog, a percentage breakdown of 94% vs. 6%.

HEROES WITH HUMBLE BEGINNINGS

The Movie Stars

Underdogs:

1. Cary Grant (2): father had a job as a pants presser in Bristol, England.
2. Fred Astaire (5): father was employed as a salesman for a brewery company in Omaha, Nebraska.
3. Clark Gable (7): father was an oil wildcatter in Cadiz, Ohio and later a small-time farmer.
4. James Francis Cagney (8): father worked as a bartender in New York City, but was often unemployed or underemployed.
5. Spencer Tracy (9): father worked for the railroads, for a corrugating concern and a truck company, mainly in Wisconsin.
6. Charles Chaplin (10): father was a vaudeville performer in London, England, divorced from his mother when Charles was young.
7. Gregory Peck (12): father worked the night shift at a drug store in San Diego, California.
8. John Wayne (13): father was a pharmacist's clerk in Iowa and then California.
9. Lawrence Olivier (14): father was a clergyman in a number of minor English parishes.
10. Gene Kelly (15): father sold phonograph records for a company based in Pittsburgh, Pennsylvania, until the Depression, when his employment became sporadic.
11. Kirk Douglas (17): father peddled junk in Amsterdam, New York.
12. James Dean (18): father worked as a dental technician for the Veterans Administration in Marion, Indiana, and then Santa Monica, California.
13. Burt Lancaster (19): father had a job as a postal clerk in New York City.
14. The Marx Brothers (20): father was a tailor in New York City.

Overdogs:

1. Humphrey Bogart (1): father was a prominent doctor and mother was a commercial artist in New York City.
2. James Stewart (3): father owned a large hardware "emporium" in Indiana, Pennsylvania.
3. Marlon Brando (4): father was a salesman for a limestone products company in Omaha, Nebraska, and then general sales manager for a calcium carbonate concern with offices in Chicago, Illinois.
4. Henry Fonda* (6): father owned a printing business in Omaha, Nebraska.

5. Gary Cooper* (11): father was a lawyer and rancher in Montana and served as state attorney general and as a judge on the state supreme court.
6. Orson Welles (16): father became wealthy when the Wisconsin company for which he worked was bought out.

Based on the above placements, the top 20 movie stars are made up of 14 Underdogs and 6 Overdogs, in percentage terms: 70% vs. 30%. If we take into account the uncertainties about categorizing Fonda and Cooper,[12] and eliminate them from consideration, there are 14 Underdogs and 4 Overdogs, a percentage breakdown of 78% vs. 22%.

The Presidents

Underdogs:

1. Abraham Lincoln (1): father was a carpenter and farmer in Kentucky and then Indiana.
2. Harry S. Truman (7): father was a real estate investor and speculator in Missouri who went bankrupt.
3. Dwight D. Eisenhower (8): father maintained the refrigeration equipment at a creamery in Abilene, Kansas.
4. Andrew Jackson (9): father, a farmer, died before Andrew Jr. was born, and mother worked as a housekeeper for her sister in North Carolina.
5. John Adams (12): father owned a small farm and worked as a cobbler in Quincy, Massachusetts.
6. Lyndon B. Johnson (16): father was a state legislator and speculator in Texas who went bankrupt.
7. Ronald Reagan (16): father worked as a shoe salesman in a variety of Illinois cities and towns.
8. Grover Cleveland (17): father served as a minister in a variety of minor congregations in Connecticut, Virginia, New Jersey and New York.
9. William McKinley (18): father was a partner in a small foundry located in Niles, Ohio, and also did carpentry and farmed.
10. William Jefferson Clinton (20): father was the parts manager in his brother's Buick dealership in Hot Springs, Arkansas.

Overdogs;

1. Franklin Delano Roosevelt (2): father was a millionaire who, apart from his inheritance, was an officer and board member of several companies.

2. George Washington (3): father was a successful farmer and major landowner in Virginia.
3. Thomas Jefferson (4): father was a planter, surveyor, map-maker and a justice of the peace in Virginia.
4. Theodore Roosevelt (5): father was a millionaire and helped run the family's New York-based business, initially in hardware, later in plate glass and real estate.
5. Woodrow Wilson (6): father, trained as a minister, taught college and presided over wealthy congregations in Virginia, Georgia and North Carolina.
6. James K. Polk (10): father began as a tobacco and grain farmer and shifted to planting cotton, operating first in North Carolina and then in Tennessee.
7. John F. Kennedy (11): father was a successful investor in coal, taxicabs and motion pictures and was named first chairman of the Securities and Exchange Commission.
8. James Madison (13): father was part of Virginia's "plantation gentry" and served as a justice of the peace and a church vestryman.
9. James Monroe (15): father was another Virginia farmer, though of the second tier, and supplemented his income doing finish carpentry.
10. John Quincy Adams (19): father was a successful lawyer and second President of the United States.

The categorization above produces 10 Underdogs and 10 Overdogs among the top 20 presidents, in percentage terms: 50% vs. 50%. If we adopt a backward cut-off of 1893, so we are considering Presidents who were near contemporaries of the ballplayers and movie stars, 6 Overdogs and 3 Underdogs drop out.[13] What is left are 7 Underdogs and 4 Overdogs, or a percentage breakdown of 64% to 36%.

Rags to Riches

When the U.S. Postal Service issued a commemorative stamp to mark the 150th anniversary of Horatio Alger's birth, *The New York Times* wrote that Alger's name "has become part of the language – when we describe a man's life as a 'Horatio Alger story' no one doubts that the man rose from poverty through virtue and hard work to achieve success and riches and thus realize the American Dream."[14]

Alger's first story appeared in 1867 in a juvenile magazine called *Student and Schoolmaster*. It was entitled *Ragged Dick, Or, Street Life in New York with the Bootblacks*. The protagonist, Dick Hunter, was a homeless and orphaned shoe-shine boy who managed through pluck and determination to rise from humble beginnings and make a mark for himself in the world. Over the next 32 years Alger published over a 100 such books for boys.[15]

WHAT OF THE AMERICAN DREAM?

Though in the world of business, populated by Alger's characters, career success is synonymous with wealth, that is not the case in every field. Not all great painters, poets, novelists, journalists, inventors and sculptors are well-paid. Nor do all great scientists, educators, generals or spiritual leaders make a lot of money. It is, therefore, necessary to examine whether the second strand of the American Dream applies to the underdogs among the top 20 ballplayers, movie stars and presidents. That is, did these men achieve wealth to accompany their celebrity?

To answer the question, I have analyzed the annual income of the underdog greats identified above and compared it with the threshold levels for the top American wage earners, as compiled by the IRS since 1917. A man is arguably "rich" if his income is at or above the level of the top 5% of U.S. workers and is certainly "rich" if he crosses the threshold for the top 1%.[16] What follows are estimates of the point in their careers when the underdog greats reached these levels, which all but one of them did. The bases for these conclusions is detailed in Appendix G.

The Ballplayers

The data, summarized below, reveal that 16 of the 17 great ballplayers who started off in metaphorical rags achieved riches early in their careers.

- Babe Ruth's salary placed him in the top 5% of American wage earners by year two of a 22-year career and in the top 1% by year six.
- Willie Mays' salary placed him in the top 5% of American wage earners in the first year of a 23-year career and in the top 1% by year five.
- Hank Aaron's salary placed him in the top 5% of American wage earners by year two of a 23-year career and in the top 1% by year four.
- Ted Williams' salary placed him in the top 5% of American wage earners in the first year of a 19-year career and in the top 1% by year two.
- Lou Gehrig's salary placed him in the top 5% of American wage earners by year three of a 17-year career and in the top 1% by year six.
- Honus Wagner's salary placed him in the top 5% of American wage earners in the first year of a 21-year career and in the top 1% by year six.
- Stan Musial's salary placed him in the top 5% of American wage earners by year two of a 22-year career and in the top 1% by year four.
- Mickey Mantle's salary placed him in the top 5% of American wage earners in the first year of an 18-year career and in the top 1% by year three.

- Walter Johnson's salary placed him in the top 5% of American wage earners by year two of a 21-year career and in the top 1% by year four.
- Joe DiMaggio's salary placed him in the top 1% of American wage earners in the first year of a 13-year career.
- Rogers Hornsby's salary placed him in the top 5% of American wage earners by year three of a 23-year career and in the top 1% by year seven.
- Cy Young's salary placed him in the top 5% of American wage earners at least by year eight of a 22-year career and in the top 1% at least by year 14.
- Tris Speaker's salary placed him in the top 1% of American wage earners at least by year seven of a 22-year career.
- Jimmie Foxx's salary placed him in the top 5% of American wage earners by year four of a 21-year career and in the top 1% by year six.
- Mike Schmidt's salary placed him in the top 5% of American wage earners by year three of an 18-year career and in the top 1% by year four.
- Lefty Grove's salary placed him in the top 5% of American wage earners in the first year of a 17-year career and in the top 1% by year four.

With respect to Josh Gibson, as an African American whose career began in the early 1930s, he came of age too soon for his prodigious talents to be properly acknowledged and appropriately rewarded.

The Movie Stars

The data, summarized below, reveal that all of the 14 great movie stars who started off humbly also became well-to-do early in their careers.

- Cary Grant's earnings placed him in the top 1% of American wage earners in the first year of his 35-year career.
- Fred Astaire's earnings placed him in the top 1% of American wage earners in the first year of his 42*-year career.[17]
- Clark Gable's earnings placed him in the top 1% of American wage earners in the first year of his 31-year career.
- James Cagney's earnings placed him around the top 5% of American wage earners in the first year of his 32*-year career and around the top 1% by year two.
- Spencer Tracy's earnings placed him in the top 5% of American wage earners in the first full year of his 37-year career and in the top 1% by year two.

WHAT OF THE AMERICAN DREAM?

- Charles Chaplin's earnings likely placed him in the top 5% of American wage earners in the fifth year of his 40-year career and in the top 1% by year eight.
- Gregory Peck's earnings placed him in the top 1% of American wage earners in the first year of his 45*-year career.
- John Wayne's earnings placed him around the top 5% of American wage earners in the first full year of his 46-year career and in the top 1% by year two.
- Lawrence Olivier's earnings placed him in the top 1% of American wage earners by the seventh year of his 52*-year career.
- Gene Kelly's earnings placed him in the top 1% of American wage earners by the second year of his 29*-year career.
- Kirk Douglas' earnings placed him in the top 1% of American wage earners by the second year of his 43*-year career.
- James Dean's earnings placed him in the top 5% of American wage earners in the second full year of his 4-year career and in the top 1% by year four.
- Burt Lancaster's earnings placed him in the top 1% of American wage earners in the first year of his 44-year career.
- The Marx Brothers' individual earnings placed each in the top 1% of American wage earners in the first year of their 15-year careers.

The Presidents

Assessing the riches achieved by the Presidents is a lot simpler because their salaries were prescribed by statute.[18] The 10 underdogs among the great Presidents are listed below in chronological order along with their salaries and the average and high 1% thresholds during their tenures.[19]

Rank	Name	Tenure		Statutory Salary	1% Threshold in Tenure	
		Term 1	Term 2		Average	High
11	John Adams	1797-1801		$ 25,000	$ 5,223	$ 5,318
9	Andrew Jackson	1829-1833	1833-1837	$ 25,000	$ 3,714	$ 3,875
1	Abraham Lincoln	1861-1865	1865	$ 25,000	$ 5,334	$ 6,838
17	Grover Cleveland	1885-1889	1893-1897	$ 50,000	$ 3,799	$ 4,027
18	William McKinley	1897-1900		$ 50,000	$ 3,514	$ 3,571
7	Harry S. Truman	1945-1949	1949-1953	$ 50,000	$ 13,374	$ 15,751
8	Dwight Eisenhower	1953-1957	1957-1961	$ 100,000	$ 18,386	$ 20,599
14	Lyndon Johnson	1963-1965	1965-1969	$ 100,000	$ 26,142	$ 30,859
16	Ronald Reagan	1981-1985	1985-1989	$ 200,000	$ 97,604	$ 132,679
20	William Jefferson Clinton	1993-1997	1997-2001	$ 200,000	$ 191,372	$ 261,991

The statutory salaries of all 10 underdogs exceeded the average 1% thresholds during their years in office. President Clinton's salary was the only one that was less than the maximum 1% threshold in certain years, though it always was above the 5% threshold. Congress increased the presidential salary to $400,000, effective 2001.

Analysis

Of the all-time great ballplayers, movie stars and Presidents, there is a varying picture of the extent to which the proportion of underdogs within each group of 20 matches the promise of the American Dream. Under our assumption that underdogs make up 75% of society as a whole, one would expect 75% of these greats to be underdogs, if the Dream were perfectly realized. The following table recaps the "statistics" tallied above. The "Base Case" reflects the initial cut of data, the "Alternate Case" reflects the result of discarding the "uncertain" overdogs among the ballplayers and movie stars and eliminating the Presidents in office before 1893.

	Percent of Underdogs	
	Cases	
	Base	Alternate
Ballplayers	85%	94%
Movie Stars	70%	78%
Presidents	50%	64%

As the table shows, the American Dream "worked" best for the top 20 ballplayers, second best for the top 20 movie stars and third best – or worst – for the top 20 Presidents. Given the extremely small sample size, it is fair to say that overall the Dream was realized at the top of all three of these fields.[20]

Other studies corroborate the conclusion that most sports stars and entertainment celebrities had humble beginnings. Suzanne Keller, who tackles the subject of elites generally, wrote that "the elites of stage, screen, sports and the arts . . . have apparently always been more accessible to lower-class individuals."[21] A 1958 survey of 156 leading actors of the 1950s found that 54% of them were "poor" and only 7% were "wealthy."[22] Two decades later, a more comprehensive analysis of the backgrounds of 129 actors defined as America's "screen elite" during the period from 1932 to 1984, resulted in a similar finding:

> None of the stars has been drawn from the upper-upper class and only one tenth from the upper-middle classes. Most performers have come from the middle (46 percent) or lower-middle (24 percent) classes. However, the percentage from the lower-lower classes has also been considerable: one fifth. . . . As a group, movie stars have come from the lower socio-economic strata . . .[23]

With respect to baseball, we have this general observation from a student of the game: "Since it first took shape in the grass of Hoboken, New Jersey, the diamond has been the Ellis Island of playing fields, offering its base paths and batter's boxes for the hungriest and readiest of able young men."[24]

As to the Presidents, two academics contend that occupants of the Oval Office come predominantly from the privileged classes, dismissing the American Dream as a myth.[25] One reason for the divergence between their conclusions and those presented here is our different approaches to classification.[26] It is unclear whether theirs has a basis in classical sociology or is idiosyncratic. Whatever the case, mine is not technical in nature.

In making a lay determination of who is an underdog, I have focused primarily on the economics side of "socio-economics," on standard of living rather than social status. I have also focused on the immediate family – parents and siblings – treating the extended family as largely irrelevant; a maternal grandmother's mercantile empire has no bearing to me unless she actually handed it down to her grandson, just as a paternal grandfather's Harvard degree, in my mind, does not affect his grandson's standing unless he too was an Ivy Leaguer. Further, I have viewed a parent's economics in absolute not relative terms; the question is whether the family was well-fixed from a national perspective, and it does not matter that its 20-acre farm was the largest in the county or that no one else in the village had indoor plumbing. Moreover, I have treated as immaterial a son's perception of his family's circumstance; that Reagan, Cagney and Aaron all felt that others had it far worse than they did is a bit surprising and quite heart-warming but of no probative significance. Finally, I have given determinative weight to a father's ultimate financial status during his son's childhood, rather than his ups and downs along the way. So, the fact that Richard Welles, Orson's father, had limited resources early on working for a Kenosha, Wisconsin, bicycle company is trumped by the fact that he received a $100,000 settlement when that company was sold, and he never had to work another day in his life. By the same token, the fact that Sam Johnson, Lyndon's father, had a big house and fancy car when his wheeling and dealing went well is eclipsed by the fact that he went bankrupt and his family became destitute when his bet on the cotton market spectacularly failed.

The point is that when the son of a clothing salesman makes it to the majors or has a role in a big-budget movie or is elected to Congress, his achievement stands as an underdog success story. It does not matter that the town held his father in esteem or that the family's annual income put it among the highest in the rural county or that a great-grandparent had owned an estate or that his parents at one time had made a bundle. The kid is still an underdog in my book.

As to the "riches" strand of the American Dream, the picture is quite simple and uniform. Virtually all of these underdog greats achieved some level of fortune to go along with their fame. Josh Gibson aside, all of the 16 underdog ballplayers had earnings above the 1% threshold for the bulk of their careers.[27] The same appears to be true for all of the 14 underdog actors, although the earnings data for Charles Chaplin, the Marx Brothers and Gene Kelly is sketchy. Finally, the statutory stipends prescribed for the 10 underdog Presidents were sufficiently large, indeed extremely generous in the 19th century, to exceed the 1% cut-off in each year that nine of the 10 were in office, and even for the 10th, Bill Clinton, his $200,000 stipend was more than the *average* 1% cut-off during his eight years in office.

B. For Others

As we have seen, the collective portrait of the top 20 ballplayers, movie stars and Presidents by and large reflects the promise of the American Dream. That is, the proportion of underdogs among the greats in these fields approximates the proportion of underdogs in American society as a whole. But can this finding be generalized? Can the same be said of the 20 great men and women in all or most enterprises or walks of life? Unfortunately, that precise question is virtually impossible to answer.

The problems begin with deciding what other careers to examine. There are the standard professions, law, medicine, engineering, business and finance, where being the "best in the business" results in admiration, recognition and perhaps celebrity. But, what about the premier scientists, psychologists, philosophers, educators and academics? What about the top missionaries, generals, architects and painters? How many careers should be examined? Should some be sub-divided? Are all lawyers lumped together or should we distinguish those who practice with firms from those who become judges from those who are legal scholars? For engineers, should we distinguish chemical from electrical from mechanical? For doctors, should we distinguish surgeons from psychiatrists from diagnosticians? For scientists, should we distinguish physicists from botanists from astronomers?

Once we somehow agree on a list of suitable careers, how do we identify the "Greats"? What are the evaluative criteria? How readily available is the information required to make the evaluation once the criteria are set? Who are the evaluators, the counterparts to the sportswriters and film critics and political pundits who ranked the ballplayers, movie stars and Presidents? That is, who can provide competent and objective assessments of quality for occupations that are esoteric and/or seldom in the public eye?

And if a set of careers can be defined and if the 20-best participants of all-time can be identified, how accessible and comprehensive is the biographical information necessary to determine the socio-economic status of their parents and how handy and reliable is the information on their earnings?

In light of these hurdles, it is simply not feasible to analyze the greats in other fields in the same way that we have analyzed the greats in the worlds of sports, entertainment and politics. Nonetheless, there is considerable general data out there about the backgrounds of notables in other careers from which we can gain a sense, and draw conclusions, about the efficacy of the American Dream in these other worlds.

Obscurity to Fame

A number of academics have examined the lives of men and women of distinction in an effort to explain the factors that caused or enabled them to so set themselves apart. Among the factors considered in some of these studies is the nature of their upbringing, including their parents' status. In 1962 Victor and Mildred Goertzel published *Cradles of Eminence,* examining the childhoods of 400 people who were deemed to have made a significant mark on society. Sixteen years later, and joined by their son Ted, the study was updated in *Three Hundred Eminent Personalities.* The 700 in the combined studies included artists, novelists, composers, poets, inventors, scientists, diplomats, explorers, labor leaders, financiers, soldiers and humanitarians. In a summary of the first 400, the Goertzels found that "[w]ealth is much more frequent than is abject poverty," calculating that nine were on public assistance, raised in orphanages or experienced extreme deprivation as compared with 21 who lived on inheritances or were extremely well-off.[28] They said that fully 358 of the 400 "could be classified as representing the business or professional classes."[29] They reached the same conclusions after evaluating the next 300, claiming that "the eminent come predominantly (80 per cent) from middle-class business and professional homes."[30] Recognizing that their figures likely include some in the business class who owned small shops and some in the professional class that taught public school, the Goertzels' work nonetheless suggests that the bulk of their "eminences" were not underdogs.

The Goertzel findings were consistent with those reached several decades earlier by Evelyn Raskin of the University of Minnesota. In a study of the backgrounds of two groups of "eminent men" from the 19th century, 120 scientists and 123 "men of letters," she concluded "that the predominance of gifted men come from the three highest socio-economic divisions, with the professional class, specifically, making the largest contribution."[31] She also concluded "that 73 per cent and 85 per cent of writers and scientists respectively are not recorded to have experienced financial hardships . . . ."[32]

C. Wright Mills studied the nearly 1,500 American businessmen, born between 1570 and 1879, who had achieved sufficient renown to be included in the *Dictionary of American Biography*. Nearly 64% of this "American business elite" were from the Upper and the Upper Middle Classes, the proportion increasing to 70.7%, if the focus is restricted to those born from 1850 to 1879. Mills also reported that over 75% of those in the next generation of business elite, with birthdates between 1879 and 1907, had fathers who were in the professions or in business. He observed that "[t]he best statistical chance of becoming a member of the business elite is to be born into it."[33] Suzanne Keller published findings complementing and buttressing those of Mills.

She calculated that 57% of business leaders in 1950 had fathers who were "businessmen (owners or managers)," with only 25% having "originated from lower-class homes."[34]

Another comprehensive study, this one by John Schmidhauser, analyzed the rarefied world of the U.S. Supreme Court. He found that from 1789 through 1957, 90% of the Justices were "overwhelmingly from the socially prestigeful and politically-influential gentry class in the late eighteenth and early nineteenth century or the professionalized upper middle-class thereafter."[35] Only a "handful" – nine when he wrote – were of "humble origin."[36]

Harriet Zuckerman analyzed another rarefied world, that inhabited by the 71 Americans who won a Nobel Prize in science. Of them 58, or 82%, had fathers who were Professionals or Managers/Proprietors, seemingly members of the privileged classes.[37] Leo Moulin conducted a broader study of 214 Nobel Prize science winners from around the globe. Though his data was more fragmentary – he only had background information for a third of them – he similarly concluded that "the social origins of the Nobel Prize winners are never 'humble' and that the fathers almost always are of very high social position."[38] His conclusion was consistent with Anne Roe's finding that "most" of the 64 distinguished physical, biological and social scientists she interviewed were "from what would be called upper middle class homes," 34 with fathers in the "Professions" and 20 with fathers in "Business."[39]

U.S. diplomats at premier postings constitute another elite. Keller studied the backgrounds of 120 Ambassadors and Ministers sent to 10 important capitals during the period from 1900 to 1953. She discovered that "[o]ne third . . . could be classified as members of a native aristocracy of old landed wealth" and "another third" could be classified "as members of a native plutocracy of financial and commercial wealth."[40] When looked at in terms of fathers' occupations, Keller found 32% were professionals and 36% had jobs she called "Proprietary and Official."[41]

Finally, there is some data on high-ranking members of the military and on preeminent members of the press corps. Morris Janowitz studied over 1,200 military leaders in all branches of service between 1910 and 1950 and found that over 65% had fathers with "Professional and Managerial" or "Business" backgrounds.[42] Only 15% had fathers who were wage earners or farmers.[43] Leo Rosten interviewed 127 journalists whose beat was Washington, D.C., prestigious newsmen whose columns appeared in nearly 200 daily papers. He concluded that "most of them came from favorable economic backgrounds," largely from professional families.[44]

The foregoing is admittedly anecdotal in nature, and there are ambiguities in the terminology used. That said, unlike the great ballplayers, movie stars and Presidents, the majority of these anonymous "greats" do not seem to be underdogs. To the contrary, these "eminences" and "elites" come mainly from privileged backgrounds, generally from the business and professional classes. As such, their successes belie that aspect of the American Dream promising that the well-born should not have any edge when it comes to the race to the top. For them, in defiance of Adams' hopes, they seem to have reached "the fullest stature" in part because of "the fortuitous circumstances" of their birth.[45]

Rags to Riches

There are two approaches to examining whether those who achieve a "better and richer life" in fields other than sports, entertainment and politics have demographic backgrounds that, in keeping with the American Dream, mirror our overall class structure.[46] The first approach involves an analysis of the relationship between affluence and education. The second looks at intergenerational studies of economic mobility.

Affluence and Education

Using 2000 as a sample year, the Decennial Census permits us to identify men in job classifications with a median income at or above the 5% level for all wage earners, a level that can fairly be described as conferring "riches."[47] The 23 specific occupations that make up the 5% slice can be grouped into five broad categories:

> ➢ Engineers (civil, mechanical, aerospace, etc.) 29%
> ➢ Computer software developers 20%
> ➢ Chief executives and public administrators 19%
> ➢ Medical and allies (doctors, dentists, etc.) 17%
> ➢ Legal (lawyers, judges) 13%

There have been no published studies of the class origins of the individuals who comprise this top tier. But there is a way of backing into such an assessment, based on other information the Census Bureau collects, data on the academic attainments of those within each occupational code.

For the year 2000, over 94% of American males in the top 5% spent some time in college, 34.2% earning bachelor's degrees and 43.2% earning either masters degrees, professional degrees or doctorates.[48] This academic profile is consistent with the conventional wisdom that the more schooling you have, the better your chances are of landing a good job.[49] To what extent did these highly-educated men who achieved this financial success rise from modest backgrounds? Or more precisely, to what extent did these men who ended up in the top 5% of wage earners begin as underdogs, such that their climb up the economic ladder fits the rags to riches paradigm? Apparently, not much. The facts are that almost from infancy, the child who grows up in an affluent family has an advantage over his un-privileged counterpart when it comes to succeeding academically. Put another way, "[S]uccess in school remains linked tightly to class"[50]

Some evidence of that linkage:

- By age 3 the children of professional parents hear three times as many words spoken to them as children of welfare parents and this "shortfall" is "at the root of the poorer kids' later failures in school . . ."[51]
- "[P]reschool attendance remains higher among children from more advantaged families."[52]
- "Test scores of more and less advantaged preschoolers show wide gaps before the children even enter school."[53]
- By fifth grade, lower class kids had reading scores that were 15% lower than those of upper class kids, the difference attributable entirely to the "learning" the upper class kids did during summer vacations.[54]
- Students from low income homes were, on average, "two or three levels behind" their wealthier counterparts by the time they were out of middle school.[55]
- "By junior high school and high school, the pupil of higher social position makes higher grades, even when I.Q. is held constant."[56]
- Fully 75% of children from "professional or managerial" families plan to attend college, the percentage declining as status does, with only 25% of families at the lowest level having college plans.[57]
- "Generally speaking, the wealthier a student's family, the higher the SAT score."[58] Students in the top 10-15% of family income have for decades scored a combined 250 points higher on the verbal and math tests than students in the bottom 10-15% of family income.

The cumulative effect of all of this is that over 80% of high school graduates from families in the highest income quartile are enrolled in colleges as compared to only about half of high school graduates from families in the lowest income quartile. Most significant is this finding: "Seventy-four percent of the students at the top 146 highly selective colleges came from families in the top quarter of the socioeconomic status scale . . ."[59] That is, almost three quarters of students attending the nation's best colleges were children of means.

It would seem likely that companies hiring young men and women right out of college for high-paying positions – those at the top 5% – would tend to recruit from the top-tier schools. If these employers did as expected, then the roughly 34% of the top five-percenters – the slice with "just" a college degree – would be composed predominantly of overdogs.[60] That is, these hires would mirror the pattern of the top-tier schools from which they came, and roughly 75% of them would come from families in the top 25% of our class system.

The bulk of the remainder of the top five-percenters, some 43%, earned an advanced degree, from a masters or PhD program or from a professional school. It would seem that most graduate schools, like most high-paying employers, would recruit heavily from the Tier 1 colleges, resulting in their student bodies being over-populated with upper-class kids.[61] There is support for this inference. In 2005, over 55% of medical school admits had parents whose income placed them in the top 20% of U.S. households. In 2011, more than 75% of students in the 20 highest-ranked law schools were from families in the top 25% of the socioeconomic scale. Taken together, these two categories of professional schools, dominated by overdogs, make up nearly 25% of the 43% of those in the top 5% holding advanced degrees. There is no definitive evidence that students in graduate programs in business or engineering come from families that are any less well-off.

The "academic" advantages that affluent parents provide their children are in part a function of hard cash: the money to buy them theater tickets, to have a home library, to sign them up for after school programs, to hire tutors and advisors to help them with their classwork, the SATs and college applications. They are a function, as well, of the fact that affluent parents are themselves frequently highly educated. As such, they naturally create a more intellectually-sophisticated and stimulating environment and can provide their sons and daughters with clearer guidance on how to effectively navigate the American school system.

Over 50 years ago, Suzanne Keller wrote: "The link between material means and education persists, and the appeal of various types of success is unequally distributed in the different strata of society."[62] That has not changed. Financial attainment is linked to education which, in turn, is linked to high social status. While the evidence is fragmentary, it is also very consistent: children from the upper classes are better students and, therefore, are more likely to replicate the "riches" of their parents.

Two final observations about affluence and education. As to affluence, the fact that well-heeled parents are more likely to raise children who will advance further in school does not mean that they are "good" parents or that their children are happy or happier than the children of the less wealthy. Soniya Luthar, a Columbia psychologist, conducted studies of high-income suburban and low-income inner-city adolescents. One showed that moneyed suburban teenagers drank, smoked and experimented with drugs at a consistently greater rate than their poorer counterparts. Another found a possible causal explanation for this elevated substance usage: students' distress resulting from "excessive achievement pressures and isolation from parents – both physical and emotional."[63] Luthar cautioned:[64]

> The American Dream spawns widespread beliefs that Ivy League educations and subsequently lucrative careers are critical for children's long-term happiness. In the sometimes

single-minded pursuit of these goals, let us not lose sight of the possible costs to mental health and well-being of all concerned.

As to education, while a college degree or more is a necessary ticket to the 23 occupational categories that produce the top 5% of wage earners, it is not a requirement for all highly-paid careers.[65] Specifically, it was not required for the ballplayers, movie stars and Presidents who are the subject of this book. The very lack of academic prerequisites may explain the public's fascination with those ballplayers and movie stars who went to Ivy League schools. Sports commentators often fill dead space with reminders that old-timers like Lou Gehrig and Eddie Collins (both infielders) went to Columbia and that newer-comers like Ron Darling and Kyle Hendricks (both pitchers) attended Yale and Dartmouth.[66] A lot more big-name movie stars had Ivy League educations. In terms of the screen legends, it is no secret that Jimmy Stewart went to Princeton or that Jack Lemmon went to Harvard. Of more recent "A-listers," Yale, Harvard and Columbia provide the affiliations that dominate. Yale claims Paul Newman, Meryl Streep, Jodie Foster, Ed Norton, James Franco, Frances McDormand and Paul Giamatti. Harvard claims Matt Damon, Natalie Portman, Ashley Judd and Tommy Lee Jones. And Columbia claims the two Gyllenhaals, Ed Harris and Julia Stiles.[67]

Even though many presidents have been highly educated, eight having advanced degrees,[68] seven of the top 20 Presidents, including four ranked in the top 10, did not go to or finish college.[69] In all, a dozen of the 45 Presidents were not college graduates. And while there have been a large number of Ivy League Presidents,[70] many went to schools that were not elite institutions.[71] The key point is that, as with the ballplayers and movie stars, there are no academic prerequisites for residing in the White House.

Given the importance of higher education to economic success and its heavy bias towards the wealthy, the fact that a university diploma never has been required to get into the major leagues or make it in Hollywood or move into 1600 Pennsylvania Avenue may be a significant reason for the prevalence of underdogs at the upper reaches of these three coveted careers.

Intergenerational Mobility

In the book *Class Matters,* a group of *New York Times* correspondents wrote: "Mobility is the promise that lies at the heart of the American Dream."[72] To test whether that "promise" has been fulfilled, economists conduct "intergenerational" studies that chart the relationship between the economic success of children and the economic success of their parents. Examining income data for parent-child pairs, these studies analyze whether children end up at the same relative income level as their parents or at different levels – whether higher or lower. If the American Dream is working, even if someone starts out at the bottom of the economic ladder, he or she should have the same chance of making it to the top as someone who starts out there.

Until 1992 there were few analyses of intergenerational mobility, and those that existed suggested little correlation between a father's and a son's income level. But in 1992 Gary Solon conducted an investigation using an improved methodology, and it revealed that a father's and son's income level *were* significantly correlated. Solon concluded that the United States had "a much less mobile society" than previously described.[73] That same year, Ellen Peters published a study which divided parent-child pairs into income quartiles and, consistent with Solon's conclusion, found that 40% of sons born into the highest income quartile remained at the top and that 42% of sons born into the lowest income quartile remained at the bottom, respectively 15% and 17% more than the 25% that would be expected in a world of perfect mobility.

A little over a dozen years later, in 2005, Bhashkar Mazumder replicated Peters' results. Reminding us that "[u]nder perfect mobility . . . . a son whose father was in the bottom quartile of the earnings distribution would be just as likely to be in the top quartile as the bottom quartile,"[74] his analysis showed that, in fact, 43% (not 25%) of children born into the top quartile remained there as adults and 38% (not 25%) of children born into the bottom quartile remained there as adults.

In 2006 Tom Hertz presented the results of his investigation, using a data set of 4,004 children. Hertz divided their parents into five income-based quintiles, rather than four quartiles, and then charted into which of the five quintiles the children ended up. If mobility were perfect, parents' income would have no bearing on that of their children, and 20% of the poorest sons would end up in each of the five quintiles, as would 20% of the richest sons. The same would be true of the sons in the three quintiles in between.

Hertz, like his colleagues, found gross imperfections in the real world.[75] He reported that nearly 42% of children born into the top quintile remain at the top as adults, more than twice the 20% probability predicted in a world of perfect mobility. The same was true, in reverse, for the bottom quintile, where about 42% of children born into it remain there as adults, also more than twice the 20% predicted in a world of perfect mobility. Only 6% of the children born in the top quintile dropped to the bottom, just as only 6% of the children born into the bottom quintile rose to the top. A child born into highest quintile had a seven times better chance of remaining there than a child born into the lowest quintile had of reaching it, 42% vs. 6%.[76]

Then, in 2012, a series of papers issued by the Pew Charitable Trusts corroborated the conclusions of Peters, Mazumder and Hertz. The Pew group said its work demonstrated "that the 'rags to riches' story is more often found in Hollywood than in reality."[77] Among the specific findings: "Forty-three percent of those who start at the bottom are stuck there as adults, and 70 percent remain below the middle quintile . . . At the other end of the ladder, 40 percent of those raised in the top stay there as adults, and 63 percent remain above the middle quintile."[78]

There is some dispute as to whether intergenerational mobility in the U.S. has gotten worse in the last few decades or whether it was always bad and it is just econometric techniques that have gotten better. That said, there is no disagreement that intergenerational mobility in this country is far from perfect or that its imperfections confound gauzy notions of the viability of the American Dream. This recognition has resulted in the spawning of books with titles like *Illusions of Opportunity: The American Dream in Question* and *Our Kids: The American Dream in Crisis*. This intergenerational research offers further confirmation that the financial success achieved by our underdog greats in their three exclusive worlds is the exception rather than the rule. Adams' optimism aside, as a general matter if you are born without much, the deck is stacked against your hitting the jackpot or even of significantly improving your station in life.

III. What the Polls Say

Given the hard evidence that beginnings *do* matter and that the chances of advancement are uneven and skewed, what does the proverbial "man on the street" think about the vitality of the American Dream? *The New York Times* first posed the question in 1983, asking "Do you think it's still possible to start out poor in this country, work hard, and become rich?"[79] Fifty-seven percent responded by saying they thought it was. Over the next three decades, the *Times* and CBS continued to pose this question, conducting 13 surveys in all. Each time, a clear majority expressed a belief in the possibility of realizing the Dream, averaging out at 73%, or nearly three-quarters of those surveyed.

Gallup, which did not start polling on this topic until 2001, raised a similar question: "Are you satisfied or dissatisfied about the opportunity for a person in this nation to get ahead by working hard?"[80] In its 14 surveys, conducted from 2001-2008 and 2011-2016, Gallup also reported that in each a majority – theirs averaging out at 64% – felt "satisfied" with opportunities in the United States for getting ahead.

In January 2017 Fox News put a series of questions to registered voters specifically focused on "Your family and the American Dream." It found that 40% felt they had already "achieved it" and another 43% said that they were "on the way." A whopping 83% expressed the belief that the American Dream could be realized. In August of 2017 the Pew Research Center put virtually the same questions to its own sample and reported an identical 83% believing they had or would realize the Dream.

A dozen years before Fox and Pew did their polling, Isabel Sawhill of Brookings had indicated that these results were nothing new: "[S]urveys find that most Americans think that they – or at least their children – will one day achieve the American dream."[81]

IV. Why It Endures

There are a variety of reasons why a majority continually profess a belief that the American Dream is achievable, despite the hard evidence to the contrary. The fact is few know of the raft of academic studies about the sluggishness of upward mobility, and lay summaries of their conclusions seldom become front page headlines or the lead story on the evening news. Because most people are in the dark about these findings, perceptions of the general probabilities of moving up the economic ladder remain inordinately optimistic.[82] Interestingly, individuals are even more bullish on the subject when asked about their own chances of making good.[83] In addition, not every American dreams of becoming rich. Some just dream of owning a home or being able to take a vacation or simply bringing home a larger paycheck than their fathers did.[84] When pollsters come calling, inquiring about the accessibility of the American Dream, people respond based on their own take on its meaning.

There may be another reason the survey results are so unvaryingly positive: the real-life accounts of underdog success. As the *Times'* staff wrote, these "success stories," amplified by "cultural mythmaking" from the media, serve to "reinforce perceptions of mobility . . ."[85] 2015 provides a recent and instructive example of the prevalence of underdogs among that year's notable professional athletes, entertainers and politicians.

As to the 2015 "newsmakers" in the world of baseball, the two Most Valuable Players both came from blue collar homes. Bryce Harper, the MVP of the National League, grew up in Las Vegas, where his father was employed as a union laborer, installing rebar in the hotels and casinos that line the strip. Josh Donaldson, the MVP of the American League, was born and raised in Pensacola, where his father worked construction until Josh was seven, when he was imprisoned for sexual battery. Salvador Perez of the Kansas City Royals was named the World Series MVP. He grew up in Venezuela and was raised largely by his mother, who supported the family by making and selling cakes, flan and lasagna. Salvador's father had abandoned the family when he was four.

Though professional basketball, like baseball, is organized into two divisions – the Eastern and Western Conferences – it chooses a single MVP. In 2015 that honor went to Steph Curry of the Golden State Warriors. Unlike his baseball counterparts, Curry's family was affluent, his father Dell having had a 16-year career in the NBA. The same cannot be said for the two next highest vote getters: Kawhi Leonard of the San Antonio Spurs, who came in second, and LeBron James of the Cleveland Cavaliers, who came in third. Leonard's father owned and ran a car wash in Los Angeles, until he was killed when Kawhi was 16. LeBron was raised in Akron by his teenaged mother. James never knew his father. The family lived in a succession of squalid apartments, making seven moves during the year he was five. By the time LeBron was 10 his mother had sent him to live with a local coach to give him at least a chance for a stable upbringing.

The NFL, like the NBA, chooses only one MVP a season, and in 2015 that honor went to the Carolina Panthers' Cam Newton. Newton spent his childhood in Atlanta, where his father was the pastor of Holy Zion Center of Deliverance, presiding with his wife Jackie over its dilapidated church.

The Emmys, Grammys, Tonys and Oscars are the principal trophies recognizing excellence in the world of the performing arts. Many who went home with statuettes in 2015 were, like their sports counterparts, underdogs. Beginning with television, Jeffrey Tambor won the Emmy for Outstanding Lead Actor in a Comedy Series for his role in *Transparent*. His father was a flooring contractor. Viola Davis won the Emmy for Outstanding Lead Actress in a Drama Series, for her role in *How to Get Away with Murder*. Her father trained horses; her mother was employed at times as a maid and at times as a factory worker.

Two of the biggest Grammy winners in 2015 were Beyoncé and Pharrell Williams, each of whom received three awards. Beyoncé grew up in Texas, where her father was a sales manager for Xerox and her mother ran a hair salon. Williams grew up in Virginia, where his father was a handyman and his mother was a teacher. Neither was disadvantaged; neither was privileged. Two perennials also took home Grammys in 2015: Eminem and Carrie Underwood. Eminem's parents were both members of a small band that played at Ramada Inns in the Dakotas, until his father left, and he and his mom shuttled back and forth between their Midwestern relatives. Underwood was raised in rural Oklahoma, where her dad worked in a sawmill and her mom taught grammar school.

When it came to Broadway, Helen Mirren was awarded the Tony for Best Performance by a Leading Actress in a Play for her role as Queen Elizabeth in *The Audience*. Mirren's father was initially a viola player, then a cab driver, then a civil servant. Her mother was one of 14 children from a decidedly working class family. Michael Cerveris was awarded the Tony for Best Performance by a Leading Actor in a Musical for his role as the patriarch in *Fun Home*. Cerveris's mother was a dancer and his father was a professor of music at a small college, both positions more prestigious than well paid. As to the Oscars, Julianne Moore was named Best Actress for her performance in *Still Alice*. Moore's father was a paratrooper in Vietnam at the time of her birth, and she spent much of her youth as an Army brat, moving frequently among far-flung bases from Alaska to Panama.

WHAT OF THE AMERICAN DREAM?

When 2015 began President Obama and Vice President Biden were still the two most highly-elected officials. Obama's underdog saga was familiar: mixed race, deserted by black father, mother a struggling student, partly raised by white grandparents of modest means. Biden's early years were also ones of financial challenge. Born in Scranton, Pennsylvania, when his father's businesses failed, the family of six was forced to move in with his maternal grandparents. As the economy in Scranton declined, Joe Sr. was underemployed. Eventually, he sold used cars and cleaned furnaces.

At the other end of Pennsylvania Avenue, John Boehner, the Republican Speaker of the House of Representatives, had faced comparable hardships growing up in Reading, Ohio. He along with his eight brothers and three sisters shared one of two bedrooms in their parents' house. His father owned a neighborhood tavern, and by the time John was eight he was up before dawn sorting bottles and mopping the floor. While Boehner's tale was perhaps the best known, his three senior congressional colleagues had their own adversities to overcome. Mitch McConnell, the Majority Leader of the Senate, had contracted polio when he was two, and his parents almost went bankrupt getting him well. Harry Reid, the Minority Leader of the Senate, grew up in Searchlight, Nevada, a town without a telephone, a television or a doctor. The Reid house was built of railroad ties, with an outhouse in the back. Harry's father was a miner. His mother took in laundry from the casinos and brothels. Nancy Pelosi, Reid's counterpart on the House side, suffered no such deprivations. Her father, Thomas D'Alesandro, Jr., had been a Congressman from Maryland and Baltimore's Mayor, and the family was reasonably prosperous. Despite these social and material assets, Pelosi's quest to become the first woman to rise to the lofty position of Speaker had been neither simple nor easy.

Hillary Clinton was trying to blaze another trail as she sought to become the first woman to occupy the Oval Office. Although she was the clear frontrunner for her Party's nomination, the barriers to realizing her goal were, as events proved, formidable. The daughter of a successful manufacturer of textiles, she tried to evoke sympathy for her underdog roots by talking about her mother's harrowing childhood. Bernie Sanders, the Vermont Senator and Clinton's Democratic rival, did not have to make up the challenges he faced. Clearly an underdog when it came to his shot at becoming the Democratic nominee, he was also an underdog when it came to his upbringing. Born in Brooklyn, Sanders' father was a Polish immigrant who made a living selling paint.

On the Republican side, the early favorite, Jeb Bush, was the ultimate overdog, the son and brother of Presidents. The same could not be said for many of his competitors. Marco Rubio, the Florida Senator, grew up in Las Vegas, where his father was employed as a bartender in a small hotel and his mother worked as a housekeeper in one of the gambling houses. John Kasich, Ohio's Governor, was the son of a mail carrier raised in a suburb outside of Pittsburgh. Ben Carson, a renowned neurosurgeon, spent his early childhood in Detroit, where his father was a laborer at the Cadillac plant. At eight his parents separated, and he moved with his mother to a tough part of Boston. For a time Mrs. Carson worked as a maid. The family relied on food stamps into his teenage years.[86]

During 2015 a number of celebrities passed away. The obituaries of some provided reminders of their underdog roots.[87]

- Mario Cuomo (died January 1). Governor of New York. Andrea Cuomo, Mario's father, was an uneducated laborer who came to America from Italy. Mario was born "in the urban equivalent of a log cabin."[88] The Cuomos lived at first in a single room with a toilet and a large stone tub, located behind the grocery store where Mario's parents worked for seven years. Eventually Andrea had a little store of his own in Queens.
- Leonard Nimoy (died February 27). Spock in *Star Trek.* Nimoy's parents escaped from Russia and settled in an ethnic neighborhood in Boston. Leonard's father owned a barbershop. To help make ends meet, Leonard peddled newspapers, shined shoes and sold vacuum cleaners.
- B.B. King (died May 14). Blues singer and electric guitarist. Albert and Nora Ella King, B.B.'s parents, were from Itta Bena, Mississippi. They were sharecroppers. When B.B. was four, his mother left his father for another man, and B.B. ended up being raised by his grandmother.
- E.L. Doctorow (died July 21). Novelist. Doctorow grew up in the Bronx. His parents were of Russian Jewish ancestry. David Doctorow, his father, operated a small music store.
- Moses Malone (died September 13). Professional basketball star. Malone was born in Petersburg, Virginia, and "grew up in poverty."[89] His mother, who never got beyond fifth grade, raised him by herself, eking out a living working in a nursing home. His father, an alcoholic, had walked out on the family when Moses was two.
- Frank Gifford (died August 9). Professional football star. Gifford spent his youth in California, where his father was an oil driller. Frank moved 29 times before entering high school, the family often sleeping in the park or the back of their car. During the Depression years, there frequently were no jobs anywhere, and at times it was so bad that the Giffords had to eat dog food.
- Yogi Berra (died September 29). Professional baseball star. Yogi was one of five children in an Italian family that lived in St. Louis, Missouri. His parents were immigrants, his dad struggling to earn a living wage as a brickmaker. Yogi quit school after eighth grade and drove delivery trucks, pulled tacks in a shoe factory and worked in a coal yard.

WHAT OF THE AMERICAN DREAM?

The point is not that all of these underdog stories were universally or even widely known, but that virtually everyone was aware of at least some of them. Whether the setting was the world of sports, arts or politics, each story showed that in this country the "fortuitous circumstances of birth or position,"[90] in Adams' language, were not a bar to fame or fortune. As such, each of these stories in its own fashion reinforced the core presumption of the American Dream.

When the son of a Baltimore saloon-keeper, who is shipped off to a reform school as an "incorrigible" at the age of seven and a half ends up being ranked the number one ballplayer of all time, and by some as the premier athlete of the 20th Century; when the son of a Bristol pants presser, who as a young teenager joins a troupe of gymnasts and ends up being ranked the number two movie star of all time and, for women and men of a certain generation, the ultimate Beau Ideal; when the son of an illiterate backwoods farmer, who had scarcely a year of schooling himself, ends up being ranked the number one President of all time, and by many as one of the world's greatest leaders; when such things occur, people believe that the prospects for advancement are limitless for anyone with talent and the drive to succeed, irrespective of how little he or she has starting out.

Some years ago, Suzanne Keller wrote

> Even though elites represent only a small fraction of the total population, their visibility and symbolic impact are enormous, and there is reason to suppose that their collective characteristics affect popular expectations about opportunities for "getting ahead." In providing a notion of what the upper limits of mobility are, elites are perceived as models to be imitated . . .[91]

Though economists tell us that the American Dream is improbable for most, we should not be blinkered by the inequalities and inequities that put it out of reach. As attested to by the biographies of our greats, enormous success can be achieved, even by those whose beginnings are humble. While their achievements may not be representative, they are inspirational and foster a stubborn belief in what some now call a myth. And that belief will persist so long as we continue to hear of the obstacles faced and overcome by the latest crop of newsmakers. After all, their stories are the stuff that dreams are made of, and even as grown-ups their fairy tales are not only a source of enchantment, but of hope.

Appendices

APPENDIX A
Listing of Notable Underdog Films By Decade

The Thirties: Depression and the New Deal

Min and Bill (1930); *Emma* (1932); *The Champ* (1932); *Lady for a Day* (1933); *Morning Glory* (1933); *It Happened One Night* (1934); *Les Miserables* (1935); *My Man Godfrey* (1936); *The Great Ziegfeld* (1936); *The Story of Louis Pasteur* (1936); *Mr. Deeds Goes to Town* (1936); *A Star Is Born* (1937); *Captains Courageous* (1937); *Good Earth* (1937); *Alexander's Ragtime Band* (1938); *Angels with Dirty Faces* (1938); *Boys Town* (1938); *Pygmalion* (1938); *The Adventures of Robin Hood* (1938); *You Can't Take It With You* (1938); *Goodbye, Mr. Chips* (1939); *Jesse James* (1939); *Love Affair* (1939); *Mr. Smith Goes to Washington* (1939).

The Forties: World War II and Return to Normalcy

Abe Lincoln in Illinois (1940); *Edison, the Man* (1940); *Grapes of Wrath* (1940); *Kitty Foyle* (1940); *How Green Was My Valley* (1941); *Meet John Doe* (1941); *Sergeant York* (1941); *They Died with Their Boots On* (1941); *Random Harvest* (1942); *Yankee Doodle Dandy* (1942); *Pride of the Yankees* (1942); *Madame Curie* (1943); *Cover Girl* (1944); *National Velvet* (1944); *A Tree Grows in Brooklyn* (1945); *Lost Weekend* (1945); *It's A Wonderful Life* (1946); *Lassie Come Home* (1946); *Sister Kenny* (1946); *The Best Years of Our Lives* (1946); *The Jolson Story* (1946); *Till the Clouds Roll By* (1946); *Gentleman's Agreement* (1947); *Great Expectations* (1947); *The Farmer's Daughter* (1947); *I Remember Momma* (1948); *Joan of Arc* (1948); *Johnny Belinda* (1948); *All the King's Men* (1949); *Pinky* (1949).

The Fifties: Korea and Buffalo Bob

All About Eve (1950); *Born Yesterday* (1950); *Cyrano de Bergerac* (1950); *Quo Vadis* (1951); *High Noon* (1952); *Roman Holiday* (1953); *Shane* (1953); *Stalag 17* (1953); *A Star Is Born* (1954); *Country Girl* (1954); *On the Waterfront* (1954); *Sabrina* (1954); *Blackboard Jungle* (1955); *Marty* (1955); *Rebel Without A Cause* (1955); *Giant* (1956); *Lust for Life* (1956); *The Ten Commandments* (1956); *An Affair to Remember* (1957); *Gigi* (1958); *My Fair Lady* (1958); *Ben-Hur* (1959); *Diary of Anne Frank* (1959); *Young Philadelphians* (1959).

The Sixties: Vietnam and Black Power

Alamo (1960); *Exodus* (1960); *Spartacus* (1960); *Sunrise at Campobello* (1960); *The Apartment* (1960); *Breakfast at Tiffany's* (1961); *West Side Story* (1961); *Lawrence of Arabia* (1962); *Gypsy* (1962); *The Miracle Worker* (1962); *The Great Escape* (1963); *Greatest Story Ever Told* (1965); *A Man for All Seasons* (1966); *Georgy Girl* (1966); *Bonnie and Clyde* (1967); *Guess Who's Coming to Dinner* (1967); *To Sir with Love* (1967); *The Dirty Dozen* (1967); *Wait Until Dark* (1967); *Charly* (1968); *Funny Girl* (1968); *Oliver* (1968); *Butch Cassidy and the Sundance Kid* (1969); *Easy Rider* (1969); *Midnight Cowboy* (1969).

APPENDICES

The Seventies: Watergate and Malaise

Great White Hope (1970); *Love Story* (1970); *The Sting* (1973); *Alice Doesn't Live Here Anymore* (1974); *The Longest Yard* (1974); *Give 'em Hell, Harry!* (1975); *A Star Is Born* (1976); *Rocky* (1976); *Star Wars* (1977); *The Buddy Holly Story* (1978); *Breaking Away* (1979); *Norma Rae* (1979); *Rocky II* (1979); *The Rose* (1979).

The Eighties: Trickle Down Economics and Iran/Contra

Caddyshack (1980); *Coal Miner's Daughter* (1980); *Nine to Five* (1980); *Raging Bull* (1980); *The Elephant Man* (1980); *The Empire Strikes Back* (1980); *Chariots of Fire* (1981); *Annie* (1982); *E.T., the Extra-Terrestrial* (1982); *First Blood* (1982); *Gandhi* (1982); *Rocky III* (1982); *The Verdict* (1982); *Return of the Jedi* (1983); *Tender Mercies* (1983); *The Outsiders (1983)*; *Places in the Heart* (1984); *The Karate Kid* (1984); *The Natural* (1984); *First Blood, Part II* (1985); *Rocky IV* (1985); *Children of a Lesser God* (1986); *Hoosiers* (1986); *First Blood, Part III* (1988); *Rain Man* (1988); *Stand and Deliver* (1988); *The Accused* (1988); *Working Girl* (1988); *Driving Miss Daisy* (1989); *Field of Dreams* (1989); *Lean on Me* (1989); *Major League* (1989); *My Left Foot* (1989).

The Nineties: The Dot Com Boom and Monica Lewinsky

Awakenings (1990); *Edward Scissorhands* (1990); *Pretty Woman* (1990); *Rocky V* (1990); *Beauty and the Beast* (1991); *Robin Hood, Prince of Thieves* (1991); *A Few Good Men* (1992); *A League of Their Own* (1992); *The Mighty Ducks* (1992); *Malcolm X* (1992); *Scent of a Woman* (1992); *Homeward Bound: The Incredible Journey* (1993); *Philadelphia* (1993); *Robin Hood, Men in Tights* (1993); *Schindler's List* (1993); *Angels in the Outfield* (1994); *Forrest Gump* (1994); *Braveheart* (1995); *Sabrina* (1995); *Sense and Sensibility* (1995); *Evita* (1996); *Jerry Maguire* (1996); *Shine* (1996); *Good Will Hunting* (1997); *Titanic* (1997); *The Rainmaker* (1997); *Life Is Beautiful* (1998); *Boys Don't Cry* (1999); *Notting Hill* (1999); *Star Wars, Episode I* (1999).

The Aughts: Nine Eleven and Recession

Billy Elliott (2000); *Erin Brockovich* (2000); *Gladiator* (2000); *Remember the Titans* (2000); *The Patriot* (2000); *A Beautiful Mind* (2001); *Ali* (2001); *Bridget Jones's Diary* (2001); *Fellowship of the Ring (2001)*; *I Am Sam* (2001); *Legally Blond* (2001); *The Princess Diaries* (2001); *Catch Me If You Can* (2002); *Maid in Manhattan* (2002); *Spiderman* (2002); *Star Wars, Episode II* (2002); *The Rookie* (2002); *The Two Towers* (2002); *Legally Blonde 2: Red, White and Blonde (2003)*; *Return of the King* (2003); *Seabiscuit* (2003); *X-Men United* (2003); *Dodgeball: A True Underdog Story* (2004); *Million Dollar Baby* (2004); *Miracle* (2004); *Ray* (2004); *Troy* (2004); *Batman Begins* (2005); *Cinderella Man* (2005); *The Longest Yard* (2005); *Star Wars, Episode III* (2005); *Walk the Line* (2005); *Dreamgirls* (2006); *Rocky Balboa* (2006); *Superman Returns* (2006); *The Pursuit of Happyness* (2006); *300* (2007); *La Vie en Rose* (2007); *Milk* (2008); *Slumdog Millionaire* (2008); *The Wrestler* (2008); *Crazy Heart* (2009); *Invictus* (2009); *Precious* (2009); *The Blind Side* (2009).

APPENDICES

APPENDIX B
Chart on the Colonization of North America

As detailed in the Source codes, the data was taken from Aaron S. Fogleman, "From Slaves, Convicts, Servants to Free Passengers: The Transformation of Immigration in the Era of the American Revolution," *The Journal of American History*, June 1998, and from Aaron S. Fogleman, "The United States and the Transformation of Transatlantic Migration during the Age of Revolution and Emancipation," in *The American Revolution Reborn*, edited by Michael Zuckerman and Patrick Spero (Philadelphia: University of Pennsylvania Press, 2016), unpublished Appendix.

Immigrants by Nationality and Number

Period	Nationality	Slaves		Convicts		Indentured		Fare Paying		Total Immigrants
1600-1699	African	14,100	a							14,100
1700-1775	African	265,800	b							265,800
Total	African	279,900								279,900
1600-1699	English			500	c	89,500	c	57,800	c	147,800
1700-1775	English			32,500	d	27,200	d	13,400	d	73,100
Total	English			33,000		116,700		71,200		220,900
1600-1699	Irish			300	c	3,000	c	1,700	c	5,000
1700-1775	Irish			17,500	d	39,000	d	52,100	d	108,600
Total	Irish			17,800		42,000		53,800		113,600
1600-1699	Scots			1,500	c	400	c	400	c	2,300
1700-1775	Scots			2,200	d	7,400	d	25,700	d	35,300
Total	Scots	-		3,700		7,800		26,100		37,600
1600-1699	Germans			-		-		1,000	c	1,000
1700-1775	Germans			-		38,100	e	73,000	f	111,100
Total	Germans	-		-		38,100		74,000		112,100
1600-1699	Other			-		3,700	c	5,400	c	9,100
1700-1775	Other			-		-		5,900	d	5,900
Total	Other	-		-		3,700		11,300		15,000
1600-1699	Total	14,100		2,300		96,600		66,300		179,300
1700-1775	Total	265,800		52,200		111,700		170,100		599,800
Grand Total	Total	279,900		54,500		208,300		286,400		779,100

Source codes
a: Unpublished Appendix at 5.
b: Unpublished Appendix at 8.
c: Journal of American History at 68, Table A.1
d: Journal of American History at 71, Table A.3
e: Unpublishe d Appendix at 7.
f: Unpublished Appendix at 6.

APPENDICES

APPENDIX C
Description of Social Class in the U.S.

Upper/Capitalist Class (1%): The smallest group numerically, it includes "Old Money," people like the Rockefellers and DuPonts, who made their fortunes a century ago, as well as "New Money" people, like Walmart's Walton and Microsoft's Gates, who made their fortunes more recently. It includes heirs, investors in the stock market and in real estate and high-salaried individuals, such as chief executives of large corporations and celebrities. Almost all went to college, many to Ivy League schools. The incomes were $500,000 or more.[1]

Upper Middle Class (14-15%): A mid-sized group, it includes corporate executives, white-collar managers, physicians, attorneys, accountants and other professionals. Many have advanced degrees. University professors may be in this group, because their prestige is high, though their incomes are often not. Similarly, prosperous owners of small businesses may be in this group, even though they have not gone to college. The incomes were $100,000 or more.

Lower Middle/Middle Class (30-33%): One of the two largest groups, it is highly diverse and includes people with significant skills, such as teachers, bank employees, mid-level supervisors, non-retail sales workers and well-paid craftsmen. Most graduated from high school and some went to college. These workers have some autonomy, but not as much as the class above. The majority, but not all, wear "white collars." The incomes ranged from $30,000 to $70,000.

Working Class (30%): The second of the largest groups, it is made up of clerical workers, retail sellers, truck drivers, machine operators and low-paid craftsmen. Most in this class are closely supervised and perform functions that are highly routine. Their jobs are relatively stable, though not as secure as those of the Middle Class. A high school diploma is typical. The incomes ranged from $16,000 to $30,000.

Lower Class/Working Poor (13-14%): Most in this group work low skill jobs at firms that have marginal stability. Pay is erratic and benefits unlikely. Lack of job security, rather than job function, distinguishes people in this class from those in the class above. Some earn so little that they qualify for government assistance. Generally members of this strata have some high school education. The incomes were $16,000 or less.

Underclass (12%):[2] It is composed of the unemployed or whose work is erratic and who rely on government assistance to survive.

APPENDICES

APPENDIX D
Ballplayers Rankings[3]

No.	Avg Rank	Listd or Top 20	Players	Team	Legue	Career	Posit	A	B	C	D	E	F	G	H	I	J	K	L
1	1.30	12	Ruth	Yankees	A	1914-1935	OF	1	1	2	1	3	1	1	L	L	1	1	1
2	3.40	12	Mays	Giants	N	1951-1973	OF	3	2	3	2	1	2	7	L	L	10	2	2
3	5.50	12	Aaron	Braves	N	1954-1976	OF	7	14	4	5	2	3	9	L	L	3	3	5
4	5.70	12	Cobb	Tigers	A	1905-1928	OF	5	4	6	3	7	4	6	L	L	9	7	6
5	5.90	12	Williams	Red Sox	A	1939-1960	OF	4	8	7	9	4	7	4	L	L	8	4	4
6	7.50	12	Gehrig	Yankees	A	1923-1939	1B	11	13	11	7	8	5	2	L	L	6	5	7
7	9.00	11	Wagner	Pirates	N	1897-1917	SS	2	3	8	14	NL	12	13	L	L	4	13	12
8	10.44	11	Musial	Cardinals	N	1941-1963	OF	10	10	22	11	5	8	11	L	L	7	10	11
9	12.67	11	Mantle	Yankees	A	1951-1968	OF	12	7	12	19	20	15	10	L	L	NL	6	13
10	7.25	10	Johnson	Senators	A	1907-1927	P	6	5	5	4	9	10	NL	L	L	NL	11	8
11	10.89	10	DiMaggio	Yankees	A	1936-1951	OF	25	11	21	12	6	6	3	L	L	5	9	17
12	14.22	10	Hornsby	Cardinals	N	1915-1937	2B	13	21	18	10	10	11	18	L	L	NL	17	10
13	17.50	8	Mathewson	Giants	N	1900-1916	P	19	41	13	8	13	13	NL	L	NL		15	18
14	13.25	7	Bonds	Giants	N	1986-2007	OF	8	6	1	6	NL	47	5	NL	NL	2	31	3
15	19.14	7	Young	Red Sox	N	1890-1911	P	16	23	42	16	NL	20	NL	L	NL	NL	8	9
16	20.78	6	Speaker	Cleveland	A	1907-1928	OF	9	12	19	29	14	27	24	L	NL	NL	39	14
17	20.89	6	Foxx	Red Sox	A	1925-1945	1B	20	27	24	17	32	14	8	L	L	NL	22	24
18	22.57	6	Schmidt	Phillies	N	1972-1989	3B	15	24	17	30	NL	16	12	L	L	NL	44	
19	17.00	5	Gibson, J	Homestead	Neg	1930-1946	C	27	9	10	20	NL	9	NL	NL	L	NL	27	
20	21.00	5	Grove	Red Sox	A	1925-1941	P	14	15	14	25	18	40	NL	L	NL	NL	NL	
28	37.38	3	Clemente	Pirates	N	1955-1972	OF	61	64	57	22	12	29	42	L	NL	NL	12	

Sources of Ballplayers Rankings

A https://bit.ly/2J7LI5B, *Top100 Players* by Bruce Grossberg edited by Steve Orinick, updated December, 2001
B *Baseball's Best 1,000* by Derek Gentile, 2008
C *Who's Better, Who's Best in Baseball* by Elliott Kalb, 2005
D Sporting News Selects *Baseball's 100 Greatest Players*, Second Edition, 2005
E *Baseball's 100* by Maury Allen, 1981
F *100 Greatest Players of the 20th Century Ranked* by Mark McGuire and Michael Sean Gormley, 2000
G *Stat One, A New System for Rating Baseball's All-Time Greatest Players* by Craig Messmer, 2007
H *100 Greatest Baseball Players of All Time* by Lawrence Ritter and Donald Honig (unranked), 1981
I *The 25 Greatest Baseball Players of All Time* by Len Berman, 2010
J https://bit.ly/2OS6Fvi, top 10 only
K https://bit.ly/2OZExGN, popularity contest downloaded 8/27/11
L https://bit.ly/2G2TPYb, Andrew Gould, 3/28/17

APPENDIX E
Presidents Rankings[4]

Rnk	Nr	Name	A	B	C	D	E	F	G	H	I	J	K	L	M	N	O	P	Q	R	S	T	U	V	Average
1	22	Abraham Lincoln	1	1	1	1	3	2	2	1	1	1	2	2	2	3	1	3	2	2	1	2	1	1	1.5
2	22	Franklin D. Roosevelt	3	3	2	2	1	1	1	2	3	2	3	1	3	3	3	1	1	3	3	3	3	3	2.3
3	22	George Washington	2	2	3	3	4	4	4	3	2	3	1	4	1	2	2	4	4	1	2	1	2	2	2.4
4	22	Thomas Jefferson	5	5	4	5	2	3	5	4	4	7	4	5	4	4	7	5	5	4	5	4	7	5	4.6
5	22	Theodore Roosevelt	7	7	5	4	5	5	3	5	6	4	5	3	5	5	4	2	5	5	7	10	4	4	5.0
6	22	Harry S. Truman		9	8	8	7	7	7	7	8	5	7	7	7	7	5	9	7	7	5	12	6	6	6.9
7	22	Woodrow Wilson	4	4	6	7	6	6	6	6	7	6	11	6	11	10	9	8	6	11	3	18	11	11	7.9
8	22	Dwight D. Eisenhower		22	11	9	11	12	8	9	10	9	9	10	8	6	8	10	10	9	24	7	5	7	9.7
9	22	Andrew Jackson	6	6	7	6	13	9	11	8	5	13	6	13	10	14	13	14	9	6	9	5	18	15	9.8
	4	Barack Obama															15					10	12	8	11.3
10	22	James K. Polk	10	8	12	11	12	13	14	11	9	12	10	11	9	9	12	12	16	10	16	14	14	20	12.0
11	20	John F. Kennedy		13	14	8	10	10	15	12	8	18	14	15	11	6	11	15	18	8	23	8	16	12.7
12	22	John Adams	9	10	9	14	10	14	12	14	16	13	13	12	15	13	17	12	13	12	9	19	14	12.9
13	22	James Madison	14	12	12	17	9	8	9	10	17	18	15	9	17	15	20	6	14	15	11	8	17	12	13.0
14	20	Lyndon B. Johnson			10	12	14	15	13	12	14	10	17	15	18	12	11	16	11	17	15	11	10	10	13.2
15	22	James Monroe	12	18	15	16	15	11	15	13	15	14	16	8	16	21	14	11	13	16	9	6	13	18	13.7
16	18	Ronald Reagan					16	22	20	26	25	11	8	16	6	8	10	18	10	8	34	15	9	9	15.1
17	22	Grover Cleveland	8	11	17	13	18	17	19	16	13	17	12	20	12	19	21	20	21	12	23	16	23	24	16.9
18	22	William McKinley	18	15	18	18	19	19	18	17	16	15	14	19	14	17	16	21	17	14	27	28	16	19	17.6
19	22	John Quincy Adams	11	13	16	19	17	16	17	18	18	19	20	17	25	16	19	19	20	20	18	25	21	23	18.5
20	16	Bill Clinton									23	20	21	18	22	23	15	13	19	24	18	13	15	13	18.6

Sources of Presidents Rankings

A Schlesinger 1948 Poll
B Schlesinger 1962 Poll
C 1982 Murray-Blessing Survey
D *Chicago Tribune* 1982 Poll
E Siena 1982 Poll
F Siena 1990 Poll
G Siena 1994 Poll
H Ridings-McIver 1996 Poll
I Schlesinger 1996 Poll
J CSPAN 1999 Poll
K *Wall Street Journal* 2000 Poll
L Siena 2002 Poll
M *Wall Street Journal* 2005 Poll
N *New York Times* 2008 Poll
O CSPAN 2009 Poll
P Siena 2010 Poll
Q USPC 2011 Poll
R *Presidential Leadership*, A Wall Street Journal Book, 2004
S *The American Presidents Ranked by Performance*, Faber and Faber, 2000
T Washington Post research, published in "Outlook" 10/2/16 at pg. 2
U CSPAN 2017 Poll
V *The 2018 Presidents and Executive Politics Presidential Greatness Survey*, Rottinghaus and Vaughn

APPENDICES

APPENDIX F
Demographic Profiles of the Top 20s

As in the text, the Underdog Greats and Overdog Greats have been grouped together, an asterisk denoting some uncertainty regarding placement. The number in parentheses following each name indicates the ranking of these men within the respective top 20s.

The Ballplayers

Underdogs

1. Babe Ruth (1): Babe's father had little formal education and trouble holding down a job. At various times he was a driver, an agent, a salesman and a harness maker. He ended up owning a small saloon where he worked till all hours with his wife. The family lived in the Pigtown section of Baltimore, a tough part of the city located near the railroad tracks. George Sr. sent his son to St. Mary's Academy, which was an institution that catered to the underprivileged.
2. Willie Mays (2): Willie was a "poor Depression-era black kid from the segregated South."[5] His father, known as Cat, started off sweeping floors and ended up working intermittently in the tool room of a wire mill in Alabama owned by a U.S. Steel subsidiary. When Willie was a baby, the family could not afford a three-cent can of milk. "Money was tight all through Willie's childhood," and sometimes he went to school without shoes.[6] Cat never earned more than $2,000 a year at the mills. For a time he was a porter for the Pullman Company.
3. Henry Aaron (3): Henry grew up in and around Mobile, Alabama, though his father Herbert began his working life in the cotton fields of Georgia. Henry first lived in Down the Bay, a neighborhood of domestic help and dockworkers. When Herbert was 25 he was hired as a boilermaker's assistant with Alabama Dry Dock and Shipping Company at a salary of 16 cents an hour. During the Depression Henry was frequently without a job, and he did not get steady work until the onset of World War II, when he became a full-time riveter. The six Aaron children always shared a bed, wore nothing but hand-me-downs and survived on a diet heavy on beans.
4. Ted Williams (5): Ted was the first child of Sam and May Williams. His parents initially lived in Los Angeles where Sam had a job as a street-car conductor. After a couple of years, the Williams moved to San Diego, and Sam opened a small photography studio. Sam's earnings were "modest" at best.[7] While his wife May gained a considerable reputation for her zealous efforts on behalf of the Salvation Army, she was unpaid. Her missionary zeal did result in a wealthy admirer forgiving the note she had taken to purchase a small bungalow.
5. Lou Gehrig (6): Lou Gehrig grew up in New York, the only surviving child of German immigrant parents. He "was raised in a dirt-poor household precariously close to the poverty level."[8] Pop Gehrig seldom worked, in part because jobs were scarce, in part because his health was bad and in part because his appetite for beer exceeded his ambition. Christina Gehrig was the principal breadwinner, earning money cooking, cleaning, taking in laundry and baking. When Lou was a high school senior, his mom was hired as a domestic at Columbia University.
6. Honus Wagner (7): The Wagners immigrated to the United States from Prussia, settling in western Pennsylvania, six miles southwest of Pittsburgh. They were uneducated and lived on a dirt road near the railroad tracks "in a poor, working-class section of town."[9] Honus's father, Peter, worked in the coal mines, as did his three older brothers and, at 12, Honus himself.
7. Stan Musial (8): Stan spent his childhood in Donora, Pennsylvania, a small industrial city south of Pittsburgh. His father Lukacs emigrated from Poland and had virtually

no formal education. He was employed by American Steel and Wire to load 100 pound bales of wire onto railroad cars. His wife Mary hired out as a maid. The Musials lived in a box-like house in a poor part of town, its two bedrooms accommodating Stan's parents, at least one grandparent and six brothers and sisters. During the Depression Lukasz was mainly out of work, and Mary found a job as a cleaning lady in a movie house. During those years the Musials survived on handouts.

8. Mickey Mantle (9): Mickey's dad "Mutt" ended his formal education before graduating from high school. He and his wife Lovell set up housekeeping in a two-room unpainted house on an unpaved road outside Spavinaw, Oklahoma. Mutt went from grading roads to tenant farming to employment as a shoveler and then as ground boss at the Eagle-Picher Zinc and Lead Company of Commerce, Oklahoma. For 10 years Mutt, Lovell and their five children lived in a 750-square-foot clapboard house, four sometimes sleeping in a single bed. For a brief period Mutt tried his hand at farming, but was defeated by unending rain and was forced to go back to the mines.

9. Walter Johnson (10): Frank and Minnie Johnson, Walter's parents, owned a 160-acre farm three miles north of Humboldt, Kansas. After 15 years of backbreaking work, the Johnsons lost the farm following a severe drought, as Walter became a teenager. The family moved into town, and for a time, Frank was only earning $1 a day. It moved again a year or so later, this time to California where Frank found a job as a teamster and loader for the Santa Fe Oil Company.

10. Joe DiMaggio (11): Joe grew up in an Italian family of Sicilian descent. Their house, filled with nine kids, was little more than a cabin on a dirt road on "the wrong side of the tracks" in Martinez, California.[10] Giuseppe, Joe's father, had limited goals: "to buy a small boat and make a living on his own."[11] And that is what he did. The boat was too small for crabbing or catching salmon or venturing beyond the Golden Gate Bridge. As a result, he only fished in the Bay, where his haul ended up as bait for the bigger fisherman or was sold to the processors. Giuseppe did "the marine equivalent of rag-picking: collecting by weight what others disdained."[12]

11. Rogers Hornsby (12): By the time Rogers was born, his parents, Ed and Mary Hornsby, had settled near Winters, Texas, on a 640-acre spread his brother gave him. Rogers was their fifth child. The Hornsbys raised a few head of cattle and harvested whatever wheat and corn they could from the inauspicious land. Ed Hornsby died in his early 40s, before Rogers turned three. For the next four years Mary and her five children moved to her parents' farm near Austin, Texas. She re-settled in Fort Worth, where the three older boys got jobs in the meat-packing plants.

12. Cy Young (15): McKenzie Young, Cy's father, was given 54 acres of farmland in Gilmore, Ohio, by his father around the time he married Rebecca Miller.[13] Over the next 20 years, the Youngs added another 120 acres to their holdings. Cy left school after completing sixth grade in order to help with the farming chores. While the Youngs met with some success, there is no indication that they ever became people of means.

13. Tris Speaker (16): "Tristram" Speaker was the sixth and youngest child of A.O. and Jenny Speaker. A.O. was a carpenter, farmer and part-owner of a dry goods shop in Hill County, Texas. The family seemed to be "reasonably well off," until A.O. prematurely died before turning 50, when Tris was only nine.[14] Thereafter, Jennie Speaker supported herself by taking in boarders and sending Tris and his older brother to work on the family farm.

14. Jimmie Foxx (17): The town of Sudlersville, Maryland, had a population of 420 in the first part of the twentieth century, when Jimmie Foxx was born. Jimmie's father was a tenant farmer on a property located three miles from the village, producing corn and dairy products.

15. Mike Schmidt (18): At the time of Mike's birth, his father, Jack, was employed by a linen supply company in Dayton, Ohio. Five years later he became the operator of a

fast-food restaurant located adjacent to the Phillips Aquatic Club, a swimming pool owned by his wife's family and where his wife worked. Mike had summer jobs as a janitor at a drive-in, a locker boy at his grandfather's pool and as a soda jerk at a pay rate of 50 cents an hour.

16. Josh Gibson (19): Josh's parents, Mark and Nancy, began their married life sharecropping in Buena Vista, Georgia. Neither had much, if any, formal education. Mark left his family when Josh was nine to go North to find a better livelihood. He was able to get a job as a steelworker at the Carnegie-Illinois mills in Pittsburgh, Pennsylvania, and after three years had saved enough to buy train fare for his wife and children. The Gibsons lived in a polluted part of the city known as Pleasant Valley. Mark Gibson never left the mills.

17. Lefty Grove (20): Robert Moses "Lefty" Grove was born in Lonaconing, Maryland, "a hardscrabble mining town" in the state's western panhandle.[15] He was the seventh of eight children. Lefty's father John spent his life working in the mines. The Groves lived in a modest, white-washed wooden house which lacked both plumbing and running water.

Overdogs

1. Ty Cobb* (4): Ty's father, William Herschel, graduated from North Georgia Military College and began life as a schoolteacher. His young bride, Amanda, was from a distinguished Georgia family. When Ty was six or so the Cobbs moved to Royston, Georgia, and William bought a two-story house and eventually a 100-acre farm on which he grew cotton and other crops to round out his teaching salary. By the time Ty was a teenager, William had founded a newspaper and been elected to the Georgia legislature. He ultimately became the town mayor as well.

2. Christy Mathewson* (13): Christy grew up in Factoryville, Pennsylvania. His parents had both attended Keystone Academy. Though his father Gilbert was a bartender, did a bit of carpentry and had a stint in the Senate post office, he saw himself as a "gentleman farmer."[16] Gilbert never worried much about money, because his wife Minerva was a Capwell, a patriarchal family which owned farmland, real estate and mills. Although the general view was that the Capwell legacy "ensured that the Mathewsons were always comfortable, if not wealthy," at some point his wife's inheritance must have run out, as she "took a boarder" and "maintained a milk route."[17]

3. Barry Bonds (14): Barry was born around the time that his 18-year-old father Bobby signed with the San Francisco Giants, beginning his career in its minor league organization. Before Barry celebrated his fourth birthday, Bobby was called up to the "Bigs." Bobby's major league contract was sizable enough for Bobby to re-locate his family to San Carlos, an upper class, virtually all-white suburb populated principally by doctors, lawyers, businessmen and university officials. Bobby earned $100,000 in 1974 and $175,000 in 1977. At 10 Barry was transferred from public to private schools, first to the Carey School and then to Junipero Serra High.

The Movie Stars

Underdogs:

1. Cary Grant (2): Neither Elias Leach nor his bride Elsie had much schooling. Elias did not have much ambition either. Aside from a six-month period in Southampton, England, when he was employed making military uniforms, Elias lived his whole life in Bristol, pressing creases into jackets and trousers at Todd's Clothing Factory. The Leaches first lived in a working class house with a toilet out back. For a time they rented a bigger

place, taking in relatives as boarders. There was never an excess of money; Archie's first pair of long pants were made, poorly and out of cheap goods, by Elsie. Archie attended an English "public" school for a while on scholarship.

2. Fred Astaire (5): Frederic "Fritz" Austerlitz had emigrated from Austria to find a better life, settling in Omaha, Nebraska.[18] After working as a cook and selling "glasses and fancy goods," he got a job with the Omaha Brewery Association.[19] By then he had married Johanna Geilus and was the father of two, first Adele, then Fred. There was not a lot of money early on, Johanna making the children's clothes and Fritz making their toys. When Fred was five and Fritz was working for the Storz Brewing Company, Johanna went to New York to pursue a dancing career for the talented Adele. Fritz stayed in Omaha, sending funds, as Adele and Fred tried to find work on the vaudeville circuit. Fritz visited once or twice a year, and, as Fred recalled, they "went to the expensive restaurants."[20] But finances deteriorated, as impending Prohibition caused a reduction in Fritz's wages and as his earnings were diverted to support a mistress. To keep afloat, Johanna periodically pawned her small diamond ring and fur coat.

3. Clark Gable (7): William Gable was an oil wildcatter who, until Clark was 16, prospected in Cadiz, Ohio. His income was erratic. He and his first wife, Addie, lived in a two-room apartment on the second floor of a clapboard house, accessed by an outside stairway. Addie died before Clark was one. Will remarried Jennie Dunlap and eventually moved to a modest three-bedroom house built by him and his brothers-in-law. Will was hardly ever home. Clark starting working at 12 at a local mill and later as a water boy for coal miners. Will changed course while Clark was in high school and purchased a small farm at which he eked out a living.

4. James Francis Cagney (8): James Cagney grew up primarily in the poorer parts of Manhattan. His father, James Sr., had little education. His mother, Carrie, quit school at 12. Though James Sr. was a bookkeeper when they got married, within a few years he took up bartending and continued to do so until he died. But for a short period when he was the proprietor of his own saloon, around the time Jim was 12, James Sr. worked for others. And but for that period, when the Cagneys rented a house in the country, they lived in a succession of drab Upper East Side apartments, often doubled up in bedrooms. While the family always had a roof over their heads, the four boys did not always have three square meals or ever have a second pair of shoes. And Santa Claus never came. James Sr. was frequently unemployed or working part-time, and even when his sons were small, they had to pick up the slack by getting odd jobs of their own. Frequently, Carrie was forced to temporarily hock her few prized possessions in order to put food on the table and pay the rent.

5. Spencer Tracy (9): John Tracy was a Notre Dame graduate from a lace-curtain, Irish-Catholic railroading family. His wife Carrie Brown was the daughter of a prominent Protestant miller and feed-store owner. Both were from Freeport, Wisconsin. Shortly after their wedding, John found a position as a bookkeeper with the St. Paul Railroad. He remained there about five years, during which time Carroll Edward and Spencer Bernard Tracy were born. John then spent 10 years with Milwaukee Corrugating, starting as a clerk and rising to the position of traffic manager. For most of the rest of Spencer's teenage years, John was employed by Sterling Motor Truck Company, initially as a sales representative and for a very brief time heading its Kansas City Office. The Tracy's lived in a series of leased apartments and houses, primarily in Wisconsin.

6. Charles Chaplin (10): Both of Charles' parents were London vaudevillians making a good living at the time of his birth. But his father separated from his mother when Charles was one, and his mother lost her voice, and livelihood, when he was five. Their situation became desperate, and they devolved into "the lower strata" and then "into poverty."[21] The rest of Charles' abbreviated childhood was unremittingly grim.

APPENDICES

The money that came in was a combination of intermittent alimony from his father, his mother's earnings from sewing, and what he and his brother could bring in from various odd jobs. He was in an out of workhouses and orphanages. His mother was committed to and released from an insane asylum. His father died just after his 12th birthday. A half-orphan before he was a teenager, necessity and tradition propelled Chaplin to a life on the stage. Before he reached 16, a Lunatic Reception Order was signed to re-institutionalize his mother, and she never recovered or was released.

7. Gregory Peck (12): Greg's father and namesake attended the University of Michigan, earning a degree in pharmacology. Over the next six years he bought a drug store, acquired the moniker "Doc," wed Bernice Ayres, lost the drug store and welcomed into the world Eldred Gregory Peck. Before Greg was one, Doc had taken a job as the night-shift druggist at Ferris & Ferris in San Diego, and by the time Greg was five, his parents were divorced. Doc never rose above the position of night-shift druggist and lived in the modest box-like bungalow willed by his mother.

8. John Wayne (13): After attending pharmacy school, Clyde Morrison and his new bride, the former Mary Brown, settled in Winterset, Iowa, where Clyde began his career as pharmacist's clerk. Throughout "Duke" Morrison's childhood, Clyde remained a pharmacist's clerk but for one year when he ran – and bankrupted – his own drug store and two and a half years when he tried, unsuccessfully, to raise corn on the edge of the Mojave desert. Other than a shack that Clyde built during the desert years, the Morrisons never owned a home, renting a tiny place in Winterset when their marriage began and a succession of tumbledown houses during the nine years they lived outside of L.A. Finances were so tight that Duke took on a series of jobs before he reached his teens.

9. Laurence Olivier (14): Laurence Olivier was born in "a modest semidetached house" in Dorking, England, a town 21 miles south of London.[22] His father Gerald had gone to university, and he and his wife Agnes started a preparatory school. When enrollment faltered, he resumed his studies and became an ordained priest. Gerald had been the curate in Dorking for three years at the time of his son's birth. Though the Oliviers moved to better houses and Gerard secured more prestigious appointments, Laurence always described the family circumstance as one of "genteel poverty."[23] Gerard was known to economize by having Laurence bathe in the water already used by his father and older brother.

10. Gene Kelly (15): Gene grew up in working class Pittsburgh, one of the five children of James Sr. and Harriet Kelly. "The neighborhood in which he lived approximated a slum."[24] James was on the road most of the time as a salesman for the Columbia Phonograph Company. In 1924 James was pushed into buying a house in a better neighborhood. But the house was heavily mortgaged, and as the Twenties progressed and free radio took hold, the record-peddling business became less and less profitable. James was fired around the time of the 1929 Crash, and he never regained his bearings or found another steady job.

11. Kirk Douglas (17): Herschel and Bryna Danielovitch were Russian immigrants who settled in New York around 1910. Totally illiterate and with no marketable skills, Herschel traveled the streets of Amsterdam, peddling metal, junk and rags, a job which placed him at the bottom of the economic ladder, even as measured by the poor. The Danielovitch house was dilapidated, uninsulated and adjacent to the mills. Food was often in short supply. All seven children went to work while still young to supplement Herschel's minimal wages.

12. James Dean (18): Denton and Mildred Dean began their married life in a boardinghouse in Marion, Indiana. Denton was employed as a dental technician at the local Veterans Administration Medical Center, molding false teeth, bridges and crowns. When James was five, Denton accepted an offer from the V.A. hospital in Santa Monica, California.

Mildred died when James was nine, and he was sent to live with his aunt and uncle on their small farm in Indiana.

13. Burt Lancaster (19): James and Lizzie Lancaster got married and moved into Lizzie's family's "long, dreary" apartment located in East Harlem, a poor section of New York City.[25] James was employed as a clerk at the General Post Office. The seven Lancasters occupied a floor of a narrow four-story brownstone, contending with the incessant noise and awful smells that were inescapable in their working class neighborhood. Burt recalled his youth in terms of "the cold" – his lack of warm clothing – and the constant "scrounging for jobs."[26]

14. The Marx Brothers (20): The Marxes lived in the Upper East Side of New York, moving, according to Groucho, "as often as a gypsy caravan" in order to evade eviction notices and rent bills.[27] Their serial households were filled with the five Marx boys, a set of parents and grandparents and an adopted sister, Polly. Sam Marx was a tailor whose weekly earnings ranged between $18 and zero. Though he was extremely hard-working, he was hopelessly inept. His customers were all one-timers, and could be identified because one sleeve or trouser leg of a Marx-made suit was shorter than the other.[28] Harpo succinctly summed up family economics: "The Marxes were poor, very poor."[29]

Overdogs:

1. Humphrey Bogart (1): A recent Bogart biography opens with the assertion that "[i]n the 150-year history of cinema, few performers have arrived with a more impressive resume of monetary privilege and social distinction."[30] Humphrey's father, Belmont DeForest Bogart, was a well-respected doctor and his mother, Maud Humphrey, a highly-successful commercial artist. Belmont had studied at Andover, Yale and Columbia. Maude had been trained in Paris. At the time they met, their combined annual income was $70,000, the equivalent of nearly $2 million in 2017. The Bogarts had two homes: a 55-acre lakeside estate in the western part of New York State and a four-story town-house in New York City. Both were staffed with live-in servants. The three Bogart children enjoyed the best that money could buy. From the time his formal education began, Humphrey attended a succession of old-line private schools.

2. James Stewart (3): Both Alexander and Elizabeth Stewart attended college and were from distinguished families, each boasting relatives who had fought in the Revolutionary and Civil Wars. His mother's ancestors were instrumental in starting a bank and a steel company in Apollo, Pennsylvania. His father's had founded a hardware store in Indiana, Pennsylvania. The "three-story emporium" carried everything for building a house, as well as equipment for hunting, gardening and automotive repair.[31] Alex Stewart purchased a one-third interest in the store when James was two, and by the time James was 15, he was its sole owner. The Stewarts lived in a handsome custom-built brick Dutch Colonial with a columned entrance.

3. Marlon Brando (4): Marlon Brando Sr. was driven to prosper. He began his married life with Dorothy Myers on the West Coast working for the telephone company shortly after leaving the army. Once the Brandos moved back to their home town of Omaha, Nebraska, Marlon Sr. became a salesman for Western Limestone Products Company, a position he had when his namesake, their third child, was born. Four years later, Marlon Sr. became general sales manager for the Calcium Carbonate Company, resettling outside of Chicago. The family always lived in rental houses, but sent Marlon Jr. away to private school when he was 17. Many thought the Brandos were upper class, because of their airs and the servants they employed, though there was talk that they were often short of money and late in paying their bills. "The Brandos weren't rich, but they were 'comfortable,' even during the worst Depression years."[32]

APPENDICES

4. Henry Fonda* (6): William Fonda was selling Uneeda Biscuits when Henry was born in Grand Island, Nebraska. The young family moved to Omaha, where William took up the printing trade, ultimately owning what became a "flourishing" business.[33] The Fondas did not become rich, but "lived comfortably" by Midwestern standards, eventually moving into a large clapboard house.[34] Nonetheless, William insisted that his son learn the value of money. Henry started working in the Fonda print shop at 12 and was required to get after-school and summer jobs. His most significant work experience was with the Northwestern Bell Telephone Company.

5. Gary Cooper* (11): Gary's father Charles was born in England and immigrated to the United States at 18, eventually settling in Montana. He became a lawyer, married another English émigré, Alice Brazier, and together they produced two sons. The Coopers' first home was a modest brick residence, and his wife recalled "we had nothing for a long, long time."[35] They later bought a "fairly elegant house with an iron fence around it" in a middle class neighborhood, though not in the richest part of town.[36] When Gary was five, Charles acquired a 2,600 acre ranch, growing alfalfa and raising cattle. When Gary was seven, Charles was appointed U.S. Attorney. At eight Gary and his older brother were sent to England to attend grammar school. According to Gary, his father "lost his shirt ranching" and while well-regarded for his legal ability, did not prosper as a lawyer.[37] As Gary was approaching adulthood, Charles was state attorney general and a judge on the Montana Supreme Court. Charles resigned before his six-year term ended in order to recoup from several "disastrous business ventures."[38]

6. Orson Welles (16): Richard Head Welles, Orson's father, was "in trade," working as treasurer and general secretary of Badger Brass, a Kenosha, Wisconsin, firm whose principal product was an acetylene bicycle lamp. Though his mother Beatrice was a social activist and butterfly, the family's financial problems caused it to move four times in 10 years, always to less expensive houses, sometimes requiring it to take in boarders. However, when Orson was two, Badger Brass was bought out by a Detroit company, and Richard received a $100,000 payout and never had to, or did, another lick of work again.

The Presidents

Underdogs:

1. Abraham Lincoln (1): Neither Thomas Lincoln nor his first wife, Nancy Hanks, had any formal education or, really, any education at all. Thomas made his living as a carpenter and farmer, initially in Kentucky. He had a reputation for accumulating property that was not very good or that he eventually lost. The Lincolns moved to Indiana when Abe was seven, living in one-room log cabins wherever they went. During the first Indiana winter the Lincolns survived on what they could hunt. At an early age Abe helped Thomas with the planting, hoeing and fence-building on their farm, but starting in his teens was hired out to work for others, giving any earnings to his father. Quoting Thomas Gray, Lincoln told a reporter that his childhood could be summed up as "[t]he short and simple annals of the poor. . ."[39]

2. Harry S. Truman (7): Harry's mother, the former Martha "Mattie" Young, had gone to Lexington Baptist Female College and was better educated than her father John, who only had limited rural schooling. John's family never had any money, and he wanted to change that. In the first six years of marriage John started a mule-trading business and worked a small farm. Neither venture was very successful, and the Trumans moved in with Mattie's family. The Trumans next went to Independence, Missouri. John resumed trading and started to do better. He was able to buy a comfortable house and hire help.

Still not wealthy, he began to invest in real estate and speculate in the grain market. When Harry turned 17, John lost it all – the nice house, his wife's land, their lifetime savings – betting on wheat futures. The family was forced to move to Kansas City, and John took a job as a night watchman. As Harry wrote later, "He got the notion he could get rich. Instead he lost everything at one fell swoop and went completely broke."[40] Harry found work as a "timekeeper on a railroad construction outfit."[41]

3. Dwight D. Eisenhower (8): David Eisenhower, Dwight's father, spent two years at Lane University, where he met his future wife Ida Stover. Right before their wedding he opened a grocery store. Three years into the marriage, the store failed. David responded by fleeing to Texas, working for over three years as a grease monkey for the railroads. He returned to his hometown of Abilene, Kansas, to tend to the refrigeration equipment at the Belle River Creamery. The pay was meager, the hours long and the responsibilities minimal, but David remained at the Creamery throughout Dwight's childhood. The Eisenhowers moved from a tiny cottage to a house on three acres when Dwight was eight. Though the new place was larger, it lacked running water and indoor plumbing and its three bedrooms had to accommodate David, Ida, their five (ultimately six) boys and a boarder. Ida made it all work by converting her sons into after-school farmhands, raising crops and animals for subsistence.

4. Andrew Jackson (9): Andrew Jackson Sr. arrived in the United States from Ireland in the spring of 1765, accompanied by his wife Elizabeth and two small sons. He came to find a better life, settling in a rural part of the Carolinas near his wife's sisters. Because the Jacksons had little money, Andrew Sr. bought a parcel in a remote location notable for its inhospitable red clay. The second year on the farm Andrew Sr. injured himself and died a month before his namesake was born. Elizabeth Jackson and her three sons, with no visible means of support, had to move in with her wealthy sister and brother-in-law. She performed the duties of a housekeeper in return for room and board for herself and her family. Though Andrew was surrounded by elegance, there was no question that he enjoyed it as a poor relation. Elizabeth died when Andrew was 14. But for a modest inheritance that Andrew received from his paternal grandfather and promptly squandered, his childhood and adolescence was dominated by economic hardship.

5. John Adams (12): Deacon John Adams did not get married until he was 43. His bride was the 25-year-old Susanna Boylston. A year after the wedding, Susanna gave birth to her first of three children, a son whom they named after her husband. Deacon John had no formal education, and Susanna was likely illiterate. From mid-March to October or so Deacon John tended his small 50-acre farm, trying to coax wheat, barley and corn out of the poor Massachusetts soil. During the rest of the year he cobbled shoes in a tiny room off the kitchen of their simple New England saltbox. The house, built a century before, was furnished in the "plainest" manner with six wooden chairs, a table, a few beds and a mirror or two.[42] Both parents toiled for all 12 months, causing a contemporary to regard Adams as having grown up in "the soil of poverty."[43] At 15 John Adams was awarded a partial scholarship to Harvard. Though Deacon John believed strongly that once acquired land be held, he sold 10 acres to fund his son's college.

6. Lyndon B. Johnson (16): Men of position were on both sides of Lyndon Johnson's family. There had also been, on both sides, a cycle of prosperity and collapse, a pattern that persisted with Lyndon's father, Sam. Sam was ambitious and tried a variety of professions and trades before he was elected to the Texas legislature. A natural at politics, he sought to work his magic with cotton futures and lost badly. Shortly after winning his second term, he met and married Rebekah Baines, a reporter who interviewed him. During Lyndon's first 12 years the Johnson's circumstances varied, early on living in ramshackle fashion in a glorified shanty in the country, then moving into the city, buying a bigger house and hiring some "girls" to help with the chores.

In both good and bad times, Lyndon took on odd jobs when school was not in session. When Lyndon turned 12, Sam bet it all on making a killing raising cotton on the old Johnson farm. The bet failed dramatically, and Sam was in debt for the rest of his life. He was also a broken man, in failing health and unable to find anything but menial and low-paying positions.

7. Ronald Reagan (16): Ronald's mother Nelle did not make it to high school, and his father Jack got no further than the sixth grade. Jack was a shoe salesman when he met and married Nelle and when his two boys arrived. And, despite Jack's aspirations of one day owning a shop of his own, he remained a shoe salesman until he lost even that job when the Depression hit. The Reagans never owned a home, renting modest places in a series of Illinois cities and towns. To make ends meet, Nelle took in boarders and did needlework, economized on food and recycled clothing for Dutch. Dutch contributed directly to family finances by caddying, hiring out as a circus roustabout and working construction.

8. Grover Cleveland (17): After graduating from Yale College, Richard Cleveland, like many of his forbears, pursued a career in the ministry. He studied theology in Baltimore, where he met his bride to be, Ann Neal. Though Ann's father was fairly prosperous, she married this "poor divinity student," knowing that she would be sacrificing the comforts she had known.[44] Over Richard's brief lifetime he served congregations in Connecticut, Virginia, New Jersey and New York. Grover was the third of their four sons and the fifth of their nine children. He later said that his father supported his large family "upon a salary that at no time exceeded a thousand dollars a year."[45] To augment Richard's scant income, at 10 Grover began doing household chores and found work outside the home. At 14 he clerked in a general store, receiving $50 for the year, plus room and board. Richard died when Grover was 16, and Grover gave up his plans for college. He hired out as a bookkeeper to help his mother care for his four younger siblings.

9. William McKinley (18): William McKinley Sr. began working at 16, without the benefit of any formal education. He was a partner in a small foundry in Niles, Ohio, forging iron and managing the blast furnaces which he bought or rented. He also built houses, mended fences, plowed fields and tended to livestock. William and his wife Nancy raised nine children in a modest frame cottage, a portion of which doubled as a store. Though William Sr. worked hard, the nature of his business and the size of his family meant they had only the barest of necessities. It was "a life of struggle and adversity."[46] Given the difficult circumstances, all of the children helped out at home. William Jr.'s chores included chopping wood, working in the yard and driving cows to and from pasture. William was able to attend grammar and high school and at 17 enrolled in Allegheny College in Meadville, Pennsylvania. He left school shortly after the beginning of his freshman year because of illness. He never returned. While William was recuperating, his father's finances had taken a turn for the worse, and the family could no longer afford his tuition.

10. William Jefferson Clinton (20): William Blythe, who was presumed to be Bill Clinton's father, was killed three months before his son was born. Four years later his mother, the former Virginia Cassidy, married Roger Clinton. Virginia worked in various health care capacities, largely as a nurse. Roger spent the first three years of his marriage in Virginia's home town of Hope, Arkansas, running a Buick dealership into the ground. He then fled to his home town of Hot Springs, Arkansas, to try his hand at farming. That too went badly. For the rest of Bill's childhood Roger was the parts manager in his brother's Buick dealership.

APPENDICES

Overdogs:

1. Franklin Delano Roosevelt (2): Franklin Roosevelt was a child of fortune, the only son of Sara Delano and James Roosevelt. The Delanos made the bulk of their money in the China trade, buying and selling goods and, it is said, dealing in opium. The Roosevelts made somewhat less money in more traditional ways, from real estate, textiles and sugar. James Roosevelt attended Union College and Harvard Law School before becoming a director of the Consolidated Coal Company of Maryland. The Roosevelts had a 17-room country estate on the Hudson River and a townhouse in New York City. Franklin was tutored at home until he was 14, by which time he had been to Europe eight times. He began his formal schooling at Groton, then went to college at Harvard and law school at Columbia. He wanted for nothing.

2. George Washington (3): George was the first son of Mary Ball, the second wife of Augustine Washington. She gave birth to him in Pope's Creek, Virginia. Augustine who began his first marriage with 1740 acres, continued to acquire land and by the time George was five owned a plantation, multiple farms and an iron furnace. When George was seven the Washingtons moved to Ferry Farm, "a livable residence of eight rooms."[47] Four years later Augustine died. He left 10,000 acres and 49 slaves to his heirs. George's half-brother Lawrence, 14 years his senior, received the largest share of the estate. George inherited Ferry Farm, 10 slaves and three lots, which was enough to make him "a planter of a second class."[48] Lawrence built a comfortable house on the Potomac called Mount Vernon, where George was always made to feel welcome, as Lawrence acted almost like a parent to him. At 15½ George earned his first fee for surveying. And while George found time to socialize, play billiards and whist and learn how to dance, "he was far from rich" such that "making a fortune came first."[49]

3. Thomas Jefferson (4): Thomas was born in "a modest frame house" in Shadwell, located in the western part of the Virginia colony.[50] His father, Peter, had expanded his original thousand-acre patent to 1,400 acres shortly before Thomas's birth. Though Peter was part of the Virginia gentry, he was not among its largest property owners. His wife Jane Randolph, however, was a descendant of one of the colony's richest and most prominent families. In addition to being "a moderately successful planter," Peter was a surveyor, map-maker and justice of the peace.[51] Upon his death, in addition to land, he had amassed 200 hogs, 70 head of cattle and 25 horses.

4. Theodore Roosevelt (5): Theodore Roosevelt Jr., the second child and first son of Theodore Roosevelt Sr. and Martha "Mittie" Roosevelt, was born into New York aristocracy. His parents lived in a five-story brownstone located in midtown Manhattan, with a domestic staff of five. Theodore Sr. had gone into the family business when he was about 20. That business, Roosevelt and Son, had been transformed by Cornelius Van Schaack – "CVS" – Roosevelt, Sr.'s father. CVS shifted the main product line from hardware to imported plate glass and began to hedge his commercial activities by accumulating real estate. His strategy paid off: in 1868 he was identified as one of only 10 true New York City millionaires. Five years later, Theodore Sr. himself had become a millionaire. Theodore Jr. enjoyed all the trappings of wealth, including two year-long Grand Tours of Europe and summers in the country. At 18 he enrolled at Harvard College.

5. Woodrow Wilson (6): Joseph Wilson, Woodrow Wilson's father, was a minister, trained at the Western Theological Seminary in Pennsylvania and the Princeton Theological Seminary in New Jersey. After five years teaching rhetoric at Jefferson College and the sciences at Hampton-Sydney College, Joseph, his wife Jessie and their two daughters moved to Staunton, Virginia, to take over the pulpit of an affluent Presbyterian congregation. They were given a 12-room house where Thomas Woodrow Wilson was born. When "Tommy," as he was called, was around two Joseph became the

minister of the First Presbyterian Church of Augusta, Georgia. The Wilsons lived in an elegant two-and-a-half-story brick manse, adjacent to a stable and servants' quarters. Joseph's initial annual salary was $2,500, $500 more than professionals were making. After roughly 12 years in Augusta, he accepted a teaching position at the Columbia Theological Seminary. When Tommy was 18, Joseph transferred to "a well-paid pulpit" in North Carolina.[52] Though "never wealthy," Joseph "was financially secure and socially accepted."[53]

6. James K. Polk (10): Sam and Jane Polk began their married life in Mecklenburg County, North Carolina. Sam started as a farmer, raising "tobacco, wheat, corn and hemp."[54] With prosperity and the advent of the cotton gin, he acquired 400 acres and shifted to planting cotton. The Polks were a family of seven by the time Sam followed his father and four brothers to an area south of Nashville, Tennessee. After the move, Sam changed his focus again, this time to real estate. He became a rich man and rose within the community, serving as a judge and civic leader.

7. John F. Kennedy (11): John Fitzgerald Kennedy was the second child of Joseph P. Kennedy and Rose Fitzgerald. By the time he was born, his father was the youngest bank president in Boston. While there are many questions about how Joe made his money during the years that followed, there is no question that he made a lot of it. He went from running a bank to running a shipyard to joining a brokerage house, and by 1919 he was on his way to earning his first million. In 1920 he purchased a 14-room mansion in a Boston suburb and his first Rolls Royce. Joe invested in, and invariably profited from, trading shares in coal, taxicabs and motion picture production companies. He perceptively was out of the stock market before Black Monday. In 1927, when Jack was 10, the Kennedys bought a summer house in Hyannis Port. By the time Jack was 12 they had moved to a 12-room colonial in Riverdale, New York. Jack went to private school at Choate in Connecticut, and while he was there, his father entered the liquor distribution business and became the first chairman of the Securities and Exchange Commission.[55]

8. James Madison (13): James Madison was born in Orange County, Virginia. His father, James Sr., was a member of the "plantation gentry," the Madison family having held property in the colony since the 1650s.[56] James Sr. consolidated his standing by marrying Nelly Conway, the daughter of another prosperous landowner. James Sr. had social position, serving as a justice of the peace and a church vestryman. He and Nelly raised seven children in Montpelier, the house they built when James was nine. The Madisons controlled 3,000 acres and had a "family" of 150, made up of freemen, dozens of slaves and "kindred 'subjects.'"[57]

9. James Monroe (15): Spence Monroe was a Virginia farmer, inheriting 500 acres from his father. With families like the Lees overseeing plantations of 20,000 acres, the Monroes were regarded as being in the "second-tier" of property owners.[58] Spence added to his farm income by working as a master carpenter, and while he was regarded as a gentleman, he was "at the lower end of the social scale."[59] He improved his economics and standing by marrying the wealthy Elizabeth Jones. James was the oldest son and second child. The Monroe home, which had to accommodate Spence, Elizabeth and five children, was relatively modest: a one-story building "topped by a half-story dormered attic," crudely crafted.[60] James, like all farm boys, had chores to perform: feeding the animals, hoeing the garden, milking the cows. Elizabeth died when James was 14 and Spence died soon thereafter. Elizabeth's wealthy brother, Judge Joseph Jones, settled the Monroe debts and helped raise the Monroe offspring.

10. John Quincy Adams (19): The year after Abigail Smith married John Adams they had their first child, a daughter whom they named Abigail. Two years later, they had their second child, a son christened John Quincy but known through childhood as Johnny. Ultimately their brood grew to five, with the addition of two more boys and another

APPENDICES

girl. John Adams had attended Harvard College and become a lawyer. The Adamses lived in a modest New England farmhouse in Quincy, Massachusetts, the brothers sharing a bed. Though John Adams was not among the truly wealthy in Massachusetts Bay, by the time Johnny was five his law practice was "prospering."[61] When his father was dispatched on diplomatic missions to Europe, Johnny accompanied him, his first trip occurring before his 11th birthday. Indeed, his second European trip, which began in mid-November 1779 lasted over five years, taking Johnny to France, Holland, Russia, Sweden and England and from boyhood to adulthood. Upon returning to the United States, he said that his father's "fortune" had "suffered" because of his service to the cause and that, as a result, the Adams children would have to make their own way.[62]

APPENDIX G
Earnings Details of the Ballplayers and Movie Stars

The Ballplayers

The detailed summaries below analyze the salaries for the 17 of the top 20 ballplayers who were categorized as Underdogs. Again, parenthetical numbers specify rank within the top 20.

1. Babe Ruth (1): In 1915, Ruth's first full year in the majors, he was paid $2,500,[63] which was more than the 5% level of $1,645. By 1919, he had been jumped to $10,000, which exceeded the 1% level that year of $7,065. For the next 15 years of his career, Ruth continued to exceed the 1% level each year by an average margin of nearly $50,000.[64] In his presumed peak year, 1931, Ruth was making $80,000, when the cut-off for 1% was $6,040.

2. Willie Mays (2): In 1951, Mays' first year in the majors, he was paid $7,500, which was more than the 5% level of $6,678. By 1956, he had been jumped to $30,000, which exceeded the 1% level that year of $18,582. For the remaining 17 years of his career, Mays continued to exceed the 1% level each year by an average margin of over $75,000.[65] In his peak and last year, 1973, Mays was making $165,000, when the cut-off for 1% was $41,744.

3. Henry Aaron (3): In 1954, Aaron's first year in the majors, he was paid $6,000, which was less than the 5% level of $7,588. By 1955, he had been jumped to $10,000, which exceeded the 5% level that year of $8,262. In 1957, he had been increased again to $22,500 which was more than the 1% level of $19,006. For the remaining 19 years of his career, Aaron continued to exceed the 1% level each year by an average margin of nearly $78,000.[66] In his peak year, 1975, Aaron was making $240,000, when the cut-off for 1% was $46,762.

4. Ted Williams (5): In 1939, Williams' first year in the majors, he was paid $4,500, which was more than the 5% level of $2,863. By 1940, he had been jumped to $12,000, which exceeded the 1% level that year of $6,579. For the remaining 17 years of his career, which was interrupted for three years by World War II, Williams continued to exceed the 1% level each year by an average margin of over $48,000.[67] In his peak year, 1950, Williams was making $90,000, when the cut-off for 1% was $14,076.

5. Lou Gehrig (6): In 1923, Gehrig's first year in the majors, he was paid $2,400, which was less than the 5% level of $3,123. By 1925, he had been jumped to $3,750, which exceeded the 5% level that year of $3,263. In 1928, he had been increased again to $25,000 which was more than the 1% level of $8,420. For the remaining 11 years of his career, Gehrig continued to exceed the 1% level each year by an average margin of nearly $21,000.[68] In his peak year, 1939, Gehrig was making $39,000, when the cut-off for 1% was $6,215.

6. Honus Wagner (7): In 1897, Wagner's first year in the majors, he was paid $1,500, which was more than the 5% level of $1,415. By 1902, he had been jumped to $3,600, which

exceeded the 1% level that year of $3,571. For the remaining 15 years of his career, Wagner continued to exceed the 1% level each year by an average margin of over $4,300.[69] In his peak year, 1908, Wagner was making $10,000, when the cut-off for 1% was $3,875.

7. Stan Musial (8): In 1941, Musial's first year in the majors, he was paid $1,800, which was less than the 5% level of $3,251. By 1942, he had been jumped to $4,500, which exceeded the 5% level that year of $3,605. In 1944, he had been increased again to $10,000 which was more than the 1% level of $9,815. For the remaining 18 years of his career, Musial continued to exceed the 1% level each year by an average margin of nearly $36,000.[70] In his peak year, 1951, Musial was making $75,000, when the cut-off for 1% was $15,616.

8. Mickey Mantle (9): In 1951, Mantle's first year in the majors, he was paid $7,500, which was more than the 5% level of $6,678. By 1953, he had been jumped to $17,500, which exceeded the 1% level that year of $15,951. For the remaining 15 years of his career, Mantle continued to exceed the 1% level each year by an average margin of nearly $51,000.[71] In his peak year, 1963, Mantle was making $100,000, when the cut-off for 1% was $22,865.

9. Walter Johnson (10): In 1907, Johnson's first year in the majors, he was paid $1,050, which was less than the 5% level of $1,600. By 1908, he had been jumped to $2,700, which exceeded the 5% level that year of $1,569. In 1910 he had been increased again to $4,500 which was more than the 1% level of $3,951. For the remaining 17 years of his career, Johnson continued to exceed the 1% level each year by an average margin of nearly $7,500.[72] In his peak year, 1925, Johnson was making $20,000, when the cut-off for 1% was $7,879.

10. Joe DiMaggio (11): In 1936, DiMaggio's first year in the majors, he was paid $8,500, which exceeded the 1% level that year of $6,251. For the remaining 12 years of his career, which was interrupted for three years by World War II, DiMaggio continued to exceed the 1% level each year by an average margin of over $39,000.[73] In his peak year, 1949, DiMaggio was making $100,000, when the cut-off for 1% was $12,924.

11. Rogers Hornsby (12): In 1915, Hornsby's first year in the majors, he was paid $1,200, which was less than the 5% level of $1,645. By 1917, he had been jumped to $3,000, which exceeded the 5% level that year of $2,085. In 1921 he had been increased again to $11,000 which was more than the 1% level of $6,178. For the remaining 16 years of his career, Hornsby continued to exceed the 1% level each year by an average margin of nearly $21,500.[74] In his peak year, 1927, Hornsby was making $40,000, when the cut-off for 1% was $8,420.

12. Cy Young (15): In 1891, Young's first year in the majors, he was paid $1,430, which was less than the 5% level of $1,539.[75] By 1899, he had been jumped to $2,400, which exceeded the 5% level that year of $1,415. In 1904, he had been increased again to $4,000 which was more than the 1% level of $3,723. In 1909 his salary was still $4,000, which was also in excess of the 1% level that year of $3,799.

13. Tris Speaker (16): In 1913, Speaker's seventh year in the majors, he was paid $9,000, which exceeded the 1% level of $3,985.[76] For the remaining 15 years of his career, Speaker continued to exceed the 1% level each year by an average margin of nearly $16,000.[77] In his peak year, 1922, Speaker was making $30,000, when the cut-off for 1% was $6,495.

14. Jimmie Foxx (17): In 1925, Foxx's first year in the majors, he was paid $2,000, which was less than the 5% level of $3,263. By 1928, he had been jumped to $5,000, which exceeded the 5% level that year of $3,287. In 1930, he had been increased again to $16,666 which was more than the 1% level of $7,325. For the next 12 years of his career, Foxx continued to exceed the 1% level each year by an average margin of nearly $14,500.[78] In his presumed peak year, 1939, Foxx was making $27,500, when the cut-off for 1% was $6,215.

15. Mike Schmidt (18): In 1972, Schmidt's first year in the majors, he was paid $13,5000, which was less than the 5% level of $20,601. By 1974, he had been jumped to $35,000, which exceeded the 5% level that year of $24,977. In 1975, he had been increased again to $65,000 which was more than the 1% level of $46,763. For the next 13 years of his career, Schmidt continued to exceed the 1% level each year by an average margin of over $1,200,000.[79] In his presumed peak year, 1988, Schmidt was making $2,250,000, when the cut-off for 1% was $132,677.
16. Josh Gibson (19): Because Gibson was only able to play in the Negro League, the salary data for him is not comparable and is largely anecdotal. In 1931 he made $125 a month, which amounts to $500 for a four-month season and $625 for a five-month season, figures well below the 5% threshold that year of $2,649. The next year his monthly salary was raised to $250 and remained at that level through 1936, yielding four- and five-month totals of $1,000 and $1,250, respectively, still shy of the 5% thresholds for those years which ranged from $1,943 to $2,642. But in 1939 a reporter for the *New York Daily News* wrote that Gibson's salaries "averaged $5,000 a year."[80] That amount exceeded the 5% thresholds for the late '30s and early '40s, but did not reach the 1% thresholds for those years.[81]
17. Lefty Grove (20): In 1925, Grove's first year in the majors, he was paid $6,500, which was more than the 5% level of $3,263. By 1928, he had been jumped to $9,000, which exceeded the 1% level that year of $8,420. For the remaining 13 years of his career, Grove continued to exceed the 1% level each year by an average margin of over $13,000.[82] In his peak year, 1934, Grove was making $45,000, when the cut-off for 1% was $4,936.

The Movie Stars

The earnings data available for motion picture actors is far spottier than that available for major league ballplayers. For most of the underdogs we do have information from Quigley Publications on their box office standings, which undoubtedly became the bargaining chip for salary negotiations.[83] With respect to more direct salary data, sometimes we have weekly numbers,[84] sometimes yearly contract amounts, sometimes general "per picture" compensation and sometimes the guarantee for a specific film.[85] The detailed summaries below analyze the income for the 14 of the top 20 movie stars who were categorized as Underdogs.

1. Cary Grant (2): Grant first appeared in the Quigley poll in 1939 and continued to rank in the top 25 in 25 of the next 29 years. In 14 of those years he was in the top 10 of male actors. When he began his career in 1932, Grant's weekly salary was $450. He made seven films in 1932, generating in total between $6,300 and $12,600, and placing him above the top 1% threshold that year of $4,658. By 1936 his weekly salary had increased almost eight-fold to $3,500 and his estimated per picture income ranged from $7,000 to $14,000 in a year when the 1% threshold was $6,251. By 1937 he was being paid $50,000 per picture when the 1% threshold was $6,474. Grant earned $150,000, plus 10% of the profits, for *None But the Lonely Heart* released in 1944, which was over 15 times higher than the 1% threshold that year. His take more than tripled to $500,000 for *The Bishop's Wife* in 1947. In the 1950s, his per picture salary ranged from a low of $300,000 for *People Will Talk* (1951) to a high of $3,000,000 for *Operation Petticoat* (1959). He made a million more than that for *That Touch of Mink* which was released in 1962. The 1% thresholds for 1947, 1951, 1959 and 1962 were $12,329, $15,616, $20,454 and $22,329, respectively.
2. Fred Astaire (5):[86] Astaire first appeared in the Quigley poll in 1935 along with his dancing partner, Ginger Rogers, and was in the top 10 of all actors, male and female, through 1937, and in the top 5 of male actors for the same period. In 1933 he signed a three-week contract at $1,500 a week, and that one contract alone exceeded the 1%

threshold that year of $4,301. Considering Astaire did two films in 1933, *Dancing Lady* and *Flying Down to Rio*, and recognizing the tremendous amount of rehearsal time required for musicals, his income was obviously many times the 1% threshold as his movie career began. In 1935, Astaire was paid an astronomical $150,000 plus a percentage of profits for performing in *Top Hat*, when the 1% cut-off was $5,290, and that ignores the fact that he also starred in *Roberta* that year. In 1937, Astaire was reported to have earned more than $211,000, over 30 times the 1% average of $6.474. For *You Were Never Lovelier*, released in 1942, he received $100,000, accepting less for *Holiday Inn*, debuting the same year. The fees of *Lovelier* alone dwarfed the 1942 threshold of $8,274 for the one-percenters. One hundred thousand dollars remained Astaire's per picture baseline for many years to come.

3. Clark Gable (7): Gable was truly box office magic for three decades, appearing in the very first Quigley poll in 1932 and, but for three years, continuing to show up in each poll through 1957. He was ranked in the top 5 for every year between 1934 and 1942. In 1931, effectively his debut year, Gable was paid $150 per week for his first picture, *The Painted Desert*, and $650 per week for the remaining six. His estimated income from all seven films ranged from $8,100 to $16,200, both figures comfortably above the 1% threshold of $4,567. His weekly salary increased to $2,000 in 1932, $2,500 in 1933, $4,000 in 1938 and $7,500 in 1940. He made at least one film each of these years, and if each required only three weeks to shoot, his annual income would have been above the respective 1% thresholds of $4,657 (1932), $4,301 (1933), $5,762 (1938) and $6,579 (1940). In 1939 Gable appeared in *Gone with the Wind*, earning $130,000, more than 20 times the 1% cut-off of $6,215. A decade later, the $241,250 he made for *Any Number Can Play* dwarfed the 1949 cut-off of $12,924. In the mid-1950s he only earned $100,000 for *Soldier of Fortune*, but the 1% cut-off was $17,123. Gable's pay rebounded dramatically with his last movie: he was paid $750,000 for *The Misfits* (1962), when the 1% cut-off was $22,329.

4. James Francis Cagney (8): Cagney showed up in the Quigley poll in 1934 and 1935 and then for six years straight from 1939 through 1944. In five of those eight years he appeared in the top 10. Cagney earned between $400 and $500 a week for the two films released his debut year of 1930. That translated into income between $1,600 and $4,000, straddling the 5% threshold of $3,001. The next year, there were five Cagney films, and his weekly salary averaged $425, resulting in annual earnings ranging from $4,250 and $8,500, straddling the 1% threshold of $6,040. By 1932, with a jump to $1,400 per week and with three pictures to his credit, Cagney's wages, ranging between $8,400 and $16,800, plainly put him among the one-percenters, the cut-off being only $4,658. He made $100,000 for *Great Guy* in 1936, when the 1% threshold was $6,251 and $150,000 for *Angels with Dirty Faces* in 1938, when the 1% threshold was $5,762. Less than a decade after *Angels*, in 1947, Cagney did *13 Rue Madeline* for a fee of $300,000 against a 1% cut-off of $12,330. In 1949, he entered into a deal with Warners which guaranteed him $250,000 for the one film he made for them a year, and permitted him to star in pictures made by his own Cagney Productions. His $250,000 Warners' guarantee compared with 1% thresholds that until 1959 never exceeded $20,000.

5. Spencer Tracy (9):[87] In the period from 1937 through 1951, Tracy appeared among the top 25 in every Quigley poll, ranking among the top 10 men in 10 of those 15 years. The contract he signed at the end of 1930 was for $750 a week. With three films shot in 1931, Tracy earned between $4,500 and $9,000 in his first full year, an amount above the 5% cut-off of $2,649 at the low end, and above the 1% cut-off of $6,040 at the high end. The next year, his weekly salary had risen to $1,000, and he appeared in seven pictures. With that level of output, his $14,000 to $28,000 placed him comfortably in the 1% stratum, which began at $4,658. Cagney entered into a contract in November 1934, promising weekly earnings of $2,250, that was superseded in April 1935 by a contract promising him $25,000 a picture, calling for five to be made annually. His fee

for a single picture was almost $20,000 more than the 1% threshold of $5,289. In 1944, a new agreement upped his per picture take to $110,000, or $100,000 more than the 1% threshold of $9,815. In 1956 he earned $156,000 for *Broken Lance*, when the 1% cut-off was $18,582. In 1960 he earned $250,000 for *Inherit the Wind*, when the 1% cut-off was $20,599. In 1963 he earned $250,000 for *It's a Mad, Mad, Mad, Mad World*, when the 1% cut-off was $22,865. And in 1967 he earned $300,000 for *Guess Who's Coming to Dinner*, when the 1% cut-off was $28,709.

6. Charles Chaplin (10):[88] As an Englishman whose career was principally in silent films, Chaplin does not register on the Quigley polls. In 1906, at the age of 17, Chaplin was earning about two and a half pounds a week, or about $12.50 weekly. Even had he worked throughout the year, his annual income would have been about $650, at a time when the top 5% of U.S. wage earners were bringing home $1,539. Two years later, in 1908, his weekly salary had increased to four pounds, or about $20. Again, even if he worked throughout the year, his annual income would have been about $1,000, at a time when the top 5% of U.S. wage earners were bringing home $1,569. In 1910, at the age of 21, Chaplin was earning $75 a week. If he worked 22 weeks he would have met the 5% cut-off of $1,600, and if he worked a full year he would have fallen just shy of the 1% cut-off of $3,951. By October 1913, his weekly salary had doubled to $150. If he worked just 11 weeks he would have met the 5% cut-off of $1,613, and if he worked a little more than half a year, he would have met the 1% threshold of $3,982. In 1914 Chaplin saw another increase, this time to $200 a week. If he worked nine weeks he would have exceeded the 5% cut-off of $1,629, and if he worked 21 weeks he would have exceeded the 1% cut-off of $4,022. It appears that by the next year, 1915, his weekly compensation had been raised "eightfold" to $1,600 a week, meaning if he were shooting for just three weeks he would have comfortably beat the 1% benchmark that year of $4,062.[89] Two decades later, in 1937, Chaplin's annual income was estimated to be $125,000, at a time when the 1% cut-off was $6,474.

7. Gregory Peck (12):[90] Beginning in 1945, Peck was recognized in the Quigley poll for 10 years in a row. He appeared again in 1956 and 1958 and in 1961 through 1963. In 1941 Peck entered into a seven-year contract, starting him at $75 per week and rising to $350 per week at the end of the period. A year later he signed a new and far-improved deal, guaranteeing him $1,000 a week for his first picture and $1,200 a week for his second. He was also given a $5,000 signing bonus. In 1943 he shot *Days of Glory*, earning $10,000, which was slightly more than that year's 1% threshold of $9,376. In November, 1943, Peck agreed to star in *Keys of the Kingdom* for $1,500 for each of 10 guaranteed weeks. *Keys* opened at the end of 1944 and, putting aside his weekly salary, the $25,000 bonus he got was, by itself, over two-and-a-half times larger than the 1% cut-off of $9,815. In 1945, Peck was paid $45,000 for *Valley of Decision*, when the threshold for 1% was $10,719, a year in which he also starred in *Spellbound*. Peck made $60,000 for *Only the Valiant*, aired in 1951, when the 1% cut-off was roughly a quarter of that amount: $15,616. Three years later, in 1954, he made somewhere between $500,000 and $700,000 in a two-picture deal, at over 30 times the $16,359 benchmark for one-percenters at the low end. Peck made $250,000 for *To Kill a Mockingbird* released in 1962, $400,000 for *Behold a Pale Horse* released in 1964, between $500,000 and $600,000 for *The Chairman* released in 1969 and $250,000 for *The Omen* released in 1976. The 1% thresholds for those four years were $22,329 (1962), $23,292 (1964), $32,253 (1969) and $49,945 (1976), meaning he made a minimum of five times the cut-off amount, irrespective of any entitlement to a share of the gross.

8. John Wayne (13): Though Wayne began making movies in 1930, he did not surface in the Quigley poll until 1945 and then as number 24 of 25 stars ranked. He disappeared for another two years, reappearing in 1948. Thereafter he then became a fixture, showing up for the next 22 years, being voted in the top five in 16 of those years and being below

number 10 only twice. Wayne made one film in 1930. He made four films in 1931, being paid $200 per week for one and $350 per week for the other three, earning between $2,500 and $5,000, the low estimate being close to the 5% cut-off of $2,649 and the high estimate approaching the 1% cut-off of $6,040. In 1932 he did two films for a flat fee of $675 each, two at $350 a week and another two at $1,500 a week, producing a minimum annual take of $8,750, $4,000 above the 1% threshold of $4,658. In 1935 Wayne received $6,000 for one of the eight movies featuring him that year, the single-picture fee alone exceeding the $5,290 1% cutoff. One source has him earning $24,000 in 1937, when the 1% threshold was $6,474. By 1942 Wayne's per picture take was up to $25,000, increasing seven-fold to $180,000 by 1949, amounts that were, respectively, three times the 1942 1% cut-off of $8,274 and nearly 14 times the 1949 1% cut-off of $12,974. In the 1950s, Wayne's income ranged from $300,000 at the beginning of the decade to $750,000 at the end of the decade; the 1% threshold ranged from around $15,000 at the beginning of the decade – 5% of Wayne's earnings – to around $20,000 at the end of the decade – 2.7% of Wayne's earnings. In the 1960s, he got paid $250,000 for two pictures, $750,000 for two pictures and $1,000,000 for two pictures. With the 1% cut-off averaging about $25,000 during the decade, Wayne was earning between 10 and 40 times the threshold amount. He continued to be paid handsomely in the 1970s, making $1,000,000 for *Rio Lobo* in 1970, when the 1% threshold was $33,673, $500,000 for *Brannigan* in 1975, when the 1% threshold was $46,763, and $750,000 for the *Shootist* in 1976, when the 1% threshold was $49,945.

9. Lawrence Olivier (14): Olivier does not appear in any Quigley polls. The $20,000 he earned for *Wuthering Heights*, released in 1939, was almost $14,000 more than the 1% threshold of $6,215. A year later he took home $50,000 for *Rebecca*, nearly eight times the 1% threshold of $6,579. In 1948, Olivier was paid 50,000 pounds for *Hamlet*, roughly $230,000, when the 1% threshold was $13,583. Between 1950 and 1985, the lowest fee he received for a picture was $100,000 – *The Devil's Disciple* (1959) – and the highest he received was $1,000,000 – *The Jigsaw Man* (1983). During this period, the 1% threshold began at $14,076 (1950) and never got higher than $97,471 (1985). Olivier's fees were always multiples of the 1% cut-offs. For example, in 1950 Olivier was paid $125,000 for *Carrie*, over eight times the 1% threshold of $14,075, in 1978 he was paid $725,000 for *The Boys from Brazil*, more than 12 times the 1% threshold of $58,755, and in 1980 he was reportedly paid $1,000,000 for *The Jazz Singer*, nearly 14 times the 1% threshold of $72,649.

10. Gene Kelly (15):[91] Kelly does not appear in any Quigley polls, and salary figures are largely unavailable. According to a database reporting on the wealth of "The Richest Celebrities, Actors . . ." Kelly had a net worth of $10,000,000 at the time of his death, some evidence that his earnings from films met the 1% threshold. When his career began in 1941, he signed a contract for $750 per week to commence at the end of the year. By the following autumn, his weekly salary had been raised to $1,000 as part of a seven-year deal. He made four movies in 1943: *Pilot No. 5, Du Barry Was a Lady, Thousands Cheer* and *The Cross of Lorraine*. Even assuming a modest four week production schedule for each film, his $16,000 of earnings would have been far above the 1% threshold of $9,376. At the end of the seven years his weekly salary was raised to $2,500. Since Kelly was most often appearing in musicals, involving extensive preparation, he was undoubtedly above the 1% cut-off of $14,076 in 1950, a year in which he worked on three movies. In 1951, the year in which he made the extremely elaborate *An American in Paris*, the threshold was at $15,616, an amount he would have exceeded after only six weeks of work.

11. Kirk Douglas (17): For the seven years between 1957 and 1963 Douglas appeared in every Quigley poll, though never rising above a ranking of 13. For *Out of the Past*, an early film released in 1947, he was paid $25,000, about double the 1% threshold of

APPENDICES

$12,329. Though his salary dropped to $15,000 for *Champion*, put out in 1949, the figure was still above the 1% threshold of $12,924. In the 1950s, he earned $175,000 for *20,000 Leagues Under the Sea* (1954), $350,000 for *Paths of Glory* (1957) and $325,000 for *Last Train from Gun Hill* (1959), when the respective 1% benchmarks were a fraction of these figures: $16,359 (1954), $19,006 (1957) and $20,454 (1959). *In Harm's Way*, a 1965 movie, brought him $400,000, more than 15 times the 1% cut-off of $24,132.

12. James Dean (18): Dean does not appear in any Quigley polls. In his tragically short career, he made three films. In his first, *East of Eden*, his salary was $1,000 a week, earning him $10,000 for the 10 weeks of shooting in 1954. His paycheck exceeded the 5% threshold of $7,588, but was less than the 1% threshold of $16,359. The same was true of *Rebel Without a Cause*, released the following year, for which Dean also earned $10,000. The respective 5% and 1% cut-offs were $8,262 and $17,123. By the time he made *Giant*, which debuted in 1956, his weekly pay had gone up to $1,500 and his income rose to $21,000, greater than the 1% benchmark that year of $18,582.

13. Burt Lancaster (19): Lancaster's name first appeared in a Quigley poll in 1950 and continued to show up in all but two years between then and 1963. But for 1956, when he ranked fourth, he never got above tenth. Lancaster's per picture fees were well in excess of the relevant 1% cut-offs. For example, he made $20,000 for *The Killers*, released in 1946, when the threshold was $11,992, $120,000 for *From Here to Eternity*, released in 1953, when the threshold was $15,951, $150,000 for *Birdman of Alcatraz*, released in 1962, when the threshold was $22,329 and a reported $750,000 for *Twilight's Last Gleaming*, released in 1977, when the threshold was $53,446.

14. The Marx Brothers (20): The Marx Brothers were recognized in the Quigley poll just once, in 1933. For two of their major hits, *A Night at the Opera* (1935) and *A Day at the Races* (1937), the group was paid $175,000 plus 15% of the gross. Assuming an equal division among Groucho, Harpo, Chico and Harpo, each made a minimum of $43,750 per movie, tens of thousands of dollars more than the 1% benchmarks of $5,290 in 1935 and $6,474 in 1937.

APPENDICES

APPENDIX H
Occupations of the Top 5% of Male Wage Earners, 2000

	Threshold	Occupation	Populace	Percentage
1	95.0	Metallurgical and materials engineers, variously phrased	41,441	0.59%
2	95.0	Civil engineers	307,670	4.38%
3	95.6	Mechanical engineers	306,089	4.36%
4	96.2	Computer software developers	1,504,125	21.43%
5	97.2	Not elsewhere classified engineers	425,087	6.06%
6	97.9	Electrical engineer	421,183	6.00%
7	97.9	Judges	69,348	0.99%
8	97.9	Sales engineers	36,823	0.52%
9	98.5	Pharmacists	231,275	3.29%
10	98.5	Air traffic controllers	42,342	0.60%
11	98.7	Aerospace engineer	129,146	1.84%
12	98.7	Airline pilots and navigators	142,278	2.03%
13	98.9	Physicists and astronomers	22,757	0.32%
14	99.1	Petroleum, mining and geological engineers	25,505	0.36%
15	99.1	Chemical engineers	73,743	1.05%
16	99.1	Actuaries	23,214	0.33%
17	99.6	Optometrists	33,571	0.48%
18	99.9	Podiatrists	12,253	0.17%
19	99.9	Lawyers	940,769	13.40%
20	100.0	Chief executives and public administrators	1,271,397	18.11%
21	100.0	Physicians	787,375	11.22%
22	100.0	Dentists	172,238	2.45%
		Totals	7,019,629	100.00%

Source: Steven Ruggles, Katie Genadek, Ronald Goeken, Josiah Grover, and Matthew Sobek. Integrated Public Use Microdata Series: Version 7.0 [dataset]. Minneapolis: University of Minnesota, 2017.

APPENDIX I
Intergenerational Mobility Study, 2006

Probability of Attaining Each Income Quintile in 1994-2000 Based on Parent's Income Quintile in 1967-71
Total Household Income

	Parental Quintiles (1967-71)	Children's Income Quintile (1994-2000)				
		1	2	3	4	5
		$0 to $32,700	$32,701 to $51,900	$51,901 to $70,800	$70,801 to $98,000	$98,001 and above
1	$0 to $29,900	41.5%	24.0%	15.5%	13.2%	5.9%
2	$29,901 to $42,000	22.6%	25.8%	23.1%	18.5%	10.0%
3	$42,001 to $54,300	18.7%	20.1%	24.1%	19.6%	16.9%
4	$54,301 to $72,300	11.1%	19.0%	20.7%	25.1%	24.0%
5	$72,301 and above	6.1%	11.1%	17.2%	23.7%	41.9%
	Expected Value	20.0%	20.0%	20.0%	20.0%	20.0%

Source: Tom Hertz, "Understanding Mobility in America," paper presented at Moving on Up? Economic Mobility in America, Center for American Progress, April 26, 2006 at 9.

For simplicity, the chart above omits a column and row from Mr. Hertz's table dealing with the top 5%. It also corrects an apparent error for the third quintile of parent's income and the second quintile of children's income by inputting a figure of 20.1%. The printed version for that cell had 25.8%, the same figure as in the cell immediately above.

Bibliography

The sources are listed below in the order in which they appear in the Table of Contents.

PART ONE: SETTING THE STAGE
Introduction

Nadav P. Goldschmied and Joseph A. Vandello, "The Future is Bright: The Underdog Label, Availability, and Optimism," *Basic and Applied Social Psychology*, 34:1 (February 2012): 34-43.

Joseph A. Vandello, Nadav Goldschmied and David A.R. Richards, "The Appeal of the Underdog," *Pers Soc Psychol Bull* 33 (2007): 1603-1616.

Cultural Conditioning and Reinforcement

bit.ly/2SZkDM6
https://nydn.us/1cITx0p
https://bit.ly/2TJmA3Y
https://bit.ly/2F4ir2v
https://bit.ly/2TwXwOk
https://bit.ly/2TsvRhv
https://bit.ly/2O1k0RG
https://bit.ly/2O1k0RG
https://bit.ly/2HfjiPR
https://bit.ly/2NYY9dg
https://bit.ly/1Py4AMk
https://bit.ly/2VQDYB2

Neal Gabler, *An Empire of Their Own, How the Jews Invented Hollywood* (New York: Doubleday, 1988).

Ben Stein, "Do Jews Run Hollywood? – You Bet They Do . . .& What of It?" E.Onlne.com. 3-13-02.

America's Roots
Colonization

Charles M. Andrews, *The Colonial Period in American History: I The Settlements* (New Haven: Yale University Press, 1934).

Marilyn Baseler, *"Asylum for Mankind" America 1607-1800* (Ithaca: Cornell University Press, 1998).

BIBLIOGRAPHY

Bernard Bailyn, *The Barbarous Years, The Peopling of British North America: The Conflict of Civilizations, 1600-1675* (New York: Vintage Books, 2012).

Bernard Bailyn, *Voyagers to the West, A Passage in the Peopling of America on The Eve of the Revolution* (New York: Vintage Books, 1988).

Herbert Eugene Bolton and Thomas Maitland Marshall, *The colonization of North America, 1492-1783* (New York: The MacMillan Company, 1921).

Aaron S. Fogleman, "From Slaves, Convicts, Servants to Free Passengers: The Transformation of Immigration in the Era of the American Revolution," *The Journal of American History*, June 1998.

Aaron S. Fogleman, "Migration to The Thirteen British North American Colonies, 1700-1775: New Estimates," *Journal of Interdisciplinary History* XXII:4 (Spring 1992).

Aaron S. Fogleman, "The United States and the Transformation of Transatlantic Migration during the Age of Revolution and Emancipation," in *The American Revolution Reborn*, edited by Michael Zuckerman and Patrick Spero (Philadelphia: University of Pennsylvania Press, 2016), including an unpublished appendix, referred to with the author's approval.

Marcus Wilson Jernigan, *Laboring and Dependent Classes in Colonial America 1607-1783* (Chicago: The University of Chicago Press, 1931).

Maldwyn Allen Jones, *American Immigration* (Chicago: The University of Chicago Press, 1960).

Herbert Klein, *Population History of the United States* (Cambridge: Cambridge University Press, 2004).

Susan F. Martin, *A Nation of Immigrants* (Cambridge: Cambridge University Press, 2001).

Robert Middlekauff, *The Glorious Cause, The American Revolution, 1763-1789* (New York: Oxford University Press, 1982).

Plimoth Plantation, Peter Arenstam. John Kemp and Catherine O'Neill Grace, *Mayflower 1620, A New Look at a Pilgrim Voyage* (Washington, DC: National Geographic, 2003).

Nathaniel Philbrick, *Mayflower, A Story of Courage, Community, and War* (New York: Viking, 2006).

Alan Taylor, *American Colonies, The Settling of North America* (New York: Penguin Books, 2001).

John Thornton, *Africa and Africans in the Making of the Atlantic World: 1400-1800* (Cambridge: Cambridge University Press, 1992).

Leaders

Benjamin Franklin
Ronald W. Clark, *Benjamin Franklin, A Biography* (New York: Random House, 1983).

Benjamin Franklin, *The Autobiography of Benjamin Franklin* (New York: Dover Publications, 1996).

Esmond Wright, *Franklin of Philadelphia* (Cambridge: The Belknap Press of Harvard University Press, 1986).

BIBLIOGRAPHY

<u>Thomas Paine</u>
Moncure Conway, *Thomas Paine* (New York: Chelsea House, 1983).

Christopher Hitchens, *Thomas Paine's Rights of Man* (New York: Atlantic Monthly Press, 2006).

Harvey Kaye, *Thomas Paine and the Promise of America* (New York: Hill & Wang, 2005).

The Life and Times of Thomas Paine (Golgathe Press, 2012)

Lepore, Jill. "The Sharpened Quill." *The New Yorker*. 16 Oct. 2006. https://www.newyorker.com/ magazine/2006/10/16/the-sharpened-quill.

Craig Nelson, *A Biography Thomas Paine, Enlightenment, Revolution, and the Birth of Modern Nations* (London: Penguin Books, 2006).

Audrey Williamson, *Thomas Paine, His Life, Work and Times* (New York: St. Martin's Press, Inc., 1973).

<u>John Paul Jones</u>
Joseph Callo, *John Paul Jones, America's First Sea Warrior* (Maryland: Naval University Press, 2006).

Michael Cooper, *Hero of the High Seas, John Paul Jones and The American Revolution* (Washington, DC: National Geographic, 2006).

Samuel Eliot Morrison, *John Paul Jones, A Sailor's Biography* (Boston: Little, Brown and Company, 1959).

Evan Thomas, *John Paul Jones, Sailor, Hero, Father of the American Navy* (New York: Simon & Schuster Paperbacks, 2003).

<u>Alexander Hamilton:</u>
Richard Brookhiser, *Alexander Hamilton, American* (New York: The Free Press, 1999).

Ron Chernow, *Alexander Hamilton* (New York: The Penguin Press, 2004).

James Thomas Flexner, *The Young Hamilton, A Biography* (New York: Fordham University Press, 1997).

Robert Hoffman, *The Founding Father's Boyhood on the Island of St. Croix* (US Virgin Islands: Southern Cross Publications, 2009).

The Revolutionary War

Herman O. Benninghoff, II, *The Brilliance of Yorktown, A March of History, 1781 Command and Control, Allied Style* (Gettysburg Pennsylvania: Thomas Publications, 2006).

Burke Davis, *The Campaign That Won America, The Story of Yorktown* (Eastern Acorn Press, 1992).

John Ferling, *Almost A Miracle, The American Victory in the War of Independence* (England: Oxford University Press, 2007).

Samuel B. Griffith, *The War for American Independence* (Chicago: University of Illinois Press, 2002).

David McCullough, *1776* (New York: Simon & Schuster Paperbacks, 2005).

BIBLIOGRAPHY

Joseph B. Mitchell, *Decisive Battles of the American Revolution* (New York: Fawcett Premier, 1962).

Andrew Jackson O'Shaughnessy, *The Men Who Lost America, British Leadership, the American Revolution, and the Fate of the Empire* (New Haven: Yale University Press, 2013).

W.J. Wood, *Battles of the Revolutionary War* (Cambridge: Da Capo Press, 1990).

PART TWO: UNDERDOG GREATS

I. On the Diamond

Josh Gibson
William Brashler, *Josh Gibson, A Life in the Negro Leagues* (New York: Harper & Row Publishers, 1978).

Carrie Golus, *Josh Gibson* (Minneapolis: Twenty-First Century Books, 2011).

John B. Holway, *Josh Gibson* (New York: Chelsea House Publishers: 1955).

Mark Ribowsky, *Josh Gibson, The Power and the Darkness* (Urbana and Chicago: University of Illinois Press, 1996).

Nick Tremlow, *Josh Gibson* (New York: The Rosen Publishing Group: 2002).

Mickey Mantle
Jane Leavy, *The Last Boy, Mickey Mantle and the End of America's Childhood* (New York: Harper Collins, 2010).

Tony Castro, *Mickey Mantle, America's Prodigal Son* (Washington, D.C.: Brassey's Inc., 2002).

Randall Swearingen, *A Great Teammate, The Legend of Mickey Mantle* (SportsPublishingLLC: 2007).

Mickey Mantle and Robert W. Creamer, *The Quality of Courage, Heroes In and Out of Baseball* (New York: Doubleday & Company, Inc., 1964).

Stan Musial
James N. Gigilo, *Musial, From Stash to Stan The Man* (Columbia: University of Missouri Press, 2001).

Jerry Lansche, *Stan The Man Musial, Born to Be a Ballplayer* (Texas, Taylor Publishing Company, 1994).

Stan Musial as told to Bob Broeg, *Stan Musial: "The Man's" Own Story* (New York: Doubleday & Company, 1964).

Ray Robinson, *Stan Musial: Baseball's Durable "Man"* (New York: G.P. Putnam's Sons, 1963).

George Vecsey, *Stan Musial, An American Life* (New York: Ballantine Books, 2011).

Ted Williams
Ben Bradlee, Jr., *The Kid, The Immortal Life of Ted Williams* (New York: Little, Brown and Company, 2013).

BIBLIOGRAPHY

Ed Linn, *Hitter, The Life and Turmoils of Ted Williams* (New York: Harcourt Brace & Company, 1993).

Leigh Montville, *Ted Williams, The Biography of an American Hero* (New York: Anchor Books, 2004).

Michael Seidel, *Ted Williams, A Baseball Life* (Chicago: Contemporary Books, 1991).

Ted Williams with John Underwood, *My Turn at Bat: The Story of My Life* (New York: Simon and Schuster, 1969).

Henry Aaron
Hank Aaron with Lonnie Wheeler, *I Had a Hammer, The Hank Aaron Story* (New York: Harper Perennial, 1991).

Howard Bryant, *The Last Hero: A Life of Henry Aaron* (New York: Anchor Books, A Division of Random House, 2011).

Al Hirshberg, *The Up-to-Date Biography of Henry Aaron, Quiet Superstar* (New York: G.P. Putnam's Sons, 1969).

Richard Scott Rennert, *Henry Aaron* (New York: Chelsea House Publishers, 1993).

Babe Ruth
Robert W. Creamer, *Babe, The Legend Comes to Life* (New York: Simon & Schuster, 1974.

Leigh Montville, *The Big Bam, The Life and Times of Babe Ruth* (New York: Broadway Books, 2006).

Babe Ruth as told to Bob Considine, *The Babe Ruth Story* (New York: A Signet Book, 1992).

Kal Wagenheim, *Babe Ruth, His Life and Legend* (New York: Henry Holt, 1974).

Roberto Clemente
David Maraniss, *Clemente: The Passion and Grace of Baseball's Last Hero* (New York: Simon & Schuster, 2006).

Bruce Markusen, *Roberto Clemente: The Great One* (Illinois: Sports Publishing Inc., 1998).

Phil Musick, *Who Was Roberto? A Biography of Roberto Clemente* (New York: Doubleday & Company, Inc., 1974).

Karl Wagenheim, *Clemente!* (New York: Praeger Publishers, 1973).

Paul Robert Walker, *Pride of Puerto Rico: The Life of Roberto Clemente* (San Diego: Harcourt Brace Jovanovich, 1988).

The Odds
Mark Armour and Daniel R. Levitt, "Baseball Demographics, 1947-2016" published in https://bit.ly/2SYxxKD

Jason Kaufman and Jay Gabler, "Cultural Capital and the extracurricular activities of girls and boys in the college attainment process." *Poetics* 32 (2004) 145-168. Print.

BIBLIOGRAPHY

II. At the Movies

https://bit.ly/2TvXwy3

Leading Men: The 50 Most Unforgettable Actors of the Studio Era (San Francisco: Chronicle Books, 2006).

Kirk Douglas
Kirk Douglas, *The Ragman's Son, An Autobiography* (New York: Simon and Schuster, 1988) at 15.

Michael Munn, *Kirk Douglas* (New York: St. Martin's Press, 1985).

John Wayne
Scott Eyman, *John Wayne, The Life and Legend* (New York: Simon and Schuster, 2014).

Carolyn McGivern, *John Wayne, a giant shadow* (Bracknell: Sammon Publishing Ltd, 2000).

Michael Munn, *John Wayne, The Man Behind the Myth* (New York: New American Library, 2003).

Randy Roberts and James S. Olson, *John Wayne, American* (Lincoln and London: University of Nebraska Press, 1995).

Donald Shepherd and Robert Slatzer with Dave Grayson, *Duke, The Life and Times of John Wayne* (New York: Doubleday and Company, 1985).

Maurice Zolotow, *Shooting Star, A Biography of John Wayne* (New York: Simon and Schuster, 1974).

Gregory Peck
Gary Fishgall, *Gregory Peck, A Biography* (New York: Scribner, 2002).

Michael Freedland, *Gregory Peck, a biography* (New York: William Morrow and Company, Inc., 1980).

Lynn Haney, *Gregory Peck, A Charmed Life* (New York: Carroll & Graf Publishers, 2003).

Tony Thomas, *Gregory Peck* (New York: Pyramid Publications, 1977).

Clark Gable
David Bret, *Clark Gable, Tormented Star* (New York: Carrol & Graf Publishers, 2007).

Warren G. Harris, *Clark Gable* (New York: Three Rivers Press, 2002).

Charles Samuels, *The King, A Biography of Clark Gable* (New York: Coward-McCann, Inc., 1962).

Lynn Tornabene, *Long Live the King, A Biography of Clark Gable* (New York: G.P. Putnam's Sons, 1976).

Jane Ellen Wayne, *Clark Gable, Portrait of a Misfit* (New York: St. Martin's Press, 1993).

Rene Jordan, *Clark Gable* (New York, Pyramid Publication, 1973).

James Cagney
James Cagney, *Cagney By Cagney* (New York: Doubleday & Company, 1976).

BIBLIOGRAPHY

Michael Freedland, *Cagney* (New York: Stein and Day Publishers, 1975).

John McCabe, *Cagney* (New York: Carroll & Graf Publishers, 1997).

Patrick McGilligan, *Cagney* (San Diego: A.S. Barnes & Company, 1975).

Doug Warren with James Cagney, *Cagney, The Authorized Biography* (New York: St. Martin's Press, 1983).

Cary Grant
Marc Eliot, *Cary Grant, A Biography* (New York: Harmony Books, 2004).

Lionel Godfrey, *Cary Grant, The Light Touch* (New York: St. Martin's Press, 1981).

Warren G. Harris, *Cary Grant, A Touch of Elegance* (New York: Kensington Publishing Corp., 1987).

Charles Higham and Roy Moseley, *Cary Grant, The Lonely Heart* (New York: Avon Books, 1989).

Graham McCann, *Cary Grant, A Class Apart* (New York: Columbia University Press, 1996)

Nancy Nelson, *Evenings with Cary Grant* (New York: William Morris and Company, 1991).

Geoffrey Wansell, *Haunted Idol: The Story of the Real Cary Grant* (New York: William Morrow, 1983).

Sidney Poitier
Carol Bergman, *Sidney Poitier* (Los Angeles: Melrose Square Publishing Company, 1988).

Carolyn H. Ewers, *Sidney Poitier The Long Journey* (New York: Signet Books, 1969).

Aram Goudsouzian, *Sidney Poitier* (Chapel Hill: The University of North Carolina Press, 2004).

David Paige, *Sidney Poitier* (Minnesota: Creative Education Children's Press, 1976).

Sidney Poitier, *The Measure of A Man, a spiritual autobiography* (San Francisco: Harper Collins Publisher, 2000).

Sidney Poitier, *This Life* (New York: Ballantine Books, 1980).

The Odds
https://bit.ly/2UspSFD

Jason Kaufman and Jay Gabler, "Cultural Capital and the extracurricular activities of girls and boys in the college attainment process." *Poetics* 32 (2004) 145-168. Print.

III. In the White House

Bill Clinton
Charles E. Allen and Jonathan Portis, *The Comeback Kid, The Life and Career of Bill Clinton* (A Birch Lane Press Book, 1992).

Bill Clinton, *My Life* (New York: Arthur A. Knopf, 2004).

BIBLIOGRAPHY

David Gallen, *Bill Clinton As They Know Him, An Oral Biography* (New York: Gallen Publishing Group, 1994).

Nigel Hamilton, *Bill Clinton: An American Journey: Great Expectations* (New York: Random House, 2003).

David Maraniss, *First in His Class: The Biography of Bill Clinton* (New York: Simon & Schuster, 1995).

Ronald Reagan
Lou Cannon, *President Reagan, The Role of a Lifetime* (New York: Public Affairs, 1991).

Dinesh D'Souza, *Ronald Reagan, How an Ordinary Man Became an Extraordinary Leader* (New York: A Touchstone Book Published by Simon & Schuster, 1997).

John Patrick Diggins, *Ronald Reagan, Fate, Freedom and the Making of History* (New York: W.W. Norton & Company, 2007).

Marc Eliot, *Reagan, The Hollywood Years* (New York: The Rivers Press, 2008).

Edmund Morris, *Dutch, A Memoir of Ronald Reagan* (New York: Random House, 1999).

Peggy Noonan, *When Character Was King, A Story of Ronald Reagan* (New York: Penguin Books, 2001).

Ronald Reagan, *An American Life* (New York: Simon and Schuster, 1990).

Ron Reagan, *My Father at 100, A Memoir* (New York: A Plume Book, 2011).

Lyndon Johnson
Robert Caro, *The Years of Lyndon Johnson, The Path to Power* (New York: Vintage Books, 1983).

Robert Dallek, *Lone Star Rising, Lyndon Johnson and His Times, 1908-1960* (New York: Oxford University Press, 1991).

Rebekah Baines Johnson, *A Family Album* (New York: McGaw Hill, 1965).

Doris Kearns, *Lyndon Johnson and the American Dream* (New York: Harper & Row Publishers, 1976).

Merle Miller, *Lyndon, An Oral Biography* (New York: Ballantine Books, 1960).

Clarke Newlon, *LBJ, The Man from Johnson City* (New York: Dodd Mead & Company, 1964).

Alfred Steinberg, *Sam Johnson's Boy, A Close-Up of the President from Texas* (New York: The MacMillan Company, 1968).

Irwin Unger and Debi Unger, *LBJ, A Life* (New York: John Wiley & Sons, Inc., 1999).

Andrew Jackson
H, W. Brands, *Andrew Jackson, His Life and Times* (New York: Anchor Books, 2006).

Augustus C. Buell, *History of Andrew Jackson* (New York: Charles Scribner's Sons, 1904).

Andrew Burstein, *The Passions of Andrew Jackson* (New York: Alfred A. Knopf, 2003).

BIBLIOGRAPHY

Marquis James, *Andrew Jackson The Border Captain* (Indianapolis: New York: Bobbs-Merrill Company, 1933).

Amos Kendall, *Life of Andrew Jackson, Private, Military and Civil* (New York: Harper & Brothers, 1843).

Jon Meacham, *American Lion, Andrew Jackson in the White House* (New York: Random House [Large Print], 2008).

Robert V. Remini, *Andrew Jackson and the Course of American Empire, 1767-1821* (New York: Harper & Row, Publishers, 1977).

https://bit.ly/2xLIypf

Dwight D. Eisenhower
Piers Brendon, *Ike, The Life and Times of Dwight D. Eisenhower* (London: Secker & Warburg, 1987).

Alfred D. Chandler, Jr., ed., *The Papers of Dwight David Eisenhower* (Baltimore, 1970).

Carlo D'Este, *Eisenhower, A Soldier's Life* (New York: Henry Holt and Company, 2002).

Dwight D. Eisenhower, *AT EASE, Stories I Tell to Friends* (New York: Doubleday & Company, Inc., 1967).

Michael Korda, *Ike, An American Hero* (New York: Harper Perrenial, 2008).

Geoffrey Perret, *Eisenhower* (New York: Random House, 1999).

Abraham Lincoln
David Herbert Donald, *Lincoln* (New York: Simon & Schuster, 1996).

Carl Sandburg, *Abraham Lincoln: The Prairie Years* (New York: Harcourt Brace Jovanovich, 1926).

Ronald C. White, Jr., *A Lincoln, A Biography* (New York: Random House, 2009).

Barack Obama
David Maraniss, *Barack Obama, The Story* (New York: Simon & Schuster, 2012).

Barack Obama, *Dreams from My Father* (Edinburg: Canongate, 2008).

The Odds
https://bit.ly/2EQTW7r

https://bit.ly/2THMHbq

Jason Kaufman and Jay Gabler, "Cultural Capital and the extracurricular activities of girls and boys in the college attainment process." *Poetics* 32 (2004) 145-168. Print.

PART THREE: HOW BEGINNINGS MATTER

I. On the Way Up

(*See* **PART TWO** for the sources related to the six previously discussed Underdogs, except as indicated.)

BIBLIOGRAPHY

B. The Movie Stars

Cary Grant
Charles Champlin, "Cary Grant." *The Movie Star,* Elisabeth Weis, editor (New York: The Viking Press, 1981).

C. The Presidents

Abraham Lincoln
Jean H. Baker, "Abraham Lincoln." *The American Presidency,* edited by Alan Brinkley and David Dyer, Houghton Mifflin Company, 2004.

Richard Carwardine, *Lincoln, A Life of Purpose and Power* (New York: Vintage Books, 2003).

Jim Collins, *Good to Great* (New York: HarperCollins Publishers, 2001).

Doris Kearns Goodwin, *Team of Rivals: The Political Genius of Abraham Lincoln* (NewYork: Simon & Schuster, 2005).

James McPherson, *Abraham Lincoln* (Oxford: Oxford University Press, 2009).

Ronald Reagan
Nigel Hamilton, *American Caesars: The Presidents from Franklin D. Roosevelt to George W. Bush* (New Haven: Yale University Press, 2010).

Gil Troy, "Ronald Reagan," *The American Presidency,* edited by Alan Brinkley and David Dyer (Boston: Houghton Mifflin Company, 2004).

Jacob Weisberg, *Ronald Reagan* (New York: Henry Holt and Company, 2016).

II. At the Top

Fred Greenstein, *The Presidential Difference, Leadership Style from FDR to Obama* (Princeton: Princeton University Press, 2000).

John D. Mayer, Peter Salovey and David R. Caruso, "Emotional Intelligence, New Ability or Eclectic Traits?" *American Psychologist* Vol. 63, No. 6 (September 2008).

III. Special Sauce.

Tom Butler-Bowdon, *50 Success Classics, Winning wisdom for work and life from 50 landmark books* (London: Nicholas Brealey Publishing, 2004).

Daniel Coyle, *The Talent Code, Greatness Isn't Born, It's Grown. Here's How* (New York: Bantam Books, 2009).

Charles Duhigg, *The Power of Habit, Why We Do What We Do in Life and Business* (New York: Random House, 2012).

Angela L. Duckworth, Christopher Peterson, Michael D. Matthews and Dennis R. Kelly, "Grit: Perseverance and Passion for Long-Term Goals," *Journal of Personality and Social Psychology,* Vol. 92, No. 6 (2007).

Angela Duckworth, *Grit, The Power of Passion and Perseverance* (New York: Scribner, 2016).

BIBLIOGRAPHY

Carol Dweck, *Mindset, The New Psychology of Success, How We Can Learn to Fulfill Our Potential* (New York: Ballantine Books, 2006).

Malcolm Gladwell, *David and Goliath: Underdogs, Misfits, and the Art of Battling Giants* (New York: Little Brown and Company, 2014).

Malcolm Gladwell, *Outliers* (New York: Little Brown and Company, 2008).

Victor Goertzel and Mildred Goertzel, *Cradles of Eminence 2nd Edition* (Scottsdale, Arizona: Great Potential Press, 2004).

John Lehrer, *I Imagine, How Creativity Works* (Boston: Houghton Mifflin Harcourt, 2012)

Dean Keith Simonton *Greatness, Who Makes History and Why* (New York: The Guilford Press, 1994).

Paul Tough, *How Children Succeed, Grit, Curiosity and the Hidden Power of Character* (Boston: Houghton Mifflin Harcourt, 2012).

PART FOUR: WHAT OF THE AMERICAN DREAM?

I. Where It Came From

James Truslow Adams, *The Epic of America* (Santa Barbara: Greenwood Press, 1931).

Jim Cullen, *The American Dream, A Short History of an Idea That Shaped a Nation* (Oxford: Oxford University Press, 2003).

II. Whether It Has Worked

Correspondents of The New York Times, *Class Matters* (New York: Henry Holt and Company, 2005)

Carmen DeNavas-Walt, Robert W. Cleveland, Marc I. Roemer, "Money Income in the United States: 2000." *Current Population Reports, Consumer Income* (U.S. Census Bureau, September 2001).

https://bit.ly/2SXWqFZ

Dennis Gilbert, *The American Class Structure in an Age of Growing Inequality* (Los Angeles: Pine Forge Press, 2008).

John E. Schwarz, *Illusions of Opportunity: The American Dream in Question* (New York: W.W. Norton & Company, 1997).

William E. Thompson and Joseph V. Hickey, *Society in Focus, An Introduction to Sociology* (Boston: Allyn and Bacon, 2002).

A. For Our Greats

Rags to Riches
Horatio Alger, *Ragged Dick Or, Street Life in New York with the Boot Blacks* (New York: Signet Classics, 2005).

F. Alvaredo, A.B. Atkinson, T. Piketty, E. Saez, and G. Zucman, *The World Wealth and Income Database* (2015), available at: http://www.wid.world.

BIBLIOGRAPHY

Analysis
E. Digby Baltzell and Howard G. Schneiderman, "Social Class in the Oval Office," *Transaction Social Science and Modern Society* Vol.25, No. 6 (September/October 1988): at 44-45. Print.

Suzanne Keller, *Beyond the Ruling Class, Strategic Elites in Modern Society* (New York: Random House, 1963).

Emanuel Levy, "The Democratic Elite: America's Movie Stars." *Qualitative Sociology*, 12(1), Spring 1989, 29-54.

Donald R. Matthews, *The Social Background of Political Decision-Makers* (New York: Doubleday & Company, 1954).

C. Wright Mills, *The Power Elite* (London: Oxford University Press, 1956).

David Nasaw, *Andrew Carnegie* (New York: The Penguin Press, 2006).

Edward Pessen, *The Log Cabin Myth* (New Haven: Yale University Press, 1984).

Leo C. Rosten, *Hollywood, The Movie Colony, The Movie Makers* Keller (New York: Harcourt, Brace and Company, 1941).

Sidney Willhelm and Gideon Sjoberg, "The Social Characteristics of Entertainers" *Social Forces* Vol. 37, No. 1 (October 1958): 71-76. Print.

B. For Others

Obscurity to Fame
Victor Goertzel and Mildred Goertzel, *Cradles of Eminence 2nd Edition* (Scottsdale, Arizona: Great Potential Press, 2004).

Mildred George Goertzel, Victor Goertzel and Ted George Goertzel, *Three Hundred Eminent Personalities* (San Francisco: Jossey-Bass Publishers, 1978).

Morris Janowitz, *The Professional Soldier, A Social and Political Portrait* (Glencoe, Illinois: The Free Press, 1960).

C. Wright Mills, "The American Business Elite: A Collective Portrait," *The Journal of Economic History* Vol. 5. Supplement: The Tasks of Economic History (December 1945): pp. 20-44. Print.

Leo Moulin, "The Nobel Prizes for the Sciences from 1901-1950 – An Essay in Sociological Analysis," *British Journal of Sociology* Vol. VI No. 3 (September, 1955) 246-263. Print.

Evelyn Raskin, "Comparison of Scientific and Literary Ability: A Biographical Study of Eminent Scientists and Men of Letters of the Nineteenth Century," *Journal of Abnormal and Social Psychology* Vol. XXXI (April-June 1936): 20-35. Print.

Anne Roe, *The Making of a Scientist* (New York: Dodd, Mead & Company, 1952).

John R. Schmidhauser, "The Justices of the Supreme Court: A Collective Portrait," *Midwest Journal of Political Science* Vol. 3, No. 1 (February 1959) 1-57. Print.

Leo Rosten, *The Washington Correspondents* (New York: Harcourt Brace, 1927).

Harriet Zuckerman, *Scientific Elite: Nobel Laureates in the United States* (New York: The Free Press, 1977).

BIBLIOGRAPHY

Rags to Riches

Affluence and Education

Sandy Baum, Jennifer Ma and Kathleen Payea, "Education Pays 2013, The Benefits of Higher Education for Individuals and Society," *College Board* 2013.

Ethan Biamonte, "The SAT and Admission: Racial Bias and Economic Inequality," November 15, 2013.

Anthony P. Carnevale and Stephen J. Rose, "Socioeconomic Status, Race/Ethnicity, and Selective College Admissions," *America's Untapped Resource, Low-Income Students in Higher Education*. Ed. Richard D. Kahlenberg (New York: The Century Foundation Press, 2004).

Correspondents of The New York Times, *Class Matters* (New York: Henry Holt and Company, 2005).

Lawrence E. Gladieux, "Low Income Students and the Affordability of Higher Education." *America's Untapped Resource, Low-Income Students in Higher Education*. Ed. Richard D. Kahlenberg (New York: The Century Foundation Press, 2004).

William J. Goode, "Family and Mobility," *Class, Status and Power, Social Stratification in Comparative Perspective* Second Edition. Ed. Reinhard Bendix and Seymour Martin Lipset (New York: The Free Press, A Division of McMillan Co., 1966).

IPUMS USA.

Soniya Luthar and Chris C. Sexton, "The High Price of Affluence," *Advances in Child Development* Vol. 32, ed. R.V. Kail (San Diego: Academic Press, 2004).

Soniya S. Luthar and Shawn J. Latendress, "Children of the Affluent, Challenges to Well-Being," *American Psychological Society* Vol. 14, No. 1 2005 (2005) 49-53. Print.

Catherine Rampell, August 27, 2009. https://nyti.ms/2qgJOzC

Steven Ruggles, Katie Genadek, Ronald Goeken, Josiah Grover, and Matthew Sobek. Integrated Public Use Microdata Series: Version 7.0 [dataset]. Minneapolis: University of Minnesota, 2017.

Isabel Sawhill, "Opportunity in America: The Role of Education," Policy Brief issued as companion piece to *Opportunity in America*, a publication of the Woodrow Wilson School of Public and International Affairs and the Brookings Institution (2005).

Joseph A. Soares, *The Power of Privilege, Yale and America's Elite Colleges* (Stanford, California: Stanford University Press, 2007).

P. Michael Timpane and Arthur M. Hauptman, "Improving the Academic Preparation and Performance of Low-Income Students in American Higher Education," *America's Untapped Resource, Low-Income Students in Higher Education*. Ed. Richard D. Kahlenberg (New York: The Century Foundation Press, 2004).

https://unc.live/2UxtGFU
https://bit.ly/2NYB22s
https://bit.ly/2UvBeZD
https://bit.ly/2EVDLpg
https://bit.ly/2XNW0Wp
https://bit.ly/2JgcN10

BIBLIOGRAPHY

Intergenerational Mobility

Emily Beller and Michael Hout, "Intergenerational Social Mobility: The United States in Comparative Perspective," *Future of Children* Vol. 16, No. 2 (Fall 2006).

Raj Chetty https://wapo.st/2ChLDB0

Tom Hertz, "Understanding Mobility in America," paper presented at *Moving on Up? Economic Mobility in America*, Center for American Progress, April 26, 2006.

Bhashikar Mazumder, "The Apple Falls Even Closer to the Tree Than We Though, New and Revised Estimate of the Intergenerational Inheritance of Earnings," *Unequal Chances, Family Background and Economic Success*, Eds. Samuel Bowles, Herbert Gintis and Melissa Osborne Groves (New York: Russell Sage Foundation, 2005).

H. Elizabeth Peters, "Patterns of Intergenerational Mobility in Income and Earnings," *Review of Economics and Statistics* 74 no. 3 (Aug. 1992) 456-466. Print.

Pew Trust's Economic Mobility Project: "Pursuing the American Dream: Economic Mobility Across Generations" (July 2012), "Economic Mobility in the United States" (July 2015) and "Economic Mobility: Is the American Dream Alive and Well?" (May, 2007).

Gary Solon, "Intergenerational Income Mobility in the United States," *American Economic Review* Vol. 82 (1992) 393-408. Print.

John E. Schwarz, *Illusions of Opportunity: The American Dream in Question* (New York: W.W. Norton & Company, 1997).

Robert D. Putnam, *Our Kids: The American Dream in Crisis* (New York: Simon & Schuster, 2015).

III. What the Polls Say

https://bit.ly/2J5ta0v
https://fxn.ws/2kkGvS7
https://pewrsr.ch/2SYABX9
https://nyti.ms/2XTiRji
https://nyti.ms/2F5oSSI

IV. Why It Endures

Congressional Quarterly News, September 25, 2015.

Harry Reid with Mark Warren, *The Good Fight: Hard Lessons from Searchlight to Washington* (New York: G.P. Putnam's Sons, 2008) at 25-26.

Robert S. McElvaine, *Mario Cuomo, A Biography* (New York: Charles Scribner's Sons, 1988).

Leonard Nimoy, *I Am Spock* (New York: Hatchette Books, 1995).

Gene Schoor, *The Story of Yogi Berra* (New York: Doubleday & Company, 1976).

Jane Mersky Leder, *Moses Malone* (Manakato, Minnesota, Crestwood House, 1955).

Frank Gifford and Harry Waters, *The Whole Ten Yards* (New York: Random House, 1993).

BIBLIOGRAPHY

https://bit.ly/2Hec1zW
https://bit.ly/2u1JOU1
https://bit.ly/2u1JOU1
https://bit.ly/2Ce19Ow
https://bit.ly/2tZYRhd
https://bit.ly/2TvwiaF
https://nyti.ms/2Hd2IAf
https://read.bi/2pgCzaY
https://nyti.ms/2SUJYqE
https://nym.ag/2CiaRzs
https://bit.ly/2TGFSGX
https://bit.ly/2TGFSGX
https://lat.ms/2EQyqQg

APPENDICES
APPENDIX F
Demographic Profiles of the Top 20s

(*See* **PART TWO** for the sources related to the 18 previously discussed Underdogs.)

The Ballplayers
Charles C. Alexander, *Rogers Hornsby, A Biography* (New York: Henry Holt and Company, 1995).

Charles C. Alexander, *Spoke, A Biography of Tris Speaker* (Dallas: Southern Methodist University Press, 2007).

Richard Bak, *Peach, Ty Cobb in His Time and Ours* (Michigan: Sports Media Group, 2005).

John Bloom, *Barry Bonds: A Biography* (Westport, Connecticut: Greenwood Press, 2004).

Reed Browning, *Cy Young, A Baseball Life* (Amherst: University of Massachusetts Press, 2000).

Richard Ben Cramer, *Joe DiMaggio, The Hero's Life* (New York: Simon & Schuster Paperbacks, 2000).

W. Harrison Daniel, *Jimmie Foxx, The Life and Times of a Baseball Hall of Famer, 1907-1967* (North Carolina: McFarland & Company, Inc., 1996).

Dennis DeValeria and Jeane Burke DeValeria, *Honus Wagner, A Biography* (New York: Henry Holt and Company, 1995).

Timothy M. Gay, *Tris Speaker, The Rough-and-Tumble Life of a Baseball Legend* (Lincoln: University of Nebraska Press, 2005).

Arnold Hano, *Willie Mays* (New York: Grosset & Dunlop, 1966).

Michael Hartley, *Christy Mathewson, A Biography* (North Carolina: McFarland & Company, Inc., 2004).

James S. Hirsch, *Willie Mays, The Life, The Legend* (New York: Scribner, 2010).

Arthur D. Hittner, *Honus Wagner, The Life of Baseball's Flying Dutchman* (North Carolina: McFarland & Company, Inc., Publishers, 1996).

Stan Hochman, *Mike Schmidt Baseball's King of Swing* (New York: Random House, 1983).

BIBLIOGRAPHY

Willie Mays with Lou Sahadi, *Say Hey, The Autobiography of Willie Mays* (New York: Simon and Schuster, 1988).

Jim Kaplan, *Lefty Grove, American Original* (Ohio: SABR, 2000).

Mary Kay Linge, *Willie Mays, A Biography* (Westport, Connecticut: Greenwood Press, 2005).

Jeff Pearlman, *Love Me, Hate Me: Barry Bonds and the Making of an Anti-Hero* (New York: HarperCollins, 2006).

Ray Robinson, *Iron Horse, Lou Gehrig in His Time* (New York: W.W. Norton & Company, 1990).

Philip Seib, *The Player, Christy Mathewson, Baseball, and the American Century* (New York: Thunder's Mouth Press, 2003).

Henry W. Thomas, *Walter Johnson, Baseball's Big Train* (Lincoln: University of Nebraska Press, 1995).

The Movie Stars
Fred Astaire, *Steps in Time, An Autobiography* (New York: HarperCollins, 2008).

Kate Buford, *Burt Lancaster, An American Life* (New York: Alfred A. Knopf, 2000).

Simon Callow, *Orson Welles, The Road to Xanadu* (New York: Penguin Books, 1995).

Gary Carey, *Marlon Brando* (New York, St. Martin's Press, 1985).

Charles Chaplin, *My Autobiography* (New York: Pocket Books, Inc., 1966).

James Curtis, *Spencer Tracy, A Biography* (New York: Alfred A. Knopf, 2011).

Donald Dewey, *James Stewart, A Biography* (Atlanta: Turner Publishing, Inc., 2007).

David Downing, *Marlon Brando* (New York: Stein and Day, 1984).

Gary Fishgall, *Pieces of Time, The Life of James Stewart* (New York: Scribner, 1997).

Michael Freedland, *Fred Astaire* (London: W.H. Allen, 1976) at 11, 12; Benny Green, *Fred Astaire* (London: Hamlyn, 1979).

Clive Hirschhorn, *Gene Kelly, A biography* (Chicago: Henry Regnery Company, 1974).

Val Holley, *James Dean, The Biography* (New York: St. Martin's Press, 1995).

Peter Manso, *Brando, A Biography* (New York: Hyperion, 1994).

Groucho Marx, *Groucho and Me* (New York: Bernard Geis Associates, 1959).

Harpo Marx with Rowland Barber, *Harpo Speaks* (London: Virgin Books, 1961).

Devin McKinney, *The Man Who Saw A Ghost, The Life and Work of Henry Fonda* (New York: St. Martin's Press, 2012).

Jeffrey Meyers, *Gary Cooper, American Hero* (New York: William Morrow and Company, Inc., 1998).

BIBLIOGRAPHY

Allen Roberts and Max Goldstein, *Henry Fonda, A Biography* (North Carolina: McFarland & Company, Inc., 1984)

David Robinson, *Chaplin, His Life and Art* (New York: McGraw-Hill Book Company, 1985)

Tim Satchell, *Astaire The Biography* (London: Hutchinson, 1987).

A.M. Sperber and Eric Lax, *Bogart* (Harper Collins Publishers, 1998).

Donald Spoto, *Laurence Olivier, A Biography* (NewYork: HarperCollins Publishers, 1992).

Donald Spoto, *Rebel, The Life and Legend of James Dean* (New York: HarperCollins Publishers, 1996).

Howard Teichmann, *Fonda, My Life, As Told to . . .* (New York: New American Library, 1981).

Stephen Weissman, *Chaplin: A Life* (New York: Arcade Publishing, 2008).

Alvin Yudkoff, *Gene Kelly, A Life of Dance and Dreams* (New York: Back Stage Books, 1999)

The Presidents
A. Scott Berg, *Wilson* (New York: G.P. Putnam's Sons, 2013).

John Morton Blum, *Woodrow Wilson and the Politics of Morality* (Boston: Little, Brown and Company, 1956).

Walter R. Borneman, *Polk, The Man Who Transformed the Presidency and America* (New York: Random House, 2008).

Alyn Brodsky, *Grover Cleveland, A Study in Character* (New York: St. Martin's Press, 2000).

Richard Brookhiser, *James Madison* (New York: Basic Books, 2011).

James MacGregor Burns, *Roosevelt, The Lion and the Fox, 1882-1940* (New York: Harcourt Brace Jovanovich, 1956).

John Milton Cooper, Jr. *Woodrow Wilson, A Biography* (New York: Vintage Books, 2011).

Noble E. Cunningham, *In Pursuit of Reason, The Life of Thomas Jefferson* (New York: Ballantine Books, 1987).

Jonathan Daniels, *The Man of Independence* (Philadelphia: J.P. Lippincott Company, 1950)

Robin S. Doak, *Profile of the Presidents, William McKinley* (Minneapolis: Compass Point Books, 2004).

Laura B. Edge, *William McKinley* (Minneapolis: Twenty-First Century Books, 2007).

Joseph J. Ellis, *American Sphinx, The Character of Thomas Jefferson* (New York: Vintage Books, 1996, 1998).

John Ferling, *John Adams, A Life* (New York: Henry Holt and Company, 1992).

Douglas Southall Freeman as abridged by Richard Harwell, *Washington* (New York: Simon & Schuster, 1992).

BIBLIOGRAPHY

Miriam Greenblatt, *James K. Polk, 11th President of the United States* (Oklahoma: Garrett Educational Corporation, 1988).

Nigel Hamilton, *JFK, Reckless Youth* (New York: Random House, 1992.

Margaret Leech, *In the Days of McKinley* (New York: Harper & Brothers, 1959)

David McCullough, *John Adams* (New York: Simon & Schuster, 2001).

David McCullough, *Mornings on Horseback* (New York: Simon & Schuster, 1981).

David McCullough, *Truman* (New York: Simon & Schuster, 1992) at 36.

Robert McElroy, *Grover Cleveland, The Man and the Statesman* (New York: Harper & Brothers Publishers, 1923).

Edmund Morris, *The Rise of Theodore Roosevelt* (New York: Coward, McCann & Geoghegan, Inc., 1979).

Paul C. Nagel, *John Quincy Adams, A Public Life, A Private Life* (New York: Alfred A. Knopf, 1997).

Charles S. Olcott, *The Life of William McKinley* (Boston: Houghton Mifflin Company, 1916).

Wendie Old, *James Monroe* (New Jersey: Enslow Publishers, Inc., 1998).

George F. Parker, *Recollections of Grover Cleveland* (New York: Century, 1909.

Robert V. Remini, *John Quincy Adams* (New York: Henry Holt and Company, 2002)

Harry Truman, *Autobiography* (Missouri: University of Missouri, 1980).

Harlow Giles Unger, *The Last Founding Father, James Monroe and a Nation's Call to Greatness* (Philadelphia: Da Capo Press, 2009).

Jeffrey C. Ward, *Before the Trumpet, Young Franklin Roosevelt* (New York: Harper & Row, Publishers, 1985).

Garry Wills, *James Monroe* (New York: Henry Holt and Company, 2002).

John K. Winkler, *Woodrow Wilson, The Man Who Lives On* (New York: The Vanguard Press, 1933)

APPENDIX G
Earnings Details of Ballplayers and Movie Stars

https://bit.ly/2yYfPho
https://bit.ly/2VOe8O8
https://bit.ly/2O1ppbq
https://imdb.to/20jEWkj
https://bit.ly/2EUBmvi
https://bit.ly/2EYIzKC
https://bit.ly/2ChH3CQ

Acknowledgments

I have been fortunate to have had a lot of support in writing this book. Olissa Oniyuke, Morgan Dowd and Livonne Moore helped me gather basic research materials which local libraries did not have. A number of scholars were more than generous with their time and expertise, including Joe Barton, Andy Beveridge, David Caruso, Aaron Fogleman, Joseph Soares and Paula Lantz, although I am, of course, responsible if I did not properly heed their guidance. Carol Henley was a wizard at locating the vintage headshots of my 21 heroes. And when it came to navigating the torturous path of obtaining permissions to use them, John Horne at the Hall of Fame in Cooperstown was invaluable in clearing the rights for the baseball images, as was Howard Mandelbaum of Photofest in New York City in enabling me to include the publicity stills of the movies stars. And despite the old adage about the irrelevance of book packaging, I hit the jackpot when Amanda Bouknight accepted the task of designing the front and back covers and when such established figures as Chris Mathews, Ann Hornaday, Tim Kurkjian and Karl Marlantes were willing to write such nice things about what I had done. While there are still undoubtedly glitches because of my constant fiddling, there would be hundreds more had Patty LaDuca not agreed to perform a thorough and painstaking edit. And at the eleventh hour, Stephanie Wang came to the rescue to convert my impossibly dense Excel spreadsheets into impossibly dense Word tables.

I was extremely lucky that old and new friends agreed to read this. At the beginning, there were Steve Brose and Norm Hile, who were given a much longer version in a jumbled order and, nonetheless, provided insightful comments and thoughtful and specific suggestions. Jim Carlsen, Frank Clifford and Michael Dockterman not only went through the manuscript, but endured hours of discussion about what points to make and how to make them. Brady Cassis, Jeremy Engle and David Fragale gave me hope that my profiles were of interest to those from younger generations. And there others who took the time to look at all or parts of the book and provide helpful and honest reactions, including Ellen Brondfield, Eve Carson, Sam Chauncey, Tom Dewey, Vince Falcone, Matt Herrington, Pantellis Michalopoulos, Mike Miller, Gwendolyn Renigar, Dave Richards, Michael Rips, Sam Stein, Preston Taylor and Hugh Wachter.

Finally, I am quite sure I never would have taken this project on or seen it through had it not been for David Maraniss. He encouraged me when all I had was the germ of an idea, followed along and poked me to find out how it was going (and how I was doing), pored through a massive and pretentious early draft, forced me to slim it down and rein it in, continuing to keep me at it until I had made it as good as I thought I could. My gratitude to David is profound.

Endnotes

Where I have relied on an author who has written multiple books or articles, the endnote will include his or her name and the first word or so of the relevant title.

PART ONE: SETTING THE STAGE

1. https://bit.ly/2w5cRcW
2. Another take on the etymology traces the term to plank-making. According to this version, the sawyer on the lower saw-pit was dubbed the underdog because he was located below the "dogs," the name for the metal brackets used to hold the logs in place. http://www.answers.com/topic/underdog
3. Goldschmeid and Vandello at 34, 37, 39, 41.
4. In exploring why it is that many think of underdogs as winners, Goldschmied and Vandello (at 35) write of the "inspirational examples" presented in "the media and popular arts (e.g., literature and cinema)." In a companion study these same authors tell of the impact of "the numerous heroic or sympathetic portrayals of underdogs in fiction and nonfiction." Vandello, Goldschmied and Richards at 1613. Among the "examples" and "portrayals" they cite are David and Goliath, Cinderella, the USA's 1980 Olympic hockey victory and the movies *Hoosiers*, *Rocky* and *Seabiscuit*.
5. Others include *A Chorus Line, Annie, Carousel, Chicago, Dream Girls, Evita, Fiddler on the Roof, Funny Girl, Gigi, Gypsy, Jesus Christ Superstar, Les Miz, Man of La Mancha, Oliver, Rent, Showboat, Sound of Music, The King and I* and *West Side Story*.
6. In addition, there were *Born Yesterday, Pygmalion, The Country Girl, The Miracle Worker* and *A Few Good Men*.
7. There are a host of other novels with underdog themes. For instance: James Fenimore Cooper's *The Last of the Mohicans*; Howard Fast's *Spartacus*; Edna Ferber's *So Big*; Kathryn Forbes' *Mama's Bank Account*; Winston Groom's *Forrest Gump*; Richard Llewellyn's *How Green Was My Valley*; W. Somerset Maugham's *Of Human Bondage*; Richard P. Powell's *The Philadelphians*; J.K. Rowling's *Harry Potter* series; Erich Segal's *Love Story*; Betty Smith's *A Tree Grows in Brooklyn*; Alice Walker's *The Color Purple*; and Robert Penn Warren's *All the King's Men*.
8. Some other non-fiction books about underdogs are: *And the Band Played On, Angela's Ashes, Awakenings, A Brief History of Time, Chaplin, A Civil Action, The Diary of Anne Frank, Gangs of New York, Into the Wild, My Left Foot, Rabbit Proof Fence, The Perfect Storm* and *Unbroken*.
9. https://bit.ly/2TsvRhv; https://bit.ly/2HfjiPR; https://bit.ly/2wyKgKk
10. To give some feel for the "reach" of movies, as compared to that of Broadway shows and books, consider the following: In 2010 the number one new movie, *Toy Story 3*, was seen by 52,200,000 people. The number one new Broadway show that season, *The Addams Family*, had an audience of roughly 925,000 and the number one new best-selling

book, *Decision Points*, sold 1.7 million copies, 1.8% and 3.3%, respectively, of the movie figure. The total number of people attending the top 20 new movies in 2010 was about 553,000,000, while the total number of attendees for the top 20 new Broadway shows was less than five million, or 1% of the movie figure. The top 20 new best-sellers sold 12.4 million copies or a little over 2% of the movie figure.

11 For me, there is a final "genre," the work of director Frank Capra. Born in Sicily, the youngest and seventh child, he came to the United States at five, travelling steerage. After arriving in New York harbor, the Capras went West and settled in an Italian ghetto on the east side of Los Angeles. Frank's father made a living picking fruit. He was on the streets hawking newspapers after school. This self-made man created a host of underdog classics, among them *It Happened One Night*, *Mr. Smith Goes to Washington* and *Lady for a Day*.

12 The data for ranking by ticket sales is excellent for the period from 1980 forward, as reported on the website "Box Office Mojo." For the period before, the sources I consulted provide data for no more than the top 20 highest grossing movies, and often for just the top 10.

13 A list of these movies, grouped by decade, can be found at Appendix A. There will obviously be quibbles about whether all the pictures I have identified are "truly" or sufficiently about underdogs, and countervailing arguments that I have left out a lot of obvious candidates.

14 There were only four years when there were no "notable" underdog movies: 1931, 1971, 1972, and 1987.

15 According to Ben Stein, things have not changed that much over time, given the prominent roles played by second- and third-generation Jews like Sumner Redstone and Sherry Lansing at Paramount, Michael Eisner and Michael Orvitz at Disney, Jeff Berg and Jim Wiatt at International Creative Management and Jack Rapke at Creative Arts Agency.

16 Gabler at 2. And Stein (at 4) wrote that the subsequent crop of Jewish moguls felt much the same way: "Yes, of course, the Hollywood product is made mostly by Jews. But these Jews are in love with America." In this connection, it is well to remember another Russian Jew, one who stayed put in New York. He was born Israel Isidor Baline. His father died when he was 13 and the next year he moved to the Lower East Side, so there would be one less mouth to feed. He lived with other homeless boys and taught himself to play piano and write songs. Irving Berlin, as he recast himself, was also in love with his adopted country. Called the "yiddishe Yankee Doodle Dandy" he gave us "God Bless America," the anthem that got us through World War II.

17 Fogleman, *The Journal of American History* at 43.

18 Data on the colonization of British North America prior to 1776 is contained in Appendix B.

19 In the 17th century the nearly 97,000 indentured servants, virtually all English, comprised 85% of servile labor. The pattern changed in the first three quarters of the 18th century, when the nearly 112,000 indentured servants comprised only about 25% of servile labor, with Germany supplying the largest contingent.

20 For example, David Clocker died owning a 320-acre spread, and Cuthbert Fenwick died as the lord of a 2,000-acre manor. Some former servants became justices of the peace, burgesses, sheriffs, councilors and militia officers, and two signed the Declaration of Independence.

21 "Clergyable offenses" were lesser crimes which, because they were "under benefit of clergy," could result in capital punishment. Martin at 22.

22 Fewer than 2,500 convicts came the century before.

23 As one eyewitness described it: "During the journey the ship is full of pitiful signs of distress – smells, fumes, horrors, vomiting, various kinds of sea sickness, fever,

ENDNOTES

dysentery, headaches, heat, constipation, boils, scurvy, cancer, mouth-rot and similar afflictions . . ." Taylor at 320.

24 Ninety-five percent came from these four countries. The English dominated the 17th century with nearly 90% of the total, while the Germans and Irish dominated the 75 years before the Revolution with over 70% of the total.
25 Taylor at 120.
26 The records were for voyages from December 1773 to March 1776. The two top categories in the occupational scale were "Gentle Occupation or Status" and "Merchandising." Bailyn *Voyagers* at 150.
27 Martin at 19. Virginia colonists were in the main a collection of "the disinherited [and] the dispossessed," just as most of those who settled in the Chesapeake region were from "the lower margins" of the English populace. Jones at 10; Bailyn *Barbarous Years* at 166.
28 Middlekauff at 31.
29 Taylor at 318.
30 The Ulster Irish included Scots who had moved to Ulster in the 17th century. I am including the Ulster Scots with the Irish, and not with the Scots, in keeping with the preferred approach of recent historiographers.
31 Baseler at 4.
32 Franklin at 6-7.
33 Franklin at 15.
34 Franklin at 16.
35 Franklin at 22.
36 Kaye (at 43) contends that "proportionally" it was "nation's greatest best-seller ever."
37 Lepore at 3. In his dotage, this most ill-tempered of the Founding Fathers referred to Paine's pamphlet as "a poor, ignorant, Malicious, short-sighted, Crapulous Mass." Lepore at 3.
38 While Hitchens (at 20) and Nelson (at 17) assert that the "stays" that Joseph made were for corsets, *Wikipedia*, citing only a dictionary of nautical terms, contends they were the thick ropes used on sailing ships. I will stick with the sources saying Joseph was in the undergarment business.
39 Hitchens at 25.
40 It was as captain of the *Richard* that Jones engaged a merchant convoy escorted by the 44-gun British naval vessel *Serapis*. According to lore, it was during this engagement that, when prematurely asked to surrender, Jones declared, "I have not yet begun to fight." Cooper at 9.
41 Morrison at 8. While Morrison (at 3) describes John Paul Jr. as having been "[b]orn in obscurity and poverty," Callo (at 6) contends that his parents were "representative of the hard-working social strata that would soon emerge as the British middle class." Whatever Callo may think, John Paul Jr. perceived himself as burdened by his humble beginnings.
42 Thomas (at 15) notes that John and Jeannie Paul were married the day before Sir William wed, that Craik had at least one illegitimate son and that John Sr.'s relationship with the master was tense. All this may have made John Paul Jr. doubt his paternity.
43 Morrison at 5. Thomas (at 16) says the cottage was "cramped" and had but two rooms, and Cooper (at 22) comes up with the same room count. Callo (at 6) contends it was a "multiroom" affair and that there was "nothing lowly" about it.
44 Although John Paul Jr. did not take the name Jones until 1774, for simplicity he shall be referred to as "Jones" from this point forward.
45 Morrison at 11.
46 Thomas at 16.

47 Because the "Ringleader" lived on the island, his friends and family would have been in the jury pool. Though Jones turned himself into the Justice of the Peace, he left Tobago before any proceedings began.
48 Morrison at 26-27. It is difficult to know how much of this story to credit, since it is based on Jones' account six years after the fact in a letter to Benjamin Franklin.
49 Thomas at 45. He later described Hewes as "the angel of my happiness." Thomas at 45.
50 Thomas at 45. Jones must have been pleased with the "Esquire," a title accorded to gentlemen.
51 Though Brookhiser (at 16) and Flexner (at 18) contend his birth year was 1757, Chernow (at 16-17) persuasively argues that adopting the later year is inconsistent with contemporaneous documents and makes Alexander just too much of a prodigy.
52 It is unclear whether he was embarrassed to be living in the city where the scandal surrounding his wife was inescapable, was weary of his constant business reversals or just no longer wanted the responsibility of a common-law family.
53 Lavien sued for a formal divorce on the grounds that Rachel had "absented herself" for nine years and had "begotten several illegitimate children." Chernow at 20.
54 Edward Stevens came to be like a younger brother to Alexander. In fact, Edward looked so much like Alexander that he could have been his real brother, or more to the point, Thomas Stevens could have been Alexander's real father. While contrary to Michael Lavien's vicious charges, Rachel was not a "whore," neither was she a saint. The doubts about Alexander's paternity, and the suspicion that he might be Thomas Stevens' son, may have been yet another explanation for James Hamilton's departure.
55 The triggering event for the fund-raising was a devastating hurricane that struck St. Croix on August 31, 1772. Alexander wrote a lengthy letter, describing in melodramatic detail the impact of the storm, sermonizing on its moral significance. The letter was published first in the local newspaper and again, at the request of the governor general of the Danish West Indies, in the more widely read *Gazette*. While purple in its prose, the letter was a testament to the precocity of the 17-year-old boy. The subscription for Hamilton's "scholarship" followed the re-publication in the *Gazette*.
56 Ferling at 569.
57 According to O'Shaughnessy (at 354) "[t]he most fundamental miscalculation" of the English was "the assumption that the loyalists were in a majority and that they would rally in support of the [English] army."
58 Senior officers during the earlier conflict dismissed colonial soldiers as the "lowest dregs" of humanity, "the dirtiest most contemptible cowardly dogs," "slothful and languid," "obstinate and perverse to the last degree." Ferling at 18-19.
59 Ferling at 563.
60 O'Shaughnessy at 353.
61 Ferling at 573.
62 Mitchell at 26.
63 Washington believed strongly that if there were to be a *battle royale*, it should take place in New York, a conviction that as late as July of 1781 led him to launch several exploratory probes. And Clinton was initially livid when Cornwallis, without orders, set up camp in Virginia earlier that May, writing him that he "shall dread . . . the consequences" of the move and "should certainly have endeavored to have stopped you" had he had any advance warning. Davis at 106-107.
64 Wood at 271, 280.
65 The so-called "long march" required the French army to cover more than 750 miles and the American army to cover more than 500 miles, distances greater than either force had previously traversed. The route was perilous and uncharted, so maps had to be created. The two armies moved separately, so communications had to be effected. The

ENDNOTES

soldiers could not carry sufficient food or water, so armories had to be built along the way and then provisioned.

66 Wood at 290.
67 The problem may not only have been a lack of urgency on the part of General Clinton, who was assembling the New York-based reinforcements. The timing of the decisive encounters was undoubtedly moved up because Cornwallis, without rebel provocation, decided to withdraw from his outer perimeter defenses, a move highly irregular in the face of a siege.
68 Ferling at 562, citing John C. Fitzpatrick, ed. *The Writings of Washington,* volume 27 at 223.

PART TWO: UNDERDOG GREATS ON THE DIAMOND

1 The calculation of the composite rankings from the 12 sources is set forth in Appendix D.
2 The four pitchers in the top 20 (Walter Johnson, Christy Mathewson, Cy Young and Lefty Grove) were excluded mainly because the information on their childhoods was scanty and not all that compelling.
3 Brashler at 2.
4 Holway at 16.
5 Ribowsky at 29-30.
6 Ribowsky at 30.
7 Ribowsky at 32.
8 Ribowsky at 33-34.
9 Ribowsky at 33.
10 Ribowsky at 33.
11 Ribowksy at 34.
12 Ribowsky at 35.
13 Ribowsky at 35.
14 Ribowsky at 35.
15 The "W.O.W." may somehow relate to the teams' sponsorship by a Western Pennsylvania "wood-working store." Ribowsky at 37.
16 Ribowsky at 39.
17 Ribowsky at 40.
18 Ribowsky at 43.
19 Ribowsky at 43.
20 Brashler at 23.
21 Brashler at 25.
22 Brashler at 31.
23 Ribowsky at 51.
24 Ribowsky at 56.
25 Ribowsky at 56.
26 Ribowsky at 57.
27 Ribowsky at 59.
28 Ribowsky at 64.
29 Ribowsky at 64.
30 Ribowsky at 61.
31 Ribowsky at 60. Brashler (at 26) says the Wilson column appeared on September 30 in the Philadelphia *Independent.*
32 Brashler at 31.
33 Brashler at 31.
34 Brashler at 30.
35 Leavy at 50.

ENDNOTES

36 Cochrane's real Christian names were Gordon Stanley, "Mickey" being a handle he had been given at college because of his prowess on the *football* field. Castro at 6.
37 Castro at 6.
38 Leavy at 39.
39 Leavy at 51.
40 Castro at 11.
41 Mantle and Creamer at 18.
42 Castro at 24.
43 Castro at 24.
44 Leavy at 55.
45 Though Leavy (at 60) says that Mickey only played "one season" of football, during the fall of 1946 as a sophomore, Castro (at 36) says "Mickey was busy playing football after school" during the fall of 1948 as a senior. This makes some sense, given the invitation from the Oklahoma scouts, who were unlikely to still be fantasizing about Mickey's exploits as a scrawny sophomore. In any event, nothing came of the trip.
46 Castro at 28.
47 Castro at 37.
48 Castro at 31.
49 Castro at 33.
50 Even when Mickey was hospitalized in Oklahoma City, one of his parents stayed with him.
51 Swearingen at 7.
52 Giglio at 5.
53 Musial at 6.
54 Since "Stashu" became "Stan" by the time he started school, we will use "Stan" from here on out. Giglio at 5.
55 123 Vecsey at 38.
56 Giglio at 10.
57 Vecsey (at 37, 39) suggests that Lukasc's drinking led him to strike Stan, but Stan never talked about this either.
58 Musial at 10.
59 Giglio at 14.
60 Giglio at 14; Musial at 13.
61 Giglio at 13-14.
62 Robinson at 14.
63 Musial at 15.
64 Vecsey at 62; Giglio at 25-26.
65 Vecsey at 63.
66 Interestingly, Musial makes no mention of this laudable incident in his autobiography.
67 Giglio at 16.
68 Musial at 28.
69 Robinson at 18.
70 Montville at 20; Seidel at 1.
71 Williams at 28.
72 *Compare* Williams at 28 *with* Bradlee at 32.
73 Seidel at 2.
74 A handwritten "Theodore" was later substituted for the typed "Teddy," and a handwritten "30" was later substituted for the typed "20." Bradlee at 37. Unaccountably, Williams says he was "not even sure where I got my name." Williams at 30. Despite his father's known fixation with the Rough Riders, Williams drew a blank on the source of "Teddy" and stated that "Samuel" was chosen to honor May's dead younger brother,

not his dad. Seidel (at 6) calls Williams' bewilderment on this score "a forgetfulness bordering on absurdity."
75 Seidel at 5.
76 Seidel at 3.
77 Seidel at 2.
78 Williams at 29.
79 Williams at 29.
80 Williams at 29.
81 Williams at 29.
82 Seidel at 5.
83 Linn at 30. May was "formally dedicated" to the Salvation Army when she was six. Linn at 30.
84 Williams at 27.
85 Williams at 33.
86 Williams at 28.
87 Williams at 19.
88 Williams at 31.
89 Though May was also not around, she was such a force of nature that she remained a presence even when she was away. As to Danny, it mattered little that he was not a source of companionship, since Williams never had any problem finding friends.
90 Seidel at 6.
91 Williams at 30.
92 Williams at 32.
93 *See* Willliams at 24, 27, 32, 33.
94 Linn at 35.
95 Williams at 22.
96 Linn at 36.
97 Williams at 23.
98 Williams at 21.
99 Bradlee at 48. In his autobiography, Williams (at 22) called it "one of those ten days you remember in your life."
100 Linn at 37.
101 Linn at 37.
102 Williams at 33.
103 Bradlee at 66.
104 In one Pomona tournament, perhaps this one, Williams hit four home runs in five games.
105 Sam had closed up his studio in 1931 to become a deputy U.S. marshal, likely through May's intercession. Three years later he was appointed inspector of prisons, and May's influence was likely again the impetus. The change in profession did not measurably improve the Williams' economics. Sam's yearly salary was $1,440 as deputy marshal and $2,160 as prison inspector. And the inspector position, based in San Francisco with requirements that he be constantly on the road, kept him away from home even more.
106 Linn at 42.
107 Bradlee (at 71) says that San Diego offered Sam "a couple of hundred bucks for signing" and that Ted would be paid for all of June, even though the agreement was reached late in of the month. Linn (at 47) says May had an understanding that if San Diego sold Williams' contract to a major league team "she would receive 10 percent of the purchase price."
108 Williams at 38.
109 Williams at 38.
110 Montville at 32.

111 Montville at 34.
112 Aaron at 23.
113 Rennert at 17.
114 Bryant at 12.
115 Bryant at 20.
116 Although Bryant (at 21) says the house had two rooms and was "owner built," Aaron (at 11) says it was a six-room dwelling that his dad paid two carpenters $100 to put up.
117 Aaron at 11.
118 Rennert at 19.
119 Aaron at 12.
120 Rennert at 19.
121 Other Mobile natives who eventually became major leaguers were Willie McCovey, Billy Williams, Cleon Jones and Tommie Agee.
122 Aaron at 27.
123 Hirshberg at 23.
124 Aaron at 19.
125 Aaron at 26.
126 An impoverished kid from Florida who dropped out of school at 12, Scott worked as a porter at Scott Paper, but his passion was managing the Bears.
127 Aaron at 33; Hirshberg at 25.
128 A tryout with the Brooklyn Dodgers that summer in Mobile did not go nearly as well. Henry was pushed out of the batter's box by some bigger kids, having hardly taken a swing, and then told by the scouts that he was just too little to play in the majors.
129 Henry was apparently credited with finishing his freshman and sophomore years at Central High and spent his junior year at Josephine Allen Institute, "a small private school" in Toulminville. Bryant at 27.
130 Aaron at 44. Indeed, the celebrated Goose Tatum had been the Clowns first baseman before moving on to the basketball court.
131 Aaron at 46.
132 Bryant at 43.
133 Aaron at 47, 53.
134 The Clowns would receive $2,500 right away and another $7,500 if Henry lasted over a month in the Braves' organization.
135 The Clowns would receive $2,500 immediately, another $2,500 if Henry were promoted to a Giants' Triple A club, a further $2,500 if he were moved up to New York and $7,500 more if he remained there for 30 days.
136 Aaron at 53.
137 According to Montville (at 6), baseball historian Jerome Holtzman said that, as of 2006, Ruth had the most biographies with 27, followed by Jackie Robinson with 25.
138 His mother died when he was a teenager. His father passed away after Ruth's second year in the majors, when he was just an exciting up-and-comer.
139 Montville at 15.
140 As late as 1944, *Current Biography* said his name was "reportedly George Herman Ehrhardt." Wagenheim at 10. That is not the name listed for Ruth's parents on his birth certificate, and Ruth always disavowed it. Ruth at 2.
141 Montville at 9.
142 Wagenheim at 11; Montville at 9.
143 Ruth at 2.
144 Ruth at 2.
145 Though Ruth (at 1) contended that his mother was "mainly Irish," because Katie is such an Irish-sounding name, Wagenheim (at 10) and Creamer (at 26) maintain that at least Katie's father, Pius Schamberger, emigrated from Germany. Mamie Ruth went further,

saying it was "nonsense" to think that her mother was anything other than German. Montville at 11.
146 Ruth at 2, 1; Creamer at 29.
147 Ruth at 2.
148 Wagenheim at 12.
149 Wagenheim at 12.
150 Creamer at 29.
151 Creamer at 30; Montville at 17.
152 Creamer at 29. Since there will be few further references to George Sr., the young Babe Ruth will from here on be simply referred to as "George."
153 Wagenheim at 12.
154 Creamer at 32.
155 Montville at 22.
156 Creamer at 32.
157 Montville at 18.
158 Montville at 17.
159 Creamer at 33.
160 Ruth at 3.
161 Creamer at 38.
162 As to George's looks, there is the familiar "dark skin, flat nose, big lips," the source of the hated nickname "Nigger Lips." Montville at 21. Brother Herman described him at 12 as "pretty big for his age", "not fleshy" but "on the wiry side" with "a mop of thick dark-brown hair." Montville at 22. Three years later he was said to be "tall and rangy, a smooth-muscled, broad-shouldered youth with long arms and long legs." Creamer at 41.
163 Montville at 22. Despite his rambunctious nature there is only one fight that gets noted: a knock down/drag out with a new boy who was acting like a bully. Montville at 23.
164 Creamer at 39.
165 Creamer at 39.
166 Creamer at 38.
167 Montville at 24; Creamer at 36.
168 Ruth at 3, 5.
169 Ruth at 4.
170 Ruth at 5.
171 Ruth at 8.
172 Creamer at 35.
173 Creamer at 35.
174 Ruth at 4.
175 Ruth at 4.
176 Ruth at 5.
177 Ruth at 5-6.
178 Ruth at 5.
179 Montville at 25.
180 Ruth at 5.
181 Creamer at 42.
182 Wagenheim at 14.
183 Wagenheim at 15.
184 Ruth at 7.
185 Ruth at 7.
186 Ruth at 7.
187 There is a less colorful story: the Red Sox pitcher was unexpectedly sidelined for some school infraction, and George asked the coach whether he could have a go at it.

ENDNOTES

188 Creamer at 45.
189 Creamer at 45.
190 Creamer at 45.
191 Creamer at 45.
192 Creamer at 46.
193 Creamer at 46.
194 Montville at 27.
195 Wagenheim at 15.
196 Creamer at 44.
197 Montville at 27; Creamer at 46.
198 Creamer at 48.
199 Creamer at 49.
200 Creamer at 51; Montville at 33.
201 Creamer at 52.
202 Musick at 52.
203 Musick at 52.
204 Musick at 54.
205 Musick at 54.
206 Musick at 55.
207 Musick at 55.
208 Musick at 57.
209 Musick at 54; Markusen at 2.
210 Maraniss at 19. Walker (at 3) agrees that Melchor made twice as much as the cane cutters, but says he earned $4 a week. Markusen (at 2) says that Melchor earned $.45 a day, when the average income in Puerto Rico "might have been" $.30 a day.
211 Musick at 53.
212 Maraniss at 18; Wagenheim at 20.
213 Maraniss at 19.
214 Musick at 55.
215 Wagenheim at 20.
216 Musick at 58.
217 Maraniss at 21.
218 Wagenheim at 13.
219 Musick at 60.
220 Wagenheim at 24.
221 Musick at 59.
222 Musick at 54.
223 Musick at 54.
224 Markusen at 5.
225 His senior year was spent at the Instituto Commercial de Puerto Rico in Hato Rey, since Vizcarrando refused to let him attend school and play semi-pro baseball.
226 Musick at 64.
227 Though he did not typically run track, he was entered into the 440-yard race in a meet against his school's "archrival" and beat the best runner on the island. Musick at 65.
228 Maraniss at 21-22.
229 Markusen at 3.
230 Musick at 55.
231 Musick at 56.
232 Wagenheim at 21.
233 Irwin had been a star in the Negro League in the 1930s, but was a bit too old to fully benefit from the breaking of the color line by Jackie Robinson in the mid-1940s. He

did play eight years in the majors from 1949 to 1956, mostly with the Giants, and he appeared in two World Series.

234 Musick at 59.
235 Markusen at 5.
236 Maraniss at 25. He went on to admit: "Of course, he quickly surpassed me." Maraniss at 25.
237 Wagenheim at 18.
238 Musick at 57.
239 Wagenheim at 23. Marin was also the godfather of Clemente's first son.
240 Wagenheim at 23.
241 Musick at 62.
242 Maraniss at 26.
243 Markusen at 9.
244 Musick at 70.
245 Wagenheim at 31.
246 Markusen at 11.
247 Maraniss at 26.
248 Wagnheim at 25; Markusen at 11.
249 Musick at 71.
250 Walker at 25.
251 In his second year with the Crabbers, Roberto was slotted in the lead-off spot and brought his average up 50 points, to a more than respectable .288.
252 Wagenheim at 32.
253 Wagenheim at 32.
254 Walker at 31.
255 Markusen at 13.
256 The 1050 figure is made up of 540 position players who appeared in at least 54 games and roughly 510 pitchers who appeared in at least 11 games. For the position players, 54 games is one third of a 162 game season. For the pitchers, 11 games approximates a third of the 32 games, which is the number in which a starter (and reliever) will appear assuming a rotating five-man staff.
257 This number is somewhat conservative since the denominator only includes American males, and in 2000 nearly 25% of major leaguers were of Latino descent, many having emigrated from the Dominican Republic and Venezuela.
258 For each of the team sports, the prescribed roster is multiplied by the same 1.4 used for MLB to reflect the fact that injury and performance results in significant churning. For each of the individual sports, 100 athletes are presumed to represent the real pros.
259 Kaufman and Gabler at 155. The impact of these revisions is to increase the numerator nearly five-fold, from 1,050 to 5,134 and to decrease the denominator by over 45% from 52,136,369 to 24,034,866.

PART TWO: UNDERDOG GREATS AT THE MOVIES

1 For example, in a poll of "regular people" only three of the AFI top 20 sneak into their top 20: Marlon Brando at 6, James Stewart at 18 and Humphrey Bogart at 20. Of the remaining 17, four do not register at all: Fred Astaire, Kirk Douglas, Gene Kelley and the Marx Brothers. Jim Carrey is ranked above Cary Grant and Bruce Willis is ranked above Lawrence Olivier. The likes of Christian Bale, Robert Downey, Jr., Sean Connery, Samuel L. Jackson, and Nicholas Cage rank above John Wayne, Gregory Peck, Spencer Tracy, Clark Gable, Henry Fonda and Gary Cooper. http://www.thebest100lists.com/best100actors/

ENDNOTES

2. Robert Osborne, the long-time host of Turner Classic Movies, provides some corroboration for this list. In the Foreword to *Leading Men: The 50 Most Unforgettable Actors of the Studio Era* he names, in alphabetical order, 18 great actors, 13 of whom are in AFI's top 13.
3. "Jewish Massacre Denounced," *New York Times*, April 28, 1903 at 6.
4. Munn at 13.
5. Douglas at 17.
6. Douglas 18.
7. Douglas at 25.
8. Douglas at 28.
9. Douglas at 20.
10. Douglas at 21.
11. Douglas at 21.
12. According to Douglas, the mills were not an option, because they did not hire Jews.
13. Douglas at 19.
14. Douglas at 20.
15. Douglas at 31.
16. Douglas at 22.
17. Douglas at 32.
18. Munn at 14.
19. Douglas at 26.
20. Douglas at 37.
21. Douglas at 41.
22. Douglas describes being kept after school one afternoon, when she clutched his hand near his thigh and being in her apartment one evening, when she kissed him while sitting on her bed.
23. Douglas at 50.
24. Douglas at 56.
25. Douglas at 56.
26. Shepherd, *et al.* at 18.
27. Roberts and Olson at 12.
28. There is an even split on the date of the wedding. Roberts and Olson (at 13), Eyman (at 17) and Shepherd, *et al* (at 18) say it took place in 1905. Zolotow (at 12), Munn (at 8) and McGivern (at 9) say it occurred in 1906.
29. Eyman at 17.
30. For a brief period, the Morrisons lived in Brooklyn, Iowa, where Clyde found an unsatisfying position at Raimsburg Drug.
31. Zolotow, Munn and McGivern, the three biographers who place the Morrison marriage on September 29, 1906, suggest that another reason for Molly's dislike of her firstborn was that under their chronology, his birth on May 27, 1907 was only eight months after the wedding, and in a small Iowa town a premature birth would have caused gossip and acute embarrassment. Zolotow at 12; Munn at 8; McGivern at 9.
32. Shepherd *et al.* (at 23) and Munn (at 10) are skeptical that Clyde's poor health had anything to do with his going out West, other than as a convenient cover story.
33. McGivern at 15.
34. Interestingly, property records show that Clyde bought and sold three houses in Glendale within three years. Likely purchased with the inheritance from his father, they did not turn much, if any, profit. Clyde was no more successful as a real estate entrepreneur than he was as a druggist or farmer.
35. Munn at 12.
36. Shepherd *et al.* at 36.

ENDNOTES

37 The studios included Fox, Vitagraph, Sierra Photoplays and Kalem. The movie star was Helen Holmes, a rival to Pearl White of *Perils of Pauline* fame.
38 That is how Wayne is quoted as recalling it (Munn at 13), though a couple of biographers write that Wayne had it backwards, and that he was the "Little Duke." McGivern at 10; Eyman 22.
39 Roberts and Olson at 45.
40 Duke was adept at chess and cards, as well.
41 Eyman at 29. Shepherd *et al.* (at 44) and Zolotow (at 40) write that though Duke did forget a few lines, the audience was nonetheless impressed by his presence, fine speaking voice and apt delivery. No sources are cited for this contrary view.
42 Eyman at 27.
43 Shepherd *et al.* at 48.
44 Eyman at 25.
45 Haney at 34.
46 Haney at 35.
47 The first film Peck recalled seeing there was *The Scarlet Letter,* starring Lillian Gish.
48 Fishgall at 38.
49 Haney at 37-38.
50 Fishgall at 30.
51 Tornabene (at 29) says Adele's parents were "of humble circumstance," while Samuels (at 15) says they were "prosperous."
52 Samuels at 27.
53 It turned out that Clark was not afraid of fighting, but was afraid of the harm he could do when he fought. He grew big early and at 14 weighed 150 pounds and at 5'9" was already as tall as his father.
54 Harris at 5. He went further: "The best day of my life was the day I met my stepmother." Harris at 5.
55 Wayne at 12.
56 Harris at 8.
57 Bret at xi-xii; Harris at 11-12; Samuels at 37-38; Tornabene at 46-47; Wayne at 16.
58 Harris at 12.
59 Harris at 12.
60 Cagney at 3.
61 Cagney at 2.
62 Cagney at 2.
63 Cagney at 3.
64 Though Cagney (at 5) says his father was "a bookkeeper" when he subbed at the bar, Jim's birth certificate describes his father as a "telegraphist." McCabe (at 5).
65 Cagney at 14.
66 McCabe at 7.
67 Cagney at 22.
68 Cagney at 21.
69 Warren at 8.
70 McCabe at 10.
71 McCabe at 8-9.
72 McCabe at 14.
73 Cagney at 4.
74 McCabe at 6.
75 Cagney at 6.
76 McCabe at 15.
77 McCabe at 22.
78 Warren at 15.

ENDNOTES

79   McCabe at 25.
80   His German teacher, Frank Mankiewicz, was the father of Joseph Mankiewicz, the famous Hollywood director, and Herman Mankiewicz, the famous Hollywood screenwriter.
81   Freedland at 22.
82   McCabe at 4.
83   McCabe (at 20), quoting Cagney, attributes the victory to the performance of Cagney and Mitchell at the plate, while Warren (at 21) says the win was more the result of their performance as a catching-pitching battery.
84   Cagney at 15.
85   Cagney at 6.
86   McCabe at 28.
87   Warren at 17.
88   McCabe at 30.
89   McCabe at 5.
90   Cagney at 2.
91   Cagney at 2.
92   Cagney at 23.
93   This is not entirely true. He had already seen a few amateur plays and vaudeville shows, and when he was visiting Aunt and Uncle Nicholson in Flatbush he got to roam the backlot and soundstages of the Vitagraph Studio, located near their home.
94   McCabe at 33.
95   McCabe at 33.
96   McGilligan at 6; Warren at 32.
97   Cagney at 11.
98   Cagney at 11.
99   Warren at xiv.
100 Higham and Moseley at 2; Godfrey at 19.
101 Godfrey at 19.
102 Wansell at 23. The other Kingdon ancestors, brewery laborers and laundresses, hardly sound "superior" to the Leaches potters and pants pressers.
103 Wansell at 23.
104 Higham and Moseley at 4.
105 Eliot at 25.
106 Quincy Jones observed that when Cary Grant was growing up "the upper-class English viewed the lower classes like black people." He went on: "Cary and I both had an identification with the underdog. My perception is that we could be really open with each other because there was a serious parallel in our experience." Nelson at 29.
107 Wansell at 27.
108 Wansell at 27.
109 Wansell at 28.
110 Wansell at 32.
111 Wansell at 29.
112 Whatever he was like with Elsie and in adult company, his cousins remembered him as "proud," "willful," "stubborn" and "given to petulance." Wansell at 28.
113 But the differences were not only about money. One autumn evening in 1909, shortly after Archie began at the Bishop Road School, Elias had friends over for some singing. He went up to his son's room, rousted him from his bed and perched him on a table to perform. Elsie disapproved of waking the five year old and making him into a spectacle. Elias pushed Elsie away when she tried to remove Archie from the table and then raised him high above his head so he was out of her protective reach.
114 Wansell at 28.

ENDNOTES

115 Wansell at 35.
116 Wansell at 36.
117 Eliot (at 31) and Higham and Moseley (at 18) claim that at some point Archie was told that his mother had died of a heart attack.
118 Wansell at 42.
119 Godfrey at 27.
120 Godfrey at 27.
121 Godfrey at 26.
122 Higham and Moseley at 19-20.
123 Eliot at 29.
124 Godfrey at 34.
125 Nelson at 37.
126 Harris at 31.
127 McCann at 33.
128 Harris at 33.
129 Nelson at 42.
130 Higham and Moseley at 18.
131 Nelson at 44.
132 Eliot at 35.
133 Harris at 37.
134 Eliot at 35.
135 Wansell at 52.
136 Higham and Moseley at 26. Archie also was responsible for opening the trap door in the million gallon pool through which the female swimmers vanished.
137 Harris at 43; Higham and Moseley at 27.
138 Harris at 43.
139 Harris at 44.
140 McCann at 41.
141 Grant would never forget how Ms. Bori suggested that they walk to and from the event, knowing he did not have money for a cab. He remembered her thoughtfulness when taxi fare had ceased to be a problem for him, helping out struggling actors whenever he could.
142 Wansell at 58.
143 Harris at 49.
144 *Better Times* had 409 performances, closing in April, 1923. During the run, Archie had his "first serious love affair," this one consummated, if somewhat haphazardly. Harris at 49. The object of Archie's affection was a showgirl in *Better Times*. They seemed to have become intimate one evening when Archie, who could not tolerate alcohol, was laid out in a bedroom at a party and his friends, thoughtfully, directed his sweetheart to join him. Grant acknowledged that while something "fumblingly" and "falteringly" happened, it was not "an occasion for song." Harris at 50. The relationship ended when he tired of taking his lady love home by subway to Brooklyn and not returning to his own apartment until dawn.
145 By the 1940s there were all-black musicals, like *Cabin in the Sky* and *Stormy Weather*, where the roles were less demeaning, but to that time no black starred in an integrated film.
146 Poitier at 3.
147 Goudsouzian at 10.
148 Poitier at 5.
149 Poitier at 5.
150 Goudsouzian at 11.
151 Ewers at 12.

ENDNOTES

152 Poitier at 8.
153 After two years, Evelyn found a cheaper, even worse rental in a noisier part of town.
154 Poitier at 16.
155 Goudsouzian at 14.
156 Ewers at 18.
157 Goudsouzian at 20.
158 Poitier at 24.
159 Poitier at 19.
160 Poitier at 25. Reginald had already had to cope with the imprisonment of his son Cedric for extortion.
161 Goudsouzian at 24.
162 Goudsouzian at 27.
163 Ewers at 24.
164 Poitier at 38.
165 Poitier at 38. She was working as a nurse's aide and Cyril was holding down three jobs.
166 Poitier at 39.
167 Poitier at 39.
168 Goudsouzian at 26.
169 Poitier at 43.
170 Poitier at 43.
171 Poitier at 43.
172 Poitier at 43.
173 Poitier at 45.
174 Poitier at 45.
175 Poitier at 45-46.
176 Poitier at 48.
177 Poitier at 49.
178 Poitier at 56.
179 Poitier at 57.
180 Poitier at 59.
181 Ewers at 38.
182 Goudsouzian at 37. James Baldwin, at the time "a young observer," agreed that the rumors of flagrant racial abuse with respect to this incident were an "invention." Goudsouzian at 37.
183 Poitier at 65.
184 Poitier at 68.
185 Poitier at 81.
186 Poitier at 81.
187 Ewers at 42.
188 Poitier at 82.
189 Poitier at 82.
190 Poitier at 83.
191 Poitier, *Measure* at 57-58.
192 Poitier at 84.
193 Goudsouzian at 44.
194 Poitier at 84.
195 Poitier at 87-88.
196 Poitier at 88.
197 Ewers at 49.
198 Poitier at 89.
199 Poitier at 89.
200 Goudsouzian at 44.

ENDNOTES

201 http://www.boxofficemojo.com/yearly/chart/?yr=2000

202 I have increased to 10 the number of featured male actors in movies, and assumed that 10 was also a conservative estimate for the number of featured male actors in television and Broadway shows. I assumed there were roughly 150 recurring tv series, including the "soaps," which may be generous, and I used the actual number of Broadway shows in 2000, 32. For singers, it seemed about 200 would roughly and plausibly reflect those who had achieved some measure of prominence.

203 Kaufman and Gabler at 155. The impact of these revisions is to increase the numerator by a factor of nearly 15, from 353 to 5,550 and to decrease the denominator by almost exactly 25% from 92,670,991 to 23,154,959.

PART TWO: UNDERDOG GREATS IN THE WHITE HOUSE

1 A chart showing the derivation of the composite rankings from the 22 surveys appears at Appendix E.
2 Hamilton. at 5.
3 Maraniss at 23.
4 Maraniss at 22.
5 Maraniss at 22, 24.
6 Maraniss at 21.
7 Clinton at 10. He also spent time with his grandfather at his second job as night watchman at a sawmill.
8 Maraniss at 31.
9 Hamilton at 52.
10 Hamilton at 52.
11 Clinton at 23-24.
12 Hamilton at 103.
13 Hamilton at 103.
14 Hamilton at 63.
15 Hamilton. at 104
16 Hamilton. at 104
17 Maraniss at 40.
18 He took Roger's last name at this point, even though Roger did not then – or ever – adopt him.
19 Clinton. at 30.
20 Gallen at 32.
21 Hamilton at 117.
22 Hamilton at 108; Clinton at 50.
23 Hamilton at 112.
24 Hamilton at 122.
25 Maraniss at 47.
26 Hamilton at 123.
27 Clinton at 60. He also knew he could never be elected Governor, because his good friend from Hope, Mack McLarty, had the job "saucered and blowed," *i.e.*, "in the bag." Clinton at 60.
28 Hamilton at 118.
29 Clinton at 62.
30 Hamilton at 121.
31 Though Clinton (at 67) claims he was accepted the second week in April, his mother, his guidance counselor and biographer Hamilton say he did not get in until some time after his graduation. Allen and Portis at 21; Gallen at 33; Hamilton at 131.
32 Maraniss at 48-49.

33 Noonan at 17.
34 Going back further, Ronald Reagan's great-great-grandfather, Thomas "O'Regan," worked the land in Doolis, Ireland, for a wealthy squire. Thomas's son Michael, Ronald Reagan's great-grandfather, left Doolis at 23 for London, where he met his future bride, Catherine Mulcahy, a gardener's laborer. Michael spent about four years employed as a soap maker before sailing to America in 1856 with his wife, three children and two older brothers, landing first in Canada and then traveling to Illinois. Michael Reagan's oldest son John was Ronald Reagan's grandfather.
35 Edwards at 26.
36 Edwards at 26.
37 Edwards at 34.
38 It took, according to Reagan, because he thought his given name "Ronald" was not "rugged enough for a young red-blooded American boy." Reagan at 21.
39 Morris at 25.
40 Reagan at 24.
41 Edwards at 39.
42 Edwards at 43.
43 Reagan at 31. Nancy Reagan attributed her husband's "emotional detachment" to his family's nomadic existence. D'Souza at 39.
44 Edwards at 50.
45 Reagan at 28.
46 Reagan at 33.
47 Reagan at 22.
48 D'Souza at 38.
49 Noonan at 17.
50 Reagan at 28.
51 Caro at 42.
52 Caro at 48.
53 For Sam Sr., they were from 1868 through 1870; for Sam Jr., they were from 1902 through 1905.
54 For Sam Sr., it was 1871; for Sam Jr., it was 1906.
55 Caro at 52.
56 Caro at 61.
57 And while on her lap, he would tell her, "I don't *like* you one bit! I just *love* you." Caro at 69.
58 Dallek at 35; Caro at 56.
59 Steinberg at 19.
60 Dallek at 42.
61 When he was 12 he missed 50 of 180 school days and was late for another 30.
62 Ungers at 8.
63 Dallek at 38.
64 Caro at 97.
65 Caro at 99.
66 Caro at 102.
67 Caro at 120.
68 Dallek at 57.
69 Caro at 124.
70 Caro at 129.
71 Dallek at 60.
72 Dallek at 61.
73 Steinberg at 30; Caro at 100.

ENDNOTES

74 According to Meacham (at 623), an early biographer wrote, "Andrew Jackson [Sr.] was very poor, both in Ireland and in America." Parton at I:47.
75 Brands at 17.
76 Bassett at 5.
77 Meacham at 14.
78 Buell at 36.
79 Buell at 36.
80 Burstein at 8.
81 Meacham at 15; Remini at 10.
82 Kendall at 25.
83 Buell at 52.
84 Brands at 27.
85 Meacham at 21.
86 Remini at 11.
87 Meacham at 23.
88 These funds, obtained in March of 1783, would have amounted to between $45,000 and $60,000 in 2017.
89 Brands at 34.
90 Remini at 28.
91 Brands at 37.
92 Brands at 18.
93 Burstein at 5. To the same effect, Kendall (at 11) wrote that Jackson owed his success "[n]ot to a long line of titled ancestors, nor to an extensive circle of influential connections, but to his own merits and energy of character," and a contemporary of Jackson's somewhat excessively observed that he "owed less to birthright and more to self-help than any other great man, not only in our history but in any other." Buell at 25.
94 Eisenhower at 56. He contrasts *"eisenhower"* with *"eisenschmidt,"* defined as blacksmith.
95 D'Este at 9.
96 Korda at 58.
97 Organized in 1862, their fundamentalist beliefs proscribed alcohol, cards, tobacco and theater and required the wearing of simple, old-fashioned garb.
98 Brendon at 15.
99 D'Este at 12.
100 D'Este at 12.
101 Korda at 60; Brendon at 15.
102 Perret at 5.
103 Jacob had sold his Pennsylvania land for $175 per acre.
104 Perret at 6.
105 Korda at 62.
106 Eisenhower at 32.
107 Eisenhower at 31.
108 Eisenhower at 31.
109 D'Este at 19.
110 Korda at 65.
111 Korda at 65.
112 Perret at 3-4.
113 Brendon at 20.
114 D'Este at 26.
115 Eisenhower at 67.
116 Eisenhower at 30.
117 Eisenhower at 82.
118 Eisenhower at 72.

ENDNOTES

119 Eisenhower at 69-70.
120 Eisenhower at 36.
121 Perret at 18; Korda at 68.
122 Brendon at 23. He remarked as well, "If we were poor – and I'm not sure that we were by the standards of the day – we were unaware of it." Eisenhower at 36.
123 Eisenhower at 31.
124 Eisenhower at 32.
125 Perret at 11.
126 Perret at 21.
127 Eisenhower at 37.
128 Perrett at 20.
129 Eisenhower at 34.
130 D'Este at 31.
131 Eisenhower at 35.
132 Eisenhower at 88.
133 Another older man who took an interest in Dwight was his across-the-street neighbor named Dudley. Supposedly a deputy in Abilene during the days when Wild Bill Hickok patrolled the town, he was a source of exciting stories about the characters and events of that bygone era. He also let Dwight accompany him and his pals when they held shooting contests at Mud Creek.
134 Eisenhower at 52.
135 Eisenhower at 52.
136 Eisenhower at 83.
137 Eisenhower at 36.
138 Eisenhower at 37.
139 Eisenhower at 94. According to Perret (at 27), Dwight weighed all of 115 pounds at the time.
140 Eisenhower at 96-97. The doctor's wife was adamant "that her husband had never recommended amputating Dwight Eisenhower's leg." D'Este at 42.
141 Eisenhower at 41.
142 Eisenhower at 40.
143 Eisenhower at 101.
144 Eisenhower at 101.
145 Eisenhower at 103.
146 Perret at 38.
147 Korda at 86.
148 Perret at 41.
149 Brendon at 27.
150 Donald at 20.
151 Donald at 21.
152 White at 11.
153 Sandburg at 21; White at 11.
154 Donald at 21.
155 As White (at 22) observed, "The previous generations of American Lincolns included Puritan courage, adventurous migration, bold commercial ventures, proud military service, and political office holding."
156 Donald at 22.
157 White at 14.
158 Sandburg at 22-23.
159 Sandburg at 23.
160 The Hankses have been described as "a prolific tribe, for the most part illiterate but respectable farmers of modest means." Donald at 19.

ENDNOTES

161 Donald at 20.
162 White at 14.
163 Sandburg at 24-25.
164 White at 14.
165 Sandburg at 23.
166 Donald at 23; White at 18; Sandburg at 26.
167 Donald at 22.
168 Sandburg at 28.
169 Sandburg at 29.
170 Donald at 22.
171 Lincoln never forgot the Saturday he spent dropping pumpkinseeds in alternate rows of a seven-acre cornfield from morning to dusk, only to see them all washed away Sunday in a big morning downpour. Donald at 23; White at 18; Sandburg at 30.
172 Donald at 23.
173 Donald at 23.
174 Sandburg at 31.
175 White at 18.
176 Sandburg at 31. Hardin County, Kentucky, had 1,238 slaves by 1816.
177 Donald (at 22) and White (at 14) both note that in 1814 Thomas ranked 15th of 98 Hardin County property owners. If their point is that Thomas Lincoln was prosperous, land holdings were merely paper wealth. Moreover, as his exit from Kentucky showed, Thomas was not exactly a real estate wizard.
178 Shortly after he was married, Thomas entered into a contract to "hew timbers" and erect a saw mill for one Denton Geoghegan. After days of effort, Geoghegan refused to pay Thomas and brought suit against him, claiming the timbers were not "hewn square." Sandburg at 27. Though Thomas prevailed, the experience did not enamor him of Kentucky justice.
179 White at 24.
180 Donald at 25.
181 Sandburg at 32.
182 Sandburg at 33.
183 White at 25.
184 White at 26.
185 Sandburg at 35.
186 Donald at 26.
187 Donald at 26.
188 Donald at 26.
189 Sandburg at 35. In fact, Thomas may have unsuccessfully courted Sarah before proposing to Nancy.
190 Sandburg at 35.
191 Sandburg at 35.
192 Sandburg at 41.
193 Donald at 28.
194 Donald at 28.
195 Sandburg at 35.
196 White at 30.
197 Donald at 28; Sandburg at 41.
198 Donald at 28.
199 Sandburg at 41.
200 Sandburg at 39.
201 Sandburg at 39.
202 Donald at 34.

203 Donald at 34.
204 Donald at 34.
205 Donald at 36.
206 Donald at 34.
207 Donald at 27.
208 Sandburg at 44.
209 White at 34.
210 White at 34.
211 Sandburg at 36.
212 Sandburg at 36.
213 Sandburg at 36.
214 Sandburg at 36.
215 Donald at 30.
216 Donald at 30.
217 Sandburg at 37.
218 Donald at 29.
219 Donald at 29.
220 Sandburg at 37.
221 Sandburg at 37; Donald 30.
222 White at 31.
223 Sandburg at 37.
224 Sandburg at 37.
225 White at 31.
226 Donald at 29.
227 White at 30.
228 Sandburg at 38.
229 Donald at 30.
230 Donald at 31.
231 White at 34.
232 Abe was "generous with his knowledge" in other ways. Donald at 30. There is the tale of the spelling bee when a classmate was stumped on the fourth letter of the word "defied," until he subtly pointed to his eye. Donald at 30.
233 Sandburg at 40.
234 Donald at 33.
235 Donald at 33; White at 30. He was regarded by some in the community as a "tinker – a piddler – always doing but doing nothing great." Donald at 32.
236 Donald at 32.
237 White at 30.
238 White at 30.
239 Sandburg at 41.
240 Donald at 28.
241 Sandburg at 37.
242 Sandburg at 37.
243 Sandburg at 38.
244 Donald at 33. Some neighbors, for example, called Abe "awful lazy." Donald at 33.
245 White at 30.
246 Sandburg at 38.
247 Sandburg at 38.
248 Donald at 20.
249 Donald at 23.
250 Donald at 20.
251 Donald at 19.

ENDNOTES

252 Obama at 14.
253 Obama at 14. Maraniss (at 24) dismisses the expulsion and principal-punching episode as pure fiction.
254 Maraniss at 32.
255 Maraniss at 68.
256 Maraniss at 89.
257 Maraniss at 125.
258 Maraniss at 127.
259 Obama at 16.
260 Maraniss at 160.
261 Maraniss at 163.
262 Obama at 5.
263 Maraniss at 175. Those who knew Barack Sr. best during this period, who spent time with him in class, at parties, at bars, were not aware that he had an American wife, much less a baby. Nor, in a wide-ranging interview with Barack Sr. upon his graduation from U of H, did he make mention of Ann or Barry.
264 Obama at 11.
265 Maraniss at 188.
266 Maraniss at 191.
267 Obama at 30-31.
268 Maraniss at 213.
269 Maraniss at 220.
270 Maraniss at 220.
271 Ironically, Lolo's "unraveling" came when things were seemingly going well. Maraniss at 231.
272 Maraniss at 231.
273 Obama at 50.
274 Maraniss at 264.
275 Obama at 60.
276 Maraniss at 162.
277 Maraniss at 268.
278 Maraniss at 283.
279 Maraniss at 283. There were a couple of other incidents. In one, an older woman contacted the manager of his grandparents' apartment house because she thought Barry was following her when he rode up with her in the elevator. In another, an assistant basketball coach reacted to a playground loss to a bunch of black men, muttering too loudly that his Punahou boys should not have lost "to a bunch of niggers" Obama at 80.
280 Maraniss at 285.
281 Obama at 75.
282 Obama at 21.
283 Maraniss at 289.
284 Maraniss at 289.
285 Maraniss at 289.
286 Maraniss at 290.
287 Maraniss at 291.
288 Maraniss at 291.
289 Maraniss at 293.
290 "Choom" is a verb, meaning "to smoke marijuana." Maraniss at 293.
291 Maraniss at 294.
292 Maraniss at 298.
293 Maraniss at 302; Obama at 95.
294 Obama at 96.

295 Maraniss at 310.
296 Maraniss at 306.
297 Maraniss at 314.
298 Maraniss at 315.
299 Obama at 91.
300 Obama at 19.
301 Obama at 18.
302 Maraniss at 317.
303 Maraniss at 318.
304 Maraniss at 318.
305 Maraniss at 319.
306 Maraniss at 319.
307 His choice was casual: "[I] settled on Occidental College in Los Angeles mainly because I'd met a girl from Brentwood while she was vacationing in Hawaii with her family." Obama at 96.
308 Maraniss at 220.
309 They were John F. Kennedy and Donald Trump, respectively.
310 The categorization of legislatures as full-time and well-paid comes from the National Conference of State Legislatures http://www.ncsl.org/research/about-state-legislatures/full-and-part-time-legislatures.aspx#side_by_side. Cities with populations over 100,000 as of 2000 are listed in http://www.census.gov/statab/ccdb/cit1020r.txt.
311 Kaufman and Gabler at 155. The impact of these revisions is to increase the numerator by a factor of over 2,700 from 1 to 2,738 and to decrease the denominator by almost a 85% from 40,514,622 to 6,513,060.

PART THREE: HOW BEGINNINGS MATTER

1   Montville at 37.
2   Ruth at 16. According to Ruth (at 15), the incident that spawned the comment involved his bribing a hotel elevator operator to allow *him* to run the new-fangled machine, sticking his head out while the doors were open on the third floor and almost getting it lopped off as he powered the lift up to the fourth.
3   Montville at 42.
4   Ruth at 28.
5   Montville at 97.
6   Montville at 100.
7   Ruth at 75-76.
8   Ruth at 27.
9   Montville at 55.
10 Ruth at 45.
11 While his morals were deplorable, Ford Frick, who knew him well, said that "he never led a young ballplayer astray and he never took advantage of an innocent girl." Creamer at 330.
12 Montville at 152.
13 As Hoyt later recalled, "His fabulous personal escapades were shaded with pathos, for the Babe no was longer sampling life. He was wolfing it down in immense, oversized doses." Montville at 206.
14 Ruth at 69-70; Montville at 87.
15 Bryant at 33.
16 Aaron at 19.
17 Aaron at 55.
18 Aaron at 57.

ENDNOTES

19 Aaron at 60.
20 Bryant at 46.
21 From Wisconsin, Henry went to Puerto Rico, and again he helped his team into a first-place finish, was selected as an All Star and garnered MVP honors. His manager in Caguas, Mickey Owen, taught Henry how to steady his hands and properly distribute his weight at the plate and shifted Henry from the infield, where he was floundering, to the outfield.
22 Aaron at 76.
23 Aaron at 79.
24 Aaron at 134.
25 The message was reinforced when he saw the name "Arron" stenciled on his locker. Aaron at 118.
26 Aaron at 118.
27 Aaron at 140.
28 Bryant at 79, 187. Two men from the Braves organization were positive forces during the Milwaukee decade. One was centerfielder Billy Bruton, who was also an African American, eight years Henry's senior. Henry described him as "my Big Brother," the man who "showed me the way." Aaron at 125; Bryant at 95. The other was publicity man/traveling secretary Donald Davidson, who was white and a diminutive four-feet tall. Aaron said he was "one of my best friends in baseball." Aaron at 142.
29 Bryant at 196.
30 Aaron at 155.
31 Bryant at 196.
32 Aaron at 155. In mid-1957 a generally favorable *Time Magazine* article ended with the left-handed observation that "Aaron is not as dumb as he looks when he shuffles around the field." Bryant at 189.
33 Aaron at 160-161.
34 Aaron at 185.
35 The relocation was inevitable. The team had begun a steady decline after its near miss of a pennant in 1959, dropping to fourth place in 1961 and never rising above fifth after that. In the six years between opening day 1960 and the final pitch of 1965, the Braves "spent just four days *total* in first place." Bryant at 296. All this was reflected in deteriorating attendance.
36 Bryant at 306.
37 Aaron at 252.
38 Bryant at 318.
39 Aaron at 257.
40 Aaron at 257.
41 Aaron at 248.
42 Aaron at 248.
43 Herman J. Mankiewicz wrote *Citizen Kane* and Joseph L. Mankiewicz directed *All About Eve*.
44 Cagney at 28. All in, he made $55 a week, not bad when a five-course meal cost a buck.
45 Willie, almost exactly Jim's age, was born on a farm in Iowa. At 16 she was shipped off by her parents to Chicago to attend teachers' college. Defying their wishes, she used the tuition money to go to New York and, after a stint waitressing, enroll in dancing classes.
46 McCabe at 43.
47 McCabe at 44.
48 McCabe at 47.
49 Cagney at 30.

ENDNOTES

50 McCabe at 46. Decades later, on the night Jim won the Oscar, he recalled that moment and said, "It couldn't have happened without you." Not missing a beat, Willie replied, "Damned right boy." McCabe at 46.
51 McCabe at 47.
52 McCabe at 52.
53 McCabe at 54.
54 McCabe at 55.
55 McCabe at 57.
56 McCabe at 57.
57 McCabe at 57.
58 McCabe at 61.
59 McCabe at 65.
60 McCabe at 68.
61 McCabe at 69.
62 He later directed such classics as *The Adventures of Robin Hood* and *The Man Who Came to Dinner*.
63 McCabe at 69.
64 McCabe at 70.
65 Nelson at 37.
66 Wansell at 59.
67 Wansell at 62.
68 Wansell at 62.
69 Wansell at 62. For a short while, he expanded his horizons and become part of a trio. The experiment ended after a *Variety* squib described the act as "two boys and a girl with a skit idea that gets nowhere." Harris at 53. When he left, his spot was filled by another up-and-comer, a red-headed dancer named Jim Cagney.
70 Nelson at 55.
71 Harris at 63.
72 Wansell at 69. She went on to admit, however, that "everybody liked him. He had charm." Wansell at 69.
73 Wansell at 70; Harris at 66.
74 Nelson at 58. Archie wore a 17½-inch collar.
75 Nelson at 66.
76 Wansell at 83.
77 Wansell at 87.
78 Grant was forever offended by West's claim to have "discovered" him, since he had already been in seven movies before he stepped with her onto the sound stage.
79 Two examples. Grant: "Haven't you ever met a man who can make you happy?" West: "Sure, lots of times." Wansell at 90. Grant: "I'm sorry to be taking your time." West: "What do you think my time is for." Godfrey at 56.
80 Harris at 99.
81 Harris at 99-100.
82 Wansell at 109.
83 Nelson at 83.
84 Even Grant recognized that Paramount had a surplus of actors "with dark hair and a set of teeth like mine." Harris at 113. There was not only Gary Cooper and Fredric March, but Bing Crosby, George Raft, Henry Fonda and Randolph Scott.
85 Donald at 39.
86 Donald at 44.
87 Donald at 39.
88 McPherson at 6.
89 Donald at 43.

ENDNOTES

90 Donald at 44.
91 One of Abe's admirers bought his survey equipment at auction and returned it to him.
92 Donald at 57.
93 McPherson at 7.
94 Donald at 97.
95 Donald at 112-113. In the midst of the congressional campaign, Logan told Abe that he wished to dissolve their partnership and go into business with his son. Abe joined forces with 26-year-old William H. Herndon. He liked Billy's energy, optimism and appetite for learning, as well as his connections to the populist wing of the Whig Party. He also liked the idea of being the senior member of his own firm.
96 McPherson at 13.
97 The consolation prize, Governor of the Oregon Territory, had little appeal, since once the territory was admitted to the Union, the strongly-Democratic electorate was unlikely to extend the tenure of a member of a rival Party.
98 Donald at 142. Abe endured two deaths during this period, that of his four-year-old son Edward, on February 1, 1850, and his father, on January 17, 1851. He did not attend Thomas's funeral.
99 Donald at 146-147.
100 Donald at 149.
101 White at 196.
102 McPherson at 23.
103 McPherson at 24.
104 McPherson at 26.
105 White at 305-306. In addition, Abe's promoters claimed he could win in Pennsylvania, Indiana and Illinois – states Frémont had lost – because, unlike Seward, Lincoln had cannily and carefully avoided a head-on collision with the "Know Nothings," the Mid-Western nativists hostile to immigrants and foreigners.
106 Weisberg at 13.
107 Reagan loved to recall the day when the telegraph failed during a Cubs-Cardinals game, and he had to make-up a 20-minute at-bat, with foul ball after foul ball after foul ball, until the wire came back to life.
108 Weisberg at 19. The initial agreement was for seven years at a salary of $200 a week.
109 Weisberg at 26.
110 Weisberg at 27.
111 Weisberg at 28.
112 Noonan at 72.
113 Weisberg at 34.
114 Noonan at 80.
115 Noonan at 80.
116 Weisberg at 38.
117 Noonan at 87-88.
118 Weisberg at 45.
119 Weisberg at 46.
120 Weisberg at 46.
121 Noonan at 95.
122 Noonan at 126, 127.
123 Weisberg at 64.
124 Weisberg at 2.
125 Some say Reagan won it with his first answer, when he looked into the camera and declared, "I believe with all my heart that our first priority must be world peace," refuting in one fell swoop the notion that he would be a reckless adventurer. Weisberg at 65. Some say he won it half way through, when Carter mistakenly accused Reagan of

opposing Medicare, and Reagan, shaking his head, genially responded, "There you go again." Weisberg at 66. And some say he won it with his conclusion, when he asked the American people, "Are you better off than you were four years ago?" Weisberg at 66.
126 In his book on *Greatness*, Dean Simonton wrote, "[I]t may require a full decade of arduous labor to acquire the expertise essential to distinction in any domain," citing research on chess grandmasters and composers to demonstrate his point. Simonton at 138, 65-68.
127 Duckworth, *Grit* at 42.
128 Duckworth, et al, *Journal* at 1087.
129 Duckworth et al, *Journal* at 1087-1088. A virtual cottage industry has grown up to satisfy the insatiable desire to find the key to raising a successful child or to becoming a successful adult. Of the half dozen I have read, three favorably cite Duckworth's findings at key points: Charles Duhigg at 131, John Lehrer at 233, and Paul Tough at 61-64 and 75-76. Carol Dweck (at 12, 137) posits a "growth mindset" as producing the resilience and persistence in the face of setbacks that are the keys to success, concepts central to Duckworth's notion of grit. Daniel Coyle (at 13-14) describes what he calls "deep practice," recognizing the progress which occurs when people "screw up" but do not give up, no matter how many times it happens, until they get the task right, a concept which sounds like Gladwell but feels like Duckworth. Even Gladwell (*David* at 149) touches on it, observing "Courage is not something that you already have that makes you brave when the tough times start. Courage is what you earn when you have been through the tough times and you discover they aren't so tough after all."

In 1894 Orison Swett Marden published a self-help book entitled *Pushing to the Front, or Success under Difficulties*, anticipating elements of Duckworth's grit by more than a century. Swett emphasized that character comes from adversity, observing, "Failure often leans a man to success by arousing his latent energy, by firing a dormant purpose, by awakening powers which were sleeping." Tom Butler-Bowdon at 205, 206. Even before that, in 1869, Galton (at 39) more than hinted at the same trait, writing that the geniuses he studied had a "nature" that "if hindered or thwarted, will fret and strive until the hindrance is overcome, and it is again free to follow its labour-loving instincts."
130 Duckworth, *Grit* at 9.
131 Simonton at 153.
132 Simonton at 153-157.
133 Simonton at 138.
134 Goertzels, *Cradles* at 215-247.
135 Goertzels *Cradles* at 247. Gladwell (*David* at 275) similarly observes, "If you take away a mother or a father, you cause suffering and despair. But one time in ten, out of that despair rises an indomitable force."
136 Goertzels *Cradles* at 342.
137 Tough at 28.
138 Tough at 28.
139 Tough at 28.
140 Tough at 34, 33.
141 The nurturing adults were "Hooks" Tinker and the Masons for Josh Gibson; Mutt and Charlie Mantle for Mickey; Joe Barbao, Ki Duda and the Labashes for Stan Musial; Rod Luscomb, Chick Rotert, John Lutz and the whole Cassie family for Ted Williams; Ed Scott for Henry Aaron; Father Mathias for Babe Ruth; and Roberto Marin for Roberto Clemente.
142 Kirk Douglas, James Cagney, Clark Gable and Cary Grant all had doting mothers, and Sidney Poitier perhaps did, as well. John Wayne had a very caring father, and Gregory Peck had his loving grandmother Kate and the highly supportive Clardy clan.

ENDNOTES

143 Tough at 84.
144 Duckworth, *Grit* at 273.
145 For a detailed discussion on the link between affluence and academic success, see pages 289-292.

PART FOUR: WHAT OF THE AMERICAN DREAM?

1 In composing Virginia's Bill of Rights, George Mason wrote "all men are by nature equally free and independent." John Locke had previously written that a "free man" was "one who was independent of others for life's sustenance." Schwarz at 22, 24.
2 Cullen at 4.
3 Adams at 404.
4 Thompson and Hickey at 207.
5 Thompson and Hickey at 199-201; Gilbert at 231. These classes are described in Appendix C.
6 Gilbert at 231.
7 For example, *under*privileged kids are the children of miners, boilermakers and ragmen, while *un*privileged kids are the children of schoolteachers, shoe salesmen and office workers.
8 Adams at 404. While, on the one hand, saying 75% of Americans are underdogs seems like a pretty easy standard to meet, on the other, it makes it more challenging to prove the American Dream has "worked," because that means that three-quarters, or 15 of each of our top 20s, would have to fit that bill.
9 Growing up, "a person's class is his parents' class." *Class Matters* at 9.
10 Sometimes the asterisk is used when a family may be doing relatively well financially, but there is doubt, or lack of clarity, as to how well they are doing in absolute terms. Sometimes it is used when a father achieves a position of respect, but there is a question as to whether that respect translates into cash earnings. And sometimes it is used when the job description or life style particulars are too vague and indefinite to make a confident classification.
11 The difficulty with William Cobb is assessing whether his holding the well-respected positions of teacher, newspaper editor, state legislator and mayor meant that the family had an upper middle class standard of living. As to the Mathewsons, the problem is determining whether the Capwell "safety-net" merely permitted Gilbert Mathewson to pose as a gentleman farmer and of what to make of the fact that at some point Minerva took in a renter and entered the dairy business, which at least suggests the Capwell legacy was exhausted.
12 The difficulty with William Fonda is there is no hard economic data on his pay and the description of the family's comparative well-being makes it unclear whether the family's income would have placed it in the top quarter of wage earners. Owning a print shop in Omaha is not clearly a ticket to the privileged class. As to Charles Cooper, there is no question that he was a professional with a fine reputation and was chosen for positions of honor. However, it appears that his prestige may not have translated into a reliable stream of income and that there were times when he was close to being broke.
13 The Overdogs who drop out are Washington, Jefferson, Madison, Monroe, Quincy Adams and Polk. The Underdogs who drop out are the first Adams, Jackson and Lincoln.
14 Alger, Meyer Introduction at *viii*.
15 Ironically, while Alger's protagonists invariably started off in rags, they never achieved riches, but "a much more modest success consisting of middle class respectability." Alger, Meyer Introduction at *viii*.

ENDNOTES

16. Alvaredo, *et al.* analyzed the IRS data and compiled it into a chart of the annual median income at the top 5% and top 1% thresholds. For years before 1917, the 5% and 1% thresholds are derived using a conversion program that makes an inflation calculation based on the U.S. consumer price index. The website I used was found at htttps://www.in2013dollars.com.
17. An asterisk means that the actor continued to make occasional films in years beyond the endpoint of the stated range.
18. The statutory levels were $25,000 from 1789-1872, $50,000 from 1873-1908, $75,000 from 1909-1948, $100,000 from 1949-1968, and $200,000 from 1969-2000.
19. Though Presidents serve four-year terms, because they take office in the calendar year after elections, their tenures are often expressed as five-year brackets. For simplicity, the threshold averages and "high points" are for the first four years, ignoring the stub period at the end. Until FDR's second term, Inauguration Day was on March 4 of the year following election. Since then, it has been on January 20.
20. That a minority of "overdogs" are in the top 20s may reflect the workings of the American Dream. It may also reflect the fact that the upper classes are still affected by lingering notions that these careers lack respectability, a throwback to the days when each was regarded as amoral, immoral or unlawful. Boxing, horseracing and contact sports were sweaty and violent and often involved gambling. Theater meant burlesque, with images of barely clad chorus girls and slapstick comedians telling bawdy jokes. Politics was synonymous with corruption and graft, the shanty Irish and Tammany Hall.
21. Keller at 206.
22. Willhelm and Sjoberg at 73.
23. Levy at 41. Leo Rosten sent questionnaires to 309 actors who performed between 1938 and 1941. Keller at 303. He concluded that almost 83% of them had fathers with "professional" or "proprietary" occupations. Rosten at 393. Since Levy finds only 129 actors qualify as "America's screen elite" over five decades, Rosten was undoubtedly considering far more than *bona fide* "movie stars," the sole focus here.
24. Aaron at 114.
25. In his book *The Log Cabin Myth*, Edward Pessen analyzes the social backgrounds of every president from George Washington through Ronald Reagan and places each in one of six social classes. As his title implies, he concludes the overwhelming majority were well-born. According to Pessen, "almost nine tenths of our highest leaders" came from families in the top three social classes which he estimates comprise 12-13% of the population at large. Pessen at 69, 63. His placement seems to be based significantly on educational attainments, community standing and the economic circumstances of the presidents' ancestors and other relatives, going far beyond their parents. He also often presents a one-sided portrayal of the facts. And so, Pessen places Harry Truman between the lower upper and upper middle class, above nearly 90% of society, because Harry's paternal great-grandfather was a successful farmer and his maternal grandfather left his mother a handsome piece of property. But he ignores the fact that the ancestral Truman wealth never made it to Harry's father, John, or that John ultimately went bankrupt and had to liquidate his wife's inheritance, as well as all his other holdings. Pessen also places Grover Cleveland between the lower upper and upper middle class because his father Richard went to Yale and Princeton, his maternal grandparents were rich, and he was taken in by his prosperous uncle when his father died. Pessen neglects to mention that Richard Cleveland never earned more than a $1,000 a year, he had to stretch that amount to care for his wife and nine children and he died penniless. Pessen even denied Abraham Lincoln's humble beginnings, noting that in one year his father Thomas was among the top 15% of taxpayers in his small community and that his paternal grandfather was a successful farmer, characterizing

Abe's parents as members of the "true" middle class. Pessen at 68. Pessen fails to disclose that under the laws of primogeniture Thomas inherited none of his father's wealth and that the titles to Thomas's own properties were under a cloud, requiring him to sell them at a loss. Dwight Eisenhower's family is also slotted into the "true" middle class, because Ike's paternal grandfather had given his father a farm and cash, Ike's mother was a college girl and the family lived in "an imposing house." Pessen at 46. He never reveals that David had a menial position of maintenance engineer, that Nelle's college was academically suspect and she attended for but a year and that the "imposing house" they lived in had primitive facilities and may have been a gift from Ike's grandfather or uncle.

I have the same reservations about the work of Balzell and Schneiderman, who endorsed Pessen's analysis and adopted his approach.

26 Others have written more generally about highly-elected officials, including Presidents, contending they come from the upper crust of society. Donald R. Matthews in *The Social Background of Political Decision-Makers* derided the notion of "log-cabin to White House" as it applies to politics generally. Matthews at 23. Looking at the 100 men who were Presidents, Vice Presidents and Cabinet members from 1789-1934, he reported that 58% of them had fathers who were "Professional" men or what he called "Proprietors & officials." Matthews at 23. Since fewer than a third of these men were in the White House, it is impossible to know how he classified Presidents alone. This is even more of an issue in evaluating the conclusions reached by C. Wright Mills in *The Power Elite*. Mills contended that most of the 513 men who through 1953 served as Presidents, Vice Presidents, Speakers of the House, Justices of the Supreme Court and Cabinet members came "from quite prosperous family circumstances." Mills at 400 n. 3. But the Presidents make up an insignificant 7% of Mills' subjects.

27 There is a caveat as to the assessment of Cy Young, since 13 years of salary information is missing.
28 Goertzels, *Cradles* at 282.
29 Goertzels, *Cradles* at 283.
30 Goertzels, *Three Hundred* at 345.
31 Raskin at 20, 27.
32 Raskin at 28.
33 Mills, "The American Business Elite . . ." at 29.
34 Keller at 294.
35 Schmidhauser at 9.
36 Schmidhauser at 6.
37 Zuckerman (at 65) was careful to point out that not all of the fathers she classified as professionals – 38 men – were necessarily highly paid, noting, for example, that some were high school teachers and clergymen. However, even after eliminating those in assumedly less-lucrative professions, the total percentage of Nobel laureates reared in America's upper strata is still a healthy majority of around 60%.
38 Keller at 296.
39 d Roe at 66, 68.
40 Keller at 297.
41 Keller at 311.
42 Janowitz at 91.
43 Keller at 311.
44 Keller at 301.
45 Adams at 404.
46 Adams at 404.
47 A chart of the top five-percenters drawn from an analysis of this census data is set forth at Appendix H.

48 Within the post-graduate category, 13.9% earned Masters degrees, 25.1% earned Professional degrees and 4.3% earned PhDs.
49 In a 2005 *New York Times* poll, 39% of respondents thought education was "essential" to "getting ahead in life" and another 46% thought it was "very important." *Class Matters* at 251. The data bear this out. According to the 2010 Census, those who did not graduate from high school had an average income of about $25,000; those with a bachelor's degree had an average income of approximately $56,000, more than double that amount; and those having a professional degree had an average income of roughly $102,000, over quadruple that amount. Baum, Ma and Payea at 11.
50 Class Matters at 2.
51 Tough at xiv.
52 Sawhill at 4.
53 Sawhill at 4.
54 Gladwell, *Outliers* at 258. The learning of the wealthier kids was attributable to the "enriched" experiences bought by affluence: museum visits, enrollment in "special programs," "classes" at summer camps, home libraries. Gladwell, *Outliers* at 258.
55 Tough at 188.
56 Goode at 591.
57 Goode at 591.
58 Rampell at 1. Biamonte (at 3) found a "causal relationship" between the differences Rampell found in SAT scores and the "preparatory materials" and "coaching programs" that wealthier families could provide for their children.
59 Carnevale and Rose at 106. In 2005, a year after the publication of these findings, reporters from *The New York Times* stated: "At 250 of the most selective colleges in the country, the proportion of students from upper-income families has grown, not shrunk." *Class Matters* at 21. Two years after that, Joseph Soares (at 4) found that 79% of students in 44 Tier 1 colleges and 64% of students in 85 Tier 2 colleges were from the highest socio-economic quartile.
60 To the extent these top flight firms will seek to recruit the best students at the best schools, I have assumed that academic performance at college does not vary significantly with the student's socio-economic background. That is, that the poor kids do not do better than the rich kids at these first tier schools. There is no body of evidence to suggest this assumption is wrong.
61 Another reason for "overpopulation" is that students from the Tier 1 colleges are far more likely to attend graduate school than the students from colleges in Tiers 2 through 4: 35% compared to 18%. Carnevale and Rose at 110. This differential is consistent with differentials in graduation rates as a function of income: 40% of students from the top quartile graduate as compared to 6% of students from the bottom quartile. Gladieux at 22.
62 Keller at 217.
63 Luthar, "High Price" at 135.
64 Luthar and Latendress, "Children of the Affluent . . ." at 52.
65 While our sample is for 2000, there is no basis for concluding that the highest paid occupations had significantly fewer overdogs in earlier periods. The 1970 census reveals that 86% of males in the top 5% of wage earners went to college and there is no data, or logic, to suggest that the most competitive schools were more democratic – accepted fewer children of privilege – back then. The 1940 census reveals only 65% of the top five-percenters had a college education, but there are indications that the elite schools – certainly those in the Ivy League – had an even greater concentration of wealthy students in those days. It also seems likely that the roughly 12% of high school graduates who had these well-paying jobs would have tended to be among the more

advantaged, since the 1940 census reflected the impact of the Great Depression, which inevitably forced those from the lower classes to leave school early.

66   Other schools represented are Princeton (Moe Berg), Brown (Bill Almon) and Penn (Doug Glanville).
67   As to the other Ivies, Princeton has Brooke Shields, Cornell has Christopher Reeve, Brown has Laura Linney and Penn has Candace Bergen.
68   Six have law degrees (Hayes, Taft, Nixon, Ford, Clinton, Obama), one has an MBA (G.W. Bush) and one has a doctorate (Wilson).
69   They are Lincoln (1), Washington (3), Truman (7), Jackson (9), Monroe (15), Cleveland (17) and McKinley (18).
70   Counting both undergraduate and graduate schools, both Adamses, both Roosevelts, John Kennedy and Barack Obama went to Harvard; both Bushes, William Howard Taft, Gerald Ford and Bill Clinton went to Yale, and James Madison and Woodrow Wilson went to Princeton.
71   For example, Warren Harding attended Ohio Central College, Lyndon Johnson attended Southwest Texas State College, Richard Nixon attended Whittier College and Ronald Reagan attended Eureka College. Three Presidents who ended up at Ivy League Schools did not start there. Wilson began at Davidson before transferring to Princeton, Obama began at Occidental before transferring to Columbia, and Trump began at Fordham before transferring to Penn.
72   *Class Matters* at 2.
73   Solon at 405.
74   Mazumbder at 92. There were at least two more pieces, also published in 2005, that touched on the "imperfections" of intergenerational mobility in the United States. In *Class Matters*, reporters for *The New York Times* wrote, "Americans are arguably more likely than they were thirty years ago to end up in the class into which they were born," quoting the "old saw" of a Berkeley economist that "the most important decision you make is choosing your parents." *Class Matters* at 4, 22. Isabel Sawhill, a senior fellow at the Brookings Institution, agreed: "Mobility is especially limited at the top and bottom of the income distribution, suggesting that the degree of one's wealth or poverty influences one's opportunities." Sawhill at 2.
75   Hertz's results are reproduced at Appendix I.
76   Hertz also examined the prospects of becoming "rich," which he – like we – "defined as attaining the top 5 percent of the family income distribution." Hertz at 3. He calculated that ". . . the chances of getting rich are about 20 times greater if you were born rich than if you were born to a low-income family." Hertz at 8.
77   Pew, *Pursuing* at 6.
78   Pew, *Pursuing* at 6.
79   *Class Matters* at 146.
80   https://news.gallup.com/poll/188780/americans-satisfaction-ability-ahead-edges.aspx
81   Sawhill at 1.
82   Three thousand respondents "overshot the likelihood of rising from the poorest quintile to one of the three top quintile by nearly 15 percentage points." https://www.nytimes.com/2015/05/03/ opinion/Sunday/ american-dream-or-mirage.html?_r=0
83   Research by Professors Kraus and Tan revealed people "believe unduly" in their "own capacity to move up the economic ladder" and to vastly "overestimate" their chances. https://www.nytimes.com/ 2015/ 05/ 03/opinion/sunday/american-dream-or-mirage.html?_r=0,
84   A 2005 survey on the meaning of the American dream elicited the following responses: Freedom/opportunity (20%), Happiness/contentment/peace of mind (19%), Financial security/steady job (19%), Have a house/home (13%), Family (7%), Successful (7%),

ENDNOTES

Health (2%), Comfortable retirement (2%), Good job (1%), "Life in America" (1%). *Class Matters* at 248.
85   *Class Matters* at 19.
86   Donald Trump's economic situation was vastly different, and his attempt to minimize his advantages – after all, he was just a kid from Queens who had only been staked a million dollars to get started – was laughable.
87   These names were culled from a *New York Times* piece entitled "Notable Deaths of 2015." Not all those deemed by *The Times* as "notable" were necessarily well-known. For example, there was Sally Gross who died on July 20 and was highly praised for her contributions to minimalist dance and choreography. Ms. Gross was one of eight children, four of whom survived into adulthood, and was raised on the Lower East Side of New York. Her father made a living peddling fruits and vegetables from a horse-drawn wagon. https://www.nytimes.com/interactive/2015/ obituaries /notable-deaths-2015.html?_r=0
88   McElvaine at 40.
89   Leder at 5.
90   Adams at 404.
91   Keller at 222, n. 11.

APPENDICES

1   The income figures for this tier and the others are as of the year 2000. They are included solely to provide a feel for the difference across the strata.
2   Thompson and Hickey (at 199-201) list five tiers, but the percentages for the five add up to 93%, implying there is a sixth tier at the bottom made up of 7% of the population.
3   Rankings are based first on the number of sources listing the player or ranking him in the top 20 and then by the average rankings of those sources that assign a numerical rank.
4   "Nr." indicates how many of the 22 sources rank a particular president.
5   Hirsch at 4.
6   Linge at 2.
7   Seidel at 5.
8   Robinson at 31.
9   DeValaria at 8.
10 Cramer at 17.
11 Cramer at 16.
12 Cramer at 20.
13 Cy Young was christened Denton True Young and did not acquire his nickname, a short form of "Cyclone," until he was 23. Browning at 8.
14 Gay at 36.
15 Kaplan at 31.
16 Hartley at 6.
17 Seib at 5; Hartley at 9.
18 Satchell at 8.
19 Satchell at 10.
20 Astaire at 23.
21 Chaplin at 15.
22 Spoto at 1.
23 Spoto at 7. His biographer disagrees.
24 Hirschhorn at 19.
25 Buford at 14.
26 Buford at 19.
27 Groucho Marx at 15.

ENDNOTES

28. Grandpa Marx helped out for a time by mending umbrellas. He gave up when his take for his first year in business was $12.50.
29. Harpo Marx at 19.
30. Kanfer at 3.
31. Dewey at 55.
32. Carey at 2.
33. Roberts and Goldstein at 6.
34. Teichmann at 27.
35. Meyers at 8.
36. Meyers at 7.
37. Meyers at 17.
38. Meyers at 20.
39. Donald at 19.
40. McCullough, *Truman* at 67.
41. Truman at 17.
42. McCullough, *John Adams* at 32.
43. Cullen at 68.
44. Brodsky at 13.
45. Brodsky at 20.
46. Leech at 4.
47. Freeman at 6.
48. Freeman at 9.
49. Freeman at 19, 26.
50. Cunningham at 1.
51. Ellis at 30.
52. Cooper at 22.
53. Blum at 7.
54. Greenblatt at 2.
55. FDR was reputed to have said, "[I]t takes a thief to catch a thief." Hamilton at 109.
56. Brookhiser at 16.
57. Wills at 12.
58. Unger at 9.
59. Old at 13.
60. Unger at 10.
61. Nagel at 7.
62. Remini at 17.
63. The salary data for the ballplayers is taken from the individual player profiles at https://bit.ly/2F6wgNW, except for Josh Gibson, where the source is Ribowsky.
64. Ruth's average salary for the period was $55,467, and the average 1% threshold was $6,821. Ruth's career extended till 1935, but there is no salary data for his last year.
65. Mays's average salary for the period was $102,941, and the average 1% threshold was $27,113.
66. Aaron's average salary for the period was $108,533, and the average 1% threshold was $30,747.
67. Williams' average salary for the period was $63,265, and the average 1% threshold was $15,246.
68. Gehrig's average salary for the period was $26,727, and the average 1% threshold was $5,975.
69. Wagner's average salary for the period was $8,333, and the average 1% threshold was $4,008.
70. Musial's average salary for the period was $53,194, and the average 1% threshold was $17,222.

ENDNOTES

71 Mantle's average salary for the period was $72,867, and the average 1% threshold was $22,118.
72 Johnson's average salary for the period was $13,382, and the average 1% threshold was $5,933.
73 DiMaggio's average salary for the period was $47,981, and the average 1% threshold was $8,813.
74 Hornsby's average salary for the period was $28,100, and the average 1% threshold was $6,665. There is no salary figure for 1924, so only 15 years are used in the numerator and denominator of the calculation.
75 The salary data for Young is extremely spotty. There is none for the years 1893-1898, 1900, 1902-1903, 1905-1908 and 1910-1911.
76 There is no salary data for Speaker's first six years in the majors, 1907 to 1912.
77 Speaker's average salary for the period was $22,357, and the average 1% threshold was $6,511. There is no salary figure for 1921, so only 14 years are used in the numerator and denominator of the calculation.
78 Foxx's average salary for the period was $20,500, and the average 1% threshold was $6,027. Foxx's career continued into 1945, but there is no salary data for his last three years.
79 Schmidt's average salary for the period was $1,292,193, and the average 1% threshold was $83,110. Schmidt's career actually extended till 1989, but there is no salary data for his last year.
80 Ribowsky at 206.
81 Between 1937 and 1943 the 5% thresholds were at a low of $2,590 and a high of $4,171. The 1% thresholds were at a low of $5,762 and a high of $8,274.
82 Grove's average salary for the period was $19,269, and the average 1% threshold was $6,142.
83 Since 1932, Quigley Publishing surveyed movie exhibitors and compiled the results of their poll, always reporting the top 10 movies stars but gathering a more comprehensive list. A Wikipedia entry reveals Quigley's top 25 male and female actors for most years between 1932 and 1965. I have included the actual Quigley ranking for stars regardless of gender and, on occasion, a derived ranking among just male actors.
84 For films made in the 1930s, it is assumed that two weeks was the shortest production time and that four weeks was a reasonable average for a shooting schedule.
85 Unless otherwise indicated, the earnings information is taken from the individual biographies on the IMDb website.
86 Salary data taken from Satchell.
87 IMDb salary data supplemented by Curtis.
88 Salary data taken from Weissman.
89 Weissman at 257.
90 IMDb salary data supplemented by Fishgall.
91 Salary data taken from Hirschhorn and Yudkoff.

Made in the USA
Middletown, DE
24 October 2024